DODGER STADIUM

Blue Heaven on Earth

Edited by Bill Nowlin
and Glen Sparks

Associate Editors Len Levin and Carl Riechers

Society for American Baseball Research, Inc.
Phoenix, AZ

Dodger Stadium: Blue Heaven on Earth

Edited by Bill Nowlin and Glen Sparks
Associate editors Len Levin and Carl Riechers

Design: Rachael E. Sullivan
Front cover photograph copyright Joe Sohn / dreamstime
Back cover images by Jon SooHoo / Los Angeles Dodgers

ISBN 978-1-960819-20-8   Dodger Stadium – Blue Heaven on Earth ebook
ISBN 978-1-960819-21-5   Dodger Stadium – Blue Heaven on Earth paper

Library of Congress Control Number: 2024905774

Cronkite School at ASU
555 N. Central Ave. #416
Phoenix, AZ 85004
Phone: (602) 496-1460
Web: www.sabr.org
Facebook: Society for American Baseball Research
Twitter: @SABR

CONTENTS

INTRODUCTION.............................. 1
by Glen Sparks

1. DODGER STADIUM 3
by Curt Smith

2. EXACTLY 56,000 SEATS???? 14
by Andy McCue

3. THE STRUGGLE TO BUILD DODGER
STADIUM 15
by Andy McCue

4. THE BATTLE OF CHAVEZ RAVINE.............. 21
by Bill Pruden

5. A MONUMENT TO THE O'MALLEYS 27
by Andy McCue

6. WHEN THE ANGELS CALLED DODGER
STADIUM................................ 31
By Kurt Blumenau

7. WHY WERE THE DODGERS TEAMS OF THE
1960S SO GOOD? 36
by John Zinn

8. REKINDLING THE LIGHT: THE JAPANESE
STONE LANTERN AT DODGER STADIUM ... 41
By Russ Speiller

9. IT'S A RED ADAMS JERSEY,
NOT A DODGERS JERSEY........................ 46
by Zak Ford

10. "VIVA, VALENZUELA!": FERNANDOMANIA
AND THE TRANSFORMATION OF THE LOS
ANGELES DODGERS.............................. 49
by Jason Scheller

11. OLYMPIC BASEBALL AT DODGER
STADIUM 56
by Tony S. Oliver

12. A WEEKEND TO REMEMBER.................... 59
CENTENNIAL OLD-TIMERS DAY
by Greg King

13. "SCULLY'S SHRINE": A BROADCASTER AND
HIS BALLPARK........................ 63
by Michael Green

14. FANS COME FIRST – A HISTORY OF DODGER
STADIUM PROMOTIONS 68
by Joey Elledge

15. THE DODGER DOG................................ 72
by Tony S. Oliver

16. DODGER STADIUM CONCERTS............... 74
by Zac Petrillo

17. DODGERS WIN WORLD SERIES IN 2020
COVID SEASON 79
by Glen Sparks

18. JANET MARIE SMITH 87
by Bob Webster

19. DODGER STADIUM RENOVATIONS.......... 91
by Bob Webster

SELECTED GAMES 95

20. DODGERS LOSE TO REDS IN DODGER
STADIUM DEBUT 97
APRIL 10, 1962: CINCINNATI REDS
6, LOS ANGELES DODGERS 3
by David Krell

21. THE GIANTS WIN THE PENNANT, PART TWO! 100
OCTOBER 3, 1962: SAN FRANCISCO GIANTS 6, LOS ANGELES DODGERS 4

by Tim Otto

22. SANDY KOUFAX'S SECOND NO-HITTER.... 103
MAY 11, 1963: LOS ANGELES DODGERS 8, SAN FRANCISCO GIANTS 0

by Marc Z Aaron

23. TOMMY DAVIS SECURES SECOND CONSECUTIVE BATTING TITLE AS DODGERS END THE 1963 SEASON WITH LOSS TO THE PHILLIES 105
SEPTEMBER 29, 1963: PHILADELPHIA PHILLIES 3, LOS ANGELES DODGERS 1

by Alan Stowell

24. "THE BEST PITCHED GAME OF THIS SUPERBLY PITCHED SERIES" 108
OCTOBER 5, 1963: LOS ANGELES DODGERS 1, NEW YORK YANKEES 0

by Andy McCue

25. KOUFAX STIFLES YANKEE BATS AGAIN AS DODGERS SWEEP WORLD SERIES........... 110
OCTOBER 6, 1963: LOS ANGELES DODGERS 2, NEW YORK YANKEES 1

by Andy McCue

26. "MILLION BUTTERFLIES" AND ONE PERFECT GAME FOR SANDY KOUFAX 113
SEPTEMBER 9, 1965: LOS ANGELES DODGERS 1, CHICAGO CUBS 0

by Mike Huber

27. WELL, GOLLY: "GOMER" CLAUDE OSTEEN GETS DODGERS BACK INTO THE SERIES .. 116
OCTOBER 9, 1965: LOS ANGELES DODGERS 4, MINNESOTA TWINS 0 (GAME THREE OF THE 1965 WORLD SERIES)

by Norm King

28. BIG D SURPASSES THE BIG TRAIN FOR CONSECUTIVE SCORELESS INNINGS MARK 118
JUNE 8, 1968: LOS ANGELES DODGERS 5, PHILADELPHIA PHILLIES 3

by Richard Cuicchi

29. STARGELL HOMERS OUT OF DODGER STADIUM 121
AUGUST 5, 1969: PITTSBURGH PIRATES 11, LOS ANGELES DODGERS 3

by Dave Lande

30. WILLIE DAVIS BREAKS 53-YEAR-OLD FRANCHISE HITTING RECORD 123
SEPTEMBER 2, 1969: NEW YORK METS 5, LOS ANGELES DODGERS 4

by Warren Campbell

31. DON SUTTON THROWS 11-INNING, 1-0 SHUTOUT AGAINST THE GIANTS 126
SEPTEMBER 22, 1972: LOS ANGELES DODGERS 1, SAN FRANCISCO GIANTS 0

by Joseph Wancho

32. NEW YORKERS LISTEN TO BASEBALL WITH THEIR BREAKFAST................................. 128
MAY 24, 1973: NEW YORK METS 7, LOS ANGELES DODGERS 3 (19 INNINGS)

by Alan Cohen

33. GARVEY, WYNN, SUTTON PACE DODGERS' ROUT OF PIRATES IN NLCS CLINCHER 131
OCTOBER 9, 1974: LOS ANGELES DODGERS 12, PITTSBURGH PIRATES 1 (GAME FOUR OF THE 1974 NATIONAL LEAGUE DIVISION SERIES)

by John Fredland

34. FERGUSON'S FANTASTIC THROW A FOOTNOTE AS OAKLAND WINS 1974 WORLD SERIES OPENER 135
OCTOBER 12, 1974: OAKLAND ATHLETICS 3, LOS ANGELES DODGERS 2 (GAME ONE OF THE 1974 WORLD SERIES)

by Mark S. Sternman

35. "RICK MONDAY ... YOU MADE A GREAT PLAY!" 138
APRIL 25, 1976: LOS ANGELES DODGERS 5, CHICAGO CUBS 4
by Jeff Barto

36. DUSTY BAKER HITS 30TH HOMER, RECEIVES FIRST-EVER HIGH-FIVE FROM GLENN BURKE IN DODGERS' LOSS TO ASTROS 141
OCTOBER 2, 1977: HOUSTON ASTROS 6, LOS ANGELES DODGERS 3
by John Fredland

37. BILL RUSSELL'S WALK-OFF SINGLE SENDS DODGERS BACK TO WORLD SERIES; GARVEY WINS NLCS MVP 145
OCTOBER 7, 1978: LOS ANGELES DODGERS 4, PHILADELPHIA PHILLIES 3 (10 INNINGS) (GAME FOUR OF THE 1978 NATIONAL LEAGUE CHAMPIONSHIP SERIES)
by Joseph Wancho

38. BOB WELCH STRIKES OUT REGGIE JACKSON TO SECURE 1978 WORLD SERIES GAME TWO VICTORY 148
OCTOBER 11, 1978: LOS ANGELES DODGERS 4, NEW YORK YANKEES 3
by Alan Stowell

39. THE 1980 ALL-STAR GAME 151
JULY 9. 1980: NATIONAL LEAGUE ALL-STARS 4, AMERICAN LEAGUE ALL-STARS 2
by Gary Sarnoff

40. DODGERS FORCE NL WEST SHOWDOWN 154
OCTOBER 5, 1980: LOS ANGELES DODGERS 4, HOUSTON ASTROS 3
by Mike Bell

41. OPENING DAY 1981 AND THE BIRTH OF FERNANDOMANIA 157
APRIL 9, 1981: LOS ANGELES DODGERS 2, HOUSTON ASTROS 0
by Jason Scheller

42. REUSS, RYAN, AND A FITTING END TO A PITCHER-DOMINATED PLAYOFF SERIES .. 159
OCTOBER 11, 1981: LOS ANGELES DODGERS 4, HOUSTON ASTROS 0 (GAME FIVE OF THE NATIONAL LEAGUE DIVISION SERIES)
by John Bauer

43. DODGERS COMPLETE HOME SWEEP OF YANKEES TO TAKE DRIVER'S SEAT IN 78TH FALL CLASSIC 162
OCTOBER 25, 1981: LOS ANGELES DODGERS 2, NEW YORK YANKEES 1 (GAME FIVE OF THE 1981 WORLD SERIES)
by Chad Moody

44. PEDRO GUERRERO SETS RECORD; STEVE HOWE ENDS DODGER CAREER 165
JUNE 30, 1985: LOS ANGELES DODGERS 4, ATLANTA BRAVES 3
by Jeff Findley

45. OCTOBER 12, 1988: DODGERS BEAT METS IN NLCS GAME SEVEN 167
LOS ANGELES DODGERS 6, NEW YORK METS 0
by Thomas J. Brown Jr.

46. KIRK GIBSON'S HOMER WINS THE FIRST GAME OF THE 1988 WORLD SERIES........ 169
OCTOBER 15, 1988: LOS ANGELES DODGERS 5, OAKLAND ATHLETICS 4 (GAME ONE OF THE 1988 WORLD SERIES)
by Darren Gibson

47. PHENOM RAMÓN MARTÍNEZ REALIZES POTENTIAL 172
JUNE 4, 1990: LOS ANGELES DODGERS 6, ATLANTA BRAVES 0
by Thomas Baird

48. FERNANDO (SORT OF) PREDICTS NO-HITTER 175
JUNE 29, 1990: LOS ANGELES DODGERS 6, ST. LOUIS CARDINALS 0
by Carter Cromwell

49. DENNIS MARTÍNEZ'S PERFECT GAME 178
JULY 28, 1991: MONTREAL EXPOS
2, LOS ANGELES DODGERS 0
by Rory Costello

50. AFTER SEASONS OF STRUGGLES, LA'S KEVIN
GROSS DAZZLES FANS BY NO-HITTING THE
GIANTS 181
AUGUST 17, 1992: LOS ANGELES DODGERS
2, SAN FRANCISCO GIANTS 0
by Andrew Harner

51. DODGERS TURN THE TABLES ON RIVAL
GIANTS 184
OCTOBER 3, 1993: LOS ANGELES DODGERS
12, SAN FRANCISCO GIANTS 1
by Tom Schott

52. NOMO TAKES THE SPOTLIGHT WITH 17
K'S ON A BIG SPORTS NIGHT IN LOS
ANGELES 187
APRIL 13, 1996: LOS ANGELES
DODGERS 3, FLORIDA MARLINS 1
by Bob Timmermann

53. FERNANDO TATÍS TATTOOS TWO GRAND
SLAMS IN THE SAME INNING 189
APRIL 23, 1999: ST. LOUIS CARDINALS
12, LOS ANGELES DODGERS 5
by Mike Huber

54. STEVE FINLEY GRAND SLAM ENDS DODGER
PLAYOFF DROUGHT 191
OCTOBER 2, 2004: LOS ANGELES DODGERS
7, SAN FRANCISCO GIANTS 3
by Carter Cromwell

55. JOSÉ LIMA SHUTOUT BREAKS POSTSEASON
DROUGHTS FOR DODGERS – AND DODGER
STADIUM 194
OCTOBER 9, 2004: LOS ANGELES
DODGERS 4, ST. LOUIS CARDINALS 0
(GAME THREE OF THE 2004 NATIONAL
LEAGUE DIVISION SERIES)
by Joal Ryan

56. DODGERS TIE PADRES WITH 4 STRAIGHT HRS
IN 9TH 197
SEPTEMBER 18, 2006: LOS ANGELES
DODGERS 11, SAN DIEGO PADRES 10
by Bob Timmermann

57. DODGERS DEFEAT ANGELS DESPITE GETTING
NO HITS 199
JUNE 28, 2008: LOS ANGELES DODGERS 1,
LOS ANGELES ANGELS OF ANAHEIM 0
by Mike Huber

58. ANDRE ETHIER HITS MAJOR-LEAGUE RECORD
FOURTH WALK-OFF HOME RUN OF THE
SEASON 202
SEPTEMBER 15, 2009: LOS ANGELES DODGERS
4, PITTSBURGH PIRATES 3 (13 INNINGS)
by Joseph Wancho

59. LORETTA'S HIT COMPLETES DODGERS' NINTH-
INNING RALLY 204
OCTOBER 8, 2009: LOS ANGELES
DODGERS 3, ST. LOUIS CARDINALS 2
(GAME TWO OF THE 2009 NATIONAL
LEAGUE DIVISION SERIES)
by Kevin Snyder

60. OPENING DAY PITCHERS' DUEL ULTIMATELY
DECIDED BY KERSHAW'S BAT 207
APRIL 1, 2013: LOS ANGELES DODGERS
4, SAN FRANCISCO GIANTS 0
by Greg King

61. URIBE HOME RUN ADVANCES DODGERS TO
NLCS 210
OCTOBER 7, 2013: LOS ANGELES
DODGERS 4, ATLANTA BRAVES 3
(GAME FOUR OF THE 2013 NATIONAL
LEAGUE DIVISION SERIES)
by Theo Tobel

62. CLAYTON KERSHAW THROWS
NO-HITTER AGAINST ROCKIES 213
JUNE 18, 2014: LOS ANGELES DODGERS
8, COLORADO ROCKIES 0
by Glen Sparks

63. VIN SCULLY BIDS FAREWELL TO LA FANS . 216
SEPTEMBER 25, 2016: LOS ANGELES
DODGERS 4, COLORADO ROCKIES 3
by Thomas Baird

64. JUSTIN TURNER HOMERS ON ANNIVERSARY
OF GIBSON'S '88 HOME RUN 219
OCTOBER 15, 2017: LOS ANGELES
DODGERS 4, CHICAGO CUBS 1
(GAME TWO OF THE 2017 NATIONAL
LEAGUE CHAMPIONSHIP SERIES)
by Glen Sparks

65. KERSHAW, TURNER, MOTHER NATURE BRING
THE HEAT TO SERIES OPENER 222
OCTOBER 24, 2017: LOS ANGELES
DODGERS 3, HOUSTON ASTROS 1
(GAME ONE OF THE 2017 WORLD SERIES)
by John Bauer

66. ROOKIE RIGHT-HANDER BEATS ROCKIES,
DODGERS WIN NL WEST TITLE 225
OCTOBER 1, 2018: LOS ANGELES
DODGERS 5, COLORADO ROCKIES 2
by Paul Hofmann

67. TWO GAMES IN ONE – DODGERS PREVAIL
OVER RED SOX IN LONGEST WORLD SERIES
GAME EVER 227
OCTOBER 26, 2018: LOS ANGELES DODGERS
3, BOSTON RED SOX 2 (18 INNINGS)
(GAME THREE OF THE 2018 WORLD SERIES)
by Bill Nowlin

68. DODGERS SMACK EIGHT HOMERS IN
RECORD-BREAKING OPENING DAY AT
HOME 230
MARCH 28, 2019: LOS ANGELES DODGERS
12, ARIZONA DIAMONDBACKS 5
by Bryan Dietzler

69. THIRD STRAIGHT GAME WITH A WALK-OFF
HOME RUN BY A ROOKIE 232
JUNE 23, 2019: LOS ANGELES DODGERS
6, COLORADO ROCKIES 3
by Joey Elledge

70. DODGERS HIT 8 HRS AND SCORE DODGER
STADIUM RECORD 22 RUNS 234
JULY 10, 2021: LOS ANGELES DODGERS
22, ARIZONA DIAMONDBACKS 1
by Paul Hofmann

71. CHRIS TAYLOR HITS THREE HOME RUNS
TO PROPEL DODGERS TO CRUCIAL WIN IN
NLCS 236
OCTOBER 21, 2021: LOS ANGELES
DODGERS 11, ATLANTA BRAVES 2
(GAME FIVE OF THE NATIONAL LEAGUE
CHAMPIONSHIP SERIES)
by Frank Ittner

72. DODGERS' UNBEATEN GONSOLIN UNABLE TO
STOP AL FROM 9TH CONSECUTIVE ALL-STAR
WIN 239
JULY 19, 2022: AL ALL-STARS 3, NL ALL-STARS 2
by Richard Cuicchi

73. DODGER STADIUM CONTRIBUTORS 242

INTRODUCTION

by Glen Sparks

"Blue heaven on earth" –
Tommy Lasorda on Dodger Stadium

Dodger Stadium is the third oldest ballpark in major-league baseball. Only Fenway Park and Wrigley Field have been hosting games longer than the House That Walter O'Malley Built. The iconic venue that sits atop a hill just north of downtown Los Angeles, with views of both the city and mountains, turns 62 years old in 2024.

This book chronicles the rich history of Dodger Stadium and the great games played there. You'll read about Sandy Koufax's perfect game, Don Drysdale's scoreless-innings streak, Dusty Baker's historic 30th home run in 1977, and much more. Of course, the book includes an account of Kirk Gibson's miraculous home run in Game One of the 1988 World Series and the 4+1 game in 2006. Some stories include quotes from the team's beloved former broadcaster Vin Scully.

The Dodgers, as most baseball fans know, have their roots in Brooklyn, New York, where they were founded in 1883. They won some pennants in the early days before suffering through a series of losing seasons and gaining the nickname of the Daffy Dodgers. They are most famous, of course, for being the "Boys of Summer," with such great players as Jackie Robinson, Duke Snider, Pee Wee Reese, Gil Hodges, and Roy Campanella. The Brooklyn Dodgers won their lone World Series in 1955. Two years later they were gone, having moved from Flatbush to Southern California.

During those first years on the West Coast, the Dodgers played at the Los Angeles Memorial Coliseum, a gigantic venue more suited for football than baseball. The *New York Daily News* lamented that the Coliseum made "a mockery of big-league baseball." The Dodgers won a World Series in 1959 with home crowds of more than 92,000 for all three games. Fans kept transistor radios pressed against their ears so they could hear Scully describe the faraway action. Owner Walter O'Malley already had a new spot picked out for his team. He supposedly spotted the Chavez Ravine site while taking a helicopter ride over the LA basin.

The Dodger Stadium origin story is a colorful one and not without controversy. This book covers not only the construction of the ballpark – and all the political events that preceded it – but also the Battle of Chavez Ravine, a protracted conflict that concluded with the destruction of a close-knit, mostly Mexican American, neighborhood.

Ground was broken for Dodger Stadium on September 19, 1959. Workers moved more than 8 million cubic yards of dirt and rocks from the rugged hillside. Nineteen giant earth movers flattened the hills and filled in the many gullies. The construction bill ran to about $23 million.

Dodger Stadium hosted its first baseball game on April 10, 1962. The home team lost to the Cincinnati Reds, 6-3. Dodgers coach and former manager Leo Durocher offered a glowing review of the new ballpark. "I had to see it to believe it," he told the *Long Beach Press-Telegram*. "It's not only beautiful, but it's also practical. All the fielders have room to move around. And there's not a bad seat in the house." Reds outfielder Wally Post said, "Nobody will get cheap homers here. The park is really beautiful, though, and sure shames some of those other dinky things we play in."

The tough one-two pitching combination of Koufax and Drysdale led the Dodgers to three pennants and two World Series titles in the 1960s. Opposing hitters battled tough pitches thrown in hazy sunshine. The 1970s Dodgers won three pennants and in 1978 were the first team to draw more than 3 million fans. Fernando Valenzuela burst onto the scene in 1981, bringing "Fernandomania" and the team's first World Series championship since 1965. The Dodgers won another title in 1988.

Fans still flock to Dodger Stadium, the home of maybe baseball's most famous concession, the Dodger Dog, and the many palm trees that sway in the soft breezes. Several improvements have been made over the years. Those include LED video displays and a better sound system, plus a children's playground, and more concession options – including Tommy Lasorda's Trattoria.

After the Dodgers won the 2020 World Series, the Centerfield Plaza opened. Fans can enjoy new sports bars and seating areas, displays of team memorabilia, and statues of Koufax and Robinson. A family area was also added. Janet Marie Smith, who worked on the construction of Oriole Park at Camden Yards and the renovation of Fenway Park among other projects, said, "We sent a clear message that this is a family-friendly place, and the kind of atmosphere here is one for all generations to enjoy." She told Bill Shaikin of the *Los Angeles Times*, "Too much is too much. You still want an intimacy. We're still here to watch the game and celebrate the Dodgers. We weren't looking to create a theme park. We were looking to create the kind of amenities that other ballparks have, but in a way that respected the original architecture of Dodger Stadium."

Former Los Angeles Angels superstar Shohei Ohtani signed a $700 million contract with the Dodgers before the 2024 season. Japanese pitcher Yoshinobu Yamamoto also signed a big deal to play for the Dodgers, who finished in first place with a 100-62 record in 2023 and boasted such great players as Mookie Betts, Freddie Freeman, and Clayton Kershaw. More than 3.8 million fans filed into the ballpark built atop a hill. The future seems bright for both the Dodgers and Dodger Stadium.

This book is the collaborative effort of 49 members from the Society for American Baseball Research.

NOTES

1   Andy McCue, *Mover and Shaker: Walter O'Malley, the Dodgers and Baseball's Westward Expansion* (Lincoln: University of Nebraska Press, 2014), 221.

2   Nathan Masters, "They Moved Mountains to Build Dodger Stadium," PBS SoCal, October 11, 2013, https://www.pbssocal.org/shows/lost-la/they-moved-mountains-to-build-dodger-stadium.

3   Hank Hollingsworth, "It's Unanimous – Dodger Plant Best," *Long Beach Press-Telegram*, April 11, 1962: 53.

4   Eric Stephen, "Dodger Stadium Upgrades Ready to Be Seen," truebluela.com, April 8, 2021, https://www.truebluela.com/2021/4/8/22373029/dodger-stadium-upgrades-center-field-plaza-shake-shack.

5   Bill Shaikin, "Commentary: Dodger Stadium Renovations Are Latest Masterpiece Designed by Janet Marie Smith," *Los Angeles Times*, April 7, 2021, https://www.latimes.com/sports/dodgers/story/2021-04-07/on-baseball-dodger-stadium-renovations-janet-marie-smith.

DODGER STADIUM

by Curt Smith

On October 8, 1957, the stockholders and directors of the Brooklyn Baseball Club announced that the franchise would move to Los Angeles for the 1958 season.[1] A welcoming parade jammed downtown LA streets.[2] On the steps of City Hall, longtime Dodgers President and owner Walter O'Malley gave Mayor Norris Poulson home plate from Ebbets Field.[3] Yet uncertainty lingered: Where would the Dodgers play?

In time, O'Malley forged Dodger Stadium, debuting in 1962 «with perfect sightlines for each of its 56,000 seats and glorious views in all directions," said noted baseball architect and urban planner Janet Marie Smith. With a nonpareil 16,000 parking spaces, it was "surrounded by Elysian Park, one of the most beautiful urban oases in America – a park within a park."[4] Exuding the charm of baseball's early-century classic sites, it avoided the later boredom of multi-sport stadiums. Fusing beauty and amenity, baseball's third-oldest major-league home still is forever young.[5]

What, though, preceded it? As a stopgap O'Malley considered the longtime Pacific Coast League's Wrigley Field, acquired by the Brooklyn franchise in February 1957[6] but housing far too few (20,450)[7] for a big-league park. Pasadena's famed football Rose Bowl (capacity 91,136)[8] was too vast for baseball. With time running out, O'Malley chose Los Angeles's 94,600-seat Memorial Coliseum[9] to house his team until a new ballpark could be built.

Opening in 1923, the Coliseum was "a football and track and field place," said Dodgers 1950-2016 radio/TV legend Vin Scully, "and football and baseball demand different configurations."[10] Left field's 250-foot foul line, later measured at 251, was the majors' shortest. To compensate, O'Malley hoisted a 42-by-140-foot screen. Center field's last bleacher row was 700 feet from the plate,[11] Angelenos bringing radios to hear Vin tell them what they couldn't see. In 1958 the seventh-place club drew 1,845,556, dwarfing Brooklyn's prior-year 1,028,258.[12] It presaged things to come.

Ahead lay "The ... Taj O'Malley,"[13] in an area of LA to which Walter already had been drawn. In May

Fans cheer on their favorite team on June 29, 2021, at Dodger Stadium.

1957 he took a helicopter ride to survey possible sites for a new park,[14] traveling two miles from downtown over a mélange of "mountains, hills, valleys, and basins."[15] At a gas station O'Malley found on a map the name of a plateau he had found especially striking on "underdeveloped city-owned ground." It was "surrounded by urbanity – freeways, a teeming population, skyscrapers, sprawl – yet in traveling up a slight but steady palm-tree-lined grade, fans had the immediate illusion, in true movie style, of a park."[16] The site's name was Chavez Ravine.

O'Malley "liked everything – the access, the vicinity, potential: the freeways above all," longtime general manager Emil J. "Buzzie" Bavasi said.[17] Later in 1957, the Los Angeles City Council voted 10-4 to accept Wrigley Field from the Dodgers, buy 300 acres of Chavez Ravine, and spend $2 million on infrastructure. LA wanted the team. "All O'Malley wanted was land. The city and county of Los Angeles had plenty of that,"[18] including Ravine hillside inhabited by "illegal Mexican immigrants."[19] To get it, O'Malley swapped his property in Watts, the site of Wrigley Field.

Aiding him was City Councilwoman Rosalind Wyman, first elected to the Council in 1953 at age 22. Believing that "people wanted sports,"[20] she vocally backed the June 3, 1958, "Dodgers Referendum" to let O'Malley buy the acreage. The vote pivoted on a five-hour June 1 KTTV "Dodger Telethon," starring baseball-loving celebrities including Jack Benny, George Burns, Ronald Reagan, Debbie Reynolds, and Joe E. Brown, chairman of the Taxpayers Committee for "Yes on Baseball." O'Malley made an eloquent plea, more than two million watching the show days before the vote. It helped the referendum pass, 351,683 to 325,898, a 25,785-vote margin.[21]

At the time, some wondered what the Dodgers don could possibly see in Chavez Ravine. Squatters'

shacks and grazing goats roamed amid the refuse. From the helicopter O'Malley had seen "dogs, possums, skunks, jackrabbits, gophers, rusty tin cans, rotting tires, moribund mattresses, and broken beer bottles."[22] The squatters included Manuel Arechiga, his wife, and four granddaughters, who were evicted in August 1957, but not before biting and bruising sheriff's deputies.[23] Other residents refused to leave until as late as 1960.[24]

Trying to block the sale, critics brought countless lawsuits, accusing O'Malley of reaping a giveaway with hidden oil and mineral rights.[25] Twice the State Supreme Court ruled in the Dodgers' favor. On September 17, 1959, groundbreaking ceremonies occurred at the Ravine. The next month the US Supreme Court ditched the protesters' last appeal. Tractors then began their work. Soon O'Malley began the task of building what he hoped would be the ultimate baseball site.[26]

On February 18, 1960, O'Malley finalized the sale, paying $494,000 to buy land, then believed to be worth $92,000,[27] to be used to build Dodger Stadium. He could afford it, that year's Dodgers drawing a National League record 2,253,887. Meantime, construction intensified. Fused: 23,000 precast concrete frames and planks. Removed: 8 million cubic yards of earth. Supervised and engineered by: Captain Emil Praeger of Praeger, Kavanagh, and Waterbury, New York. Constructed by: Vinnell Constructors of Alhambra, California.[28]

Used: 19 giant earth-movers, 80,000 tons of asphalt and paving for parking lots and roads, 546 tons of cast iron, 40,000 cubic yards of concrete, 3 million pounds of reinforced steel, 3 tons of aluminum nuts and bolts, and 375,000 feet of lumber. Employed: Up to 342 workers at peak. Busted: the budget, $23 million, about twice the original estimate. Crucial was O'Malley's passion to outdo any park ever built – to Scully, the "Golden Gulch";[29] to the public, "Dodger Stadium" or "Chavez Ravine – used interchangeably – involving him at every level.

In the Dodgers' 1956 tour of Japan, Walter had discovered ground-level suite seating – "dugout boxes" – built by connecting "the roof of the first-base dugout with the roof of the third-base dugout,"[30] patrons and players getting the same up-close view. Mentally, O'Malley listed this and other features that he felt the new park should have like Santa Ana Bermuda grass, red infield and warning track clay, and palm trees beyond the outfield. Praeger preferred an 85,000-seat enclosed site with a center-field fountain.

O'Malley craved a grand location and scenic park, meriting "enormous credit for declining to enclose the outfield."[31]

Instead, Walter approved single-tier bleachers, five-tier seating (a baseball first) just past each line, and perpendicular bullpens to separate the bleachers from foul-line seats. Parking spaces held "cars on 21 terraced lots at five different levels. Seating and parking levels were color-coordinated for fan convenience"[32] – top (sky blue), loge (tangerine orange), Stadium Club and dugout box (red, yellow, and blue), reserved (sea foam green), and field (yellow) – each minimizing a need for elevators, escalators, stairs, and lengthy treks after parking.[33]

Janet Marie Smith has related an "urban legend I believe to be true" about LA's kinship with its ubiquitous symbol: the car. Chavez Ravine's Club level – itself a baseball first – had a very wide concourse. Until officials ruled that gasoline-powered autos "would be unsafe inside an occupied stadium,"[34] O'Malley hoped Club level members could drive to their seats, cars parked behind them. In 1960 an aerial photo showed "Dodger Stadium beginning to take shape,"[35] several decks faintly evident of the first privately financed park since Yankee Stadium opened in 1923.

As Smith, an adviser to the Orioles (Camden Yards), Red Sox (Fenway Park), and Dodgers (since 2012), observed in her essay, "Ballpark Diaries: Notes from the Field," the "glorious setting, carved into the hillside of Chavez Ravine," enchants.[36] At first glance, it might seem that O'Malley positioned the park to "capitalize on the views of the snowcapped San Gabriel mountains and the green of Elysian Park to the north and the downtown skyline to the south." In fact, in 1962 "downtown's only tower was City Hall to the East."[37] The city grew with the team, the ballpark's third-base line fixed due north on the field to curb interference from the sun.

From any perspective, O'Malley believed in the Dodgers park and his Westward-Ho, claiming history would redeem him. By the end of 1961, the Coliseum had lured 7,974,738 since 1958,[38] vindicating the trek from Brooklyn. Jerry Doggett, a 1956-87 Dodgers announcer, recalled how the first time "I came out of the dugout [in 1962] and looked up, I talked with Walter, and he was as pleased as a person could possibly be."[39] Having survived landslides and lawsuits, O'Malley and Rosalind Wyman walked through the Club level the night before 1962's Opening Day,[40] marveling at the result.

The next afternoon, April 10, after a parade passed through Center City, squeaky-clean Dodger Stadium opened with two temporary gaffes: Emil Praeger forgot to include water fountains – ironic given his design – and foul poles were in foul ground. For 1962, the NL ruled them fair. Doggett remarked, "It was almost like the club's Brooklyn past,"[41] crystallized by a 1926 game against the Braves when three Dodgers occupied third base.[42] In 1963 the team relocated home plate slightly so that each pole became fair.[43] Consequently, the Ravine's most visible landmark is not foul-ball homers but a 10-story elevator shaft bearing the team's logo rising behind home plate atop the upper deck.

Most found dimensions fair: lines, 330 feet; alleys, 380 (370 in 1969 and 385 in 1983); left- and right-center, 395; and center, 410 (400 in 1969). The top deck linked first to third base, other decks reaching past the poles. Unique: upturned concrete sunscreen poured in place on the top deck, a zig-zag wavy pavilion roof using folded corrugated metal, and four hexagonal scoreboards: two field-level auxiliary boards, baseball's largest message/out-of-town board in left, and an in-game information board in right. A 10-foot (8 in 1973) fence tied left- and right-center.[44] The 1000 Elysian – Greek for "paradise" – Park Avenue address hailed baseball's first park, Elysian Fields in Hoboken, New Jersey.[45]

In Brooklyn O'Malley had telecast each home set; in LA, almost none. Since many felt that "here was the finest sports palace ever conceived,"[46] they were happy to pay in person. The change profited radio: hence Scully. Atypically, the Ravine opener was locally televised, Vin emceeing the pregame rite. Attendance was 52,564: Trapped in traffic, some gave up and went

The Jackie Robinson statue stands near the Center Field Entrance at Dodger Stadium.

home. O'Malley's wife, Kay, tossed out the first ball. Johnny Podres lost, 6-3, to Cincinnati's Bob Purkey. First hit/run: The Reds' Eddie Kasko. Homer: mate Wally Post. Dodgers hit: Duke Snider. LA run: Jim Gilliam. "Reds Crash Stadium Party," wrote the *Los Angeles Times*.[47]

When Dodger Stadium opened, it had far more foul turf than now: "as much as multipurpose parks, presumably so a 50-yard line for football would fit," Smith wrote in another essay, "How the Firsts Have Fared."[48] Architect Edward H. Fickett's drawings at the University of Southern California even suggested placing "the outfield seating on wheels so it could be moved to alter the center field for football or other uses."[49] Ultimately, O'Malley was wise enough to see the folly of a multisport yard. By 1999, then-owner Fox Entertainment Group even axed the "1962 dugout suites ... and minimized foul territory to create a [solely baseball] premium seating area in front of the field box seats."[50]

O'Malley Sr. resigned as president in 1970, remaining owner and chairman till his death in 1979. On January 4, 1997, his successor, son Peter, met at the park with Scully, by 1976 fan vote named "most memorable personality" in LA Dodgers history.[51] Learning that O'Malley Jr. and sister Terry meant to sell the franchise, Vin felt "a ... closure of a major portion of my life."[52] Next year media czar Rupert Murdoch's News Corp. bought the team for $311 million.[53] In 2004 Fox sold it to Frank McCourt, who went bankrupt, yielding to Guggenheim Baseball Management LLC in 2012, after which continuity again became a Dodgers rite.

Almost from the start the Ravine became a magnet. "People poured in from all over California, western Canada and northern Mexico, even Hawaii to marvel at the sheer grandeur of the place," Frank Finch wrote.[54] Pitching became a theme; speed, another, as in Dodgers shortstop Maury Wills stealing a record 104 bases in 1962. "It'd been [at Brooklyn] all power," Wills said. By contrast, now "I'd steal second and ... Gilliam sacrificed me to third and I'd come home on an infield out." Said Mets skipper Casey Stengel: "He's the most amazin' slider I ever saw."[55]

What has been amazin' – at least indelible – about Dodger Stadium? In 1962 the ex-Brooks lost a tie-breaking playoff to the Giants but drew a big-league record 2,755,184 against the American League Angels' 1,144,063 in the latter's first of four years of tenancy. Sandy Koufax no-hit the Mets. Next year he went 25-5, tossed his second of four no-nos, and won two

games in the Dodgers' World Series sweep of the Yankees. "When Sandy was in top form, I became a fan out there on the field," said 1962-63 batting titlist Tommy Davis. "You sometimes forgot you're playing baseball because Sandy's controlling the whole game."[56]

LA took the 1965 Series, enduring Sandy's next-year retirement from an arthritic elbow: "I don't regret for one minute the 12 years I've spent with baseball, but I could regret one season too many."[57] Koufax finished 165-87, leading the NL thrice in victories (high, 27), four times in strikeouts (best, 382), and five years in ERA (at or below 2.54). The Ravine evokes Don Drysdale, too, Big D copping 1962's 25-9 Cy Young Award and in 1968 pursuing Walter Johnson's record for consecutive scoreless innings: 56 in 1913. By May 31, Don had 44 straight. "Curve – hit him!" Vin Scully etched a no-out bases-full ninth-inning pitch to Dick Dietz, the streak ending, or had it? "Hold everything!" – the umpire gesturing "as if to say Dietz stuck his arm in front of the pitch."

Drysdale escaped the jam, his streak reaching 58⅔ innings, then tore his rotator cuff, retiring in 1969 with a 209-166 record.[58] He broadcast for several teams and networks, the last six years with the Dodgers. On July 3, 1993, Don, 56, had a fatal heart attack in Montreal. That night Scully, a close friend, disclosed it during the game: "Never have I been asked to make an announcement that hurts me as much as this one," Vin said. "And I say it to you as best I can with a broken heart."[59]

Dodger Stadium also evokes history – in 1969 Willie Stargell belted the first homer out of the park, estimated at 506 feet 6 inches over the pavilion roof. (He later encored at 470 feet.) Others: Ronald Acuña Jr., Giancarlo Stanton, Mark McGwire, Dodger Mike Piazza, and Fernando Tatis Jr.[60] – and heroism. In 1976 two men left the bleachers. One laid the US flag out, spreading lighter fluid. The other lit a second before Cubs outfielder Rick Monday raced to take it "away from him!" exclaimed Scully, a World War II veteran. "That guy was going to set fire to the American flag! ... Rick will get an ovation, and properly so. ... And now, a lot of the folks are standing. And now the whole ballpark!"[61]

Chavez Ravine conjures Hollywood. "Forget the glitz," said longtime vice president of player personnel Al Campanis. "It's TV-film tradition that matters." Movie scenes have been filmed at Dodger Stadium. TV in the 1960s lured Dodgers Koufax, Drysdale, and coach Leo Durocher, among others, Big D appearing on *The Rifleman* and variety shows with Red Skelton, Groucho Marx, and Steve Allen. In a 1963 episode of *Mister Ed*, a series based on a talking horse, Ed offered hitting advice to Durocher.[62] Celebrities like Benny and Cary Grant regularly visited the ballpark,[63] as stars like Arsenio Hall, Jennifer Lopez, and Matthew McConaughey did in later years.[64]

The Ravine includes rites like the best-selling Dodger Dog, the "Peanut Guy" Roger Owens, 1954-76 manager Walter Alston's "solidity," and and 1976-96 skipper Tommy Lasorda's wit: "Baseball is like driving, it's the one who gets home safely that counts."[65] Scout Mike Brito was another institution, approached by Campanis in 1979 when pitcher Bob Welch began struggling. Al: "What are you doing tonight?" Brito: "Nothing special. Why?" Campanis: "I want you to go down to field level." Standing behind the plate in a dugout box, Mike used a radar gun to judge pitches. His "The Straw-Hat Man" attire made the cigar-chomping Brito famous.[66]

Dodger Stadium recalls precedent. In 1967 it braved the ballpark's first rainout after 737 games.[67] The '78 Angelenos became the first team to draw 3 million or more in attendance.[68] In 1980 the Ravine debuted a large screen, high-definition left-field Electric "Diamond Vision Scoreboard" with line score, lineup, and replay; shortly, most of baseball followed. In turn, it was replaced in 2013 by a new state-of-the-art video board.[69] In 1984 Dodger Stadium unveiled a star-spangled precedent, hosting part of that year's Summer Olympics, the first privately financed Games.[70]

Another first buoyed Opening Day 1981: 20-year-old rookie Fernando Valenzuela, found in 1977 in Mexico by Dodgers scout Corito Varona, hurling a shutout in his first big-league start. "Got him swinging! And a little child shall lead them!" Vin cried. "Fernandomania included arguably baseball's first Spanish-speaking broadcaster translating English into Spanish for Valenzuela, then back: Ecuador-born Jaime Jarrin arrived in LA in 1955, began play-by-play in 1959, and got the 1998 Hall of Fame Ford C. Frick Award for broadcast excellence, joining Scully and past Dodgers Red Barber and Ernie Harwell. He retired in 2022.[71]

In time, O'Malley had Scully do TV as well as radio. Other announcers ferried play-by-play, too. After René Cárdenas trained Jarrin, he went to Houston, returning to LA in 1982-96. From 1977 to 2004, Ross Porter shared radio/TV, using statistics like Roy Acuff did a fiddle. In 1989 Vin waived a road trip, Drysdale away. The game finally ended in the 22nd inning, LA winning, 1-0. By then, even statistics looked good. In 2005 Brooklyn native Charley Steiner joined Scully, so wowed by Vin as a child that Mom bought him a right-handed mitt at 6, assuming that her left-handed son's glove would fit that hand. Steiner, a future five-time Emmy Award winner,[72] soon found where his future lay: above the field, not on it.[73]

Dodger Stadium recalls defeat. "Big Blue" (a Dodgers moniker) trailed 1985's best-of-seven League Championship Series to St. Louis but led Game Six, 5-4, in a one out and two Cardinals on base ninth inning. Lasorda and reliever Tom Niedenfuer communed on the mound, deciding to pitch to Jack Clark, who promptly homered: Redbirds win, 7-5. Later, the Dodgers manager consoled a shattered Niedenfuer, saying, "We wouldn't be there without your [19 regular-season] saves. ... [you] should talk to the media – be a Dodger."[74]

The Ravine also evokes victory. An injury to each leg made Kirk Gibson ostensibly unable even to pinch-hit in 1988's Series opener. In the ninth, A's up 4-3, Kirk told Lasorda he could hit. Eyeing a monitor, NBC TV's Scully said, "And look who's coming up!" Barely able to swing, fouling off pitches, Gibson worked a 3-and-2 count. Then: "High fly ball into right field! She is gone!" Vin glittered, silent another 67 seconds, letting the crowd hold sway. Finally: "In a year that has been so improbable, the impossible has happened!"[75] Lasorda, who called the park "Blue Heaven on earth," levitated.[76] Kirk pumped fists like pistons. Next day NBC ran an elegiac feature tying the plot to film's *The Natural* – except that by contrast even fiction paled.

Three years earlier lanky right-hand pitcher Orel Hershiser had gone 19-3 in his second full major-league season. Now, in World Series Game Five, up 5-2, he faced Oakland's Tony Phillips. "Got him!" Scully said of Orel's second 1988 Classic triumph. "They've done it! Like the 1969 Mets, it's the Impossible Dream revisited!" The previous month Hershiser had lived another dream, forging 59 straight scoreless innings to break Drysdale's 1968 record.[77] Thrice leading the NL in innings, Orel pitched for LA through 1994, spent five years with three other clubs, then returned in 2000 to Chavez Ravine, retiring at age 42 with a 204-150 record.[78]

In its seventh decade, Dodger Stadium respects age. Don Sutton pitched for Los Angeles in 1966-80 and then for four other teams, returning to the Ravine for a final year in 1988. Retiring at 43, he was, as of his death in 2021, LA's all-time leader in innings pitched, wins (233), shutouts, and strikeouts.[79] (Clayton Kershaw passed him in K's in 2022.[80]) By comparison, in 1992, Eric Karros launched the Dodgers' record of five consecutive Rookies of the Year, preceding Mike Piazza, Raul Mondesi, Hideo Nomo, and Todd Hollandsworth.[81] Youth had been served.

Even in a pitching-friendly park, offense can rule. In 2000 Gary Sheffield tied Duke Snider's then-single-season home-run mark (43): the sole Angeleno to top .300 (.325) with at least 30 homers, 100 runs batted in, 100 walks, and 100 runs for a second straight year.[82] LA's single-season best includes Tommy Davis's 153 RBIs and 230 hits (both 1962) and Shawn Green's 49 home runs (2001).[83] Career highs include Sheffield's on-base percentage (.438), slugging percentage (.643), and OPS (1.081).[84]

Like Koufax, Big D, Hershiser, and Sutton, Kershaw symbolized artistry on the mound: NL 2014 MVP, 2011-13-14 Cy Young Award honoree, thrice league-best in wins, first to lead baseball in ERA four straight years (2011-14), and as Steve Garvey had and Justin Turner would, received the Roberto Clemente Award in 2012 for exemplifying "extraordinary character, community involvement, philanthropy, and positive contributions, both on and off the field"[85] – the same kind of service that lets the Los Angeles Dodgers Foundation programs help 2.3 million children each year.[86]

LADF grants and programs generously support such projects as "Dodgers Dreamfields," "LA Reads," and "Dodgers RBI [Reviving Baseball in Inner Cities]."[87] Such charity has been contagious. In his 2000-04 Chavez Ravine career, outfield alumnus Green donated $1.5 million to the Dodgers' Dream Foundation, backed four local Dodgers "Dreamfields," and broke his 415-consecutive-game streak to honor the Jewish holy day of Yom Kippur, not playing on September 5, 2001.[88]

Dodger Stadium has shared sorrow. On September 11, 2001, four planes were seized by terrorists and crashed into New York City, the Pentagon, and rural Pennsylvania, killing nearly 3,000 Americans. Six days later the Dodgers played their first post-9/11 game, at the Ravine. In a pregame video, President George W. Bush asked the nation to "go back to work." Scully then spoke: "And so, despite a heavy heart, baseball gets up out of the dirt, brushes itself off, and will follow his command, hoping in some small way to inspire the nation to do the same."[89]

Chavez Ravine has known joy. On September 18, 2006, the NL West title at stake, LA trailed San Diego, 9-5, in the ninth inning. Traffic exited while Jeff Kent, J.D. Drew, and Russell Martin then went deep. As cars U-turned, Marlon Anderson homered – a fourth straight homer: 9-all. Scully beamed: "Can you believe this inning? In fact, can you believe this game?" San Diego regained a 10-9 10th-inning edge, whereupon Kenny Lofton walked in the home half and Nomar Garciaparra "hits a high fly ball to left field! It is away out and gone! The Dodgers win it, 11 to 10! Unbelievable!"[90]

Dodger Stadium means change. In 2008 the team moved its longtime Florida spring-training site from Vero Beach to Arizona. To salute a half-century on the West Coast, the Dodgers that March played an exhibition against the Boston Red Sox – the Coliseum's first baseball since 1961 and game's largest-ever crowd, 115,300. Permanent seats cut left field by 50 feet to 201, the screen rising from 18 feet to 60 to compensate. The Red Sox won, 7-4.[91] That year a $412 million project to build a Dodgers museum, shops, and restaurants around the Ravine was also disclosed.

In person or on TV, the Ravine defines living color. In 2012 Frank McCourt sold the team to Guggenheim Baseball Management, which modernized the park, yet preserved the past. It matched new signage and seating with the original seating color scheme, assigned by Emil Praeger to "mimic the LA sunset."[92] The next year, investing "over $150 million,"[93] Guggenheim hired D'Agostino Izzy Quirk Architects to serve a public that bought food, beer, caps, and shirts from LA's official store and brought children to "play areas." New President and CEO Stan Kasten was addressing the Average Joe.

Kasten's view resonated because while "suites and premium areas ... had been added,"[94] concourses gave Joe Fan little chance to change seating levels, walk around the park, or be entertained. So right- and left-field boards and ultimately other message boards were replaced by "state-of-the-art [high-definition] video boards," restoring their former hexagon shape but "22 percent larger with 66 percent more active viewing area."[95] Renovation brought wider concourses, "companion seats," and "improved wheelchair-access areas."[96] New standing-room areas gave "fans a unique view of the game."[97] A better sound system also muted echo.

Meanwhile, flashing strobe arcs were making the Ravine a better-lighted place, later replaced by even brighter LED lights that went on instantly, not gradually, changing the "game experience,"[98] Kasten said. A "state-of-the-art wi-fi network and cellular antenna system upped cellphone and internet connectivity from mobile devices." Change brought brighter signage and more picnic areas,[99] new and expanded restrooms, concessions, indoor home and away batting cages, better training and conditioning facilities, and a larger footprint of the Dodgers clubhouse, as Kasten had vowed.

Once he asked, "Where, oh where, is the memorabilia? This is the Dodgers!" – a team proving Faulkner's saw "The past is never dead. It's not even past."[100] Yearbooks and media guides were hung for public perusal. Staff re-created "MVP Awards, Gold Gloves, Silver Sluggers, the decades of program covers ... enlarged and framed like artwork."[101] New entry plazas housed autographed baseballs, life-size bobbleheads, and five-foot replicas of Dodgers Cy Young winners.[102] Another change became past "[logos being] ... painted onto different areas" from Brooklyn's only world title in 1955 to "1959 Dodgers 50th Anniversary."[103] Wrote Janet Marie Smith: "There is something about an anchor to the past that makes this a great game today."[104]

Outside, in 1962, $6 million in landscaping included planting three palms beyond center field: to Vin, "The Three Sisters."[105] In 2012 they were moved to allow new power in buried duct banks under them, then next year to build the plaza and bullpen-overlook bars. Officials unsure if roots would survive in "burlap bags during construction"[106] shifted trees to a temporary site, then planted and dug them up again. The trees now "grace the Dodgers bullpen" – where better to ensure saves? – "carefully replanted" to realign their trunks.[107]

"More than 3,400 trees cover[ed] the 300 acres of beautiful landscape" in 2001, "maintained by a full-time staff."[108] A decade later each tree displaced for plazas at a ballpark entry was replanted and more than 100 added. Old highway signs were replaced by corrugated metal signs in 1962's hexagonal scoreboard shape. Red bougainvillea matched the color of the Dodgers' home uniform number.[109] Befitting a camera-phone age, in 2015 Dodger Stadium became the second most Instagrammed site in the world.[110]

By then, many performers had sung in a park largely defined by Scully's tenor. Among them: David Bowie, Eric Clapton, Michael Jackson, Elton John, KISS, The Beatles, The Bee Gees, The Rolling Stones, and U2. In 1994 Jose Carreras, Placido Domingo, and Luciano Pavarotti gave a one-night-only concert performance at Dodger Stadium: "Encore – the Three Tenors." Paul McCartney later starred, with Ringo

Starr as guest performer, singing 38 songs in "an epic three-hour concert."[111] Less secularly, Pope John Paul II celebrated Mass there on September 16, 1987.[112]

"Never say Dodger fans do not love their history," Smith attests, the franchise's music between the lines among baseball's most inspiring.[113] Prior to 2022, the uniform numbers of eight players and two managers had been retired: 1 (Pee Wee Reese), 2 (Lasorda), 4 (Snider), 19 (Gilliam), 20 (Sutton), 24 (Alston), 32 (Koufax), 39 (Campanella), 42 (Jackie Robinson), and 53 (Drysdale). Gil Hodges' number 14 was retired in 2022, Valenzuela's 34 a year later. All were Baseball Hall of Famers save Gilliam, who died in the 1978 season, and Fernando.[114]

In 2012-20, Guggenheim's LA baseball debut, Big Blue each year but the first won the NL West. In 2017 it became the first team to go 43-7 in a 50-game period since the 1912 Giants,[115] but lost a seven-game Fall Classic to Houston, notably the Astros' 13-12 10-inning Game Five victory deemed "one of the greatest World Series games ever."[116] Ten Dodgers including Reese, Campy, and Big D comprised the Ravine's third-deck Ring of Honor. In May, Scully became the 11th, a mic, not a number, on his plaque.

A year earlier, more than 24,000 at the annual "FanFest" hailed the man who perhaps more than anyone defined Ravine and Dodgers history. "As the Legend said Goodbye, the World of Baseball Paid Loving Tribute," the 2017 Dodgers Yearbook wrote of Vin's last radio/TV year.[117] On April 11, 2016, LA's Elysian Park Avenue address was renamed "1000 Vin Scully Avenue." That September 23, Vin Scully Appreciation Day, he got a key to the City of Los Angeles, tributes from Koufax and Kershaw, actor Kevin Costner, and fellow mic men Jarrin and Steiner, and a Dodgers blue carpet exit for Vin and wife Sandi.[118]

Scully won a lifetime Emmy, aired 25 World Series, made every major radio/TV Hall of Fame, and was named "Top Sportscaster of All Time" by the American Sportscasters Association. His record 67 years with the Dodgers made Vin integral to the Ravine. At his last home game, a sellout crowd and Dodgers and Giants players, tipping their caps, said so long. After Vin's last game a week later in San Francisco, he bade farewell, quoting an Irish poem: "May God give you for every storm, a rainbow, For every tear, a smile, For every care, a promise, And a blessing in each trial. For every problem life sends, A faithful friend to share, For every sigh, a sweet song, And an answer for each prayer."[119]

In 2017 Fox Television's Joe Davis became LA's lead TV play-by-play man, Hershiser on color. Today, Garciaparra, Karros, Jessica Mendoza, José Mota, Stephen Nelson, Tim Neverett, Steiner, Valenzuela, Kirsten Watson, Dontrelle Willis, and Pepe Yñiguez also buoy Dodgers radio/TV.[120] In 2018 Jaime Jarrin entered the Ring of Honor[121] and Walker Buehler started the franchise's first combined no-hitter. Chavez Ravine lists 13 no-nos, the first by the Angels' Bo Belinsky and eight by the Dodgers' Koufax (three), Bill Singer, Valenzuela, Kevin Gross, Ramón Martinez, and Kershaw.[122] In Series Game Three against Boston, Max Muncy's 18th-inning blast gave LA a victory after the longest postseason set of 7 hours and 20 minutes.[123]

In 2019 Dodgers attendance peaked at 3,974,309, the team also breaking the NL season record with 279 home runs.[124] The 2020 Angelenos outlasted the 29 other teams – and COVID pandemic. In March baseball canceled spring training. In July it ordained a 60-game season, sans spectators.[125] The Dodgers' 30-10 start was the best since the 31-9 2001 Mariners.[126] Los Angeles ended the regular season 43-17, its winning percentage a post-1960 expansion high .717. Extrapolated to 162 games, LA's 116 victories would tie the 1906 Cubs and 2001 Mariners.[127] Mookie Betts, acquired from Boston, and A.J. Pollock led in home runs (16), Corey Seager and Justin Turner in average (.307), and Kershaw in victories (6) and ERA (2.16).[128]

The pandemic extended postseason, the Dodgers sweeping Milwaukee in the wild-card series. They ousted San Diego in the best-of-five Division Series, edged the Braves in the LCS, and beat Tampa Bay in the 2020 Fall Classic.[129] Seager won the Series MVP Award.[130] LA's director of baseball operations Andrew Friedman was named Major League Baseball Executive of the Year[131] and his team Baseball America's Major League Organization of the Year[132] for winning the bicoastal franchise's seventh world title since 1955 and first since 1988.

Since then, it has tried to top the topper. In 2021 Los Angeles lost the West for the first time since 2012, but made the postseason a record ninth straight year – 106 victories the most for a team that hadn't won its division or league.[133] A year later, the Ravine hosted the All-Star Game, six Dodgers chosen including starting pitcher Kershaw. LA won a franchise-high 111 sets but lost the 2022 Division Series to San Diego, not advancing despite the divisional era's best regular-season record. "It's crushing," said NL 2016 Manager of the Year Dave Roberts.[134]

The 2023 Dodgers went 100-62, 16 games ahead of second-place Arizona, but again stumbled in October. In the Division Series, the D-backs tamed Big Blue at Dodger Stadium, 11-2 and 4-2. In Game Three at Phoenix, Arizona became the first big-league team to hit four postseason home runs in an inning.[135] After three batters had gone deep, Gabriel Moreno's drive was ruled a homer, then reversed by instant replay. Unfazed, Moreno smashed a drive "to the moon," cried TBS broadcaster Bob Costas. It presaged another 4-2 LA loss for the club with the most wins (317) in three years (2021-23) not to make a World Series.[136] Brooklyn's ancient cry, "Wait Till Next Year," rarely seemed so poignant.

Despite that, by 2023 a $100 million center-field plaza renovation at Chavez Ravine included a children's playground, relocation there of Jackie Robinson's statue from the left-field entrance, and display feting "The Legends of Dodger Baseball." It hailed Steve Garvey, Kirk Gibson, Orel Hershiser, Fernando Valenzuela, Maury Wills, 1949-58 Dodgers pitcher, 1956 Cy Young Award recipient, and founder of baseball's first community relations department Don Newcombe, and LA's 1969-80 and 1982 nonpareil pinch-hitter and 1980-2012 coach Manny Mota.[137]

In 2015 Stan Kasten and Dodgers Chairman and part-owner Mark Walter had commissioned a statue to be unveiled on the 70th anniversary of Jackie Robinson's breaking the color line – the Ravine's first. Oakland-based Haitian-American artist Branly Cadet[138] was named to create it, prior works including public figures like Congressman Adam Clayton Powell Jr. in New York City and educator Octavius Catto in Philadelphia. They showed, said Janet Marie Smith, "the power of a bronze to tell the story of a man."[139]

Working with widow Rachel and daughter Sarah Robinson, Smith was struck by how the statue heightened the effect of Jackie sliding into home plate. On the sculpture's base lie several Robinson quotes, the most familiar "A life is not important except for the impact it has on others."[140] On April 15, 2017, 20 years after the pioneer's number 42 was retired by baseball, Cadet's statue was unveiled. Baseball's first Black owner, Magic Johnson, said that "Jackie paved the way"[141] for him to invest in the Dodgers, Robinson's impact having helped end segregation.

On June 18, 2022, another graceful Cadet statue showing Sandy Koufax's classic leg kick[142] was dedicated in the "Legends" area flanking Jackie's. "As teammates, we were bound together by a single interest and common goal. To win," the pitcher's quote read. "Nothing else mattered and nothing else would do."[143] Koufax spoke modestly at the event, saying, "I think my only regret today is that so many are no longer with us," including the ailing Scully, who died on August 2.[144] Sandy's big-league career began with the 1955-56 Dodgers, Robinson's last two years before retiring. Vin broadcast each. Any definition of the franchise must accent all three.

When Elysian Park Avenue was renamed in 2016, the Dodgers "planted a double row of trees and firestick plants along the street to celebrate," Smith wrote.[145] Yearly the palms and lilacs blossom as if to coincide with Opening Day: apt for Scully, who helped each season bloom with poetry and gentle humor, and baseball, each year renewing its need for courage and resilience, Vin once musing of an injured player, "He's listed day to day. Aren't we all?"

The book *A Baseball Century* wrote, "More difficult than imagining America without baseball is imagining baseball without the Dodgers."[146] As difficult is imagining the Dodgers without the wonder of Chavez Ravine.

SOURCES

Thanks to the sources cited under "Interviews by author." Grateful appreciation is made to reprint play-by-play and color radio text courtesy of The Miley Collection. In addition to sources cited in the Notes, especially the Society for American Baseball Research, the author consulted the Baseball-Reference.com and Retrosheet.org websites, box scores, season, and team pages, batting and pitching logs, and other material relevant to this history. FanGraphs.com provided statistical information. Beyond the sources cited in the Notes, the author consulted:

Reidenbaugh, Lowell. *The Sporting News Take Me Out to the Ball Park* (St. Louis: Sporting News Publishing Co., 1983).

Wood, Bob. *Dodger Dogs to Fenway Franks: And All the Wieners in Between* (New York: McGraw-Hill Publishing Co., 1988).

Interviews by author:

Emil J. "Buzzie" Bavasi, 1978.

Jerry Coleman, 2010.

Bob Costas, 1988.

Jerry Doggett, 1992.

Dick Enberg, 2014.

Pat Hughes, 2022.

Jorge Iber, 2022.

William Johnson, 2005.

Jon Miller, 1991.

Phil Mushnick, 2007.

Vin Scully, 1986 and 1992.

Charley Steiner, 2007.

George Vecsey, 2012.

NOTES

1   Gene Schorr. *A Pictorial History of the Dodgers: From Brooklyn to Los Angeles.* (New York: Leisure Press, 1985), 104.

2   Frank Finch, *The Los Angeles Dodgers: The First Twenty Years.* (Virginia Beach, Virginia: Jordan & Company, 1977), 16.

3   Finch, 17.

4   Janet Marie Smith, "How the Firsts Have Fared" (speech, NINE Conference, Phoenix, Arizona, March 2016.)

5   Thomas Harrigan, "Every Ballpark, from Oldest to Newest," MLB.com, February 22, 2022. https://www.mlb.com/news/mlb-parks-from-oldest-to-newest.

6   Jim Gordon, "Wrigley Field (Los Angeles)," SABR.org. https://sabr.org/bioproj/park/wrigley-field-los-angeles/.

7   https://www.ballparksofbaseball.com/ballparks/los-angeles-wrigley-field/.

8   https://uclabruins.com/facilities/the-rose-bowl/1.

9   Philip J. Lowry, ed., *Green Cathedrals: The Ultimate Celebration of Major and Negro League Ballparks* (New York: Addison-Wesley, 1992), 170.

10   Vin Scully interview, 1992.

11   *Green Cathedrals*, 168-70.

12   Finch, 24.

13   Finch, 41.

14   Emil J. "Buzzie" Bavasi interview, 1978.

15   Steven Travers, *A Tale of Three Cities: The 1962 Baseball Season* (Washington: Potomac Books, 2009), 9.

16   Travers, 25.

17   Bavasi interview, 1978.

18   Travers, 9.

19   Travers, 25.

20   "Blue Heaven," *2018 Los Angeles Dodgers Yearbook* (New York: Professional Sports Publications), 10.

21   https://www.walteromalley.com/en/features/chavez-ravine/Timeline.

22   Finch, 13.

23   *Green Cathedrals*, 52.

24   https://www.walteromalley.com/en/features/chavez-ravine/Overview/view-all.

25   Finch, 14.

26   https://www.walteromalley.com/en/features/chavez-ravine/Overview/view-all.

27   Matt Borelli, "This Day in Dodgers History: Walter O'Malley Buys Land to Build Dodger Stadium," dodgerblue.com, February 18, 2022. https://dodgerblue.com/this-day-dodgers-history-walter-omalley-completes-purchase-land-build-dodger-stadium/2022/02/18/.

28   https://www.walteromalley.com/en/dodger-stadium/construction-facts/Page-1.

29   https://www.walteromalley.com/en/dodger-stadium/construction-facts/Page-1.

30   Smith, "How the Firsts Have Fared," 12.

31   Bruce Adams and Margaret Engel, *Baseball Vacations* (New York: Fodor's Travel Publications, 2000), 312.

32   Adams and Engel, 312.

33   Randi Radcliff, "Dodger Stadium's History, Facts, and Nostalgia," dodgersway.com, June 6, 2017. https://dodgersway.com/2017/06/06/dodgers-stadium-history/.

34   Smith, "How the Firsts Have Fared," 13.

35   Finch, 45.

36   Janet Marie Smith, "Ballpark Diaries: Notes from the Field," *NINE: A Journal of Baseball History and Culture* 30(1): 16-17.

37   Smith, "Ballpark Diaries: Notes from the Field," 17.

38   https://www.baseball-reference.com/teams/LAD/.

39   Jerry Doggett interview, 1992.

40   *2018 Los Angeles Dodgers Yearbook* (New York: Professional Sports Publications), 10.

41   Doggett interview.

42   L. Robert Davids, "Three Men on Third," *Baseball Research Journal* (SABR), 1977. https://sabr.org/journal/article/three-men-on-third/.

43   *Green Cathedrals*, 53.

44   *Green Cathedrals*, 52.

45   John Thorn, "The Elysian Fields of Hoboken," OurGamemlblogs.com, December 2, 2014. https://sabr.org/latest/thorn-the-elysian-fields-of-hoboken/.

46   Travers, 1.

47   Finch, 41.

48   Smith, "How the Firsts Have Fared," 12.

49   Smith, "How the Firsts Have Fared," 12.

50   Smith, "How the Firsts Have Fared," 12.

51   Rowan Kavner, "Vin Scully Was Dodger Baseball," foxsports.com, August 2, 2022. https://www.foxsports.com/stories/mlb/vin-scully-was-dodger-baseball.

52   Larry Stewart, "There's No Change in the Booth," *Los Angeles Times*, March 20,1998, https://www.latimes.com/archives/la-xpm-1998-mar-20-sp-30847-story.html.

53   Thomas Heath and Paul Farhi, "Murdoch Adds Dodgers to Media Empire," *Washington Post*, March 20, 1998, https://www.washingtonpost.com/archive/politics/1998/03/20/murdoch-adds-dodgers-to-media-empire/4cc70d40-801d-4e53-8a8d-0af1626f0f9e/.

54   Finch, 41.

55   Finch, 42.

56   *2013 Los Angeles Dodgers Yearbook* (New York: Professional Sports Publications), 14.

57   Finch, 67.

58   Finch, 97.

59   "Don Drysdale, Hall of Fame Dodger Pitcher, Dies at 56," New York Yankee Fans Forum, July 3, 1993, https://nyyfansforum.sny.tv/forum/forum/general-baseball-forums/history-trivia-memorabilia/12613008-july-3-1993-don-drysdale-passes-away.

60   Andrew Simon, "Acuña's Derby Blast Leaves Dodger Stadium," MLB.com, July 18, 2022, https://www.mlb.com/news/home-runs-hit-out-of-dodger-stadium.

61   *Gene Schoor, A Pictorial Picture of the Dodgers: From Brooklyn to Los Angeles* (New York: Leisure Press, 1985), 202-203.

62   https://www.imdb.com/title/tt0649836/.

63   Travers, 72-73.

64   *2019 Los Angeles Dodgers Yearbook* (New York: Professional Sports Publications), 143, 145.

65   https://www.brainyquote.com/quotes/tommy_lasorda_139446.

66   Charley Steiner interview, 2007.

67   Finch, 95.

68   Schoor, 219.

69   Scott Andes, "Farewell Sweet Diamond Vision," Dodgers Way, January 21, 2013, https://dodgersway.com/2013/01/21/farewell-sweet-diamond-vision/.

70   "Peter Victor Ueberroth," Encyclopedia.com, May 29, 2018, https://www.encyclopedia.com/people/sports-and-games/sports-biographies/peter-victor-ueberroth.

71   A Martinez, "Veteran Baseball Broadcaster Jaime Jarrin Says Goodbye," NPR.org, October 14, 2022, https://www.npr.org/2022/10/14/1129001701.

72   https://www.mlb.com/dodgers/team/broadcasters.

73   Steiner interview, 2007.

74   Richard Justice, "Lasorda Doesn't Dodge Rehashing Fateful Pitch to Cardinals' Clark," *Washington Post*, February 14, 1986, https://www.washingtonpost.com/archive/sports/1986/02/14/lasorda-doesnt-dodge-rehashing-fateful-pitch-to-cardinals-clark/6ac83422-0a40-4677-b9b0-6aa1a48779a7/.

75   https://www.youtube.com.com/watch?v=jeGFSEIONyA.

76   Matthew Moreno, "Tommy Lasorda Receives Lifetime Achievement Award at 17th Annual LA Sports Awards," dodgerblue.com, March 9, 2022. https://dodgerblue.com/dodgers-tommy-lasorda-lifetime-achievement-award-los-angeles-sports-awards/2022/03/09/.

77   Matthew Moreno, dodgerblue.com, September 28, 2022, https://dodgerblue.com/this-day-dodgers-history-orel-hershiser-breaks-don-drysdales-record-59-consecutive-scoreless-innings/2022/09/28/.

78   https://www.baseball-reference.com/players/h/hersho01.shtml.

79   Matt Kelly, "Sutton's Numbers Still Boggle the Mind," MLB.com, January 19, 2021, https://www.mlb.com/news/don-sutton-facts-and-figures#:~:text=While%20the%20Dodgers%E2%80%99%20history%20is%20as%20overflowing%20with,pitched%20%283%2C816%20I%2F3%29%2C%20shutouts%20%2852%29%20and%20strikeouts%20%282%2C696%29.

80   https://www.youtube.com/watch?v=1onmbbAQktg.

81   Luke Norris, "Remember When the LA Dodgers Had 5 Rookie of the Year Winners in a Row?" sportscasting.com, October 21, 2020, https://www.sportscasting.com/remember-when-the-la-dodgers-had-5-rookie-of-the-year-winners-in-a-row/.

82   *2001 Los Angeles Dodgers Yearbook* (Los Angeles: Los Angeles Dodgers, Inc.), 55.

83   https://www.baseball-reference.com/teams/LAD/leaders_bat_season.shtml.

84   https://www.baseball-reference.com/teams/LAD/leaders_bat_season.shtml.

85   https://www.mlb.com/news/roberto-clemente-award-2023-nominees.

86   *2019 Los Angeles Dodgers Yearbook* (New York: Professional Sports Publications), 154.

87   *2019 Los Angeles Dodgers Yearbook* (New York: Professional Sports Publications), 154.

88   Alan Schwarz, "Green to Sit Out on Yom Kippur," espn.com, September 5, 2021, https://www.espn.com/mlb/news/2001/0905/1248286.html.

89   https://www.mlb.com/video/scully-s-touching-speech-c18652293.

90   www.mlb.com/video/dodgers-win-on-homer-fest-c20006559.

91   Eric Stephen, "Dodgers vs. Red Sox LA Coliseum Exhibition," truebluela.com, June 20, 2020, https://www.truebluela.com/2020/6/20/21293920/dodgers--red-sox-coliseum-exhibition-2008.

92   Smith, "Ballpark Diaries," 18.

93   Smith, "How the Firsts Have Fared," 14.

94   Smith, "How the Firsts Have Fared," 15.

95   *2013 Los Angeles Dodgers Yearbook* (New York: Professional Sports Publications), 8.

96   *2013 Los Angeles Dodgers Yearbook* (New York: Professional Sports Publications), 6.

97   *2013 Los Angeles Dodgers Yearbook* (New York: Professional Sports Publications), 7.

98   Matthew Moreno, "Stan Kasten: New Dodger Stadium Lights Change 'Game Experience,'" dodgerblue.com, March 20, 2023, https://dodgerblue.com/stan-kasten-new-dodger-stadium-lights-change-game-experience/2023/03/30/#:~:text=President%20and%20CEO%20Stan%20Kasten%20revealed%20news%20of,on%20and%20off%20and%20full%20color%2C%E2%80%9D%20Kasten%20said.

99   *2013 Los Angeles Dodgers Yearbook* (New York: Professional Sports Publications), 8.

100   https://www.goodreads.com/work/quotes/2041161-requiem-for-a-nun.

101   Smith, "Ballpark Diaries," 13.

102   *2013 Los Angeles Dodgers Yearbook* (New York: Professional Sports Publications), 8.

103   *2013 Los Angeles Dodgers Yearbook* (New York: Professional Sports Publications), 7.

104   Smith, "Ballpark Diaries," 13.

105   Smith, "How the Firsts Have Fared," 15.

106   Smith, "How the Firsts Have Fared," 15.

107   Smith, "Ballpark Diaries," 17.

108   *2001 Los Angeles Dodgers Yearbook* (Los Angeles: Los Angeles Dodgers, Inc.), 89.

109   Smith, "Ballpark Diaries," 18.

110   Smith, "How the Firsts Have Fared," 14.

111   Katie Atkinson, "Paul McCartney Spreads Love with Ringo Starr, Plus More Highlights from Epic Final Tour Stop at Dodger Stadium." *Billboard*, July 14, 2019, https://www.billboard.com/music/rock/paul-mccartney-dodger-stadium-concert-recap-8519795/.

112   *2001 Los Angeles Dodgers Yearbook* (Los Angeles: Los Angeles Dodgers, Inc.), 89.

113   Smith, "Ballpark Diaries," 13.

114   Ken Gurnick, "Dodgers' All-Time Retired Numbers," MLB.com, December 1, 2021, https://www.mlb.com/dodgers/history/retired-numbers.

115   *2018 Los Angeles Dodgers Yearbook* (New York: Professional Sports Publications), 25.

116   *2018 Los Angeles Dodgers Yearbook* (New York: Professional Sports Publications), 36.

117   *2017 Los Angeles Dodgers Yearbook* (New York: Professional Sports Publications), 17.

118   *2017 Los Angeles Dodgers Yearbook* (New York: Professional Sports Publications), 32.

119   *2017 Los Angeles Dodgers Yearbook* (New York: Professional Sports Publications), 38.

120   https://www.mlb.com/dodgers/team/broadcasters.

121   *2019 Los Angeles Dodgers Yearbook* (New York: Professional Sports Publications), 55.

122   https://www.nonohitters.com/dodger-stadium-no-hitters/.

123   *2019 Los Angeles Dodgers Yearbook* (New York: Professional Sports Publications), 39.

124   Ken Gurnick, "Dodgers Set NL Single-Season Mark for Homers," MLB.com, September 5, 2019, https://www.mlb.com/dodgers/news/dodgers-set-single-season-nl-home-run-record.

125   Mark Feinsand, "Play Ball: MLB Announces 2020 Regular Season," MLB.com, July 6, 2020, https://www.mlb.com/news/mlb-announces-2020-regular-season.

126   Eric Stephen, "Battle of the Bullpens Tilts Toward Dodgers in Late Home Run Derby with Rockies," trubluela.com, September 4, 2020, https://www.truebluela.com/2020/9/4/21423734/dodgers-home-run-derby-rockies-bulllpen-recap.

127   Do-Hyoung Park, Andrew Simon, and Chad Thornburg, "Which Teams Won the Most Games in a Season?" MLB.com, October 5, 2022, https://www.mlb.com/news/most-mlb-wins-in-a-season-c289159676.

128   https://www.baseball-reference.com/teams/LAD/2020.shtml.

129   Anthony Castrovince, "Wait Is Over! Dodgers Win 1st WS since '88," MLB.com, October 28, 2020, https://www.mlb.com/news/dodgers-win-2020-world-series?game_pk=635886.

130   Richard Justice, "World Series MVP Seager 8th in Special Club," MLB.com, October 28, 2020, https://www.mlb.com/news/corey-seager-named-2020-world-series-mvp.

131   Ken Gurnick, "Friedman Wins Executive of the Year Award," MLB.com, November 17, 2020, https://www.mlb.com/dodgers/news/andrew-friedman-2020-executive-of-the-year-award.

132   Bill Plunkett, "2020 MLB Organization of the Year: Los Angeles Dodgers," baseballamerica.com, November 30, 2020, https://www.baseballamerica.com/stories/2020-mlb-organization-of-the-year-los-angeles-dodgers.

133   Blake Williams, "Dodgers' Streak of NL West Titles Snapped at 8 Years by Giants," dodgerblue.com, October 3, 2021, https://dodgerblue.com/dodgers-streak-eight-nl-west-titles-snapped-giants-division/2021/10/03/.

134   Juan Toribio, "LA's Historic Season Ends in NLDS Heartbreak," MLB.com, October 16, 2022, https://www.mlb.com/dodgers/news/dodgers-lose-nlds-to-padres-eliminated-from-2022-postseason.

135   Associated Press, "Diamondbacks 1st Team to Homer 4 Times in Postseason Inning with Big 3rd vs. Dodgers," October 11, 2023, https://apnews.com/article/diamondbacks-homers-perdomo-marte-walker-moreno-a04d774b4b90d40e5dbc20de7ca3ed81.

136   AJ Gonzales, "Dodgers Set MLB Record Without 2023 World Series Appearance," msn.com, October 13, 2023, https://www.msn.com/en-us/sports/mlb/dodgers-set-mlb-record-without-2023-world-series-appearance/ar-AA1iaNZW.

137   Eric Stephen, "Orel Hershiser & Manny Mota to Join 'Legends of Dodger Baseball' in 2023," truebluela.com, February 10, 2023, https://www.truebluela.com/2023/2/10/23594616/orel-hershiser-manny-mota-legends-baseball-honor-2023.

138   https://www.branlycadet.com.

139   Smith, "Ballpark Diaries," 14.

140   *2018 Los Angeles Dodgers Yearbook*, "Paving the Way" (New York: Professional Sports Publications), 155.

141   *2018 Los Angeles Dodgers Yearbook*, "Paving the Way" (New York: Professional Sports Publications), 155.

142   Juan Toribio, "'One of a Kind' Koufax Immortalized With Dodger Stadium Statue," MLB.com, June 18, 2022, https://www.mlb.com/news/sandy-koufax-statue-unveiled-at-dodger-stadium.

143   https://www.branlycadet.com/sandy-koufax-monument.

144   Anthony Castrovince, "Vin Scully, Legendary Broadcaster, Dies at 94," MLB.com, August 3, 2022, https://www.mlb.com/news/vin-scully-legendary-announcer-dies.

145   Smith, "Ballpark Diaries," 18.

146   Jeremy Friedlander, ed., *A Baseball Century: The First 100 Years of the National League* (New York: Rutledge Books, 1976), 177.

EXACTLY 56,000 SEATS????

by Andy McCue

For over six decades, the Dodgers have maintained that the capacity of their stadium is exactly 56,000, despite a number of renovations over the years. The original dugout seats were removed. The bottom level was extended into foul territory. Seats were added at the front of the outfield pavilions. Still, the team kept to that unlikely 56,000 figure.

The number is tied to the conditional-use permit the city issued, which called for 16,000 parking spaces (another suspiciously round figure) with a ratio of 3.5 people to each parking space. Janet Marie Smith, who has been supervising Dodger Stadium upgrades, declined to give a current figure but said exiting capacity, restrooms, and concessions have always been kept up to the 56,000 standard.

A few months after Dodger Stadium opened, Sid Ziff of the *Los Angeles Times* reported that it contained exactly 55,792 seats, but the Dodgers would not confirm that.[1] After the 1963 World Series, when they reported ticket sales to the commissioner's office, they said they had sold 57,206 tickets for both Game Three and Game Four. Some temporary seats had been added to the front edge of the lower deck for these games.

Over the last decade, the Dodgers have announced several sellouts, but no crowd over 54,307. Yet, the capacity is still listed at a nice, round 56,000.

NOTES

1   Sid Ziff, "Dupas Bout Was Close," *Los Angeles Times*, July 17, 1962: C3.

THE STRUGGLE TO BUILD DODGER STADIUM

by Andy McCue

It's easy to look up at the stadium on its hill over-looking Los Angeles and see nothing but easy – the location, the design, and, above all, the year-after-year attendance. But the process of winning the right to build Dodger Stadium was a four-year grind through dogged opponents and naïve and dilatory politicians.

In the beginning, it did seem easy. In February 1957, Walter O'Malley announced he had paid $3 million for the Pacific Coast League's Los Angeles Angels and their ballpark, Wrigley Field. Under baseball rules, this gave him the rights to the Los Angeles market. Within two weeks, Los Angeles Mayor Norris Poulson and LA County Supervisor Kenneth Hahn organized a six-person delegation to meet O'Malley at the Dodgers' Vero Beach, Florida, training site.

It was a lopsided meeting. The Los Angeles delegation, brimming with enthusiasm and frustrated after nearly two decades of misses in their desire for major-league baseball, were willing to discuss anything. O'Malley, a veteran of stadium operations and major-league politics, knew what he wanted – land to build a stadium and parking lots he could control. He suggested multiple possibilities – a city-built stadium, a long-term lease for the land, government-provided grading, freedom from property taxes, $1 annual rent on the Los Angeles Coliseum while the stadium was built. Every time he suggested something, including 500 acres near downtown, the local politicians indicated it was very possible.

Poulson emerged from the meeting full of smiles. O'Malley was less fulsome, taking the podium after the mayor and saying, "I'll take the edge off that right now." Both described the talks as throwing out ideas and said the discussion was far too preliminary to make public.[1] Poulson continued to ooze confidence, saying all problems were solvable. Upon his return to Los Angeles, he was quoted as saying, "We've got the Dodgers," but he quickly backed away.[2]

It would become clear over the next months that the two parties really had not communicated. When the Los Angeles delegation got home, reality set in. The city attorney pointed out that the Los Angeles Coliseum Commission, which controlled the facility, had not been represented in Vero Beach and would not have to honor any promises. There were still questions about the city's title to the Chavez Ravine acreage O'Malley wanted. The federal government had given it to the city with the restriction it had to be used for a "public purpose." Robert Moses had used similar limits on federal money to deny O'Malley's desire for aid in putting together a ballpark site in Brooklyn.[3] Los Angeles officials had to go to Washington, D.C., for assurances that a deal for the land was legal. Other issues appeared.

Over the next few months, O'Malley clarified his list of desires and the city named former Eisenhower administration official Chad McClellan to work out an agreement. By September the major issues had been settled. The city would provide "about" 300 acres in the Chavez Ravine area and up to $2 million in city and county investments, mostly in infrastructure near

SABR: The Rucker Archive.

Los Angeles County supervisor Kenneth Hahn and Los Angeles City Councilwoman Rosalind Wyman welcome Walter O'Malley at Los Angeles International Airport on October 23, 1957, as O'Malley arrives to set up headquarters for the Los Angeles Dodgers.

Los Angeles Mayor Norris Poulson presents key to city to the Dodgers' Walter O'Malley.

the ballpark. In return, the Dodgers would turn over the Wrigley Field property, which the city wanted for a public park, and lease 40 acres on the stadium site for another park and spend up to $500,000 for building facilities on that site, plus $60,000 in upkeep annually for 20 years. The Dodgers would also give up half the mineral rights on the site.

In the Los Angeles area at that time, mineral rights were a hot-button issue. In earlier decades, oil finds in Signal Hill and Santa Fe Springs had given some people backyard wealth and others dreams of it. In the stadium negotiations, the rights became an issue that far exceeded reality. The city council bloc opposed to the contract demanded that a site within the acreage be set aside for drilling. O'Malley had checked with oil industry people who had told him the potential of Chavez Ravine was negligible. He stood to lose little but was getting exasperated, saying he was getting the feeling he wasn't wanted, just as he felt in New York.[4] He demanded half the profits any wells might produce but said the money would go to youth sports programs.

On Sunday, October 6, 1957, Councilwoman Rosalind Wyman, the point person in attracting the Dodgers, called O'Malley in Brooklyn. She described the uncertain political situation for a final vote scheduled for the next day. She said the Dodgers' case could be strengthened if O'Malley promised that a favorable vote would guarantee that the team would come. O'Malley refused. The council did approve the contract and the next day O'Malley said the team would move.

For much of Los Angeles, the move was a momentous validation of its status as a "major league" city. O'Malley's reception at the airport later in October

was rapturous. As the Dodgers organization ramped up later in the year, ticket requests were overwhelming.

But the opposition was not going away. At the airport, a man shouldered his way to O'Malley in front of the TV cameras. He presented O'Malley with a summons. There was already a taxpayers' lawsuit even before the city council had agreed on its final offer. By December 5, it was announced that a referendum challenging the contract had qualified for the ballot in June 1958.

The opposition was a grab-bag of interests. The public face was City Councilman John Holland, whose highly conservative politics were offended by any public money being spent on a private enterprise. Other councilmen, from distant districts in the spreadeagled city, saw the stadium as a ploy to build up downtown Los Angeles to the detriment of their areas, a view echoed by some of the suburban newspapers. Movie theater owners saw the Dodgers as competition.

Holland argued that the city was losing a valuable piece of land near the city center. While tax records showed a higher value for the Wrigley Field parcel than for the Chavez Ravine land, there was no doubt that the stadium parcel had much more potential. But Holland's attempts to promote a "world scientific exposition" or a cemetery for the site found little support.[5]

The antis weren't making much progress in the city council, but they did persuade the California State Assembly's Interim Committee on Governmental Efficiency and Economy to hold hearings. One day of testimony saw both sides reiterate their positions on the contract. The only new wrinkle was John Smith, owner of the minor-league San Diego Padres and a major financier of the antis' effort, who made an offer to pay the city for the oil rights. When the city took him up on the offer, he began putting conditions on it, and no other oil company stepped forward to accept the terms. Profitable levels of oil have never been found under the stadium land. The Assembly committee never issued a report.

At first, Poulson and O'Malley decided to ignore the referendum campaign, especially when their polls indicated that two-thirds of voters supported the contract. But the drumbeat of criticism and the Assembly hearings were having their effect. Polls showed that support had fallen to 37 percent. O'Malley and Poulson began pressing the case.[6]

Speeches to civic groups multiplied. Poulson declared a Dodger Week. In April, O'Malley backed off his refusal to televise Dodgers games, scheduling the broadcast of a series in San Francisco in early May.[7] The *Los Angeles Times* redoubled its support in both editorial and news columns. On the Sunday before the vote, the Times-owned Channel 11 staged a five-hour "Dodgerthon" with celebrities joining O'Malley in supporting the stadium contract. It worked, barely, with the stadium deal affirmed by 51.8 percent of voters.

O'Malley's fears of further legal entanglements for his stadium were confirmed all too quickly. On Wednesday, June 4, 1958, with the win for Proposition B confirmed, O'Malley was talking of construction work within a month. On Friday, June 6, Superior Court Judge Kenneth Newell issued a preliminary injunction blocking the city from transferring the Chavez Ravine land to the Dodgers.

The referendum had asked voters if the stadium deal was good for the city; the taxpayers' lawsuit alleged that the deal was illegal. The key issue raised by the taxpayer suit's attorney, Phill Silver, was highly similar to the argument Robert Moses relied on in New York – whether aiding a private corporation constituted a "public purpose." The Los Angeles trial was unusual because there were few issues of fact involved.

It would focus on whether the provisions of the city council's contract with the Dodgers conformed to law.

As the trial progressed, Judge Arnold Praeger forced the lawyers for the city, the Dodgers, and Silver to focus on whether the contract gave the team too much authority in deciding exactly how to spend city money and whether the city could close public streets for the benefit of a private corporation. He also raised the broader "public purpose" issue.[8] On July 14 his decision came down squarely against the Dodgers. It was illegal, he ruled, for the city to transfer land formerly designated for public housing (a public purpose) to the Dodgers, a private corporation. It was illegal for the city to pledge to spend public money to acquire more land in the area to be given to the Dodgers, to close streets for the benefit of a private corporation, to delegate to the club decisions on exactly how to spend public money provided for grading, and how to spend the money for parks raised by any oil revenues. On the public-purpose issue, he said the city council had exceeded its authority.

"I remain an optimist," O'Malley said. "This is just another hurdle which we will have to take in stride. What hurts is the delay. Our timetable is out the window and I'm afraid San Francisco will have its new

Dodger Stadium, opened in 1962, is located just north of downtown Los Angeles.

stadium first."[9] With fans still bringing their money to the Coliseum, *Time* magazine said Los Angeles was the "Garden of Eden and the Black Hole of Calcutta rolled into one" for O'Malley.[10]

The first decision to be made was how to use the appeals process. The city and the Dodgers' attorneys calculated that an appeal couldn't be completed before 1960. With construction time tacked on after that (and the unspoken thought that any California decision might be appealed to the US Supreme Court), it looked unlikely that the Dodgers could have their stadium until late in the 1962 season. Instead, the Dodgers/city team made the decision to seek a writ from the California Supreme Court to prohibit enforcement of Praeger's decision.

On October 15, 1958, the California Supreme Court granted the city and the Dodgers a temporary writ of prohibition, but didn't render a final decision until January 13, 1959, when it unanimously overturned Praeger's decision. The justices looked at the contract in an entirely different way than Praeger had. "In considering whether the contract made by the city has a proper public purpose, we must view the contract as a whole," wrote Chief Justice Phil S. Gibson. "The fact that some of the provisions may be of benefit only to the baseball club is immaterial, provided the city receive benefits which serve a legitimate public purpose."[11]

O'Malley was bubbling. Groundbreaking for the new stadium, he said, would happen within 30 days. It would be open for the 1960 season, although it might have only 32,000 of its seats at that point, with more being added as time went on.[12] By the next day, reality had set in again. City Attorney Roger Arnebergh said O'Malley had been "extremely optimistic," noting that it would take a minimum of 60 days to clean up the paperwork and get the city/Dodgers contract signed. Only then could the Dodgers begin the process of submitting documents to the City Planning Commission. County Supervisor Frank Bonelli predicted that the stadium wouldn't open until 1964 as opponents would keep throwing up roadblocks. Silver said he would appeal.

In February and again in April, the top California court rejected Silver's pleas – first for a rehearing and then to overturn the earlier decision. The latter was the last gasp in state courts, but Silver indicated he was willing to appeal to the US Supreme Court. Since the Supreme Court didn't even come back into session until October, the delay would stretch for months more. The city/Dodgers contract was formally signed on June 3, 1959, the first anniversary of the referendum victory and 20 months after the city council first approved its terms. Barely three weeks later, on the eve of O'Malley's proposed July 1 groundbreaking, Silver appealed to the US Supreme Court.

On Monday, October 19, 1959, the Supreme Court sped up the process enormously. It declined to hear Silver's appeal, giving no reason. O'Malley, pleased but properly chastened after nearly 2½ years of fighting for what he thought he'd been promised in February 1957, said he hoped there would be no more "political" delays. Delay, he said, already had added to the projected cost of the stadium and pushed its debut far beyond Opening Day 1960 as he had planned.[13] He hoped the ballpark would be ready for Opening Day 1961, with maybe some games late in 1960.

By Wednesday morning, O'Malley had Dick Walsh deliver stadium plans to the city to support a request for necessary zoning changes on the Chavez Ravine land. Immediately, there were problems. The plans weren't as specific as City Councilman Ransom Callicott, chairman of the council's planning committee, wanted. Callicott also noted that the plan included a number of commercial enterprises – a gas station, a car wash, and several restaurants – that had not been anticipated. Callicott, who'd been a consistent Dodgers supporter on all the earlier votes, indicated that he was troubled by these unexpected additions.[14] Within a few days, more exact maps came back. The car wash was gone. The restaurants – a fast-food outlet, an outdoor luau-type arrangement, and a sit-down restaurant – had been moved inside the stadium structure. The gas station was still there. O'Malley said it had been requested by city planners as there were no others in the immediate area.

The changed plans won the zoning approval requested, but not before another uncomfortable afternoon in city council chambers. After the council dithered through several procedural issues, O'Malley rose to say that the referendum and the lawsuits already had pushed the stadium back so far that the cost had risen by $3 million. "I cannot afford to have this drag on," he concluded. The council voted approval.[15]

The city's dilatory ways had already created another controversy, one that still echoes to this day.

In May 1959, sheriff's deputies evicted a Mexican American family named Arechiga from their home on the Chavez Ravine property and tore the house down. The scene, with dramatic film, played big on Los Angeles' television stations.[16]

If a picture is worth a thousand words, these needed a thousand words of context. The Chavez Ravine property had been designated for public housing in 1950. The Los Angeles Housing Authority began eminent-domain proceedings against the landowners, including the Arechigas, and $10,050 was deposited in an escrow account while title was transferred to the city. By 1953, the Chavez Ravine community, which once had numbered 1,100 families, was down to the Arechigas and perhaps 20 other holdouts.

Events had overtaken the Housing Authority. Conservative groups around Los Angeles, including the real estate industry, the Chamber of Commerce, and the *Los Angeles Times*, rallied against public housing. The city council abrogated its contract with the Housing Authority. In a June 1952 ballot measure, 60 percent of voters said they wanted no part of public housing.

In 1953 the Arechigas sued to regain title, citing the death of the public-housing proposal. The resulting court battle was decided in the city's favor. The Arechigas, still hoping to retain their home, did not accept the money. And the city, uncertain what the land could be used for, did nothing to enforce the judgment and take over the property. The incident went into public memory as poor Mexican Americans thrown into the streets to build Dodger Stadium even though the land had originally been taken for public housing.[17]

Work picked up. But by early 1960, it was clear that yet another of the city's casual procedures was about to cause problems. As with the Arechigas and their neighbors, this was a fistful of property owners whom the city hadn't dealt with as promised. They owned homes and one small store, that hadn't been included in the Housing Authority's land. They should have been bought as part of the city's 1957 deal with the Dodgers. The city had started eminent-domain proceedings but dropped them.[18] There had been some desultory bargaining but that had stalled. The city didn't want to budge too far from the pre-Dodgers' assessed value and the homeowners knew that with the bulldozers tearing up the hill above them, their properties had skyrocketed in value.

Caught between the city's casual attitude and his timetable, O'Malley bit his tongue and paid. There were a dozen lots involved. All the property owners had hired the same attorney and promised that none would break ranks. The dozen lots had been assessed at $82,850 during the eminent-domain proceedings. O'Malley paid $494,400.[19]

By the time escrow closed on these houses, O'Malley was forced to concede that the stadium wouldn't be ready for Opening Day 1961. For another month, he held out hope for July 1961, but then agreed it would take at least until Opening Day 1962. "I can't tell you when we can open the park. It depends on how long are the delays that may be caused by our dedicated opponents," he said. Asked if the Dodgers could learn anything from the problems popping up at the newly opened Candlestick Park in San Francisco, he said, "The way things are going, we will have more than ample time."[20]

He did. As every Dodger-related piece of paper entered the city council, John Holland and his supporters found a way to delay. When the question of closing city streets in the Chavez Ravine area arose in August 1959, everybody in the council except Holland treated it as pro-forma. Holland voted no.[21] The lack of a unanimous vote automatically forced a second reading and a delay of another two weeks. In May 1960 it was approval of a tract map for the stadium. In June it was an appropriation to buy a former elementary school site on the property from the school district. In July O'Malley's supporters on the council were finally able to get an escrow on the Chavez-Ravine-for-Wrigley-Field exchange set up and approved. In August the city granted a conditional-use permit for the property, which would automatically turn into a building permit 10 days later unless an appeal was filed. With 15 minutes left in the appeal period, Silver filed one. A little over a week later, the appeal was overturned, but August had been lost to construction as well. In October the Dodgers and the city finally swapped land titles. In December the council gave approval to the final tract map, with Holland voting doggedly against each of the four necessary motions. The key vote was 18 to 1, Holland's remaining supporters having thrown in the towel.[22]

It was the October 1960 swap of land titles that had really allowed construction to get going. But even as construction progressed, there were further difficulties with the city. A stadium hadn't been built in Los Angeles since Wrigley Field in the 1920s, noted Dodgers executive Fresco Thompson, and nobody in the city inspector's office had any experience with a stadium project. With the knowledge that Holland and other opponents were looking for issues to jump on, the inspectors had to be very thorough. They insisted that a sewer line be increased in size because a zoo might be built in neighboring Elysian Park. (It wasn't.) They required that each car be given a separate parking slot so people could leave easily during games (the two major arenas where the city had a voice, the Coliseum and the Hollywood Bowl, both allowed parking cars bumper to bumper).[23] "We had almost as many city officials swarming over the park as we did contractors' workmen. You couldn't tell 'em without a scorecard," Thompson said.[24]

Then there was the phantom road. The city insisted that a route across the construction site be kept open even though it would disappear once the stadium opened. In fact, the city required the Dodgers to build a finished road, complete with curbs and streetlights. The road was used for 109 days before being torn up. It cost the Dodgers $59,742.[25]

Finally freed from the processes of the city, construction progressed. Dodger Stadium finally opened on April 10, 1962, two years later than O'Malley had planned.

As the construction process stumbled to its end, O'Malley was fed up. "One of the biggest mistakes I made when I came West was taking Western politicians at their word. I had been informed that a Western politician was a hearty, candid fellow whose handshake was his bond. I learned otherwise," he said years later. "I didn't expect a double-cross."[26]

NOTES

1   Frank Finch, "L.A. Officials Hopeful After Secret Session," *Los Angeles Times*, March 7, 1957: C1.

2   Frank Finch, "Bum-Giant Feud Due to Move Here," *Los Angeles Times*, March 10, 1957: 1.

3   Neil Sullivan, *The Dodgers Move West* (New York: Oxford University Press, 1987).

4   H.C. McClellan, "McClellan Tells 'Full Truth' of Dodgers' Coming to L.A.," *Los Angeles Times*, August 25, 1963: J1.

5   "Chavez Ravine Baseball Foes Present Ideas," *Los Angeles Times*, January 14, 1958: C1.

6   "O'Malley Sees Start on Park by July 5," *Los Angeles Times*, June 5, 1958: C1.

7   Televising only road games in San Francisco would remain the team's policy for nearly two decades.

8   Gene Blake, "Judge Questions Chavez Contract," *Los Angeles Times*, June 25, 1958: 2.

9   Frank Finch, "Extra-Inning Legal Tussle Looms Over Dodger Park," *The Sporting News*, July 23, 1958: 10.

10   "Ravine Roadblock," *Time*, July 28, 1958: 55.

11   Gene Blake, "High Court Approves Dodgers Chavez Pact," *Los Angeles Times*, January 14, 1959: A1.

12   Mal Florence, "Dodgers to Open '60 Season at Chavez Ravine," *Los Angeles Times*, January 14, 1959: C1.

13   Carlton Williams, "Supreme Court Approves Dodger Chavez Park," *Los Angeles Times*, October 20, 1959: A1.

14   Frank Waldman, "Dodger Plan for Chavez Draws Fire," *Los Angeles Times*, October 22, 1959: A1.

15   Frank Waldman, "Council Votes Chavez Ravine Zone Changes," *Los Angeles Times*, November 6, 1959: A1. A few days later, *New York Times* sports columnist Arthur Daley would portray this as the council caving in as O'Malley cried wolf. He noted the team's attendance and asked, "O'Malley walk out on such a windfall? He ain't that crazy." Daley, evidently unfamiliar with the continuing battle, didn't recognize that the 9-to-5 vote in favor of the zoning changes reflected the consistent split on Dodger issues during that time period. Nobody's mind had been changed either by the opponents' or O'Malley's rhetoric. Arthur Daley, "Sports of the Times: Sounding the Lupine Alarm," *New York Times*, November 11, 1959: 47.

16   "Sit-down Strike in Ruins Begun by Chavez Evictees," *Los Angeles Times*, May 10, 1959: B1.

17   "Arnebergh Explains Background of Eviction," *Los Angeles Times*, May 9, 1959: 3. See also Eric Nusbaum, *Stealing Home: Los Angeles, the Dodgers, and the Lives Caught in Between* (New York: Public Affairs, 2021).

18   Sullivan, *The Dodgers Move West*, 175.

19   "Dodgers Near Finish of Chavez Purchases," *Los Angeles Times*, February 12, 1960: 2; "Dodgers Put 3 Chavez Properties in Escrow," *Los Angeles Times*, February 13, 1960: B1; Final Eight Homes Sold to Dodgers," *Los Angeles Times*, February 19, 1960: B1.

20   Paul Zimmerman, "Hope Vanishes for Dodgers to Be in Chavez Ravine by 1961," *Los Angeles Times*, April 26, 1960: C1.

21   Andy McCue, *Mover and Shaker: Walter O'Malley, the Dodgers and Baseball's Westward Expansion* (Lincoln: University of Nebraska Press, 2014), 252-3.

22   "Final Steps Taken on Dodger Baseball Park," *Los Angeles Times*, December 23, 1960: B1.

23   McCue, *Mover and Shaker*, 253.

24   Fresco Thompson with Cy Rice, *Every Diamond Doesn't Sparkle* (New York: David McKay Co., 1964), 197.

25   McClellan, "McClellan Tells Full Truth ..."

26   Bob Oates, "It's Goat Hill, Not Chavez Ravine – O'Malley," *Los Angeles Times*, February 18, 1969: D1.

THE BATTLE OF CHAVEZ RAVINE

by Bill Pruden

When eternal Dodgers hero Johnny Podres threw the first pitch to Cincinnati Reds shortstop Eddie Kasko on April 10, 1962, it marked the official opening of Dodger Stadium as the new home of the Los Angeles Dodgers.[1] Less recognized and certainly less celebrated was how it represented the definitive end of what has come to be called the Battle of Chavez Ravine.

The Battle was a multifaceted conflict, one that offered insight into the business side of baseball as well as the distinctive demographics that characterized Los Angeles and indeed all of California, while also reflecting the tenor of the times, the decade of the 1950s. These two forces were bridged by the political realities in California, soon to be the nation's most populous state. At the same time, while the Battle of Chavez Ravine had its roots in actions that predated any plans the Dodgers had to relocate to the West Coast, much less build their new ballpark in that location, it was, nevertheless, a political, social, and cultural battle in which the Dodgers played no small role.

Indeed, the controversy split the Los Angeles area while also leaving the Dodgers to spend more than two decades trying to woo and then placate a part of the local populace, the Mexican Americans who should have been enthusiastic boosters but instead resented what they saw as an insensitive money-grubbing power play. Only with the arrival of Fernando Valenzuela in 1981 would fences begin to be mended in a way that allowed the major leagues' largest attendance base to include the thousands of fans whose fellow Mexican Americans had at one time resided in what would become the team's geographic home.[2]

One of the great ironies of the whole saga is that the central elements of the conflict predated the team's decision to leave New York, much less to build a stadium in Chavez Ravine. In fact, when the conflict began, Dodgers owner Walter O'Malley was in the midst of an almost decade-long battle, one that began in the late 1940s, with New York power broker Robert Moses over the possibility of building a new ballpark that would allow the Dodgers to remain in New York.[3]

Indeed, the Battle of Chavez Ravine had its roots in the 1950 decision by Los Angeles authorities to use federal money made available to local municipalities under the Federal Housing Act of 1949 to build public housing in the suburban area outside of the city known as Chavez Ravine.[4] While technically a part of greater Los Angeles, the semirural area, made up of three neighborhoods – La Loma, Palo Verde, and Bishop – was a distinctive area, and the home to a predominantly Mexican American population. Indeed, it was an area that city officials had never quite known what to do with, but as they contemplated where to use the expected infusion of federal funds, Chavez Ravine seemed to check every box for the new project that would "have to be sited in a thoughtful way to fit with planned freeway construction, potential rezoning, and perhaps most importantly, the remaking of downtown LA into a business and cultural hub befitting the city's ruling class."[5]

And while downtown was fully accessible, the construction of the 110 freeway served to physically separate the area from downtown Los Angeles.[6] But more importantly, and reflective of an often overlooked or at least unacknowledged cultural bias, not to mention political disconnect, while most residents of Los Angeles viewed Chavez Ravine as basically at best "antiquated and backward," and at worst a slum, often referring to it as an "eyesore" and a "vacant shantytown," its residents, many of whom had moved there to escape the discrimination they had experienced elsewhere in the city, saw it as something very different.[7] For those who lived there it was home, "a self-sufficient and tight knit community, a rare example of small town life with in a large urban metropolis."[8] They took pride in it, having developed the area into a vibrant, thriving community, one that included its own church, elementary school, and recreational center, and where they grew much of their own food.[9]

But all of this was set to be upended when city planners, led by Frank Wilkinson of the Los Angeles Housing Authority, targeted the area for redevelopment as part of an effort to turn Chavez Ravine into

Elysian Park Heights, a public housing project that would cover 54 acres. The initial plans called for the construction of 163 one-story buildings that would provide 3,600 low-cost apartments.[10] The notification of the intended plan was received by the residents of Chavez Ravine in July 1950.[11]

The letters explained the city's plan and not only ensured residents that if they were eligible for public housing they would not only have "top priority to move into any [Los Angeles] public housing development," but promised that once the new development was completed they would "have the first chance to move back into the Elysian Park Heights Development."[12] The letters also announced the opening of three area offices to which residents could come for help and guidance in getting relocated.[13] While rumors of such a possibility had "been whispered for years," to the many families for whom the area had long been a community it was nevertheless a crushing, and still unexpected, blow, especially given the reality that since most of the area residents were undocumented, they did not meet the eligibility requirements for residency in the new project.[14] The city's efforts to console the soon-to-be-transplanted residents represented little more than idle promises.

The real trouble began soon after the notices arrived as many families, recognizing that they were not eligible to continue living there, and fearing that they would lose everything, took low offers for their homes and began to move out. With each departure the community was diminished, while at the same time those who remained lost whatever political leverage they might have retained. The exodus was large and fast. By the summer of 1952, Chavez Ravine was, in the words of one commentator, "essentially a ghost town."[15]

But in another ironic twist, at the same time that the land was being prepared for the creation of Elysian Park Heights, the proposed project was upended by politics – both national and local. First, in 1952 Frank Wilkinson, the city planner leading the effort to build the public housing, became a victim of the developing power of the Cold War anti-Communist movement.[16]

While most commonly labeled "McCarthyism" on the national level, in fact, the California Senate Factfinding Subcommittee on Un-American Activities, commonly known as the Tenney Committee, after its chairman, Jack Tenney, a state version of the US House Un-American Activities Committee (HUAC), was already a powerful force in the state, one whose influence was in full bloom before US Senator Joe McCarthy arrived on the scene waving his list of alleged Communists in the federal government.[17]

Indeed, with battles raging over alleged Communist influence in the movie industry, as well as loyalty oaths in the state universities, the public's concerns in the Golden State predated the national fears that were embodied in McCarthy. Consequently, when it was discovered that Wilkinson had once been involved in radical politics, he was not only fired from his job (and subsequently tried and found guilty of contempt of Congress for refusing to testify before HUAC, a conviction for which he would ultimately serve time in prison after losing an appeal in the US Supreme Court), but opponents sought to use Wilkinson's taint to discredit the whole public housing effort.[18] Although the city council's attempt to cancel the contract for the project ran into a legal roadblock, when longtime California politician Norris Poulson, running on a platform that sought to bar the construction of any new public housing projects – efforts that were seen by conservatives as radical efforts that ran counter to solid capitalist principles as well as being spending that they characterized as "un-American" – was elected as mayor of Los Angeles, ousting incumbent Fletcher Bowron, a staunch proponent of the Elysian Park Heights project, by a 53-47 percent margin, the project's fate was essentially sealed.[19]

With the Elysian Park Heights project clearly dead and the federal government looking to cut its losses, once Poulson took office, his administration was able to buy from the federal government the land intended for the Elysian Park Heights project at a significantly reduced price. The only stipulation, one that would later prove to be a sticking point when the area was identified as a potential site for the Dodgers' new home, was that the land needed to be used for a public purpose.[20]

While the political landscape was changing, a group of boosters of Los Angeles, including members of the city council led by Roz Wyman and Ed Roybal, the only Mexican American on the council, were seeking to launch the city into the ranks of the nation's top metropolitan areas, an effort they believed would be greatly enhanced if they could land a major-league sports team.[21] Despite being the third-largest city in the United States, Los Angeles could lay claim only to the NFL's Rams, who had moved from Cleveland in 1946. The city now sought to expand their number, believing that being the home of a pro franchise was a sign of true big-league status as New York, Chicago, Boston, and Detroit, among others, all claimed teams in the major sports and in some cases multiple franchises in the same sport. Meanwhile, back in New York, despite the Brooklyn Dodgers having finally broken through years of frustration to win the 1955 World Series in seven games over their longtime rivals the New York Yankees, O'Malley's efforts to get any help or support from Robert Moses or New York City Mayor Robert Wagner in his quest to build a new stadium continued to meet nothing but opposition.[22] Consequently, he turned his attention west, where Los Angeles officials, although previously rebuffed, were ready to welcome him and the Dodgers.[23]

Yet as enticing as Los Angeles officials had made the proposition appear – and upon agreeing to come to Los Angeles, O'Malley had convinced New York Giants owner Horace Stoneham to join him in the cross-country move, with Stoneham, who had been considering a relocation for several years, planning to make San Francisco his team's new home – O'Malley discovered that not all of Los Angeles was ready to welcome him and the Dodgers with open arms. At least not as far as a decision on a home for the Dodgers was concerned.[24]

Indeed, while Chavez Ravine had been one of many places mentioned as a possible site for a new stadium, in the years since Poulson's election and the death of Elysian Park Heights, a number of ideas had been proposed on how to best use the now all-but-deserted area. One popular suggestion was to turn it into a zoo, an option that all agreed satisfied the public-use condition attached to the city's purchase from the federal government.[25] Meanwhile, all but ignoring that potential problem, some city council members were offering O'Malley Chavez Ravine as a possible stadium site. The prospect became all the more enticing after the Dodgers owner was treated to a helicopter ride over the city, where the aerial view made clear the site's potential, its location ideally situated near the developing freeway, a factor that would make for easier stadium access, a critical consideration in a city and culture that was increasingly based in automobile travel.[26] Finally, in 1957, after continued wrangling and many debates about what constituted public use, the city council approved the transfer of the Chavez Ravine land to the Dodgers. But organized opposition halted the transfer, successfully petitioning for a public referendum to determine whether the transfer could be made.

Meanwhile, on April 18, 1958, the former Brooklyn Dodgers began life as the Los Angeles Dodgers, starting a new chapter in team history by defeating

their fellow West Coast transplant, the San Francisco Giants, 6-5, before 78,672 fans at the Los Angeles Memorial Coliseum.[27] But hanging over the games and the early part of their inaugural season was the impending June 3 referendum. The campaign was a no-holds-barred affair featuring many of the city's power brokers, while the opposition was led by a group that called itself the Citizens Committee to Save Chavez Ravine for the People.[28] Led by Councilman John Holland, who had a record both as an opponent of public housing as well as bringing baseball to Los Angeles, and John Arnholt Smith, the owner of the Pacific Coast League's San Diego Padres, the opposition forces also included small homeowners and small businesses unhappy with the way the city had handled the Dodgers move.[29]

For the most part the opposition reflected not so much a problem with baseball as a deep resentment at the "sweetheart deal [offered] a New York businessman at the expense of the LA taxpayer."[30] They did not understand why, based on other local stadiums, O'Malley needed so much land.[31] The answer, of course was for parking, but that did not address the other complaint about why the city had also promised millions of dollars in land improvement that would benefit a single private business.[32] These were arguments based, for the most part, in economics and public policy. Interestingly, its name notwithstanding, the people for whom they sought to save Chavez Ravine were not the remaining residents. Too, the committee that had in fact begun collecting signatures to force a referendum to challenge the proposed stadium deal even before the Dodgers officially announced their planned move, ignored the amount that O'Malley was in fact investing and the business risks he was taking.[33]

In contrast, the supporters of the stadium deal included the city's top political figures as well as a collection of Hollywood figures excited at the arrival of another form of entertainment. With the powerful *Los Angeles Times* squarely behind the deal, supporters mounted a high-priced advertising campaign with the slogan "Vote B for Baseball."[34] National League President Warren Giles threatened to pull the franchise if the vote went against the ballclub, and while O'Malley, who had stayed on the sidelines in the campaign's early going, contradicted Giles' threat, it nevertheless hung over the campaign.[35]

The effort culminated on June 1 with a five-hour telethon on KTTV. Besides a supportive stream of celebrities that included Dean Martin, Jerry Lewis,

George Burns, Jack Benny, and former baseball radio announcer and actor Ronald Reagan, the program featured Walter O'Malley sitting at a desk, taking questions from callers, offering "witty, charming answers."[36] *Sports Illustrated* reported that O'Malley "gave viewers warmth and dignity, and using a blackboard and pointer, he gave them O'Malley style facts."[37] The magazine added that the often "imperious" Dodgers owner "created an image of a gentle, kindly, fatherly type, who wanted nothing in this world (at this moment) but 300 acres of city property to build happiness and parking spaces for all."[38] The well-orchestrated event culminated with a live feed of the Dodgers arriving at the airport after a road trip that included a final victory over the Chicago Cubs, greeted by thousands of fans who had heeded the show's urging that they head to the airport and greet the team.[39]

Two days later, on June 3, 1958, in a heavy turnout, especially for an offyear election, the city's voters made their decision. By the slim margin of 25,000 votes out of 677,000 cast, the effort to block the transfer was defeated.[40] O'Malley, sitting in the owner's box at the Coliseum, received news updates as he watched the Dodgers lose to the Cincinnati Reds, 8-3.[41] By the end of the game, his electoral victory was clear.

However, there remained one final legal hurdle. Just days before the referendum, activist lawyers had filed suits contesting the legality of the city council's action.[42] A hearing was held in Los Angeles Superior Court just weeks after the vote and on July 14 Judge Arnold Praeger ruled that neither the city council nor the voters had the right to change the public-purpose clause of the deed to the Elysian Park Heights site.[43] The ruling was appealed to the California Supreme Court.[44]

The 1958 season had not been what the Dodgers had wanted. They finished 12 games under .500, their first sub-500 season since 1944, and in seventh place. At the same time, all of the legal hassles aside, the team had clearly been well received with their attendance being almost double their final year in Brooklyn and their best since 1947, the year Jackie Robinson broke the color line in modern major-league baseball.[45] Determined to turn things around in 1959, the club got good news on January 13 when the California Supreme Court unanimously ruled in favor of the Dodgers and the city, removing the final legal obstacle to the deal and clearing the way for building Dodger Stadium.[46]

Unhappily for the Dodgers, one final hurdle remained before construction could begin. It was a hurdle that, notwithstanding the long and convoluted process that had preceded the Dodgers' acquisition of the land, would for years, if not forever, leave the team stamped as the ultimate bad guys in the destruction of the Mexican American community that had long made Chavez Ravine their home.

Despite the fact that the original notices had been mailed in 1950 and despite the fact that so much of what had made the area a community had been demolished or at least rendered inoperable, of the more than 300 families that had received the notices back in 1950, by 1957 only 20 remained, still living in their homes, in a virtual "ghost town," even after all those years.[47] And with the dust having finally settled and demolition followed by construction set to begin, the final vestiges of the Chavez Ravine community had to be evicted. And so, it was done.

By this point, with all legal avenues exhausted, city officials came in and longtime residents or their descendants were simply carried out, in some cases literally kicking and screaming. On May 9, 1959, a day former residents refer to as "Black Friday," the last residents of Chavez Ravine were evicted.[48] One of the longest-tenured residents, Aurora Vargas, a war widow, who had vowed, "They'll have to carry me out," in fact suffered that fate, being "physically removed from her home, manhandled by four officers and rammed into a squad car" while later being briefly jailed and fined for her efforts.[49] With the date of eviction having long ago been announced, there was a heavy media presence ready to document the final act in the long-running drama.[50] And when the forcible evictions lit up the television screens, they reawakened the bleak memories that had been buried for almost a decade, going back to when the first letters had arrived, while also leaving a legacy that would long color the relationship between the Dodgers and the local Mexican American population.[51] It was a public-relations disaster for both the Dodgers and the city and the back story and all that had preceded these televised evictions meant nothing to a populace that saw the final nails being driven into the coffin of a once-vibrant community, one whose emotional pull had only grown as the community itself diminished.

After months of clearing and preparing the grounds, an effort that included knocking down the ridge that separated the Sulfur and Cemetery ravines before filling them in, burying Palo Verde Elementary School in the process, on September 17, 1959, ground was broken for Dodger Stadium.[52]

Like so much history, the Battle of Chavez Ravine, as well as its impact, remains open to debate and discussion. While the optics of the final event were by any measure horrible, some have noted that by that point the defiant refusal of the remaining families to leave was little more than a series of small symbolic actions, the final shots in a long-lost battle, and did not represent the admittedly diminished community, but it did make for good effect in an era increasingly attuned to the images that television could share.[53]

Of course, the evictions are well remembered and were a public-relations black eye for the team. Yet there can be no denying that for the most part, the response to the arrival of the Dodgers and the new stadium was overwhelmingly positive toward both the stadium and the team that had already claimed a World Series crown since its arrival in Los Angeles.[54] But to paraphrase the aphorism about people voting with their feet, in assessing the impact of the Battle of Chavez Ravine, one cannot ignore the fact that despite efforts by the team that included Spanish-language radio broadcasts almost from the beginning of their time in LA, there was initially little support from the Mexican American community.[55] It was not until the arrival of the Mexican-born pitching phenom Fernando Valenzuela – and the accompanying Fernandomania in 1981 –that the Dodgers began to see the type of Mexican American attendance one could have expected given the demographics of the region.[56]

In the end, there can be little doubt that the Battle of Chavez Ravine offers interesting and instructional lessons about the intersection of sports, business, ethnicity, and culture in an ever-changing and sports-obsessed United States.

NOTES

1. Cincinnati Reds vs. Los Angeles Dodgers, box score, April 10, 1962, Baseball-Reference.com, https://www.baseball-reference.com/boxes/LAN/LAN196204100.shtml.

2. See Erik Sherman, *Daybreak at Chavez Ravine: Fernandomania and the Remaking of the Los Angeles Dodgers* (Lincoln: University of Nebraska Press, 2023) for a full discussion of the issues the Dodgers had with the Mexican American community and the way the emergence of Fernando Valenzuela in 1981 changed the dynamic.

3. Eric Nusbaum, *Stealing Home: Los Angeles, the Dodgers and the Lives Caught in Between* (New York: Public Affairs, 2020), 210-211.

4. Thomas S. Hines, "The Battle of Chavez Ravine," *Los Angeles Times*, April 20, 1997.

5. Nusbaum, 135.

6. Nusbaum, 141.

7. Zinn Education Project, "Chávez Ravine: A Los Angeles Story," https://www.zinnedproject.org/materials/chavez-ravine#:~:text=Ch%C3%A1vez%20 Ravine%3A%20A%20Los%20Angeles%20Story%20tells%20the%20 story%20of,in%20an%20early%20self%2Dportrait.

8. Zinn Education Project.

9. Zinn Education Project; Nusbaum, 132.

10. "The Battle of Chavez Ravine," Historias Unknown, July 16, 2022, https://www.historiasunknown.com/blog/the-battle-of-chavez-ravine/.

11. Nusbaum, 142-143.

12. Nusbaum, 143.

13. Nusbaum, 143.

14. Nusbaum, 142; "The Battle of Chavez Ravine," Historias Unknown.

15. Zinn Education Project.

16. Nusbaum, 179-80.

17. Edward L. Barrett Jr., *The Tenney Committee: Legislative Investigation of Subversive Activities in California* (Ithaca, New York: Cornell University Press, 1951).

18. Nusbaum, 179, 219-220.

19. Hines; Elina Shatkin, "The Ugly, Violent Clearing of Chavez Ravine Before It Was Home to the Dodgers," *LA History*, October 17, 2018; https://laist.com/news/la-history/dodger-stadium-chavez-ravine-battle.

20. Shatkin.

21. Nusbaum, 201-204, 208.

22. Paul Hirsch, "Walter O'Malley Was Right," *The National Pastime* (Phoenix: SABR, 2011).

23. Nusbaum, 208-211.

24. Nusbaum, 221-222.

25. Nusbaum, 204.

26. Nusbaum, 212-213.

27. San Francisco Giants vs. Los Angeles Dodgers, box score, April 18, 1958, Baseball-Reference.com, https://www.baseball-reference.com/boxes/LAN/LAN195804180.shtml.

28. Nusbaum, 222.

29. Nusbaum, 222.

30. Nusbaum, 223.

31. Nusbaum, 223.

32. Nusbaum, 223.

33. Nusbaum, 223.

34. Nusbaum, 225.

35. Nusbaum, 226.

36. Nusbaum, 226.

37. Nusbaum, 226.

38. Nusbaum, 226-227.

39. Nusbaum, 227.

40. Nusbaum, 227.

41. Nusbaum, 227.

42. Nusbaum, 227.

43. Jerald Podair, "How the California Supreme Court Saved Dodger Stadium and Helped Create Modern Los Angeles," *California Supreme Court Historical Society Newsletter*, Fall/Winter 2018: 3.

44. Nusbaum, 228.

45. Nusbaum, 240.

46   Nusbaum 240; Podair, 5.

47   Shatkin.

48   Taeler Kallmerten, "Dodger Stadium's Decade Long Battle Over Chavez Ravine," SustaintheMag, https://www.sustainthemag.com/culture/dodger-stadiums-decade-long-battle-over-chavez-ravine.

49   "Chavez Ravine: Displaced Communities under Dodger Stadium," ReflectSpace; https://www.reflectspace.org/post/chavez-ravine-displaced-communities-under-dodger-stadium#:~:text=May%209%2C%20 1959%2C%20is%20a,by%20Los%20Angeles%20County%20Sheriffs; "This Day in Los Angeles History: April 10, 1962, California Historical Society, April 10, 2023; https://californiahistoricalsociety.org/blog/this-day-in-los-angeles-history-april-10-1962-first-game-at-dodger-stadium/.

50   Nusbaum 258.

51   Nusbaum, 258-260; Janice Llamoca, "The Battle Over Chavez Ravine," latinousa.org, January 22, 2019; https://www.latinousa.org/2017/11/03/battle-chavez-ravine/.

52   Shatkin.

53   Nusbaum, 256-259.

54   Sherman, 19.

55   Sherman, 19.

56   As noted above, Erik Sherman offers a comprehensive treatment of the way Fernandomania turned the tide in the early 1980s and added a whole new dimension to the Dodgers' active fan base.

A MONUMENT TO THE O'MALLEYS

by Andy McCue

To Walter O'Malley, Dodger Stadium was never just a building, or a place to sell tickets. It was "a monument to the O'Malleys."[1] As such, he took an almost obsessive interest in its design and construction, from innovations in precast concrete to the details of the benches in the dugouts.

It was the first stadium built solely for major-league baseball since Yankee Stadium 40 years earlier.[2] It was the last stadium for 30 years built with private money and designed for baseball. It would be succeeded by multipurpose stadiums built with public funds. Although it was adjacent to downtown Los Angeles, it was truly the first "suburban" stadium, with limited public transport, surrounded by extensive parking lots, and framed by three freeways.

The stadium's first innovation was molding its design to its hilly terrain. It would be built into the hillside, something O'Malley and his architect, Emil Praeger, had already done on a small scale in Holman Stadium at the Dodgers' Vero Beach training camp. Using the hillside as support reduced the cost and made it easier to build the stands using cantilevered construction, an idea Praeger had championed. Cantilevers – giant versions of the horizontal brackets that support wall-mounted bookshelves – replaced pillars for supporting the decks of a stadium. Their usage in ballparks dated back to Philadelphia's Baker Bowl in 1895 but had not been widely adopted.

Other baseball parks used pillars, which created obstructed views, and O'Malley constantly touted the lack of obstructions as a selling point. But the cantilevers also meant that upper decks had to be set back at least a bit from the first deck. As a result, patrons would have unobstructed views, but, in all but the lowest deck, their seats would be much farther from the action than comparable seats in older ballparks with pillars.[3] Praeger and O'Malley compensated by designing the decks like arms embracing the pitching mound. As the stands moved beyond the bases, the decks, and more so the seats, curved so they faced the pitcher rather than straight forward.

While Dodger Stadium has the size and heft of a "stadium," its design, especially the orientation of seats to the pitching mound, gives it the more intimate feel of a "ballpark," says Janet Marie Smith, who oversaw the mold-breaking design of Camden Yards and as of 2023 ran Stadium redesign initiatives for the Dodgers.[4] "It had details distinctive to the era, but very simple, and that's why it didn't age," she said.

The hillside design also allowed for two other innovations. The parking lots behind the ballpark were terraced with the idea that patrons could park on the same level as their seats.[5] It also allowed the team to provide limited access among the stadium's four decks. Theoretically, patrons would enter at the level of their seats, and access between decks was limited to one interior stairway and two elevators. None of the large ramps, stairs, or escalators that connected the decks of other stadiums would be available. The

Dodgers owner Walter O'Malley brought his team out west in 1958.

problem of people moving to claim upgraded seats was severely limited.

Decks were designed with large concourses, either at the top of the seating areas or behind the stands, offering stunning views of the city and the sunsets of night games. For the bottom two decks, patrons could stroll to concession stands or restrooms while still keeping an eye on the action. The flexible design would allow for the introduction of luxury boxes when that trend arrived.

While these major design elements owed a great deal to Praeger and Vinnell Constructors, the construction firm, the details of the ballpark were heavily O'Malley. All were part of O'Malley's philosophy of trying to make a ballgame a pleasant experience for the fan, whether the home team won or not. "Why should we treat baseball fans like cattle? I came to the conclusion years ago that we in baseball were losing our audience and weren't doing a damn thing about it," he said.[6] "Race tracks are way ahead of us in imagination, planning, showmanship."[7]

Peter O'Malley said his father was influenced greatly by Disneyland, the new Southern California tourist attraction, which had opened in 1955. After his first visit, Peter recalled, O'Malley came home and said, "You just have to see that place – the presentation of it, the restrooms, the food. He realized the standard had been set by Disneyland."[8] He ordered his stadium executives to go to Disneyland and take notes.

O'Malley did not want to be way behind anybody, especially in attracting fans. Madison Avenue had cottoned to the symbolism and uses of color many years earlier. Industrial engineers had seized on its uses for subconsciously guiding the eye and making connections. O'Malley would code his whole ballpark in color. Each of the four main decks would have different-colored seats, and correspondingly colored signs would guide the fan there. Tickets would be the same color as the correct seats. In the parking lots the baseball-shaped signs marking the various areas would be color-coded to the appropriate deck.

As with the parking plan, some of O'Malley's innovations were designed into the stadium. Using an idea he had picked up on the team's 1956 postseason trip to Japan, the Dodgers would build an arc of seats at the same level as the dugouts.[9] For players, the outfield walls were built of plywood rather than concrete. For women performers in fashion shows and other pregame events, the design team provided a separate dressing area.[10] For the media, which overwhelmingly meant newspaper reporters in those days, the press box would contain showers, large workspaces, and a small restaurant. It was also where visiting club officials, scouts, and other baseball people could eat for free, giving the reporters access to people with knowledge and stories.

Dodger Stadium would cater to those who were willing to pay more. There would be deluxe boxes with food service. There also would be a large stadium club at the same level as the press box, but far down the right-field line. With a $250 membership on top of a $265 season box seat, a customer could dine on swordfish or rack of lamb served on china while watching the game.

But the hot-dog set would be served as well. The 47,964 seats ordered from the American Seating Company of Grand Rapids, Michigan, would range between 19 and 22 inches in width. The standard stadium seat of the time was 17 to 18 inches wide, the company said.[11] There would be 48 bathrooms, with 26 being set aside for men after studies of the fan base. Two thousand pairs of seats, dubbed love seats, would be fitted with retractable armrests between them. "This was Walter's idea. He's all for compatibility," said Dick Walsh.[12] Spaces for wheelchairs were designed at the playing-field edge of each deck's concourse, right behind the top row of seats. There was a map of stadium access routes and the parking lot design on the back of each ticket. The main benefit for the average fan, however, would be that ticket prices would be maintained at the same level as at the Los Angeles Memorial Coliseum, where the Dodgers had played for their first four seasons. In fact, they were maintained at the Coliseum level through 1975.

Once fans were in the stands, they would find a large scoreboard above the right-field pavilion that would display the lineups as well as the score, count, time of day, and umpires. Above the left-field pavilion was another innovation – a message board. O'Malley said it would allow the Dodgers to post statistical notes and other interesting material.[13] It would also permit the Dodgers to recognize visiting groups, lead cheers, and plug coming events.

Aside from the round Union Oil sign perched atop the message board, the plugs for coming events and Dodger souvenirs would be the only advertising in the stadium.[14] O'Malley would eschew several sources of revenue and keep prices low to maintain the aura of a pristine place to take the family for wholesome entertainment. He planned to reinforce that almost rural feel of the ballpark with extensive landscaping, indulging in another of his passions with color-coordinated displays of flowers.[15] For a while he even considered trying to coordinate the flowers with the colors of the various decks.

Not all the ideas got in. There was the plan for a 40-foot waterfall behind the fence in center field. When a Dodger hit a home run, the water would shoot up like a fountain while colored lights played over it. When the city required a water-retention basin during construction, O'Malley talked about landscaping it as a permanent lake on-site.[16] There was talk of building the stadium in the shape of the city seal, or orienting it so fans could see both the mountains surrounding Los Angeles and the city skyline, an idea with geographic difficulties.[17] He also kicked around a milk and ice-cream bar for kids, a chuck wagon restaurant, staff living quarters, an air-pumped flag pole to keep the flag waving, a zoo as part of the recreation area, a helipad, infrared heating near the seats, a bowling alley, a moving sidewalk, a miniature golf course, and a monument with a large crossed bat with a ball on top at the Top of the Park parking lot.[18]

O'Malley looked at a number of systems, modeled on Disneyland, for transporting people from the distant sections of the parking lots to the stadium. In the 1958 team yearbook they were called "mule trains" and featured a drawing of a nineteenth-century locomotive pulling tram cars. By early 1961 the drawings showed blunt-nosed open-air cars with a driver's seat in the front row.[19] In the months before the stadium opened, O'Malley was in talks with Lockheed Corporation about providing a monorail system to move the fans.[20] None was built, presumably because of cost and the terraced design of the parking lots.

In the spring of 1960 Candlestick Park opened in San Francisco, and the Dodgers began to learn all kinds of negative lessons quickly. Some were gleefully learned, as the Dodgers' political opponents had held up Candlestick as the model for Los Angeles during the 1958 referendum campaign. After Candlestick opened, Dodgers officials and team brochures would talk about the lack of wind up in Chavez Ravine, although they would mention a nice breeze.[21]

O'Malley, Praeger, and officials from Vinnell Constructors made several trips to scout out possibilities, and the Dodgers instituted a parking-control operation after watching the postgame exit from the San Francisco ballpark. Dodger Stadium became the first one built with traffic signals inside the park.[22]

O'Malley's trips to Candlestick were only one part of his almost obsessive involvement in the ballpark. He would interrupt vacations and the spring sojourn

in Vero Beach for visits to the stadium site. When visitors came to town, he would take them up himself, pointing out all the wonders and, as construction progressed, driving a car through the stadium's concourses to show different features. O'Malley himself would drive up to Chavez Ravine almost every day, often on his own. He would walk the site, kicking the tires, worrying about details, dreaming.[23]

O'Malley's focus on the project was intense, with his engineering experience coming out as he surveyed the details. Touring the Dodgers' dugout during the last week of construction, he decided the players' bench should be pulled out a couple of inches farther from the rear wall to allow a backrest.[24]

O'Malley was there constantly. "Here's the gent again," said one plasterer. "We've seen more of him than we have our own boss."[25]

On the day itself the 52,564 paying fans arrived early, and, inevitably, not everything worked. The color scheme, at first, could not overcome fans' expectations of ballpark design. In other stadiums they had visited, you arrived behind home plate. When you did this at Dodger Stadium, you arrived at the top of the ridge behind general admission seating for the fourth deck. To get to seats in the three lower decks, they had to use either the elevators, one of which failed, or an inadequate internal staircase. Lines for the elevator reached 40 minutes. The kitchen was not finished, so the food was catered and served buffet style. Approached by a woman asking how she could get a drink, O'Malley said, "If I knew, I would have one myself."[26]

One *Los Angeles Times* reporter said half the seats were empty when the first pitch was thrown because the fans were still wandering and gawking.[27]

The "monument to the O'Malleys" was not monumental in its details yet. From the embarrassing to the merely delayed, Walter O'Malley spent the next four years cleaning up both his stadium and the residue of his agreements with local officials.

Three days after the stadium opened, *Los Angeles Times* columnist Sid Ziff reported that his personal investigation still had not found a drinking fountain there. Dodgers public-relations people said they did not know if the stadium had any.[28] Two days later Ziff reported one of his readers had been told to get her drink from the tap water in the bathrooms.[29]

The immediate assumption was that the "greedy" O'Malley had deliberately left the drinking fountains out to sell more beer and soda.[30] The city, which had approved the stadium design, now ordered the installation of an "adequate" number of water fountains. Two more or less official explanations emerged over time. The first was that, as Ziff's reader had been told, drinking water was available in the restrooms, with color-coded paper cups provided. But when the controversy arose, the city said drinking facilities had to be a certain distance from any toilets or urinals.[31] The second version was that it had simply been overlooked.[32]

Much of this was inevitable. O'Malley outlined a "typical" fan letter to Ziff. "Dear sir: We congratulate you on a perfectly beautiful stadium. We're so proud of it and we're so happy with it. But–" the writer starts. "And then," shuddered O'Malley, "the writer of the letter will go on to state some very valid complaints."[33] Answering a complaint letter from comedian Milton Berle, O'Malley wrote, "We opened a new park which was not completed, with elevators that were not running properly, with a traffic program that left much to be desired, and with an entirely green staffing crew."[34] He kept promising the team would deal with the problems.

Eventually, it did.

NOTES

1   Roger Kahn, *The Boys of Summer* (New York: Harper & Row, 1971), 430.

2   In the interim, Baltimore and Kansas City had refurbished minor-league stadiums. Milwaukee had taken a minor-league stadium being built with the hope of attracting a major-league team and upgraded it. All three also hosted NFL teams.

3   Homer T. Borton, "Stadium Design Is a Challenge," *Consulting Engineer*, August 1956: 48.

4   Interview, Janet Marie Smith, Dodger Stadium, April 28, 2023.

5   While this worked very well for the bottom deck and the outfield pavilions, the number of parking spaces at the levels of the upper decks did not quite match and some uphill climbing was usually necessary.

6   "Walter in Wonderland," *Time*, April 28, 1958: 58.

7   Robert O. Shaplen, "O'Malley and the Angels," *Sports Illustrated*, March 24, 1958: 62.

8   John Helyar, *Lords of the Realm: The Real History of Baseball* (New York: Villard, 1994), 60.

9   These seats were removed in the 1999 renovation. The idea was incorporated into the Guardians' ballpark in Cleveland and into Angel Stadium in Anaheim.

10 Andy McCue. *Mover and Shaker: Walter O'Malley, the Dodgers and Baseball's Westward Expansion* (Lincoln: University of Nebraska Press, 2014), 263.

11 Bob Hunter, "Workmen Start Installing Seats at Dodger Park," *The Sporting News*, November 29, 1961: 15.

12 McCue, *Mover and Shaker*, 263.

13 Sid Ziff, "Dan Reeves Can Smile," *Los Angeles Times*, February 27, 1962: B3.

14 Union Oil also had a gas station in the parking lots, part of its deal to help O'Malley finance the stadium after political machinations had delayed construction and inflated costs.

15 Jeane Hoffman, "Model of Chavez Park Prepared," *Los Angeles Times*, March 30, 1958: C6.

16 Jeane Hoffman, "No Jumpers, Please," *Los Angeles Times*, March 12, 1961: N6.

17 The stadium opened to the north, with the view of mountains, but downtown was south, behind the seats.

18 https://www.walteromalley.com/en/biography/reference/Construction-of-Dodger-Stadium, retrieved October 13, 2023.

19 "What's Ahead for Dodger Fans," team brochure, Allan Roth papers, Western Reserve Historical Society, Cleveland.

20 McCue, *Mover and Shaker*, 264.

21 "What's Ahead for Dodger Fans."

22 Sid Ziff, "It's the Greatest," *Los Angeles Times*, April 11, 1962: B4.

23 Interview, Chandler Van Wicklen, March 19, 1998. Van Wicklen worked for the company that supplied the infield dirt for the stadium.

24 Walter Bingham, "Boom Goes Baseball," *Sports Illustrated*, April 23, 1962: 21.

25 "Boom Goes Baseball."

26 "Even O'Malley Stuck: Traffic Jam in Stadium Club, Yet," *Los Angeles Times*, April 11, 1962: B8.

27 Jim Murray, "Where's the Jam," *Los Angeles Times*, April 11, 1962: B1.

28 Sid Ziff, "Battle of Statistics," *Los Angeles Times*, April 13, 1962: B3.

29 Sid Ziff, "Debut of a Rookie," *Los Angeles Times*, April 15, 1962: C3.

30 Jim Murray, "H2O'Malley," *Los Angeles Times*, April 19, 1962: B1.

31 "Better Water Facilities at Park Ordered," *Los Angeles Times*, April 18, 1962: B1.

32 Interview with Los Angeles sportscaster Gil Stratton, January 17, 2000, with Stratton recounting a conversation with O'Malley.

33 Sid Ziff, "Letters to O'Malley," *Los Angeles Times*, August 5, 1962: H3.

34 Letter, O'Malley to Berle, June 8, 1962, https://www.walteromalley.com/en/historic-documents/Personal-Correspondence/146/1, retrieved September 20, 2023.

WHEN THE ANGELS CALLED
DODGER STADIUM HOME

By Kurt Blumenau

History students who want to learn about uneasy détente during the 1960s could study the tense Cold War between the US and other democratic nations on one side, and the USSR and other "Iron Curtain" Communist nations on the other.

Or they could just look at the smiles-out-front, scowls-in-private relationship between the Los Angeles Dodgers and Los Angeles Angels during the four seasons – 1962 to 1965 – that the National and American League teams shared Dodger Stadium.

The teams' disagreements began with the name of the ballpark. Trying to establish their own identity, the fledgling Angels famously insisted on referring to the ballpark as Chavez Ravine when they played there.[1] From the start this gave the Dodgers-Angels relationship the same feel as two rival nations squabbling over the size and shape of the negotiating table in a conference room.

The Battle of Dodger Stadium was a losing effort for the expansion Angels, who consistently ran a distant second to their landlords before they departed for nearby Anaheim in 1966. But the junior team authored some moments that still echo in stadium lore. The first pitcher to throw a no-hitter at the ballpark was an Angel. So was the first batter to hit for the cycle. And some 60 seasons later, a few of Dodger Stadium's record-setting or most noteworthy performances still belong to the Angels, not the Dodgers.

THE SINGING COWBOY RENTS A RAVINE

When Brooklyn Dodgers owner Walter O'Malley moved his team to Los Angeles after the 1957 season, he had to have known that he wouldn't have sunny, glamorous, populous, and affluent Southern California to himself forever. Still, he was displeased when the American League advanced plans after the 1960 season to award an expansion franchise to the city he'd occupied just two years earlier.[2]

Using his influence on Commissioner Ford Frick, O'Malley pushed through an agreement that compensated him nicely for the intrusion on his territory. The new team, to be called the Angels, would pay O'Malley $350,000 for the privilege of playing in Los Angeles.[3] After playing the 1961 season in Wrigley Field – a former Pacific Coast League bandbox the Dodgers had passed up – the Angels would become O'Malley's tenants in the new Dodger Stadium. The annual rent would be 7½ percent of paid admissions, or a minimum of $200,000; the Angels would receive half the concessions, but no money from parking.[4] (O'Malley had a knack for spreading his business costs to his new competitors: The Angels leased the Dodgers' team plane, too.[5])

O'Malley thanked Angels owners Gene Autry and Robert Reynolds for supporting the Dodgers' move west, adding: "These are people who are good for the game. I am delighted that they were awarded the franchise."[6] Autry and Reynolds stifled any objections they might have had. The agreement that brought the Angels into existence was settled only four months before Opening Day 1961, leaving the ownership team with little time to argue, negotiate, or seek other arrangements. Autry, famed as a Hollywood singing cowboy, simply told reporters that owning a team was "the realization of a lifetime dream."[7]

The tenants made headlines in November 1961 by staking a small but important claim to their own identity. Autry announced that the Angels would refer to their new home as Chavez Ravine in all settings, rather than Dodger Stadium. "Our relations with the Dodgers up to now have been the finest," Autry assured reporters. "Using a different name for the same stadium is not to be construed as an objection to the Dodgers' name for their park. We just want to use our own identity." An unnamed Dodgers spokesman took the high road with the team's response, while reminding the Angels where they stood: "A tenant has

Klamath Falls (Oregon) Herald and News, *November 16, 1961.*

the privilege of calling the ballpark whatever he wants when he's using it."[8]

After drawing just 603,510 fans at Wrigley Field in 1961, second lowest attendance in the AL, the Angels moved into Dodger Stadium – or Chavez Ravine – on schedule. They opened with a 5-3 loss to the Kansas City Athletics on Tuesday night, April 17, 1962. Only 18,416 attended. Those early adopters were the first of 3,292,244 fans who saw the Angels play at home during their four seasons in their rented ravine.

One of the Angels' chronic squawks about their landlords developed that July, after Angels outfielders struggled on a reseeded and over-watered field. One of their number, Gordie Windhorn, accused O'Malley of building a $20 million stadium and a 10-cent field. A perceptive reporter added, "It will be noted with interest that this work wasn't done just before the Dodgers were to play in Chavez Ravine."[9] Autry expanded on the point in a later outburst, calling O'Malley a "difficult landlord" and noting that the Dodgers only had the field resodded when the Angels were occupying the ballpark.[10]

Autry went public with complaints about the ballpark's parking arrangements for fans and visiting teams in 1963, noting that New York Yankees manager Ralph Houk had demanded improvements to the parking setup. Autry also regretted the fact that fans couldn't roam the entire ballpark, but had to stay in the area where they'd bought a ticket. "As a tenant, however, these are matters he has to live with," a reporter wrote. "He has no control over them."[11]

The Angels had no control over the ballpark's signage, either, which favored the Dodgers and the National League. "When I came into the park today there was nothing that told me the American League plays here," Angels farm director Roland Hemond said.[12]

Also in 1963, a proposal was floated to build a 55,000-seat domed ballpark adjacent to the Los Angeles Memorial Coliseum – a far cry from the lopsided field the Dodgers had jerry-rigged for use at

the Coliseum between 1958 and 1961. The proposal occurred at the same time as a tax dispute between O'Malley and Los Angeles County that underlined the importance of the Angels' rent payments to O'Malley's pocketbook.[13] Autry, perhaps trying to make his landlord break a sweat, said he would "listen with interest" to the pitch. It came to nothing.[14]

Rumors about a potential move elsewhere in Southern California had gained steam by the spring of 1964. While Autry said relations with the Dodgers were "cordial," he added, "You can never be anything more than a stepchild to the people you rent from." He went on to take another dig at the "ridiculous" parking at Chavez Ravine, adding that he believed the Angels could build a better ballpark of their own.[15]

The Dodgers held their tongue throughout these rough patches. The Angels periodically downplayed any tension as well. And once the Angels' interest in Anaheim was confirmed in April 1964, concord came firmly to the forefront. "Mr. O'Malley had tremendous courage to buck the odds and give our area major league representation," Reynolds said in June of that year. "Our departure from Chavez Ravine is not based on personal animosity with the Dodger president but to build ourselves a better mousetrap."[16]

WINS ON THE FIELD, LOSSES IN THE STANDS

In another time or place the Angels might have fared better in close rivalry with another team, because they were fairly competitive by the standards of expansion teams.

The 1961 Angels, playing at Wrigley Field, posted 70 wins. As of 2023, no first-year expansion team has won more. Playing at Chavez Ravine the following season, the Angels won 86 games, held first place as late as the Fourth of July, and finished third in the AL. It was a distant third, 10 games back, but third nonetheless, and skipper Bill Rigney won *The Sporting News'* Manager of the Year award.

The Angels fell out of the running in subsequent seasons. They finished ninth in 1963 at 70-91, fifth in 1964 at 82-80, and seventh in 1965 at 75-87, and made no significant runs at first place. Still, the Angels remained a cut above the majors' other 1961-62 expansion teams, the New York Mets, Houston Colt .45s/Astros, and Washington Senators. Only the Senators managed to win as many as 70 games in a season during this period, going 70-92 in 1965.

Rigney's team even outperformed the Dodgers at home in 1964: The Angels went 45-36 at Chavez Ravine, while the Dodgers went 41-40. It was the only year of the teams' co-tenancy that the AL team managed a better home record.

The Angels boasted stars and recognizable faces for fans to watch and follow. Pitcher Dean Chance won the AL Cy Young Award in 1964 and finished fifth in MVP voting. He led the AL in ERA, complete games, shutouts, and innings pitched, and tied for the league lead with 20 wins.[17] Outfielder Leon Wagner contributed 37 home runs in 1962 and 26 in 1963, placing fourth in Most Valuable Player voting in '62 and making All-Star teams in both seasons. Albie Pearson, AL Rookie of the Year in 1958, resurrected his sagging career as the new team's spark-plug center fielder. Shortstop Jim Fregosi, just 20 years old in his rookie season in 1962, emerged as an infielder with pop and an All-Star. And colorful pitcher Bo Belinsky made his own distinctive impact, which we'll get back to shortly.

But against the star power and established success of Sandy Koufax, Don Drysdale, Maury Wills, and Walter Alston, none of it mattered.

A famous axiom of military success says, "Get there firstest with the mostest," and the Dodgers had the unbeatable twin advantages of early arrival and strong performance.[18] The Dodgers had wrapped up LA's first World Series title in 1959, before the Angels' creation, and delivered two more in 1963 and 1965. They led the NL in attendance every season from 1962 to 1965 and crushed their tenants at the box office by a larger margin each year.

The 1962 Angels were fourth in the AL with 1,144,063 paying fans. That was respectable by most teams' standards, but less than half of the Dodgers' remarkable 2,755,184 attendance. By 1965, LA's junior team was drawing less than one-quarter the attendance of its senior team. The Angels attracted just 566,727 fans – eighth in the 10-team AL – while the Dodgers drew 2,553,577.

WON-LOST RECORDS AT DODGER STADIUM/CHAVEZ RAVINE

Season	Dodgers	Angels
1962	54-29	40-41
1963	50-31	39-42
1964	41-40	45-36
1965	50-31	46-34
Total	195-131 (.598)	170-153 (.526)

YEARLY ATTENDANCE AND RANK IN LEAGUE

Season	Dodgers (NL)	Angels (AL)
1962	2,755,184 (1st)	1,144,063 (4th)
1963	2,538,602 (1st)	821,015 (6th)
1964	2,228,751 (1st)	760,439 (7th)
1965	2,553,577 (1st)	566,727 (8th)
Total	10,076,114	3,292,244

Sagging attendance in the Angels' final two seasons might also have been a reflection on the team's lame-duck status in Los Angeles, as the team had confirmed its plans to move to a new, 45,000-seat stadium in Anaheim.[19]

The Angels played their final home games at Chavez Ravine on September 22, 1965, in a Wednesday day-night doubleheader. Just 3,353 fans turned out to see the Angels sweep the Boston Red Sox, 10-1 and 2-0. George Brunet won the second game with a complete-game two-hitter, one of five he pitched in his 15-season major-league career. (Jerry Stephenson, who opposed Brunet and took the loss, was an Anaheim High School graduate.)

Angels players expressed mixed emotions about the move. Fregosi said he wouldn't miss the spacious dimensions of Chavez Ravine, adding, "Having our own park with our own fans will mean a great deal to team pride. There won't be 10,000 fans in the stands listening to the Dodgers." Pitcher Bob Lee was more circumspect: "The bigger the better and Dodger Stadium is the best park in the majors for a pitcher. It was a paradise for me. I could come in dead tired, throw the ball right down the middle and still end up all right."[20]

Dodgers general manager Buzzie Bavasi attended the final games, presenting Autry and Angels general manager Fred Haney with a ballpark-shaped cake bearing the slogan "Good Luck California Angels."[21]

Amid the bonhomie, Bavasi recalled a comment Autry had made about O'Malley. News writers said the wisecrack was good-humored, but decades later, it seems sharp-edged. "O'Malley said nothing was too good for us," Autry said, "and nothing is what we got."[22]

HISTORY WRITTEN IN RED: STADIUM RECORDS AND NOTEWORTHY GAMES

Perhaps the most memorable Angels home game at Chavez Ravine took place a scant month into the team's residence there. On May 5, 1962, rookie left-hander Belinsky no-hit the Baltimore Orioles, 2-0. It was only Belinsky's fourth major-league game and the Angels' 11th at their new home. A freewheeling night-hawk, Belinsky briefly became a national sensation but lacked the discipline to be a consistent winner. He left the majors in 1970 with a 28-51 lifetime record.[23] Belinsky claimed the park's first no-hitter by a margin of less than two months, as Koufax threw the first of his three no-hitters at Dodger Stadium on June 30, 1962.

Fregosi was as committed to baseball as Belinsky was carefree, and had a longer career as a result. The San Francisco native played 18 seasons in the majors and managed for 15 more. He played in six All-Star Games, won a Gold Glove in 1967, and skippered the 1993 Philadelphia Phillies to the NL championship. And on July 28, 1964, in front of 35,976 fans at Chavez Ravine, Fregosi recorded the park's first cycle. Hitting against Stan Williams and Hal Reniff of the Yankees, Fregosi collected a first-inning double, a third-inning homer, a sixth-inning triple, and an eighth-inning single. Los Angeles won 3-1.

Earlier that season on June 6, 1964, Chance pitched 14 innings of three-hit-shutout ball, also against the Yankees. As of May 2023, this outing remained the Dodger Stadium single-game record for innings pitched. (Angels relievers Willie Smith and Dan Osinski coughed up two runs in the 15th and the Yankees won 2-0.) The Angels' Ken McBride hit four batters in a game on April 23, 1964, setting a less de-sirable stadium record that has since been tied by two other pitchers.[24] Similarly, the Angels' Rudy May is one of seven pitchers who have walked nine batters in a game at the stadium.[25]

Two Cleveland Indians pitchers opposing the Angels at Chavez Ravine also claimed spots in the stadium record book. As of May 2023, no pitcher had allowed more hits in a single game than Barry Latman, who surrendered 16 in 10⅔ innings in a com-plete-game loss on September 22, 1962. And Sudden Sam McDowell's four wild pitches in a game on July 10, 1965, stood alone as a ballpark record for 52 sea-sons until Adam Ottavino of the Colorado Rockies tied it on June 25, 2017.

Angels Don't 'Dig' Dodger Stadium Bit

Headline Kenosha Evening News, November 16, 1961.

Other games became noteworthy with the passage of time. On September 13, 1963, 300-game winner and future Hall of Famer Early Wynn made his final big-league appearance, 24 years to the day after his first, in front of just 7,363 fans at an Indians-Angels game. Relieving Jack Kralick in the sixth inning of an eventual 7-6 Indians win, Wynn gave up an RBI single to Fregosi, then retired Charlie Dees on a line drive to shortstop to end the inning.

The 9,737 fans who attended the Orioles-Angels game of September 4, 1964, could boast years later that they'd seen the big-league debut of Lou Piniella, future AL Rookie of the Year and NL and AL Manager of the Year. Piniella, then 21 years old, pinch-hit for Robin Roberts and grounded to second base. More than a decade later Piniella returned to the ballpark as a participant in three Yankees-Dodgers World Series in 1977, 1978, and 1981.

One of the saddest stories in Sixties baseball un-folded at Chavez Ravine on Friday, April 13, 1965. Hard-throwing rookie pitcher Dick Wantz made the Angels as a nonroster player,[26] and in his first ap-pearance, he allowed three hits and two runs in an inning of work against Cleveland. Shortly afterward, he told the team doctor he was suffering from extreme headaches, which were initially diagnosed as a virus.[27] Further testing revealed a fast-spreading cancerous brain tumor. Exactly one month after his only big-league game, Wantz died at age 25 following surgery in a Los Angeles hospital.[28]

One other Angels game lives on in Dodger Stadium annals, though not many fans could tell you about it firsthand. On Thursday, September 19, 1963, the Angels and Orioles played a day game to make up for a rainout two days earlier. Only 476 fans attended. As of summer 2023, this remained the smallest offi-cially announced crowd in Dodger Stadium history, excluding the COVID-19 pandemic season of 2020.[29] Belinsky scattered five hits in a complete game as the Angels romped, 7-2. It might have been the definitive example of Dodger Stadium's junior tenants putting on a show while Los Angeles's collective back was turned.[30]

SOURCES

In addition to the sources identified in the Notes, the author consulted other news articles from Los Angeles-area newspapers. He also consulted Baseball-Reference and Retrosheet for basic background information on teams, seasons, games, and players.

NOTES

1   Alex Kahn (United Press International), "New Stadium Slated to Have Two Names," *Ogden* (Utah) *Standard-Examiner,* November 16, 1961: 10C.

2   Unless otherwise specified, the background on the creation of the Angels and the business agreement between Walter O'Malley and Gene Autry is based on the SABR biographies on O'Malley (by Andy McCue) and Autry (by Warren Corbett), accessed May 2023.

3   According to a Consumer Price Index inflation calculator made available online by the US Bureau of Labor Statistics, $350,000 in December 1960 had the same buying power as more than $3.5 million in April 2023.

4   "Will Angels Transfer to Coliseum?" *Long Beach* (California) *Press-Telegram,* July 18, 1963: C1; Joseph A. St. Amant (United Press International), "Angels Say Goodbye to Dodger Stadium," *Alexandria* (Indiana) *Times-Tribune,* September 23, 1965: 6; George Lederer, "Baseball Treaty Reached, L.A. Angels Play Next Year," *Long Beach Independent,* December 8, 1960: D1.

5   Melvin Durslag, "Critics Tell O'Malley 'Get Out of Town,'" *San Francisco Examiner,* June 19, 1962: 47.

6   Lederer, "Baseball Treaty Reached, L.A. Angels Play Next Year."

7   Jeanne Hoffman, "Autry Set to Build Angels in 120 Days," *Los Angeles Times,* December 13, 1960: IV-5. Autry had stepped in to replace Hall of Famer Hank Greenberg, who withdrew his interest in ownership of the proposed AL expansion team due to O'Malley's request for payment.

8   Kahn, "New Stadium Slated to Have Two Names"; Ross Newhan, "Dodger Stadium – Not to Angels," *Long Beach Press-Telegram,* November 16, 1961: C1; Hank Hollingsworth, "Autry Still Fast on Draw," *Long Beach Press-Telegram,* November 16, 1961: C1.

9   Maxwell Stiles, "Styles in Sports," *Los Angeles Evening Citizen-News,* July 14, 1962: 13.

10   Al Carr, "When and Will Angels Move?" *Los Angeles Times,* February 9, 1964: 14.

11   Sid Ziff, "Money Makers," *Los Angeles Times,* February 20, 1963: III: 3.

12   Wells A. Twombly, "That Old Sweet Song," *North Hollywood Valley Times,* September 9, 1963: 8.

13   Paul Zimmerman, "Some Strange Site Changes," *Los Angeles Times,* July 19, 1963: III: 2.

14   United Press International, "Angels Baseball Club May Leave Chavez Ravine," *Redlands* (California) *Daily Facts,* September 10, 1963: 1; Melvin Durslag, "Will Angels Quit Ravine?" *San Francisco Examiner,* September 10, 1963: 49; Associated Press, "Angels Hinting at Coliseum," *San Bernardino County* (California) *Sun,* September 11, 1963: A8.

15   Ross Newhan, "Angels Admit They're Moving," *Long Beach Press-Telegram,* March 30, 1964: C1.

16   Maxwell Stiles, "Bob in Tomorrowland," *Los Angeles Evening Citizen-News,* June 29, 1964: B2.

17   Chance also led the league in numerous advanced statistical categories, such as Fielding Independent Pitching, Base-Out Runs Saved, and Adjusted Wins. While these are significant accomplishments, they're not mentioned here because they wouldn't have brought fans to the ballpark in 1964.

18   The phrase "Get there firstest with the mostest" is incorrectly attributed to Nathan Bedford Forrest, a Confederate general during the US Civil War. Forrest, who had a clear command of English, instead used the grammatically correct "Get there first with the most men." Forrest was a slave trader and Grand Wizard of the Ku Klux Klan, and public tributes and monuments to him have been removed or challenged, but the saying associated with him is embedded in the American vernacular. "Nathan Bedford Forrest," Encyclopedia Britannica, accessed May 26, 2023. https://www.britannica.com/biography/Nathan-Bedford-Forrest.

19   United Press International, "Angels Sign Contract to Transfer Franchise," *Kingsport* (Tennessee) *Times-News,* August 9, 1964: 3C.

20   Ross Newhan, "No Tears by Rig on Move," *Long Beach* (California) *Independent,* September 23, 1965: C1. Sure enough, while Lee's won-lost record and ERA remained solid in 1966, his Wins Above Replacement declined from 4.1 in 1965 – second-best on the team – to 1.2 in 1966.

21   "Fond Farewell" (photo and caption), *Los Angeles Times,* September 23, 1965: III: 1. According to Baseball-Reference, the Angels changed their name from the Los Angeles Angels to the California Angels in September 1965, late in their tenure at Chavez Ravine.

22   Bob Myers (Associated Press), "So Long LA, It's Good Knowin' Ya," *San Pedro* (California) *News-Pilot,* September 23, 1965: 10.

23   Gregory H. Wolf, "Bo Belinsky," SABR Biography Project, accessed May 2023.

24   The other two pitchers were Orel Hershiser of the Dodgers against the Houston Astros on April 19, 2000, and Lance McCullers of the Astros on November 1, 2017, in Game Seven of that season's World Series.

25   "Top Individual Performances at Dodger Stadium," Retrosheet, accessed May 1, 2023. https://www.retrosheet.org/boxesetc/L/PKTP_LOS03.htm

26   John Hall, "It's Cimoli, Si! Satriano, No as Angels Pare Their Team," *Los Angeles Times,* April 8, 1965: III: 3.

27   John Hall, "Chance Labors, but Still Beats 'Pigeon' Yanks, 6-3," *Los Angeles Times,* April 25, 1965: III: 1; John Hall, "Chance Loses Stuff as Angels Blow One, 5-4," *Los Angeles Times,* April 29, 1965: III: 1.

28   "Angels' Dick Wantz Succumbs to Brain Tumor," *Los Angeles Times,* May 15, 1965: III: 1.

29   Based on the author's review of Dodgers attendance figures from 1962 through 2022 and Angels attendance from 1962 through 1965 on Retrosheet's year-by-year game logs, accessed May 2023. The author did not find any examples of an officially announced Dodgers home attendance of fewer than 1,000 fans between 1962 and 2022. The smallest official attendance on record for a Dodgers game at Dodger Stadium is 6,559, for a doubleheader against the Atlanta Braves on September 13, 1976, that was rescheduled from two days earlier due to rain. Major-league ballparks were closed to fans throughout the 2020 season because of COVID-19 safety restrictions.

30   The Dodgers returned home the following night for a regularly scheduled Friday-night game and drew an officially announced crowd of 40,476 against the Pittsburgh Pirates.

WHY WERE THE DODGERS TEAMS OF THE 1960S SO GOOD?

by John Zinn

Readers will be excused if their knee-jerk answer to the above question is just two words – Sandy Koufax. Since the left-hander went 111-34 over his last five seasons with a 1.95 ERA, it's a perfectly understandable response. But even though baseball may be more of an individual game than other team sports, success at the highest level requires more than one or two great players. And so it was with the Los Angeles teams that in the same five-year period won three pennants, lost another in a tiebreaker and won two World Series. Perhaps surprisingly, the key to understanding the Dodgers' success can be found in the wreckage of the team's epic 1962 failure or rather in how they

responded to that failure. While the 1962 team had Koufax for roughly only half of a season, the rest of a strong staff led by Don Drysdale, along with an offense that averaged five runs per game, put the Dodgers four games ahead with only seven to play. Needing just two wins to clinch the pennant, Los Angeles managed only one victory, enabling the Giants to gain a tie on the season's final day.

After splitting the first two tiebreaker games, the Dodgers rallied to take a 4-2 lead after seven innings of the deciding game. When Los Angeles reliever Ed Roebuck faced only three Giants hitters in the eighth, it looked as though the Dodgers were

L to R: Don Drysdale, Claude Osteen, Johnny Podres, and Sandy Koufax, 1964.

home free. However, disagreements broke out in the Dodgers' dugout, with players and third-base coach Leo Durocher arguing that Walter Alston should bring in Drysdale to get the final three outs. According to Maury Wills, Alston refused solely because it was Durocher's idea.[1] The chaos in the dugout spread to the field, where the Giants were handed four runs on only two hits, thanks to four walks, an error, and some controversial defensive positioning.[2] While longtime Dodgers fans may consider 1951 worse, veteran sportswriter Dick Young, who covered both, claimed 1962 was "much worse." Indeed, Young called it "the biggest apple [choke up] in the history of big-league ball."[3] The sentiment was echoed by his colleague Jimmy Powers, who said the Dodgers "choked" so badly that there was "no euphemistic way of saying it."[4]

What's important for our purposes is Powers' further comment that the Dodgers lost because of an "almost incredible exhibition of futile major league baseball."[5] In 1951, it could be argued, the Giants won the pennant, while in 1962 the Dodgers lost it. It would not have been at all surprising for such an epic failure to have a damaging carryover effect. In this case, however, the lessons learned from the 1962 disaster enabled the Dodgers to find an identity that helped them win three pennants and two World Series in four years. It was an identity built first on pitching excellence that began with, but was not limited to, Koufax. Pitching excellence that was strengthened and complemented by Buzzie Bavasi's strategic roster-building, Walter Alston's managing, Maury Wills' leadership, and "finishing" crucial games.

The 1962 disaster notwithstanding, Los Angeles, with a healthy Koufax, plus Drysdale, Podres, and Perranoski, already had a good pitching staff. However, general manager Bavasi used the 1962 off-season to begin building something special by replacing Stan Williams with Bob Miller. Williams, who walked in the winning run in the third playoff game, had, deservedly or not, become the poster boy for the 1962 failure. His wildness at that crucial time, however, was symbolic of his consistently inconsistent control. According to Drysdale, Alston couldn't abide a lack of control so a pitcher would "either throw strikes or be gone."[6] While getting rid of Williams was understandable, replacing him with Miller and his 1-12 record and 4.89 ERA did nothing to impress Frank Finch of the *Los Angeles Times,* who sarcastically said the trade "fell far short of upsetting the balance of power in the National League."[7] Bavasi, however, had

liked Miller for several years, an opinion supported by Dick Young, who saw Miller on a regular basis and dubbed him "the best 1-and-12 pitcher in baseball."[8] Bavasi's faith in Miller was rewarded as the right-hander proved a competent fourth starter in 1963 and went on to become an important part of the Dodgers' very deep bullpen. Nor was this the last time Bavasi found overlooked or undervalued talent.

Los Angeles redeemed the 1962 failure by winning the 1963 National League pennant and the World Series, but a year later, the Dodgers finished in a disappointing sixth-place tie. In response, Bavasi demonstrated beyond any doubt his belief that pitching excellence was the team's core identity. In a trade with the Washington Senators, Bavasi gave up power (Frank Howard and Ken McMullen) for pitching and defense (Claude Osteen and John Kennedy). Not appreciating or understanding what Bavasi was doing, Sid Ziff of the *Los Angeles Times* wrote that the Dodgers general manager "went bear hunting again and came back with a couple of squirrels."[9] In response, the Dodgers GM argued that "[i]f you can improve your defense and pitching you can accomplish the same thing [as adding more power].[10] While Kennedy was not the answer at third, Osteen stepped in just as Johnny Podres' career was winding down. On three occasions in 1965, Osteen was an invaluable stopper, especially in the World Series, when his third-game shutout saved the Dodgers from a possible insurmountable three-games-to-none deficit.

Bavasi's final major pitching acquisition appeared to be so insignificant that it understandably attracted little attention. After winning the 1965 pennant and World Series, he traded Dick Tracewski to Detroit for right-hander Phil Regan. In a six-year major-league career as a starter, Regan had a mediocre 42-44 record with an ERA over 4.00. His performance was so underwhelming that he spent most of 1965 in the minors. As with Bob Miller, however, Bavasi saw something others missed.[11] Regan, whom *Los Angeles Times* columnist Jim Murray called "just another faceless American League spot starter," performed so well for the 1966 Dodgers pennant-winning team that he received the National League Comeback Player of the Year Award.[12] Bavasi and the Dodgers also strengthened their pitching staff from within, especially through the 1966 addition of future Hall of Famer Don Sutton.

While Los Angeles' major acquisitions primarily strengthened the pitching staff, there was another trade whose value exceeded everyone's expectations, most likely including Bavasi. In April of 1964, the Dodgers traded Larry Sherry to Detroit for Lou Johnson, the ultimate journeyman who played for so many teams it's hard to keep track. Johnson was considered of so little significance that the deal was described as the "sale of relief pitcher Larry Sherry."[13] When Tommy Davis, the Dodgers' best hitter, suffered a season-ending injury on May 1, 1965, Johnson took his place. He went on to hit .320 in "close and late games" and .300 against the Giants and Reds, the two teams immediately behind the Dodgers. His contributions also included a game- winning home run in the stretch run and a key homer in the seventh game of the World Series. Johnson and home-grown players like Wes Parker and Jim Lefebvre were not superstars, but they still made important contributions to the Dodgers success.

Just how excellent was the Dodgers pitching? In winning three pennants, Los Angeles hurlers led the league in ERA and shutouts while finishing near the top in strikeouts, fewest home runs allowed, and complete games. Also important was the durability of the four-man starting rotation. In 1963 the top four started 86 percent of the team's games, which grew to 90 percent in 1965 and a hard-to-imagine 95 percent in 1966. During those last two seasons, the top four starters of the Giants, the Dodgers' main rival, managed only 72 percent and 76 percent respectively of games started. It was a major advantage for Los Angeles in two pennant races that were decided on the last weekend of the season.

And when the starters didn't deliver a victory, the team could rely on relievers who not only saved games but won when the starters couldn't finish the job. In 1963 and 1966 Perranoski and Regan contributed not only saves (21 each), but wins, 16 by Perranoski in 1963 and 14 by Regan in '66.. In over 75 percent of those wins, the two Dodgers relievers entered the game either with the score tied or their team behind. They were effectively carrying on almost like a second starter until the offense scored enough runs. It was an invaluable additional form of depth for a team built on pitching excellence.

There is no better illustration of the LA pitching staff's excellence than the 1965 and 1966 pennant races. On September 15, 1965, the Dodgers were in third place, 4½ games out of first with just 16 games to play. Los Angeles then won 14 of its next 15 games to come from behind and win the pennant. During that streak, Dodgers pitchers threw seven shutouts and allowed just 14 earned runs for an ERA of 0.90. Surprisingly, the worst performance was by Koufax, who allowed

five of the 14 runs in one game. Drysdale had the best ERA among the starters at 0.28, while Perranoski in 20⅔ innings of relief didn't allow a single earned run. While the 1966 performance wasn't quite as dominant, it was just as effective. In third place on September 7, Dodgers pitchers threw four straight shutouts to begin an eight-game winning streak with a combined staff ERA of 1.11. The streak put the Dodgers in first to stay.

Winning the pennant was, of course, not the ultimate challenge. That came in the World Series, especially in 1963 when the Dodgers faced a Yankees dynasty that had won nine Fall Classics in 14 years. Koufax knew exactly what he was up against when he saw how "pre-series reports, especially in New York, had become a tribute to the Yankee dynasty."[14] His challenge in the first game was "to show myself and my team, and the Yankees too, that they were just a team of baseball players, not a pride of supermen."[15] The challenge couldn't have been met any more completely. The Dodgers ace struck out the first five Yankees on the way to setting a World Series record of 15 K's in a game.[16] Koufax's dominating performance set the tone for the Dodgers' four-game sweep, in which the Yankees managed only four runs. The task in 1965 was far more difficult, especially after the Twins defeated both Drysdale and Koufax in succession. At this point, the Dodgers' pitching depth came to the rescue when Osteen shut out Minnesota in Game Three, only the fourth time the Twins were shut out all season. Having avoided the abyss, the Dodgers won three of the next four, featuring two Koufax shutouts. The Dodgers staff shut out the Twins as many times in one week as the entire American League did in a season.

No pitching staff, even one like the Dodgers, runs itself. According to Drysdale, Alston ran the Los Angeles staff, and ran it well. If "the greatest strength a manager can have is knowing his pitchers," the Dodgers right-hander said "… Walt knew us like the back of his hand."[17] While the Dodgers always had a pitching coach, Alston supposedly took charge of the pitching staff once the regular season began.[18] Just one example of how Alston effectively handled his pitchers is his visit to the mound when Koufax was struggling in the seventh game of the 1965 World Series. Rather than telling his ace what to do, the Dodgers skipper simply reminded Koufax to "pitch your normal way" in order to avoid the mistakes that pitchers often make when they "try too hard."[19]

Much of the praise given to Alston came after the Dodgers manager received scathing criticism for his handling of the team's pitchers in the ninth inning of the deciding game of the 1962 playoffs. Roseboro, Durocher, and – according to Durocher – Koufax, Drysdale, and Podres all criticized Alston for allowing Roebuck to start the ninth inning, for not taking him out sooner and for bringing in Williams instead of Perranoski or Drysdale.[20] According to both Durocher and Roseboro, Alston "played everything conservatively" and "by the book."[21] Alston himself, in an interview a few years later, said he thought of himself as "a 'percentage' manager."[22]

Whether Alston modified his approach after 1962 or he wasn't as conservative as some claimed, he could and did manage aggressively. A case in point is a crucial September 1, 1963, game with the Giants at Dodger Stadium. After using some unorthodox moves to help his club gain a 5-3 lead going to the ninth, Alston not only brought in Podres in relief for the first time in two years, he did so against four consecutive right-handed hitters. The move worked, earning Alston praise from Curley Grieve of the *San Francisco Examiner,* who wrote that the manager's moves were "why the Dodgers won their biggest game of the season."[23] The loss left the Giants reeling and on their way out of pennant contention.

Despite his overall success as Dodgers manager, Alston had no shortage of critics, including some of his own players. Roseboro at least partially addressed such criticism when he declared that he "never knew a player who wasn't critical of his manager."[24] What's more impressive, however, is the consistent refrain of players like Drysdale and Roseboro as well as Bavasi about how easy it was to play for Alston. As Drysdale put it, "[I]f you couldn't play for Walt, you might as well pack up your gear and find another line of work."[25]

While winning pennants with dominant pitching and limited offense was not the preferred approach of the 1960s, it had been successful in earlier times. In retrospect, the Dodgers of that period were something of a throwback to the Deadball Era, 1901-1919. As such, Los Angeles was extremely fortunate to have an on-the-field leader in Maury Wills, who would have fit right in during the early twentieth century. According to sportswriter Bud Furillo, Wills "revolutionized baseball" by "[bringing] back the stolen base" along with "speed and daring."[26] In 1960 the Dodgers shortstop led the league with 50 stolen bases, which today may not seem that extraordinary. It was, however, the first time a National League player had reached the half-century mark since Max Carey 37 years earlier,

in 1923. During those years, the average stolen bases for the league leader was a mere 30. In the same time frame going forward, the average jumped more than twice to 72, demonstrating that Wills' "revolutionary" strategy was no temporary fad.[27]

Wills' basestealing was crucial to the Dodgers' offense, but his overall contributions to the Dodgers' success cannot be measured by statistics alone. Wills' approach to the game was like that of Hall of Famer Johnny Evers, one of the great players of the Deadball Era. In Wills' book *On the Run*, he said that when he and Roger Craig were in the minors together, "We worked out plays on the bus from the hotel going to the ballpark. We talked about them in the dugout and the clubhouse.[28] Those words are eerily similar to Evers' lament in 1925 about how the game had "deteriorated" from the days when "we used to spend hours doping [figuring out] plays.[29] Among Wills' common practices was watching the other team take infield and outfield practice, something he claimed other players stopped doing once they reached the majors.[30] His self-stated goal was to play baseball "not as well as *I* could play, but as well as *it* could be played."[31] Wills, the Dodgers' captain in 1965 and 1966, had no bigger fan than Koufax, who said, "We cannot win without Maury Wills in the lineup."[32]

While it's harder to quantify than the other explanations of the Dodgers' success, the team's achievements in the mid-1960s can also be attributed to another lesson learned from the 1962 disaster. Reflecting on that failure, John Roseboro wrote, "We spent so much time looking at the scoreboard to see how the Giants were doing, we stopped doing for ourselves."[33] In the final analysis, the 1962 Dodgers failed to "finish" the job twice. First, by scoring only two times in their last three regular-season games when they needed only one win to "finish" the 1962 pennant race. And then, to make matters worse, needing only three outs to "finish" the playoff series with the Giants, chaotic decision-making and poor pitching lost the pennant for a second time.

It's hard to envision a more painful lesson, and the Dodgers learned it well. During the 1963 pennant race, Los Angeles won crucial games against the Giants and the Cardinals where a loss would have allowed their opponents to stay in the race. In the September 1 game mentioned earlier and a September 18 game with the Cardinals, Los Angeles won close contests without either Koufax or Drysdale. The two wins "finished" the opposition and avoided the need of any last-week-end dramatics. In 1965 and 1966, as in 1962, on the last weekend of the season, the Dodgers needed one win to "finish" the pennant race, and in both cases, they got it. Both times Koufax was on the mound, but it's worth noting that in the 1966 game against Philadelphia, his teammates staked their ace to a 6-0 lead. As painful as the 1962 debacle was, it was a lesson well learned.

The decline of the 1960s Dodgers began when Sandy Koufax announced his retirement shortly after Los Angeles was swept by the Baltimore Orioles in the 1966 World Series. While it's unlikely that the Dodgers could have quickly rebuilt or reloaded, management decisions greatly limited any such possibilities. At the top of the list was trading Maury Wills due to his leaving the team without permission during the ill-advised Japan trip. Although it happened earlier, insisting that Tommy Davis return prematurely from an injury that probably required a two-year recovery period was also a mistake. The Dodgers dropped quickly into the second division, and it wasn't until 1971 that they again competed for a title. While the Dodgers of the 1960s were not a dynasty like the Yankees, they compare favorably to other dominant National League teams like the Cubs (1906-1910), the Giants (1921-1924), the Cardinals (1942-1946), and their Brooklyn counterparts (1952-1956). More than anything else, they were successful because they found their identity and fully embraced it.

NOTES

1   Steve Delsohn, *True Blue – The Dramatic History of the Los Angeles Dodgers, Told by the Men Who Lived It* (New York: Harper Collins, 2001), 54; Leo Durocher with Ed Linn, *Nice Guys Finish Last* (Chicago: University of Chicago Press, 1975), 18-20.

2   David Plaut, *Chasing October The Dodgers-Giants Pennant Race of 1962* (South Bend, Indiana: Diamond Communications, 1994), 183-84.

3   Dick Young, "Dodgers Lose, Giants Win to Force Playoff," *New York Daily News*, October 1, 1962: 44, 47.

4   Jimmy Powers, "The Clubhouse," *New York Daily News*, October 4, 1962: 83.

5   Powers, "The Clubhouse."

6   Don Drysdale with Bob Verdi, *Once a Bum, Always a Dodger* (New York: St. Martin's Press, 1990), 168.

7   Frank Finch, "Burright, Harkness Swapped for Miller," *Los Angeles Times*, December 2, 196: 58.

8   "Burright, Harkness Swapped for Miller," Dick Young, "Mets Snare Burright, Harkness for Miller," *New York Daily News*, December 2, 1962: 146.

9   Sid Ziff, "Who Got Slickered?" *Los Angeles Times*, December 7, 1964: 45.

10 "Who Got Slickered?"

11 "Dodgers Trade Tracewski to Tigers," *Los Angeles Times*, December 16, 1965: 49.

12 Jim Murray, "Phil Regan, the Man Who Came to 'Vulch,'" *Los Angeles Times*, September 2, 1966: 41.

13 Frank Finch, "Dodgers May Add Brewer to Roster," *Los Angeles Times*, April 10, 1964: 49.

14 Sandy Koufax with Ed Linn, *Koufax* (New York: Viking Press, 1966), 191.

15 Koufax, 191.

16 Bob Gibson set a new record of 17 strikeouts in a game in the 1968 Series.

17 Drysdale, 174.

18 Drysdale, 174.

19 Michael Leahy, *The Last Innocents: The Collision of the Turbulent Sixties and the Los Angeles Dodgers* (New York: Harper Collins, 2016), 327.

20 Durocher, 19; John Roseboro with Bill Libby, *Glory Days with the Dodgers and Other Days with Others* (New York: Atheneum, 1978), 224.

21 Durocher, 16; Roseboro, 223.

22 Paul Zimmerman, "Dodgers' Quiet Man Gets Job Done," *Los Angeles Times*, September 23, 1966: 42.

23 Curley Grieve, "Alston's Juggling Act Trips Dark," *San Francisco Examiner*, September 2, 1963: 49.

24 Roseboro, 224.

25 Plaut, 29; Drysdale, 167; Roseboro, 226.

26 Delsohn, 49.

27 https://www.baseball-reference.com/leaders/SB_leagues.shtml.

28 Maury Wills and Mike Celizic, *On the Run The Never Dull and Often Shocking Life of Maury Wills* (New York: Carroll & Graf, 1991), 83.

29 "Game Has Deteriorated Says Evers," *Pittsburgh Press*, August 1, 1925: 9.

30 Wills, 129

31 Wills, 22.

32 Koufax, 245.

33 Roseboro, 202.

REKINDLING THE LIGHT: THE JAPANESE STONE LANTERN AT DODGER STADIUM

By Russ Speiller

For decades, the most intriguing and significant Dodger Stadium structure resided not inside the ball-park itself, but just beyond Parking Lot 6 (formerly parking lot 37) on a hill outside Dodger Stadium. On that hill lies a Japanese garden and, within that garden, stood a large stone lantern symbolizing the relationship between Japanese and United States baseball cultures. On some nights you might have even seen the soft yellow glow of the lantern emanating beyond right field.

The story of how this lantern came to be at Dodger Stadium begins with a 1956 Brooklyn Dodgers tour of Japan. Based on both the success of previous US team tours of Japan and the Brooklyn Dodgers claiming victory as the 1955 World Series champions, Japanese baseball officials reached out to owner Walter O'Malley to attract the team to come to their country to play a series of exhibition games after the 1956 season. The timing was perfect, as O'Malley was looking to increase the size of the Dodgers' worldwide audience; hence, he jumped at the opportunity to take his team's brand to Japan.[1]

On the Japanese side, the two instrumental men who arranged for these tours were Matsutarō Shōriki (正力 松太郎) and Sotaro Suzuki (鈴木 惣太郎. Born on April 11, 1885, Shōriki rose to become a media mogul as owner of the *Yomiuri Shimbun* newspaper, as well as owner of the Yomiuri Giants baseball team, leading to his ultimate recognition as the "father of Japanese professional baseball."[2]

Upon introduction of professional baseball in Japan, Suzuki became an acclaimed sportswriter for the *Yomiuri Shimbun*, reporting on American baseball. He wrote several books, notably *Baseball in*

Frank Ego visits the Japanese lantern outside Dodger Stadium.

America in 1929 and *Babe Ruth* in 1948. Having been partially educated in the United States at Columbia University, Suzuki helped Shōriki arrange visits of US all-stars to Japan, including Charlie Gehringer, Jimmie Foxx, Lou Gehrig, and Babe Ruth in 1931 and 1934. After World War II, believing it would help heal his country, Suzuki worked tirelessly to ensure that Japanese baseball resumed. Shōriki sent him to New York to meet with O'Malley about organizing the 1956 tour. Suzuki's importance to Japanese and US baseball relations was commemorated in 1968 with his induction into the Japanese Baseball Hall of Fame.[3]

The success of the 1956 tour went beyond just the record of the Dodgers' team, which finished with 14 wins, 4 losses, and 1 tie, as it spurred a long-standing relationship between the Dodgers and Japan, beginning with O'Malley and Shōriki.[4] In the spring of 1957, a small contingent from the Yomiuri Giants, accompanied by Sotaro Suzuki, accepted O'Malley's invitation to train with the Dodgers at their Vero Beach, Florida, Dodgertown spring-training complex.

Afterward, Suzuki and O'Malley continued to correspond. O'Malley invited Sotaro and his wife, Toku, to attend the grand opening of Dodger Stadium on April 9, 1962. Suzuki's appreciation for both the VIP invitation and the relationship with the Dodgers was so great that he wanted to give the team a significant and meaningful gift. Inspired by a photograph of a stone lantern observed at a friend's home in Japan, Suzuki commissioned the Kasuga ("*springtime*" in Japanese) stone lantern, which was placed as the centerpiece in the Japanese garden on the Dodger stadium grounds.

In a May 19, 1965, letter to O'Malley, Sotaro Suzuki wrote:

My Dear Mr. O'Malley:

I have been very busy since I came back to Japan, but I feel great and have found everything o.k.

After thorough investigation and research, I have found a reliable manufacturers of the "Toro" (stone lantern) to be dedicated to the Dodger Stadium in memory of our being invited to the Grand Opening on April 9th, 1962 as guests, which Toku and myself are always thinking one of the greatest honored prouds in our life. The manufacturers are in Nagoya Prefecture who are very popular of their skill and good workmanship to make that kind of Stone Lantern and are regarded one of the best in Japan. I have ordered of them a Lantern about 8 feets high a few days ago. It takes about 3 months to be complete. So I figure that the Lantern will arrive in Los Angeles in about four

months. This is just a brief information I can tell you about our dedication of the lantern to the Stadium, but will give you some more informations very shortly. Tomorrow we are going to our country home, where we will stay about 5 days to rest and to attend some private affairs. I have to write letters to Terry and Peter, but will do it after I come back Yokohama home again.

Trusting this letter will find you and Mrs. O'Malley and every one of your family in the very best humor and spirits,

Yours very truly,
Sotaro[5]

Constructed by the well-known Shimizugumi Stone Works Company stone-carving business, located in the Aichi prefecture of Japan, the stone lantern gift for the Dodgers was sculpted in Okazaki City, near Nagoya.

In Japanese culture, "Toro are traditional lanterns made from either wood, stone, or metal. In their original form, stone lanterns embody the five elements of Buddhist cosmology. The closest piece to the ground represents the earth (chi); the next part on top of it represents water (sui). The portion encasing the lantern's light represents the fire (ka). The air (fu) and the spirit (ku) are symbolized by the two upper sections that are close to the sky. Such lanterns are also a metaphor for the ephemerality of life: after death, our physical bodies will go back to their elemental and original form."[6]

Fully constructed, the Kasuga stone lantern was 8 feet tall, weighed 3,921 pounds and needed to be shipped to Los Angeles in six sections during the winter of 1965. Inscribed on the back of the lantern base were the words "*To commemorate the opening of Dodger Stadium on April 9, 1962. Donated by Sotaro and Toku Suzuki, Guests.*"[7] The traditional-style Japanese garden in which the stone lantern was housed was designed and maintained by award-winning head landscaper Mitch Inamura, who handled many of the Dodger Stadium landscaping projects.[8] Reaching the garden meant climbing a steep hill where one would encounter river-rock paths, Japanese-style cut pine trees, and two cherry blossom trees.

For many years, O'Malley visited the garden on a regular basis, sitting on a bench that faces the ballpark and clearing his head. O'Malley had plants and trees from the Vero Beach facility planted around the lantern.[9]

During the 1990s, a Los Angeles resident, Frank Ego, made weekend visits to help maintain and care for the Japanese garden.[10] (Ego died in April 2000.)

What compelled him to make these visits? In an email interview in May 2023, his daughter, Kimi, shed light on her father's deep love for and connection to the garden.

Born in Long Beach, California, on May 31, 1921, Frank Ego made several trips back and forth between Japan and California throughout his youth. When Japan and the United States went to war, like many other Japanese Americans on the West Coast, he was interned, at the Manzanar Internment Camp in Independence, California.

Returning to Japan in 1946 after World War II ended, Ego followed Japanese baseball and attended Yomiuri Giants games. He also read the sports columns of *Yomiuri Shimbun's* sportswriter Sotaro Suzuki. It was during a visit to Suzuki in his office in Yokohama in the late 1940s that Frank's life changed forever.

Returning to the. United States in the 1950s, Frank settled in Gardena, California, with his wife and three children. He continued communicating with Suzuki, who would mail Frank the Yomiuri sports pages for over 10 years. In 1962 Frank Ego attended the Dodger Stadium opening day ceremony alongside Suzuki.

Sotaro introduced Ego to Walter O'Malley and his son Peter. Ego and the O'Malley family bonded over a love for horticulture, culminating in a visit by Frank to the O'Malley home, where he later planted cherry blossom trees. Upon retiring from gardening,

Ego became a volunteer caretaker for the Japanese garden and stone lantern throughout the 1990s. He made the 20-mile trip from his home in Gardena to Dodger Stadium each weekend. Proud of his work as a gardener, he cherished his time alone in the Japanese garden, planting cherry blossom (*sakura*) and pine trees.[11]

In 1998 Walter O'Malley's son Peter sold the Dodgers to the Fox Entertainment Group, headed by Robert Murdoch. Five years later, the stone lantern was rededicated in a ceremony that posthumously recognized Frank Ego for his work maintaining the garden and stone lantern. Former Dodgers manager Tommy Lasorda spoke during the ceremony, recalling that Walter O'Malley used to picnic at the Japanese garden site.[12]

In 2004 the Fox Entertainment Group sold the Dodgers to Frank McCourt, who later stood next to the stone lantern and proclaimed, "The lantern contains a light, and the light is a symbol of our enduring relationship with Japan."[13]

In 2012 the Guggenheim Baseball Management group purchased the Dodgers from McCourt. The new owners continued to honor Japanese-American ties, most notably via annual heritage days held at Dodger Stadium. Festivities over the years have included jersey giveaways for fans, an exhibition titled "Baseball's Bridge to the Pacific: Celebrating the

Courtesy Todd Anton.

The Japanese garden symbolized the strong relationship between the Japanese and USA baseball cultures. Fenced off, 2023.

Legacy of Japanese American Baseball," and performances by Japanese drumming ensembles.[14]

However, while the relationship between the Dodgers and Japan has remained strong since 2012, maintenance of the Japanese garden has not. Recent pictures and fan chatter depict a hidden (secret) garden surrounded by a fence with a "No Trespassing" sign on the gate. Online references to the garden, such as Reddit chats, give the impression that existence of the garden and lantern have become something of an urban legend.[15]

One possible explanation for the lack of maintenance might be found in the fact that the current Dodgers ownership group doesn't own the parking lots outside the ballpark or the land where the garden and lantern reside. Those lots were retained in ownership by former owner McCourt.[16] There also were issues of accessibility and security under the Americans with Disabilities Act.

In 2016 Japanese American mystery writer Naomi Hirahara published the novel *Sayonara Slam*, in which the main character, elderly gardener Mas Arai, is told of the Dodger Stadium Japanese garden.[17]

"I'm Smitty Takaya." The white-haired man extended his right hand.

"Mas. Mas Arai."

"Maybe you can take a look at our Japanese garden someday?" Mas frowned. Maybe his ears weren't working either. Who ever heard of a Japanese garden in Dodger Stadium?

"One was dedicated out there past the edge of the parking lot. You could draw a line from home plate to centerfield and you'll find it out there."

Later in the novel, Mas Arai goes to the garden. …

When he finally reached the edge, he came face to face with a tall, black iron fence with a sign that was menacing in its simplicity: "No Trespassing." The gate, which was too high for him to scale, had a simple lock that was probably easy to pick. But he didn't have to go to such lengths, because with one jiggle, the gate opened.

He was able to see the broken cement stairs that took him up the dried-out hill. Did they ever bother to water this area?

When he finally reached the top, Mas felt weak in the knees. It wasn't the climb that did it. It was what he saw. Dead, uprooted pine trees. Stones thrown haphazardly like giant dice. Dead grass. If a garden could bleed, this one would be covered in blood.

A toro, a Japanese stone lantern, was the only evidence that something artful had once lived here. It was large, maybe ten feet tall. These things were not cheap; Mas knew because he'd acquired smaller versions for the "Oriental" gardens some of his customers had requested in the past. With the fallen trees beside it, the toro seemed like a lone survivor in a war zone.

Mas felt the loneliness creep into his bones. Who had ravaged — or perhaps, more appropriately, ignored — this Japanese garden? He stumbled around the bleak area one more time while the sky quickly lost light.

In late March of 2024, as this essay reached final printing status, the Dodgers announced that the Japanese stone lantern has been moved to a prominent location on the top deck of Dodger Stadium. Dodgers president Stan Kasten stated that "The Los Angeles Dodgers are extremely excited to display a remarkable monument from our past that showcases our long-term relationship with Japan and Japanese baseball. Now that we are making the lantern more visible and more accessible, our fans will have a wonderful opportunity to connect with this part of our history on a personal level."[18]

SOURCES

The author would like to greatly thank Brent Shyer, vice president of special projects for O'Malley Seidler Partners LLC, who provided both documentation on the stone lantern and Japanese garden, as well as a soon-to-be-published biography of Sotaro Suzuki. Mr. Shyer also provided numerous photographs of the Japanese garden and stone lantern.

The author would also like to thank Kimi Ego, whose correspondences by email provided valuable information on her father, Frank Ego, a gentleman who poured love and care into the Dodger Stadium Japanese garden until his passing.

NOTES

1   Mark Langill, "Virtual Talk – 1956 Dodgers' Tour of Japan: Setting the Stage for Nomo," YouTube Video, July 3, 2020, Japanese American National Museum Talk, 3:09 to 3:35, https://www.youtube.com/watch?v=UrH5iGNW-hc.

2   https://www.baseball-reference.com/bullpen/Matsutaro_Shoriki

3   Brent Shyer, "Sotaro Suzuki Bio," May 2023. Unpublished.

4   Don Daijiro Kanase, "The Dodgers' Japan Connections: From the 1956 Japan Tour to Hideo Nomo." *Discover Nikkei, Nikkei Chronicles #9 – More Than a Game: Nikkei Sports*, July 9, 2020, https://discovernikkei.org/en/journal/2020/7/9/dodgers-tour/.

5   Brent Shyer, "Stone Lantern Is Focal Point of Traditional Japanese Garden at Dodger Stadium," www.walteromalley.com.

6   Ann Walther "What Are Toro? Discovering Japanese Lanterns," January 7, 2022, https://japanobjects.com/features/japanese-lanterns.

7   Shyer, "Stone Lantern Is Focal Point of Traditional Japanese Garden at Dodger Stadium."

8   Shyer, "Stone Lantern Is Focal Point of Traditional Japanese Garden at Dodger Stadium."

9   Carter Cromwell, "Japanese Stone Lantern Is a Dodger Stadium Hidden Gem," *JapanBall*, May 31, 2023, https://japanball.com/articles-features/baseball-around-the-world/japanese-stone-lantern-is-a-dodger-stadium-hidden-gem/. Accessed December 21, 2023.

10   Shyer, "Stone Lantern Is Focal Point of Traditional Japanese Garden at Dodger Stadium."

11   Kimi Ego, email correspondence with author pertaining to Frank Ego, May 29, 2023.

12   Rafu staff and wire reports, "An Appetite for Life, Amore, for All Things Dodger Blue." *Rafu Shimpo*, January 11, 2021, https://rafu.com/2021/01/an-appetite-for-life-amore-for-all-things-dodger-blue/.

13   Carter Cromwell, "Japanese Stone Lantern Is a Dodger Stadium Hidden Gem," *JapanBall*, May 31, 2023, https://japanball.com/articles-features/

baseball-around-the-world/japanese-stone-lantern-is-a-dodger-stadium-hidden-gem/. Accessed December 21, 2023.

14   Rico Cabrera Sr., "Dodgers Celebrate Japanese Heritage Night." *East LA Sports Scene*, June 14, 2022, https://eastlasportsscene.com/dodgers-celebrate-japanese-heritage-night/.

15   Captain Dana, "The Abandoned Japanese Garden Out in the Parking Lot," *Reddit*, February 2023, https://www.reddit.com/r/Dodgers/comments/112qgjd/the_abandoned_japanese_garden_out_in_the_parking/.

16   Jeff Snider, "Former Dodgers Owner Frank McCourt Is Trying to Build Apartments Close to Dodger Stadium," *Dodgers Nation*, February 10, 2023, https://dodgersnation.com/former-dodgers-owner-frank-mccourt-is-trying-to-build-apartments-close-to-dodger-stadium/2023/02/10/.

17   Naomi Hirahara, *Sayonara Slam: A Mas Arai Mystery* (Los Angeles, Prospect Park Books, 2021), Loc 384, 391, 396, 403 [Kindle Edition].

18   Mark Langill, "Historic Japanese Lantern Tops Park," *Dodger Insider*, March 27, 2024, https://dodgers.mlblogs.com/historic-japanese-lantern-tops-park-7367267e8588. Accessed March 31, 2024.

Mark Langill / Los Angeles Dodgers

The historic Japanese stone lantern was moved to a more prominent location at Dodger Stadium's Top Deck before Opening Day 2024.

IT'S A RED ADAMS JERSEY, NOT A DODGERS JERSEY

by Zak Ford

Dodger Stadium is a special place for me. While this statement isn't unique, I feel conflicted making it as a Giants fan.

I have a divided extended family. My grandma had pumped blue blood since listening to Vin Scully call Dodger games from Brooklyn. For some reason, my dad chose the Giants, and his preference was passed down to me.

My conflict grew deeper as a teenager when I befriended Red Adams. Adams was a "baseball lifer" whose career included 33 years with the Dodgers in numerous scouting and coaching roles. He spent 12 seasons as the team's pitching coach, 1969-1980, when the Dodgers won three pennants and six team ERA titles. I found his baseball résumé very impressive. However, I found who he was as a man even more impressive.

I met Adams through my great-uncle, Larry Powell. Larry and Red were teammates with the Los Angeles Angels of the Pacific Coast League in 1947 and 1948 and kept in touch. Since I loved baseball and lived relatively close to Red, Larry suggested I reach out to him. Red was always very accommodating. We talked on the phone occasionally, regularly traded letters, and I was a guest at his home multiple times. We often joked about our preferred teams. Early conversations focused on baseball, but as I got older, they evolved into more important life topics.

For nearly a decade, while I began my career and started my family, we lost regular contact. We spoke by phone in mid-2015, and that fall his birthday card was returned. I attempted a call in early September of 2016, but his number was disconnected.

Giants fan Zak Ford wore his Red Adams jersey to Dodger Stadium in 2018.

Shortly after, on the evening of Friday, September 23, 2016, I watched Vin Scully Weekend festivities begin at Dodger Stadium while at my house in Northern California. I was overcome with emotions thinking of my late grandma's love for the Dodgers, and Red's deep ties to the team. That night I decided to make the journey to Dodger Stadium for Scully's last two games in Los Angeles. For some reason, I brought one of my most prized possessions – Red's 1980 game-used home jersey.

I arrived at Dodger Stadium and was quickly caught up in my surroundings. For the first time in my life, I put on Dodgers apparel. However, I told myself it wasn't as much of a Dodgers jersey as it was a Red Adams jersey. I also figured it was a fitting way to retire the jersey and say goodbye to Red, as I never expected to see him again.

Being at Dodger Stadium for Scully's last two home games will always remain among my top baseball memories. The appreciation for one of baseball's all-time greatest ambassadors superseded any team affiliation that weekend. I could feel the presence of baseball gods when Scully's final call before the home crowd was a walk-off homer in the 10th inning by Charlie Culberson. The ball landed in the Dodgers bullpen, where Red spent much of his time. Despite the homer clinching the National League West, I could instantly appreciate the moment. When Scully took the microphone and said goodbye to the Dodger Stadium crowd, I cried.

Upon returning from that nostalgic and emotional Dodger Stadium trip, I decided I'd attempt to track Red down, despite how unlikely my success would be. After a few days of online searches and calls, I connected with his oldest daughter, who informed me he was in an assisted-living and memory care home in Fresno.

I am thankful that in the last three months of his life, we enjoyed four visits. Despite not remembering many details of his baseball career, Red was the same man. He hadn't lost his sense of humor nor his welcoming nature and ability to lift everyone around him up with his encouraging personality. I was able to thank him for the positive impact he had on my life and even introduce him to my wife and kids. During those visits, we didn't talk much about his experiences in baseball. That was no longer important. We talked about what was important to him at his core as a man.

After his passing in early 2017, I decided that wearing a Red Adams jersey at Dodger Stadium would

Zak Ford first met Red Adams in the winter of 1993.

become an annual tradition. I call it my annual "It's a Red Adams Jersey, Not a Dodgers Jersey" game. Crediting my year as a cutout in 2020, I haven't missed a season.

While I haven't experienced anything quite as magical as that first 2016 trip, each visit creates another special memory of Dodger Stadium. More importantly, each visit rekindles old memories of Red.

Red Adams, 1921-2017, was a professional baseball pitcher, scout, and pitching coach. Adams pitched 19 seasons professionally (1939-1942, 1944-1958), before a long scouting and coaching career with the Dodgers (1959-1991).

As a minor-league pitcher, primarily in the Pacific Coast League, Adams compiled a 179-172 record. He posted his best record, 21-15, in 1945 with the Los Angeles Angels, which resulted in a promotion to the Chicago Cubs the following year. He saw only brief big-league action, posting a 0-1 record over eight games in relief during the 1946 season. At the time of his passing, he was the oldest living Cub.

Zak Ford enjoys a visit with Red Adams at a Fresno assisted-living home in 2016.

After his playing days, Adams spent 33 years with the Dodgers, 1959-1991, in numerous scouting and coaching roles. His time with the Dodgers included 12 seasons as their pitching coach, 1969-1980. In seven seasons (1972-1978), the Dodgers led the National League in ERA six times (1972-1975, 1977-1978). During this time, the Dodgers won three pennants (1974, 1977, 1978). He was praised by many Dodgers pitchers for his coaching abilities. In Don Sutton's Hall of Fame induction speech, he stated, "Red Adams is the standard by which every pitching coach should be measured. No person ever meant more to my career than Red Adams. Without him, I wouldn't be standing in Cooperstown today."

In 2019 Red's grandson, Eric Adams, self-published the book Red and Blue, which details Red's life and career, and includes insights from numerous prominent Dodgers figures. The book is available through Amazon.

"VIVA, VALENZUELA!": FERNANDOMANIA AND THE TRANSFORMATION OF THE LOS ANGELES DODGERS

by Jason Scheller

In May of 1957, Dodgers owner Walter O'Malley took a helicopter ride over Chavez Ravine, the eventual home of his iconic new ballpark. In Brooklyn he had loaded the team with Italian and African American players to reflect the demographics of that borough. He wanted his team to reflect the large Mexican American population in Los Angeles, so he put the word out to his scouts to find him the Mexican Sandy Koufax. While seemingly impossible to many in the Dodgers organization, the team's longtime Spanish language broadcaster Jaime Jarrin said, "He had a vision. He knew that eventually that market would grow and would be a very important part of the business for the Dodgers."[1]

Though he would not live to see Fernando Valenzuela's Dodgers debut – O'Malley died in 1979 – his dream became a reality when the Mexican native was signed by Dodgers scout Mike Brito in 1979. The left-hander was sent to Lodi of the Class-A California League. Valenzuela worked with Dodgers reliever Bobby Castillo to develop an off-speed pitch that eventually became the screwball. He picked it up faster than anyone in the Dodgers organization could have imagined. Called up to the majors on September 15, 1980, Valenzuela made 10 relief appearances. He

Fernando Valenzuela won the NL Cy Young Award and Rookie of the Year honors in 1981.

pitched 17⅔ scoreless innings with a 0.00 ERA mostly in relief for the Dodgers' playoff run, which was ended by the Houston Astros in a one-game tiebreaker for the National League title.[2]

Valenzuela came to Los Angeles when it boasted the highest concentration of Mexican Americans in the world. Approximately 2 million of the 7½ million residents of Los Angeles County were of Mexican American descent.[3] While there had been Mexican American or Dominican players for the Dodgers, including Bobby Castillo, José Peña, Sergio Robles, and Manny Mota, none had the impact that Valenzuela had, and Mexicans for the most part stayed away from Dodger Stadium. The 1981 season finally brought the Dodgers the player they had been hoping for and ignited a passion among the Mexican American population as one of their own was finally taking the mound at Dodger Stadium.

On Opening Day in 1981, the Dodgers found themselves in the peculiar position of needing a starting pitcher. Jerry Reuss, the 1980 National League Cy Young Award runner-up and the ace of the Dodgers' rotation, was a late scratch because a calf muscle he had strained the day before left him unable to walk. The number-two starter, Burt Hooten, had just had a procedure to remove an ingrown toenail, which took him out of contention for the starting job. The third man in the Dodgers' rotation, Bob Welch, was recovering from a bone spur in his right elbow; and the two men at the bottom of the rotation, Dave Goltz and Rick Sutcliffe, were healthy scratches. Both had pitched in an exhibition series against the California Angels before the season opener.[4] That left Valenzuela as the lone option to start against the formidable Astros.

Additionally, the Astros had acquired former Dodgers pitching great Don Sutton in the offseason, a move that Dodgers manager Tommy Lasorda seemed to take in stride: "We knew there was a possibility of losing Don Sutton (who played out his option and signed with Houston as a free agent), so we had to plan ahead." Speaking of Valenzuela, Lasorda said, "We were looking at him as the replacement for Don."[5]

Valenzuela was 20 years old and the first rookie to start on Opening Day in the team's history. Many in the crowd of 50,511 had to wonder why he was pitching. He warmed up, then went into the training room for a nap before jogging out to the bullpen and then onto the field as the Opening Day festivities got underway.

Making the situation arguably more comical, Valenzuela threw a screwball, a pitch that no one else

had thrown with regularity since Carl Hubbell in the 1930s. Hubbell used that pitch in the 1934 All-Star Game to strike out, in order, Babe Ruth, Lou Gehrig, Jimmie Foxx, Al Simmons, and Joe Cronin, all future hall of famers.[6] Regarding Valenzuela, Hubbell, who had retired in the 1940s, told reporters, "He's got the best screwball since mine."[7]

Valenzuela was opposed by Joe Niekro, who had pitched the Astros to a 7-1 victory in the 1980 tiebreaker.[8] The Astros were unfazed by Valenzuela. "When we heard that Reuss wasn't going to start and that we were going up against a rookie, we felt we had a much better chance against [Valenzuela] than the veteran All-Star," said Houston pitcher Joe Sambito.[9]

The Astros were ready to pounce on the largely untested rookie, but they were in for a surprise. Valenzuela's delivery befuddled them. With his hands clasped, he reached toward the sky, while simultaneously lifting his right leg and his eyes toward the heavens, as if to ask for divine intervention, before delivering his pitch. Valenzuela threw a screwball to Astros leadoff hitter Terry Puhl, who hit a grounder to shortstop for the first out of the game. Valenzuela proceeded to pitch an almost flawless game, coaxing Astros hitters into groundballs, or occasional singles, but not giving up a run. He fanned Dave Roberts on a screwball for the final out to complete a five-hit, 2-0 shutout.[10]

Speaking of his screwball afterward, he said, "That's my pitch, and when I need the big outs that's what I go to."[11] While that victory provided a measure of retribution for the playoff loss in 1980, the game is better remembered as the birth of "Fernandomania." It marked the beginning of a string of victories that made Valenzuela the star of the league and a hero to the legions of Dodgers fans the world over. Sportswriter Paul Oberjuerge summed up fans' feelings when he stated, "Enroll me in the Fernando Valenzuela fan club. Any guy who can get people out despite that Pillsbury Doughboy physique is all right in my book."[12]

That first win also ignited the local Mexican American community in Los Angeles, who wanted to see someone who reflected their background pitch for the Dodgers. That same community had once sworn not to attend Dodgers games when the ballpark opened in 1962 because of the way the evictions for the remaining Chavez Ravine families had been handled in 1959. The win would, in the words of Erik Sherman, "spark a phenomenon in which this remarkable young Mexican pitcher would begin to heal a long-fragmented relationship between the Dodgers, the city of Los Angeles, and a largely marginalized Latino community."[13]

After the Opening Day series against Houston, the Dodgers went on the road. When Valenzuela's second start came around, they were 4-0 and off to their fastest start since 1955. Unfazed by the frigid winds of Candlestick Park, Valenzuela pitched another gem of a game, allowing four hits and striking out 10 in a 7-1 victory over the Giants. He gave up a run, which he hadn't done since his time with San Antonio in the minors. "I didn't get tired, but I was a little stiff the last few innings because of the cold," Valenzuela said.[14]

His next game was on April 18, in San Diego. The Dodgers won 2-0. Valenzuela pitched a five-hit shutout to improve his record to 3-0. Since his debut in September the season before, Valenzuela had allowed just one run in 44⅔ innings pitched. The win gave Valenzuela his second shutout and third straight complete game of the season. Valenzuela spoke modestly of his performance after the game, saying, "I don't know if this is a streak. I've always pitched like this."[15]

His next start came against Houston in the Astrodome. Before a crowd of 22,830, Valenzuela faced off against the man he was brought to Los Angeles to replace, Don Sutton. Both pitched well. While Sutton scattered six hits and allowed one run over seven innings, he was no match for the Dodgers phenom. Valenzuela threw yet another complete game, with 11 strikeouts en route to a seven-hit shutout. He also supplied his own run support, slapping a single off Sutton in the fifth inning to score Pedro Guerrero for the only run of the game. "When I got the hit, I was pleased to get the hit, but thankful to get ahead in the game," Valenzuela said.[16] With the win, Valenzuela now led the league in wins (4), strikeouts (36), complete games (4), shutouts (3), and innings (36), with an ERA of 0.25.[17] Speaking of Valenzuela after the game, Sutton said, "He'll come back to earth someday and give up an earned run or two."[18]

Valenzuela returned April 27 to a hero's welcome at Dodger Stadium. Throngs of fans burst through the turnstiles to welcome him back home against the Giants. The Dodgers hired Spanish-speaking ushers, and many in the crowd waved Mexican flags. Vendors hawked Fernando Valenzuela paraphernalia, mariachi bands played, and Mexican Americans showed up in force to support their freshly adopted favorite. "The fan demographics of Dodger Stadium changed in a month," said Peter Schmuck. "It was stunning to pull your car into the parking lot and drive by mariachi bands. Sure, Mexican Americans came to games, but

not like that. It was so much fun, just a wonderful, unbelievable circus."[19] Pitching in front of 49,478 fans, Valenzuela gave them what they came to see, beating the Giants 5-0 to secure his fifth straight victory and fourth shutout. "Webster has no words to define him," Dodgers second baseman Davy Lopes said. "He owns this city right now. He's entitled to all this acclaim. He's a super kid and a great pitcher."[20]

While Valenzuela's seven strikeouts catapulted him to first place in the National League with 43, and the seven hits in his past 11 plate appearances ballooned his batting average to .438, it all paled in comparison to the woman who ran onto the field that night. In the ninth inning, Norma Echevarra, a young Mexican American woman wearing a "Valenzuela 34" raglan T-shirt. grasped Valenzuela's shoulders and kissed him on the right cheek. Afterward, she raised her arms into the air and jumped up and down on the pitcher's mound before being escorted from the ballpark by security.

Echevarra's kiss was symbolic of the Mexican American community's recognition of Valenzuela. It became, in the words of Erik Sherman, "a lasting image and symbol of the love and adoration being bestowed by millions of Mexican and other Latino fans on their new hero – Fernando Valenzuela."[21] Her kiss was emblematic of the transformative effect he had on the Dodger fanbase.

While the Dodgers possessed other high-profile pitchers, Valenzuela outdrew all of them in 1981. At home he drew an average 48,431 while everyone else on the pitching staff drew 40,941. For road games he pitched in, he averaged 32,273 people in attendance while other Dodgers pitchers garnered 14,292, a difference of 18,981.[22] The Dodgers' veteran Spanish-language announcer Jaime Jarrin summarized Valenzuela's effect best by saying, "I truly believe that there is no other player in major league history who created more new fans than Fernando Valenzuela. Sandy Koufax, Don Drysdale, Joe DiMaggio, even Babe Ruth did not. Fernando turned so many people from Mexico, Central America, South America into fans. He created interest in baseball among people who did not care about baseball."[23]

There were so many interview requests that the Dodgers were forced to hold pregame press conferences in the locker room of every ballpark they visited. Back in Los Angeles, fans bought Valenzuela T-shirts or made their own bootleg versions to sell. Newspapers were hungry for more stories about Valenzuela, and the local newspapers were cranking out stories about him, his mysterious beginnings, and every facet of his life as fast as they could. Even the Los Angeles Police Department became part of the mania, ordering 100,000 Dodgers baseball cards with the LAPD insignia to hand out to children in the areas they patrolled.[24] "Everyone was clamoring for Fernando stories, and it was just so unbelievable the amount of attention he was getting," said former Dodgers director of publicity Steve Brener. "I can't remember one player who captured the fantasy of the fans and the media the way Fernando did."[25]

With Fernandomania now in full swing, the Dodgers traveled north of the border to take on the Montreal Expos on May 3, 1981. Valenzuela retired 21 straight batters after allowing a single to start the game. In the eighth inning, Chris Speier hit a single scoring pinch-runner Tom Hutton to tie the game, 1-1. Up to that point, Valenzuela had gone 36 innings without allowing a run. Manager Lasorda brought in Reggie Smith to pinch-hit for Valenzuela in the top of the 10th inning, while the Expos stuck with Tom Gullickson, who gave up five runs in the 10th inning to give Valenzuela a 6-1 victory. Valenzuela was 6-0, and it was only the second time he had been scored upon all season. Lasorda put the momentous victory in perspective saying, "It's good for the Dodgers, the city of Los Angeles, for the country of Mexico and for baseball all over."[26]

Valenzuela pitched next at Shea Stadium against the New York Mets on May 8. Up to that point he had six games, six wins, and four shutouts while allowing only two earned runs. He also had become the biggest draw in the major league. The Mets' attendance numbers certainly reflected that. "39,848 fans – not bad for a team that averaged 11,300," said sports artist LeRoy Neiman, who was on hand to sketch Valenzuela's portrait before the game.[27]

Fans at Shea Stadium, just like fans who watched Fernando at other ballparks, waved Mexican flags and many wore sombreros. Valenzuela had certainly had a profound effect on baseball in Los Angeles and Latino culture throughout the United States. "I really do believe Fernando's significance, in terms of what he did to give Mexicans a feeling of belonging, and of telling Americans that 'we're here,' was remarkable," said José de Jesus Ortiz, the first Latino to serve as president of the Baseball Writers Association of America. "So, he took us out of the shadows and introduced us to a country that didn't realize we were here in such large numbers."[28]

With all the adoration heaped on the visiting Valenzuela, the Mets felt like strangers in their own stadium. "I get a little tired when I look up at our own scoreboard and see constant plugs for a visiting team and visiting pitcher," said Mets manager Joe Torre.[29] Many Mets players agreed with Torre. "I'm sure the kid's doing a super job," second baseman Doug Flynn said, "and you've got to respect him. But I'd like to see the Mets promote our own club instead of visiting players. We'd like to think we've got a good selling product, too. We don't want all those people coming in here hoping the guy will shut us out."[30] The Mets finished 21 games under .500 in 1981. With no good news of their own to report they used other teams' best players to promote their club.

Despite the Mets' best efforts, Valenzuela pitched his fifth shutout of the season, striking out 11 and dropping his earned-run average to 0.29. The Dodgers won 1-0, and Fernando improved to 7-0. "I had no control the first three innings," he said after the game. "I wasn't following through. I was throwing straight. My screwball wasn't breaking, and my fastball was out of the strike zone."[31] Valenzuela was now on pace to set the rookie record for shutouts, and it seemed possible to all who watched him pitch that he would do it. Valenzuela was asked if he could pitch his entire career undefeated. He wryly answered, "It is difficult, but not impossible."[32] The victory left Valenzuela one away from the record of eight consecutive wins to begin his rookie season set by Boston Red Sox rookie pitcher Boo Ferriss in 1945, and three shy of the all-time rookie shutout record set by the Chicago White Sox pitcher Reb Russell in 1913.[33] Ferriss began his rookie season with the Boston Red Sox in 1945 pitching 22⅓ consecutive scoreless innings, over nine games, he recorded eight consecutive victories.[34] While many attributed Ferriss's success to facing lineups weakened by the absence of players in World War II, his manager, Joe Cronin, said, "That boy is no wartime ballplayer. He'd be outstanding in any era."[35]

A week after the Mets game an action shot of Valenzuela pitching appeared on the cover of *Sports Illustrated* with the caption "UNREAL" in block letters. It was the pinnacle of magazine covers for a professional athlete, reserved only for the best, and he had made it after only seven games! In that same week he appeared on the covers of *Sport Magazine*, *The Sporting News*, and *Baseball Digest*.

Valenzuela took the mound on May 14, 1981, against the Expos in a Thursday night game that had been sold out for a week. A crowd of 53,906, the most for a Dodgers regular-season home game since 1974, showed up to cheer on their new hero. To accommodate the large number of Mexican American fans, the Dodgers hired ushers who spoke Spanish. The flags flying in the crowd that night no longer represented just Mexico. "Every Latin American county seemed to be represented. Not only Mexico. I'm talking El Salvador, Nicaragua – there were so many different flags," recalled Dusty Baker.[36] Valenzuela seemed human for the first time in his career, giving up three hits and two runs. Pedro Guerrero hit a tie-breaking solo home run to win it for the Dodgers, 3-2. While Valenzuela's record increased to 8-0, it was the first time he had pitched from behind all season, as well as the first time he had given up more than one run in a game. He now had eight consecutive wins, tying the rookie record set by Boo Ferriss in 1945, seven complete games, 68 strikeouts, and a 0.50 ERA. The game marked the first time Valenzuela's incredible streak might be in danger of ending. "Right now, I'm winning, and I hope it continues. But if I do lose, I'm prepared to deal with it," Valenzuela said.[37]

Pitching on three days' rest, Valenzuela next appeared against the Philadelphia Phillies at Dodger Stadium. His parents had flown in from Mexico to see him pitch in front of 52,439 fans. Despite all that, Valenzuela lost his first game of the season thanks to a home run by Mike Schmidt and a three-run fourth inning that propelled the Phillies to a 4-0 victory over the Dodgers. "I don't think it will affect me. You win some games, and you lose some games. Tonight, I just lost. That's all there is to it," Valenzuela said afterward.[38] During the game, the LAPD received a teletype message from the Savannah, Georgia police department asking, "Could you advise how Valenzuela is doing?" After the game was over, the LAPD passed along the news that Valenzuela had lost to the Phillies, 4-0. A spokeswoman for the Los Angeles Police Department noted that it was not usual to use police communications for unofficial business.[39]

By June 11, 1981, Valenzuela's record stood at 9-4. In his six starts after posting an 8-0 record he went 1-4 with a 6.16 ERA.[40] Then a players strike deprived fans of Valenzuela's magic until August 10, when the games resumed. Valenzuela, who was named the starting pitcher for the National League All-Star team, returned from the strike strong, pitching three shutouts and pushing his total to eight, tying Reb Russell's record. Attendance again attested to Valenzuela's popularity as 46,168 people turned out to watch the game on September 17 against the Atlanta Braves, despite

competition from a televised pro football game.[41] Valenzuela won four of his last nine starts and finished the regular season with a 13-7 record.

In the National League West Division Series against the Astros, the Dodgers came back from two games down to win the five-game series behind the brilliant pitching of Valenzuela. Game One was a pitchers' duel for the ages as the Astros' Nolan Ryan and Valenzuela faced off. The two did not disappoint, as a capacity crowd of 44,836 filled the Astrodome to watch Ryan pitch a two-hitter, walking one and striking out seven. Valenzuela equaled his effort, striking out six and walking two over eight innings. Each man gave up one run. In the top of the ninth, Jay Johnstone pinch hit for Valenzuela. Fernando was replaced by Dave Stewart, who gave up a two-run home run to Astros catcher Andy Ashby as Houston edged out the Dodgers, 3-1.

A sellout crowd of 55,983 filled Dodger Stadium to witness Game Four. Pitching on three days' rest, Valenzuela held the Astros in check through eight innings before giving up one run on four hits to win the game, 2-1. "There was no way I was going to take Valenzuela out of the game in the ninth inning," Lasorda said. "It didn't even enter my mind."[42]

The Dodgers beat the Expos three games to two in the League Championship Series. In Game Two Valenzuela found himself on the wrong side of a shutout, losing to the Expos 3-0. In Game Five, Valenzuela was masterful, pitching 8⅔ innings, scattering three hits, and allowing only one run. The game was famous for Rick Monday's clutch two-out home run in the top of the ninth to give the Dodgers the victory, 2-1.[43]

After the victory over the Expos, the stage was set for the 11th World Series matchup between the Yankees and Dodgers. The Dodgers had been on the losing end of eight of the first 10, with the most recent one in 1978.[44] In this one, the Dodgers came back from a two-games-to-none deficit to knock off the Yankees.

In Game Three of the World Series, Valenzuela pitched to his largest crowd ever as 56,236 fans, a team record, filled Dodger Stadium. Sandy Koufax threw out the first pitch to a chorus of cheers from the crowd. Valenzuela threw 147 pitches en route to a complete game as the Dodgers beat the Yankees, 5-4. It was not vintage Valenzuela as he struggled mightily, almost being taken out more than once. But Lasorda stuck with him, and he finished the game. "It was my most difficult game ever," Valenzuela said afterward.[45]

At the end of the season, Valenzuela received the Cy Young Award, edging out Cincinnati's Tom Seaver,

70 points to 67 points, and becoming the youngest pitcher in history to be given the award.[46] He was also named the National League Rookie of the Year, and he won the Silver Slugger Award as the best batter at his position. It was certainly the year of Fernando Valenzuela, and, more than anything, the mania that followed him that season was justified.

Valenzuela played nine more seasons with the Dodgers and made five more All-Star teams. He won 21 games in 1986. He played a total of 17 seasons for six teams and won 173 games. He completed 113 games and threw 31 shutouts. On June 29, 1990, he threw a no-hitter against the St. Louis Cardinals.

After retiring as a player, Valenzuela joined the Dodgers' Spanish-language radio broadcast alongside Jaime Jarrín. In 2011 he was inducted into the Latino Baseball Hall of Fame and in 2013 the Caribbean Baseball Hall of Fame. In 2015 he became a US citizen, joining 8,000 others at the naturalization ceremony in Los Angeles.[47] While he could have had a private ceremony, he opted instead to join others who had made a similar journey to their citizenship. In 2023 the Dodgers retired his number 34.[48]

Valenzuela's statistics, as great as they are, would not be enough to enshrine him at Cooperstown, but the impact he has had on Mexican American culture would. He brought approximately 9,000 more fans to the games at which he pitched. He increased the Mexican American fan base of the Dodgers from around 10 percent when he started playing to 50 percent as of 2024.[49] He was a tireless advocate for encouraging boys and girls to stay in school and visited countless elementary schools during his career to inspire the youth. He was appointed by President Barack Obama in 2015 as a presidential ambassador for citizenship and naturalization.

More than anything, Valenzuela helped bring the Mexican Americans who had been marginalized by perceived mistreatment and brutal removal from Chavez Ravine back to the ballpark. In the process, he gave them a feeling that they belonged there because one of their own was on the mound, and that somehow, he represented their dreams of what was possible. He fundamentally altered the composition of the Dodgers fan base by what he accomplished in his rookie season and continues to do as a former player and broadcaster today. He is beloved by those who saw him play and by new generations who listen to him broadcasting Dodgers games over the radio.

Valenzuela blazed the trail for future Dodgers greats like Hideo Nomo, as well as new Dodgers Shohei Ohtani and Yoshinobu Yamamoto. One could make a compelling case that Valenzuela belongs in the Hall of Fame not because of his impact statistically, but his impact culturally. For both Dodgers fans and Mexican Americans alike, Valenzuela will remain a baseball and cultural legend.

SOURCES

In addition to the sources cited in the Notes, the author consulted Baseball-Reference.com, Retrosheet.org, BaseballAlmanac.com, and the Fernando Valenzuela player file at the National Baseball Hall of Fame.

Thanks to Jorge Iber, Dodgers team historian Mark Langill, Rachel Wells, and Roger Lansing at the National Baseball Hall of Fame, as well as Pat and Joy Scheller, Holly Scheller, and Greg Fowler for their support.

NOTES

1   Dylan Hernandez, "Fernando Valenzuela Was a Game-Changer for the Dodgers, Baseball, and Los Angeles," *Los Angeles Times*, March 30, 2011, https://www.latimes.com/sports/la-xpm-2011-mar-30-la-sp-0331-fernandomania-20110331-story.html, accessed November 14, 2023.

2   Hernandez.

3   Jason Turbow, *They Bled Blue: Fernandomania, Strike Season Mayhem, and the Weirdest Championship Baseball Had Ever Seen: The 1981 Los Angeles Dodgers* (Boston: Houghton Mifflin Harcourt, 2019), 76.

4   Erik Sherman, *Daybreak at Chavez Ravine: Fernandomania and the Remaking of the Los Angeles Dodgers* (Lincoln: University of Nebraska Press, 2023), 55.

5   Mike Davis, "Valenzuela Crafts 5-hitter, Blanks Astros in 1st Start," *San Bernardino County* (California) *Sun*, April 10, 1981: 64.

6   Stew Thornley, "July 10, 1934: Carl Hubbell Strikes Out Five Hall of Famers in a Row at All-Star Game," https://sabr.org/gamesproj/game/july-10-1934-carl-hubbell-strikes-out-five-hall-of-famers-in-a-row-at-all-star-game/, accessed November 24, 2023.

7   Jerome Crowe, "A Screwball Chain of Events Led the Dodgers to Fernando Valenzuela," *Los Angeles Times*, March 28, 2011: C-2

8   "Chubby Rookie Blanks Astros, 2-0," *Santa Cruz* (California) *Sentinel*, April 10, 1981: 48.

9   Sherman, 56.

10   Turbow, 53.

11   Logan Hobson (United Press International), "Dodger Rookie Baffles Astros," *Ukiah* (California) *Daily Journal*, April 10, 1981: 4.

12   Paul Oberjuerge, "Fernando Has Dodgers in Fat City," *San Bernardino County Sun*, April 15, 1981: 21.

13   Sherman, 60.

14   "Dodgers Rookie Sensation Stumps Giants on Four-Hitter," *Santa Cruz Sentinel*, April 15, 1981: 18.

15   "Ole! Fernando Does It Again, 2-0 Over S.D.," *San Bernardino County Sun*, April 19, 1981: 19.

16   "Valenzuela's Magic Dazzles Astros, 1-0," *New Braunfels* (Texas) *Herald-Zeitung*, April 23, 1981: 7.

17   "Valenzuela Beats the Odds, Astros Again: He Pitches, Hits Dodgers Past Sutton, Astros, 1-0," *San Bernardino County Sun*, April 23, 1981: 73.

18   "Valenzuela's Magic Dazzles Astros, 1-0."

19   Turbow, 78.

20 "Los Angeles' Valenzuela Stills Giants," *Santa Cruz Sentinel*, April 28, 1981: 11.

21 Sherman, 61.

22 Vic Wilson, "Fernandomania," https://sabr.org/journal/article/fernandomania/, accessed November 30, 2023.

23 Wilson.

24 Sherman, 90.

25 Jesse Sanchez, Nathalie Alonso, and David Venn, "Fernandomania Still Resonates Decades Later," https://www.mlb.com/news/featured/remembering-fernandomania-40-years-later, accessed November 30, 2023.

26 Mike Tully, "Valenzuela Finally Scored Upon," *Ukiah Daily Journal*, May 4, 1981: 6.

27 Turbow, 81.

28 Sherman, 85.

29 Joseph Durso, "The Buildup for Valenzuela Annoys Some of the Mets," *New York Times*, May 9, 1981: 15.

30 Durso

31 "Valenzuela Does It Again…," *Greenwood* (South Carolina) *Index-Journal*, May 9, 1981: 9.

32 Turbow, 81.

33 "Valenzuela Does It Again…."

34 Richard Cuicchi, "June 6, 1945: Boo Ferriss Wins Record 8th Straight Game to Start Career," https://sabr.org/gamesproj/game/june-6-1945-boo-ferriss-wins-record-8th-straight-game-to-start-career/, accessed December 23, 2023.

35 Ed Rumill, "The Ferriss Wheel," *Baseball Digest*, August 1945: 39-42.

36 Sherman, 89.

37 Mike Davis, "Fernando (8-0) Wins but Gives Up 1st HRs," *San Bernardino County Sun*, May 15, 1981: 50.

38 "Phils End Valenzuela's Winning Streak on Shutout," *Ukiah Daily Journal*, May 19, 1981: 4.

39 Associated Press, "Loss wired to Georgia cops," New *Orleans Times-Picayune*, May 20, 1981, Section 2: 9.

40 Turbow, 93.

41 "Valenzuela Equalled Rookie Shutout Mark," *Iola* (Kansas) *Register*, September 19, 1981: 7.

42 "Valenzuela's Four-Hitter Paces Dodgers Over Astros," *Santa Cruz Sentinel*, October 11, 1981: 42.

43 David Leon Moore, "Dodgers, Monday Leave the Expos Feeling Blue, 2-1," *San Bernardino County Sun*, October 20, 1981: 44.

44 "Recapping the Greatest World Series Rivalry," *San Bernardino County Sun*, October 20, 1981: 44.

45 David Leon Moore, "Fernando Comes Back; Yanks Don't: Dodgers Survive Slow Start for 5-4 Victory," *San Bernardino County Sun*, October 24, 1981: 33.

46 Jack Lang, "Valenzuela Nips Seaver for 'Cy,'" *New York Daily News*, November 12, 1981: 1.

47 Steve Dilbeck, "Dodgers' Fernando Valenzuela Becomes a U.S. Citizen," *Los Angeles Times*, July 22, 2015. latimes.com/sports/dodgers/dodgersnow/la-sp-dn-dodgers-fernando-valenzuela-us-citizen-20150722-story.html, accessed November 30, 2023.

48 "Dodgers to Retire Fernando Valenzuela's No. 34 in August," https://www.espn.com/espn/print?id=35590016, accessed November 30, 2023.

49 Sherman, 240.

OLYMPIC BASEBALL AT DODGER STADIUM

by Tony S. Oliver

Though baseball's history as an "official" Olympic event is short and fragmented (1992-2008, 2020, 2028), the sport was the roster as an "exhibition" game for various decades.

Although a dozen nations competed in the 1904 St. Louis Olympic Games, the baseball competition only had American teams, making the competition parochial rather than global.[1]

In 1912 Stockholm's baseball game featured US athletes from other sports, including Jim Thorpe, and renowned nineteenth-century player George Wright as an umpire.[2] The Nazi-sponsored 1936 Olympiad did little to advance the sport, and even less to promote civility as the globe soon plunged into World War II. Officially, about 114,000 spectators witnessed portions of the game between Australians and US military personnel in the Pacific Theatre in Melbourne.[3] However, this 1952 exhibition preceded the marquee track-and-field competition, so few purposely came to see the Americans' 11-5 victory in the cavernous venue.[4]

The Japanese had acquired a taste for baseball in the twentieth century, but the sport was not "official" for the 1964 Tokyo Olympics. A squad of US collegiate players handily defeated the host nation, 6-2.[5] Eight future major leaguers[6] suited up for the Americans, but afterward the sport would experience a two-decade hiatus, missing the Mexico City (1968), Munich (1972), Montreal (1976), and Moscow (1980) Olympics. During this absence, the game's popularity grew in the Caribbean, Mexico, Canada, South Korea, Japan, and pockets of Europe. The creation of the International Baseball Association helped position the sport back in the Olympic sights.

Dodger Stadium hosted the Olympic baseball tournament in 1984. Japan beat the USA in the championship game.

The sport's true competitive debut – as a "demonstration" sport, per the parlance of the International Olympic Committee (IOC), took place in Los Angeles during the 1984 Olympics. The amateur US team featured future big leaguers Mark McGwire, Barry Larkin, Cory Snyder, Will Clark, B.J. Surhoff, Chris Gwynn, and Oddibe McDowell, chosen from 100 eager tryout attendees.[7] Major-league teams drafted 20 of these US Olympians in the 1984 and 1985 amateur drafts.

Italy, Chinese Taipei,[8] the Dominican Republic, Japan, South Korea, Nicaragua, and Canada joined the United States in the eight-country tournament. Perennial amateur superpower Cuba withdrew from the competition in solidarity with the Soviet Bloc's boycott of the games, a tit-for-tat response to the United States' protest of the 1980 Moscow Olympics due to the USSR's invasion of Afghanistan. American manager Rod Dedeaux, longtime skipper of the USC Trojans, acknowledged the threat posed by the Cubans. "They've got pitching, power, and defense," he said.[9] They also had a seemingly unfair advantage, as they were amateurs in name only: Castro's revolution had outlawed "professional" baseball, though few of the Cuban players held other jobs beyond those on the diamond.

The 16 games drew a total of 385,285 spectators.[10] The preliminary round was held from July 31 to August 5 at Dodger Stadium, with two daily games. The United States and Taipei dominated the "White Division," while Japan and South Korea advanced in the "Blue Division."

On August 6, Team USA (first in the White Division) defeated South Korea (runner-up in the Blue Division), 5-2. McDowell clubbed a two-run home run in the third inning to give the Americans an early lead. South Korea countered with an unearned run in the fourth inning and a home run in the fifth to tie the game. Gwynn's single and a double by Snyder drove in a trio of runs in the sixth inning to put the Americans ahead for good.[11]

Japan (first in the Blue Division) bested Chinese Taipei (White Division runner-up), 2-1, in extra innings. A single up the middle by Yukio Arai scored Kozo Shoda, who had doubled.

The Bronze Medal game treated spectators to a thrilling pitchers' duel. Chinese Taipei scored three runs in the top of the 14th inning to slip by South Korea, 3-0, and win the Bronze. The Gold Medal game attracted 55,235 fans who saw the locals take a 1-0 lead on Shane Mack's home run.[12] The Japanese

tagged American starter John Hoover for two runs in the fourth inning and another one in the fifth to take the lead, 3-1. The American offense, which had scored 35 runs in four games, sputtered. A seventh-inning three-run home run by Katsumi Hirosawa made the score 6-1. Snyder's ninth-inning two-run blast cut the deficit, but the Americans were unable to come from behind.[13]

Hoover, who did not enjoy a long big-league career, tossed a complete game on the first day against Chinese Taipei but may have been tired in the late innings against Japan. "I was a member of probably the best amateur baseball team ever," Hoover said. "That alone, being in the Olympics with that team, was unbelievable, overwhelming."[14] Will Clark, though disappointed by the outcome, fondly recalled the experience. "We were not only playing for ourselves, but for the guys who came after us," he said."[15]

Dedeaux focused on the greater picture. "We caught the imagination of the whole baseball world in '84," he said. "I always felt that winning or losing was secondary to the fact that we showcased baseball to the world. The name of the game was selling international baseball."[16]

Displaced from their ballpark, the Dodgers played 13 games on the road (7-6). They returned with a 59-59 record but finished four games under .500, their first losing season since 1979. The organization graciously thanked "the International Olympic Committee, the Los Angeles Olympic Organizing Committee and its thousands of volunteers, the fans who supported Olympic Baseball at Dodger Stadium, and (to) the amateur baseball officials and players from throughout the world" for creating "baseball's greatest moment in the history of the Olympic Games."[17] Baseball was the only Olympic competition held at Dodger Stadium.

The major-league-baseball connection did not end after the Games. Peter Ueberroth, lauded for his stellar organizational job, was selected as the sixth commissioner of baseball. He held the job from October 1, 1984, to April 1, 1989, when Bart Giamatti succeeded him.

Baseball remained an exhibition sport for the 1988 Seoul Olympics. Cuba, winner of the 1985 International Cup, the 1986 World Baseball Championship, and the 1987 Pan American Games, again sat out the Olympics, this time in support of North Korea's boycott. Future major leaguers Robin Ventura, Jim Abbott, Andy Benes, Tino Martínez, and Ben McDonald led the Americans. In a rematch, the United States beat

Japan for the Gold Medal while Puerto Rico knocked off host South Korea for the Bronze.

Baseball became an official sport in 1992 (Barcelona), and Cuba won the Gold Medal. The Caribbean nation would revalidate its prize in 1996 (Atlanta).[18]

The 2000 Games (Sydney) were the first to allow professional players, though no active US major leaguers participated. Managed by Tommy Lasorda, the US team avenged its prior defeat to Cuba, but four years later, when the preliminary tournaments conflicted with the regular baseball season, the United States failed to qualify for the Games. South Korea won the 2008 Gold Medal, the last one contested as an official Olympic sport until the 2020/2021 Beijing Games.[19]

While Major League Baseball and team owners have allowed big-league players to participate in the World Baseball Classic (WBC), the tournament's typical schedule interrupts only spring training, not the regular season. Although the National Hockey League has set a precedent of pausing its regular-season schedule for global competition, it is unlikely that Major League Baseball will follow suit for the 2028 Los Angeles Olympics, though it is possible that clubs will allow their top minor-league prospects to compete.

NOTES

1   Pete Cava, "Baseball in the Olympics," 1991, https://digital.la84.org/digital/collection/p17103coll10/id/3005/rec/4.

2   Cava.

3   The game was held at the Melbourne Cricket Ground. Capacity limits have changed through the years, with a record 143,500 in attendance for Billy Graham and crowds in excess of 90,000 for cricket matches in the twentieth century. However, it is high unlikely that many watched the baseball game, as the true event that day was track and field.

4   Cava.

5   Cava.

6   The eight players: Alan Closter, Dick Joyce, Chuck Dopson, Jim Hibbs, Ken Suarez, Mike Epstein, Shaun Fitzmaurice, Gary Sutherland.

7   Los Angeles 1984: Dodger Salute to Olympic Baseball, https://www.youtube.com/watch?v=GDiCv7i_m9g.

8   "Chinese Taipei" is the name used by the Republic of China (Taiwan) in international sporting competitions.

9   Cava.

10   Ross Newhan, "A Silver Lining: Talented '84 U.S. Baseball Team Didn't Get the Gold, but the Sport Proved to Be an International Winner," *Los Angeles Times*, July 22, 1992, https://www.latimes.com/archives/la-xpm-1992-07-22-sp-4198-story.html.

11   Brendan Macgranachan, "A Look Back at the '84 Olympic Baseball Tournament," Seamheads, July 11, 2008, https://seamheads.com/blog/2008/07/11/a-look-back-at-the-84-olympic-baseball-tournament/.

12   Macgranachan.

13   Macgranachan.

14   Newhan.

15   Newhan.

16   Newhan.

17   Paid advertisement, *Los Angeles Daily News*, August 12, 1984: 13.

18   Eric Goodman, "Baseball 101: Olympic History," NBC Olympics, March 15, 2021, https://www.nbcolympics.com/news/baseball-101-olympic-history.

19   The 2020 Beijing Olympic Games were delayed until 2021 because of the COVID-19 global pandemic.

A WEEKEND TO REMEMBER

Centennial Old-Timers Day

By Greg King

A third of a century has passed since the Dodgers commemorated their centennial – 100 years since joining the National League in 1890, the year they consider their founding. The anniversary was highlighted by a midsummer Old-Timers Weekend held at Dodger Stadium, which included a private luncheon for former players and coaches on Saturday, June 30, and an exhibition on Sunday, July 1, 1990, before the regularly scheduled game against the St. Louis Cardinals. The largest number of former Dodgers to appear at an Old-Timers Game, before or since, assembled that weekend. The specific theme was a salute to the Dodgers' 21 National League pennant-winning teams. Players from 16 teams who went to the World Series between 1941 and 1988, including six that won the Series, attended.[1]

The first group of retired players began to show up at the ballpark on Friday evening, June 29, a night that would go down in Dodger annals. Carl Erskine and Rex Barney were among those looking on as Fernando Valenzuela, the 1981 National League Rookie of the Year and Cy Young Award winner, on this summer evening twirled a no-hitter, something both Erskine and Barney had accomplished with Brooklyn. Then in his 10th season with the ballclub, Valenzuela beat St. Louis Cardinals pitcher José DeLeón, 6-0. The Dodgers offense was sparked by a three-hit night from Lenny Harris and home runs by Hubie Brooks and Juan Samuel.[2]

Valenzuela's was the 20th no-hitter in Dodgers history, and the first thrown by a Dodgers pitcher since Jerry Reuss held the Giants hitless in 1980. It also was the first at Dodger Stadium since Bill Singer denied the Phillies a hit on July 20, 1970.[3] Valenzuela's gem nearly evaporated in the top of the ninth inning. With a runner on first and one out, former Dodger Pedro Guerrero hit a grounder that Valenzuela deflected with his glove and second baseman Samuel converted into a game-ending double play. With the last out recorded, Dodgers broadcaster Vin Scully advised listeners, "If you have a sombrero, throw it to the sky!"[4]

Remarkably, earlier in the day, Valenzuela's former teammate and friend, Dave Stewart, of the Oakland Athletics, hurled a no-hitter against the Toronto Blue Jays. As of 2023, this was the only time in big-league history that two no-hitters were thrown on the same day. And on Sunday, Andy Hawkins of the New York Yankees pitched an eight-inning no-hitter against the Chicago White Sox but in a losing cause, 4-0; in 1991 he also "lost" the no-hitter, when a major-league rule change asserted that a game must go at least a full nine innings to be classified as a no-hitter.[5]

On Saturday afternoon, June 30, the Dodgers hosted a private luncheon for former players and coaches in the posh Stadium Club, perched high above right field, where old acquaintances were renewed and days of glory recalled. Erskine kidded with Dodgers President Peter O'Malley's sister Terry Seidler: "Peter paid for a hotel room, meals, plane tickets, game tickets, and chauffeur service to get me here. That's more than your dad (Walter O'Malley) paid me to play for him."[6] Don Drysdale, who was by this time a member of the Dodgers broadcasting crew, served as the luncheon's emcee, and after viewing a four-minute video encapsulating a century of the team's history, told those gathered, "I wish I could put everything in a time capsule and keep it just the way it was."[7]

Sunday afternoon was set aside for the Old-Timers Game. There was nothing particularly new about Old-Timers Games. In fact, MLB historian John Thorn traced the earliest one to have been played at Elysian Fields in Hoboken, New Jersey, in 1875.[8] The Yankees have famously held an annual Old-Timers Day continuously since 1947 and as of 2023 were the only big-league team that carried on the tradition. It appears the Dodgers held their first Old-Timers Game at Ebbets Field in August 1932, and held another in September 1936, the latter ostensibly to mark the 60th anniversary of the founding of the National League.[9] Four years later, in September 1940, the Dodgers brought back nearly 40 of their former players for a three-inning old-timers exhibition. It was the last one held in Brooklyn.[10]

Thirty-one seasons passed before the Dodgers hosted their next Old-Timers Day. In their 14th season on the West Coast, in 1971, the Dodgers brought 34 of their former players back to Chavez Ravine.[11] It became an annual promotion for the next 25 seasons, often centered on a specific theme or commemoration of an anniversary, such as their first year in Los Angeles, a World Series championship team, their first year in Dodger Stadium, the retirement of a uniform number, and so forth. The 1990 event, in fact, was the 20th consecutive season the Dodgers staged an Old-Timers Game. There would be five more through 1995.

By 1990, Equitable Insurance had not only become a sponsor of the Dodgers Old-Timers Game but held one in each big-league ballpark.[12] On July 1, 1990, fans cheered on their favorite players of seasons past at Dodger Stadium. Before a crowd of just under 40,000 fans, 86 Dodgers alumni from both the Brooklyn and Los Angeles eras emerged from the dugout and stood along the baselines and were introduced to the crowd, and assembled afterward for a team photo. Veteran backstop Rick Dempsey, age 40, was summoned from the dugout to join the group photograph to represent the 1988 champions.[13]

Tom Pagnozzi and Bob Tewksbury were among the Cardinals collecting autographs from some of the famed Dodgers, and Tewksbury, an amateur artist, recorded the day in his sketch pad. Cardinals coach and Hall of Famer Red Schoendienst was asked about his impressions in seeing many of his old rivals on the field again. "Those old goats used to slide into my legs and knock me down. My legs started hurting when I got here, so I knew there was going to be an Old-Timers game," he joked.[14]

Then it was time to play ball. The Dodgers divided into two teams and, amid all the on-field antics expected of them, somehow played three innings. For those interested, the highlights included Derrell Griffith's (1963-66) clutch double to drive in Al Ferrara (1963; 1965-68), and Tommy Davis's (1959-1966) RBI single. It was fitting that both Ferrara and Davis had been born in Brooklyn. Seventy-four-year-old Mickey Owen (1941-45), the catcher who dropped the third strike with two outs in the ninth inning of Game Four in the 1941 World Series against the Yankees, made solid contact for a hit and drove in a run. Sandy

Koufax (1955-1966) received the loudest ovation, and retired the two batters who faced him: Maury Wills (1959-1966; 1969-72) grounded out to third baseman Ron Cey (1971-82) and Ted Sizemore (1969-70; 1976) flied out to left fielder Lou Johnson (1965-1967). Dodgers manager Tommy Lasorda took to the mound and received the crowd's cheers while running over to cover first base on a dribbler hit by Dick Nen (1963). Lasorda was so excited about nipping the runner that in attempting to whip the ball around the infield, threw the ball wildly into the outfield.[15]

In the regular-season game that followed, the Dodgers took an early 5-0 lead against St. Louis. Dempsey arguably had his best performance all season – smashing two doubles and going 3-for-4 – in seeming defiance of time. But the Dodgers' fortunes quickly changed, and the players began to resemble their "Daffiness Boys" antecedents rather than any of those league championship teams they had just finished honoring. In this game, the 1990 Dodgers exhibited mental lapses and committed physical errors, with a wild pitch, an errant pickoff throw, and strange baserunning thrown into the mix. Lenny Harris was picked off base for the first time in his major-league career – by, of course, a former Dodger, now Cardinal, Ricky Horton. Rubbing salt into the wound was another former Dodgers pitcher, Tom Niedenfuer, who, like Horton, shut the door on his old chums. The Cardinals came back to win, 6-5.[16]

The Dodgers shelved the annual Old-Timers Games after 1995. When asked why, the organization offered no official comment. After an 18-year absence, the Dodgers resumed Old-Timers Day for five seasons, between 2013 and 2017, but as of 2023 have not scheduled one since. Though every Old-Timers Game is special, those fortunate enough to attend the special event in the summer of 1990 were witness to the greatest assemblage of former Dodger players in their history before or since.[17]

ROSTER OF PLAYERS AND COACHES INTRODUCED AT DODGER STADIUM ON JULY 1, 1990

Red Adams

Don Drysdale

Tommy Lasorda

Dick Schofield

Joey Amalfitano	Gene Hermanski
Carl Erskine	Claude Osteen
Don LeJohn	Steve Yeager
George Shuba	Al Campanis
Sandy Amoros	Ben Hines
Chuck Essegian	Mickey Owen
Bill Loes	Geoff Zahn
Ted Sizemore	Jim Campanis
Bob Aspromonte	Burt Hooton
Joe Ferguson	Danny Ozark
Ken McMullen	Ron Cey
Reggie Smith	Tommy John
Monty Basgall	Ron Perranoski
Al Ferrara	Eddie Chandler
Mike G. Marshall	Lou Johnson
Duke Snider	Joe Pignatano
Rex Barney	Chuck Churn
Herman Franks	Tom "Spider" Jorgensen
Carmen Mauro	Johnny Podres
Dick Teed	Dolph Camilli
Jim Baxes	Von Joshua
Augie Galan	Doug Rau
Joe Moeller	Pete Coscarart
Darrel Thomas	Clyde King
Joe Beckwith	Phil Regan
Al Gionfriddo	Willie Crawford
Manny Mota	John Kennedy
Arky Vaughan	Pete Richert
Carroll Beringer	Mark Cresse
Dick Gray	Clyde King
Dick Nen	Ed Roebuck
Ben Wade	Tommy Davis
Joe Black	Sandy Koufax
Derrell Griffith	John Roseboro
Don Newcombe	Willie Davis
John Werhas	Clem Labine
Ralph Branca	Jerry Royster
John Hale	Al Downing
Nate Oliver	Lee Lacy
Maury Wills	Bill Russell
Bobby Bragan	Norm Larker

NOTES

1   The Dodgers announced that their season-long 1990 Centennial Celebration would include the largest promotional program ever launched in the organization's history. Among these were a 100th-anniversary logo patch worn on uniforms all season long, a museum-quality exhibit on Dodgers history circulating through area malls, and a team sponsorship of special art and essay contests in the local school system, two separate fan balloting programs: one to select the greatest players in the team's history and another to select the greatest moment in the club's history. One of the most popular promotions, in conjunction with Target retail stores, was the distribution of a set of over 1,000 baseball cards featuring a photograph of every Dodger player in their history.

2   Bill Plaschke, "The Night of Two No-Hitters: Fernando Pitches One for the First Time as He Stymies Cardinals," *Los Angeles Times*, June 30, 1990: C-1; Matt McHale, "Valenzuela Closes No-Hitter Night," *Orange County (California) Register*, June 30, 1990: D1; Terry Johnson, "Fernando Never Lost Respect of Teammates," *Torrance Daily Breeze*, July 1, 1990: C1; Rick Hummel, "Valenzuela 'Predicted' Gem," *St. Louis Post-Dispatch*, July 1, 1990: F1.

3   A chronological list of no-hitters can be found at https://www.retrosheet.org/nohit_chrono.htm.

4   John Jeansonne, "Vin Scully, 1927 – 2022, Melodic Voice of Dodgers," *Newsday* (Long Island, New York), August 4, 2022: A46.

5   But they were far from the only no-hit major-league games pitched during the 1990 season. In April, the Angels' Mark Langston and Mike Witt combined to no-hit the Seattle Mariners. In June, two more no-hitters were tossed: the Mariners' Randy Johnson against Detroit and the Rangers' Nolan Ryan against Oakland. Nor were Stewart's and Valenzuela's no-hitters the last of the season. The Phillies' Terry Mulholland pitched a no-hitter against San Francisco in August, and the Blue Jays' Dave Steib threw the final no-hitter of the season, in September against Cleveland.

6   Allan Malamud, "Notes on a Scorecard," *Los Angeles Times*, July 3, 1990: C3.

7   Woody Woodburn, "Dodgers Old-Timers Go to BAT," *Ventura County Star* (Camarillo, California), July 1, 1990: C1.

8   In 1875 the *New York Clipper* reported the "largest gathering of old ball-tossers seen at the classic ground at Hoboken" for a game played on September 26, 1875, to commemorate the 25th anniversary since James Whyte Davis played his first game with the Knickerbockers. "The Knickerbocker Club: Baseball in the Olden Time," *New York Clipper*, October 9, 1875: 222. This information was generously provided by John Thorn in an email communication to the author dated December 12, 2023.

9   Among former Brooklyn players participating in the 1932 game were Harry McIntyre, Tommy Griffith, Cy Barger, and Rube Bressler. William McCullough, "Dodgers Trim Reds Twice," *Brooklyn Times Union*, August 21, 1932: 2A; Thomas Holmes, "Dodger Data," *Brooklyn Eagle*, August 21, 1932: C1. The roster of Dodgers suiting up for the 1936 game included Zack Wheat, Casey Stengel, Otto Miller, Bill Scanlan, Jimmy Hickman, Al Mamaux, Eddie Zimmerman, Tex Erwin, Lew Malone, Ed Phelps, Gus Getz, Clise Dudley, Mickey Welsh, Harry Lumley, George Bell, Larry Cheney, Charlie Hargreaves, George Smith, Val Picinich, Jack Warner, and legendary Dodger scout Larry Sutton, who signed Zack Wheat and Jake Daubert among others. In honor of the occasion of the National League's "60th birthday," the three-inning exhibition was played according to 1876 rules. Lee Scott, "Buck Wheat Steals Show as Old Timers Frolic in Grand Reunion Party," *Brooklyn Citizen*, September 11, 1936: 6; Bill McCullough, "Stars of Yesteryear Relive Old Days in League Celebration at Ebbets Field," *Brooklyn Times Union*, September 11, 1936: A1; Tommy Holmes, "Zack Wheat is Still the Idol of Veteran Brooklyn Baseball Fans," *Brooklyn Eagle*, September 11, 1936, 24.

10   Dodgers who made an appearance in the 1940 reunion game included Zack Wheat, Tommy Griffith, Hy Myers, Dazzy Vance, Rube Marquard, Burleigh Grimes, Tim Jordan, Rabbit Maranville, Fresco Thompson, Ivy Olson, Casey Stengel, Ed Konetchy, Andy High, Del Bissonette, Otto Miller, Rube Bressler, Bernie Neis, Chuck Ward, Hank DeBerry, Sherry Smith, Leon Cadore, Larry Cheney, Nap Rucker, Al Mamaux, Jack Coombs, Ernie Krueger, Lew Malone, Gene Sheridan, Jimmy Hickman, Waite Hoyt, Jesse Petty, Owen Carroll, Val Picinich, Joe Stripp, Horace Ford, Jack Fournier, Jimmy Johnston, Gus Getz, and Milton Stock, and former manager, Bill Dahlen. Tommy Holmes, "'Old Timers' Enjoy Romp at Ebbets Field," *Brooklyn Eagle*, September 19, 1940: 15; "Spectators Get Big Thrill as 'Oldtimers' Play," *Brooklyn Citizen*, September 23, 1940, 6; "Dodger Old-Timers Beat Older Timers," *New York Daily News*, September 23, 1940: 42. In August 1954, a Dodgers Old-Timers Day was proposed to take place in the 1955 season, but no record of it having been staged could be found. "Buy Your Ticket and Name All-Time Team," *Brooklyn Record*, August 27, 1954: 1.

11   Among retired players honored in 1971 were Carl Furillo, Sandy Koufax, Don Drysdale, Andy Pafko, Jim Gilliam, Charlie Neal, Andy Carey, Babe Herman, George Shuba, Maury Wills, Norm Larker, Dick Tracewski, John Roseboro, Casey Stengel, Wally Moon, Roger Craig, Don Demeter, Bill Skowron, Dixie Walker, Ed Roebuck, Joe Pignatano, Gil Hodges, Cookie Lavagetto, Sal Maglie, Johnny Podres, Don Newcombe, Gene Hermanski, Larry Sherry, Pee Wee Reese, Larry Burright, Chuck Essegian, Joe Black, Duke Snider, and Ralph Branca. For good measure, former major-league umpires Al Passarella, Jocko Conlon, Beans Reardon, and Pat Orr participated in the festivities. http://www.ladodgertalk.com/2022/02/15/old-timers-game. Accessed September 2023.

12   In 1990, as it had for the previous four seasons, the Equitable Life Insurance company sponsored the Old-Timers Series, Old-Timers games played in each big-league ballpark; the company donated $10,000 to the Baseball Assistance Team (BAT), a nonprofit organization currently affiliated with Major League Baseball to assist former major-league (including the Negro Leagues) players and umpires, for each game played. The Dodgers announced they would also donate to BAT in 1990. Woody Woodburn, "Dodgers Old-Timers Go to BAT," *Ventura County Star* (Camarillo, California), July 1, 1990: C1; *Dodgers Line Drives*, Volume 33, No. 3: 1. But 1990 would also mark the final year of Equitable's corporate sponsorship. Mike Terry, "AL President Says Showers Would Postpone Game 24 Hours," *San Bernardino County Sun*, July 10, 1990: C4. In December 1990, the Upper Deck Company, then based in Orange County, California, signed a five-year contract to take over the campaign, rebranding it as the Heroes of Baseball Series, and likewise donating $10,000 to BAT where each Old-Timers Game was played. "County Firm to Back Games," *Los Angeles Times*, December 4, 1990: C13. Though they started with a full slate with each ballpark initially in 1991, by 1994 and 1995, the company was sponsoring only a handful of games, though it did sponsor games in Dodger Stadium each season. Upper Deck dropped its sponsorship of the program after 1995 and the Dodgers likewise stopped scheduling the Old-Timers Games.

13   Steve Dilbeck, "Dodgers Drop Another, 6-5 to Cards," *San Bernardino County Sun*, July 2, 1990: C4.

14   Rick Hummel, "Oquendo's June Boom Nets 15 RBIs," *St. Louis Post-Dispatch*, July 2, 1990: 4C.

15   Bill Plaschke, "Dodgers Throw Game Away and Cardinals Catch It," *Los Angeles Times*, July 2, 1990: C10; Mike Waldner, "The Boys of Autumn Return," *San Pedro News-Pilot*, July 2, 1990: B1.

16   Terry Johnson, "Dodger Win Not in These Cards," *San Pedro News-Pilot*, July 2, 1990: B1; Rick Hummel, "Saving Grace for Cards," *St. Louis Post-Dispatch*, July 2, 1990: C1.

17   The Dodgers hosted an Old-Timers Game in 2013 for the first time since 1995 to mark the 50th anniversary of their four-game sweep of the Yankees in the 1963 World Series. It was played when the Yankees were at Dodger Stadium for an interleague series. Jim Peltz, "Puig Can't Save Dodgers This Time," *Los Angeles Times*, June 23, 2013: C6; Advertisement for Dodger Stadium ticket promotions, *Los Angeles Times*, May 4, 2014: C5; Steve Dilbeck, "Koufax: Kershaw Will Be Just Fine," *Los Angeles Times*, May 16, 2015: D3; Mike DiGiovanna, "Dodgers Report," *Los Angeles Times*, July 3, 2016: D5; and Andy McCullough, "Seager's Walk-off Double Does the Job," *Los Angeles Times*, June 11, 2017: D5.

"SCULLY'S SHRINE": A BROADCASTER AND HIS BALLPARK

by Michael Green

For 55 of his 67 years as a broadcaster for the Dodgers, Vin Scully went to work at the same place: Dodger Stadium. In 2001 the area from which he broadcast became the Vin Scully Press Box. In 2016, his final season, the Los Angeles City Council changed the name of the street leading to the ballpark from Elysian Park Avenue to Vin Scully Avenue. In 2017, the year after he retired, the Dodgers added his name to the "Ring of Honor" of Hall of Famers with retired numbers, representing him with "Vin" and a "microphone." Those honors speak to Scully's history with the team and the ballpark, and how their interconnections remain after his death in 2022.

Several of Scully's ties to Dodger Stadium, and harbingers of how inseparable they would become, originated before anyone with the team had even heard of Chavez Ravine or built a ballpark there. Scully realized the connection between a ballpark and its team when he grew up going to New York Giants games at the Polo Grounds in the late 1930s and early 1940s: After its destruction in the early 1960s, he saw an oil painting of the Polo Grounds and "felt like I had been kicked in the stomach."[1] He became especially aware of those links, and how they included the announcer, when he joined the Brooklyn Dodgers in 1950 at the age of 22. Red Barber, who chose him for the job, was a beloved figure in Brooklyn, and Scully discovered how intimate Ebbets Field was. One day as he sat next to Barber in the broadcasting booth, Scully heard Hilda Chester, a fan legendary for ringing her cowbell and hectoring the opposition, bellow, "Vin Scully, I love you!" When Scully looked down in embarrassment, he heard, "Look at me when I'm talking to you."[2]

When the Dodgers moved to Los Angeles, they spent four years at the far less intimate Memorial Coliseum, where Scully's legend really began before they moved, as Scully put it, to "this golden palace on the other side of the horizon."[3] The Coliseum was

built for the 1932 Olympics and then used mainly for football, reconfigured for baseball with a 250-foot left-field line with a high screen. Not only did many of those fans have to strain to see the field and the players, but they had little experience with major-league baseball, other than postseason play and weekend network telecasts on CBS and NBC. Many of the fans knew about major-league baseball but had rarely seen it or its players. As Don Drysdale recalled of the team's move and the Coliseum's configuration, "From the bottom to top row of seats, it must have been a good block. The fans didn't only need Vin Scully on the radio to find out what was happening. They needed telescopes."[4] Scully became so well known for fans

SABR / The Rucker Archive.

Vin Scully served as Dodgers broadcaster from 1950 through 2016.

bringing their radios to the park that for a major *Sports Illustrated* profile of Scully in 1964, Robert Creamer and his editors titled the article "The Transistor Kid." Scully said, "I got lucky. I came along about the same time as the transistor radio," but another sportswriter said, "A lot of people mention that Vin benefited from the transistor radio, but really the transistor radio benefited from Vin."[5]

As Scully and the team eagerly awaited the move to Chavez Ravine, he played a role in Dodger Stadium before he started doing play-by-play there. When O'Malley chose September 17, 1959, for the ceremony to begin construction, Scully served as the emcee. As many as 5,000 brought shovels to take home souvenir dirt in boxes the Dodgers provided, and watch the starting lineup run out to the places where they eventually would stand after the stadium's completion. On Opening Day 1962, Scully emceed the ceremonies dedicating Dodger Stadium, though his prediction that one day it would be expanded to 80,000 seats with space for 25,000 cars has yet to be realized. After the pregame events, he moved to his new home on the third-tier club level next to the press box, a booth that included a seating area in the back and a table built into the front with room for Scully, his colleague Jerry Doggett, and the engineer.

The transistor tradition moved from the Coliseum to Dodger Stadium when it opened in 1962. Scully had to switch from using a microphone to wearing a headset, and his engineer had to adjust the microphones in the booth and around the park to avoid hearing the feedback from the radios in the stands. The Dodgers encouraged the phenomenon: Promotions director Danny Goodman started selling radios at the souvenir stands, and a *Los Angeles Times* columnist guessed that of 52,000 fans at one game, about 40,000 had radios.[6] Fans grew so accustomed to listening to his account of what they saw that Red Patterson, the team's longtime vice president for public relations, recalled the night a fan called the stadium switchboard from a phone booth in the left-field pavilion and said, "Will you please notify [manager Walt] Alston immediately the men in the bullpen are making too much noise popping pitches into the catcher's glove? I can't hear Vin Scully and Jerry Doggett on my transistor."[7] Alston's successor, Tom Lasorda, said, "Davey Lopes hits a line drive off the wall, comes flying around second and slides head-first into third and not one person in the stadium believes it until Vinnie tells them it's true."[8]

This connection to the fans in the stands may well have made Scully an even better broadcaster than he already was. As Scully explained, "I tell you one thing, it keeps you on your toes. When you know that just about everybody in that ballpark is listening to you describe a play that they're watching, you'd better call it right. You can't get lazy and catch up with a pitch that you've missed. You can't fake a play that you've called wrong."[9] He took pride that he had never heard from fans that his descriptions had been incorrect.

Even those on the field became part of the transistor tradition. Catcher Norm Sherry recalled sitting in the Dodgers bullpen and being able to hear Scully's broadcasts from the transistors. When the Cincinnati Reds came to Dodger Stadium in 1969, reliever George Culver, a Californian who later became a Dodger himself, took a radio to the bullpen to listen to Scully and Doggett, and manager Dave Bristol allowed a radio in the dugout. During the game, a pitcher began to throw in the Reds bullpen down the right-field line behind the stands, just out of Scully's view. Thinking the pitcher was Wayne Granger, and knowing about the radio, Scully said on the air, "George, if that's Granger warming up, give us a wave." Culver moved into view and did as Scully had asked.[10]

Players in the middle of the action also heard Scully's voice echoing through the ballpark. Nearly a decade before he joined the team, Jerry Reuss pitched at Dodger Stadium for the first time for the St. Louis Cardinals. With the crowd around 20,000, he could recall hearing Scully and figuring out that he was in the middle of a story. "As a courtesy to the best in the business," he took some time, used the rosin bag, and returned to the rubber. When the crowd laughed, Reuss knew that Scully had finished and resumed pitching. Later, when Reuss broadcast for the Dodgers, he recounted the story to Scully, who "had a laugh about it."[11]

Although Scully famously encouraged the Coliseum crowd to wish umpire Frank Secory a happy birthday, he also found ways to involve the Dodger Stadium faithful. In 1963 National League President Warren Giles ordered umpires to enforce the balk rule more stringently, including that a pitcher had to come set for at least one second. The number of balks rose, as did the number of arguments about them, including one at Dodger Stadium that April 24. As Reds manager Fred Hutchinson argued with the umpires, Scully discussed the balk rule, eventually noting how hard it is to figure out exactly how long one second is. He said, "Hey, let's try something. I'll get a stopwatch from the engineer." Then he said, "I'll push the stopwatch and say, 'One!' and when you think one full second has elapsed, you yell, 'Two!' Ready? One!" The crowd of more than 19,000 screamed, "Two!" Scully said, "I'm sorry. Only one of you had it right. Let's try it again. One!" Again, they yelled, "Two!" Someone from the dugout called the booth to find out what was going on.[12]

Scully also found other ways to include the Dodger Stadium crowds. When the Dodgers clinched the 1965 pennant at home on the next-to-last day of the season, Alston told Scully that since the next game didn't matter, "How about managing? You tell me on the air what to do. I'll listen in the dugout, with earphones on, and give directions to the guys," who were recovering from a night of celebrating their victory. When Ron Fairly, who was not noted for speed, reached first, Scully said, "For those of you with radios, let's have Fairly steal. Watch Fairly's face when he … gets the sign." Scully said that Fairly did a double-take and "sloshed to second, but had to retreat to first after a foul ball.[13]

Even without being in on strategy, fans in Dodger Stadium played an important role in any Scully broadcast. In a 1966 profile, after Doggett said, "Six minutes until game time," the author asked, "Are you just a little bit nervous, Vin?" Scully replied, "Not after 17 years. But just wait until a key play – just wait – and my arm will be covered with goose bumps."[14] He often spoke of his love for the roar of the crowd, and the Dodgers' success in attendance –climbing well above 3.5 million fans in the later years of his tenure – meant that the crowd's roar would be in evidence. Further, the Dodgers' success – the team had only 13 losing seasons in Scully's 67 years with the team – meant that fans had ample reason to make noise during his broadcasts. And Scully became well known for what broadcasters referred to as "laying out" – enabling listeners to enjoy the excitement of the fans in the ballpark and "to let the crowd noise tell the story." Scully said, "On the road, it's slightly different. In Milwaukee, when the Braves first landed there, the crowds would react to a good Dodger play with stony Prussian silence. You don't know what silence is until you've heard a Milwaukee crowd react to a home run by Duke Snider. I'm captivated by crowd noises – like, oh, when an L.A. crowd boos Juan Marichal as if he were a landlord not giving enough steam heat in the winter."[15]

Scully admitted to one time when the Dodger Stadium crowd carried him into an emotional reaction he apparently never repeated. Although he said, "I am not neutral. You cannot travel with and live with

Courtesy Todd Anton.

Fans at Dodger Stadium were given a commemorative Vin Scully microphone in 2014.

and become friends with members of a team and not want them to do well," he prided himself on his on-air objectivity.[16] On at least one occasion, though, he had to find a way to vent his support for the Dodgers. He recounted to the *Los Angeles Times* that after a Dodger delivered a key hit in a game against the Giants, "[s]uddenly, that tremendous animal roar of the crowd got to me. I felt like I was going to explode. I had to do something. I leaned out of the booth and started pounding my fist on the façade of the stadium. None of the listeners knew what I was doing, though. I'd at least pressed the cough button on the mike, the only time I ever did that. When I finally got the fist-pounding out of my system, I resumed announcing as calmly as I could. One of the letters I got later asked how in the world I could be so cool and detached during such an exciting game."[17]

Scully's connection with the fans in the stands became well known beyond his home ballpark and even entered popular culture. Terry O'Neil, who as CBS Sports' executive producer based in New York helped prompt Scully to leave the network for NBC's *Game of the Week* when he denied him the chance to broadcast the Super Bowl, wrote that his "great respect" for Scully included having "joined his worshipers for the 'transistor stereo rites' one evening in Dodger Stadium."[18] Dodgers fans became known for leaving the game early, and Dick Young, the *New York Daily News* columnist who often criticized the Dodgers and their fans, praised his old friend Scully when he suggested that they left the stadium early because "they feel they can walk out, listening, without missing a thing."[19]

In another example of Scully's impact, Kevin Fagan, who grew up in Southern California and has drawn the comic strip *Drabble* since 1979, paid tribute to him in numerous strips. One Sunday strip captured how the tradition of listening to Scully at the ballpark continued. In his later seasons, Scully broadcast only on television, with the first three innings simulcast on radio. Fans still sought access, as Fagan wryly noted. At the beginning of Scully's final season in 2016, Fagan depicted the family wondering where the father, Ralph, had been for the past three innings. They found him in the men's room with several other people, looking at the monitor, where they heard, "Did I ever tell you about the time Jackie Robinson and I raced on ice skates?"[20] That was not unusual: Fans continued to bring their radios to Dodger Stadium for the rest of his tenure, and would congregate around monitors spread throughout the concession areas to watch and listen.

When Scully retired at the end of the 2016 season, the connection between him and the ballpark remained. A retirement ceremony attracted a full house. After the final regular-season game, manager Dave Roberts spoke to him from the field and Scully addressed the crowd from the booth, where a banner said, "I'll miss you," signed, "Vin." Scully returned for ceremonial occasions – to throw out a first ball and for two inductions into the Ring of Honor: his own and that of his friend Jaime Jarrín, the team's Spanish-language voice for 64 years (only three fewer than Scully). After Scully died on August 2, 2022, at the first home game afterward, Roberts addressed the crowd, the pitcher's mound included "Vin" and a microphone embedded in the dirt, and his television successor, Joe Davis, joined analyst Orel Hershiser in dropping a banner from his old booth saying, "Vin – We'll miss you! Dodger Fans." More than ever, Dodger Stadium had become what sportswriter Rick Reilly called it in 1985: "Scully's shrine."[21]

Yet Scully saw it as a shrine of a different sort. He had been close to the longtime owners, the O'Malleys. Walter O'Malley had hoped Dodger Stadium would be "a monument to the O'Malleys."[22] Scully told Kirk McKnight, "The biggest thing about Dodger Stadium – certainly in July, August, September – when the air is clear and you are looking out beyond the pavilions, you would see the mountains, and you would remember the words from the song and the words 'the purple mountains' majesty' and that's out there for all the world to see. It's a beautiful ballpark." He recalled the effort that O'Malley put into planning and building the ballpark. "Mr. O'Malley loved the earth. He loved flowers, and so we have a lot of that as well," Scully said. He concluded, "It's a great tribute to the game,

it's a great tribute to baseball, and it's a great tribute to Walter O'Malley, so, all in all, it's a rather sacred place for me."[23] Scully helped make it into a marvelous place for Dodger fans.

ACKNOWLEDGMENTS

The author would like to thank his friends and fellow SABR members David Tanenhaus and Rob Sheinkopf for their comments on this article.

NOTES

1   Rich Wolfe, *Vin Scully: I Saw It on the Radio* (N.P., A Tribute Book, 2006), 197-98.

2   Ken Burns and Lynn Novick, *Baseball* (Florentine Films, 1994), Episode 6 at 42:29.

3   Tom Hoffarth, "Scully Recalls Culture Shock of L.A. Move 50 Years Ago," *San Bernardino* (California) *Sun*, March 28, 2008, https://www.sbsun.com/2008/03/28/scully-recalls-culture-shock-of-la-move-50-years-ago/.

4   Don Drysdale with Bob Verdi, *Once a Bum, Always a Dodger: My Life in Baseball from Brooklyn to Los Angeles* (New York: St. Martin's Press, 1990), 78.

5   Robert Creamer, "The Transistor Kid," *Sports Illustrated*, May 4, 1964, https://vault.si.com/vault/1964/05/04/the-transistor-kid.

6   Don Page, "The Radio Beat: Transistor Testimonial to Scully," *Los Angeles Times*, June 16, 1963: B30.

7   Dick Kaegel, "Even Writers Toss Bouquets at Scully, Dodger Ace on Air," *The Sporting News*, July 16, 1966: 36.

8   Rick Reilly, "Vin Scully: In 36 Years as Voice of the Dodgers, He's Never Been at Loss for Words," *Los Angeles Times*, April 8, 1985: D1, 10-11.

9   Creamer, "The Transistor Kid."

10 Wolfe, *Vin Scully*, 148; Charles Maher, "Help from the Bullpen," *Los Angeles Times*, September 18, 1969: Part III, 2.

11 Ron Kantowski, "The Night Jerry Reuss Helped Vin Scully Finish a Story," *Las Vegas Review-Journal*, August 6, 2022, https://www.reviewjournal.com/sports/sports-columns/ron-kantowski/the-night-jerry-reuss-helped-vin-scully-finish-a-story-2619202/; Jerry Reuss, *Bring in the Right-Hander! My Twenty-Two Years in the Major Leagues* (Lincoln: University of Nebraska Press, 2014), 57.

12 Creamer, "The Transistor Kid"; Kaegel, "Even Writers Toss Bouquets at Scully."

13 Curt Smith, *Pull Up a Chair: The Vin Scully Story* (Washington: Potomac Books, 2010), 102-03; Rich Wolfe, *Vin Scully: I Saw It on the Radio*, 128. Scully's recollection after the foul ball had Fairly stealing the base, but Fairly did not end up stealing a base in the game in question. See https://www.retrosheet.org/boxesetc/1965/B10030LAN1965.htm.

14 Donald Freeman, "Scully: Old Pro of the Dodgers," *San Pedro* (California) *News-Pilot*, May 27, 1966: 10.

15 Freeman.

16 Bill Libby, "Vin Scully: How I Announce a World Series," in Zander Hollander, ed., *The Complete Handbook of Baseball: 1975 Edition* (New York: Associated Features and New American Library, 1975), 8.

17 John Hall, "Vin or the Egg?" *Los Angeles Times*, July 1, 1970: Part III, 2. Scully's memory was legendary, and he demonstrated it here: He thought he had reacted to a key triple by outfielder Lee Walls. The only triple Walls hit with the Dodgers was not in a crucial situation and occurred against the Philadelphia Phillies in the seventh inning, when Doggett would have been broadcasting; that hit did give the Dodgers the lead. But in the second

game of the 1962 playoff against the Giants, with the Dodgers needing to win to force a third game and starting the inning down 5-0, Walls doubled in the sixth, scoring two runs and advancing to third on the throw, and giving the Dodgers a 6-5 lead. See https://www.retrosheet.org/boxesetc/1962/B08090LAN1962.htm; https://www.retrosheet.org/boxesetc/1962/B10020LAN1962.htm.

18   Terry O'Neil, *The Game Behind the Game: High Stakes, High Pressure in Television Sports* (New York: Harper & Row, 1989), 93.

19   Smith, *Pull Up a Chair*, 91.

20   http://www.laobserved.com/archive/2013/10/drabble_cartoonists_tribu.php; https://drabble.substack.com/p/this-day-in-drabble-history-vin-scully?sd=pf.

21   Reilly, "Scully."

22   Roger Kahn, *The Boys of Summer* (New York: Harper & Row, 1972), 389.

23   Kirk McKnight, *The Voices of Baseball: The Game's Greatest Broadcasters Reflect on America's Pastime* (Updated edition, Lanham, Maryland: Rowman & Littlefield, 2023), 26.

FANS COME FIRST – A HISTORY OF
DODGER STADIUM PROMOTIONS

by Joey Elledge

The Los Angeles Dodgers are one of the most popular and influential brands in sports. Walter O'Malley moved his team from Brooklyn to LA despite it clearly not being popular with Brooklyn fans. On April 13, 1958, five days before the Dodgers' first game in Los Angeles, Mayor Norris Poulson declared that week to be "Welcome Dodgers Week."[1] Fans gathered in the streets of LA to greet their future team. The excitement for the team was just beginning. O'Malley and the Dodgers knew their top priority would be to build a solid and loyal new fan base.

The fans were a large part of O'Malley's daily concern.[2] Baseball, of course, had to be the primary focus. The Dodgers also wanted to ensure a family-friendly environment at a comfortable, safe, and clean Dodger Stadium. If a fan reached out by telephone or mail,

Dodgers staff were expected to reply. It is said that with the help of his secretary, O'Malley read and answered every letter he received during his ownership.[3] O'Malley was a constant presence with fans and even developed a newsletter as another way to communicate with fans. Not only did fans know that O'Malley was available, but O'Malley made sure baseball games at Dodger Stadium were affordable.

Prices remained unchanged at 75 cents to $3.50 for 18 years. Dodger Stadium was thus viewed by many as a family-affordable and entertaining experience. The Dodgers set records for attendance, breaking the major-league record in 1962 with 2,755,184. In 1978 the Dodgers became the first team to surpass 3 million fans in a season. Fans have been treated to memorable promotions since the opening of Dodger Stadium.

Some of the recent additions to Dodger Stadium include these larger-than-life bobbleheads.

DANNY GOODMAN'S INFLUENCE ON DODGER STADIUM PROMOTIONS

Danny Goodman, a leader in the Dodgers organization for 25 years, is considered one of the best business minds in baseball history. Goodman was an innovative businessman for his time and brought in many of the promotion's baseball teams continue to use. In 1958, before the Dodgers were in Dodger Stadium, Goodman's efforts contributed more than $200,000 to the club's profits with his souvenir ideas and innovation. Goodman is credited with bringing one of the most sought-after souvenir items to major-league baseball – the bobblehead doll.[4]

The Dodgers were one of the first teams to adopt bobbleheads for promotional giveaways. In 1974 Goodman created his brand of bobbleheads, called Bobbing Heads. These bobbleheads did not just feature the Dodgers logo. Fans could shop for Bobbing Heads from all 24 major-league teams at Dodger Stadium.

Additionally, Goodman is credited with bringing Hollywood to Dodger Stadium. His visionary initiatives led to a natural relationship between the Dodgers and movie and television celebrities. Goodman created "Hollywood Stars Night."[5]

Celebrities and baseball players competed in the Hollywood Stars softball game. The first games were held when Goodman worked for the Hollywood Stars of the Pacific Coast League at Gilmore Field, where he suggested celebrities join the game. When the Dodgers relocated to Los Angeles, O'Malley and Goodman wanted to have a baseball game for celebrities at Dodger Stadium. The Dodgers held the first Hollywood Stars Game in 1958. A prelude to a Dodgers game, it ran annually through 2009.

While this was largely an event for publicity, it was fun for Dodgers players, fans, and celebrities, sometimes drawing a crowd of 48,000. Actor and filmmaker Rob Reiner exhibited warning-track power by nearly hitting a home run twice in these games. Celebrities and Dodgers shared the locker room and created memories for all. From 1958 to 2009 and in sporadic years since 2009, a wide range of celebrities have participated in this game.[6] Due to the spacious foul territory at Dodger Stadium, some celebrities entered the field in automobiles, among them Dean Martin arriving in a limo for his at-bat.

One of the biggest celebrities involved in Hollywood Stars night was Kareem Abdul-Jabbar. The 7-foot-2-inch Los Angeles Lakers center was a dominating presence on and off the court. Poking fun at his height, two stars would carry an oversized bat for Abdul-Jabbar to swing.

LATINO PROMOTIONS AND "THE BATTLE OF CHAVEZ RAVINE"

The Dodgers have had a strong Latino fan base since the early 1980s. Originally, though, there was considerable opposition from Latinos to the Dodgers because construction of the ballpark uprooted many Latino families. In the 1950s, eminent domain was used to evict three largely Mexican American neighborhoods for a housing project that ultimately failed.[7] With the abandoned land and the Dodgers' need for a new home, Chavez Ravine seemed a perfect fit. Dodger Stadium was built despite the initial pushback from the metro area's Latino population, which grew to 4 million.[8]

The Dodgers' efforts to engage Latinos have been ongoing since the 1980s with programs like Hispanic Heritage Month. When asked in 2012 how important the Latino fan base is to the Dodgers, club President and CEO Stan Kasten said, "Our Latino fans and every single one of our fans are top of mind year-round. We do want to take this opportunity, however, to express our pride in the Dodgers' history and future in Latin America and the countless Latino Dodgers past and present that have made an impact on the game and on this city."[9] This led to the creation of "Viva Los Dodgers!"

Since 1997 Viva Los Dodgers! is hosted on the last Sunday of each month during the season, culminating in "La Gran Fiesta" at the end of the season. Latino artists such as Louie Cruz Beltran, a master percussionist, in 2019, and Banda La Maravillosa, a Mexican regional-style band in 2018, have performed at the event.

The Dodgers drew on their Latino fans to add to the Viva Los Dodgers! promotion. To Mexican Americans, the team was the "Doyers" because the Spanish language has no "J" sound.[10] In the September 2023 event, the club featured Viva Los Doyers™ on its website.

In 2023 the promotion also featured players of Latino heritage – Luis Avilán, Pedro Báez, Carlos Frías, Yimi García, Adrián González, Yasmani Grandal, Álex Guerrero, Kiké Hernández, Juan Nicasio, Joel Peralta, and Ronald Torreyes, as well as other Latino employees.

Courtesy Todd Anton

Dodger bobbleheads decorate Todd Anton's classroom in southern California.

What began with initial pushback from the Latino residents of Los Angeles, has been transformed into diehard fandom in support of their home team.

THINK BLUE

In 1997 the club added a "Think Blue" sign outside Dodger Stadium designed to mimic the city's famous Hollywood sign. The sign was initially put up for the promotion "Think Blue Week."[11] In view of overwhelming fan support, the Dodgers made it a staple. In December of 2011 the wind blew down some of the letters and the sign read "Ink Bl je." The Dodgers had the sign taken down, but judging from numerous petitions and websites, fans wanted it returned.

2006 – GOLDEN FLEECE: FANS FLOCK TO DODGER STADIUM FOR FREE BLANKETS

On May 9, 2006, Dodger Stadium hosted what was at the time the second-largest crowd in Dodger Stadium history – 55,992 fans on a Tuesday night for a baseball game. The reason was not a playoff game, not a World Series game, but for a free Dodger-blue fleece blanket commemorating the 25th anniversary of the team's 1981 World Series title.[12] It was estimated that an extra 20,000 tickets were sold thanks to the blankets, which were provided by Dodgers sponsor Toyota. These types of promotions are considered beneficial both for the team and the sponsor.

RE-OPENING DAY

In March 2020, the sports landscape came to a crashing halt due to the COVID-19 pandemic. The baseball season was curtailed, and fans were not allowed to attend games as a public health precaution.

On June 15, 2021, Dodger Stadium hosted what was called "Re-Opening Day" with 52,078 in attendance.[13] The first 25,000 fans received a Justin Turner bobblehead, and country singer Brad Paisley sang the National Anthem. The 2020 World Series champion Dodgers were honored for the first time by the 2021 team wearing special gold-trimmed jerseys and hats.

SISTERS OF PERPETUAL INDULGENCE

June 16, 2023, at Dodger Stadium, was supposed to be the Pride Night celebration. Among the invitees were the Sisters of Perpetual Indulgence, a nonprofit organization that raises funds and volunteers in the LGBTQ+ community. The group wears apparel similar to Catholic nuns' robes, leading many to view them as anti-Catholic.

Some players spoke out against the Sisters being invited to Dodger Stadium, saying it went against the Dodgers' code of conduct for their players, which prohibited support for anything that would disparage one's religion. Pitcher Clayton Kershaw spoke out against the group and urged the team to reinstate Faith and Family Night, which before the pandemic had been a longstanding annual promotion.[14] (It was last held in 2019.) Kershaw said he was not bothered by the Sisters' support of the LGTBQ+ community, but rather their perceived mocking of Christian beliefs. Some politicians spoke out against the group, saying the invite was anti-Catholic. Former Vice President Mike Pence said on social media, "Having been raised in a Catholic family, the Dodgers decision to invite the Sisters of Perpetual Indulgence, a hateful group that blatantly mocks Catholicism, to their event next month is deeply offensive."[15] Senator Marco Rubio of Florida, in a letter to Commissioner Rob Manfred, voiced his opposition to the group. Because of the backlash, the Dodgers disinvited the Sisters from Pride Night. However, the backlash for disinviting the group proved to be severe as well.

Because the Sisters were disinvited, other groups, including the Los Angeles LGBT Center, the ACLU of Southern California, and LA Pride, withdrew from the event. The LGBT center issued an ultimatum to the Dodgers: cancel Pride Night or reinvite the Sisters. A few days later, the Dodgers reversed themselves. LA Pride, a longtime collaborator on the Pride Night event, said: "The Dodgers have taken a good first step toward their commitment to the LGBTQ+ community by renewing their invite to the Sisters of Perpetual Indulgence at next month's Pride Night. We fully support the Sisters receiving their much-deserved

Community Hero Award and will stand in solidarity with them at Pride Night. They continue to inspire us with their grace."[16]

On June 17, the Sisters were honored with the Dodgers' Community Hero Award on Pride Night. The Catholic League urged Dodgers fans who were Catholic to not attend the event and not be in the ballpark when the Sisters received their award. Archbishop José Gomez hosted a Mass before the game "for healing due to the harm caused by the Dodgers decision to honor a group that intentionally denigrates and profanes the Christian faith."[17]

If one asks fans who are Catholic, fewer people attended the game. If one asks fans who supported the Sisters, there was only love and support for the group inside the ballpark.[18] There was a protest outside Dodger Stadium that led to the Dodgers closing the main entrance.

LAKERS NIGHT – 2023

Kobe Bryant is a beloved figure in the Los Angeles sports world. Bryant led the Lakers to five NBA championships and frequently attended Dodgers games. When Bryant was killed in a helicopter crash in January 2020, the sports world was determined to continue his legacy. Bryant was honored at "Lakers Night" in September 2023 when fans who bought a special ticket package received a crossover jersey for the Dodgers, featuring both Lakers and Dodgers branding with Bryant's jersey numbers 8 and 24.[19]

In addition to the jersey, Dodgers fans were treated to Bryant's daughter Natalia throwing out the ceremonial first pitch, the team making a $100,000 donation to the Mamba and Mambacita Sports Foundation, and to a special drone show that honored Bryant's career and life. In addition, the Dodgers players stood along the foul line while wearing Bryant jerseys.

Over the years, Dodger Stadium has had a variety of promotions, some larger and more successful than others. As times change, and new ideas come forth, it will be interesting to see what forms future promotions may take.

NOTES

1   Shelly Kale, "This Day in Los Angeles History: April 10, 1962 — First Game at Dodger Stadium," California Historical Society, https://californiahistoricalsociety.org/blog/this-day-in-los-angeles-history-april-10-1962-first-game-at-dodger-stadium/.

2   Brent Shyer, "Walter O'Malley's Legacy," https://www.walteromalley.com/en/biography/short/Walter-OMalleys-Legacy.

3   Shyer

4   Andy McCue, "Danny Goodman," SABR BioProject, https://sabr.org/bioproj/person/danny-goodman/

5   Mark Langill, "The (Movie) Hollywood Stars Game," SABR.org, 2011. https://sabr.org/journal/article/the-movie-hollywood-stars-game/.

6   City News Service, "Dodgers to Hold First Hollywood Stars Game Since 2009," *Los Angeles Daily News*, June 6, 2015. https://www.dailynews.com/2015/06/06/dodgers-to-hold-first-hollywood-stars-game-since-2009/.

7   Eric Nusbaum, *Stealing Home: Los Angeles, the Dodgers, and the Lives Caught in Between* (New York: Public Affairs, 2020).

8   United States Census Bureau, https://data.census.gov/profile/Los_Angeles_County,_California?g=050XX00US06037

9   CBS Los Angeles, "Dodgers Celebrate Hispanic Heritage Month," 2012. https://www.cbsnews.com/losangeles/news/dodgers-celebrate-hispanic-heritage-month/.

10 Gustavo Arellano, "How LA's "Los Doyers" Fans Turned a Racist Insult into a Point of Pride," *REMEZCLA*, October 26, 2017. https://remezcla.com/features/sports/los-angeles-doyers-chavez-ravine/.

11 Ron Cervenka, "'Sign-Stealing' Nothing New for Dodger Fans," *ThinkBlue. Com*, January 21, 2020. https://thinkbluela.com/2020/01/sign-stealing-nothing-new-for-dodger-fans/.

12 David Nusbaum, "Golden Fleece: Fans Flock to Dodger Stadium for Free Blankets," *Los Angeles Business Journal*, May 22, 2006

13 MLB.com, "Dodgers to Celebrate Reopening Day Tomorrow," MLB.com, June 14, 2021. https://www.mlb.com/press-release/press-release-dodgers-reopening-day-6-15-21.

14 Isabel Gonzalez, "Dodgers Pride Night Controversy Explained: Clayton Kershaw Speaks Out Against Sisters of Perpetual Indulgence," CBS Sports, June 15, 2023. https://www.cbssports.com/mlb/news/dodgers-pride-night-timeline-club-re-invites-sisters-of-perpetual-indulgence-to-lgbtq-celebration/.

15 Gonzalez.

15 Sonja Sharp & Jeong Park, "The Dodgers Booted the Sisters of Perpetual Indulgence. Then Came a Big-League Backlash," *Los Angeles Times*, May 19, 2023. https://www.latimes.com/california/story/2023-05-19/sisters-of-perpetual-indulgence-dodgers-pride-night.

17 City News Service, "LA Archbishop Expresses 'Dismay and Pain' as Dodgers Set to Honor Sisters of Perpetual Indulgence," 2023. https://abc7.com/dodgers-pride-sisters-of-perpetual-indulgence-catholic/13381504/.

18 Jordan Mendoza, "Sisters of Perpetual Indulgence Cheered at Dodgers Pride Night: 'I Did Not Hear a Single Boo,'" *USA Today*, June 16, 2023. https://www.usatoday.com/story/sports/mlb/dodgers/2023/06/16/sisters-of-perpetual-indulgence-dodgers-pride-night-honor/70331982007/.

19 Noel Sanchez, "Multiple Dodgers Stars Rock Kobe Bryant Merch on Lakers Night," si.com, September 1, 2023. https://www.si.com/nba/lakers/news/multiple-dodgers-stars-rock-kobe-bryant-merch-on-lakers-night-ns2002.

THE DODGER DOG

by Tony S. Oliver

*"A hot dog at the park is better
than a steak at the Ritz."*
—Humphrey Bogart [1]

"Take Me Out to the Ballgame" may mention peanuts and Cracker Jack, but the hot dog is the cleanup hitter of the baseball stadium lineup.

The quintessential ballpark meal is believed to have been born in the nineteenth century and soon found itself an American staple. But how did the Dodger Dog – not invented until 1962, in a city better known for fusion food than beef – become the most popular of all the franks?

Harry M. Stevens introduced hot dogs to New York ballparks in 1905, allegedly to replace poor-selling ice cream during an early season game. Known as "red hots," the sausages sold well enough to merit a permanent place in the concession roster, especially as a double-play partner to the lucrative beer.[2] The portability of the food, and its ability to be consumed with one hand, without utensils, added to the appeal.[3]

Upon leaving Brooklyn for Los Angeles in 1958, the Dodgers franchise wished to honor its New York borough traditions and simultaneously establish a fresh identity in California. Thomas Arthur, manager of concessions, sought to sell a footlong sausage modeled after the Coney Island hot dogs of his youth, but the offering was two inches short of the promised 12.

Branding and ingenuity solved that problem. According to hot-dog historian Bruce Kraig, "people are more receptive to a hot dog if it is slightly longer than its bun," so Arthur opted for a shorter roll.[4] With the alliterative "Dodger Dog" name, a culinary star was born. Arthur, who died in 2006, ran the Dodgers' food operations from the ballpark's 1962 opening until his retirement in 1991.[5] In a town where idea ownership is often contested, former team owner Peter O'Malley has said "the Dodger Dog (w)as Tom's idea."[6]

Vin Scully and Jerry Doggett promoted the Dodger Dog on television and radio, further cementing the relationship between the snack and the stadium. Scully, the quintessential Dodger, noted, "The ones they have here are as good as I've ever tasted. Without a doubt."[7] Hot dog connoisseurs are less sanguine. Bruce Kraig, author of *Man Bites Dog: Hot Dog Culture in America*, states matter-of-factly that "First, it's marketing. And secondly, it's marketing. And the third thing? Oh yes, marketing."[8]

Players were not immune to its appeal: Rick Sutcliffe once sat in the bullpen enjoying a Dodger Dog before he was summoned to the mound to replace an injured starter. Manager Tommy Lasorda hectored the hungry hurler once he noticed the mustard and relish on Sutcliffe's uniform.[9]

Even celebrities are star-struck by the concession champion. Emmy Award winner Bryan Cranston confided that "there's something about the environment of being here at Dodger Stadium. ... [Y]ou know what it's like? When you go to a movie theater, you have to have popcorn. You've *got* to have popcorn. When

Celebrating the Dodger Dog.

Courtesy Todd Anton

you come to a Dodger game, you've got to have a Dodger Dog."[10]

Though sales figures were not officially reported, the National Hot Dog and Sausage Council calculated that 1.7 million Dodger Dogs were sold during the 2005 season.[11] *Sports Illustrated* estimated that 2.7 million yearly dogs were consumed from 2015 to 2019, more than twice the runner-up Yankees' 1.2 million annual sales.[12] Commercial success was buoyed by critical acclaim: Baseball fan Bob Wood rated it A-plus in his 1985 book *Dodger Dogs to Fenway Franks: And All the Wieners in Between*, perhaps the only authoritative book on the subject.[13]

Although the Dodgers, like most baseball teams, have expanded their culinary offerings to include other fare, the Dodger Dog still remains king. The team briefly boiled the dogs in the early 1990s but soon reverted to grilling them after fan uproar.[14] At the start of the 2023 season, the club offered plant-based dogs, bacon-wrapped dogs, and a rotating offering based on the visiting team, in addition to the standard pork-based Dodger Dog and the beef-based "super dog."[15]

According to the retail package of Dodger Dogs, each 75-gram link contains 200 calories, 8 grams of protein, 17 grams of fat, and 40 milligrams of cholesterol, though fans may not be too focused on the statistics.

In 2020 Farmer John and the Dodgers did not renew their contract and Papa Cantrella's became the official hot-dog provider of the franchise. Though the terms of the divorce were not divulged, press reports cited Occupational Safety and Health (OSHA) investigations on worker safety shortcomings.[16] Smithfield, parent company of Farmer John, announced the closure of its Vernon, California, plant in 2023.[17]

Rookie Papa Cantrella's eagerly played up its Southern California roots: "[L]ike the Dodgers, our history and community ties run deep in Los Angeles. We could not be more proud to be partnering with this iconic brand and product."[18] Founded in 1980, Papa Cantrella's continues to sell the iconic sausage in both Dodger Stadium and LA-area grocery stores.[19] As a testament to the fans' devotions, the Dodger Dog received its very own statue outside of Dodger Stadium, and bobbleheads of its likeness have been a constant presence among Dodgers game promotions.

Team historian Mark Langhill noted that "it's simply a hot dog but there's a romance about that title – the Dodger Dog. It's part of the organ music, the souvenirs, saving your ticket stub. The Dodger Dog was a major part of growing up as a Dodger fan in Los Angeles."[20] This love affair is bound to continue, as Dodger Stadium executive chef Christine Gerriets noted before the 2023 season: "It's the world famous dog, Dodger Dog, if you will. It's a fan favorite, and that's you know, one item that will always be here to stay."[21]

NOTES

1   A clip of Bogart on baseball is available on YouTube: https://www.youtube.com/watch?v=Rp1U7LnMs3A .

2   Jari Villanueva, "Hot Dog and Baseball," Taps Bugler Website, July 20, 2021, https://www.tapsbugler.com/hot-dogs-and-baseball/.

3   Chris Landers, "Everyone Gets a Hot Dog at Games … but Why?" MLB.com, April 3, 2020, https://www.mlb.com/news/history-of-iconic-mlb-ballpark-food-explained.

4   Emma Baccellieri, "The Most Iconic Hot Dog in Baseball," SI.com, July 19, 2022, https://www.si.com/mlb/2022/07/19/dodger-dog-daily-cover.

5   Arthur's company also ran the food business at the LA Coliseum.

6   Elaine Wood, "Thomas G. Arthur, 84: Made Dodger Dogs a Staple of L.A.," *Los Angeles Times,* June 27, 2006, https://www.latimes.com/archives/la-xpm-2006-jun-27-me-arthur27-story.html.

7   Frank Shyong, "Great Read: For the Nostalgic, the Dodger Dog Is a Home Run," *Los Angeles Times,* October 6, 2014, https://www.latimes.com/local/great-reads/la-me-c1-dodger-dog-20141006-story.html.

8   Shyong.

9   Matt Borelli, "Dodgers New: Vin Scully, Rick Sutcliffe Share Farmer John Dodger Dog Memories," *Dodger Blue,* May 3, 2021, https://dodgerblue.com/dodgers-news-vin-scully-rick-sutcliffe-farmer-john-dodger-dog-memories/2021/05/03/.

10   Baccellieri, "The Most Iconic Hot Dog in Baseball."

11   Wood, "Thomas G. Arthur, 84: Made Dodger Dogs a Staple of L.A."

12   Baccellieri, "The Most Iconic Hot Dog in Baseball."

13   Bob Wood, "Dodger Dogs to Fenway Franks: And All the Wieners in Between" (New York: McGraw-Hill, 1988).

14   Haldan Kirsch, "What Makes the Dodger Dog So Unique," *Tasting Table,* July 12, 2022, https://www.tastingtable.com/925309/what-makes-the-dodger-dog-so-unique/.

15   Matthew Kang, "The Eater Guide to Dodger Stadium," *LA Eater,* March 29, 2023, https://la.eater.com/2023/3/29/23660976/where-to-eat-dodger-stadium-best-food-los-angeles.

16   Elina Shatkin, "Meet Your New Dodger Dog, Los Angeles: Papa Cantella's," *LAist,* May 11, 2021, https://laist.com/news/food/meet-your-new-dodger-dog-los-angeles-papa-cantellas.

17   Kevin Smith, "Farmer John's Laid-Off Workers Offered Free Training, New Prospects," *Los Angeles Daily News,* February 16, 2023, https://www.dailynews.com/2023/02/16/farmer-johns-laid-off-workers-offered-free-training-new-prospects.

18   "Papa Cantella's Named Proud Partner of Los Angeles Dodgers," Papa Cantella's Press Release, https://papacantella.com/about/press-release/.

19   "Papa Cantella's Named Proud Partner of Los Angeles Dodgers."

20   Julia Paskin, "A Frank History of the Dodger Dog," *LAist,* June 25, 2018, https://laist.com/news/entertainment/a-frank-history-of-the-dodger-dog-a.

21   Sophie Flay, "Opening Day Means Plenty of Food Options for Dodger Fans," ABC7, March 29, 2023, https://abc7.com/los-angeles-dodgers-opening-day-2023-dodger-stadium/13045002/.

DODGER STADIUM CONCERTS

by Zac Petrillo

Baseball parks contain an aura and grandiosity that seem ripe for events beyond the game. Yet their odd angles, inconsistent dimensions, and strange sightlines have made them a historic challenge as a site in which to pull off a concert.[1] Still, some of the most famous shows on American soil took place somewhere between a diamond and outfield grass. At Shea Stadium, The Beatles touched down in 1964 for the first show of their momentous American tour. Billy Joel sent Shea off into the sunset with a classic performance in 2008 that saw guests, including Paul McCartney, offer their farewells. Bands like Pearl Jam have pulled off successful shows while encased in the history of Wrigley Field and Fenway Park. Yankee Stadium has routinely hosted acts like Metallica and Jay-Z.

Dodger Stadium, with its scenic view of the San Gabriel Mountains and its proximity to the stars, seems the perfect venue for a night of popular music. However, with competition from some of the most famous venues on earth, from the intimate Troubadour to the outdoor stunners – such as the Hollywood Bowl and the Rose Bowl – Dodger Stadium has often sat vacant when the home team is away. As of 2023, Dodger Stadium has held 110 concerts, 77 of which have happened in the twenty-first century. By contrast, Fenway Park has hosted nearly 150 concerts since 2003.

The ballpark opened its doors for its first-ever baseball game on April 10, 1962, in front of 52,564 fans. It didn't host a concert until 1966. On August 28 of that year, a small group from Liverpool called The Beatles played the next to last concert of their last tour ever.[2] The show wasn't a sellout, with about 45,000 fans filling a stadium that proved ill-equipped to contain them. The following night, fewer people showed up to see the group's final official concert. Perhaps believing the juice wasn't worth the squeeze, organizers didn't put on another show at Chavez Ravine until 1975, when Elton John fronted two epic shows that locked the singer and the ballpark into history forever. Still, only a handful of other acts took the field through the rest of the 1970s and 1980s before a very different kind of

concert, performed by the Three Tenors to honor a sporting event other than baseball, solidified Dodger Stadium as a backdrop for some of the most storied musical acts on American soil.

THE GREAT ESCAPE
THE BEATLES – AUGUST 28, 1966

By 1966, Beatlemania was past its apex, even if the band remained popular. In March John Lennon said they were bigger than Jesus, which coincided with an evolution of the band that ultimately led to their breakup. For now, they were still an event. Before the Dodger Stadium show, the band fielded questions, including some about the Jesus quip. Their response was combative, including Paul saying, "I think most sensible people took it for what it was … and it was only the bigots that took it up and thought it was, you know, on 'their' side … thinking, 'Aha! Here's something to get them for.'"[3]

As talk of the group's decreased popularity grew, the group's manager, Brian Epstein, worked to sell the idea that the chatter was greatly exaggerated. "It's much better all round this year, from the point of view of increased interest, and we are actually playing to bigger audiences," Epstein said. "People have been saying things about diminishing popularity, but all one can go by is attendances, which are absolutely huge."[4] Epstein also mentioned that a 1967 concert at Shea Stadium (that never occurred) was already on the books. The band was paid $120,000 apiece for its performance.

The hometown Dodgers beat the rival Giants 5-2 in San Francisco that afternoon, with the game ending just about the time that music fans were taking their seats back in Los Angeles. To keep the crowd of 45,000 under control, concert promoters hired only 102 security guards. "As soon as we heard they were coming to the stadium, we started working with the (Los Angeles) Fire Department and a lot of people to see what we could do to keep the crowd from taking over the field, which they had done in a lot of other places," said Bob Smith, manager of Dodger Stadium.[5] Gates opened ahead of the 8:00 P.M. time on the ticket, and fans were introduced to a stage built behind second base. "It was absolutely magical," remembered Barb Cabot, who attended the concert with friends. "We all looked alike – long straight hair parted in the middle and bell bottoms."[6]

Three opening acts, The Ronettes, The Remains, and The Cyrkle, warmed up the crowd. With no fans allowed on the field, The Beatles emerged from the third-base dugout and strode out to the outfield grass like ballplayers taking their positions. Los Angeles radio station KRLA hosted the event, as evidenced by the sparking white K-R-L-A letters affixed to the front of the stage's shiny blue curtain. The band stood on the square stage as if grouped in the middle of a boxing ring without ropes. Beyond the platform, with a clear path to the center-field fence, a tent housed a Lincoln Continental in which the band was expected to leave via the outfield gate once the show ended.

The Beatles opened their set at 9:30 P.M. with a cover of Chuck Berry's "Rock and Roll Music." They played 11 songs for just 27 minutes, highlighted by original songs like "Yesterday," "Day Tripper," and "Paperback Writer." "Honestly, I didn't hear one song. … It didn't matter," Cabot said about the screaming crowd.[7] As the set wrapped up with a cover of Little Richard, fans started to push forward toward the stage. "Even before the group started Little Richard's "Long Tall Sally," hundreds of fans invaded the field and surrounded our getaway car," said Tony Barrow, the Beatles press officer. The limited security proved ill-equipped to hold back the hordes of bodies. "By the time the Beatles left the stage, and we were ready to pull away, many hundreds if not thousands more had positioned themselves across our path," Barrow said. As the vehicle moved toward the center-field fence, they were surrounded and had no choice but to back up across the diamond. "Our driver yelled: 'Hold very tight, folks!' Then he slammed his gears into reverse, and we sped backwards across the field at breakneck speed," Barrow recalled.[8]

The group jumped from the Continental and went back through the third-base dugout into the Dodgers clubhouse. They decided to take an armored car out through the typical player entrance, but someone had let the air out of the car's tires during the show, so it was immovable. On the Dodgers broadcast on the 50th anniversary of the concert, Vin Scully remembered:

"So, they decided, 'OK, how to sneak the Beatles out?' And they got an ambulance …

the Beatles were put into the ambulance; they were covered with blankets, with lights flashing, sirens blaring. The ambulance seemed a reasonable bet to get through the crush of kids beyond center field. And the plan was, once they got through the kids, they would get out to the 76 Station, they would get out of the ambulance, into the armored car, now with fully inflated tires. … Again, something went wrong; the driver had navigated through the fans, hit the gas, and the ambulance ran over a speed bump, and, would you believe, the radiator fell out of the ambulance."[9]

The band was rushed out of the ambulance and into the armored car, but fans swarmed the vehicle. "The truck was just piled with girls and unable to move without injuring someone," said Bob Eubanks, the young radio host who promoted the show (and gained fame hosting television's *The Newlywed Game*). "Lord knows where they came from but all of a sudden a bunch of Hells Angels surrounded the truck and got the Beatles out of Dodger Stadium," Eubanks said.[10]

After "one of the most chaotic nights in rock and roll history,"[11] the Dodgers flew across the country to face the Mets in the ballpark where the Beatles first made their mark on America. The Fab Four took the Dodgers' place in San Francisco as they headed up to Candlestick Park, where crews were prepping the field for what turned out to be their final concert for a live audience on August 29.

A LEGEND IS CROWNED
ELTON JOHN - OCTOBER 25-26, 1975

Nine years went by before Dodger Stadium retried its hand at a musical event and invited arguably the biggest star on the planet for the comeback. By October of 1975, at 28 years old, Elton John had made a half-dozen records that reached number one on the US *Billboard* 200 chart. His newest album, *Rock of the Westies*, was also headed for number one. On the night of October 24, Elton John had friends and family over to a pool party at his Beverly Hills estate in Los Angeles. "And that," John wrote in his memoir, "was when I decided to commit suicide."[12] John reportedly swallowed "a load of Valium" and dove headfirst into a pool in full view of guests, including his mother, Sheila. John later said he wasn't trying to kill himself. John's longtime songwriter, Bernie Taupin, said, "It wasn't that big a deal. Just our boy putting on a dramatic show for friends and relatives. He was very good at that!"

Two days earlier, John, sporting a lime-green suit and matching bowler hat, had received a star on the Hollywood Walk of Fame.[13] "Unless one actually lived through that time period, it's almost impossible to imagine just how big a phenomenon John was in 1975," music writer Doug Fox said. "He was littering the rock landscape with hit after hit en route to delivering a couple of No. 1 albums per year. His concerts, complete with outrageous costumes and stage antics, were already the stuff of legend."[14] Privately, John was struggling with his sexuality, and with the spotlight of the planet on him. He also was battling addictions to drugs, sex, and food. But for two nights, he captured lightning in a bottle and put on iconic shows that are not only etched into the history of Dodger Stadium but linked the performer to the stadium for the rest of his life.

"Our relationship with LA has always been sacrosanct," said Taupin. "It was here we flourished and found our sweet spot. LA embraced us before anyone, so we're indebted."[15]

Before the concert John said that flying his friends and family to Los Angeles for the shows "was a total shock to [him]." Of Hollywood, he said, "When I first came here, I was impressed. … It wears thin. … People knock it for its phony [people], but if you know that, that's all you have to worry about." As 55,000 fans filed into Dodger Stadium to view the stage much in the same spot as it had been for The Beatles, John's mother waited with anticipation, "I have butterflies, but then I know he doesn't worry about anything," she said. "If I thought that he was nervous, then I'd be a bundle of nerves."[16] This time, fans were allowed on the field (for a $10 general admission ticket), taking seats lined up between short center field and home plate, covering most of the baseball diamond.

John had photographer Terry O'Neill document the event in real time. "At the time, they were the largest outdoor concert events ever done by a single artist," O'Neill said. "On the first night, I went all the way to the top of the back of the stadium so I could get shots of what it looked like from above. I couldn't believe it when I got there – how enormous the stadium was, what 55,000 people looked like."[17]

Gates opened at 10:00 A.M., and John made his way to the stage around 1:00 P.M. for the feature presentation. He played a 10-song opening set that began with "Your Song," a slower ballad that was a number-one single. As noted in *Ultimate Classic*

Rock, "The opening piano notes preceding the rise of the curtain, and his piano starting at the back left of the stage and slowly moving to the front as the song progressed." The following nine songs featured several tracks from his new album. He then left the stage and returned wearing perhaps his most famously outrageous outfit in a lifetime of them: a now-iconic sequined Dodger uniform with his name and the number 1 embroidered on the back. The back half of the show was filled with his known hits of the time, including "Funeral for a Friend," "Goodbye Yellow Brick Road," and "Bennie and the Jets."

Backup singer Cidny Bullens recalled a magical moment from the second concert: "We were singing 'Don't Let the Sun Go Down on Me.' The sun was going down behind Dodger Stadium, and we were onstage watching it go down, and everyone in the crowd had their Zippo lighters out. You could feel the hairs go up on everyone's necks. I've done a lot of concerts in 50 years. That was the most profound moment I've ever had onstage." According to Bullens, "Elton cried after the concert was over."[18]

Offstage, John often wore a T-shirt with tennis star Billie Jean King's face and the score to her famous "Battle of the Sexes" win over Bobby Riggs. The LA shows were capped by King jumping onstage and bouncing around with John as she sang backing vocals for "Philadelphia Freedom." Taupin, who rarely appeared on stage with John, assisted with "Don't Let the Sun Go Down," adding flair to the memorable moment.

As to how John was able to captivate over 100,000 people over two nights in Hollywood: "It wasn't Elton sitting still. … It was Elton flying around," O'Neill said. "There's a great contact sheet we found where Elton is standing at the top of the piano, the next frame he's in-flight, the next he's landed and, a second later he's back at the piano!"[19]

"He never short-changed people with his shows," O'Neill recalled. "So given this opportunity to play at that stadium – the first musical act to do so since The Beatles – I knew it was going to be special."[20] "Those are the gigs you live for," John summed up years later. "It was a pinnacle."[21]

OPERA GOES POP
THE THREE TENORS – JULY 16, 1994

On the surface, the third most unforgettable concert in Dodger Stadium couldn't be more different from the other two. The Three Tenors: Luciano Pavarotti, from

Italy, and José Carreras and Plácido Domingo, both from Spain, were world-famous but not yet pop stars. Yet, there's a certain synergy between the Hollywood ending of The Beatles and the coming-out party of Elton John, with these classical musicians who, often to the frustration of traditional music purists, made opera into popular music. The concert was fittingly in the world's entertainment capital as it ushered in future popular acts like Josh Groban and Andrea Bocelli.

In 1990, just before the FIFA World Cup Final, the Three Tenors came together for their first performance as a group. Pavarotti commented that the famed trio had been asked to perform together "at least 50 times" before finally agreeing.[22] What brought them together at this moment was their shared love of soccer. After the success of their 1990 show, promoter Tibor Rudas put together the plan for them to repeat the performance at the following World Cup, this time away from Europe, where soccer is far and away the most popular sport, but in America, where the effort to popularize the game was in full swing. The three performers were each paid $1 million plus royalties for the show. As the Rose Bowl was prepared for the final game between Brazil and Italy, the concert further bridged the gap between European culture and America by taking place in a baseball park.

The Los Angeles concert was determined to be a star-making special, ultimately turning the three classical artists into traveling moneymakers. Tickets for the event ranged from $15 to $1,000. Rather than position general admission on the field, seats were sold to VIPs. Placing the event in Hollywood meant many celebrities were in attendance, including some of the biggest names of the 1990s, like Arnold Schwarzenegger, Dennis Hopper, and Dustin Hoffman, along with some of the stars from Hollywood's Golden Age like Charlton Heston and Gregory Peck. The production design was far more resplendent than anything constructed for The Beatles or Elton John. The enormous stage took up the entirety of the outfield and was decorated with two dozen fake columns, palm trees, shrubbery, and waterfalls. The souvenir stands sold merchandise that ranged from seat cushions to baseballs autographed by the singers, and the event ultimately grossed over $12 million.

Gates opened at 5:00 P.M., and the show began just as the sun went down at 8 o'clock. After "The Star-Spangled Banner" and an Overture by the composer/orchestra leader Leonard Bernstein, Carreras kicked off the set with "O souverain, ô juge, ô père" from the French opera *Le Cid* for the 56,000 people in attendance. Backed by the Los Angeles Philharmonic and the Los Angeles Opera, Indian conductor Zubin Mehta shaped the roughly hour-and-a-half show, which included classic opera arias and Neapolitan tunes, along with a handful of American pop hits. The inclusion of show tunes roiled some traditional critics. While most songs in the set were performed by individual members of the group, the pop songs were each performed together. Perhaps playing to the Hollywood crowd, the Tenors sang "America" from *West Side Story* (scored by Bernstein) and "Singin' in the Rain" from the Gene Kelly musical of the same name. They also performed a cover of Frank Sinatra's "My Way," with the glassy-eyed Chairman of the Board himself getting a standing ovation from the audience.

Music critic Martin Bernheimer was frustrated by the show, including aspects related to the stadium experience. He arrived late due to a traffic jam leading to the venue. He complained that the sound system and audiovisual presentation was "a little time warp," making for a poor-quality image coming from the stadium's screen. "Their televised visages lagged disconcertingly behind their ever-echoing voices," Bernheimer complained.[23] Critical of the capitalist intentions behind the event, he called it a "megatenor show" and called the singers "contenders for the universal Golden-Larynx award." "In the final analysis, the singing seemed virtually irrelevant," Bernheimer concluded. "This was a night for celebrating personalities and personality-cults."[24]

Bernheimer and the *Los Angeles Times* were inundated with letters either agreeing with or denouncing the writer's pan. However, no matter the intention or purity, by virtually every barometer the concert was an enormous success. An estimated 1.3 billion people watched the live television broadcast. The CD of the concert finished second among all classical albums on the *Billboard* charts at the end of the year and has gone on to sell over 8 million units internationally. The DVD of the event continued to sell into the next decades. The concert made the Three Tenors a sensation, and they took their show across the globe. Imitators even spawned internationally, including the Irish Tenors and the Three Chinese Tenors.[25] On the original group's worldwide tour, they received $500,000 per show plus a percentage of merchandising and royalties. "Is it good money?" Pavarotti said. "By God, it's good money."[26] The trio continued the World Cup tradition, singing at the 1998 event in Paris and, finally, the 2002 event in Yokohama.

Given the relative scarcity of shows in Dodger Stadium's 60-plus-year history, the proximity to the media industry has provided some of the most memorable and career-shaping (and industry-altering) concerts ever. Since the Three Tenors' 1994 show, Dodger Stadium has seen an uptick in concerts taking place on the field. Acts like Madonna, Jay-Z and Beyonce, Fleetwood Mac, and Bruce Springsteen have all performed to huge crowds. In 2019 Paul McCartney returned to the stadium, this time for two solo performances. On November 19, 2022, Elton John came back to the place that cemented his legend for the final performance on what he announced as his final tour. Roughly 50,000 people attended his last show, which went for nearly three hours and was streamed live to millions of viewers on Disney+.

NOTES

1   Forgotten Places, "Why Baseball Stadiums Make Terrible Concert Venues," YouTube, https://www.youtube.com/watch?v=nTViQum19hU, June 14, 2023.

2   This was the group's third-to-final live performance ever and next to last in front of a live audience.

3   "Beatles Interviews Database: Beatles Press Conference: Los Angeles 8/24/1966," *The Beatles Ultimate Experience*, https://www.beatlesinterviews.org/db1966.0828.beatles.html (last accessed December 2, 2023).

4   "Live: Dodger Stadium, Los Angeles," The Beatles Bible, https://www.beatlesbible.com/1966/08/28/live-dodger-stadium-los-angeles/ (last accessed December 2, 2023).

5   "Los Angeles – Sunday, August 28, 1966," *The Paul McCartney Project*, https://www.the-paulmccartney-project.com/concert/1966-08-28/ (last accessed December 4, 2023).

6   Chris Erskine, "In 1966, The Beatles Brought a Whole New Ballgame to Dodger Stadium," *Los Angeles Times*, August 26, 2011, https://www.latimes.com/sports/la-xpm-2011-aug-26-la-sp-erskine-beatles-20110827-story.html (last accessed December 6, 2023).

7   Erskine.

8   "Los Angeles – Sunday, August 28, 1966," *The Paul McCartney Project*.

9   Adrian Garro, "Vin Scully Weaved a Story about The Beatles Escaping Dodger Stadium into His Play-by-Play," MLB.com, August 28, 2016, https://www.mlb.com/cut4/vin-scully-recounts-the-beatles-escape-from-dodger-stadium-in-1966-c198222742 (last accessed December 4, 2023).

10 Erskine.

11 Joe Daly, "The Night The Beatles Were Guarded by Christ and Moses," *Louder*, July 14, 2023, https://www.loudersound.com/features/beatles-christ-moses-us-tour-1966 (last accessed December 4, 2023).

12 Craig Marks, "Elton John Will Take His Final Bow at Dodger Stadium. So Let's Time Travel Back to His Legendary 1975 Concert," *Los Angeles Times*, November 16, 2022, https://www.latimes.com/entertainment-arts/music/story/2022-11-16/elton-john-dodger-stadium-concert-1975-farewell-yellow-brick-road (last accessed December 6, 2023).

13 Marks.

14 Doug Fox, "Inside Elton John's Historic Sold-Out Shows at Dodger Stadium, *Ultimate Classic Rock*, October 25, 2015, https://ultimateclassicrock.com/elton-john-dodger-stadium/ (last accessed December 4, 2023).

15 Marks.

16 Philip Anness, "Elton John – Dodger Stadium Documentary from 1975," YouTube, https://www.youtube.com/watch?v=57JYxacBnrk, October 12, 2017.

17 Interview with Terry O'Neill, "October 25-26, 1975: Elton Knocks It Out of the Park at Dodger Stadium," EltonJohn.com, October 24, 2015, https://www.eltonjohn.com/stories/october-25-26-1975-elton-knocks-it-out-of-the-park-at-dodger-stadium (last accessed December 4, 2023).

18 Marks.

19 Interview with Terry O'Neill.

20 Interview with Terry O'Neill.

21 Marks.

22 Anastasia Tsioulcas, "How the Three Tenors Sang the Hits and Changed the Game," National Public Radio, July 16, 2014, https://www.npr.org/sections/deceptivecadence/2014/07/16/330751895/how-the-three-tenors-sang-the-hits-and-changed-the-game (last accessed December 4, 2023).

23 David Ng, "A Look Back at the Three Tenors Concert at Dodger Stadium," *Los Angeles Times*, July 16, 2014, https://www.latimes.com/entertainment/arts/culture/la-et-cm-three-tenors-dodger-stadium-20140714-story.html (last accessed December 6, 2023).

24 Ng.

25 Tsioulcas.

26 Tsioulcas.

DODGERS WIN WORLD SERIES
IN 2020 COVID SEASON

by Glen Sparks

The Los Angeles Dodgers began the 2020 regular season – finally – on July 23. A worldwide COVID-19 pandemic, coupled with prolonged negotiations on how the games could safely be played, delayed Opening Day by nearly four months. Not until summer had taken hold and August was nearly a week away did major-league baseball finally start, albeit not in the typical fashion

Dodger Stadium sat nearly empty as the home team met its longtime rival the San Francisco Giants. No one hailed the beer man or ordered even a single Dodger Dog. Rather than 50,000 fans filing into the ballpark and cheering for big hits and strikeout pitches, "a few thousand" cardboard cutouts – featuring photos of fans or, in some cases, the dogs and cats of fans – filled the seats, including those of Hollywood celebrities Mary Hart, George Lopez, Rob Lowe, and Bryan Cranston.[1]

Los Angeles Times columnist Bill Plaschke wrote about this most unusual of openers. "The coronavirus transformed this traditionally festive occasion into something that felt like a sandlot game played in the middle of a ghost town. There was no joyous noise. There was no popcorn smell. There was none of the annual sweaty buzz of a crowded concourse celebrating a spring rebirth."[2]

Keith Williams sang "a wonderful national anthem," Plaschke continued, but instead of standing next to home plate, "he was a mere speck somewhere beyond the center field fence." During a pregame ceremony, players stood six feet apart – socially distanced – on the foul lines, and "instead of waving to a crowd that wasn't there, they mostly looked down at their hands." Even the ever-upbeat Los Angeles third baseman Justin Turner acknowledged, "There's a lot of strange going on right now."[3]

Photograph by Scott Carter

Social distancing restrictions were still in place for COVID-19 for this game on May 29, 2021.

Several months earlier, in December 2019, "a cluster of patients" in Wuhan, China, underwent treatment for a pneumonia-like illness. On January 7, 2020, Chinese public health officials blamed the outbreak on a "novel coronavirus." The World Health Organization (WHO) began referring to the virus as 2019 nCoV or COVID 19. By January 19 four countries (China, Thailand, Japan, and South Korea) had reported coronavirus cases. On February 6 Patricia Dowd of San Jose, California, became the first US resident to die from COVID-19.[4]

Worldwide COVID deaths reached 1,013 on February 10,[5] the date pitchers and catchers reported to spring training in Arizona and Florida. Other players reported February 14, and Cactus League and Grapefruit League games began on February 22. Six days later, WHO officials elevated the global COVID-19 threat level from "high" to "very high."[6]

The Dodgers arrived at Camelback Ranch in Glendale, Arizona, with hopes of winning a World Series for the first time since 1988, the year of pitcher Orel Hershiser's magical run and Kirk Gibson's epic homer off Oakland A's reliever Dennis Eckersley. Los Angeles secured a pennant but lost the World Series in 2017 to the Houston Astros and in 2018 to the Boston Red Sox. In 2019 the Dodgers won 106 games before losing the Division Series to the eventual champion Washington Nationals.

LA had traded for one of baseball's superstars on February 10. The Red Sox sent outfielder Mookie Betts along with pitcher David Price to Los Angeles in exchange for outfielder Alex Verdugo, catching prospect Connor Wong, and infield prospect Jeter Downs. Betts, a six-year veteran and four-time All-Star, won the American League MVP award in 2018, the year he posted a 10.7 Baseball-Reference WAR. Dylan Hernandez wrote in the *Los Angeles Times*, "The Dodgers heard the cries of their fans, and now they have an all-world outfielder in Mookie Betts. ... A franchise that valued roster balance finally splurged on a superstar."[7]

By March 11, the number of COVID-19 cases had reached 118,000 in 114 countries, with 4,291 deaths. The WHO declared a COVID-19 pandemic.[8] Most of the sports world shut down over the next few days. The NBA and NHL suspended their seasons, while the NCAA canceled both the men's and women's basketball tournaments as well as the College World Series, still nearly three months away.

Major League Baseball decided on March 12 to delay the 2020 season by at least two weeks. The Dodgers kept their spring-training complex open although players could go home if they chose. Andrew Friedman, the Dodgers' president of baseball operations, said team employees based in Los Angeles should begin telecommuting. He expected Dodger Stadium renovation work to continue.[9]

On March 16 MLB pushed back the start of the regular season until mid-May at the earliest. Over the next few weeks, series planned for 2020 in San Juan, Puerto Rico, and in London were canceled.[10]

The federal government discouraged gatherings of 10 people or more, and restaurants and bars closed. Nonessential workers stayed away from the office. Government officials wanted "as few people as possible in close contact with one another in order to slow the pandemic." On March 22 the *New York Times* reported, "The United States is already falling into deep contraction: It is producing far fewer goods and services now than it did a month or a quarter ago."[11] The next day, the World Health Organization reported 300,000 COVID-19 cases worldwide.[12] By March 25, the United States had recorded nearly 55,000 cases, with 781 deaths.[13]

Dodgers infielder Max Muncy and his wife, Kellie, binge-watched *Lost* and other TV programs during the quarantine. Ace pitcher Walker Buehler and his future brothers-in-law completed some remodeling projects, while utility man Chris Taylor did a little surfing. Manager Dave Roberts shucked 100 oysters as part of a belated Mother's Day present for his wife, Tricia.

Betts bought groceries for customers at a Nashville, Tennessee supermarket and pizza for employees. He also worked with a nonprofit to help people obtain face masks, hand sanitizers, and similar products.[14]

On May 26, a COVID-19 testing site opened at Dodger Stadium. About 6,000 Angelenos could be tested there every day, making it three times larger than any other testing site in Los Angeles County. Mayor Eric Garcetti said, "Dodger Stadium is a place where Angelenos usually rally around a common goal of victories on the field – and today it is uniting us around a mission to save lives."[15]

Negotiations had begun in mid-May between MLB and the Players Association on how to complete a modified, shortened season. The two sides debated COVID testing frequency, protections for high-risk players, and sanitation protocols. Players, for instance, wanted to shower at the ballpark, something owners worried might spread the virus.[16]

Arguments also broke out over the proposed length of the season. Owners wanted a sprint – maybe just 50 games – while the players hoped for something much longer. In mid-June, Commissioner Rob Manfred said, "I'm not confident" about a season starting. Tom Goldman, a sports reporter for National Public Radio, said players were "through trading proposals. They're angry. … Players don't like (a 50-game season). They want more games, which translates to more money."[17]

On June 23 a 60-game schedule was approved, plus an expanded postseason to include 16 teams. No fans would be allowed at games. Spring training "2.0," or, as some called it, "summer camp," would begin July 1, and players would earn a prorated amount of their full salary, or 37 percent for a 60-game schedule. (The Players Association had proposed a 114-game season on May 31 and, after the owners' rejection, countered June 9 with an 89-game season. The owners also had wanted to pay players 70 percent of their prorated salaries due to financial worries because of all those empty seats.)[18]

Games would be played using the minor-league rule for extra innings, having a runner on second base to begin each half-frame. That runner would be the player who made the final out the previous inning. A designated hitter would be used in all games.

Each side agreed to several health and safety protocols – no high-fives, hugs, or fist bumps, and no chewing or spitting tobacco or sunflower seeds. Baserunners, fielders, umpires, and coaches would be required – as much as possible – to keep safe social distances from one another.[19] Players also agreed to have their temperatures checked multiple times every day and be tested for COVID-19 several times a week. Anyone testing positive would be quarantined until they had two negative tests.

Eager to get going, players reported to Dodger Stadium "in waves" on July 3.[20] First, their temperatures were taken. Once on the field, they were separated into three groups. Dave Roberts wore a mask throughout the practice, as did all the team's coaches. Dodgers President Stan Kasten expected the season to proceed unless the number of positive COVID tests surpassed "an acceptable level of incidents."[21] Later that day, MLB canceled the 2020 All-Star Game, scheduled for Dodger Stadium. Baseball awarded the 2022 game to the Dodgers.

In late June, the Dodgers had submitted a list of 51 players eligible for the 2020 MLB season. . The list included everyone on the 40-man roster plus all the non-roster invitees. Players not on the active roster were assigned to the team's alternate site at the University of Southern California, about six miles from Dodger Stadium, where they could get individual instruction from a handful of coaches and stay fresh if needed on the Dodgers. (MLB canceled the minor-league season on June 30.)

Not surprisingly, some players around the league opted out of the 2020 season. Among them were Giants catcher Buster Posey, Nationals third baseman Ryan Zimmerman, and the Dodgers' Price, who released a statement through social media that read in part, "I have decided it is in the best interest of my health and my family's health for me not to play this season."[22]

Inevitably, there was talk that any World Series won in such a shortened season would be a "diminished" championship. Turner and Clayton Kershaw disagreed. "People are going to say whatever they're going to say, but if there's an opportunity to win a championship, we're going to show up every day and work toward that goal," Turner said.[23] Kershaw said, "To say there's an asterisk on it or things like that, I don't think that's fair. … I think if you win this season, it's going to feel good no matter what."[24]

Although MLB gave permission for radio crews to travel, the Dodgers opted to keep all their broadcasters in Los Angeles. Joe Davis would do television play-by-play for most of the games, while Hershiser would offer his analysis, at Dodger Stadium. The pair would call games off a universal monitor that they would not manage, "giving them little control over where to steer the broadcast." Davis said, "How can you call it with conviction? I don't know."[25]

Charley Steiner and Rick Monday would handle radio broadcast chores, Steiner doing play-by-play and Monday providing analysis. Rather than sitting side by side in a ballpark broadcast booth as they had in past years, Steiner would work games from his home in the Brentwood section of Los Angeles, while Monday and producer Duane McDonald would be stationed at Dodger Stadium. "I'm a low-hanging curveball in the day of COVID-19," said Steiner, who was 71 years old and diabetic. The Dodgers built Steiner a makeshift booth at his house, complete with three flat-screen televisions, including one with a feed from the TV broadcast truck. Early on, Steiner said, "I'm doing something in my career that I never thought humanly or technically possible."[26]

Many wondered what a major-league game would look like without fans. More to the point, what would it sound like? Quiet. Maybe too quiet. "There's going to be crowd noise pumped in, but it's not going to be the same," Joe Davis said. "I don't think there's any way for anybody to truly appreciate how weird it's going to be."[27] Buehler worried that the broadcasts might pick up his salty language from the pitcher's mound.[28]

Tim Neverett shifted between television and radio broadcasts. A native New Englander, Neverett joined the Dodgers broadcast team in 2019. During the quarantine, while hiking near the White Mountains in northern New Hampshire, with his wife, Jess, he decided to chronicle the 2020 baseball season, whenever it began. "I said (to Jess) 'I think I should journal it every day because it's going to be such a unique experience."[29] That journaling turned into the book *Covid Curveball*, published by Permuted Press in 2021.

On July 22, the day before the season began, Betts signed a 12-year contract extension worth $365 million, including a $65 million signing bonus. "I'm here to bring back some rings to LA," Betts told the *Times*. "I know that the Dodgers are going to be good for a long time."[30]

Betts went 1-for-5 against the Giants with a single and run scored in his Los Angeles debut. He struck out twice. Dustin May, a young fireballer with a shock of curly red hair, got the starting pitching assignment for the Dodgers in place of an injured Kershaw. The Dodgers broke a 1-1 tie with five runs in the seventh inning and two more in the eighth to win 8-1. Enrique "Kiké" Hernández, who knocked a two-run single in the seventh, added a two-run homer the following inning. During a pregame video conference call, Justin Turner had said, "This is a day that if I'm being completely honest, I wasn't 100 percent sure we were going to see happen this year."[31]

The next day the Dodgers won 9-1. Turner, Muncy, and Will Smith each drove home two runs. Ross Stripling pitched seven innings and struck out seven. The Giants got even over the next two days, taking both games.

As fate and schedule makers made it, the Dodgers began their first road trip of the shortened season in Houston. On November 12, 2019, *The Athletic* broke a story that confirmed many rumors: The Astros illegally stole signs throughout the 2017 season and the postseason, including against the Dodgers in the World Series.[32] Houston's general manager Jeff Luhnow and field manager A.J. Hinch were suspended for the 2020 season. No players were disciplined, and MLB decided against vacating the Astros' World Series title.

Thanks to a five-run fifth inning, the Dodgers won the first game, 5-2. A benches-clearing exchange broke out in the sixth inning after Los Angeles reliever Joe Kelly threw some close pitches to Houston infielder Carlos Correa, one of the culprits named in the cheating scandal. "The sequence was a reminder that that the Dodgers were not going to let the Astros' cheating in 2017 slide," Jorgé Castillo wrote in the *LA Times*.[33] Los Angeles won the second game, 4-2, in 13 innings on an Edwin Rios two-run homer.

Being on the road meant taking extra precautions. There was no going out to restaurants after games. Instead, players called on hotel room service for meals. "We are doing what we can to make this season happen," outfielder Joc Pederson said. "Wearing mask and gloves on the plane is one thing. Don't use the remote control or pick up the phone at the hotel is another. We have to take every precaution to stay safe. … Some people think this thing (COVID 19) is fake, but it is definitely real."[34] Players were being tested for the virus every 48 hours. Through July 24, only the Florida Marlins had any positive tests.[35]

The Dodgers won five of the remaining seven games on the trip, facing the Arizona Diamondbacks and San Diego Padres. Kershaw made his 2020 season debut on August 2 and looked great on the road versus Arizona. He threw 5⅔ shutout innings and the Dodgers prevailed, 3-0.

Unfortunately, the number of COVID cases around MLB began to creep up. Another Marlins player tested positive for the virus as did two St. Louis Cardinals. The Philadelphia Phillies also had some positive tests. Commissioner Manfred told Tony Clark, head of the Players Association, "Get your players in line now or we risk having to shut the season down." The Dodgers "re-emphasized the rules" and decided to go "above and beyond MLB's protocol." Offensive coaches could not remain in the dugout while the Dodgers were in the field, and defensive coaches could not be there when the team was batting. A player not in the game could not sit in the dugout.[36]

LA knocked off the Padres 11-2 on August 13 as Betts belted three home runs, added a single, and had five RBIs. Mookie also scored four times. It was the sixth three-homer game of Betts's career, tying him with Sammy Sosa and Johnny Mize for the most ever. "I put in so much work," Betts told the *Times*. "I work a lot. To see some success is definitely a sigh of relief. But I have a lot more work to do."[37] Los Angeles improved to 13-7 and moved into a virtual tie with the Rockies for first place. Neverett could sense some tension evolving in this season. "One win equals 2.7 wins in a normal season," he wrote in *Covid Curveball*. "A single loss is like 2.7 losses. Many games now, even without fans in the stands, can have a postseason feel."[38]

Neverett stayed during the two-month season at the downtown Bonaventure Hotel. Rick Monday, a Florida resident in the offseason, set up his home away from home much closer to the ballpark. The former big-league outfielder (241 career home runs for the Dodgers and other teams) rented an RV in 2020 and – with the team's permission – parked it outside Dodger Stadium.

Often, Neverett and Monday pulled up some chairs outside the RV and enjoyed a beer or two after the game. At least one time, a coyote joined the party, or at least wandered onto the parking lot and looked Neverett right in the eye. "I found it weird that I was standing, basically a long par five from downtown Los Angeles, but there was a coyote just hanging out close to the stadium having a staring contest with me," he wrote. Coyotes roam around in the upper reaches of the hills surrounding the ballpark. "Rick Monday can hear the coyotes howling every night from his camper in Lot E, he tells me," Neverett wrote. "He hears the owls also, but he tells me the sprinklers coming on and hitting the side of his camper at 4:30 a.m. is the only sound that bothers him."[39]

Neverett explained some of the difficulties in broadcasting baseball games during the year of COVID. "It was challenging in a lot of ways, mostly when the team was on the road," he said. "We had very limited contact with the players. There were some prearranged opportunities with a player or two pregame on Zoom and then we had a manager's meeting on Zoom each day. We could not go on the field, in the dugout or near the clubhouse. … With empty stadiums and artificial crowd noise and cardboard cutouts of fans (we only saw the backs of them, and they were all plain white pieces of cardboard), it was really hard to replicate what it feels like to be in a stadium with fans. It was artificial, but it was the best we had and what we had to deal with."[40]

The Dodgers ended the first half of their schedule by knocking off the Rockies, 11-3, on August 23 and improving to 22-8. Betts drove home three runs, as did Hernández. The game was dedicated in memory of former Lakers superstar Kobe Bryant on what would have been his 42nd birthday. Bryant had died in a helicopter crash on January 26 in Calabasas, California, along with his 13-year-old daughter, Gianna, and seven others.

"Bryant was ever present from the start," Jack Harris wrote in the *Times*. Highlights of his basketball career were posted on the Dodger Stadium scoreboard between innings. Former Dodgers broadcaster Vin Scully narrated a pregame video tribute. "We lost Kobe a little too soon," "Kiké" Hernández said. "For us to be a part of something like that before the game is really meaningful. I'm glad that we …On were able to win that game for him. It's probably one that I'll always remember."[41]

Over the next 15 games, six at home and nine on the road, the Dodgers went 10-5 and improved to 32-13 but led the NL West by just 3½ games over the San Diego Padres. The Astros came to town for a two-game series starting September 12, and Dodgers fans greeted them as expected. Many stood near the ballpark entrance on Vin Scully Avenue, off Sunset Boulevard, and banged trashcans as the Houston team buses rolled by. Some fans held signs mocking the former champions. Dave Roberts supported the protest. "I loved it. I loved it," he said. "I think they have every right to do whatever they feel to express their feelings, and I thought it was great."[42] The Dodgers lost the first game, 7-5, and won the second, 8-1. Chris Taylor drove in a combined five runs.

As he had the past few years, Taylor often stuck his hands into the air and shook his fingers following a hit, acting as though his hands hurt from being jammed. Teammates in the dugout mimicked the gesture, which meant "barrels are overrated." Taylor even shook his fingers after a hard hit. He did it more than ever in 2020. Other players did similar gestures. "That kind of stuff is important when there are no fans in the stands," Taylor said. "We have to create energy somehow. That's our way of making the game fun."[43]

The regular season ended at home. LA won two out of three games against Oakland and took all three versus the Angels, prevailing in the finale, 5-0. A.J. Pollock hit two home runs and May earned his third win.

The Dodgers finished with a major-league-best 43-17 won-lost record (a 116-win pace over a 162-game schedule). They won the NL West by six games over the runner-up Padres. Pollock and Betts tied for the team lead with 16 home runs, while Corey Seager led in RBIs (41) and matched Turner for the highest batting average (.307). Kershaw won the most games (six), struck out the most batters (62), and posted the lowest ERA among starters (2.16). Kenley Jansen saved the most games (11).

"For 60 games, (the Dodgers) plowed through the opponents placed in front of them, inferior foes west of the Mississippi in both leagues, from beginning to end, and avoided a Covid-19 outbreak to complete the demolition without a hitch," Jorgé Castillo wrote in the *L.A. Times*. Even so, Pollock said, just a few paragraphs later, "When the season's closed out, and we start the playoffs, none of it means anything and we start over, and everything goes back to zero."[44]

The Dodgers began their postseason run at home, where they won the first two games of a best-of-three Wild Card Series against the Milwaukee Brewers. Betts drove in three of LA's seven total runs. After that, it was off to Globe Life Field in Arlington, Texas, the first-year home of the Texas Rangers.

Baseball had decided in early September to schedule the later postseason rounds in neutral-site "bubbles" as a way to limit travel and protect players' health. According to reporter Matt Snyder, MLB wanted to "avoid teams playing in their actual homes."[45] That made Globe Life an ideal choice. The Rangers struggled throughout the 2020 season and finished in fifth place. Dodger Stadium meanwhile, hosted one other playoff series in 2020, an American League Division Series between the Houston Astros, of all teams, and the Oakland A's. Houston prevailed three games to one.[46]

The Dodgers' traveling contingent, which included family members in some cases, spent 25 straight days at the Four Seasons Resort and Club Dallas at Las Colinas. Once again, snacks and meals were ordered through room service. According to reporter Pedro Moura, "Players could swim, play ping-ping, play video games, play cornhole." They could not, however, play golf on the resort's immaculate course. Instead, they "convened on one balcony (overlooking the 18th hole), chipped balls toward the hole, and asked a young player to scamper out undetected and recover them."[47]

L.A. beat the Padres in the NL Division Series and edged the Atlanta Braves in the league Championship Series. Muncy hit two home runs and had six RBIs in seven games against Atlanta pitching. A socially-distanced crowd watched the action. Approximately 11,500 tickets went on sale for each game at Globe Life, which seats 40,300.[48]

The Dodgers took six games to knock off the American League champion Tampa Bay Rays in the World Series, again at Globe Life, and once again in front of a sparse crowd.[49] Seager batted .400 with two home runs and earned Most Valuable Player honors. "This team was incredible all throughout the year, all throughout the postseason, all throughout (the quarantine)," Seager said. "We never stopped." Kershaw

said, "I've been saying 'World Series champs' in my head over and over again."[50]

As for asterisks, Roberts said, "There should not be an asterisk. I stand by that."[51] *Times* sportswriter Jack Harris pointed out that while the season was shorter than ever, the playoffs were longer. No team had ever won 13 games in one postseason.[52] Also, while Dodgers boasted the game's best record, they got none of the benefits (no home-field advantage, for instance, with a full ballpark and a raucous crowd). "There was less travel, but more stress," Harris wrote. The Dodgers won a championship while a global health crisis raged. "I think for us, off the field was a bigger challenge," Kiké Hernández said. A native of Puerto Rico, Hernández hadn't seen his family "in a really long time. ... Besides baseball, the most challenging part was dealing with the daily life as it is."[53]

Baseball went back to a 162-game schedule in 2021, with some restrictions still in place for the early going. Before the home opener on April 9, the Dodgers held a ring ceremony with a limited, sold-out crowd of 15,036 (and no cardboard cutouts). Players were introduced by their childhood baseball heroes, who presented special messages on the video board. Jimmy Rollins introduced Betts, for instance, and Chase Utley introduced outfielder Cody Bellinger.

Will Clark, former star first baseman for the Texas Rangers and other teams, introduced Kershaw, who grew up in the Dallas area. Presented his ring, the pitcher exclaimed, "Woo-hoo! Let's see this thing!" He put on the championship jewelry – featuring 232 diamonds and 53 sapphires – and thrust his left fist into the sky as fans applauded.[54]

Dodger Stadium returned to full capacity on June 15. More than 52,000 attended a game pitting the home team against the Philadelphia Phillies. Betts went 3-for-5, drove in a pair of runs, and led the Dodgers to a 5-3 victory. Betts hadn't played in front of fans at Dodger Stadium since he was with the Red Sox during the 2018 World Series. "Finally playing in a full Dodger Stadium on the right team is definitely something I've been looking forward to," Betts said afterward. "And being able to play a good game was the cherry on top."[55]

The Dodgers boasted a 106-56 won-loss mark in 2021 but still finished one game behind the Giants in the NL West. They beat the St. Louis Cardinals, 3-1, in the wild-card game and got their revenge by knocking off San Francisco in the Division Series. The Braves ended the Dodgers' season in the NLCS, winning in six games. The Dodgers led the majors in regular-season home attendance with a mark of 2,804,693.

NOTES

1   Jorgé Castillo, "Betts Money in the Opener," *Los Angeles Times*, July 24, 2020: B6.

2   Bill Plaschke, "It's More Like an Echo Park," *Los Angeles Times*, July 24, 2020: A1.

3   "It's More Like an Echo Park."

4   David Debolt, Fiona Kelliher, and Jason Green, "'She Held the Family Together': San Jose Woman Is First Known U.S. Covid-19 Death," *San Jose Mercury News*, April 23, 2020, https://www.mercurynews.com/2020/04/23/she-held-the-family-together-san-jose-woman-is-first-known-u-s-covid-19-death/.

5   https://www.cdc.gov/museum/timeline/covid19.html.

6   Adriana Rodriguez, "Coronavirus Updates: WHO Increases Risk to 'Very High,' Tells Government to 'Wake Up,'" *USA Today*, February 28, 2020.

7   Dylan Hernandez, "Dodgers Give Fans Star They Wanted," *Los Angeles Times*, February 11, 2020: D1.

8   https://www.cdc.gov/museum/timeline/covid19.ht.

9   Jorgé Castillo and Maria Torres, "MLB Players Are Allowed to Return Home," *Los Angeles Times*, March 14, 2020: D6.

10 Dayn Perry, Katherine Acquavella, and R.J. Anderson, "Timeline of How the COVID-19 Pandemic Has Impacted the 2020 Major League Baseball Season," CBSSports.com, July 26, 2020. https://www.cbssports.com/mlb/news/timeline-of-how-the-covid-19-pandemic-has-impacted-the-2020-major-league-baseball-season/.

11 Jim Tankersley, "The U.S. Shut Down Its Economy. Here's What Needs to Happen in Order to Restart," *New York Times*, March 22, 2020. https://www.nytimes.com/2020/03/22/us/politics/coronavirus-economy-shutdown.html.

12 "Coronavirus Timeline: Tracking the Critical Moments of Covid-19," NBC.com, https://www.nbcnews.com/health/health-news/coronavirus-timeline-tracking-critical-moments-covid-19-1154341.

13 "Coronavirus Timeline: Tracking the Critical Moments of Covid-19."

14 Jorgé Castillo, "Playing Country Hardball," *Los Angeles Times*, July 18, 2020: D2.

15 "Dodger Stadium Housing New Covid 19 Test Site," MLB.com, May 26, 2020, https://www.mlb.com/news/dodger-stadium-housing-covid-19-test-site.

16 R.J. Anderson, "MLB Players Union Responds to Coronavirus Safety Proposal for 2020 Season," cbssports.com, May 21, 2020, https://www.cbssports.com/mlb/news/mlb-players-union-responds-to-leagues-coronavirus-safety-proposal-for-2020-season/.

17 Tom Goldman, "Major League Baseball and Players Argue over the Start of the Season during Pandemic," *All Things Considered*, NPR.org, June 16, 2020. https://www.npr.org/2020/06/16/878853031/major-league-baseball-and-players-argue-over-the-start-of-the-season-during-pand.

18 "MLB Players Union Responds to Coronavirus Safety Proposal for 2020 Season."

19 For a look at how major-league umpires worked during the pandemic, see Bill Nowlin, "Major-League Umpiring during the Pandemic of 2020," *Baseball Prospectus*, April 8, 2021. https://www.baseballprospectus.com/news/article/66026/major-league-umpiring-during-the-pandemic-of-2020/.

20 Jorgé Castillo, "Finding It Hard to Mask Their Excitement," *Los Angeles Times*, July 4, 2020: D5.

21 "Finding It Hard to Mask Their Excitement."

22 Alden Gonzalez, "Dodgers Pitcher David Price Says He Won't Play 2020 Season, ESPN.com, July 4, 2020, https://www.espn.com/mlb/story/_/id/29410895/dodgers-pitcher-david-price-says-play-season.

23 Jorgé Castillo, "Dodgers Say Forget Asterisk," *Los Angeles Times*, July 6, 2020: B7.

24 "Dodgers Say Forget Asterisk."

25 Jorgé Castillo, "Pandemic Has Broadcasters on Road to nowhere," *Los Angeles Times*, July 19, 2020: B11.

26 Jorgé Castillo, "It'll be a home run for Steiner," *Los Angeles Times*, July 21, 2020: B7.

27 Castillo, "Pandemic has broadcasters on road to Nowhere."

28 *Off Air with Joe and Orel* podcast, May 21, 2020, https://podcasts.apple.com/us/podcast/episode-7-walker-buehler-dodgers/id902521814?i=1000490177865.

29 "Los Angeles Dodgers Broadcaster Tim Neverett Chats About His Book 'Covid Curveball," https://www.youtube.com/watch?v=MACevtipoXA.

30 Bill Plaschke, "L.A.'s New Contract Player," *Los Angeles Times*, July 23, 2020: A1.

31 Plaschke, "It's More Like an Echo Park."

32 Ken Rosenthal and Evan Drelich, "The Astros Stole Signs Electronically in 2017 – Part of a Much Broader Issue in Major League Baseball," *The Athletic*, November 12, 2019.

33 Jorgé Castillo, "Kelly's Close Calls Lead to Benches-Clearing Spat," *Los Angeles Times*, July 29, 2023: B6.

34 Tim Neverett, *Covid Curveball: An Inside View of the 2020 Los Angeles Dodgers World Championship Season* (New York: Permuted Press, 2021), 49.

35 Neverett, 49.

36 Neverett, 61.

37 Jack Harris, "Betts' Smashing Night Leaves Mark," *Los Angeles Times*, August 14, 2020: B7.

38 Neverett, 73.

39 Neverett, 77.

40 Twitter/X exchange between the author and Tim Neverett, December 3, 2023.

41 Jack Harris, "Dodgers' Slam Show Honors Kobe," *Los Angeles Times*, August 24, 2020: B9.

42 Jorgé Castillo, "Jansen Is No Relief for Dodgers," *Los Angeles Times*, September 14, 2020: D3.

43 *Off Air with Joe and Orel* podcast, September 24, 2020, https://podcasts.apple.com/us/podcast/episode-24-chris-taylor-dodgers/id902521814?i=1000492397807.

44 Jorgé Castillo, "Finale Is Just the Beginning for Dodgers," *Los Angeles Times*, September 28, 2020: D1.

45 Matt Snyder, "MLB considering two playoff bubbles and neutral-site World Series at Rangers' Globe Life Field, per report," cbssports.com, September 8, 2020. https://www.cbssports.com/mlb/news/mlb-considering-two-playoff-bubbles-and-neutral-site-world-series-at-rangers-globe-life-field-per-report/

46 https://www.baseball-reference.com/bullpen/2020_Postseason.

47 Pedro Moura, *How to Beat a Broken Game: The Rise of the Dodgers in a League on the Brink* (New York: Public Affairs, 2022), 198.

48 Mike Axisa, "MLB Will Allow Fans to Attend 2020 World Series, NLCS at Texas Rangers' Globe Life Field," cbssports.com, https://www.cbssports.com/mlb/news/mlb-will-allow-fans-to-attend-2020-world-series-nlcs-at-texas-rangers-globe-life-field/.

49 The Dodgers went the entire 2020 season without a player testing positive for COVID-19 until the sixth game of the World Series. A lab doing the

COVID-19 tests for Major League Baseball reported that Justin Turner's test one day earlier was inconclusive. The result of Turner's test on the day of Game Six was positive, and Turner was pulled from the game in the eighth inning. The popular third baseman later went back onto the field to join the celebration after the Dodgers won the Series against the Tampa Rays. ESPN, "Justin Turner of Los Angeles Dodgers Pulled from World Series after Positive COVID-19 Test," ESPN.com, October 28, 2020, https://www.espn.com/mlb/story/_/id/30206824/justin-turner-los-angeles-dodgers-pulled-world-series-positive-covid-19-test.

50   Jorgé Castillo, "'We Won a World Series,'" *Los Angeles Times*, October 28, 2020: D2.

51   Jack Harris, "Shorter Season Didn't Make Winning Title Easier," *Los Angeles Times,* October 28, 2020: D6.

52   The Texas Rangers became the second team to win 13 games in a single postseason when they qualified as a wild card and went on to win the 2023 World Series. 2023 MLB playoff bracket: Scores, results as Rangers win first World Series with defeat of Diamondbacks – CBSSports.com.

53   "Shorter Season Didn't Make Winning Title Easier."

54   Mike DiGiovanna, "Dodgers Receive Rings That Are Fit for Kings," *Los Angeles Times*, April 10, 2021: D4.

55   Bill Shaikin, "Huge Reopening Crowd Treated to Thrilling Win," *Los Angeles Times*, June 21, 2021: B10.

JANET MARIE SMITH

by Bob Webster

Besides her work on the renovations of Dodger Stadium, Janet Marie Smith is well known for her work in building Oriole Park at Camden Yards in 1992 and the renovation of Fenway Park, a 10-year effort begun in 2002.

Smith was born in Mississippi, the daughter of Thomas Henry and Nellie S. Smith. Thomas was an architect for 56 years; most of his work was on civic buildings like schools and courthouses. Nellie was a medical records technician for a hospital and worked into her 80s. Janet has one sister, Susan Elliott.[1]

Smith grew up in Jackson, Mississippi. She earned a degree in architecture at Mississippi State University and a master's degree in urban planning from the City College of New York.[2] When asked how she chose her career path, Smith replied,"My dad's love of architecture and public buildings and her mother's work ethic guided me to succeed in my professional career."

Her first venture into making the world a better place was as coordinator of architecture and design for the Battery Park City Authority in New York City. Smith said of the project, "The 92-acre site on the tip of lower Manhattan was slated for commercial and residential development. The first major success was the four-tower World Financial Center, and closely following that the first phase of the residential development, Rector Place. The signature feature of the site was the waterfront public esplanade and the parks and plazas that set the standard for the contextual development. The master plan departed from earlier efforts in that it was conceived to be an extension of Lower Manhattan rather than an isolated project. Following the New York City development, Smith moved to Los Angeles and worked on the renovation of historic Pershing Square. The project was part of a larger effort at downtown revitalization."

L to R: Mookie Betts, Janet Marie Smith, and David Price tour the outfield construction work at Dodger Stadium.

In 1988 the Baltimore Orioles and the State of Maryland committed to build a new ballpark in downtown Baltimore on the site of the Camden railroad yards. It was the first time a baseball team had committed to be a part of an urban development in more than 50 years.[3] Larry Lucchino, then working for Orioles owner Edward Bennett Williams, had convinced the elected officials that separating baseball and football facilities would ensure long-term success. Under new owner Eli Jacobs, Lucchino became the Orioles' president and CEO. He was concerned that the initial designs looked too much like the baseball version of the cookie-cutter stadiums of the 1960s and '70s. Lucchino was especially adamant about building a baseball-only ballpark that would look like a park from the early 1900s. Lucchino saw Smith's résumé and liked the idea that she was an architect and urban planner. He hired her as the club's vice president of planning and development.

When Smith arrived for an interview, Lucchino quickly asked her one question: "Which league has the designated hitter?" She shot back, "I'm offended by that question." She added that she loved baseball. Lucchino later said, "It was the best free-agent signing the Orioles had in 1989.[4] Moreover, the two had an instant rapport and Lucchino felt confident that Smith could not only coordinate the needs of the baseball team and communicate them to HOK Sport, the architects for the Maryland Stadium Authority, but that she could help translate his vision of capturing the character of the "old fashioned ballpark" and work with the team to achieve a design that would set a new paradigm for major-league baseball.

Creating the ballpark included saving the historic 100-year-old B&O Warehouse. He also wanted an "inside the ballpark street" known as Eutaw Street, which with a row of vendors would be open to the public outside of game times. Smith's success in carrying out Lucchino's plans helped spawn a new generation of baseball parks in urban settings.

Jacobs said, "It was Janet Marie and I. It's my basic vision and Janet Marie's attention to detail – luck was shining on us the day she appeared on the scene. She's just remarkable. The strategic part – the large part – is mine. The technical is hers."[5] Jacobs, Lucchino, and Smith all shared the same vision of wanting an old-fashioned ballpark with modern amenities. "They all had one thing in common. They all loved old-fashioned, walkable cities, and the traditional baseball parks that were often a part of them," said architectural writer Paul Goldberger.[6]

Stan Kasten, then president of the Atlanta Braves, toured Camden Yards and was so impressed with Smith that he hired her to lead the 1996 transformation of Olympic Stadium into Turner Field. Kasten said, "It was obvious she had a command of both the game and the business. She had a real passion for it."[7] Kasten, who was also president of the NBA Atlanta Hawks, made Smith responsible for the design and construction of the new Philips Arena in Atlanta. Philips Arena, known as State Farm Arena since 2018, has a unique design, with the upper deck 60 feet closer to the court than in any other modern arena.[8] The Philips Arena was part of a larger Turner Broadcasting commitment to downtown Atlanta. Smith was president of Turner Sports and Entertainment Development and vice president of planning and development for the Braves from 1994 to 2000.

Lucchino, who had moved to the presidency of the San Diego Padres, got Smith to assist with the plans for Petco Park, which opened in 2004.[9] Her primary contribution was siting the project near the historic Gaslamp district and helping to script the urban development that would take shape around Petco Park.

Lucchino, John Henry, and Tom Werner bought the Boston Red Sox after the team was put up for sale in 2001. Of the six groups interested in purchasing the ballclub, theirs was the only one interested in keeping Fenway Park. The 1912 ballpark had been declared too small and insufficient in structural integrity and modern amenities to renovate, and the ownership group had focused solely on a new Fenway Park, which failed to gain traction, leaving the door open for the rescue effort of Henry, Werner, and Lucchino.

Lucchino hired Smith to oversee the preservation, expansion, and remodeling of Fenway Park in 2002. She wanted to move food prep and other nonbaseball operations to adjacent buildings and open more concourse space and adding seats above the Green Monster, the 37-foot-high wall in left field. She said that the "renovations" were only part renovation and part expansion into adjacent buildings owned by the team but used for offices and parking.[10] The renovations were done in offseasons from 2002 through 2012 and were completed in time for Fenway Park's 100th anniversary.[11] One of the particular challenges of this project was that all work had to be approved by the city, state, and the National Park Service. (The ballpark is listed on the National Register of Historic Places.) Smith often cited the working relationship with these agencies as a collaborative, learning experience that made the ballpark better as a result of their input. Smith brought DAIQ Architects of Somerville, Massachusetts, to the Fenway Park project largely due to their work on reuse of older buildings.

She was back with the Orioles from 2009 to 2012 as vice president of planning and development under owner Peter Angelos and responsible for upgrading the earlier designs at Camden Yards, particularly focusing on the 20-year-old food and beverage locations and adding a bar and seating on top of the batters eye. She was also responsible for the renovations and expansion of the Orioles spring-training camp in Sarasota, Florida, at the Ed Smith Stadium and Buck O'Neil Complex.

In August 2012, Kasten, by then president of the Dodgers, hired Smith again, this time as senior vice president of planning and development. In her first eight months with the club, she oversaw a $100 million renovation of Dodger Stadium's clubhouses and fan areas. The renovations continued during each successive offseason. The signature project of the 2.5-acre Centerfield Plaza, "Dodger Stadium's New Front Door," as Stan Kasten calls it, was completed in 2020. Smith was also in charge of the expansion of the Dodgers' Dominican Republic facility to include training, housing, and education for teenage players across Latin America. Campos Las Palmas was the first Major League Baseball facility in the Dominican Republic and the renovations coincided with the 40th anniversary of MLB's presence.

In the press announcement for the Dodger Stadium renovation in 2012, Kasten said of Smith, "Dodger Stadium is one of the most iconic venues in sports and Janet Marie is one of the few people I would trust with its future. … She respects baseball's tradition and knows how to retain a ballpark's distinctive charms while providing fans with the amenities and comfort they've come to expect. Any fan that has walked through the gates at Oriole Park at Camden Yards, the renovated Fenway Park, or Atlanta's Turner Field has been a beneficiary of her understanding of what a ballpark means to its community."[12]

In December 2020 Smith was promoted to executive vice president of planning and development for the Dodgers.[13]

In 2023 Smith and her business partner, Fran Weld, founded Canopy Team, a Baltimore-based, women-led, multi-disciplinary practice that partners with sports teams, education and training programs, and cultural and civic institutions to build facilities that transcend their primary purpose into community gathering points and civic treasures.[14]

(Weld had been the senior vice president of strategy development for the San Francisco Giants.) They work with organizations on large scale capital projects and developments to create sponsorship and seating concepts, graphics, colors, and artwork, added Smith.

With new ballpark designs as well as renovations, Smith strives to combine nostalgic aspects of classic ballparks with modern technology and comforts.

"I've always been an orchestra conductor. I don't play any instruments. I just conduct the orchestra," said Smith. "I always shudder when I read 'she was the designer of something.' I don't feel like I'm ever actually the designer because I always have someone else who produces things. I don't act as the architect. Often I put together a design team that I know will hear what I'm saying, but I don't actually draw those things, I guide it."[15]

Said Stan Kasten: "As a conductor, she knows the role of every single instrument. That's what makes her so good at what she does."[16]

Smith has worked on multiple ballpark projects with Younts Design Inc., an architectural firm in Baltimore. Ronnie Younts, founder of the firm, said of Smith, "In my opinion, the thing that makes her projects so successful and memorable is that she believes that these buildings have their own history and their own soul, that they need to be celebrated in their own way, separate from the teams that play there." He added, "These buildings and these public spaces have a history, a life of their own. She truly knows the importance of finding the soul in every project. To me, this is what makes all of her projects so special."[17]

Jacob Pomrenke, SABR's director of editorial content, said, "The overall fan experience at every ballpark since Camden Yards has been enhanced by her work." Pomrenke used Cincinnati's Great American Ballpark as an example. "Look at the difference in Cincinnati, all those little touches like the homage to Crosley Field's 'Sun Deck' and the open view of the Ohio River and the walking bridge and Power Stacks in right-center field," he said. He added that similarities between Great American Ballpark and Camden Yards include how the city's backdrops and skyline are included in the ballparks' landscape and footprint. The thing that jumps out at me is how 'cookie-cutter' the old Riverfront Park and all of the parks built in that era (the 1960s and 1970s) were, and even the newer ballparks that she had nothing to do with were touched by her design ideas."[18]

Said the baseball writer Rob Neyer, "Just about anything written on ballparks and ballpark construction in the last 20 to 30 years begins with a reference to Oriole Park at Camden Yards, with or without mentioning Smith by name." He added, "She is a devotee of writer Jane Jacobs, who wrote about the life of a city and what it should be for its people. And that's a big part of what Smith does. In some places, they tried to put these 'retro-style' ballparks in the suburbs, but if you don't do it in the city, it's not the same."[19]

Writer George Will wrote of Smith's accomplishments, "The three most important things that have happened in baseball since the Second World War were Jackie Robinson taking the field in Brooklyn in 1947, free agency arriving in 1975, and Oriole Park at Camden Yards opening in 1992."[20]

Janet Marie Smith will go down in history as the person whose work replaced the cookie-cutter stadiums built in the 70s with the retro-style ballparks beginning with Oriole Park at Camden Yards and every ballpark built or renovated since then.

Smith was inducted into the Mississippi Sports Hall of Fame in 2020 and was named one of the 30 Most Powerful Women in Sports by Adweek.com.[21] She has received multiple honors from *Sports Business Journal,* including Class of Champions in 2017, Power Player in 2016, and the inaugural class of Game Changers in 2011. WISE named her one of their 2014 Women of Inspiration.

Smith and her husband, Bart Harvey, live in Baltimore and have three children – Bart IV, Nellie, and Jack.[22] Bart is the former CEO of the Enterprise Community Partners.

SOURCES

In addition to the sources cited in the Notes, information regarding family, architectural collaborations, and various projects was received from Janet Marie Smith through email correspondence in December 2023 and January 2024.

NOTES

1 Thomas Henry Smith Obituary, www.legacy.com/us/obituaries/clarionledger/name/thomas-smith-obituary?id=21091496.

2 Janet Smith, Mississippi Sports Hall of Fame Inductee, https://msfame.com/inductees/janet-marie-smith/.

3 Email from Janet Marie Smith, December 2023.

4 Joe Mock, "Otherwordly Janet Marie Smith charts her own course," Ballparks.com. Retrieved from: / https://baseballparks.com/essays/janet-marie-smith/

5 Peter Richmond, *Ballpark: Camden Yards and the Building of an American Dream* (New York: Simon & Schuster, 1993), 160.

6 Paul Goldberger, *Ballpark: Baseball in the American City* (New York: Penguin Random House, 2019), 210.

7 Mock.

8 Mock.

9 Mock.

10 Email from Janet Marie Smith, December 2023.

11 Sarah Tarbet and Sarah Laliberte, "Project Relevance: Collaborative Approaches to Contextual Integration. Discovering Mutual Benefits to the Renovation of Fenway Park," https://issuu.com/neuarchitecture/docs/fenway_park_case_study_final.

12 Brenda Levin, "LA Dodgers Janet Marie Smith Views Sports as a Means for Urban Revitalization," retrieved from: https://www.planningreport.com/2014/12/09/la-dodgers-janet-marie-smith-views-sports-means-urban-revitalization.

13 "Transactions," *Boston Globe,* December 11, 2020: C7.

14 https://canopyteam.com/

15 Charlie Vascellaro, "Love That Retro Look of your Ballpark? Thank Janet Marie Smith," October 1, 2019, https://globalsportmatters.com/business/2019/10/01/love-that-retro-look-of-your-ballpark-thank-janet-marie-smith/.

16 Mock.

17 Vascellaro.

18 Vascellaro.

19 Vascellaro.

20 George F. Will, *A Nice Little Place on the North Side* (New York: Crown Archetype, 2014), 167.

21 Mississippi Sports Hall of Fame; Vascellaro.

22 Andre F. Shashaty, "Industry Bids Fond Farewell to a Leader," *Affordable Housing Finance News,* June 1, 2008, https://www.housingfinance.com/news/industry-bids-fond-farewell-to-a-leader_o

DODGER STADIUM RENOVATIONS

by Bob Webster

The foul poles at Dodger Stadium were in foul territory, there were only two drinking fountains (one in each dugout), and no one had installed electrical outlets in the clubhouses.[1] Besides fixing those design issues after the 1962 opening season, no real renovations to the ballpark were made until 1975 when new, space-age plastic-colored seats replaced the memorable rainbow-colored wooden chairs at the ballpark.

The O'Malley family had owned the club since 1950 and after Walter O'Malley died in 1979, his children, Peter O'Malley and his sister, Terry Seidler, took over. They sold the team to Fox in 1998, when O'Malley cited "estate planning" as the reason for the sale.[2] Fox added suites on the club level, a feat made possible by Walter O'Malley's effort to have a concourse wide enough that fans could drive their cars directly to their club-level seats – an idea nixed by the City Council, which didn't want gasoline-powered vehicles in the ballpark, but evidence of the forward-thinking approach that defined Walter O'Malley's West Coast creation. Fox also added dugout club seats at field level, replacing the field-level suites from 1962 and reducing the foul territory that had defined the ballpark as a pitchers' park.[3]

From 2003 through 2005, LED video displays were added. Seating was again replaced in the mid-2000s, going back to the 1962 colors.[4] Frank McCourt bought the Dodgers from Fox in 2004, and restoring the midcentury-modern look was one of the most visible changes to the ballpark during his ownership. McCourt, though, ran out of money before he could complete other planned renovations, which would have cost $412 million.[5] He wanted to build a plaza with restaurants beyond center field and create easier access to all levels of the ballpark from the parking lot.[6]

The Guggenheim Baseball Management group bought the Dodgers from McCourt in May 2012. Guggenheim was headed by principal owner Mark Walter and included Dodgers President and CEO Stan Kasten and part-owners Todd Boehly, Peter Gruber, Magic Johnson, and Bobby Patton.

The ballpark needed remodeling, but its condition was considered solid and promising and there was never any threat to leave the iconic stadium.[7] "We bought that," Kasten told a journalist, his hand sweeping toward the mountains beyond the outfield walls. "That classic vista. The bleachers, the palm trees, the San Gabriel Mountains. We'll never screw with that."[8]

Kasten had hired Janet Marie Smith as vice president of planning and development of the Atlanta Braves after the 1996 Olympics in Atlanta and asked her to turn Olympic Stadium into Turner Field. Kasten had toured Oriole Park at Camden Yards upon its completion in 1992 and liked what she had done there. Smith had substantial input on the Olympic Stadium design as the Atlanta Braves representative, and oversaw the post-Olympic transformation to Turner Field with the addition of the plaza, retail store, Chop House, Scouts Alley, Braves Museum, and 755 Club.[9]

Kasten took over as president of the Washington Nationals in 2016 and kept in touch with Smith during her time with the Boston Red Sox. Kasten was so impressed with Smith that he hired her again in August 2012, to oversee the Dodger Stadium renovations, and challenged her to complete an unprecedented amount of work by the start of the 2013 season. Club Chairman Mark Walter said, "We only have one chance to make a good impression," and he authorized $100 million of renovations to be designed and constructed that offseason. Most notably, according to Smith. this included expansion of the clubhouses, accomplished by excavating under the field-level seats to create a new level for batting cages and conditioning spaces and expanding the plazas on all of the public areas to accommodate new restrooms, concessions, retail, and most importantly, space for the 56,000 fans at Dodger Stadium to move around easily.[10]

"What we all agree on is we don't want to change the look of Dodger Stadium," Kasten said.[11]

Soon after Kasten joined the Dodgers, he said of Dodger Stadium, "It's a place that's superb for sitting in your seat for nine innings and watching baseball – and not much else. ... Modern fans want, deserve, and will support you more if there are other things to get them excited at the ballpark. If what you want to do is sit in your seat for nine innings and watch baseball, great. We want to be the best place to do that. If you might want something else while you're here – to get you to come early, to get you to come more often – we want to provide that."[12]

So Smith went to work, and during the 2012-13 offseason, improvements to the outfield video boards, clubhouses and weight rooms, restrooms, concession stands, the sound system, and batting cages were completed.[13] The video boards kept the original hexagon shape and with the viewing area 22 percent larger than before, this allowed for more video content and stats to be shown. The new sound system can be heard in the concourses and restrooms. An improved wi-fi and cell antenna system helps fans using their mobile devices at the ballpark.[14]

New field-level entrances were created, and the concourses were widened by removing a couple of rows of seats in each level, creating new bar seating, and building children's play areas beyond the outfield.[15] Fans with tickets in the field, loge, and club levels can now circle the field inside the ballpark, while stopping in lounge areas overlooking bullpens.

A new plaza was created in 2014 near the left- and right-field gates with team stores and concessions areas. "Fans now expect more than just get their tickets scanned and go directly to their seats," Smith said.[16]

After the 2015 season, more standing room was created in the top deck area and more memorabilia displays were added throughout the ballpark.[17]

A statue of former Dodgers great Jackie Robinson, designed by sculptor Brandly Cadet, was unveiled on April 15, 2017, near the left-field reserve entrance, where most fans enter the ballpark. Club Chairman Mark Walter commissioned the statue. "[Walter] felt it was an idea whose time had come," said Smith.[18] The sculpture was moved in 2020 to the new center-field plaza which became the most popular entrance to Dodger Stadium.[19] More premium seating was added that year in the field level, while the suite and club levels were remodeled to accommodate larger groups, and additional memorabilia was put on display throughout the ballpark.

Club-level seats were returned to the original red, blue, and yellow colors from 1962, as well as new bar seating in left field and more concession stands in 2018.[20]

A remodeling of the "Top of the Park" store occurred during 2019, near the "Retired Numbers Plaza"

which now includes five-foot microphones honoring Vin Scully and Jaime Jarrín.[21]

A second $100 million offseason project was completed in 2020. This project included a new Centerfield Plaza, known as the ballpark's "front door."[22] This includes almost two acres of a children's play area, new food offerings, and more social and standing areas. Fans can watch the game from above a newly constructed batter's eye bar above the wall. The plaza is also home for the "Legends of Dodger Baseball" plaques.[23] A bar, which Smith called a "speak easy," was added. All of the furniture, fixtures, and décor look like the Stadium Club as it was when the ballpark opened in 1962.[24] The second bar under the left-field stands, the Gold Glove Bar, displays not only the Gold Gloves won by every Dodger awarded that honor, but also a mural designed by Nights of Neon in L.A.[25]

The left- and right-field pavilions were also renovated, including new restrooms, enclosed bars with views into the bullpens, standing room on top of each section, and "home run seats" just beyond the outfield wall. Elevators and bridges were installed to connect the new pavilion level decks to the rest of the ballpark. A new sound system replaced the speaker towers provides more direct sound inside the ballpark.[26]

Referring to the new Centerfield Plaza, Smith said, "Too much is too much," and added, "You still want an intimacy. We're still here to watch the game and celebrate the Dodgers. We weren't looking to create a theme park. We were looking to create the kind of amenities that other ballparks have, but in a way that respected the original architecture of Dodger Stadium."[27]

A Sandy Koufax statue joined the Jackie Robinson statue in the Centerfield Plaza on June 18, 2022. Other upgrades included new memorabilia exhibits throughout the ballparks. Murals were also added to the left- and right-field sides of the ballpark, featuring not only Jackie Robinson, but the 60th anniversary logo of Dodger Stadium. Club seats, including the Stadium Club, Baseline Club, Dugout Club, and Home Run Seats were all rebranded for the 2022 season. New seats and other amenities are featured.[28]

Manny Mota and Orel Hershiser were added to the Legends of Dodger Baseball display in 2023, and Fernando Valenzuela's number 34 was retired on August 11. Upgrades were made to the Stadium Club and Reserve Level.[29]

A new LED system was added in 2023 to provide better visibility for both the players and the fans and even those watching on television. The new lighting has color-changing technology for on-field celebrations and concerts.[30]

A new display case behind the Vin Scully Press Box is accessible to all fans. The case includes some of Scully's most significant awards, including five World Series rings (1955, 1963, 1981, 1988, and 2020), his All-Star Game ring, his two Emmy awards, and his 2016 Medal of Freedom Award given to him by President Barack Obama.[31]

Kasten and Smith were very careful not to disturb the view beyond the outfield wall of the mountains. "The beauty of the new plaza is what it has added for the fans, and we haven't touched the postcard view," Kasten said. "It's so important that the people who have been sitting here for 60 years feel as comfortable as they ever had, but with 21st century amenities."[32]

SOURCES

Much of the information came from the Dodgers website under "Dodger Stadium Upgrades," which went back as far as 2013. Other information was gathered and listed in the Notes section.

NOTES

1 Jim Carlisle, "Dodger Stadium Celebrates Its 50th Anniversary Today," *Ventura County Star* (Camarillo, California), April 10, 2012: 1.

2 Associated Press, "O'Malley Cites Estate Planning as Why He Wants to Sell Dodgers," *Deseret News* (Salt Lake City), https://www.deseret.com/1997/1/7/19288019/o-malley-cites-estate-planning-as-why-he-wants-to-sell-dodgers.

3 Janet Marie Smith, email correspondence, December 1-10, 2023.

4 "Dodgers History: Timeline of Dodger Stadium Renovations," www.dodgerblue.com/dodgers-history-timeline-dodger-stadium-renovations/.

5 "Dodgers History: Timeline of Dodger Stadium Renovations."

6 Jayne Kamin, "Dodgers History: Timeline of Dodger Stadium Renovations,"DodgerBlue.com, https://dodgerblue.com/dodgers-history-timeline-dodger-stadium-renovations/.

7 Janet Marie Smith.

8 Anthony Rieber, "New Owners Fully Intend to Upgrade Dodger Stadium," *Newsday* (Long Island, New York), July 1, 2012: A79.

9 Janet Marie Smith.

10 Janet Marie Smith.

11 David Hernandez, "Stadium Renovations to Begin in Winter," *Los Angeles Times*, August 7, 2012: 25.

12 Bill Shaikin, "Sitting, Watching Is So Passe," *Los Angeles Times*, May 20, 2012: 51.

13 "Dodgers History: Timeline of Dodger Stadium Renovations."

14 Beth Harris, "Dodgers Tweak Stadium," *Fresno* (California) *Bee*, January 9, 2013: B5.

15 *Dodger Blue,* "Dodgers History: Timeline of Dodger Stadium Renovations."

16 Mike Hiserman, "Dodgers Hope for Smooth Opening," *Los Angeles Times*, April 4, 2014: 29.

17 "Dodgers History: Timeline of Dodger Stadium Renovations."

18 Charlie Vascellaro, "Love that Retro Look of Your Ballpark? Thank Janet Marie Smith," globalsportsmatters.com, October 1, 2019, www.globalsportsmatters.com/business/2019/10/01/love-that-retro-look-of-your-ballpark-thank-janet-marie-smith.

19 Janet Marie Smith.

20 "Dodgers History: Timeline of Dodger Stadium Renovations."

21 "Dodger Stadium Upgrades," www.mlb.com/dodgers/ballpark/stadium-upgrades.

22 Janet Marie Smith.

23 "Dodger Stadium Upgrades."

24 Joe Mock, "Otherwordly Janet Marie Smith Charts Her Own Course," Ballparks.com, Retrieved from https://baseballparks.com/essays/janet-marie-smith/.

25 Janet Marie Smith.

26 "Dodger Stadium Upgrades."

27 Bill Shaikin, "Commentary: Dodger Stadium Renovations Are Latest Masterpiece Designed by Janet Marie Smith," *Los Angeles Times*, April 7, 2021. https://www.latimes.com/sports/dodgers/story/2021-04-07/on-baseball-dodger-stadium-renovations-janet-marie-smith.

28 "Dodger Stadium Upgrades."

29 "Dodger Stadium Upgrades."

30 Michael Duarte, "Dodgers Opening Day 2023: Here's All the New Additions for Fans at Chavez Ravine," nbclosangeles.com, March 24, 2023, https://www.nbclosangeles.com/news/sports/dodgers-opening-day-2023-heres-all-the-new-additions-for-fans-at-chavez-ravine/3121661/.

31 Duarte.

32 Mock.

SELECTED GAMES

DODGERS LOSE TO REDS IN DODGER STADIUM DEBUT

April 10, 1962: Cincinnati Reds 6, Los Angeles Dodgers 3

by David Krell

Walter O'Malley is a bane or a blessing dependent upon which coast the person describing him resides.

In Brooklyn, baseball fans remember O'Malley with contempt for transporting their beloved Dodgers to Los Angeles after the 1957 season. LA baseball fans are proud that O'Malley's decision not only made the city a major-league metropolis, but also opened the Western region to expansion: Angels in 1961; Padres in 1969; and Mariners in 1977. In the 1990s, the Diamondbacks and Rockies debuted.

While the Dodgers displaced the city's two Pacific Coast League teams – the Hollywood Stars and Los Angeles Angels (no connection to the American League squad) – they needed a major-league ballpark of their own. From 1958 to 1961, they played in Los Angeles Memorial Coliseum.

In 1962 O'Malley unveiled his vision for a modern ballpark befitting the fans who immediately embraced Dodger Blue as their favorite color in the spectrum. Dodger Stadium debuted on April 10, ushering in a new era for Southern California baseball. But it began on somewhat of a sour note: The Dodgers lost the Opening Day game to the '61 NL champion Reds. Score: 6-3.

This new edifice eclipsed the stadiums built in days of yore because of design, comfort, and luxury commanding respect, excitement, and awe.

Sportswriting legend Jack Murphy wrote, "Never has the game of rounders been played amid such splendor. The Dodgers new park is so plush that I wouldn't dare remove my coat or loosen my tie while writing this essay; surely an usher would evict me immediately."[1]

Johnny Podres had the honor of being the Dodgers' first starting pitcher in the new ballyard, which drew 52,564 fans on this special day. They sat in seats with muted colors of yellow, orange, turquoise, and blue.

With the increasing use of color television, Dodger Stadium would be a visual lure for TV viewers. Groundskeepers had painted the grass green.[2]

The home team faced a 1-0 deficit in the top of the first. Vada Pinson got the first RBI off the southpaw, scoring Cincinnati's leadoff batter Eddie Kasko, who had smacked a double and taken third base on Cookie Rojas's sacrifice.

LA responded with two runs in the bottom of the fourth, courtesy of Ron Fairly's two-run double, scoring Jim Gilliam and Duke Snider. Gilliam had begun with a single and moved to second base on Wally Moon's grounder to second baseman Rojas. Snider's infield single gave Gilliam a path to third base, putting runners at the corners.

After John Roseboro grounded out and gave Snider the opportunity to take second, Fairly's swat gave Dodgers fans something to cheer about in their new ballpark.

The Reds evened the score in the top of the sixth.

Pinson led off with a walk followed by two outs, Frank Robinson's foul out to Fairly at first base and Wally Post's fly ball to Willie Davis in center. Gordy Coleman's single gave Pinson second base; Tommy Harper's single to Dodgers stalwart Snider in right field scored him and pushed Coleman to third. Harper extended his journey to second base when Snider fired the ball.[3]

Podres loaded the bases with an intentional walk of Johnny Edwards to face Reds hurler

Bob Purkey. The strategy proved valid. Purkey struck out. When the Reds came up next, they added three runs. Podres got two outs on Kasko's grounder to third baseman Daryl Spencer and Rojas's fly to Moon in left. Then Cincinnati commenced a two-out rally. Pinson doubled; Robinson got an intentional walk; and Post smashed a three-run homer.

Alston admitted that his strategy of walking Robinson came from apprehension of his prowess. "Well, Robinson has always been a thorn in our side," explained the Dodgers manager, beginning the ninth of 23 seasons at the helm. He was the league's Most Valuable Player last year and you know he got a hit the next time he came up."[4]

Podres retired Coleman on a fly out to Davis, sending the Dodgers to bat with a 5-2 gap.

Walter Alston changed pitchers in the top of the eighth, after Podres gave up singles to Harper and Purkey. Larry Sherry came into the game with one out, then retired Kasko on a fly ball and pinch-hitter Jerry Lynch on a called third strike.

When Dodger Stadium's new occupants loaded the bases in the bottom of the eighth, Cincinnati changed pitchers.

Purkey had gotten Tim Harkness – pinch-hitting for Sherry – out on a grounder to Harper. Maury Wills drew a walk, which was never good for opposing NL squads in '62. He broke Ty Cobb's stolen-base record of 96 in a single season with 104 thieveries. Here, he stayed in the vicinity of first base until Gilliam's single sent him to second and Moon's walk advanced him to third.

Cincinnati left-hander Bill Henry came in from the Reds bullpen and faced Tommy Davis pinch-hitting for Snider. To the frustration of fans from Moorpark to Mission Viejo, Davis grounded to Kasko for a double play.

The Reds amplified their lead with a sixth run in the top of the ninth. Ron Perranoski relieved Sherry. (LA's ace reliever led the majors with appearances in 70 games that season.) Pinson and Robinson hit back-to-back singles; Pinson scored on flies by Post and Coleman to center field.

Cincy's offense shone brighter than klieg lights at a Hollywood premiere. Pinson had a 4-for-4 day with three runs scored, a walk, and an RBI. Post went 3-for-5; Harper also notched three hits.

What made the victory more splendid than usual was the lack of rest for the victors. According to Lou Smith of the *Cincinnati Enquirer*, "less than five hours of sleep" graced the visiting squad, a result of an extended plane flight lasting more than nine hours and a 4:00 A.M. arrival in Los Angeles. Smith wrote that "strong headwinds" caused the expanded length.[5]

It was Podres' first loss on his journey to a 15-13 record in 1962.

Besides his team's inaugural loss, O'Malley faced some glitches with elevators and parking. With parking-lot sections exceeding 50, chaos emerged. "The opening day crowd had all kinds of trouble determining where their parking areas were located – and even the attendants often were confused in giving directions," explained reporter Hank Hollingworth. "One Long Beach party wasted one hour after reaching the parking lot entrance before landing in the proper parking section."[6]

Elite fans and the press had access to two elevators. One went kaput in the middle of the game. But an array of 10 buttons made the job of the operators confusing at best for the other elevator.[7]

Traffic was predicted to be a hassle. It wasn't. A highly significant factor was the buildup of a perceived crisis that inspired fans to jaunt to the ballpark as early as 9:30 A.M. for a 1:00 P.M. start. LAPD Chief William H. Parker said, "We expected this to be one of the biggest traffic problems we have had to face."[8]

Los Angeles Times reporter Paul B. Zimmerman observed that the parking lots were empty within a half-hour after the game ended.[9]

But the new ballpark in Chavez Ravine did not have a smooth path toward completion. Indeed, O'Malley had to navigate challenges in the political, social, and public relations. In his book *Stealing Home: Los Angeles, the Dodgers, and the Lives Caught in Between*, SABR 2021 Seymour Medal winner Eric Nusbaum tackles the complexities involving Hispanic families living in Chavez Ravine balanced against the civic goals of a baseball hallmark. Public housing vs. public relations. Nusbaum writes of O'Malley: "[H]e was acquiring the hangover from the war over public housing that had made this land available in the first place."[10]

Dodger Nation had an aura of excitement in '62. In addition to Dodger Stadium setting a new standard for ballparks and Wills's exemplary performance on NL basepaths, Don Drysdale went 25-9 and won the Cy Young Award. The Dodgers tied the Giants for the NL title, then lost two out of three in a playoff. The Yankees defeated the Giants in seven games to win the World Series.

SOURCES

In addition to the sources cited in the Notes below, the author relied on pertinent information from Baseball-Reference.com and Retrosheet.org, including the box scores.

This article was fact-checked by Laura Peebles.

https://www.retrosheet.org/boxesetc/1962/B04100LAN1962.htm
https://www.baseball-reference.com/boxes/LAN/LAN196204100.shtml

NOTES

1   Jack Murphy, "Park Lights Glow, Starlights Dim at New Dodger Stadium," *Monrovia* (California) *Daily News-Post,* April 11, 1962: 4.

2   George Lederer, "Daffy Day At Chavez (?) Ravine," *Long Beach* (California) *Independent,* April 11, 1962: C-2.

3   Retrosheet's account does not say if Snider threw the ball home or to third base.

4   Associated Press, "Wally Moon Sums It Up: Good Game, Wrong Finish," *San Bernardino Daily Sun*, April 11, 1962: 8. Robinson led the National League in slugging percentage from 1960 through 1962. For two of those years, he led the majors.

5   Lou Smith, "Dodgers' New Stadium Utmost in All Respects," *Cincinnati Enquirer,* April 11, 1962: 23.

6   Hank Hollingworth, "Dodger Fans Find Parking, Not Traffic, Is Headache." *Long Beach Independent,* April 11, 1962: 1.

7   "Dodger Fans Find Parking, Not Traffic, Is Headache."

8   Paul Zimmerman, "Stadium Opener Lost by Dodgers," *Los Angeles Times,* April 11, 1962: 1.

9   "Stadium Opener Lost By Dodgers."

10   Eric Nusbaum, *Stealing Home: Los Angeles, the Dodgers, and the Lives Caught in Between* (New York: Public Affairs, 2020), 279

THE GIANTS WIN THE PENNANT, PART TWO!

October 3, 1962: San Francisco Giants 6, Los Angeles Dodgers 4

by Tim Otto

On September 22, 1962, the second-place San Francisco Giants trailed the Los Angeles Dodgers by four games, with seven contests remaining in the regular-season schedule.

One week later the Giants had closed the deficit to one game. In the final game on September 30, Willie Mays' eighth-inning home run gave San Francisco a 2-1 victory at home against Houston, while Los Angeles was losing at home to St. Louis, 1-0. Gene Oliver's eighth-inning homer sent the Dodgers to their fourth straight defeat and sixth loss in their last seven games. Second in the league to San Francisco in runs scored, they were in the midst of a batting slump and hadn't scored in 21 innings.[1]

Maury Wills broke the MLB record with 104 stolen bases in 1962. The NL MVP winner was caught just 13 times.

A three-game playoff would decide the winner of the National League pennant.[2] Dodgers manager Walter Alston selected Sandy Koufax as his starting pitcher for the first playoff game, at Candlestick Park on October 1. Koufax, sidelined in mid-July because of numbness in his left index finger, had been ineffective since returning in mid-September. Mays hit a two-run homer in the first inning,[3] and San Francisco went on to win, 8-0.

The teams moved to Dodger Stadium the next day. The score was 5-0 in San Francisco's favor when Los Angeles finally broke its scoring drought with seven runs in the sixth inning. The Giants tied the game in the eighth, but the Dodgers won, 8-7, when Maury Wills scored the winning run in the ninth on a sacrifice by Ron Fairly.

For the decisive third game, Dodgers coach Leo Durocher, who had managed the 1951 Giants to their dramatic playoff victory over the Dodgers when both teams were in New York, brought the same T-shirt he wore 11 years earlier when Bobby Thomson hit his pennant-winning home run. Current Giants manager Alvin Dark, Durocher's starting shortstop in 1951, was asked if he had brought anything from that game. He replied, "Yeah, Willie Mays."[4]

Johnny Podres, pitching on two days' rest for the first time in his career,[5] held the Giants scoreless in the first two innings, allowing only a single by leadoff hitter Harvey Kuenn. Wills singled to start the bottom of the first, but he was the only baserunner allowed by San Francisco starter Juan Marichal in the initial two frames.

José Pagán singled to open the top half of the third. Podres fielded Marichal's bunt and threw past second base into center; Pagan took third on the error. Pagan scored on Kuenn's single to left, with Marichal holding at second.

Chuck Hiller missed a bunt attempt. Marichal was caught off second on the play, but John Roseboro's throw sailed into center for another error, putting Marichal at third.

Hiller flied out to left. Marichal bluffed for home, and Duke Snider's throw was cut off by third baseman Tommy Davis, who threw to Jim Gilliam at second, catching Kuenn in a rundown. Kuenn scrambled back toward first; Gilliam's throw hit him in the back. Kuenn was safe at first, and Marichal scored on Los Angeles's third error of the inning for a 2-0 lead.

In the Dodgers' half of the third, Wills singled with two outs and stole second. He was stranded there after Gilliam's fly out. Consecutive two-out singles in the fourth put Giants runners on first and second, but Kuenn fouled out to the catcher, ending the threat.

Snider doubled to start the Dodgers fourth and advanced to third on a single by Tommy Davis. One out later, Frank Howard grounded to third. Davis slid hard into second base, breaking up a potential double play and allowing Snider to score. The Giants' lead was down to 2-1.

In the sixth, the Giants loaded the bases with no outs on Orlando Cepeda's line-drive single to right, Ed Bailey's smash off Wills's glove, and Jim Davenport's bunt single. Ed Roebuck, making his sixth appearance in the Dodgers' last seven games, relieved Podres. Pagan grounded to Wills, who threw home for the force out. Marichal hit into a groundball double play; the Dodgers escaped, still training by only a run.

Roebuck's clutch relief looked like a turning point after Snider led off the Dodgers' half of the sixth with a single. Tommy Davis hit a 3-and-1 pitch deep into the left-center-field seats, putting the Dodgers in front, 3-2.[6]

The Giants failed to score in the seventh, leaving runners stranded at first and second, and the Dodgers added a run in the bottom of the inning. With one out, Wills hit his fourth straight single and stole second on Marichal's first pitch to Gilliam, who then flied out to left. Wills stole third on the first pitch to the next batter, Larry Burright, and came home when Bailey's errant throw bounced past Davenport into left field.[7] Los Angeles now led 4-2.

Roebuck kept the Giants scoreless in the eighth. In the Dodgers half of the inning, Marichal, after throwing three pitches to Tommy Davis, all balls, was relieved by Don Larsen, whose first pitch was a low curve for ball four. A sacrifice by Fairly moved Davis to second. He stole third on Frank Howard's swinging strikeout. Larsen intentionally walked the next two batters, bringing up the pitcher. Roebuck grounded

out, but the Dodgers were three outs from the World Series.

Matty Alou, pinch hitting for Larsen, singled on Roebuck's first pitch in the top of the ninth. Kuenn forced Alou at second on a grounder but beat the throw to first, avoiding a double play. Pinch-hitter Willie McCovey walked on four pitches, then Felipe Alou walked on a 3-and-2 count to load the bases.

Alston visited the mound, but left Roebuck in the game. Mays lined a single off Roebuck's glove, scoring Kuenn to cut the gap to 4-3.

Stan Williams relieved with the bases still loaded. Cepeda's sacrifice fly to right tied the score, with Felipe Alou advancing to third.

Williams threw a strike to Bailey, then sailed a high pitch over Roseboro's glove. Alou held at third as Mays advanced to second on the wild pitch. Alston called for an intentional walk to Bailey, and the bases were again loaded.

Davenport walked on five pitches, sending Alou home with the go-ahead run.

Ron Perranoski relieved Williams, and Jose Pagan hit a grounder toward second. Burright, a defensive replacement in the seventh, bobbled the ball for an error – Los Angeles' fourth error of the game. Mays scored for a two-run lead.

After watching his team score four runs on two hits, four walks, an error, and a wild pitch to take the lead, 6-4, Billy Pierce relieved and retired the Dodgers in order in the home half of the ninth. The Giants were headed to the World Series for the first time since moving to California after the 1957 season.

The Dodgers kept the press out of their locker room for nearly an hour after the loss. Team captain Snider, one of the few to dress in order to congratulate the Giants, said, "Don't hold it against the guys. They just want to cool off. They agreed they didn't feel like talking. They're still in a daze."[8]

A stunned Roebuck let Wally Moon explain to reporters what happened on the line drive hit by Mays in the ninth. "Ed told me the ball just hit the web of his glove and he didn't see it."[9]

Alston said he let Roebuck hit in the eighth with the bases loaded and two out because Roebuck was the best pitcher to protect the Dodgers' two-run lead. Stating that his pitchers finally "ran out of gas," Alston added, "We just came close, that's all. Ed Roebuck did one helluva job as long as he lasted. I think everybody gave it everything he possibly could."[10]

Dark defended his counterpart's strategy. "Maybe some will think he should have taken Ed Roebuck out of the game earlier in the ninth inning, but I don't think he could have, the way Roebuck was pitching," Dark said. "When McCovey went to bat with a man on first, Alston could have called in Ron Perranoski, his lefthander, but he knew that my next three batters after McCovey were righthanders, so he couldn't take a chance with a lefthanded pitcher in a spot like that."[11]

San Francisco and the New York Yankees split the first six games of the 1962 World Series. Down 1-0 in the bottom of the ninth in Game Seven, the Giants had runners on second and third with two outs and McCovey at the plate. Their hopes of another comeback were silenced when McCovey's line drive was caught by Bobby Richardson.

Despite speculation that he would be replaced by either Durocher or Pete Reiser,[12] Alston signed his 10th one-year contract to manage the Dodgers the day after the World Series ended.[13] Koufax made a complete recovery in 1963, winning 25 games and the Cy Young Award.[14] He was also named the National League's Most Valuable Player. Los Angeles held off a late-season challenge by the St. Louis Cardinals to win the pennant. San Francisco finished in third place. The Dodgers swept the Yankees in the 1963 World Series.

SOURCES

The author accessed Baseball-Reference.com and Retrosheet.org. for box scores/play-by-play information, player, team, and season pages, pitching and batting game logs, and other data:

https://www.baseball-reference.com/boxes/LAN/LAN196210030.shtml

https://www.retrosheet.org/boxesetc/1962/B10030LAN1962.htm

The author also accessed YouTube's *Classic Baseball on the Radio* for NBC's national broadcast of this game by Al Helfer and George Kell:

https://www.youtube.com/watch?v=3jHOlcH1GiM

NOTES

1   Dan Hafner, "Stunned Dodgers Can't Believe It," *Los Angeles Times*, October 1, 1962: C4.

2   It was the fourth time the NL season ended with two teams tied for first place, necessitating a best-of-three-games playoff to decide the pennant winner. In 1946 the Dodgers and Cardinals tied, with St. Louis winning the first two playoff games. In 1951 the Dodgers and Giants needed three games to determine a winner, with Bobby Thomson's home run in the bottom of the ninth giving the Giants the pennant. In 1959, the Dodgers won the first two playoff games against the Braves. Dodgers outfielder Duke Snider and Giants center fielder Willie Mays were the only active players remaining from the 1951 playoff. Leo Durocher, now a coach for Los Angeles, managed the Dodgers in 1946 and the Giants in 1951. Current San Francisco manager Alvin Dark and coaches Whitey Lockman, Wes Westrum, and Larry Jansen all played for the Giants in 1951.

3   Results of the playoff games counted in the players' season statistics. At the end of the 162-game schedule, Mays led the National League in home runs, with 47, but Harmon Killebrew of the American League's Twins led the majors with 48. In addition to his first-inning home run, Mays hit one off Larry Sherry in the sixth inning, giving him a major-league-leading total of 49.

4   "Playoff Pearls," *The Sporting News*, October 13, 1962: 10.

5   Bob Hunter, "Dodger Slab Staff Cracks in Showdown," *The Sporting News*, October 13, 1962: 7.

6   The two RBIs gave Davis 153 for the season, tops in the majors. Davis started the game with a .344 batting average, two points ahead of Cincinnati's Frank Robinson. He ended the day with a .346 average after two hits and a walk in four plate appearances.

7   Wills had four steals in the playoff series, bringing his season total to 104, a major-league record at the time. He edged out Mays for the National League MVP award (209 points with 8 first-place vote to 202 points with 7 first-place votes for Mays).

8   "Dodgers Want to Be Alone," *San Francisco Examiner*, October 4, 1962: 65.

9   "Dodgers Want to Be Alone."

10 "Dodgers Want to Be Alone."

11 "Playoff Pearls," *The Sporting News*, October 13, 1962: 10.

12 Sid Ziff, "Walt Will Be Back," *Los Angeles Times*, October 11, 1962: B3.

13 Paul Zimmerman, "Alston Keeps Job, OK's Durocher Stay," *Los Angeles Times*, October 18, 1962: B3.

14 Until 1967, only one Cy Young Award, covering both the National and American Leagues, was given.

SANDY KOUFAX'S SECOND NO-HITTER

May 11, 1963: Los Angeles Dodgers 8, San Francisco Giants 0

by Marc Z Aaron

It was a great pitching match-up as the fifth-place Los Angeles Dodgers (15-15) hosted the National League-leading San Francisco Giants (19-11) on May 11. It was a great pitching match-up: Juan Marichal (4-2) and Sandy Koufax (3-1).

Koufax had missed two weeks at the end of April into May with stiffness in his shoulder. A couple of weeks later, he said, "Guess I'm getting old. I'm just falling apart, piece by piece."[1]

In Koufax's first no-hitter, the season before, the Dodgers supported him with four runs in the first inning. Koufax had not had great control, going to full counts on nine New York Mets batters and walking five while striking out 13.

This game was a much different story. Going to the bottom of the sixth inning, the score was 1-0 in favor of the Dodgers. The lone run was produced by a Wally Moon fly-ball home run down the right-field line. Koufax had not yet walked a batter. He only had one three-ball count – in the first inning to Willie Mays, who then flied out to center. Koufax was perfect through six. The only close play came in the fifth when Orlando Cepeda hit a slow roller that shortstop Dick Tracewski barehanded to throw out Cepeda at first.

In the bottom of the sixth, Junior Gilliam lined a single to right to open the inning. Ron Fairly tried to advance Gilliam with a bunt but popped it to first base for the first out. Tommy Davis singled to right and then Wally Moon lined a run-scoring single to right and advanced to second on the throw from the outfield. With runners on second and third and one out, Frank Howard was intentionally walked. John Roseboro, with a career average under .200 against Marichal, lined a single to center, scoring Davis and Moon. After an infield hit by Tracewski loaded the bases, Marichal was replaced by John Pregenzer, who struck out Koufax and got Willie Davis on a groundball.

At the start of the seventh, Nate Oliver went in to play second base. Second baseman Gilliam moved to third and Tommy Davis switched from third base to left field, replacing Wally Moon, who came out of the game.

This turned out to be a key move. Koufax ran into lady luck in the seventh inning when Harvey Kuenn smashed a liner to right, but squarely into the mitt of Frank Howard. Felipe Alou, the league's leading hitter, then sent a high, hard shot to left. Tommy Davis took it about two feet short of the stands. Next, Willie Mays cracked a blistering liner that Jim Gilliam stabbed behind the third base bag."[2] When Davis caught Alou's ball, the bullpen kept yelling, "You got room, you got room."[3]

Don Larsen, the last man to pitch a perfect game, was watching from the San Francisco bullpen.[4]

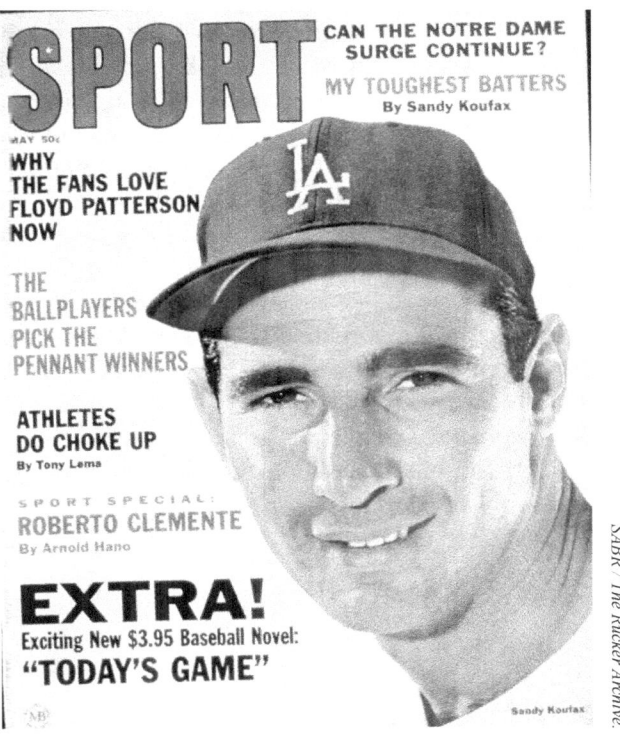

SABR / The Rucker Archive.

Sandy Koufax was the youngest player ever elected to the Baseball Hall of Fame.

None of the players on the bench said anything about the possible no-hitter but Koufax was aware all the time and knew he was close to a perfect game.[5]

Leading off the eighth, Orlando Cepeda hit a hot shot off Koufax's glove to second baseman Nate Oliver, who threw out Cepeda by a step.[6] The next man up was catcher Ed Bailey. Bailey had not much success previously against Koufax. Bailey took three balls, then two hard, straight fastballs for strikes before fouling one off. The pressure was agonizing.[7] "Finally, he threw one I couldn't reach," Bailey said later, "and he walked me."[8] Koufax, aware of the no-hitter all the way, kicked the mound and thumped his glove as the perfect game got away.[9] Then Bailey was taken off the basepaths as Jim Davenport grounded into a double play.

It was ladies night at Dodger Stadium. The crowd of 55,350 (49,807 paid) was the largest of the season thus far in the major leagues.[10] From the sixth inning on, fans were aware of the no-hitter and a possible perfect game. They applauded every time Koufax retired a batter.[11]

In the bottom of the eighth with one out, Roseboro and Tracewski singled. As Koufax approached the plate he received a standing ovation from the crowd.[12] He drew a walk and scored the sixth run of the game on a double by Ron Fairly.

In the ninth Joe Amalfitano popped out to first baseman Fairly. José Pagán flied out to Willie Davis in deep center. Willie McCovey pinch-hit for Pregenzer and walked on four pitches. Koufax got one strike on Kuenn, who hit a bouncer right back to him. Koufax carefully lobbed the ball over to Fairly after running almost to first for the putout.

Koufax was mobbed by his teammates as the crowd roared and sent a shower of seat cushions onto the field.[13] Koufax could be seen anxiously looking for his parents, who had recently relocated to the West Coast, but they were not to be seen as Koufax had forgotten to leave them tickets.[14]

Koufax believed that in his first no-hitter he had exceptional stuff, but did not think he had overpowering stuff this night. It was good but not great. Strikeouts tell the story. In his first no-hitter he had 13, but against the Giants only four, and none after the sixth inning.[15] He threw 111 pitches, relying more on breaking balls.[16]

When it was all over, Koufax had become the only active pitcher other than Warren Spahn with two no-hitters. He also joined Carl Erskine as the second pitcher in Dodgers history to pitch two no-hitters. It was the third no-hitter pitched at Dodger Stadium.[17]

Notably, Koufax had not yet allowed a run at Dodger Stadium in 1963 after having pitched 24⅔ innings.

The victory was the second and final time Koufax beat Marichal.

NOTES

1 Bob Hunter, "Koufax' No-Hit Voodoo Kayoes Injury Hex," *Los Angeles Herald-Examiner*, May 25, 1963: 5.

2 Frank Finch, "Sandy's Finger, Arm OK ---And How!! Dodger Lefty Retires First 22 Batters in 8-0 L.A. Win," *Los Angeles Times*, May 12, 1963: 11.

3 United Press International, "Koufax Triumphs on No-Hitter, 8-0," *New York Times*, May 12, 1963: S1.

4 Melvin Durslag, "Perfecto Larsen Viewed Sandy's Classic Curving," *Los Angeles Herald-Examiner*, May 25, 1963: 4. Larsen was a relief pitcher for the Giants in 1963.

5 "Koufax Rates 2nd No-Hitter First," *New York Times*, May 13, 1963: 52.

6 Joe McDonnell, "Dodger Stadium's Most Memorable Moments … Koufax's Three No-Hitters," *1987 Dodger Scorebook*; Durslag.

7 Durslag.

8 Jane Leavy, *Sandy Koufax, A Lefty's Legacy* (New York: HarperCollins, 2002), 123.

9 Hunter.

10 Finch.

11 "Koufax Rates 2nd No-Hitter First."

12 Finch.

13 Finch.

14 Leavy, 122.

15 Sandy Koufax with Ed Linn, *Koufax* (New York: Viking Press, 1966), 181-183.

16 "Koufax Rates 2nd No-Hitter First."

17 Bo Belinsky pitched a no-hitter for the Los Angeles Angels in Dodger Stadium on May 5, 1962.

TOMMY DAVIS SECURES SECOND CONSECUTIVE BATTING TITLE AS DODGERS END THE 1963 SEASON WITH LOSS TO THE PHILLIES

September 29, 1963: Philadelphia Phillies 3, Los Angeles Dodgers 1

by Alan Stowell

In late September 1963, the pennant races were winding down and it seemed likely that the Los Angeles Dodgers would meet the New York Yankees in the World Series. Only some individual honors were yet to be determined on the final day of the season – including whether Tommy Davis would claim his second consecutive National League batting title for the Dodgers.

The league batting race was the source of a good deal of drama as the season wrapped up in late September, with seven players involved. On Tuesday, September 17, Roberto Clemente of the Pittsburgh Pirates moved into a narrow lead over the St. Louis Cardinals' Dick Groat with a mark of .3231 to .3227. Davis was third at .3219.[1] Others in the chase were Orlando Cepeda of the San Francisco Giants, Vada Pinson of the Cincinnati Reds, Hank Aaron of the Milwaukee Braves, and Tony González of the Philadelphia Phillies.

On Friday, September 20, Davis went 3-for-4 in a 2-0 win over the Pirates to move ahead of Groat, .324 to .322.[2] Clemente had dropped to .320. Davis led the rest of the way but it wasn't easy. By September 22, Davis had dropped a point to .323 with Cepeda and Groat close on his heels at .320.

Yet with only a week remaining in the season and the pennant not yet clinched, the Dodgers had to focus on the standings, not the batting race. On September 24 the Dodgers clinched the pennant before taking the field as the second-place Cardinals lost a day game in Chicago to the Cubs, 6-3. In their night game in Los

Angeles, the Dodgers handled the New York Mets, 4-1, but Davis was hitless in three at-bats.

The next day three Dodgers pitchers shut out the Mets, 1-0, as Davis went 2-for-3. Davis was not in the lineup on September 26 but returned on Friday against the Phillies to go 2-for-3. In his final regular-season game, on September 28, Davis hit a two-run home run in the first inning. After flying out in his next at-bat,

Tommy Davis.

Davis left the game and the club to travel with his wife to New York following the death of his mother-in-law.[3] The Dodgers lost the game, 12-3.

Over his final eight games, Davis collected 11 hits in 28 at-bats, a .393 clip, to separate himself from Clemente, Groat, and Aaron in the batting race. Davis's mark of .326 gave him the batting title ahead of Clemente at .320, and Groat and Aaron tied at .319. Davis's average won not just the NL title. He also led the majors as Carl Yastrzemski topped the American League with a .321 average.[4]

On September 29 the Dodgers hosted the Philadelphia Phillies to close out the regular season. Los Angeles had clinched the National League flag five days earlier, and by some accounts used the finale as a World Series tuneup with a chance to rest some of its regulars. At that point, Davis seemed assured of winning the batting title and his early departure from the team for family reasons was not an issue.[5]

Despite the absence of their hitting star, the Dodgers still had reason to do more than just show up for the final game. The team was sitting on 99 wins for the season, and starter Don Drysdale was going for his 20th victory.

In the bottom of the first inning, a double by shortstop Maury Wills, a steal of third, and a sacrifice fly from center fielder Willie Davis gave Drysdale a quick 1-0 lead. Drysdale was solid for "five scoreless innings [and] probably could have rolled on to win his 20th,"[6] but manager Walter Alston was taking no chances in the 102-degree heat and turned to Pete Richert and Bob Miller to close out the game.

The Phillies were quiet until shortstop Bobby Wine tied the game in the top of the seventh with a solo home run off Richert. Pitcher Chris Short helped his own bid for a victory by following Wine's shot with a single to center. A walk to second baseman Tony Taylor sent Short to second. Right fielder Johnny Callison then gave Philadelphia a 2-1 lead when his double to left sent Short home.

Philadelphia added an insurance run in the ninth inning on a single by third baseman Don Hoak, two groundouts that moved Hoak along the basepaths, and a run-scoring single by Taylor.

The Dodgers were unable to score after the first inning; they were held in check by pitchers Art Mahaffey, Jack Baldschun, and Short, who earned the win. LA managed only six hits, all singles except for Wills' double leading off the first inning for the Dodgers.

The loss was the Dodgers' third straight to the Phillies to close out the regular campaign. Philadelphia finished in fourth place in the National League, 12 games back of the Dodgers. With the win, the Phillies finished 11-7 against the Dodgers for the season, including "seven out of nine at Dodger Stadium."[7] Despite their strong finish, the Phillies fell one game short of overtaking the San Francisco Giants for third place, while the St. Louis Cardinals claimed second place.

Clearly the Dodgers could have used Davis's bat in the lineup for the season-ender. In addition to the batting championship, Davis finished the season with 181 hits, 16 homers, and 88 runs batted in, and was a major reason the team advanced to the World Series. At age 24, Davis was the youngest to ever win two straight NL batting titles. Davis had hit .346 for the Dodgers in 1962 while pounding out 230 hits.[8] Jake Daubert in 1913-14 was the only other Dodger to win back-to-back league batting titles. The last player to accomplish the feat prior to Davis was Stan Musial, who won three straight hitting crowns from 1950 to 1952.[9]

Davis's performance was even more impressive considering that he started the season with a pulled "hamstring muscle behind the knee of the right leg" incurred in a March 31 exhibition game. Improvement in the leg was so slow that Davis was admitted to the hospital April 18 "to assure complete rest" while being treated for the injury.[10] After spending over a week in the hospital, Davis returned to action on April 29 as a pinch-hitter. He appeared in 146 of the Dodgers' 162 games during the season.[11]

For Tommy Davis, 1962 and 1963 marked the peak of what looked to be a promising career. The batting titles, combined with power and speed, showed the potential star power of the young outfielder. What seemed like the beginning of a Hall of Fame career ended suddenly on the basepaths in 1965. On May 1, the Giants were in Dodger Stadium. Davis was running from first to second on a groundball but slid awkwardly and snapped his ankle.[12] The injury ended his season and altered his career, which never got back on its promising track, although he did play 18 seasons for 10 teams and had a career .294 batting average.

Blue Heaven on Earth

SOURCES

In addition to the sources cited in the Notes, the author consulted Baseball-Reference.com and retrosheet.org.

https://www.baseball-reference.com/boxes/LAN/LAN196309290.shtml

https://www.Retrosheet.org/boxesetc/1963/B09290LAN1963.htm

NOTES

1   "Clemente New Bat Leader for NL," *Napa Valley Register* (Napa, California), September 18, 1963: 10.

2   "Baseball's Top Ten," *San Francisco Examiner*, September 21, 1963: 42.

3   "Southpaws to Start in First Series Game," *Stockton* (California) *Daily Evening Record,* September 30, 1963: 29.

4   John Thorn, Phil Birnbaum, and Bill Deane, *Total Baseball, 8th Edition* (Toronto: SPORT Media Publishing, 2004).

5   John Hall, "Dodgers Lose 'Tuneup'; T. Davis Tops Batters,*" Los Angeles Times*, September 30, 1963: 47.

6   Hall.

7   Hall. The *Los Angeles Times* erroneously reported that the Phillies won six out of nine at Dodger Stadium in 1963 but according to retrosheet.org the Phillies in fact won seven.

8   Davis also led the major leagues in hitting in 1962 as Pete Runnels of the Boston Red Sox led the American League that season with a .326 average. Thorn and Birnbaum.

9   "Tom Davis, Yastrzemski Capture Batting Crowns," *Allentown* (Pennsylvania) *Morning Call,* September 30, 1963: 8.

10   "Tommy Davis Lost to L.A. for Week," *Oakland Tribune*, April 20, 1963: 11.

11   Thorn and Birnbaum.

12   Paul Hirsch/Mark Stewart, SABR BioProject, https://sabr.org/bioproj/person/tommy-davis-2/.

"THE BEST PITCHED GAME OF THIS SUPERBLY PITCHED SERIES"

October 5, 1963: Los Angeles Dodgers 1, New York Yankees 0

By Andy McCue

Depending on who you listened to, the New York Yankees were either shell-shocked or coolly determined as they approached the third game of the 1963 World Series. The venue had shifted across the continent to Los Angeles, but the pall of the Yankees' losses to the Los Angeles Dodgers in the first two games of the Series hung over the 1962 World Series champions.

No team had ever lost the first two games of the World Series at home and come back to win. New York Mayor Robert Wagner assessed their chances and decided not to join them in Los Angeles.[1]

The *Los Angeles Times* found the Yankees rocked to their soles. "The glum, grimly-determined Yankees held a star-chamber session in the clubhouse before working out at Dodger Stadium Friday," wrote Frank Finch. Yankees manager Ralph Houk downplayed the glum and the grim, saying the meeting was a standard review of the opposition after the first two games of any series. "There was no 'Let's win one for the Gipper oration' by me," he said.[2]

Veteran Yankees third-base coach Frank Crosetti summed up the company line. "We've been two down before and come back to win. There's no reason why we can't do it again."[3]

The move from the left-handed-pitcher-loving Yankee Stadium to the pitcher-loving Dodger Stadium had both managers choosing to start their lead right-handers. Jim Bouton had emerged that season for the New Yorkers, winning 21 games with a team-leading 2.53 earned-run average. Bouton had pitched five times in Dodger Stadium against the Los Angeles Angels. It was a sterling record of two starts, including a five-hit shutout, and three relief appearances – a total of three earned runs surrendered in just over 25 innings.

For the Dodgers, Don Drysdale took his deceptive 19-17 record to the mound. His 2.63 earned-run average was a better indicator of how he had pitched. The Dodgers' anemic offense seemed to be even worse when Drysdale took the mound. In nine of his losses, the team's hitters had scored one run or been shut out. The previous Sunday, attempting to win his 20th while tuning up for the Series, Drysdale had pitched five shutout innings. The offense had scored once and the bullpen had given up three runs to the Phillies, leaving Drysdale with a no-decision.

The managers made small accommodations to the lineups, reflecting that they were now facing right-handers. John Blanchard replaced the injured Roger Maris in right field for the Yankees. Ron Fairly took over right field from Frank Howard for the Dodgers. Normally, Fairly would have played first base, but Dodgers manager Walt Alston chose to stick with Moose Skowron as the streaky veteran seemed to be on one of his streaks.[4] The crowd of 55,912 came out in 74-degree weather and were treated to one of the great pitching duels of World Series history.

The offense can be summarized quickly. In the Dodgers' first inning, Jim Gilliam drew a one-out walk. He moved to second on a wild pitch by Bouton. After a line out by Willie Davis, National League batting champion Tommy Davis came to the plate and hit a hard shot up the middle. It eluded Bouton, received a mild deflection from the edge of the pitcher's mound and ricocheted off Bobby Richardson's shin into short right field. Gilliam scored.

Richardson said he lost sight of the ball after Bouton lunged at it. The deflection and the bank of white shirts in the stands behind home plate did not help. "I just plain old didn't see it," said Richardson. "Who would think a little play like that so early in the game would be so decisive."[5] Two of the three official scorers ruled it a hit.[6]

The end of offense served to ratchet up the tension in the ballpark. Bouton gave up only three more singles in six more innings, leaving the game well within the range of Yankee hitters. He blamed himself. "I walked too many," he said. None of the rest scored.[7]

Drysdale, meanwhile, battled a powerful Yankees lineup that was always one swing away from a tied game. "Drysdale pitched with a swaggering confidence that bordered on insolence," wrote *New York Times* columnist Arthur Daley.[8]

The Yankees tried to shake that confidence. In the sixth inning, with Crosetti complaining loudly about spitballs, home-plate umpire Larry Napp went to the mound. Tony Kubek was on third and Mickey Mantle at the plate. Napp ordered Drysdale to wipe his fingers after every visit to his mouth. Drysdale struck out Mantle.[9]

In the late innings, poor Dodger baserunning ruined a chance to give Drysdale a better cushion. Johnny Roseboro led off the seventh inning with a single and with the Yankees' Clete Boyer drawn in expecting a bunt, Dick Tracewski slapped the ball past him. Roseboro beat the throw to third and Tracewski took second. Drysdale bounced to Richardson and Roseboro faked going home. Richardson threw out Drysdale at first, but Tracewski had misread Roseboro's fake and joined him on third, where he was tagged out. The Dodgers had gone from runner on second and third with no outs to a runner on third with two outs. A Maury Wills groundout ended the seventh. In the eighth, Gilliam was gunned down by Elston Howard trying to steal third with one out.

Drysdale continued to dominate. After his brush in the sixth inning, he surrendered only one single. The tension grew another notch with two outs in the ninth. Joe Pepitone hit a high fly ball to deep right that brought hearts into throats. "I was scared," Drysdale admitted.[10] But then he saw Fairly would catch it just in front of the Yankees' bullpen gate.

"It was a normal Drysdale game in that his teammates got him that one run and left the rest of the job up to him," wrote *Los Angeles Times* sports editor Paul Zimmerman.[11] "Koufax and Podres were great, but I don't think I've ever seen Drysdale any better," echoed Alston.[12]

From a more neutral vantage point, *Sports Illustrated*'s William Leggett wrote: "In two hours and five minutes Don Drysdale pitched the best pitched game of this superbly pitched series. The Dodgers gave him one cheap, lucky, idiotic, precious run, and he defended it."[13]

For bettors, the Dodgers were now listed at 15-1 favorites.[14] But Houk kept his stiff upper lip.

"The last game is the toughest to win. Nothing is impossible," he said.[15]

When asked about starting Game Five, Johnny Podres joked, "I'll be happy if I don't have to pitch again. I'd like to make other plans for Monday."[16]

SOURCES

In addition to the sources mentioned in the Notes, the author consulted Baseball-Reference.com, Retrosheet.org, and the following books, video, and digitized box scores:

Spink, C.C. Johnson, compiler. *Official Baseball Guide for 1964* (St. Louis: Charles C. Spink & Son, 1964).

"Major League Baseball Presents the World Series of 1963" (retrieved August 17, 2020, at youtube.com/watch?v=HFjFvooJagA)

baseball-reference.com/boxes/LAN/LAN196310050.shtml

retrosheet.org/boxesetc/1963/B10050LAN1963.htm

NOTES

1 "It Looks Bad, so N.Y. Mayor Stays Home," *Los Angeles Times*, October 5, 1963: A3.

2 Frank Finch, "Grim Yankees Hold Meeting Before Drill," *Los Angeles Times*, October 5, 1963: A3.

3 Braven Dyer, "We've Come Back Before, Says Crosetti," *Los Angeles Times*, October 5, 1963: A3.

4 John Drebinger, "Maris Considered Unlikely to Play," *New York Times*, October 5, 1963: 41.

5 John Hall, "Richardson Has No Alibi for T. Davis 'Hit,'" *Los Angeles Times*, October 6, 1963: I2.

6 Frank Finch, "Big D Cuts Off Yank Power Again, 1-0," *Los Angeles Times*, October 6, 1963: I1.

7 Finch, "Big D Cuts Off Yank Power Again."

8 Arthur Daley, "On the Edge of the Cliff," *New York Times*, October 6, 1963: 198.

9 Dan Hafner, "Teammates Feel Drysdale Best Series Hurler of All," *Los Angeles Times*, October 6, 1963: I2.

10 Finch, "Big D Cuts Off Yank Power Again."

11 Paul Zimmerman, "Dodgers Push Yanks to Brink of World Series Humiliation," *Los Angeles Times*, October 6, 1963: G1.

12 Hafner.

13 William Leggett, "KooFoo the Killer," *Sports Illustrated*, October 14, 1963: 23.

14 "Dodgers Now 15-1 to Hit the Jackpot," *Los Angeles Times*, October 6, 1963: I5.

15 Hall.

16 Hafner.

KOUFAX STIFLES YANKEE BATS AGAIN AS DODGERS SWEEP WORLD SERIES

October 6, 1963: Los Angeles Dodgers 2, New York Yankees 1

By Andy McCue

As the New York Yankees arrived at Dodger Stadium for the fourth game of the 1963 World Series, they knew no team had ever come back from a three-game deficit to win. "The knowledge of defeat could not be disguised in the quiet but calm Yankee clubhouse," wrote the *New York Times*'s Leonard Koppett after the third game.[1]

Days before, as the Yankees' team bus left for the airport and Los Angeles, third baseman Clete Boyer joked that what the Yankees needed was more Jewish holidays. "You mean like Yom Koufax," said Mickey Mantle.[2] Now they would have to face Sandy Koufax, the Los Angeles Dodgers' Jewish left-hander who had set a strikeout record beating them in Game One. Before they left their hotel that morning, the Yankees packed their bags, at once a standard practice and a foreshadowing.[3]

A mild fall afternoon with temperatures in the high 70s greeted Koufax and the Yankees' Whitey Ford, meeting in a rematch. With the exception of Héctor López, subbing for the injured Roger Maris in right field for the Yankees, it was the same lineup as that game, a 5-2 Dodgers victory.

Hidden from the Yankees was an open sore between the last two toes of Koufax's left foot, the one he used to push off from the mound. A corn had torn off two days before and had not healed. Dodgers team physician Robert Kerlan had given the area a shot of novocaine and the trainer was primed to give him more if needed. It was not.[4]

As with all the games in this Series, there was a premium on runs. As the Dodgers came up in the bottom of the fifth, they had managed one single. The Yankees had a single and a double. Nobody had any runs. With one out, Frank Howard came to the plate and launched the first home run ever hit into the second deck down the left-field line, a blow estimated at 450 feet.[5]

Koufax set the Yankees down in the sixth and got Tom Tresh to pop out leading off the seventh. But Mickey Mantle, limited to a fluke bunt single so far in the series, launched a Koufax fastball over the 380-foot sign in left-center to tie the score. It was Mantle's 15th World Series home run, tying him with Babe Ruth for the most round-trippers in Series history. The Yankees had never led a game the entire Series and now had barely edged into a tie.

The tie lasted five batters. Koufax shut out the Yankees in the rest of the seventh inning. Jim Gilliam led off the Dodgers' seventh with a high bouncer to Boyer, who leapt high in the air to glove the ball, came down, and launched a belt-high throw across the diamond. The throw hit first baseman Joe Pepitone on inside of his right forearm and bounced down along the right-field stands. Gilliam wound up at third and scored on Willie Davis's sacrifice fly to give the Dodgers a 2-1 lead.

"It was a perfect throw. I didn't see it. It got lost in the shirts behind third base. It hit me on the side of the glove and wrist and went on by," said Pepitone of the game's crucial play.[6]

There was one final bit of drama in the Yankees' ninth. With two outs and Bobby Richardson on first, Elston Howard hit a groundball to Maury Wills, who threw to Dick Tracewski for the force out. Koufax leapt off the mound, hands high in the air, nearly reaching third base before realizing Tracewski had dropped the short hop and Richardson was safe. Koufax returned to the mound and got Héctor López to ground slowly to Wills. This time, Tracewski held on to the throw. This time Koufax kept leaping and was joined by his teammates.

"I don't feel anything – I'm numb," said Koufax afterward.[7] His teammates were focused on a larger picture. "They won't call us choke artists any more," said Gilliam, harking back to the Dodgers' epic collapse at the end of the 1962 season, which had haunted them through 1963.[8] "This makes up for last year," echoed Johnny Podres. Asked to compare this game with his victory over the Yankees in the seventh game of the 1955 World Series, Podres exclaimed: "Damn right it's better than '55. Why, you just can't beat those guys four straight."[9]

Los Angeles Times columnist Jim Murray gloated: "There's been a bunch of guys out here masquerading as the New York Yankees. It's the clumsiest impersonation I've ever seen."[10]

The Sporting News was awed. It was "pitching that bordered on the fantastic," wrote Fred Lieb, "[w]hile Ralph Houk's versatile New York Yankees entered the Series as odds-on favorites, the Dodger victory was hardly an upset. The sweep, though, came as a shocker."[11] The Dodgers weak offense had taught them how to manufacture runs against good pitching. It was a skill the Yankees had never had to learn.

Mickey Mantle joined in the praise. "I never saw pitching like that. In our league, we see good pitching for a game or two, but never for four straight games. These guys are the best I have ever seen."[12]

Those guys were also few in number. Alston used only 13 players in the four games – eight basic position players plus Ron Fairly, three starting pitchers and one inning of relief from Ron Perranoski. With the pinch-hitters and relief pitchers necessary for come-from-behind tactics, Houk used 20. The four games took a total of 8 hours and 17 minutes.

The 55,912 people in the stands that day pushed total series attendance to 247,279 and total gate receipts to $1,995,189.09, There was also $3.5 million from NBC and Gillette for television rights.[13] The players' share came to $1,017,546.43 with the Dodgers passing out full shares worth $12,794 and Yankees disbursing $7,874.32 per share.[14] Both were the largest ever. Because the Series went only four games, the commissioner's office, and the two leagues would not participate in the receipts. The teams would take home smaller amounts. Nevertheless, Dodgers owner Walter O'Malley would describe the sweep as his greatest thrill in baseball.[15]

Summed up Red Smith: "An hour and a quarter after the game, the eleganti still lapping it up in the stadium club overlooking right field saw a gaggle of young men in business suits emerge from the dugout and trudge toward an exit gate. Most of the Yankees, for it was indeed they, wore black. All walked ever so slowly as to – hell, write your own simile."[16]

Courtesy of Bob Webster

The Dodgers swept the New York Yankees in the 1963 World Series.

DODGER STADIUM

SOURCES

In addition to the sources mentioned in the Notes, the author consulted Baseball-Reference.com, Retrosheet.org and the following books, video, and digitized box scores:

"Major League Baseball Presents the World Series of 1963" (retrieved August 17, 2020, at youtube.com/watch?v=HFjFvooJagA)

baseball-reference.com/boxes/LAN/LAN196310060.shtml

retrosheet.org/boxesetc/1963/B10060LAN1963.htm

NOTES

1 Leonard Koppett, "It Isn't Dodgers Pitching, Says Houk, It's a Yankee Batting Letdown," *New York Times*, October 6, 1963: 198.

2 Jane Leavy, *The Lost Boy* (New York: HarperCollins, 2010): 262.

3 "Yanks Packed Their Bags Before Game, Just in Case," *New York Times*, October 7, 1963: 38.

4 "Sandy Won Decider with Ulcerated Toe," *Los Angeles Times*, October 8, 1963: B2. In *The Sporting News* of October 19, 1963, Bob Hunter reported that the drug used was morphine. The information is on page 2 in a story that begins on page 1 with the headline "Couldn't Be Done – But Dodgers Did It."

5 William Leggett, 'Koo-foo the Killer," *Sports Illustrated*, October 14, 1963: 24.

6 John Hall, "'It Was a Perfect Throw. … I Didn't See It' – Pepitone," *Los Angeles Times*, October 7, 1963: B4.

7 Bill Becker, "Manager Praises Koufax's Hurling," *New York Times*, October 7, 1963: 38.

8 Bob Hunter, "Couldn't Be Done – but Dodgers Did It," *The Sporting News*, October 19, 1963: 1. In 1962 the Dodgers had a four-game lead as late as September 17, then faded into a tie with the San Francisco Giants. The Giants won a three-game tiebreaker series to take the 1962 NL pennant.

9 Dan Hafner, "'We've Made Up for Last Year,'" *Los Angeles Times*, October 7, 1963: B2.

10 Jim Murray, "Bring on the Yanks!" *Los Angeles Times*, October 7, 1963: B1.

11 Frederick G. Lieb, "Review of Series," in *Official Baseball Guide for 1964* (St. Louis: Charles C. Spink & Son, 1964): 177.

12 Dick Young, "Yanks in for Razzing; They Won't Forget It," *Los Angeles Times*, October 7, 1963: B4.

13 Bob Burnes, "Unbelievable! That's Story of Dodger Sweep," *The Sporting News*, October 19, 1963: 5. The NBC and Gillette figures are in Clifford Kachline, "'Broadcasting' Says Sponsors Will Rush to Back Fetzer Plan," *The Sporting News*, October 19, 1963: 14.

14 "Splitting Swag," *The Sporting News*, October 26, 1963: 6.

15 Bob Oates, "O'Malley's Top 10 and 20," *Los Angeles Times*, March 2, 1977: E1.

16 Red Smith, quoted in *The Sporting News*, October 19, 1963: 22. Héctor López

"MILLION BUTTERFLIES" AND ONE PERFECT GAME FOR SANDY KOUFAX

September 9, 1965: Los Angeles Dodgers 1, Chicago Cubs 0

By Mike Huber

On September 9, 1965, Sandy Koufax became the "no-hittingest pitcher of all time,"[1] the first major-league pitcher to throw four no-hitters.[2] His record-setting accomplishment was a 1-0 perfect game against the Chicago Cubs. In front of a relatively small crowd of 29,139 fans at Dodger Stadium, Koufax, who came into the contest with a 21-7 record, locked in a pitchers' duel with a fellow lefty, Bob Hendley. Koufax had been unsuccessful in his previous five starts in winning his 22nd game.

Hendley had just been recalled from the minors. After four seasons with Milwaukee and San Francisco, he had been traded on May 29, 1965, from the Giants (with Harvey Kuenn and Ed Bailey) to the Cubs (in exchange for Dick Bertell and Len Gabrielson). Hendley also pitched a brilliant game, giving up only one hit, and the only run scored off him was unearned. Koufax went him one better.

Cubs center fielder Don Young, in his major-league debut, led off the game. Koufax's first pitch was "a curve ball that bounced in the dirt."[3] After that, his control was nearly perfect, as he retired Young with a popout to second baseman Jim Lefebvre. Koufax then struck out Glenn Beckert and Billy Williams looking. Hendley was equally sharp, getting the first three Los Angeles batters in order. Koufax was in top form, striking out at least one Chicago batter in every inning. Future Hall of Famer Ernie Banks struck out three times, all swinging. According to Dodgers radio announcer Vin Scully, the first Banks strikeout came in the second inning on a forkball. Every Cubs batter except shortstop Don Kessinger struck out at least once. On the other side, Hendley had only three strike-outs, Koufax and Lefebvre (twice).

Hendley was in no danger though the first four innings. The only run of the game came in the fifth. Lou Johnson led off with a walk and advanced to second on a sacrifice by Ron Fairly. Hendley might have had a play at second base when he fielded the bunt, but he dropped the ball and got the sure out at first. With Lefebvre batting, Johnson stole third base and then continued home as Cubs catcher Chris Krug made a throwing error. The run was unearned, and Hendley still had not allowed a hit.

The Cubs had a chance in the sixth inning, when Krug hit a groundball to shortstop Maury Wills. Wills' throw to first was in the dirt, but Wes Parker dug the ball out for the first out of the inning, preserving the string of consecutive outs. This was the only threat to Koufax's perfect game. Kessinger then hit a grounder to third and was just erased, as third baseman Jim Gilliam was playing in for a possible bunt. Koufax then struck out Hendley to end the inning.

Both pitchers had no-hitters intact until the seventh inning, when Koufax retired the side on a strikeout and two fly outs. That's when Koufax "really started to feel as though I had a shot at [the perfect game]."[4] In the home half, the Dodgers had several exciting at-bats. Lead-off batter Gilliam hit a grounder to third baseman Ron Santo, who fielded the high bouncer and just threw out Gilliam at first. Willie Davis followed with a slow grounder to first. Banks fielded the ball and then tagged out Davis, who tried sliding into the bag to avoid the tag. Johnson then hit a ball past first base that barely made it to the outfield grass before rolling into foul territory. By the time Banks retreated to field it, Johnson had motored to second base for a two-out double. However, he was stranded there as Fairly grounded out to short, and the Dodgers did not score, but Hendley's bid for a no-hitter was gone.

In the top of the eighth inning Koufax, facing the middle third of the Cubs' order, struck out Santo looking and Banks and Byron Browne swinging. The Dodgers tried to add a run in their half of the eighth, but Jeff Torborg's long fly to left was caught by Browne in front of the bullpen gate.

Before the ninth inning, Vin Scully told his producers, "Let's make a recording."[5] Fans can still hear Scully call the final three outs. The Cubs had sent up two pinch-hitters. After Krug struck out, Joey Amalfitano pinch-hit for Kessinger and struck out swinging. The broadcast climaxed when Scully exclaimed, "Swung on and missed, a perfect game!" as Harvey Kuenn, who batted for Hendley, struck out to end the game.[6] The game lasted one hour and 43 minutes. The final six Chicago batters (and seven of the final nine) went down on strikes.

The next day, *Los Angeles Times* writer Frank Finch started his story with, "A Michelangelo among pitchers, Sandy Koufax produced his masterpiece when he pitched a perfect no-hit, no-run game against the Chicago Cubs."[7] After the historic game, Koufax had told reporters, "I had a real good fastball, and that sort of helps your curve."[8] He added, "The last three innings I had the best stuff I threw all night, and perhaps all year."[9]

With his accomplishment, Koufax surpassed the record of three career no-hitters held by three different pitchers: Larry Corcoran, Cy Young, and Bob Feller.[10] This was just the eighth perfect game pitched in major-league history.[11]

As of the beginning of the 2023 season, this was the only perfect game thrown by a Dodgers pitcher.[12] Further, this marked the fourth consecutive season in which Koufax had pitched a no-hit game. His record of four career no-hitters stood for 16 years, until Houston Astros fireballer Nolan Ryan pitched his fifth no-hit game on September 26, 1981, against the Los Angeles Dodgers.[13]

Hendley faced only 26 batters in his eight-inning gem. On any other day, his performance would have grabbed the top headlines. Five days after Koufax's perfect game, on September 14, 1965, he and Hendley faced each other again, this time at Chicago's Wrigley Field. The Cubs prevailed, as Hendley beat Koufax 2-1.

The Cubs had only three groundball outs. Koufax's 14 strikeouts were the highest strikeout total in a perfect game (equaled by Matt Cain on June 13, 2012). Koufax finished the season with 382 strikeouts, which bested Rube Waddell's twentieth-century record of 349 set in 1904. But Ryan topped this mark eight years later, striking out 383 in 1973.

Koufax finished the 1965 campaign with a record of 26-8. His earned run average was 2.04, and he pitched 27 complete games out of 41 starts. He was the unanimous choice for the 1965 Cy Young Award and finished second in the NL's Most Valuable Player Award voting.[14]

AUTHOR'S NOTE

This game was reminiscent of another pitchers' duel, when Chicago's Hippo Vaughan and Cincinnati's Fred Toney pitched a double no-hitter through regulation on May 2, 1917. Vaughan held the Reds hitless for 9⅔ innings, before two hits produced a run. Meanwhile, Toney pitched 10 hitless innings for the win and part of history.

An abridged version of this article was published in SABR's book *No-Hitters* (2017), edited by Bill Nowlin. As Scully described Krug's ninth-inning at-bat against Koufax, the future Hall of Fame broadcaster uttered the timeless phrase, "There's 29 thousand people in the ballpark and a million butterflies."[15]

SOURCES

In addition to the sources mentioned in the Notes, the author consulted Baseball-Reference.com, MLB.com, Retrosheet.org, SABR.org and the following sources:

"The Cubs haven't been no-hit since Sandy Koufax pitched," https://ftw.usatoday.com/2013/08/the-cubs-havent-been-no-hit-since-sandy-koufax-pitched.

"Sandy Koufax pitches perfect game," http://history.com/this-day-in-history/sandy-koufax-pitches-perfect-game.

Click here to listen to Vin Scully call the final three outs of Sandy Koufax's perfect game on September 9, 1965.[16]

https://www.baseball-reference.com/boxes/LAN/LAN196509090.shtml

https://www.retrosheet.org/boxesetc/1965/B09090LAN1965.htm

NOTES

1   "Sandy Now No. 1 on No-Hit Parade," *Los Angeles Times*, September 10, 1965: 46.

2   Koufax's other no-hit games were pitched on June 30, 1962, May 11, 1963, and June 4, 1964.

3   "Koufax Eyed 'Perfection' All the Way," *Chicago Tribune*, September 10, 1965: 53.

4   Charles Maher, "Even Koufax Admits Game 'Nearly Perfect," *Los Angeles Times*, September 10, 1965: 45.

5   "Recorded History: Vin Scully Calls a Koufax Milestone," found online at https://www.npr.org/2007/04/23/9752592/recorded-history-vin-scully-calls-a-koufax-milestone. Accessed January 2023.

6   Harvey Kuenn, who struck out to end the perfect game, also made the last out in Koufax's 1963 no-hit game against the San Francisco Giants. In that game, Kuenn grounded out to the pitcher, Koufax.

7   Frank Finch, "Hendley Loses, 1-0, on 1-Hitter," *Los Angeles Times*, September 10, 1965: 45.

8   Maher.

9   "Koufax Eyed 'Perfection' All the Way."

10   The first to achieve this total was Chicago White Stockings hurler Larry Corcoran, whose no-nos took place on August 19, 1880, against the Boston Red Caps; September 20, 1882, against the Worcester Worcesters; and June 27, 1884, against the Providence Grays. Next was Cy Young, who pitched his first no-hitter as a member of the Cleveland Spiders on September 18, 1897,

against the Cincinnati Reds; followed by two as a pitcher for the Boston Americans and Red Sox on May 5, 1904, against the Philadelphia Athletics; and June 30, 1908, against the New York Highlanders. Cleveland Indians star Bob Feller was the third pitcher to tie the mark, on April 16, 1940, against the Chicago White Sox; April 30, 1946, against the New York Yankees; and July 1, 1951, against the Detroit Tigers.

11   For the complete list, see https://www.mlb.com/news/all-time-perfect-games. Accessed January 2023.

12   "Los Angeles Dodgers no-hitters," found online at http://nonohitters.com/los-angeles-dodgers-no-hitters/. Accessed April 2015.

13   "Baseball Sisco Kid Style: Sandy Koufax Becomes the First Pitcher to Throw 4 No-Hitters September 9, 1965," http://baseballsiscokidstyle.blogspot.com/2014/09/sandy-koufax-becomes-first-pitcher-to.html. Accessed April 2015.

14   In 1965, Koufax led the majors in victories (26), earned-run average (2.04), innings pitched (335⅔) and strikeouts (382). He received all 20 first-place votes for the Cy Young Award. Koufax finished second to San Francisco's Willie Mays in the MVP race, receiving six first-place votes (177 vote points) to Mays' nine first-place votes (224 vote points). Before 1967, only one pitcher was awarded the Cy Young Award. Koufax won his third Cy Young Award in 1966, the season before MLB began the practice of awarding a winner from each league.

15   Found online at https://ia800701.us.archive.org/16/items/VinScullyCallsThe9thInningOfSandyKoufaxsPerfectGame/VinScully-1965-KoufaxPerfectGame9thInning_64kb.mp3. Accessed April 2015 and January 2023.

16   To hear Vin Scully call just the final strike, click here (from mlb.com).

WELL, GOLLY: "GOMER" CLAUDE OSTEEN GETS DODGERS BACK INTO THE SERIES

October 9, 1965: Los Angeles Dodgers 4, Minnesota Twins 0
(Game Three of the 1965 World Series)

By Norm King

People of a certain age may remember a television show from the 1960s called *Gomer Pyle, USMC*, about a country hick who joins the Marines and drives his sergeant crazy. It's a good bet, though, that people didn't know that Gomer also pitched for the Los Angeles Dodgers.

"Gomer" was the nickname bestowed on Claude Osteen, the Dodgers' starter in Game Three of the 1965 World Series, because of his (rather unfortunate) resemblance to the television character. And while the television Gomer was a goof, the real live one was

Claude Osteen, nicknamed Gomer, won 20 games twice as a Dodger.

anything but. Osteen was a solid major-league pitcher, a three-time All-Star in an 18-year major-league career, who went 15-15 with a 2.79 ERA in 1965. His won-loss record is misleading, as the Dodgers scored only 28 runs in his 15 defeats.

The Dodgers' star pitchers, Sandy Koufax and Don Drysdale, overshadowed Osteen in the media. But on this day he didn't take a back seat to anyone, shutting down the powerful Minnesota Twins with a 4-0 complete-game victory, giving the Dodgers new life in the fall classic.

This was a typical Dodger win, with speed and pitching complementing their 10-hit attack. Shortstop Maury Wills, who led the world in stolen bases in 1965 with 94, stole his first sack of the Series, as did first baseman Wes Parker (who stole third), and even catcher John Roseboro. (Parker and Roseboro combined on a double steal in the fourth.) Five of the Dodgers' hits were doubles.

The Twins' starter, Camilo Pascual, was no slouch either. He had a 9-3 record during the season with a 3.35 ERA. During his career he was a five-time All-Star and led the American League three times each in complete games and shutouts.

The game got off to a bad start for the Twins in general and catcher Earl Battey in particular. Shortstop Zoilo Versalles led off the first inning with a ground-rule double to left. Center fielder Joe Nossek grounded to the right side, allowing Versalles to reach third with one out. After a groundout by right fielder Tony Oliva and a walk to third baseman Harmon Killebrew, Battey came to the plate. Twins third-base coach Billy Martin flashed the hit-and-run sign, but Battey missed it.

What followed was the pivotal play of the game and, perhaps, the Series. Killebrew was supposed to head for second and draw a throw from Roseboro, at which point Versalles would take off for home. Killebrew was supposed to run to second but stopped. Wills saw Versalles breaking for the plate and threw back to Roseboro, who threw to third baseman Jim Gilliam, who applied the tag; 6-2-5 for you who score.

"That was the big play," said Osteen. "If they score they have a big advantage. Getting a run early makes a team confident and more aggressive. They would have been tougher to pitch to."[1]

"Earl missed the sign," said Martin. "He usually protects the runner pretty good."[2]

The game remained scoreless until the fourth inning. Right fielder Ron Fairly led off the Dodgers' half with a double to left and moved to third on a sacrifice by left fielder Lou Johnson. Second baseman Jim Lefebrve got an infield hit, but Fairly had to stay at third. Pascual then did what he didn't want to do; he walked Parker to load the bases. Up came number-eight hitter John Roseboro and he didn't disappoint, driving in two runs with a single to right. The Dodgers had broken through and went into the fifth ahead 2-0. The only downside to the inning came when Lefebvre bruised his heel crossing the plate. Dick Tracewski replaced him for the rest of the Series.

The Dodgers added to their lead in the fifth. Fleet-footed center fielder Willie Davis singled to center and went to second on a Fairly groundout. Johnson came up again and smacked a double to left-center field, scoring Davis.

With the Twins down by three and the pitcher's spot due up first in the top of the sixth, Twins manager Sam Mele chose to pinch-hit for Pascual with Rich Rollins, who was the Twins' regular third baseman during the season but saw duty only as a pinch-hitter in the Series. Rollins grounded back to Osteen, but had he gotten on base, the Twins may have gotten back into the game, because Versalles and center fielder Joe Nossek followed with singles. However, with runners on first and third, Osteen induced right fielder Tony Oliva to hit into a double play to end the Twins' last serious threat of the game.

Jim Merritt replaced Pascual on the mound and Parker greeted him with a base hit to center. Roseboro flied to right, and then Dodgers manager Walter Alston ordered the next batter, Osteen, to attempt a sacrifice with one out. The move worked, as Osteen successfully bunted over Parker, who then scored on a double by Maury Wills. Merritt got a measure of revenge by picking Wills off second to end the inning.

Battey's horrid day continued in the bottom of the seventh. While chasing a foul pop off Jim Gilliam, he smashed into the fence next to the Twins' dugout, bruising his neck and jaw. Jerry Zimmerman replaced Battey behind the plate. The doctor who examined Battey after the game would not allow him to talk unnecessarily, which was fine with him after the bad day he had.

"Gomer," who got the nickname from Tracewski, piled up the zeroes the rest of the way and earned a 4-0 complete-game win. The victory was impressive because the power-laden Twins had been shut out only three times all season, but at the same time Osteen seemed to have their number, having compiled a 5-0 record against them when he pitched for the Washington Senators from 1961 to 1964.

"I just feel I know how to pitch to them," he said. "Except for Zoilo Versalles, all the hits they got off me were on bad pitches. "When I got the ball where I was supposed to, they didn't hit me."[3]

SOURCES

In addition to the sources cited in the Notes, the author consulted baseball-reference.com, dodgers.mlblogs.com, and the *Kingsport* (Tennessee) *Times-News*.

NOTES

1   Jack Mann, "Dodgers Down – and Up," *Sports Illustrated*, October 18, 1965.

2   Lew Ferguson, "Missed Hit-and-Run Sign Throttles Minnesota," *San Bernardino* (California) *Sun*, October 10, 1965.

3   Joe Reichler, "Gomer's Luck Finally Changes," *San Bernardino* (California) *Sun*, October 10, 1965.

BIG D SURPASSES THE BIG TRAIN FOR CONSECUTIVE SCORELESS INNINGS MARK

June 8, 1968: Los Angeles Dodgers 5, Philadelphia Phillies 3

by Richard Cuicchi

Los Angeles Dodgers pitcher Don Drysdale was known to inflict fear in batters. At 6-feet-5-inches tall, he was intimidating on the mound, unafraid to plunk a batter with one of his fastballs. He often used his baseball persona to his advantage, and it likely never came in handier than when he turned in one of the most dominating stretches by a pitcher – a consecutive scoreless innings streak that broke a long-standing record held by Hall of Famer Walter Johnson.

Drysdale was one of the last holdovers from the Dodgers team that moved from Brooklyn to the West

Hall of Famer Don Drysdale won 209 games and hit 154 batters. He won the Cy Young Award in 1962

Coast in 1958. He was in the majors in 1956 as a 19-year-old. He quickly became an innings-eater, a strikeout king, and an equally capable complement to another Dodgers fireballer, Sandy Koufax.

Drysdale developed a reputation as a brushback pitcher, in the style of notoriously intimidating pitchers like Sal Maglie and Early Wynn, who were in their prime in the 1950s.[1] Drysdale, whose nickname was "Big D," not only relied on an occasional brushback to move batters off the plate; he hit more batters (154) than any other major-league pitcher between 1956 and 1969. He was also suspected of using foreign substances to give himself an added advantage over batters.[2]

By 1968 Drysdale had been a Cy Young Award winner (1962), appeared in eight All-Star Games, and was a key contributor to three World Series championship teams (1959, 1963, and 1965). Still only 31 years old in his 13th season, he was no stranger to hurling shutouts. From 1956 to 1969 he led all major-league pitchers with 49 whitewashes. In the process of breaking Johnson's 56-inning scoreless streak, set in 1913, he threw six straight shutouts, also a record. His streak became the crowning achievement in his Hall of Fame career.

Drysdale's streak began on May 14 against the Chicago Cubs. Over the next 20 days, he threw five more shutouts, defeating Houston (twice), St. Louis, San Francisco, and Pittsburgh. Among the pitchers who opposed him were future Hall of Famers Ferguson Jenkins, Bob Gibson, and Jim Bunning. In all but one of the six games, he threw on three days' rest.

In his autobiography *Once a Bum, Always a Dodger*, Drysdale recalled that he was the beneficiary of umpire Harry Wendlestedt's favorable call in the game against the Giants. With the bases loaded in the ninth inning, Drysdale grazed Dick Dietz's left elbow.

That should have scored a run and ended his streak. But Wendlestedt ruled that Dietz made no effort to get out of the way of the pitch, thus negating the hit-by-pitch call. Drysdale ended up retiring Dietz and the next two Giants batters to preserve his streak.[3]

Along his historic journey, Drysdale passed several other pitchers with significant stretches of scoreless innings. One of them occurred earlier in the 1968 season when Cleveland Indians pitcher Luis Tiant recorded 41 shutout innings. Others Drysdale passed included Cy Young (45 innings in 1904), Doc White (45 in 1904), Sal Maglie (45 in 1950), Carl Hubbell (45⅓ in 1933), and Jack Coombs (53 in 1910).

The Phillies were in Los Angeles on Saturday, June 8, to play the Dodgers. A Ladies Night sellout crowd of 50,060 showed up at Dodger Stadium to witness Drysdale's pursuit of Johnson's record.[4] Drysdale's streak was at 54 innings, two behind Johnson.

Dodgers players wore black armbands on their left sleeves in memory of Senator Robert Kennedy, assassinated two days before at the Ambassador Hotel in Los Angeles while campaigning for the presidential nomination.[5]

Veteran right-hander Larry Jackson drew the starting assignment for Phillies manager Gene Mauch. The Phillies were in fourth place, 3½ games out of first place.

With his nerves perhaps getting the best of him, Drysdale had a shaky start in the first inning, throwing seven balls in his first eight pitches. But he regained his composure to keep his streak intact.[6]

In the second inning, Drysdale retired Bill White, Tony Taylor, and Clay Dalrymple, tying Johnson's 55-year-old record.

In the top of the third, leadoff batter Roberto Peña hit a slow, high bouncer to third baseman Ken Boyer, who cleanly fielded the ball and carefully threw to first baseman Wes Parker for the out. With the record then broken, the jam-packed crowd let loose loud ovations for Drysdale's accomplishment. Drysdale stood on the mound with his back to home plate and tried to soak in the moment. Later, when questioned about what he was thinking at the time, he said, "Thank God, it's over with."[7]

After the side was retired, plate umpire Augie Donatelli intercepted Drysdale on his way to the dugout. At the request of Mauch, the umpire asked Drysdale to remove his cap so he could check him for the use of foreign substances. He ran his fingers through Drysdale's hair and confirmed Mauch's suspicion. He ordered Drysdale to stop using the greasy

substance. Then before the start of the fourth inning, Donatelli confronted him again on the mound and told him not to touch the back of his head or under the bill of his cap, or he would face automatic ejection. The *Los Angeles Times* surmised that Mauch was well aware of Drysdale's pursuit of the innings record and waited until after he passed the milestone before registering his complaint with Donatelli.[8]

The Dodgers had taken a 1-0 lead in the first inning, when Boyer singled to score Willie Davis. In the bottom of the fourth Tom Haller doubled and Boyer singled. The combination of a fielder's choice, a Phillies error, and a sacrifice fly added three more Dodger runs.

The Phillies started the fifth inning with singles by Taylor and Dalrymple. Peña struck out, but not before Drysdale caused him to hit the dirt. Howie Bedell, who played his first game with the Phillies two days earlier after not having appeared in the majors since 1962, pinch-hit for Jackson.[9] Bedell stroked a fly ball to left field that scored Taylor from third, ending Drysdale's streak at 58⅔ innings.

Drysdale gave up a solo home run to White in the sixth inning. After an RBI single by Cookie Rojas in the seventh made the score 4-3 and left runners on second and third, Dodgers manager Walter Alston pulled Drysdale. Reliever Hank Aguirre rescued the Dodgers by retiring the next two batters. The final run of the game came on Parker's solo home run off Turk Farrell in the seventh inning. The final score was 5-3.

Drysdale was credited with his eighth win of the season. The Dodgers' win was their ninth in their past 10 games. They were in second place, 2½ games behind the first-place St. Louis Cardinals. Jackson gave up four runs in four innings and took the loss to run his record to 6-6.

After retiring to the clubhouse, Drysdale admitted that it had been a harrowing experience throughout the stretch. He said breaking the streak "was bound to happen sooner or later." He acknowledged he and his family had been disturbed by the death of Robert Kennedy, a family friend. He added, "This was just one of those nights, the kind when you just run out of steam."[10]

Johnson pitched for the Washington Senators from 1907 to 1927. There were similarities between the former and new record-holders. Both had made their major-league debuts at age 19. Both had reputations for being menacing pitchers, mainly relying on their intimidating fastball. Johnson was a side-arm pitcher, while Drysdale frequently mixed in side-arm deliveries in his repertoire. At the time of Drysdale's retirement, Johnson was the all-time leader in strike-outs (3,509). Drysdale was eighth on the list (2,486).

Partially overlapping Drysdale's streak was another one involving the St. Louis Cardinals' Bob Gibson. From June 2 to June 26, Gibson pitched 47 consecutive scoreless innings, in the midst of a 15-game winning streak. Gibson won both the Cy Young Award and Most Valuable Player Award that season.

Drysdale finished the season with a 14-12 record, as the Dodgers ended up in seventh place. Suffering from shoulder problems that had bothered him in earlier seasons, he retired late in the 1969 season at the age of 33 after making only 12 appearances. He was elected to the National Baseball Hall of Fame in 1984.

Dodgers pitcher Orel Hershiser broke Drysdale's mark in 1988. He pitched 59 consecutive scoreless innings, composed of the last four innings of a game on August 30, five shutouts, and 10 shutout innings on September 28.

SOURCES

Lewis, Allen. "Dodgers Beat Phils; Drysdale Breaks Mark," *Philadelphia Inquirer*, June 9, 1968: Section 3, 1.

Daley, Arthur (New York Times Service). "Big Train: Fastest Moundsman of All," *Long Beach* (California) *Press-Telegram*, June 9, 1968: S-1.

Schlossberg, Dan. "Flashback: Orel Hershiser's 1988 Season," *Baseball Digest*, June 2003 (Vol. 62, No. 6): 48-51.

NOTES

1   Joe Goddard, "Are Brushback Pitchers a Dying Breed?" *Baseball Digest*, September 1978: 43.

2   Emil Roth. "When Drysdale's Shutout Streak Ended," *Baseball Digest*, December 1973: 63.

3   Don Drysdale and Bob Verdi. *Once a Bum, Always a Dodger* (New York: St. Martin's Press, 1990), 142.

4   The June 9, 1968, edition of the *Los Angeles Times* reported the total attendance as 55,017, with 50,060 as paid.

5   Dwight Chapin, "Boyer Carefully Handles Slow Hopper for Record," *Los Angeles Times*, June 9, 1968: Section D, 1.

6   Dan Hafner, "Drysdale Sets Record (58⅔), Then Gets KO'd," *Los Angeles Times*, June 9, 1968: Section D, 1.

7   Chapin, Section D, 6.

8   Chapin, Section D, 1.

9   Hafner.

10 Chapin, Section D, 1.

STARGELL HOMERS OUT OF DODGER STADIUM

August 5, 1969: Pittsburgh Pirates 11, Los Angeles Dodgers 3

by Dave Lande

"On a muggy, overcast night in Chavez Ravine," the Pittsburgh Pirates defeated the Los Angeles Dodgers 11-3, a game highlighted by Willie Stargell's home run in the seventh inning that was the first ever hit out of Dodger Stadium. "It appeared to be Apollo 12," one observer noted as the baseball landed in the parking lot behind the right-field pavilion.[1]

The Pirates scored the first run of the game in the top of the second inning off Dodgers starting pitcher Don Drysdale. Roberto Clemente was safe on an error by shortstop Maury Wills and went to second base on a passed ball by the Dodgers catcher, Tom Haller. After Al Oliver was hit by a pitch and Manny Sanguillen was safe on a bunt to load the bases, Gene Alley drove in Clemente from third base on a single to left field. With the bases still loaded, Bill Mazeroski struck out and the next batter, Steve Blass, flied out to Andy Kosco in left field. Oliver tagged up from third base and appeared to have scored the second run of the inning. However, he was ruled out on a successful appeal by the Dodgers who claimed he left third base early.[2]

Pittsburgh jumped ahead 2-0 in the top of the third inning. Matty Alou singled to center field, took second and third on successive infield outs, and scored when Clemente singled to left field.

Sanguillen gave the Pirates a 3-0 lead in the top of the sixth inning when he hit a home run into the left-field seats, his third homer of the season.[3]

After being held to two singles though five innings by Pirates starting pitcher Blass, the Dodgers tied the game in the bottom of the sixth inning. The second batter of the inning, Wills, singled to center field and Willie Davis followed with a single to left. Len Gabrielson reached when he hit into a force play at second. Wills and Gabrielson scored when Kosco hit a 400-foot home run over the center-field wall, his 15th homer of the season. Blass commented after the game, "It was a very hittable pitch. I would have been surprised if he hadn't hit it out."[4]

The top of the seventh inning was the scene for Stargell's memorable home run. Alan Foster had relieved Drysdale, who left the game for a pinch-hitter in the bottom of the sixth inning. With one out, Foster threw a curveball that Stargell hammered over the right-field pavilion, his 18th home run of the season that "brought the crowd up gasping. …" Stargell wasn't visibly impressed after the game. He said, "… I had no idea it was going to go that far. I wasn't trying to hit one. Every time I try, I can't do it."[5]

One writer estimated the distance of the home run to be between 480 and 500 feet[6] and another wrote that it traveled as much as 525 feet.[7] The ball easily cleared the 50-foot-high ceiling of the pavilion, which has a back fence that is 450 feet from home plate.[8] Another writer declared that the ball was still rising as it cleared the pavilion.[9] Quipped a visiting writer, "Willie Stargell's muscles have now joined Jack Benny's violin, Bob Hope's nose and Raquel Welch's anatomy as all-time great conversation stimulators here in the neon capital of the Western world."[10]

The Pirates waited until the ninth inning to blow the game open. They exploded for seven runs, all charged to former Pirates pitcher Pete Mikkelsen, who had relieved Foster to start the inning. Blass opened with a single and moved to third base on a single by Alou. Blass and Alou both scored when Richie Hebner's groundball bounced off first baseman Tom Hutton's glove for an error.[11]

After Stargell struck out, Clemente singled to left field and Hebner scored when Kosco bobbled the ball and overthrew home plate. Clemente reached third base and scored when the next batter, Oliver, doubled to the right-field corner. Oliver came home on Sanguillen's single to center field. Gene Alley grounded out, then Sanguillen scored on Mazeroski's homer down the left-field line.[12] As one visiting writer wrote, "The Pirates did win, 11-3, but their big stretch drive was as anticlimactic as stitches after open heart surgery."[13]

Blass held the Dodgers scoreless in the bottom of the ninth to finish his complete-game win, his 11th victory of the season in 18 decisions. "I've been struggling to find my slider all year," said Blass after the game. "I still have some rough edges, but I'm slowly getting back into the groove."[14] It was his second complete-game win of the week over the Dodgers.[15]

Stargell, surrounded by reporters after the game, said, "They don't pay you any more for distance. If I hit one that barely goes out and we win, that's the real thrill. They don't mean anything if you don't win." Asked if this was his best home run, Stargell said "No, the best home run I ever hit was the one over the roof at Forbes Field this year off (Mets pitcher Tom) Seaver."[16]

"If Stargell during recent years had been playing anywhere but Forbes Field," said Pirates manager Larry Shepard, "he might have challenged the home run records of Babe Ruth and Roger Maris." Hitting well at Dodger Stadium was not uncommon to Stargell, who slugged three homers there in a game in 1965.[17]

Among Clemente's two hits in the game was the 2,500th of his 15-year career.[18] "I can't remember my first major league hit," Clemente said. "I can't even remember hits I had a few weeks ago. But I'm happy to be hitting again and helping the team."[19]

This was the first game in two months in which all of the Pirates regulars played. Stargell had missed some playing time with a swollen thumb[20] and Mazeroski, for the first time in a month, was a regular in the lineup. "I'm just up from York," kidded the delighted second baseman, who was struggling through an injury-marred campaign. "That one sure felt good. I'm like a kid with a new toy." This game was the first since June 10 in which the Pirates' starting lineup was intact.[21]

Drysdale acknowledged that he was pitching with pain in his shoulder. He said, "The pain is still there, but it's something I'm going to have to learn to pitch with."[22]

"Funny," said Walter Alston, the Dodgers manager, "but Foster had great stuff tonight. I thought he was throwing the ball better than he had in some time."[23] He blamed the two Dodgers errors in the ninth for erasing any chance LA had of catching the Pirates in the game.[24]

The teams combined for 14 runs, 22 hits, and three errors in a game that lasted 2 hours 11 minutes. Attendance at Dodger Stadium on this Tuesday evening was 22,604.

SOURCES

In addition to the sources cited in the Notes, the author consulted Baseball-Reference.com and Retrosheet.org.

https://www.baseball-reference.com/boxes/LAN/LAN196908050.shtml

https://www.retrosheet.org/boxesetc/1969/B08050LAN1969.htm

NOTES

1   Ross Newhan, "Apollo 12? Stargell's Blast Flattens Dodgers," *Los Angeles Times*, August 6, 1969: 39, 42.

2   Charlie Feeney, "'Coasted' Pirates Use Homers to Top Dodgers," *Pittsburgh Post-Gazette*, August 6, 1969: 18.

3   Feeney.

4   Phil Musick, "Stargell Leads Pirates Bombing," *Pittsburgh Press*, August 6, 1969: 68-69.

5   Musick.

6   Newhan.

7   Feeney.

8   Newhan.

9   Musick.

10   Musick.

11   Feeney. On July 30, Blass had beaten the Dodgers, 4-2, at Forbes Field.

12   Feeney.

13   Musick.

14   Musick.

15   Newhan.

16   Musick.

17   United Press International, "Can LA Forget Stargell's Shot?" *Pomona (California) Progress Bulletin*, August 6, 1969: 41.

18   Feeney.

19   United Press International.

20   Feeney.

21   Musick.

22   Newhan.

23   Newhan.

24   United Press International.

WILLIE DAVIS BREAKS 53-YEAR-OLD FRANCHISE HITTING RECORD

September 2, 1969: New York Mets 5, Los Angeles Dodgers 4

by Warren Campbell

Throughout the month of August 1969, the Los Angeles Dodgers were battling for the National League West Division crown. All season the NL West had been a close race between five teams, everybody except the expansion San Diego Padres. Nobody had been hotter for the Dodgers in August than veteran center fielder Willie Davis.

William Henry Davis was born in Arkansas but went to high school just three miles away from Dodger Stadium. He was a high-school track star but loved baseball and was signed by Dodgers scout Kenny Myers upon graduating from Theodore Roosevelt High School.[1] Within two years he became the starting center fielder, replacing Duke Snider, in 1960.

The first year of the new National League West Division was a wild one, with five of the six teams within 3½ games of first place on August 1. The Dodgers entered the month in second place, two games behind Atlanta. Coming into August play, Willie Davis was hitting .260, and had just struggled through an 0-for-6 game vs. Pittsburgh on July 31. The next game he borrowed teammate Ken Boyer's larger 40-ounce bat, hoping to get more wood on the ball. His usual bat was 30 ounces and he had to choke up about four inches on Boyer's bat. As well, he stood back farther from the plate and told reporters, "I've cut down on my swing."[2]

A month later, Davis had hit in 30 straight games, tying the Dodgers' 53-year-old franchise record for the longest hitting streak, set by Zack Wheat of the 1916 Brooklyn Dodgers. He batted .459 for the month and was the NL Player of the Month. If he got a hit in the September 2 game against the Mets, he would own the record.

It was a pleasant 76 degrees for the afternoon game against the Mets who were losing ground to the East

Division-leading Chicago Cubs. Even Dodgers owner Walter O'Malley was getting caught up in the excitement. "When Koufax pitched his no-hitters, we gave him $500. When Drysdale pitched the 56 consecutive scoreless innings, we gave his wife a string of 56 pearls. We will have something very appropriate for Willie should he break the National League record," O'Malley said, adding, "This season is going to be his financial turning point."[3]

Mets first baseman Donn Clendenon started the scoring early with a first-inning blast into the right-field seats off Dodgers starter Don Sutton (15-12). The

Dodgers center fielder Willie Davis won three Gold Gloves and hit in a franchise-record 31 straight games in 1969.

previous night the Dodgers had exploded for five runs in the first inning and made sure starter Jerry Koosman didn't get past the fifth batter. Mets starter Gary Gentry (9-11) was a much different proposition.

Through the first five innings the Dodgers hitters were unable to put much offense together. Gentry scattered three hits and walked one. In the first inning Davis grounded out to shortstop and in the fourth inning he struck out.

In the Mets' fourth, Clendenon hit his second home run of the game (his 11th of the year) and was providing all the offense in the game until the sixth inning, when the bats started to show for both teams. Mets third baseman Wayne Garrett led off the top of the inning with a single to center field. Clendenon grounded out and Garrett took second. Sutton intentionally walked Art Shamsky. Second baseman Ken Boswell followed with a single to right field. With the bases loaded, Mets right fielder Ron Swoboda doubled to right-center. Garrett and Shamsky scored easily, but Boswell was thrown out at the plate by center fielder Tommy Agee, and Jerry Grote flied out. It was 4-0, Mets after 5½ innings.

The top of the Dodgers' batting order was now coming up, and the LA fans were hoping to see some offense. But Maury Wills grounded out and Manny Mota flied out. That brought up Davis making his third attempt to break Zack Wheat's record. Davis wasted no time breaking the Dodgers record and tying Stan Musial for the longest National League hitting streak in the last 30 years. He hit Gentry's first pitch to left-center field for a double. The Dodger Stadium crowd roared, and the scoreboard showed this note:

"BEFORE TONIGHT'S GAME WILLIE DAVIS GOT A WIRE WHICH READ 'CONGRATULATIONS – KEEP GOING YOU HAVE DONE A REAL JOB'

IT WAS FROM SUNRISE BEACH-MO AND WAS SIGNED 'ZACK WHEAT.'"[4]

Wheat, 81 years old at the time, told Dodgers vice president Red Patterson that he was rooting for Davis to break his record. Wheat reminded Patterson that during his streak he was robbed of a hit by the first-base umpire in game 30 and then went on to get hits in the next 11 games. "I should have reached 41 games," he said.[5]

The next batter was first baseman Wes Parker, whose single to center scored Davis with the Dodgers' first run. Left fielder Willie Crawford followed with a single, but catcher Bill Sudakis grounded out to Boswell, ending the inning.

The Mets went down in order in the seventh. The bottom half started with promise for the Dodgers with a single up the middle by catcher Tom Haller. The next three hitters – second baseman Ted Sizemore, pinch-hitter Len Gabrielson, and Wills – were not able to make anything happen.

In the top of the eighth Clendenon got his third hit, a single to left off reliever Joe Moeller with one out. He stole second base and scored two batters later on Boswell's single to center field, giving Mets starter Gentry a 5-1 cushion.

In the Dodgers' eighth, Gentry continued to dominate, making quick work of Mota, Davis, and Parker.

Moeller returned to the Dodgers mound for the ninth and kept the score unchanged after a groundout by catcher Jerry Grote, a walk to shortstop Bud Harrelson, a foul third-strike bunt by Gentry, and a groundout to third by center fielder Tommie Agee.

Willie Crawford opened the Dodgers' ninth with a walk. Bill Sudakis popped out, but Tom Haller singled to right field. Von Joshua, making his major-league debut, ran for Haller. Mets manager Gil Hodges pulled Gentry and brought in righty reliever Ron Taylor, who was having a very productive season in the Mets bullpen. Taylor got Sizemore to ground out but then gave up singles to pinch-hitter Jim Lefebvre (pinch-runner Bobby Valentine, also making his major-league debut, ran for him), Maury Wills, and Andy Kosco. This sudden awakening of Dodgers bats brought in three runs and made the score 5-4, bringing up Willie Davis to face Mets closer Tug McGraw.

Davis was not able to solve McGraw, who earned his 10th save of the season by getting Davis to foul off two pitches and then swing and miss on a low curveball. "The pitch was low," said Davis. "He threw me a breaking ball inside. Last time he did that I hit it. I don't know how I missed. I just wish we could have won the game."[6]

After the game Davis was asked about challenging Joe DiMaggio's 56-game streak. His reply: "You don't fool with Joe D."[7]

The streak continued for one more game when Davis doubled in the winning run off Mets reliever Jack DiLauro in the bottom of the ninth the next day. It ended the day after when San Diego pitchers Dick Kelley and Gary Ross held the Dodgers to four hits and none for Davis. "It was great while it lasted," Davis said. "All I can do now is start again tomorrow and hit in every game for the rest of the season."[8]

Davis's 31-game hitting streak had been the longest in the majors since Dom DiMaggio of the Boston

Red Sox hit in 34 consecutive games 20 years before. Davis's streak as of 2024 was still the longest in the 140-year history of the Dodgers franchise.

SOURCES

In addition to the sources cited in the Notes, the author consulted Baseball-Reference.com and Retrosheet.org.

https://www.baseball-reference.com/boxes/LAN/LAN196909020.shtml

https://www.retrosheet.org/boxesetc/1969/B09020LAN1969.htm

NOTES

1   Stephen Booth, "Willie Davis: Disappointment or Misunderstood?" Fangraphs.com, May 26, 2011. https://tht.fangraphs.com/willie-davis-disappointment-or-misunderstood/.

2   Mike Bryson (Associated Press), "Wondrous Willie Davis Extends Hitting Streak," *Durham* (North Carolina) *Sun*, September 1, 1969: 18.

3   Ross Newhan, "Davis Ties Mark as Dodgers Win," *Los Angeles Times*, September 2, 1969: 39.

4   AP Wirephoto caption, "Message From the Past," *Stockton* (California) *Record*, September 3, 1969: 41. The text reads as it was presented on the message board.

5   "Dodger Notes," *Los Angeles Times*, September 3, 1969: 46.

6   Associated Press, "Davis Sets Hitting Mark, but Fans in Crucial Spot," *Tucson Daily Citizen*, September 3, 1969: 31.

7   William F. McNeil, *The Dodgers Encyclopedia* (New York: Sports Publishing, 2012), 380.

8   Ross Newhan, "Padres Shut Out Davis, Dodgers," *Los Angeles Times*, September 5, 1969: III-1, 4.

DON SUTTON THROWS 11-INNING, 1-0 SHUTOUT AGAINST THE GIANTS

September 22, 1972: Los Angeles Dodgers 1, San Francisco Giants 0

by Joseph Wancho

The 1972 major-league season was winding down. Unfortunately for the San Francisco Giants and Los Angeles Dodgers, the year did not go as they might have planned. In 1971 the Giants (90-72) won the National League West Division by one game over the second-place Dodgers (89-73).

Now in 1972 the Dodgers (77-67) were in third place, 12 games behind first-place Cincinnati. San Francisco was 63-82, nestled in fifth place in the division, 26½ games off the pace. So when both teams got together for a three-game series beginning September 22 at Dodger Stadium, it may have been a

Dodgers right-hander Don Sutton holds numerous team records, including career wins (233) and shutouts (52).

mild surprise that 20,622 patrons pushed their way through the turnstiles.

Both teams had made trades to strengthen their starting rotations. Los Angeles sent third baseman-outfielder-first baseman Dick Allen to the Chicago White Sox for pitcher Tommy John and infielder Steve Huntz. Not only was Allen versatile in the field, but he was the offensive leader of the Dodgers in 1971. He batted .295 and led the team in home runs (23), RBIs (90), and walks (93). Although the loss of Allen was sure to leave a void in the Dodgers' lineup, Tommy John would prove to be a reliable pitcher for years to come.

The Giants also gambled, sending pitcher Gaylord Perry and shortstop Frank Duffy to Cleveland for Sam McDowell. While Sudden Sam was one of the great pitchers in the American League during the 1960s, his career had then taken a downturn, and the trend continued while he hurled for San Francisco.

The Dodgers were a team in transition. Steve Garvey, Bill Russell, Ron Cey, and Steve Yeager were ready to take over as everyday players, while Maury Wills, Jim Lefebvre, and Wes Parker were playing their last seasons in the big leagues. One new player making his major-league debut on this day was Dodgers second baseman Davey Lopes. The newest keystone man batted .317 at Triple-A Albuquerque to earn his first shot at big-league pitching. Together with Garvey, Cey, and Russell, the quartet formed one of the greatest infields in major-league history for the next nine seasons.

The Giants were not without young talent themselves. Center fielder Garry Maddox, shortstop Chris Speier, and third baseman-first baseman-outfielder Dave Kingman provided some excitement for the San Francisco fans. Outfielder Gary Matthews, who had made his big-league debut earlier that month, would be a fixture in left field at Candlestick Park for several years.

The pitching matchup for game one of the series was San Francisco's Jim Willoughby (6-2, 2.15 ERA) vs LA's Don Sutton (16-9, 2.22 ERA), who entered the game with 99 career wins. Willoughby, a rookie, was attempting to end the Giants' five-game losing streak. Sutton began the year with eight straight victories and had established himself as one of the best hurlers in the NL.

San Francisco threatened to score in the top of the first inning. Speier reached first base on a fielding error by shortstop Russell. Sutton then walked Willie McCovey and Kingman, but Dave Rader grounded out to end the inning.

Lopes led off the bottom of the first inning and in his first official at-bat grounded out to short. Bill Buckner followed with a walk and Willie Davis singled to right field. Willoughby uncorked a wild pitch and the runners moved up a base. But the Giants' starting pitcher gave in no further, striking out Tom Paciorek and getting Cey to fly out to right field.

With one down in the top of the second, Maddox reached on an error by Dodgers' third baseman Cey and stole second. On a single to left field by Bobby Bonds, Maddox tried to score. But a perfect relay throw from Paciorek to Cey to Yeager cut him down to keep the game scoreless.

After the Giants got their first two players on base to start the third inning, Sutton got McCovey to ground out, struck out Kingman, and retired Rader on a liner to right field. Sutton, known for having one of the game's best curveballs, set the Giants down in order over the next five innings.

Los Angeles was not having much better luck against Willoughby. The Giants starter retired the Dodgers in the third, fourth, and fifth innings before giving up a one-out single to Buckner in the top of the sixth.

The game progressed through nine innings with the score knotted at 0-0. Both Willoughby and Sutton remained on the mound. Both teams went down in order in the 10th inning. The Giants continued that trend in the top of the 11th frame.

With two down in the home half of the 11th, Paciorek beat out a high hopper to shortstop for an infield single. He took third base on Cey's single to right. Willoughby, after throwing two wide ones to LA pinch-hitter Manny Mota, put him on intentionally to load the bases. Dodgers manager Walter Alston called for Wes Parker to bat for Russell. On an 0-and-2 count, Willoughby plunked Parker in the back. The hit-by-pitch forced Paciorek home with the winning run. The Dodgers won 1-0.

It was the first time Parker had been hit all season. "I think that pitch was the hardest ball Willoughby threw all night," said Dodgers coach Danny Ozark.[1]

"He ducked into it," said Willoughby.[2]

The victory raised Sutton's season record to 17-9. He struck out 11, walked four, and gave up three hits. It was his eighth shutout of the year and the 100th victory of his career. "I just made up my mind to go out and challenge the Giants," said Sutton. "They've been batting me around pretty good lately. I just tried to have good control and hit the spots. Against the Giants, I figured 'What do I have to lose.'"[3]

Willoughby struck out seven, walked three, and surrendered seven hits, all singles. His record now stood at 6-3.

The Dodgers swept the three-game series. LA (85-70) and Houston (84-69) finished in a virtual tie for second place in the NL West, 10½ games, behind Cincinnati. San Francisco (69-86) was a distant fifth, 26½ games behind.[4]

The game had historical significance. For the first time in National League history, an African American was the home-plate umpire. Art Williams called balls and strikes. "I can't remember him missing a pitch," said Willoughby.[5] "He was great," said Rader, the Giants backstop.[6]

SOURCES

In addition to the sources cited in the Notes, the author consulted Baseball-Reference.com and Retrosheet.org.

https://www.baseball-reference.com/boxes/LAN/LAN197209220.shtml

https://www.retrosheet.org/boxesetc/1972/B09220LAN1972.htm

NOTES

1   "First for Parker Makes 100 for Sutton," *The Sporting News*, October 7, 1972: 26.

2   Bucky Walter, "Giants Bow in 11th, 1-0," *San Francisco Examiner*, September 23, 1972: 29.

3   "First for Parker Makes 100 for Sutton."

4   The start of the 1972 season was delayed by a player strike that lasted from April 1 to April 13. After the strike ended, the major leagues decided not to reschedule the games that were missed, and some teams' game totals differed.

5   Walter, "Giants Bow in 11th, 1-0."

6   "Giants Bow in 11th, 1-0."

NEW YORKERS LISTEN TO BASEBALL WITH THEIR BREAKFAST

May 24, 1973: New York Mets 7, Los Angeles Dodgers 3 (19 innings)

by Alan Cohen

"The law of averages had to catch up with you."
– Rusty Staub, May 25, 1973, after driving in the decisive run in a very long game.[1]

Marathon games dot the histories of the New York Mets and the Los Angeles Dodgers. The Brooklyn Dodgers played 26 innings against the Boston Braves on May 1, 1920. The game was called due to darkness with the score tied 1-1. The Mets, on May 31, 1964, fell to the San Francisco Giants, 8-6, in 23 innings, and in the second game of a doubleheader no less.

On May 24, 1973, the Mets and Dodgers went well past most newspaper deadlines. Joe Durso of the *New York Times* filed his story after 11 innings. Ross Newhan of the *Los Angeles Times* filed his in the middle of the 14th inning, at which time the score was tied, and the teams had collectively stranded 26 runners.[2] Numbers were piling up, both for success and futility. There were wasted opportunities galore,

TOMMY JOHN

LOS ANGELES Dodgers ®

Tommy John won 87 games for the Dodgers and underwent the career-saving surgery that bears his name.

SABR / The Rucker Archive.

and by time the game ended, the teams had stranded 40 runners (Mets 18, Dodgers 22).

Manny Mota, though, was 0-for-9 in the game, his batting average tumbling from .352 to .320, yet Dodgers manager Walt Alston said that his left fielder was "the only guy to hit the ball hard in critical conditions, but right at somebody."[3]

The Mets won with four runs in the 19th inning.

The Mets' starting pitcher was Tom Seaver (5-3), who had defeated the Dodgers 13 times since coming into the NL in 1967, losing only four times. Seaver came up short, by his standards. He left the game for pinch-hitter Jim Fregosi, the ex-Los Angeles Angel, in the seventh inning with the Mets trailing 3-2 and two runners in scoring position.

Many of the Los Angeles spectators left the game around the time that Dodger starter Tommy John (3-2) departed in the seventh inning. They did not really need to worry about traffic on this night. By the time the game ended, it was 1:35 A.M., and there were probably more fans listening on radios in New York as they were having breakfast at 4:35 A.M. (the game was not televised) than watching from the stands in Los Angeles.

The Dodgers got to Seaver for two tainted runs in the second inning. Willie Davis singled, advanced to second on Joe Ferguson's grounder, and scored when Mets first baseman Jim Beauchamp was unable to handle a grounder by Willie Crawford. Crawford advanced to third on a hit by Ron Cey and scored on Bill Russell's fly ball.

The Mets got a run back in their half of the third. Seaver singled and advanced to third on Wayne Garrett's single. Seaver scored when Félix Millan hit into a double play. The double play was one of four pulled off by the Dodgers in the game. The Mets turned five, including two after the ninth inning.

In the bottom of the third, Bill Buckner singled, took second on a groundout by Mota, and scored on Davis's second hit in as many innings.

The Mets made it 3-2 in the seventh. With one out, Tommy John surrendered a double to Bud Harrelson that scored George Theodore. Theodore had singled and advanced to second on a single by Jerry May. It was May's first game appearance with the Mets. The former Pirate had been acquired from Kansas City 10 days earlier. After Harrelson's double, Pete Richert came on in relief. Richert temporarily stopped the bleeding.

Phil Hennigan, who had been with Cleveland for four seasons, came on to pitch the seventh inning for the Mets, retiring the side in order.

Neither Richert nor Hennigan survived the eighth inning. In the top of the inning, the Mets tied things up at 3-3. Cleon Jones doubled and came home on singles by Staub and Theodore. Richert was replaced by George Culver, who pitched a double-play ball to Duffy Dyer. Dyer had replaced May behind the plate in the seventh inning after May was pulled for pinch-runner Ted Martinez.

Hennigan's second inning was problematic. He allowed a single to Willie Davis, who finished the game with a modern National League record-tying six hits. Davis then stole second base and advanced to third when Dyer's throw went into center field. After Ferguson walked, Mets manager Yogi Berra made a pitching change.

Tug McGraw came into the game with two runners on and pitched in and out of trouble for five innings. He stranded three runners in the eighth and left the bases jammed in the 10th inning after loading them with none out. With the bases full and two out, Alston sent up the well-traveled former Met Chris Cannizzaro to pinch-hit for pitcher Jim Brewer. With the Mets in 1964, he had caught all 23 innings of the Mets-Giants marathon. He grounded out, and the game continued. McGraw, after retiring the side in order in the 11th inning, stranded two runners in the 12th.

After the game, Alston allowed, "You have to give the Mets credit for getting out of that many jams."[4]

The Dodgers were changing pitchers at a rapid rate. Culver left for pinch-hitter Ken McMullen in the bottom of the eighth. Brewer worked the ninth and 10th innings without incident before leaving for Cannizzaro. Charlie Hough brought his knuckler to the mound in the 11th.

George Stone came on to pitch for the Mets in the 13th and held the Dodgers scoreless until the Mets rallied in the top of the 19th. He matched zeros with Hough through the 15th inning.

In the 14th inning, the Mets looked to push across a run. With one out, Ed Kranepool, who had played all 23 innings of the 1964 marathon, singled to the opposite field. Garrett hit a ball to right field that was misplayed by Crawford. It rolled to the wall, and Crawford chased it down. Kranepool, who had gone halfway on the play (assuming the ball would be caught), sprinted around the bases as fast as his slow legs would take him. Third-base coach Eddie Yost waved Kranepool home, but the relay from Crawford to Davey Lopes to catcher Ferguson arrived at home well before Kranepool.

Hough, after five innings of work, was removed for pinch-hitter Steve Garvey. Doug Rau came on to pitch for the Dodgers in the 16th inning. In his first three innings of relief, Rau struck out four batters.

The Mets reached Rau in his fourth inning of relief. Jones singled and was driven home by Staub's double down the left-field line. Staub said, "I was just trying to poke the ball somewhere; keep it in play."[5] Staub took third on Mota's throw home. Ken Boswell, pinch-hitting for Stone, singled to score Staub and moved to second on a bunt by Theodore. Dyer walked, and Kranepool, who had replaced Beauchamp at first base in the eighth inning, put the icing on the cake with a two-run double, scoring Boswell and Dyer.

Jim McAndrew pitched the bottom of the 19th to close out the Mets' win, and was credited with a save. He was the 21st Met to appear in the game. After retiring the first two batters, he yielded a single to pinch-hitter Von Joshua (the 18th Dodger in the game), but retired Lopes on a grounder to send the remaining fans home. Stone was credited with his first win of 1973. His six shutout innings lowered his ERA to 0.69.

"I wore out two gloves," Mets shortstop Harrelson said afterward. He had gone through his fielding glove and the golf glove he wore at the plate.[6]

"Just woke up. Reading you fine" – Telegram to Mets radio broadcasters from fan in Connecticut as the clock passed 4:00 A.M. in New York.[7]

The game was the longest in the history of Dodger Stadium in terms of both time (5:42) and innings played (19).

The record for time stood until Game Three of the 2018 World Series, when the Dodgers and Red Sox completed 18 innings in 7 hours and 20 minutes. The record for the longest regular-season game, in terms

DODGER STADIUM

of time, stood until March 29, 2019, when the Dodgers and Diamondbacks played for 6 hours and 5 minutes.

The Mets had limped into town with several wounded players. Jones went 3-for-9 in the game while nursing a wounded wrist and was replaced by Jim Gosger after scoring the lead run in the 19th. Millan played the entire game with a bad ankle. John Milner had a pulled hamstring. He appeared as a pinch-hitter, walked, and was promptly removed for pinch-runner Jon Matlack, who was scheduled to pitch the next game. The catching situation was a mess. Jerry Grote was out with an injury, Neither Dyer nor May was hitting the batboy's weight.

The Dodgers dropped to 24-19, while the Mets improved to 20-17, and fans in New York got to hear broadcaster Bob Murphy's happy, if somewhat sleepy, recap.

SOURCES

In addition to the sources shown in the Notes, the author used Retrosheet.org Baseball-Reference.com, and the following:

Associated Press. "Mets Outlast L.A. in a.m. Marathon," *Journal News* (Rockland County, New York), May 25, 1973: 1D.

Durso, Joseph. "Mets-Dodgers Tied at 3-3, After 11 Innings on Coast," *New York Times*, May 25, 1973: 29.

United Press International. "Mets Defeat Dodgers in 19 Innings over Period of 5 Hours, 42 Minutes," *Buffalo Evening News*, May 25, 1973: 46.

https://www.baseball-reference.com/boxes/LAN/LAN197305240.shtml

https://www.retrosheet.org/boxesetc/1973/B05240LAN1973.htm

NOTES

1   Associated Press, "Mets Supply Fans with Breakfast Juice," *Evening Press* (Binghamton, New York), May 25, 1973: 6-B.

2   Ross Newhan, "Dodgers and Mets Tied in 14th, 3-3; 25 Left Stranded," *Los Angeles Times*, May 25, 1973: C1, C9. Although the headline says 25, the actual number in the middle of the 14th inning was 26. The Dodgers stranded two runners in their half of the inning.

3   Gordon Verrell, "Mets Win 5-Hour 42-Minute Struggle," *Long Beach* (California) *Press Telegram,* May 25, 1973: C1.

4   Verrell.

5   Joe Donnelly, "Mets, 7, Dodgers 3," *Newsday* (Long Island, New York), May 25, 1973: 144.

6   Donnelly.

7   Verrell.

GARVEY, WYNN, SUTTON PACE DODGERS' ROUT OF PIRATES IN NLCS CLINCHER

October 9, 1974: Los Angeles Dodgers 12, Pittsburgh Pirates 1
(Game Four of the 1974 National League Division Series)

by John Fredland

The Los Angeles Dodgers, returning to the postseason after an eight-year absence, beat the Pittsburgh Pirates twice on the road to open the 1974 National League Championship Series. When the action moved to California, the Pirates rallied with a shutout win, but the relentless Dodgers shrugged it off, riding Pittsburgh's record-setting wildness, Jim Wynn and Steve Garvey's power hitting, and Don Sutton's second dominant start of the NLCS to a pennant-clinching 12-1 Game Four win on October 9 at Dodger Stadium.

After four straight second-place finishes in the NL West Division, manager Walter Alston's 21st Dodgers team held off the Cincinnati Reds in 1974 for their first-ever division title and first postseason berth since the 1966 World Series.[1] Los Angeles had transformed its roster during the early 1970s with younger players taken in the amateur draft (such as first baseman Garvey, second baseman Davey Lopes, third baseman Ron Cey, and shortstop Bill Russell)[2] and veterans acquired in astute trades (such as starting pitcher Andy Messersmith, relief ace Mike Marshall, and center fielder Wynn).[3] Sutton, who had blossomed into one of the NL's top starters in his late 20s, linked the revamped Dodgers with their pennant-winning predecessors of 1966, his rookie year.[4]

The 102-win Dodgers faced the 88-win Pirates in the best-of-five NLCS. Pittsburgh had struggled for a season and a half after star right fielder Roberto Clemente's death in a plane crash on New Year's Eve 1972.[5] But the '74 Pirates won 30 of 45 games from July 14 through September 10 to surge from fourth place to first in the NL East,[6] then conjured up just enough experience, firepower, and luck to outlast the

St. Louis Cardinals for their fourth division title in five seasons.[7]

Pittsburgh had won eight of 12 regular-season games against the Dodgers,[8] but Los Angeles went ahead in the NLCS with two wins at Three Rivers Stadium. Sutton, a 19-game winner in 1974, outdueled lefty Jerry Reuss with a four-hit shutout in the October 5 opener, limiting Pittsburgh to just one runner in

Steve Garvey played on 10 All-Star teams for the Dodgers and Padres and holds the National League record for playing in 1,207 consecutive games.

scoring position.[9] Messersmith's strong start and three eighth-inning runs against the Pirates' bullpen were decisive in Game Two.[10]

For the first half of the season, the Dodgers had a third frontline starter, left-hander Tommy John. John's 13-3 record and 2.59 ERA included a shutout of Pittsburgh on June 4.[11] But John had not pitched since tearing a ligament in his elbow in July,[12] leading to reconstructive surgery on September 25.[13]

Without John, Alston opted for Doug Rau over Al Downing in Game Three at Dodger Stadium.[14] The Pirates battered Rau for five first-inning runs, highlighted by Willie Stargell's three-run homer, and rolled to a 7-0 win.[15]

Game Four was a rematch between the 29-year-old Sutton, whose only defeat in his previous 15 decisions had come against Pittsburgh on August 16,[16] and the 25-year-old Reuss, the Pirates' leader in wins and starts.[17]

Under brilliant midday sunshine on Dodgers owner Walter O'Malley's 71st birthday, the Pirates went down in order in the first. Joe Ferguson hauled in Al Oliver's drive at the wall in right for the third out, and Oliver pounded his fists in disappointment.[18]

Reuss's control troubles began right away. Lopes, whose bases-loaded walk produced the only run against Reuss in Game One, took three straight balls, then drew a five-pitch leadoff walk. Two more balls preceded Bill Buckner's popup to shortstop Mario Mendoza.[19]

Wynn was the third straight Dodger to get ahead 2-and-0. On the second ball, Lopes – second in the majors with 59 steals, trailing only the Cardinals' record-setting Lou Brock[20] – slid into second ahead of catcher Manny Sanguillén's throw.[21]

Three pitches later, the 32-year-old Wynn, the Dodgers' most productive player after coming from the Houston Astros in an offseason trade,[22] ripped former Houston teammate Reuss's offering 390 feet off the fence in left-center. The double scored Lopes for a 1-0 Los Angeles lead.

Three more Dodgers – Garvey, Ferguson, and Cey – batted in the first; Reuss fell behind each with two balls. Garvey's groundout pushed Wynn to third and Ferguson walked on four pitches. But Stargell's running, reaching, sun-splashed catch of Cey's extra-base bid near the 360-foot sign in left ended the inning and kept it a one-run game.

Sutton dismissed mild threats in the second and third. Dave Parker reached on an infield single with one out in the second,[23] but Sanguillén hit into a double play. The third inning began with six straight balls, as Ed Kirkpatrick walked and Sutton fell behind Mendoza 2-and-0. But Mendoza flied out and, after Reuss sacrificed Kirkpatrick to second, Sutton denied Rennie Stennett an RBI single by grabbing the Pittsburgh second baseman's bouncer and throwing to first for the third out.

Reuss pitched a one-two-three second inning. He started the third with two groundouts before his control vanished again. Wynn walked on four pitches and Garvey, headed for NL Most Valuable Player honors at age 25, took three more balls. After a strike, Garvey connected on a line drive to right-center – "I don't think I've ever hit a ball harder to right center," he said afterward.[24] The ball, which initially looked as though it would hit the wall,[25] cleared it for a two-run homer. Wynn jumped for joy while rounding the bases.[26] The Dodgers led, 3-0.

Before the inning was over, Reuss had issued his fourth walk of the game,[27] and manager Danny Murtaugh called on lefty Ken Brett in relief. Brett, a NL All-Star who had missed five weeks in August and September because of an elbow injury,[28] retired Cey for the third out.

Sutton, known throughout his career for a fast-dropping knuckle curveball,[29] made it nine outs in a row with clean innings in the fourth and fifth. Murtaugh asked home-plate umpire John McSherry to check Sutton's glove for pine tar before the Pirates batted in the fifth, but McSherry found nothing illegal.[30]

"The truth is that some of Sutton's pitches *were* funny looking," the *Los Angeles Times* observed. "Stargell and Al Oliver both struck out on pitches that broke so sharply they hit into the ground."[31]

Parker threw out Lopes trying to stretch a single to right into a double to end the fourth, but the Dodgers' attack of patience and power hitting returned in the fifth. Wynn walked with one out and Garvey pulled Brett's inside slider into the seats in left between the foul pole and the Dodgers bullpen.[32] Garvey's second homer of the game gave Los Angeles a 5-0 lead.

The Dodgers turned it into a rout with three more multi-run innings against Pittsburgh's bullpen. With Larry Demery on the mound in the sixth, Lopes tripled in Steve Yeager and continued home when Stennett's relay throw to third went into the dugout.

After Stargell's second home run in two days put the Pirates on the board in the seventh, the Dodgers answered with two runs against Demery and Dave Giusti. Russell's line-drive single to left scored Garvey, and Sutton – who received standing ovations when he batted in both the sixth and seventh innings – drove in Russell on a bloop to right, the ball dropping beyond Stennett's grasp for a single.

Three eighth-inning runs off Giusti made the Dodgers the first team with 12 in a League Championship Series game.[33] Ferguson singled home Wynn, and Russell singled in Garvey and Ferguson. For the afternoon, Garvey had four hits, four runs, and four RBIs.

Alston let Sutton walk to the plate in the eighth before replacing him with pinch-hitter Manny Mota.[34] The crowd of 54,424 gave Sutton another ovation.

"I'm not an emotional guy, but I got chills when [the ovation] happened," Sutton said.[35]

Marshall went in for the ninth.[36] On his way to the NL Cy Young Award and a third-place finish in the league's MVP voting, the 31-year-old right-hander had appeared in a major-league record 106 games in 1974. He set down the side, fanning Richie Hebner on a screwball for the final out.

Los Angeles had a date with the two-time defending champion Oakland A's in baseball's first-ever all-California World Series.[37] An LCS-record 11 walks[38] – six of which led to runs – provided a steady supply of Dodgers baserunners, and Wynn and Garvey's early-game slugging forged a formidable lead. Sutton's 82-pitch masterpiece, closing out his NLCS ledger at 17 innings of 7-hit, 1-run, 13-strikeout pitching, ensured that the Pirates would get no closer.[39]

The highest postgame praise was for Sutton, who went on to record the Dodgers' only win in the World Series.[40]

"Don Sutton won two of three Dodger victories over the Pirates," Al Abrams noted in the *Pittsburgh Post-Gazette*. "He had to be the hero of the series."[41]

"I can't remember two better pitched games in a row by one of our guys," Alston said.[42]

ACKNOWLEDGMENTS

The author thanks SABR members Gary Belleville and Kurt Blumenau for their comments on an earlier draft of the article.

SOURCES

In addition to the sources cited in the Notes, the author consulted Baseball-Reference.com and Retrosheet.org for pertinent information, including the box score and play-by-play. The author also reviewed game coverage in the *Los Angeles Times*, *Pittsburgh Post-Gazette*, and *Pittsburgh Press* newspapers, and a recording of the KDKA-AM (Pittsburgh) radio broadcast posted on YouTube by the Classic Baseball On The Radio account.

https://www.baseball-reference.com/boxes/LAN/LAN197410090.shtml

https://www.retrosheet.org/boxesetc/1974/B10090LAN1974.htm

https://www.youtube.com/watch?v=9NW0nxC_PZ8

NOTES

1   In 1973 the Dodgers led the Reds by 8½ games on July 17 but fell out of first by losing 11 of 12 games from August 31 through September 12. Los Angeles finished second to Cincinnati by four games. The 1974 Dodgers had a 10½-game lead on July 10, only to see the Reds close the gap to 1½ games on September 14. Los Angeles' 7-1 win over Cincinnati on September 15, with Sutton pitching a complete game and Garvey and Wynn hitting home runs, proved the turning point, as the Dodgers went on to clinch the division on the next-to-last day of the season. Ron Rapoport, "The Dodgers' Swoon: From 8½ Games in Front, Los Angeles Has Fallen 3 Games Back Due to Prolonged Batting Slump, Injuries, Inexperience of Youth," *Los Angeles Times*, September 10, 1973: III, 1; Jeff Prugh, "A Toy Cannonade: Wynn Slams Reds, 7-1; Lead Now 2½," *Los Angeles Times*, September 16, 1974: III, 1; Jeff Prugh, "Dodgers Finally Run It Up Flagpole," *Los Angeles Times*, October 2, 1974: III, 1; Ross Newhan and Jeff Prugh, "How the Dodgers Won the West: Change in Alston's Psychology Helped Motivate the Club," *Los Angeles Times*, October 3, 1974: III, 1.

2   Of the Dodgers' top 11 players in Wins Above Replacement in 1974, as determined by Baseball-Reference.com, seven were amateur draft selections from 1966 through 1968: Cey (June 1968), Garvey (June 1968), Lopes (January 1968), catcher-right fielder Joe Ferguson (June 1968), left fielder Bill Buckner (June 1968), Russell (June 1966), and catcher Steve Yeager (June 1967).

3   The Dodgers obtained Messersmith in a seven-player deal with the California Angels in November 1972. During baseball's winter meetings in December 1973, Los Angeles acquired Marshall from the Montreal Expos for outfielder Willie Davis, and Wynn from the Houston Astros for pitcher Claude Osteen. Ron Rapoport, "Dodgers Trade Robinson to Angels: Messersmith, Valentine, Singer Also Switch Teams in 7-Player Deal," *Los Angeles Times*, November 29, 1972: III, 1; Ross Newhan, "Davis and Dodgers Get the Trade They Wanted: Captain's Split With Alston Said to Be Factor in Marshall Deal," *Los Angeles Times*, December 6, 1973: III, 1; Ross Newhan, "Wynn No Longer Has Roof Over His Head … He's Happy: Dodgers Give Up Osteen and Free the Toy Cannon from Astrodome," *Los Angeles Times*, December 7, 1973: III, 1.

4   The Dodgers relocated from Brooklyn to Los Angeles in 1958 and won the World Series in 1959, 1963, and 1965. They won another NL pennant in 1966 but were swept by the Baltimore Orioles in the World Series.

5   The Pirates, who had won three NL East Division titles and the 1971 World Series from 1970 through 1972, finished third in the division in 1973 with an 80-82 record. In 1974 Pittsburgh was in last place in its six-team division as late as June 12, and the Pirates were 12 games under .500 at 37-49 after losing the first game of a July 14 doubleheader with the Reds. Bob Smizik, "The Autopsy: Bucs Weren't a Very Good Team," *Pittsburgh Press*, October 3, 1973: 71; Bob Smizik, "Here Are the Answers to All Those Pirate Questions," *Pittsburgh Press*, June 30, 1974: D-4.

6   Jeff Samuels, "Pirates Sweep Into First, 4-1, 10-2," *Pittsburgh Press*, August 26, 1974: 24.

7   In the season's final three weeks, Pittsburgh had a six-game losing streak and fell out of first place twice. The Pirates finally broke a tie with the Cardinals, beating the Chicago Cubs with late-inning rallies in the final two games of the season. Bob Smizik, "Plunge of '74: Can Pirates Climb Back?" *Pittsburgh Press*, September 17, 1974: 27; Jeff Samuels, "Cards Fight Off Death, Stagger Pirates, 13-12," *Pittsburgh Press*, September 26, 1974: 32; Bob Smizik, "Robertson's Shot Wounds Cardinals: Pirates Near Title, 6-5," *Pittsburgh Press*, October 2, 1974: 65; Bob Smizik, "Pirates Blunder Into Division Title," *Pittsburgh Press*, October 3, 1974: 35.

8   Jeff Samuels, "Pirates Figure They Have Dodgers' Number," *Pittsburgh Press*, October 4, 1974: 38.

9   Bill Shirley, "Sutton Gives the Pirates Nothing for Openers, 3-0: Dodgers Go 1 Up in NL Playoffs Behind Right-Hander's 4-Hitter," *Los Angeles*

Times, October 6, 1974: III, 1; Bob Smizik, "Sutton Muzzles Pirates, 3-0," *Pittsburgh Press*, October 6, 1974: D-1.

10   Bill Shirley, "Dodgers (2-0) Have the Last Cey in Pittsburgh, 5-2: L.A. Comes Home, Needs One More," *Los Angeles Times*, October 7, 1974: III, 1; Bob Smizik, "Dodgers Leave Pirates for Dead: Buc Hitters, Giusti Fail in 5-2 Defeat," *Pittsburgh Press*, October 7, 1974: 24.

11   In two starts against the Pirates in 1974, John allowed one run in 16 innings for an 0.56 ERA. Bob Smizik, "Pirates No Match for the Kids of Summer," *Pittsburgh Press*, June 5, 1974: 34; Ross Newhan, "Wynn Is Ailing ... So Are Dodgers: L.A., Sagging, Loses Again; Center Fielder May Need Surgery," *Los Angeles Times*, June 19, 1974: III, 1.

12   Jeff Prugh, "John Hurt as Dodgers Lose to Expos, 5-4; Lead Now 5½," *Los Angeles Times*, July 18, 1974: III, 1.

13   Ross Newhan, "Tommy John: Portrait in Blue," *Los Angeles Times*, October 3, 1974: III, 1. After a second operation in December 1974, John spent the 1975 season rehabilitating. He returned to the mound for the Dodgers in April 1976 and pitched in the major leagues until the 1989 season, retiring at age 46. Dr. Frank Jobe's pioneering procedure, which involved harvesting a tendon from John's right wrist and using it to replace the ruptured ulnar collateral ligament in John's left elbow, became commonly known as Tommy John surgery.

14   Bill Shirley, "Stargell and the REAL Pirates Get off the Deck, 7-0," *Los Angeles Times*, October 9, 1974: III, 1.

15   "Pittsburgh scored five runs so fast it looked as if they got them off Tommy John, the disabled Dodger left-hander, who had the honor of throwing out the first pitch right-handed," the *Los Angeles Times* remarked. Shirley, "Stargell and the REAL Pirates Get off the Deck, 7-0."

16   Jeff Prugh, "Dodgers Keep the Pressure on ... Themselves," *Los Angeles Times*, August 17, 1974: III, 1.

17   Pittsburgh had obtained Reuss from the Astros in an October 1973 trade for catcher Milt May.

18   Al Abrams, "Sidelights on Sports: Contrasting Heroes, Sutton and Garvey," *Pittsburgh Post-Gazette*, October 10, 1974: 15.

19   Frank Taveras, in his first full major-league season after September call-ups in 1971 and 1972, was Pittsburgh's regular shortstop going into the NLCS. He was sidelined after Messersmith hit him on the thumb with a pitch in Game Two, and Mendoza, who made his big-league debut by appearing in 91 games with the Pirates in 1974, started at shortstop for the rest of the series. Charley Feeney, "Pirates Holding Out for One Small Miracle," *Pittsburgh Post-Gazette*, October 8, 1974: 14.

20   Brock stole 118 bases in 1974, setting a major-league record that Rickey Henderson broke with 130 steals in 1982.

21   Lopes had two steals against Reuss at Dodger Stadium in June. Ross Newhan, "John Stops Pirates on 5 Hits, 5-0, First NL 9-Game Winner," *Los Angeles Times*, June 5, 1974: III,1.

22   Wynn led the Dodgers in runs scored (104), home runs (32), on-base percentage (.387), and slugging percentage (.497). Baseball-Reference credited him with 7.7 Wins Above Replacement, the most of any Dodger.

23   Parker, in his second major-league season, started in right field instead of Richie Zisk, who led the Pirates with 100 RBIs but went 0-for-4 with three strikeouts against Sutton in Game One.

24   Bob Smizik, "Sutton Death: Dodgers Don NL Title Garb," *Pittsburgh Press*, October 10. 1974: 32.

25   "Garvey's vicious smash did not look as if it was going out, but if it hadn't cleared the wall it would have gone through it," reported the *Los Angeles Times*. Bill Shirley, "Garvey Hits 2 Home Runs; Sutton Superb as L.A. Routs Pirates, 12-1," *Los Angeles Times*, October 10, 1974: III, 1; Charley Feeney, "Sutton Death for Bucs; L.A., 12-1," *Pittsburgh Post-Gazette*, October 10, 1974: 15.

26   Abrams, "Sidelights on Sports."

27   Pittsburgh traded Reuss to the Dodgers in April 1979. In nine seasons with Los Angeles, Reuss had an 86-69 record, pitching a no-hitter against the San Francisco Giants in 1980 and finishing as runner-up to Steve Carlton of the Philadelphia Phillies in the 1980 NL Cy Young Award voting. When the Dodgers won the World Series in 1981, Reuss had two postseason victories, including a shutout in the decisive Game Five of the National League Division Series against the Astros and a one-run complete game in Game Five of the World Series against the New York Yankees. He also appeared in postseason games for the Dodgers in 1983 and 1985.

28   Bob Smizik, "Brett's Elbow OK as Bucs Handle Cubs, 12-4," *Pittsburgh Press*, September 11, 1974: 59.

29   Jim Murray, "Two Young for Curves," *Los Angeles Times*, April 25, 1967: III, 1.

30   John Hall, "Pirates Go Home Without a Bang ... or a Whimper," *Los Angeles Times*, October 10, 1974: III, 1.

31   Shirley, "Garvey Hits 2 Home Runs." Sutton was frequently accused of "doctoring" balls during his 23-season Hall of Fame career; in 1978 he was ejected from a Dodgers-Cardinals game for what umpire Doug Harvey labeled "pitching a defaced baseball." Neal Russo, "Cardinals 'Scuff Up' Outraged Sutton, Dodgers," *St. Louis Post-Dispatch*, July 15, 1978: 5A.

32   Fred Antman, "Sports Hotline," *Palm Springs* (California) *Desert Sun*, October 10, 1974: B3.

33   The Dodgers held the LCS record until the Yankees scored 13 runs against the Oakland A's in Game Two of the 1981 American League Championship Series; the 1984 Chicago Cubs were the first team to score 13 runs in an NLCS game. As of 2023, the record for runs in an LCS game was 19, set by the New York Yankees in the 2004 ALCS. The Dodgers have the NLCS record with 15 runs against the Atlanta Braves in 2020.

34   Juan Pizarro, in the final appearance of an 18-season major-league career, relieved Giusti and got Mota to hit into a double play to close out the eighth.

35   Smizik, "Sutton Death."

36   Bill Christine, "Except for Cey, Dodgers React Calmly to Clincher," *Pittsburgh Post-Gazette*, October 10, 1974: 15.

37   Oakland defeated the Dodgers in the World Series, four games to one.

38   As of 2023, Los Angeles' 11 walks drawn remained an LCS record. On the same day as this game, the A's drew 11 walks against the Orioles, and the Cleveland Indians issued the Yankees 11 walks in Game Five of the 1998 ALCS. The postseason record for walks in a game is 12, first allowed by the Astros in the 14-inning Game Three of the 2005 World Series against the Chicago White Sox and equaled by the Yankees in Game Two of the 2020 American League wild-card series against the Indians.

39   The author determined Sutton's pitch count by reviewing a recording of the game's radio broadcast.

40   The NL did not implement a LCS MVP Award until the 1977 season.

41   Abrams, "Sidelights on Sports."

42   Smizik, "Sutton Death."

FERGUSON'S FANTASTIC THROW A FOOTNOTE AS OAKLAND WINS 1974 WORLD SERIES OPENER

October 12, 1974: Oakland Athletics 3, Los Angeles Dodgers 2
(Game One of the 1974 World Series)

by Mark S. Sternman

The first-ever all-California World Series pitted two contrasting teams. The two-time defending American League (and World Series) champion Oakland A's featured a new manager and experienced teammates. The National League champion Los Angeles Dodgers, back in the Series for the first time since 1966, had a skipper in his 21st season with a team and a starting lineup with only one player in his 30s. Oakland took the first game thanks to one big blast, one small bunt, and three clutch but unusual pitching outings despite one memorable throw by a Dodger outfielder.

LA ace Andy Messersmith set down the A's in order in the top of the first. Facing Ken Holtzman, the first pitcher to start three consecutive World Series since the Yankees' Whitey Ford opened four (1961-1964), the Dodgers got the game's first baserunner via a one-out single by Bill Buckner. With two outs, Holtzman picked Buckner off.

Reggie Jackson led off for Oakland in the top of the second. Jackson hit the first of nine homers he would hit against the Dodgers in four different World Series to put Oakland up 1-0. Joe Rudi singled before Messersmith retired the side.

Los Angeles had a promising start to the bottom of the second with Steve Garvey's single and a walk to Joe Ferguson. The rally fizzled when Ron Cey hit into a 6-4-3 double play and Bill Russell grounded out.

With the advent of the designated hitter in 1973, Holtzman had only one regular-season plate appearance (a walk) in the two regular seasons since

– although he doubled twice in the 1973 World Series. Leading off the third, Holtzman walked. After Bert Campaneris sacrificed, Messersmith struck out the next two batters.

In the bottom of the third, the first two hitters for the Dodgers reached again. Steve Yeager singled and Messersmith, who had a career-high .240 batting average in 1974, one-upped Holtzman by doing the same.

Right fielder Joe Ferguson's first career assist came on a key throw to home plate in the 1974 World Series.

135

But Holtzman retired the top three hitters in the LA order to maintain Oakland's 1-0 lead.

Messersmith worked around a leadoff walk to Jackson in the top of the fourth, and Holtzman once again pitched into and out of trouble by getting Yeager on a force out after two-out singles by Cey and Russell.

In the top of the fifth, the A's started a rally thanks to a double down the third-base line by World Series doubles-machine Holtzman (three two-baggers plus a homer in seven Series), who reached with one out. Messersmith wild-pitched Holtzman to third. Then, shockingly, "Campy dumped a two-two pitch to … Messersmith's left. … Holtzman, off with the pitch[,] slid across home plate but he didn't have to, because Messersmith had the play only at first base."[1] (Campaneris had finished seventh in the American League in 1974 with 11 sacrifices.)

"We play for two or three runs," Jackson said after the game. "That's why the squeeze was a good play at that time."[2] After the successful suicide squeeze, Bill North walked, but Yeager threw out the Oakland speedster, who had led the American League in stolen bases by a wide margin but was also caught stealing more than any other player.

Shoddy Oakland defense helped the Dodgers close the gap in the fifth. Campaneris's error with one out allowed Davey Lopes to reach. Buckner singled to right, and Jackson's error allowed Lopes to score from first. Holtzman walked Jim Wynn to push Buckner to second. First-year Oakland manager Al Dark had already displayed his boldness in the top of the frame with a suicide squeeze. He did so again by quickly taking out Holtzman, who had thrown just 71 pitches, and calling on closer Rollie Fingers.

In 76 appearances in 1974, Fingers had entered the game in the fifth inning or earlier only three times. Tellingly, two of those had happened in September, the last time on September 15 against Texas, Oakland's closest competitor in the AL West. In that game, Fingers pitched the final 4⅔ innings. He earned the win, giving up three hits. Fingers performed similarly in this game with much more at stake.

Vin Scully said Fingers "looks like a man in search of a barbershop quartet."[3] He began his extended adventure by striking out Garvey before plunking Ferguson, a surprising development given that Ferguson had not been hit by a pitch in 430 plate appearances that season, and Fingers had faced 483 batters in 1974, hitting just Dave Chalk back on May 26. Fingers got Cey to fly out, concluding a consequential fifth inning with the A's up 2-1.

Messersmith retired Oakland in order in the sixth and got his second bloop single in the bottom of the frame although he died on first. Gene Tenace singled to open the seventh. Dark's sacrificial strategy failed when Ray Fosse bunted foul with two strikes. The move looked particularly peculiar since the two following batters, Dick Green and Fingers, seemed unlikely to drive Tenace home from second base. The game remained 2-1 heading into the seventh-inning stretch.

For the only time in the game, LA went down in order in the seventh. The A's took a 3-1 lead in the eighth via Campaneris's single, North's sacrifice, and a throwing error by third baseman Cey that eluded Garvey, who hesitated after retrieving the ball. As a result, Sal Bando went to third, which set up the most superlative play of the game. Jackson skied to medium-deep right-center, apparently far enough to score Bando. Ferguson prevented the run. The right fielder cut in front of center fielder Wynn to make the catch and started a double play with a laser throw to Yeager, who blocked the plate. Remarkably, Ferguson had played 52 career games in right field for the Dodgers from 1972-1974 without an assist.

"It could possibly have been the greatest throw from such a deep position," said Ferguson's admiring manager, Walter Alston.[4] Ferguson said, "I just couldn't make a better throw. If it's not perfect, Bando scores. [Yeager] didn't have to move. Bando was out. But he gave Yeager a pretty good bump."[5]

The managerial wheels picked up speed in the eighth. Dark replaced right fielder Jackson, who was nursing a hamstring injury, with Claudell Washington. Fingers walked Cey with one out before striking out Russell. Willie Crawford batted for Yeager and singled Cey to third. Von Joshua pinch-hit for Messersmith and grounded to Green, leaving the tying runs at the corners.

The indefatigable Mike Marshall, who had appeared in a record 106 games out of the bullpen during the regular season, relieved Messersmith for the ninth. Oakland threatened without hitting the ball out of the infield. Rudi bunted for a single. Tenace sacrificed Rudi to second. Fosse walked. With Green due, Dark brought in Jim Holt, who popped out. Marshall fanned Fingers, who needed just three more outs for the win.

Fingers got the first two on fly balls before Wynn "hit a drive that cleared the left field fence for a home run. [Rudi and North] leaped … and it was so close that both looked in North's glove after the leap."[6] The game had nearly ended, but LA now trailed just 3-2.

Garvey singled, and Tom Paciorek ran for him. Fingers had thrown an astounding and effective 68 pitches in relief. Dark decided that sufficed and replaced him. Four pitchers had earned saves for Oakland in 1974: Fingers (18), Paul Lindblad (6), Darold Knowles (3), and Blue Moon Odom (1). Ignoring Lindblad, Knowles, and Odom, Dark tapped Catfish Hunter, who had won 25 games in 1974 as a starter.

Hunter's only career save in the regular season (and the only one in his 15-year career) had come in the second game of a doubleheader against Baltimore on June 16, 1968. He came in with one out in the eighth with Oakland up 6-4, got Frank Robinson to hit into a double play, and retired all three hitters in the ninth. Here, Hunter needed to get just one out albeit in his first relief appearance of any sort in nearly two years. "It was the seventh game of the World Series in '72," he said, "and I came in in the fourth … with the bases loaded, two outs. The first pitch hit the wall, the second one reached it – only … Rudi jumped and caught it. That's the kind of reliever I was."[7]

Hunter faced Ferguson. An Oakland scribe described the scene: "The first two pitches missed for balls as the 55,974 fans – largest crowd in the history of Dodger Stadium – roared with anticipation. The next pitch, a strike. The next pitch, right down the middle of the plate, a fastball capable of going great distances, instead fouled back by the muscular Ferguson. The last pitch, another fastball. Ferguson swung. And missed."[8] Hunter's second and last career save sealed another World Series win for the A's. Dark's "brilliant"[9] maneuverings and the big-time performances of stars Fingers, Hunter, and Jackson proved critical in the road win over the Dodgers, who, with 12 men left on base, fell one big hit short of victory.

SOURCES

In addition to the sources cited in the Notes, the author consulted Baseball-Reference.com.

https://www.baseball-reference.com/boxes/LAN/LAN197410120.shtml

https://www.retrosheet.org/boxesetc/1974/B10120LAN1974.htm

NOTES

1 Ray Fitzgerald, "LA Caught in Squeeze," *Boston Globe*, October 13, 1974: 45.

2 George Ross, "Dodgers Undone by Telegraphed Squeeze," *Oakland Tribune*, October 13, 1974: 31.

3 The NBC broadcast of the game is available at youtu.be/xkdv1lBIXCE (accessed June 10, 2023).

4 Lowell Reidenbaugh, "Brawling A's Land One on L.A. Chin," *The Sporting News*, October 26, 1974: 3.

5 Ed Levitt, "Dodgers Take Loss In Stride," *Oakland Tribune*, October 13, 1974: 33.

6 Peter Gammons, "A's Mix It Up – Homer, Squeeze, Error – Win Opener, 3-2," *Boston Globe*, October 13, 1974: 45.

7 Peter Gammons, "Catfish Feared 'Gopher,' Avoided Same," *Boston Globe*, October 13, 1974: 46.

8 Ron Bergman, "The Fighting A's Win First Round," *Oakland Tribune*, October 13, 1974: 31.

9 Ed Levitt, "Last Series Here?" *Oakland Tribune*, October 13, 1974: 31.

"RICK MONDAY ...
YOU MADE A GREAT PLAY!"

April 25, 1976: Los Angeles Dodgers 5, Chicago Cubs 4

by Jeff Barto

The Chicago Cubs' center fielder played well on April 25, 1976. He collected three hits, scored two runs, and drove in another. His efforts helped the Cubs to rally from a three-run deficit and tie the game, even if they did not prevent a 5-4 loss to the Los Angeles Dodgers in 10 innings.

But his greatest "play" on this Sunday afternoon won the hearts of 25,167 opposing Dodger fans, as well as millions of others who read about it in the next day's newspapers. In the middle of the fourth inning, the Cubs' Rick Monday made a career-best "put out." Though it didn't appear in the box score, Monday's saving grab stayed with him for the rest of his life.[1]

The Bicentennial season was less than three weeks old when the Dodgers hosted the Cubs in the finale of a three-game weekend series at Dodger Stadium.[2] The early innings gave little indication that anything especially memorable was in store. Right-hander Rick Rhoden started for the Dodgers and set down the Cubs in order in the first inning. In the second, he allowed a one-out walk to Andre Thornton and a single by Manny Trillo but stranded both runners.

Cubs righty Steve Stone started strong, retiring the first five Dodgers before his shoulder tightened.[3] He left the game with two outs in the second inning and right-hander Ken Crosby got the third out.[4]

Monday laid down a one-out bunt single in the Cubs' third. After taking second on José Cardenal's groundout, he opened the scoring on Bill Madlock's line-drive single.

Crosby held the Dodgers in check in the third. Though Bill Russell reached on a bad throw by short-stop Dave Rosello, Crosby struck out Bill Buckner to end the threat.

The Cubs failed to score in the fourth. While warming up before the Dodgers batted in the bottom of the inning, Monday noticed two intruders lurking in shallow left field. "I had seen the two guys jump the fence and run on the field and I thought they were going to shake hands with [left fielder] José [Cardenal]."[5]

As they headed toward center, Cardenal noticed one of them fumbling with something in his pocket. "I thought he might have a knife or a gun. You never know with those crazy people. And they were high on dope, really doped out."[6]

Monday noticed the older one spreading out an American flag like a picnic blanket. With their backs to him, Monday edged closer to the pair. He soon smelled lighter fluid being poured on the flag.

Monday planned to knock them over. But when the wind blew out the first match, he got close enough to snatch the drenched flag before the second match could be lit. The would-be fire bug failed miserably in trying to hit Monday with an awkward toss of the empty can.

Monday handed the flag to Dodgers pitcher Doug Rau. The fans, stunned at first, instinctively reacted to the organist and began to sing "God Bless America."[7]

When play resumed, Crosby retired the first two batters, and then the Dodgers' dormant bats erupted. Steve Garvey singled and stole second, and Ron Cey walked.

Henry Cruz was in center field for the Dodgers while Dusty Baker rested a sore hamstring.[8] Cruz provided two-out lightning with a shot to right field, eight rows deep, for a three-run homer, his first in the majors. After the game, Cruz sighed, "I wish I could get the ball back and keep it forever. My wife just got here from Puerto Rico ... and I dedicated the home run to her."[9]

Steve Yeager followed with a single and a stolen base. Russell singled to center to drive him home for a 4-1 lead.

The Cubs began their comeback when Pete LaCock opened the fifth inning with a home run, pinch-hitting for Crosby.[10]

Monday batted next, and the fans roared with a standing ovation. The scoreboard then read, "Rick Monday … you made a great play!"[11]

After the ovation faded, Monday singled. Cardenal drew a walk, giving the Cubs two on with no outs. Rhoden retired Madlock and Jerry Morales, but Thornton made it 4-3 as he singled Monday home. Trillo walked to load the bases, but Cey turned Steve Swisher's grounder into an unassisted force at third, and the Dodgers held on to their one-run lead.

Right-hander Óscar Zamora relieved Crosby and kept the game close with three scoreless innings. Rhoden shut down the Cubs in the sixth, but when Cardenal walked to open the seventh, Dodgers manager Walter Alston made a double switch.[12] Catcher Joe Ferguson replaced Rhoden and batted ninth while right-hander Mike Marshall replaced Yeager and batted seventh.

After Madlock greeted Marshall with a single, the Cubs tested the Dodgers' new catcher. Cardenal took off on a steal of third, and Madlock made a delayed dash to second. Ferguson met the challenge, throwing to second to trap Madlock in a rundown for the first out. Marshall then fanned Morales and Thornton to strand Cardenal at third.

Marshall returned for the eighth, and Trillo led off with a double. Cubs manager Jim Marshall called for a sacrifice, but Mike Marshall fielded Swisher's bunt and threw Trillo out at third. After a walk to Rosello pushed Swisher into scoring position, Jim Marshall went to his bench, pinch-hitting Champ Summers for Zamora and sending in Joe Wallis to run for the slower Swisher.

Chicago's bad luck with tactical moves continued, as Summers struck out. But Monday connected on his third single, and Wallis's fresh legs carried him home from second, tying the game, 4-4.

Right-hander Mike Garman relieved Zamora in the eighth.[13] After a double, a wild pitch, and a walk, the Dodgers had runners on first and third with no outs. It was their first serious scoring threat since the four-run fifth, but they could not push a run across. Garvey and Cey popped up. After an intentional walk to Cruz loaded the bases, Ed Goodson, batting for Marshall, grounded out to second baseman Sizemore.

Knuckleballer Charlie Hough replaced Marshall to pitch the ninth. After yielding an infield single to Madlock, he retired Morales, Thornton, and Trillo in order. Garman pitched a quiet bottom half, sandwiching a fly ball between two groundouts.

Hough and Garman remained in the game for the 10th. Hough got the Cubs out quickly in the top of the frame. But Garman cracked in his third inning of relief. Sizemore reached when first baseman Thornton bobbled Rosello's throw for an error. John Hale sacrificed Sizemore to second.

The Cubs walked Garvey intentionally, but Cey's single scored Sizemore for a 5-4 walk-off Dodgers win. Los Angeles had the second win of what turned out to be a 12-game winning streak.

Afterward the biggest headlines belonged to Monday. He had served as a Marine reservist for six years, and the American flag meant much to him. An agitated Monday declared, "If he's going to burn a flag, he better do it in front of somebody who doesn't appreciate it. I've visited enough veterans hospitals and seen enough guys with their legs blown off defending the flag."[14]

Many questions about the two intruders remain unanswered. Discrepancies in basic facts – such as their names, ages, where they were from, and what sentence the older man received – riddled coverage of the game and its aftermath.[15] The historical record is inconclusive on what was being protested, but speculation has included treatment of Indigenous people, the Vietnam War, and the older man's wife's experience in a mental institution.[16]

Immediately after the incident, no journalist interviewed the intruders to sort out the confusion. Years later, journalist David Davis located both, but father and son refused to discuss it. "I'm not interested in reliving that time period," the son told Davis. "I don't see any good from rehashing that situation. I don't feel it necessary to go over this."[17]

A famous photo captures Monday's celebrated moment. *Los Angeles Herald-Examiner* photographer James Roark snapped the image of the flag rescue.[18] It remains a prominent reminder of the post-Vietnam years; it received a Pulitzer Prize nomination.[19] Monday soon began to receive invitations to be an honored guest at patriotic functions, and continued to receive them in the decades since. He often tours the events with Roark's iconic snapshot and the original flag given to him by Dodgers general manager Al Campanis.[20]

Campanis had often tried to land Monday in a trade, and finally dealt for him in January 1977.[21] Perhaps gifting Monday the flag and appreciation by the Dodgers fans helped. Regardless, Monday earned his second All-Star berth that year. He spent the last eight seasons of his career with the Dodgers, contributing to four NL West crowns, three pennants, and a World Series championship. His biggest hit came in the last game of the 1981 NLCS. His tie-breaking ninth-inning home run shocked the Montreal Expos and propelled the Dodgers to the World Series. To this day, Expos fans call that game Blue Monday.[22]

In 2006 the National Baseball Hall of Fame voted Monday's flag rescue among the 100 classic moments in baseball history.[23] Whether speaking at a VFW post, waving in a Memorial Day parade, or answering a war veteran's letter, Monday will remain best known for his patriotic act more than any highlight from his 19-year career. As his teammate Cardenal affirmed, "Now we've got three great patriots. George Washington, Abraham Lincoln, and Rick Monday."[24]

ACKNOWLEDGMENTS

This article was fact-checked by Kevin Larkin and copy-edited by Len Levin.

SOURCES

In addition to the sources cited in the Notes, the author consulted Baseball-Reference.com and Retrosheet.org for pertinent information, including the box score and play-by-play

https://www.baseball-reference.com/boxes/LAN/LAN197604250.shtml

https://www.retrosheet.org/boxesetc/1976/B04250LAN1976.htm

NOTES

1   In 1965 Monday was the first player selected in baseball's first-ever amateur player draft.

2   As it happened, both teams had already been involved in notable games. Los Angeles' Tommy John had returned to the mound on April 16, 19 months after undergoing a first-of-its-kind elbow surgery. On April 17, Chicago had lost a historic slugfest to the Philadelphia Phillies, victimized by Mike Schmidt's four home runs.

3   Paul Hagen, "Cancel the Funeral – Dodgers Win in 10, 5-4," *San Bernardino County (California) Sun*, April 26, 1976: 23.

4   This game was the 11th of only 16 major-league games Crosby pitched over two seasons.

5   Rick Young, "Patriotism Lives," *Alabama Journal* (Montgomery, Alabama), June 22, 1976: 10.

6   Associated Press, "Monday's 'Great Play' Saves Flag. Burns Would-Be Firebugs," *San Bernardino County Sun*, April 26, 1976: 23.

7   Kathy Boccella, "Honoring Move to Save Flag from Desecration," *Philadelphia Inquirer*, August 26, 2008: B7.

8   Don Bradley, "Dodgers Enjoy Winning Streak," *Pomona* (California) *Progress Bulletin*, April 26, 1976: 16.

9   Bradley.

10   LaCock was the son of Ralph Pierre LaCock, better known as Peter Marshall, the host of the *Hollywood Squares* game show from 1966 to 1981.

11   Associated Press, "Monday: 'I Wasn't Trying to Be a Hero,'" *Dayton* (Ohio) *Journal Herald*, April 28, 1976: 5.

12   Alston soon announced his retirement after this season. Tommy Lasorda replaced him.

13   Garman followed Monday to the Dodgers when both were traded by the Cubs for Bill Buckner, Ivan DeJesus, and minor leaguer Jeff Albert.

14   United Press International, "Monday Saluted," *Moline* (Illinois) *Dispatch*, April 27, 1976: 18.

15   The intruders were an unemployed father and his unnamed juvenile son. Discrepancies among sources included the name of the father (William Errol Thomas or William Morris), the age of both (father as 35 or 37 years old, the son as 11 or 15), and where they lived (Eldon, Missouri, or Old Town, Maine). United Press International, "Cubs' Monday Is a Hero," *Holland* (Michigan) *Evening Sentinel*, April 28, 1976: 3.

16   David Davis, "When Rick Monday Saved the American Flag from Being Burned at Dodger Stadium," VICE Sports, April 25, 2016. https://www.vice.com/en/article/3dgq4b/when-rick-monday-saved-the-american-flag-from-being-burned-at-dodger-stadium.

17   Davis.

18   Roark died in 1995 from injuries he received from a beating by four men while walking home from a Portland restaurant.

19   Bob Baum, "Man, Beaten to Death, Travelled Social Spectrum," *Iola* (Kansas) *Register.* October 21, 1995: 1.

20   Dave Daniel, "Monday Has His Day Again," *Santa Monica-Southside Advertiser and Penny Pincher*, May 6, 1976: 11.

21   Associated Press, "Dodgers Get Rick Monday From Chicago. *Ironwood* (Michigan) *Daily Globe*, January 12, 1977: 16; Associated Press, "Buckner Traded to Cubs," *San Bernardino County Sun*, January 12, 1977: 47.

22   David Leon Moore, "Dodgers, Monday Leave the Expos Feeling Blue, 2-1," *San Bernardino County Sun*, October 20, 1981: 44.

23   Kathy Boccella, "Honoring Move to Save Flag from Desecration."

24   William H. Weldon, "America's New Hero," *Jefferson City* (Missouri) *Daily Capital News*, April 29, 1976: 4.

DUSTY BAKER HITS 30TH HOMER, RECEIVES FIRST-EVER HIGH-FIVE FROM GLENN BURKE IN DODGERS' LOSS TO ASTROS

October 2, 1977: Houston Astros 6, Los Angeles Dodgers 3

by John Fredland

His career curtailed by prejudice, his life by AIDS, Glenn Burke hit just two home runs in four seasons of part-time play with the Los Angeles Dodgers and Oakland A's, but the circumstances of his first big-league homer made it significant, decades before the major leagues recognized him as the first openly gay player. As Burke's playoff-bound Dodgers closed out 1977's regular season with a 6-3 loss to the Houston Astros on October 2, he greeted a milestone-making Dusty Baker home run with what is recognized as history's first high-five – then followed with his own homer.

A celebrated high-school basketball player in Berkeley, California, Glenn Lawrence Burke tried his hand at basketball and baseball at four different colleges before the Dodgers drafted him in June 1972.[1] He climbed Los Angeles' system steadily, demonstrating power, speed, and a strong arm.[2]

Burke made it to the majors in 1976 as an injury replacement and September call-up.[3] At Triple A to open the 1977 season, he was recalled in June and remained with Los Angeles, contributing as a reserve outfielder and boosting morale with his high-octane personality, as the Dodgers regained NL West supremacy from the Cincinnati Reds.[4]

"Teammates loved his enthusiasm and gap-toothed grin, the laughter he brought to the locker room, the funky music blasting from his boom box," Burke biographer Andrew Maraniss wrote.[5] "With his broad chest, muscular legs, and seventeen-inch biceps, other players marveled at his strength and physique. He had an energy and toughness to match, never backing away from a fight."[6]

But there was more to the 24-year-old Burke than the public saw. Burke was gay, something known by few in the Dodgers' organization and elsewhere, at a time when, Maraniss noted, "[n]ot only were there no openly gay athletes in Major League Baseball, the National Football League, or the National Basketball

Before his 26 seasons as a major-league manager, Dusty Baker played 2,039 games as an outfielder. He made two All-Star teams with the Dodgers.

Association, but most Americans would have found the notion far-fetched."[7]

Harder to miss was the Dodgers' 1977 renaissance under first-year manager Tom Lasorda. A distant second in 1975 and 1976, Los Angeles had a 10½-game lead on the division by May 6 and never looked back, clinching the title on September 20, with 11 games remaining.[8]

Dodger strengths included a quartet of power-hitting veterans: First baseman Steve Garvey, third baseman Ron Cey, right fielder Reggie Smith, and left fielder Dusty Baker. One by one, as September progressed, they reached the 30-home-run milestone. Garvey was first, hitting his 30th homer off Cincinnati's Manny Sarmiento on September 14.[9] Four days later, Cey hit number 30 off Atlanta's Mickey Mahler; Smith equaled him that same game with a blast off Dave Campbell.[10]

Baker's 29th homer came off the Astros' Joe Niekro on September 25, but over the next five games he went homerless, missing the milestone blast by mere feet with a double on October 1.[11] Going into the season's final day, Baker had just one more chance to complete baseball's first-ever foursome of 30-homer teammates.

The finale's pitching matchup appeared to tilt the odds against him. Flamethrowing Houston starter J.R. Richard was as hard to homer against – or just bat against – as anyone in baseball. The 27-year-old, 6-foot-8 righty, seeking his 18th win of the season, was on his way to finishing second in the league in strikeouts and seventh in ERA; entering this game, only four NL starters had allowed home runs less frequently.[12]

With 46,501 on hand for Fan Appreciation Day,[13] Houston leadoff hitter José Cruz shattered his bat fouling off Bobby Castillo's first pitch of the game. The splintered barrel struck Dodgers catcher Steve Yeager in the back of the head. Yeager – who had narrowly escaped fatal injury a season earlier when hit in the neck by the jagged end of a broken bat – remained on the ground for several minutes before walking off. Johnny Oates replaced him.[14]

The Astros tested Oates right away. Cruz singled and attempted to steal second, but Oates threw him out. Enos Cabell followed with another single, and César Cedeño doubled, but the Dodgers gunned down Cabell at home for the second out. Houston finally broke through when Bob Watson singled Cedeño home for a 1-0 lead.

Richard protected the lead with a steady stream of strikeouts. Vic Davalillo – back in the majors at age 38 after 3½ seasons in the Mexican League – and Garvey

bookended the first by striking out around Baker's single. All three Dodgers batters fanned in the second inning, and Richard recorded two more strikeouts in the third.

Watson led off the fourth with a home run against the 22-year-old Castillo, who was making his first major-league start after winning 19 games in the Mexican League in 1977.[15] Richard continued to dominate with the 2-0 lead, holding the Dodgers hitless in the fourth and fifth innings, adding single strikeouts in each inning to increase his total to nine.

In the middle innings, Lasorda began to substitute for his regulars. Burke entered in center in the fifth.

With Castillo due to lead off the sixth, Lasorda sent up 38-year-old Manny Mota. Almost exclusively a pinch-hitter since 1974, Mota had not homered since June 1972.

The Astros shifted, anticipating the right-handed Mota slapping the ball the other way. Mota surprised everyone[16] by yanking Richard's second pitch into the bullpen in left for a home run, breaking up the shutout with his first homer in 777 plate appearances.[17]

Richard regrouped to retire the next two Dodgers; Rafael Landestoy was his 10th strikeout. Baker batted with two outs.

The first pitch sailed over Baker's head to the backstop, and Richard then got ahead 1-and-2. Baker drove the next delivery toward the 395-foot marker in left-center. Cedeño went back, then stopped as it cleared the fence. Baker had 30 home runs; the Dodgers had their historic foursome.

Baker leapt in the air and clapped his hands several times while rounding the bases. His teammates met him at home plate.

The first to reach him was Burke, direct from the on-deck circle. As the frenzied crowd gave a standing ovation, Burke raised his right hand high, shouting, "Way to go!" and encouraging Baker to slap it. Baker did.[18]

With the game now tied, Burke took a fastball for a ball. Richard came back with another fastball, and Burke belted it over the left-field fence. Baker welcomed him in the dugout with another high-five.[19] With two high-fives, three home runs, and four teammates with 30 homers, Los Angeles had a 3-2 lead.

Lasorda entrusted the advantage to right-hander Dennis Lewallyn, called up from Triple A when the rosters expanded in September. Lewallyn opened the seventh by retiring Roger Metzger and Richard on grounders. But Cruz singled and Cabell walked.

Cedeño's single drove in Cruz with the tying run, as Cabell took third.

With second base open and Watson up, Lasorda ordered an intentional walk, loading the bases for Dennis Walling, a 23-year-old appearing in only his 15th major-league game. Walling foiled the strategy with a triple to right, sending Cabell, Cedeño, and Watson home to put the Astros back up, 6-3.

Richard breezed through the last three innings against a reserve-heavy Los Angeles alignment with little in common with the lineup the Dodgers had fielded to start the game. He added two strikeouts in the seventh and two more in the eighth to finish with 14. Lee Lacy's seventh-inning walk was Los Angeles' only baserunner after Houston regained the lead. Richard completed a four-hitter for his 18th win – with three of those hits Mota, Baker, and Burke's sixth-inning homers.

Two days later, the Dodgers opened the National League Championship Series against the Philadelphia Phillies, and Burke started in center against Steve Carlton.[20] In Game Two, Baker slugged a grand slam, and Burke greeted him with another high-five, this one captured in a *Los Angeles Times* front-page photo.[21] Los Angeles won the NLCS but lost the World Series to the New York Yankees; Burke started Game One in center.

But the game soon turned against him. In the 1977-78 offseason, with speculation about his personal life increasing, Dodgers management reportedly offered Burke a raise if he got married.[22] Then, more rumors,[23] a trade to the A's in May 1978,[24] slurs in Oakland,[25] and the end of his professional career by 1980. In 1982 Burke revealed his sexuality during a nationally televised interview.[26] He contracted AIDS and died at age 42 in 1995.[27]

Baseball's official recognition of Burke's life and career waited until years after his death, as sport and society's inclusiveness gradually increased over time. Major League Baseball saluted his pioneering status at the 2014 All-Star Game, while announcing an initiative to support the game's gay, lesbian, bisexual, and transgender community.[28] The A's celebrated him on Pride Night in 2015; the Dodgers followed in 2022.[29]

But some acts require no official blessing to conquer the world. So it was for Burke's initial high-five, conceived in exuberance, and inspired by a record-setting moment involving three players – Baker, Richard, Burke – whose respective stories reflect the dazzling promise and heartbreaking limitations of baseball's inclusiveness after Jackie Robinson. The high-five's rapid, universal spread and enduring popularity ensured Burke's worldwide impact, long before baseball acknowledged his trailblazing legacy.

ACKNOWLEDGMENTS

This article was fact-checked by Bruce Slutsky and copy-edited by Len Levin. The author was inspired to write about Glenn Burke after reading Andrew Maraniss's 2021 biography, *Singled Out: The True Story of Glenn Burke.* He also acknowledges Erik Sherman, who collaborated with Burke on the posthumously released autobiography, *Out At Home: The True Story of Glenn Burke,* for his work in documenting Burke's life story. SABR members Gary Belleville and Kurt Blumenau provided insightful comments on an earlier version of this article, and Jeff J. Snider contributed valuable research assistance.

SOURCES

In addition to the sources cited in the Notes below, the author consulted Baseball-Reference.com and Retrosheet.org for pertinent information, including the box score and play-by-play. He also reviewed game coverage in the *Houston Chronicle* and *Los Angeles Times* newspapers and SABR Baseball BioProject biographies of several players involved in this game, especially Rory Costello's Vic Davalillo and Manny Mota biographies.

https://www.baseball-reference.com/boxes/LAN/LAN197710020.shtml

https://www.retrosheet.org/boxesetc/1977/B10020LAN1977.htm

NOTES

1   Andrew Maraniss, *Singled Out: The True Story of Glenn Burke,* (New York: Philomel, 2021), 23, 27-28.

2   Maraniss, 44.

3   Ross Newhan, "Lopes Is Out of Dodger Opener … If There Is One," *Los Angeles Times,* April 9, 1976: III, 2; Steve Kennedy, "Maturing Burke Relishes Spring," *Independent and Gazette* (California), September 23, 1976: 34.

4   Toby Zwikel, "Basketball Remains First Love of Dodgers' Burke," *Valley News* (Fallbrook, California), June 9, 1977: 4, 3.

5   Maraniss, 4-5.

6   Maraniss, 5.

7   Maraniss, 55. In 1975, a year before Burke's major-league debut, retired professional football player Dave Kopay became the first athlete from a major professional team sport to announce publicly that he was gay. Stan Farber, "Gay Kopay Happy, but Coaching Doors Shut," *Tacoma News Tribune,* May 3, 1976: C-2.

8   Jason Turbow, *They Bled Blue: Fernandomania, Strike-Season Mayhem, and the Weirdest Championship Baseball Had Ever Seen* (New York: Houghton Mifflin Harcourt, 2019), 14-17.

9   Ross Newhan, "Lasorda Lets John Do It – He Doesn't: Reds Overcome 8-3 Deficit for a 9-8 Victory," *Los Angeles Times,* September 15, 1977: III, 1.

10   Ross Newhan, "Dodgers Fail to Get Relief, Miss Clincher: Bullpen Collapse Gives Braves 9-8 Win; L.A. Assured of Tie Despite Defeat," *Los Angeles Times,* September 19, 1977: III, 1.

11   Ross Newhan, "Reggie Smith Regains Drive Just in Time," *Los Angeles Times,* October 2, 1977: III, 1.

12   Entering his final start of the 1977 season, Richard had allowed 0.523 home runs per nine innings pitched. The only NL pitchers ahead of him were Rick Reuschel of the Chicago Cubs, Jerry Reuss of the Pittsburgh Pirates, Steve Rogers of the Montreal Expos, and Tommy John of the Dodgers. By

allowing three home runs in this game, Richard's season figure increased to 0.607, allowing Burt Hooton of the Dodgers to pass him.

13 The Dodgers' season attendance total of 2,955,087 broke their own record, set in 1962, the first year of play at Dodger Stadium. Ross Newhan, "The Gang of Four," *Los Angeles Times*, October 3, 1977: III, 1.

14 Newhan, "The Gang of Four." The *Philadelphia Daily News* reported Lasorda wanted Yeager to catch five innings in a playoff tuneup. "I never even got to catch one pitch," Yeager said. Stan Hochman, "Nobody Ever Promised Yeager a Rose Garden," *Philadelphia Daily News*, October 4, 1977: 67. X-rays showed no injury, and Yeager caught the Dodgers' NLCS opener on October 4. Newhan, "The Gang of Four."

15 Turbow, *They Bled Blue*, 60-61.

16 The *Los Angeles Times* reported that in the Dodgers dugout, Lasorda had turned to second baseman Davey Lopes and said, "Wouldn't it be great if Manny hit a pinch-hit homer?" "If he hits a home run, I'll buy everyone on the team a steak dinner," Lopes responded. When Mota hit his home run, Lopes "collapsed on the top step of the dugout in a feigned faint." Newhan, "The Gang of Four."

17 "When I saw the outfield swing to the right today, I said to myself, 'OK, take one pitch and see if you can pull it, see if you can hit it hard,'" Mota said afterward. "It was a great feeling to run clear around the bases for the first time in five years." Newhan, "The Gang of Four." It was the last of Mota's 31 career homers over 20 major-league seasons.

18 Maraniss, 112. A 1990 *Atlanta Journal* column by Terence Moore corroborates this origin story: "[T]his high-five madness that currently dominates society began in 1977 during the first year of 'The Good Ship Lasorda.' Whenever Dusty Baker and Glenn Burke were pleased with an accomplishment by a fellow member of the Los Angeles Dodgers, they would slap hands in the air." Terence Moore, "A Totally New Wave: Why Not Start a Fad Against Fads in Sports?" *Atlanta Journal*, June 20, 1990: E-3. A 2019 *Business Insider* article on the history of the high-five adds, "slapping hands as a type of handshake dates back to at least the 1920s, [but] there was something different about the way Burke and Baker did it that instantly

caught the public's attention." Mark Abadi, "Today Is National High Five Day – This Photo from 1977 Shows the First High Five," BusinessInsider.com, April 18, 2019, https://www.businessinsider.com/where-does-the-high-five-come-from-origin-2017-4.

19 Maraniss, 115.

20 When asked by the media why he was starting Burke in center over veteran Rick Monday, Lasorda responded, "Glenn Burke had four hits in six at-bats against Carlton this year with two RBI and a double." Don Merry, "Dodger Lefty Recalls Playoff Role in 1974," *Los Angeles Times*, October 4, 1977: III, 1. Burke was hitless in three at-bats in Los Angeles' 7-5 loss.

21 "Give Him a Hand," *Los Angeles Times*, October 6, 1977: I, 1.

22 Maraniss, 133-136.

23 Maraniss, 143-145.

24 Ross Newhan, "Burke Trade Stops the Music," *Los Angeles Times*, May 21, 1978: III, 2.

25 Maraniss, 171-175, 183.

26 Maraniss, 201-212.

27 Michael Bamberger, "Grip of AIDS Leaves Burke Clinging to Life," *Austin American-Statesman*, February 14, 1995: C2.

28 Maraniss, 255-256. MLB's announcement followed Jason Collins's coming out as the National Basketball Association's first openly gay player in 2013 and Michael Sam of the University of Missouri announcing he was gay shortly before the 2014 National Football League draft. As of 2022 no active major-league baseball player has publicly announced he was gay.

29 "Glenn Burke's Family at Game as A's Honor Him on Pride Night," *Sacramento Bee*, June 18, 2015: B6; Scott Miller, "The Dodgers Embrace the Family of a Player They Once Shunned," *New York Times*, June 2, 2022, https://www.nytimes.com/2022/06/02/sports/baseball/glenn-burke-dodgers-pride.html.

BILL RUSSELL'S WALK-OFF SINGLE SENDS DODGERS BACK TO WORLD SERIES; GARVEY WINS NLCS MVP

October 7, 1978: Los Angeles Dodgers 4, Philadelphia Phillies 3 (10 innings)
(Game Four of the 1978 National League Championship Series)

by Joseph Wancho

The Los Angeles Dodgers and the Philadelphia Phillies were meeting for the second consecutive year in the 1978 National League Championship Series. LA took the series in 1977, ousting the Phillies in four games. "Three is my lucky number," said Philadelphia manager Danny Ozark. "I wear number 3 and this is our third time here. It'll be a three-game series and we're going to win it."[1]

Las Vegas certainly disagreed with Ozark and chose the Dodgers as the favorites to win the World Series even before the first pitch was thrown in the LCS.[2] According to oddsmakers, a fan with a sporting interest in the outcome would have been wise to follow them as opposed to Ozark's "Lucky Three" concept.

The first two games of the best-of-five series were played at Veterans Stadium in Philadelphia. In the opener, the Dodgers smacked four home runs that accounted for seven runs in their 9-5 victory. Steve Garvey belted two of the round-trippers and drove in four runs. In Game Two, Davey Lopes hit his second home run of the series, in addition to a triple, and drove in three runs as the Dodgers won 4-0. Starting pitcher Tommy John went the distance, yielding four hits and totaling four strikeouts for the win.

The series moved to Dodger Stadium for Game Three, and, if necessary, games Four and Five. The pitching matchup highlighted a pair of future Hall of Famers. Steve Carlton for the Phillies and Don Sutton for LA. The Phillies jumped on Sutton in the top of the second, scoring four runs. Three came on a home

run off the bat of Carlton. It was his only postseason home run. The Phillies added three runs in the top of the sixth and coasted to a 9-4 win. Carlton pitched a complete game, striking out eight Dodgers. For the Dodgers, Garvey slugged his third home run of the series, a solo shot in the bottom of the eighth. The Phillies now trailed Los Angeles, two games to one.

Game Four was played on October 7 at Dodger Stadium. The starting pitchers were a pair of left-handers: the Dodgers' Doug Rau (15-9, 3.26 ERA regular season) and the Phillies' Randy Lerch (11-8, 3.96).

In the top of the first inning, Mike Schmidt led off with a double to left field. Larry Bowa walked and Garry Maddox followed with a single to right field. The Phillies were in business with the bases loaded and nobody out. But Rau bore down. He struck out Greg Luzinski, got José Cardenal to line to short, and retired Jerry Martin on a popout to the catcher. It was a golden opportunity, but the Phillies failed to cash in. "I think that was the key to the whole ballgame," said Lerch. "But when you leave the bases loaded with none out, you deserve to lose."[3]

The Dodgers leapt ahead in the bottom of the second inning. With one down, Ron Cey doubled to left field and scored on a single by Dusty Baker.

The Phillies jumped ahead 2-1 in the top of the third inning. Luzinski smashed a two-run homer to left-center field. It was his second homer of the series. But their advantage lasted only until the bottom of the fourth, when Cey unloaded on a 3-and-2 pitch from

Lerch and drove it to left field for his first home run of the series, knotting the score at 2-2.

In the top of the sixth inning, Dodgers manager Tommy Lasorda went to his bullpen, replacing Rau with right-hander Rick Rhoden. In his five innings pitched, Rau had given up two runs on five hits, struck out one, and walked two.

The Dodgers and Phillies proceeded to exchange solo home runs. With one down in the bottom of the sixth, Garvey reached the left-field seats for his fourth home run of the series. The blast signaled the end of the day for Lerch. The Phillies starter exited the game having surrendered three earned runs on seven hits. In 5⅓ innings of work, Lerch had neither walked nor struck out a batter.

Lerch's replacement was Warren Brusstar. The right-hander gave up a two-out double to Baker and walked Bill Russell intentionally, but retired Steve Yeager on a groundout to third.

With two down in the top of the seventh inning, Bake McBride pinch-hit for Brusstar. McBride came through, smacking a Rhoden pitch into the right-field seats for a home run, tying the score again, 3-3.

The score remained tied through nine innings. Terry Forster came on for the Dodgers to pitch the top of the 10th inning. Forster led LA with 22 saves during the regular season. He was coming in to keep the Phillies off the scoreboard, albeit not a save opportunity. He gave up a harmless single to Bowa before retiring the side.

Los Angeles came to bat in the home half of the 10th inning against Philadelphia reliever Tug McGraw. With two down, McGraw walked Cey. "I wasn't going to let him take me out of the ballpark," said McGraw after the game. "I was extremely conscious of how they've beaten us in the past with the long ball. So I wasn't all that upset when I did walk him, even though that turned out to be my biggest problem."[4]

Dusty Baker was next up. He sent a liner to center field. Maddox, who was one of the better-fielding center fielders in all of baseball, charged in and dropped the baseball. As a result of the error, Cey moved up to second base. "The ball was right in my glove," Maddox said later. "I don't think it was a tough play. Definitely it was a routine line drive that should have been caught any way you look at it. I missed the ball. I cost us a heckuva chance to be world champions. I'll never forget it the rest of my life. ..."[5]

Russell stepped into the batter's box. The Dodgers shortstop was confident he could deliver a hit. "A lot of times you go to the plate and you're nervous or not comfortable," said Russell, "but this time I wasn't nervous and I felt good. I knew immediately it was a hit when I hit it, I was just hoping there was no play at the plate. It was just a matter if Ronnie could score."[6]

Indeed, Russell sent a slider from McGraw to center field. Maddox charged the ball, but the ball skidded under his glove and rolled to the wall. "I was three-fourths of the way home," said Cey, "and I saw (Phillies catcher Bob) Boone drop his head and put his hands on his knees."[7]

Cey crossed the plate unimpeded, clinching the series and the pennant for the Dodgers. The final score was 4-3. This was one "3" that was not lucky for Ozark.

Forster got credit for the win, pitching one inning in relief. McGraw was the hard-luck loser. Baker collected four hits in five at-bats, with an RBI. But it was Garvey, who smacked four home runs and drove in seven runs and batted .389 in the series, who was named MVP.

The Dodgers had played the game with heavy hearts. On September 16, first-base coach and hitting instructor Jim Gilliam suffered a cerebral hemorrhage. He underwent surgery that evening but died one day after Game Four.

Gilliam had been a Dodgers player from 1953 to 1964. He transitioned to a player-coach in 1965 for two years before becoming a full-time member of the Dodgers' coaching staff in 1967.

"I know you hear a lot of that corny stuff in sports, that 'win one for the Gipper' stuff. But Jim Gilliam really did play a part in this ... for all of us," said Rau.[8]

For the Phillies, the third time was not a charm. They fell short in the NLCS for the third straight year. The Dodgers, meanwhile, faced the New York Yankees in the World Series. For the second straight year, LA lost in six games to the Yankees.

SOURCES

In addition to the sources cited in the Notes, the author consulted Baseball-Reference.com and Retrosheet.org.

https://www.baseball-reference.com/boxes/LAN/LAN197810070.shtml

https://www.retrosheet.org/boxesetc/1978/B10070LAN1978.htm

NOTES

1   Larry Eichel, "Phils Confident for Game Tomorrow," *Philadelphia Inquirer*, October 4, 1978: C1.

2   "Dodgers Favored," *Philadelphia Daily News*, October 4, 1978: 66.

3   Larry Eichel, "To Lerch, the Season Was Over after the Top of the First," *Philadelphia Inquirer*, October 8, 1978: 10-F.

4   Larry Eichel, "Dodgers Take Phils, 4-3, in 10th," *Philadelphia Inquirer*, October 8, 1978: F1.

5   Frank Dolson, "Maddox to be Remembered for What He Can't Forget," *Philadelphia Inquirer*, October 8, 1978: F10.

6   Scott Ostler, "Russell Keeps Flag Flying for Dodgers," *Los Angeles Times*, October 8, 1978: 3-12.

7   Ostler, 3-12.

8   Earl Gustkey, "Sadness Amid Dodger Cheer: Jim Gilliam," *Los Angeles Times*, October 8, 1978: 3-15.

BOB WELCH STRIKES OUT REGGIE JACKSON TO SECURE 1978 WORLD SERIES GAME TWO VICTORY

October 11, 1978: Los Angeles Dodgers 4, New York Yankees 3

by Alan Stowell

The path to the 1978 World Series was not an easy one for the Los Angeles Dodgers, and there was speculation that an August 20 clubhouse brawl might hurt their postseason chances. In the well-publicized incident, star first baseman Steve Garvey and standout starting pitcher and future Hall of Famer Don Sutton ended up on the Shea Stadium clubhouse floor in a dispute over remarks Sutton had made to *Washington*

Right-hander Bob Welch pitched 10 years for the Dodgers and struck out Reggie Jackson to end Game Two of the 1978 World Series.

Post sportswriter Tom Boswell. According to published reports, Sutton claimed Reggie Smith was the team's best player while taking a shot at Garvey and his Golden Boy image. The wrestling bout left both players with scratches and bruises.[1]

The Dodgers won the August 20 contest with the New York Mets and actually widened their division lead over the San Francisco Giants. Sutton apologized a few days later and it seemed the Dodgers may have dodged a bullet. But at least one writer thought the fight showed division on the team that could only help the Cincinnati Reds and the Giants, the Dodgers' closest division rivals.[2]

But the team remained focused and won the National League West championship by 2½ games over the Reds. In fact, in the month after the "Grapple in the Big Apple," the Dodgers won 22 games while losing only 11 and on September 16 led the division by nine games. They clinched on September 24.[3] After the Dodgers clinched the division title behind Bob Welch, they turned to the National League Championship Series, where they defeated the Philadelphia Phillies three games to one. It took an unearned run in the 10th inning for the Dodgers to prevail in Game Four at Dodger Stadium on October 7 and send them to the World Series.

In a repeat of the 1977 World Series, the 1978 Series matched the Dodgers and the New York Yankees. In the first game, on October 10, the Dodgers defeated the Yankees, 11-5. Two home runs by Davey Lopes and another by Dusty Baker led the LA attack. Pitcher Tommy John earned the victory for the Dodgers but he did surrender a solo home run to Reggie Jackson.

But before the Dodgers could take the field for Game Two, the team and all of baseball paused to honor longtime Brooklyn and LA Dodger player and coach Jim Gilliam. Gilliam suffered a stroke and lapsed into a coma on September 15. He never emerged from the coma and died on October 8 at the age of 49. Gilliam broke in with the Brooklyn Dodgers in 1953 and earned National League Rookie of the Year honors after batting .278 with a .383 on-base percentage. After being a player-coach in 1965 and 1966, Gilliam became a full-time coach in 1967.[4]

Gilliam's funeral was the morning of October 11, just hours before the second game of the World Series. It was undoubtedly an emotional and inspiring moment for the Dodgers. Tommy Lasorda, who had just completed his second full season as manager, delivered one of the eulogies.[5] The Dodgers had dedicated the National League pennant to Gilliam.

Several hours after the funeral, the team took the field at Dodger Stadium for Game Two. Jim "Catfish" Hunter started for the Yankees and Burt Hooton got the call for the Dodgers.

In the top of the first inning, the Dodgers avoided a potential Yankees run when catcher Steve Yeager threw out center fielder Gary Thomasson trying to steal second. Yankee catcher Thurman Munson followed with a double – a harmless double as it turned out as the bases were empty. Designated hitter Reggie Jackson then struck out to end the Yankee first.

The Dodgers would not be as fortunate in the third inning. Jackson came to the plate after left fielder Roy White singled and stole second, and Munson walked. Jackson's double to right brought both runners home and the Yankees were up 2-0. In the bottom of the fourth, the Dodgers cut New York's lead in half as right fielder Reggie Smith reached on a fielder's choice, moved to second on Garvey's single, and made it home on third baseman Ron Cey's base hit to center field.

As it turned out, Cey was just getting started. Second baseman Lopes opened the bottom of the sixth inning with a single, and another single by Smith put runners at the corners. After Garvey fouled out, Cey lined a Hunter pitch into the left-field bleachers to give the Dodgers a 4-2 lead.

Jackson was not quite finished, either. White got his second single of the night to start the Yankees seventh. A pitching change brought in Terry Forster to replace Hooton. Forster was greeted with a double by pinch-hitter Paul Blair that sent White to third. After Munson struck out, Jackson grounded out second to

first. But White raced home on the play and Jackson had his third RBI of the game.

The Yankees got no more runs in the seventh or eighth innings off Forster, and Goose Gossage, in relief of Hunter, retired the Dodgers in order in the seventh and eighth. The game entered the final frame with the Dodgers clinging to a 4-3 lead.

Bucky Dent, whose homer in a tiebreaker game against the Boston Red Sox was instrumental in getting the Yankees to the World Series, started the ninth inning with a single to left field. White grounded out pitcher to first on a play that put Dent, the tying run, in scoring position. A walk to Blair by Forster brought Lasorda to the mound. The skipper changed pitchers and brought in rookie Bob Welch to try to hold the Dodgers' slim lead. Welch, the Dodgers' first-round draft pick in 1977, induced Munson to fly out to right. With two out, the capacity crowd of 55,982 roared as Jackson approached the plate.

The Yankees were down to their final out. There was no exaggerating the importance of the matchup – Welch, the untested rookie, against Jackson, the veteran slugger. "The Babe of Summer," as one writer labeled him,[6] against Mr. October, who had earned his title with three home runs in the final game of the 1977 World Series.

Nine pitches, nothing but fastballs, Welch later recalled.[7] Welch's first five offerings were a swinging strike, a ball high inside, and three straight fouls. A ball outside, another foul, and another ball outside and the count was full at 3-and-2. One last fastball, a giant swing and a miss by Jackson, and the game was over.

Welch earned a new nickname after the encounter, The Iceman.[8] For his part, a frustrated Jackson could only be philosophical. "I battled him as long and as hard as I could," he said of Welch. "He beat me. The ball was up and in. It was good pitching. If he had got it out over the plate, I would have gotten him."[9]

As United Press International sports editor Milton Richman put it: "When the dust had settled, it was the Dodger rookie who was standing there triumphantly in the middle of the street with his gun still smoking and the mighty Reggie Jackson lying wounded on the ground."[10] The Dodgers owned a 2-0 Series lead with the action switching from Dodger Stadium to New York.

SOURCES

In addition to the sources cited in the Notes, the author consulted Baseball-Reference.com and Retrosheet.org.

https://www.baseball-reference.com/boxes/LAN/LAN197810110.shtml

https://www.retrosheet.org/boxesetc/1978/B10110LAN1978.htm

DODGER STADIUM

NOTES

1. Scott Ostler, "Suddenly, the Hugging Turns to Punching," *Los Angeles Times*, August 21, 1978: 32. Sutton's entire quote, as republished in the *Los Angeles Times* was as follows: "This nation gets infatuated with a few names. All you hear about on our team is Steve Garvey, the All-American boy. Well, the best player on this team for the last two years – and we all know it is – is Reggie Smith. As Reggie goes, so goes us. Reggie doesn't go out and publicize himself. He doesn't smile at the right people or say the right things. He tells the truth, even if it sometimes alienates people. Reggie is not a façade or a Madison Avenue image. Reggie and Richie Allen are the two most totally misrepresented players I ever met. They're wonderful people with wrong reputations."

2. Marc Maturo, "Dodger Blue Turns Red During 'Family' Scrap," *White Plains* (New York) *Reporter Dispatch*, August 21, 1978: 25.

3. Gordon Verrell, "Garvey-Sutton Tussle Ignited Dodger Express," *The Sporting News*, October 14, 1978: 35.

4. "Dodger Coach Jim Gilliam Dies," *Modesto* (California) *Bee*, October 9, 1978: 17.

5. "More Than 2,000 Attend Gilliam Funeral, *Los Angeles Times*, October 12, 1978: 67.

6. Ross Newhan, "Cey Magnifique and So Is Welch," *Los Angeles Times*, October 12, 1978: 54.

7. Milton Richman, "Welch's 11 Pitches Frustrate Yankees," *Buffalo Evening News*, October 12, 1978: 6.

8. Ostler, 32.

9. Hal Bodley, "Rookie Reliever Welch Strikes Out Jackson with Two on in Ninth to Wrap Up 4-3 Win," *Battle Creek* (Michigan) *Enquirer*, October 12, 1978: 19.

10. Richman.

THE 1980 ALL-STAR GAME

July 9. 1980: National League All-Stars 4, American League All-Stars 2

by Gary Sarnoff

"Here they have the All-Star Game, and they are holding it for the first time in Dodger Stadium, where more people see baseball games than anywhere else in the country," wrote the *Chicago Tribune's* Richard Dozer.[1] The Chicago sportswriter noted that being close to Hollywood fit this game perfectly, because Steve Stone, a mediocre pitcher until this season, would be the American League's starter.

Steve Stone said when you are a .500 pitcher, you don't receive honors. "All of the sudden, I'm the player of the week, the pitcher of the month, and the All-Star starter," Stone said.[2] Before the start of the 1980 baseball season, the Orioles right-handed pitcher had a 78-79 lifetime record. "I used to go to the mound determined to avoid losing," said the veteran hurler, who was six days away from his 33rd birthday. "Now, I go out to win. I know I'm going to win."[3]

The starting pitcher for the National League was Astros ace J.R. Richard, who was 10-4 and owned a 1.96 ERA with 115 strikeouts in 110⅓ innings pitched. "My attitude has always been that I've got a job to do," said Richard. "And it doesn't matter who I am pitching against or what time of day it is."[4] The time of day was expected to help Richard and his blazing fastball. This All-Star Game was scheduled to start at 5:40 P.M., when the batters would be looking directly into a glaring sunset. In addition, Richard had a 7-2 lifetime career record at Dodger Stadium. But all was not good for Richard. He had been forced to leave nine of his 16 starts this season because of arm, shoulder, and back discomforts. "I called to ask J.R. if he was able to pitch and he said nothing was wrong and he'd be ready to go three innings," said National League manager Chuck Tanner.[5] To be safe, Astros manager Bill Virdon asked Tanner to remove Richard after two innings.

Would the AL finally win for the first time since 1971? Would it snap its eight-game losing-streak and 16 losses in the previous 17 midsummer classics?

If things weren't bad enough, three would-be starters were injured. "What could be worse for a manager than having George Brett, Jim Rice, and Paul Molitor on your bench and not be able to use them," said American League President Lee MacPhail.[6] The National League would also be minus a starter. Mike Schmidt was injured and would not play.

Before a Dodger Stadium record crowd of 56,088, the first batter of the game, Willie Randolph, grounded out, but Rod Carew followed with a walk, stole second, and advanced to third on another groundout. With a runner on third and two outs, Reggie Jackson came to the plate. After falling behind, 3-and-1, Richard threw two sliders past Jackson to end the inning.

Stone took the mound in the bottom of the first knowing he had an advantage with the opposing batters having to face the sun. Throwing primarily fastballs, Stone retired the National Leaguers in order. In the top of the second, a walk and a base hit by Bucky Dent sandwiched two outs to put runners on the corners, but Richard struck out Stone to end the inning. In the bottom of the second, Stone once again worked a three-up-three down inning.

As requested, Chuck Tanner replaced Richard after two innings. "My arm feels great," Richard said after his outing. "I could have thrown three innings, easily."[7] Willie Randolph greeted new pitcher Bob Welch with a single to lead off the inning, and then, with Carew at the plate, he proceeded to get picked off. "Nobody told me Welch had a good move," Randolph complained after the game.[8] The pickoff proved costly. Carew followed with a double down the left-field line and moved to third on a wild pitch. Then Fred Lynn struck out and Jackson walked, but Ben Oglivie struck out to end the inning.

In the bottom of the third, Stone retired the National League in order. He had faced nine batters and retired all nine on just 30 pitches.[9] "I couldn't look at this lineup as a group," explained Stone. "I had to face each one as a single entity. As a group, it would have seemed too big a task. But, one by one, I was able to handle each guy."[10] In the bottom of the fourth, Tommy John replaced Stone and, like Stone, he retired the National League in order.

The American Leaguers had put a baserunner on third base in the first three innings but failed to score. They went down in order in the top of the fourth, but in the top of the fifth they finally scored. After Welch retired the first two batters, Carew singled for his second straight hit and Lynn launched a 340-foot fly ball down the right-field line and into the seats for a home run. As Lynn trotted around the bases, the National Leaguers talked to one another. "I guess we can see the ball now," said NL outfielder Reggie Smith.[11]

Tommy John retired the first two batters in the National League fifth to extend the National League's streak to 4 1/2 innings without a baserunner. But according to the next batter, Ken Griffey, who had a .422 lifetime batting average against John, the streak was about to end. "I'm going up there and will hit a home run," he told a teammate.[12] And as he had predicted, he drove one over the 395-foot marking on the right-center-field fence to cut the American League lead to 2-1.

Jerry Reuss took the hill for the National League in the top of the sixth and struck out the side. With one out in the bottom of the inning, Ray Knight singled and Phil Garner reached base on a grounder mishandled by second baseman Randolph. "It was not an easy play but a play the Yankees second baseman had probably made many times in the past," wrote Ken Nigro of the *Baltimore Sun*.[13] "That ball was hit like a bullet. It shot by me," said Randolph.[14] George Hendrick followed with the third straight hit of the inning to advance the baserunners two bases and score Knight to tie the game, 2-2. Now with runners on first and third and one out, AL manager Earl Weaver called on White Sox reliever Ed Farmer to face Padres slugger Dave Winfield, who grounded a ball that Randolph mishandled for an error. Garner scored from third on the misplay for a 3-2 National League lead. "It was a difficult play," Weaver said in defense of Randolph.[15] "It came to me like a knuckle ball," said Randolph. "I tried to short hop it, but the ball shot over me."[16]

After Pirates pitcher Jim Bibby retired the American League in order in the top of the seventh, Ken Griffey, on his way to the game's Most Valuable Player Award, began the National League seventh with his second straight hit. Reds shortstop Dave Concepción followed by grounding into a force out at second base, but a wild pitch, a passed ball, and another wild pitch by Dave Steib propelled Concepción around the bases for a 4-2 NL lead. In the top of the eighth, Cubs closer Bruce Sutter, who had allowed no runs and struck out five while pitching 3⅔ innings in the previous two All-Star Games, took the mound for the NL. "Having Sutter in there at the end of the game is like having an insurance policy," said Cardinals All-Star first baseman Keith Hernandez.[17] As expected, Sutter set the American League down in order in the top of the eighth, retired the junior circuit in the ninth inning, and struck out Lance Parrish for the game's final out. Once again the National League prevailed, in a 4-2 win.

"It's very disappointing when you lose, especially when you're managing," said American League manager Weaver. "We did everything we could to win, and there's not much you can say except accept defeat."[18]

"Even when behind I wasn't worried," NL manager Chuck Tanner said in the victorious team's locker room. "I knew we had the bats to blow it open any time."[19]

"My pitches weren't moving well," Tommy John said about his performance. "I was probably throwing a little harder than I should have. In an All-Star Game you get pumped up and you tend to throw balls a little harder."[20]

In the National League's locker room, Reuss handed Sutter the game ball. Sutter tossed it back. "You won it; you keep it," Sutter said. Reuss then asked Sutter to sign it for him.[21]

SOURCES

In addition to the sources cited in the Notes, the author consulted Baseball-Reference.com and Retrosheet.org.

https://www.baseball-reference.com/allstar/1980-allstar-game.shtml

https://www.retrosheet.org/boxesetc/1980/YAS_1980.htm

NOTES

1   Richard Dozer, "Stone Adds Hollywood Touch to All-Stars," *Chicago Tribune*, July 8, 1980: 6-1.

2   Ken Nigro, "Birds' Stone Faces Astros' Richard in All-Star Game Tonight in L.A.," *Baltimore Sun*, July 8, 1980: C-7.

3   Dozer, 6-3.

4   Ross Newhan, "Richard Named Starting Pitcher for NL Tonight," *Los Angeles Times*, July 8, 1980: 3-6.

5   Harry Shattuck, "Arm 'No Problem' for All-Star Starter Richard," *Houston Chronicle*, July 8, 1980: 2-1.

6   Nigro, "Birds' Stone Faces Astros' Richard in All-Star Game Tonight in L.A."

7   Harry Shattuck, "J.R. Shows He Can Still Hurl Fine," *Houston Chronicle*, July 9, 1980: 2-1.

8   Ed Fowler, "Defense Key to NL Win," *Houston Chronicle*, July 9, 1980: 2-1.

9   Baseball-Reference.com shows 30 pitches. According to *Baltimore Sun* sportswriter Ken Nigro, "Stone threw only 24 pitches and was ahead of almost every National League batter." See "Stone Perfect, but NL Beats AL Stars, 4-2," *Baltimore Sun*, July 9, 1980: C-5.

10   "Stone Perfect, but NL Beats AL All Stars, 4-2."

11   Richard Hoffer, "NL's Dominance a Matter of Talent, Not Luck – Smith," *Los Angeles Times*, July 9, 1980: 3-10.

12   "Griffey, Reds Shine as NL Tops AL Again, 4-2," *Cincinnati Enquirer*, July 9, 1980: C-1. Before this game Griffey had a .422 batting average against Tommy John. During his career Griffey batted .431 against John.

13   Nigro, "Stone Perfect, but NL Beats AL All Stars, 4-2."

14   Murray Chass, "National League Rallies to Win 9th Straight All-Star Game, 4-2," *New York Times*, July 9, 1980: D17.

15   Richard Dozer, "NL Saves Its Best for Last," *Chicago Tribune*, July 9, 1980: 5-5.

16   Chass.

17   Joseph Durso, "Pitching Credited for Triumph," *New York Times*, July 9, 1980: D17.

18   Nigro, "Stone Perfect, but NL Beats AL All Stars, 4-2."

19   Fowler, "Defense Key to NL Win."

20   Chass, "National League Rallies to Win 9th Straight All-Star Game, 4-2."

2   Richard Dozer, "NL Saves Its Best for Last."

DODGERS FORCE NL WEST SHOWDOWN

October 5, 1980: Los Angeles Dodgers 4, Houston Astros 3

by Mike Bell

Going into the final weekend of the 1980 season, both National League division races were yet to be decided. In the East, Mike Schmidt of the Philadelphia Phillies took care of business with one swing of the bat in an extra-inning game against the second-place Montreal Expos on the season's final Saturday. Out West, the Los Angeles Dodgers were trailing the visiting Houston Astros by three games. Houston manager Bill Virdon's hungry team needed to win one game to clinch the first pennant in their 19-year history. They were in first place for 102 days during the season but could not shake off the Dodgers, who never trailed Houston by more than 3½ games.

By early October it looked as though the Astros might finally pull away, having won 9 of 12 games

Outfielder Manny Mota played the last 13 years of his career as a Dodger and excelled as a pinch-hitter.

going into the final series with the Dodgers. The Dodgers would have to sweep the series to keep their season alive and force a one-game playoff with Houston to decide the division title. Second baseman Joe Morgan, in his second tour with the Astros, provided the swagger by saying before the Friday opener, "There's no way they can win four games in a row from us."[1] He ended up being right in the long run, but not before a near-epic collapse under the pressure of meaningful late-season baseball in the hostile confines of Dodger Stadium.

The series began with a Friday night game that ended on a line-drive home run hit by Joe Ferguson into the left-field pavilion on the first pitch of the bottom of the 10th inning, giving the Dodgers a come-from-behind 3-2 victory. Game two featured Dodgers lefty Jerry Reuss against Houston's Nolan Ryan, whom the Astros had signed as a free agent in the offseason. This time it was All-Star Steve Garvey driving a Ryan fastball into the bleachers in the bottom of the fourth inning, giving the Dodgers a 2-1 lead that Reuss protected with a gutsy, complete-game victory.

The largest crowd of the season, 52,339, showed up to witness the final showdown. The Astros struck first, knocking out Dodgers starter Burt Hooton in the second inning, scoring two runs on three hits and an error committed by Hooton himself. Dodgers manager Tom Lasorda brought in long reliever Bobby Castillo, who grew up two miles from Dodger Stadium. He pitched out of a two-on, no-out jam with no further damage.

Astros starter Vern Ruhle gave way after yielding a leadoff single to Derrel Thomas (also a Los Angeles native) in the top of the third. Virdon summoned Joaquín Andújar, who blanked the Dodgers for two innings. Houston scored a run in the top of the fourth off Castillo on a two-out double by Terry Puhl, scoring Alan Ashby. The Astros led 3-0 after four innings.

Castillo put down the Astros in order in the top of the fifth, his fourth crucial inning of work. The Dodgers broke through in the bottom half off Andújar. With one out, Thomas, pinch-hitter Gary Thomasson, and leadoff hitter Davey Lopes hit consecutive singles leading to Los Angeles' first run. Joe Sambito relieved Andújar and threw one pitch, which Mickey Hatcher hit into an inning-ending double play. The Astros had a 3-1 lead after five innings.

In the sixth inning, Lasorda brought in 19-year-old Fernando Valenzuela, who had yet to ignite the phenomenon known as Fernandomania. The young lefty coolly shut down the Astros over the next two innings. Sambito was ambushed by the lower part of the Dodgers order in the seventh. Singles by Pedro Guerrero and Ferguson and a bunt by Thomas put runners on second and third with one-out. Lasorda opted not to pinch-run for the slow-footed Ferguson even though he had speedy Rudy Law on the bench. He told reporters after the game, "If we had lost the game, I would have hung myself and you guys would have been the pall bearers."[2]

Dodgers legend Manny Mota had retired after the 1979 season, his 18th in the big leagues and his 11th with the Dodgers. He spent 1980 as their first-base coach. With the season on the line, the coach became the player once more. He was activated for the September pennant chase.

Batting for Valenzuela, Mota worked the count to 2-and-2, then slapped a soft liner into short right field for the Dodgers' second run. Guerrero scored, Ferguson went to third, and Mota took second on the throw. It was Mota's 150th career pinch hit and the last of his long career.[3]

Frank LaCorte relieved Sambito and snuffed out the fire. Astros 3, Dodgers 2 after seven. Dodgers rookie reliever Steve Howe came on in the eighth inning. He got through the inning with no damage. Garvey led off the bottom of the eighth with a grounder to third that Enos Cabell could not handle and was safe at first on the error. This brought up wounded warrior Ron Cey. The stocky third baseman was asked to bunt Garvey to second. With a sore hamstring tightly taped, the nearly immobile Cey flailed at his two bunt attempts and was quickly down two strikes. A few pitches later, he had worked up a full count against the right-hander LaCorte. Cey fouled off three straight high fastballs, the first one off his front foot requiring a staggering, grimacing walk around the batter's box before he stepped back in and fouled the next two straight back. Then, on the 10th pitch of the at-bat, LaCorte threw

one a little lower in the zone and Cey launched it into the left-field pavilion for a 4-3 Dodgers lead.

As Cey limped around the bases, the Dodger Stadium crowd's celebration rattled the ballpark. LaCorte was able to get through the rest of inning, and Howe went to the mound in the top of the ninth to close the game. He got the first out, but two singles and a groundout later put Astros on the corners with two outs and pinch-hitter deluxe Denny Walling coming to the plate.

Two stories offer insight on what happened next. In another unconventional move, Lasorda went to the mound with the season on the line, took out his young reliever and brought in the veteran Don Sutton. Sutton had pitched eight strong innings two days before and was not expecting to pitch in this game, being spared to start in Philadelphia should the Dodgers pull off the four-game sweep. Dodgers historian Mark Langill relates one version of the events: At some point in the game Sandy Koufax, of all people, went looking for Sutton and found him in the clubhouse relaxing and about to imbibe in a glass of wine. Before Sutton drank, Koufax suggested that he refrain and stay loose in case he was needed in a pinch.[4] Another report indicates it was the injured Reggie Smith, not able to play, who suggested to Lasorda that Sutton stay ready. Either way, the 35-year-old owner of 230 career Dodgers victories and exactly four career saves was ready in the bullpen when Lasorda needed him.[5]

It took two pitches to induce Walling into a game-ending groundout and unleash utter pandemonium at Chavez Ravine. The Dodgers had done what they needed to do; they swept the Astros three straight and forced the fifth season-ending tiebreaker in National League history. At Anaheim Stadium that afternoon, where the Los Angeles Rams were trouncing the San Francisco 49ers, the game had to be stopped three times because of crowd noise. Fans listening to Vin Scully broadcast the Dodgers game on radio were roaring so loudly that the quarterback could not be heard calling plays on the field.[6]

Sutton, who had also pulled a stint as first-base coach when Mota came into the game, said, "It's about time I slammed the door, after all the times they've done it for me."[7] The 1980 National League ERA leader would be a free agent after the season, ending his 15-year run with the Dodgers on a very high note.[8]

Turns out it was an anticlimactic high note. The next day, in the Los Angeles sun and smog and in front of another huge crowd, Dodgers starter Dave Goltz was shelled early, and despite more stellar relief from the young trio of Castillo, Valenzuela, and Howe, Astros knuckleballer Joe Niekro shut down the Dodgers lineup – minus Cey – for his 20th win of the season. The Astros were not, in fact, beaten four times in a row by "that team" as Joe Morgan predicted. Instead Houston ended the 163-game 1980 regular baseball season with a very quiet 7-1 defeat of the Dodgers.[9]

AUTHOR'S NOTE

I was at the first of these three games (October 3) and I can attest to how exciting they were. I credit that series, along with the advent of the new full-color video scoreboard (Diamond Vision, unveiled at the 1980 All-Star Game), with creating an entirely new fan experience at Dodger Stadium that has only got better over the years.

SOURCES

In addition to the sources cited in the Notes, the author consulted Baseball-Reference.com and Retrosheet.org.

https://www.baseball-reference.com/boxes/LAN/LAN198010050.shtml

https://www.retrosheet.org/boxesetc/1980/B10050LAN1980.htm

NOTES

1   Gordon Verrell, "Astros Escape Dodger Clutches in Playoff," *The Sporting News,* October 18, 1980: 35.

2   David Leon Moore, "Another Day, Another Dodger Miracle," *San Bernardino* (California) *Sun,* October 6, 1980: C4.

3   Mota had previously broken Smoky Burgess's pinch-hit record on September 28, 1979, with his 146th career pinch hit. Mota's final record of 150 pinch hits was surpassed by Lenny Harris of the New York Mets on October 6, 2001. (Harris finished his career with 212 pinch hits.)

4   Ron Cey (host), "We'll See About That with Ron Cey," Podcast Episode 21 Mark Langill, March 28, 2023. https://wewillseeaboutthatcey.blogspot.com/2023/03/blog-post.html.

5   David Leon Moore, "Thanks to Sutton, L.A. Breathes Sigh of Relief," *San Bernardino Sun,* October 6, 1980: C4.

6   Paul Oberjuerge, "Powerhouse Rams Blow Away 49ers, 48-26," *San Bernardino Sun,* October 6, 1980: C4.

7   Moore, "Thanks to Sutton, L.A. Breathes Sigh of Relief."

8   Sutton returned to the Dodgers in 1988. He won three games and lost six for the eventual World Series champions before being released on August 10.

9   The Philadelphia Phillies beat the Astros in the best-of-five National League Championship Series.

OPENING DAY 1981 AND THE BIRTH OF FERNANDOMANIA

April 9, 1981: Los Angeles Dodgers 2, Houston Astros 0

by Jason Scheller

On Opening Day in 1981, the Los Angeles Dodgers found themselves in the peculiar position of needing a starting pitcher. Normally, they would have gone with a veteran who would – they hoped – mow down opposing batters while Dodgers fans looked on in awe, cheering their team to victory. This day was different.

Jerry Reuss, the 1980 National League Cy Young Award runner-up and the ace of the Dodgers' rotation, was a late scratch after a calf muscle he had strained the day before left him unable to walk. The number-two starter, Burt Hooten, had just had a procedure to remove an ingrown toenail, which took him out of contention for the starting job. The third man in the Dodgers' rotation, Bob Welch, was recovering from a bone spur in his elbow, while the two men at the bottom of the rotation, Dave Goltz and Rick Sutcliffe, were healthy scratches for the opener. Both had pitched in an exhibition series against the California Angels just prior to the season opener.[1] That left southpaw Fernando Valenzuela as the lone option to start the game against the formidable Houston Astros, who had ended the Dodgers' season the previous year in a one-game tiebreaker.

Additionally, the Astros had signed former Dodgers pitching great Don Sutton in the offseason, a move that Dodgers manager Tommy Lasorda seemed to take in stride. "We knew there was a possibility of losing Don Sutton (who played out his option and signed with the Astros), so we had to plan ahead." Speaking of Valenzuela, Lasorda said, "We were looking at him as the replacement for Don."[2] Valenzuela made quite a debut after getting promoted to the Dodgers in September 1980. He threw 17⅔ shutout innings, allowed just eight hits, and struck out 16. The native of Etchohuaquila, Sonora, Mexico, went 2-0.

The April 9 game was a David vs. Goliath matchup. Valenzuela was 20 years old and the first rookie to start on Opening Day in the team's history. To make matters worse, many in the crowd of 50,511 struggled to understand why he was pitching. Blissfully unaware of the fans' apprehension, Valenzuela pitched batting practice, then went into the training room and took a nap before jogging out to the bullpen and then onto the field as the Opening Day festivities began.

Making the situation even more comical, Valenzuela threw a screwball, a pitch that no one else had thrown with regularity since Carl Hubbell in the 1930s. Hubbell used that pitch in the 1934 All-Star Game to strike out, in order, Babe Ruth, Lou Gehrig, Jimmie Foxx, Al Simmons, and Joe Cronin, all future Hall of Famers.[3]

Valenzuela was opposed by Joe Niekro, who together with his brother and fellow knuckleball pitcher Phil, would eventually post a total of 539 wins, the most by any pair of brothers in the major leagues.[4] The previous season, Niekro had pitched the Astros to a 7-1 victory over the Dodgers in a one-game tiebreaker for the National League West title.[5] The Astros were unfazed by Valenzuela. Astros pitcher Joe Sambito said, "When we heard that Reuss wasn't going to start and that we were going up against a rookie, we felt we had a much better chance against [Valenzuela] than the veteran all-star."[6]

When Valenzuela took the mound to start the game, the Astros were ready to pounce on the untested rookie, but they were in for a surprise. Valenzuela's delivery befuddled everyone, including Astros hitters. With his hands clasped he reached toward the sky, while simultaneously lifting his right leg and his eyes toward the heavens, as if to ask for divine intervention, before delivering his pitch. Valenzuela threw a screwball to Astros leadoff hitter Terry Puhl, who hit a grounder to shortstop for the first recorded out of the game. Craig Reynolds then singled to center field, but Valenzuela retired the next two batters. Niekro held the Dodgers hitters in check in the bottom of the first inning. Davey Lopes flied out to left field to start the inning. Ken Landreaux doubled, but Niekro got Dusty Baker and Steve Garvey to fly out.

Valenzuela walked Art Howe to start the second, and Howe got to second when Dave Roberts flied out to center field and to third with two outs on Dickie Thon's groundball to second. But Luis Pujols' popup to first retired the side. Niekro dealt with a threat of his own in the second. After Pedro Guerrero singled to right field and stole second, Niekro struck out Mike Scioscia and got Bill Russell to ground out to shortstop to end the inning. With two innings down, both sides seemed equally matched, and both pitchers settled in for the long haul.

Valenzuela and Niekro pitched scoreless third innings. In the top of the fourth, Valenzuela recorded his first strikeout of the game, against César Cedeño. The Dodgers broke the ice when Garvey tripled to right field in the bottom of the fourth and scored on Cey's fly to left field.

Pitching with a 1-0 lead, Valenzuela worked around an infield hit by Pujols in the fifth, striking out pitcher Niekro to retire the side. Niekro allowed a walk and a single in the bottom of the fifth inning but Landreaux's fly ball ended the inning.

"Fernando was using mostly his fastball and curve in the first few innings, then started working the screwball in," Dodgers catcher Scioscia said after the game. "From the sixth through the ninth he had awesome command of everything."[7] Valenzuela's only trouble came in the top of the sixth inning, when Reynolds smacked a one-out single into center field and Cedeño doubled to put runners in scoring position. But Valenzuela retired José Cruz on a lineout to shortstop and followed that by collecting Howe's comebacker and throwing him out to end the inning.[8]

In the bottom of the sixth, Garvey hit a one-out single to left field. Cey blooped a hit that bounced off home plate, Astros catcher Pujols grabbed the ball and threw out Cey as Garvey went to second base. On a wild pitch to Pedro Guerrero, Garvey took third base. Guerrero then walloped a line drive to left field just of Cruz's reach, scoring Garvey making the Dodgers' lead 2-0.

Niekro was replaced by Dave Smith to start the eighth; Smith blanked the Dodgers. In the Astros'

ninth, Valenzuela gave up a two-out single to Howe, then ended the game with a screwball to strike out Dave Roberts. After retiring 11 of the last 12 batters to post a five-hit shutout, Valenzuela said, "I mixed in the fastball, slider, and screwball early but the last three innings it was almost all screwballs. … That's my pitch, and when I need the big outs that's what I go to."[9]

While the victory over the Astros provided a measure of retribution for the playoff loss in 1980, the game is better remembered as the birth of "Fernandomania." It marked the beginning of a string of victories that made Valenzuela the star of the league and a hero to Dodgers fans. Sportswriter Paul Oberjuerge summed up fans' feelings when he wrote, "Enroll me in the Fernando Valenzuela fan club. Any guy who can get people out despite that Pillsbury Doughboy physique is all right in my book."[10] In this Opening Day victory, a star was born for the Los Angeles Dodgers, one that would continue to shine brightly for many years to come.

SOURCES

In addition to the sources cited in the Notes, the author consulted Baseball-Reference, Retrosheet, Baseball Almanac, Stats Crew, and the Fernando Valenzuela player file at the National Baseball Hall of Fame.

Thanks to Dodgers team historian Mark Langill and Rachel Wells at the National Baseball Hall of Fame, as well as Joy and Pat Scheller, Holly Scheller, and Greg Fowler for their support. In memory of Rick Bush.

https://www.baseball-reference.com/boxes/LAN/LAN198104090.shtml

https://www.retrosheet.org/boxesetc/1981/B04090LAN1981.htm

NOTES

1   Erik Sherman, *Daybreak at Chavez Ravine: Fernandomania and the Remaking of the Los Angeles Dodgers* (Lincoln: University of Nebraska Press, 2023), 55.

2   Mike Davis, "Valenzuela Crafts 5-hitter, Blanks Astros in 1st Start," *San Bernardino County* (California) *Sun*, April 10, 1981: 64.

3   Stew Thornley, "July 10, 1934: Carl Hubbell Strikes Out Five Hall of Famers in a Row at All-Star Game," https://sabr.org/gamesproj/game/july-10-1934-carl-hubbell-strikes-out-five-hall-of-famers-in-a-row-at-all-star-game/, accessed November 24, 2023.

4   Sherman, 56.

5   "Chubby Rookie Blanks Astros, 2-0," *Santa Cruz* (California) *Sentinel*, April 10, 1981: 48.

6   Sherman, 56.

7   "Valenzuela Crafts 5-hitter, Blanks Astros in 1st Start."

8   Sherman, 58.

9   Logan Hobson (United Press International), "Dodger Rookie Baffles Astros," *Ukiah* (California) *Daily Journal*, April 10, 1981: 4; Jason Turbow, *They Bled Blue: Fernandomania, Strike Season Mayhem, and the Weirdest Championship Baseball Had Ever Seen: The 1981 Los Angeles Dodgers* (Boston: Houghton Mifflin Harcourt, 2019), 53.

10 Paul Oberjuerge, "Fernando Has Dodgers in Fat City," *San Bernardino County Sun*, April 15, 1981: 21.

REUSS, RYAN, AND A FITTING END TO A PITCHER-DOMINATED PLAYOFF SERIES

October 11, 1981: Los Angeles Dodgers 4, Houston Astros 0
(Game Five of the National League Division Series)

by John Bauer

The Los Angeles Dodgers and Houston Astros played several high-stakes, season-deciding games in 1980 and 1981. In 1980 the Dodgers needed a sweep of the Astros over the final weekend to force a playoff. They got the sweep but lost the tiebreaker game, and Houston qualified for its first postseason. The split-season format resulting from the 1981 players strike led to a division series between the winners of the two halves. The Cincinnati Reds had the best overall record, but the NL West Division championship would be decided between the Dodgers and Astros.

Houston opened with two wins at the Astrodome before the series shifted to Dodger Stadium, and Los Angeles required another sweep. The Dodgers won the next two, setting up a deciding Game Five.

The Game Five pitching matchup suggested that runs would be at a premium. Nolan Ryan had been masterly against the Dodgers in two prior outings. On September 26 Ryan no-hit the Dodgers while registering 11 strikeouts. In Game One of the Division Series, Ryan allowed two hits and a single run for the win. Before the game, Ryan exhibited the confidence of the proverbial man in the arena. He said, "I love these situations. I'm a lot happier being a participant than a spectator. … The Dodgers aren't going to beat me."[1] Ryan's previous starts were made at the Astrodome, however, and he entered Game Five with a 0-5 career record at Dodger Stadium.

Jerry Reuss was not the same sort of pitcher as Ryan. Reuss never racked up large strikeout totals; instead, he relied on groundballs easily vacuumed up by the Dodgers infielders. Former teammate and current Astros starter Don Sutton commented, "Jerry has had one of the great invisible seasons any pitcher has

ever had."[2] His quiet efficiency had perhaps been lost amid the excitement around Fernando Valenzuela's rookie campaign, but the Astros should have taken note. In addition to going 10-4 with a 2.30 ERA, Reuss had pitched 26 innings against Houston in 1981 and allowed only two runs, including nine scoreless frames in a Game Two loss in extra innings. Before Game Five, Reuss mused, "Everybody thinks about a situation like this where everything comes down directly to your performance."[3]

In the top of the first, Reuss set down the Astros in order with two fly balls and a groundout. In the Dodgers first, a Phil Garner two-out error allowed Dusty Baker to reach base, but Steve Garvey's grounder to Art Howe ended the inning. The pitchers' duel was on.

Reuss worked out of some jams in the next two innings, and it seemed likely that the occasion had him amped up. He later observed, "The ball was all over the place, The ball was jumping around. I might just have been too damn excited."[4] In the second, José Cruz singled to left with one out and Denny Walling reached base on shortstop Bill Russell's error. Reuss, though, recovered to get grounders from Dickie Thon and Alan Ashby to retire the Astros. Reuss walked Ryan to open the third, followed by a fielder's choice with Terry Puhl at bat. Puhl stole second to get into scoring position. Again, Reuss induced grounders when he needed them as Garner and Tony Scott bounced balls to third baseman Pedro Guerrero. Meanwhile, Ryan walked Guerrero in the Dodgers second; Guerrero worked his way to third before Russell's fly ball to Cruz in left field ended the inning. In the Dodgers third, Davey Lopes's one-out single and Thon's throwing error on a groundball from Ken Landreaux placed Dodgers at second and third with one out. The inning ended without further incident as Thon cleanly fielded a popup from Baker and a grounder from Garvey.

After five scoreless frames, the first crooked number arrived on the scoreboard in the sixth. Initially, it seemed the Astros might take the lead. Reuss allowed a leadoff walk to Scott, but the Astros center fielder was thrown out attempting to steal second base with Howe at bat. Howe singled to right and Houston fans had to wonder if Scott would have scored had his theft attempt been successful. Reuss gave up another walk, this time to Cruz. With two on and one out, Reuss dodged another threat. Catcher Mike Scioscia claimed Walling's pop fly in foul territory and Russell gathered Thon's grounder to force Cruz at second.

After Landreaux led off the Dodgers sixth with a fly out, Baker and Ryan squared off in a nine-pitch battle. With the count full, Ryan's eighth pitch resulted in a pop foul, but a potentially decisive one. Walling, playing first base after César Cedeño pulled a hamstring in Game Four,[5] drifted into foul territory but lost the ball in the sun. He turned and pointed upward as if to direct the sprinting Garner to the ball. Garner, though, was unable to cover enough ground from second base as the ball landed on the warning track. Ryan's next pitch was low and Baker claimed first base. Afterward, Ryan called the walk the "turning point."[6]

Baker attempted three times to steal second base, but Garvey fouled off pitches each time. With a 2-and-2 count and Thon cheating toward second base, Garvey's grounder found a hole between Howe and Thon. Dodger Stadium came alive with runners at the corners and Rick Monday coming to the plate. Monday hit a liner into right, allowing Baker to score the game's first run and advancing Garvey to second. After Guerrero popped up to Garner for the second out, Scioscia whacked a first-pitch curveball into center field to score Garvey for a 2-0 lead. The Dodgers added one more run when Russell's chopper to Howe led to an off-balance throw that required Walling to reach for the ball in the direction of the charging Russell. The resulting contact caused the ball to roll away and scored Monday from second. The Dodgers led, 3-0. Ryan struck out Reuss for the third out, but it seemed inconsequential. When Reuss came out for the seventh, he was in a more relaxed frame of mind. He said, "When we got that field goal, I was happy as hell."[7]

Ashby started the seventh by hitting a hopper to Guerrero, who muffed the play, allowing Ashby

to reach on the error. Ryan's afternoon was confirmed over as Astros manager Bill Virdon opted for pinch-hitter Joe Pittman. He flied out to Baker in left, while Puhl's grounder to Garvey and Garner's fly to Landreaux left Ashby stranded. After the stretch, Dave Smith took the mound for Houston, but his appearance would not last long. Smith struck out Lopes for the first out before Landreaux drilled a pitch into Smith's left ankle. The comebacker had such force that the ricochet bounced into foul territory and was claimed by a fan reaching into the field. The result of the play was a ground-rule double, and Smith limped off the field. Virdon handed the ball to right-hander Frank LaCorte. After Baker flied to Scott for the second out, Garvey crushed LaCorte's pitch into deep left field. Cruz appeared to fight the glare in tracking the ball. As he sprinted toward the warning track, he reached out to make the catch. The ball bounced off Cruz's glove and away from him. Garvey was credited with an RBI triple as Landreaux scored to make it 4-0. Following an intentional walk to Monday, LaCorte struck out Guerrero to end the inning.

The remaining innings passed largely without incident, as Reuss prevented the Astros from mounting a comeback. With two outs in the ninth, Reuss struck out pinch-hitter Dave Roberts. The ball rolled away from Scioscia, though, and toward the backstop while Roberts headed to the dugout. With fans streaming onto the field, Scioscia chased down the ball as Roberts realized the situation and made a beeline for first base. The ball arrived before the runner, sparing Scioscia any blushes. Scioscia recalled the 1941 World Series in noting, "I was thinking shades of Mickey Owen there for a while."[8]

In postgame interviews, the anemic Astros offense and Reuss's incredible performance were the primary topics. Although it was generally accepted that Ryan was not at his best, the Astros ace opined, "If I pitch a shutout, we're still out there playing."[9] On the Dodgers side, Reuss had needed time to settle into the game, and he and his teammates knew it. Assessing his performance, Reuss observed, "I was struggling early. I was very keyed up. … We wanted to beat the team that beat us last year. After the team got three runs, I settled down and was able to put the ball anywhere I tried to."[10]

The Dodgers enjoyed a raucous clubhouse celebration that featured several players pouring beer down manager Tom Lasorda's pants. They would have to refocus in less than 48 hours. After winning their Division Series against Philadelphia in a decisive fifth game, the Montreal Expos headed to Dodger Stadium with the NL pennant at stake.

SOURCES

also consulted Baseball-Reference.com and Retrosheet.org, and viewed the NBC broadcast of the game, accessible at youtube.com.

https://www.baseball-reference.com/boxes/LAN/LAN198110110.shtml

https://www.retrosheet.org/boxesetc/1981/B10110LAN1981.htm

https://www.youtube.com/watch?v=6kZDWz7ZS1c

NOTES

1   Mike DalNegro, "The Gang of Four Shoots to the Top," *Sports Illustrated*, October 19, 1981: 44-45.

2   Mike Littwin, "Dodgers Get Even, but Are Astros Ahead?" *Los Angeles Times*, October 11, 1981: Part III, 11.

3   Littwin, "Dodgers Get Even, but Are Astros Ahead?"

4   Mark Heisler, "This Time Dodgers Get to Keep the title," *Los Angeles Times*, October 12, 1981: Part III, 1.

5   George Vecsey, "Dodgers Win, 4-0, Take Western Crown," *New York Times*, October 12, 1981: C1.

6   Vecsey.

7   Heisler.

8   Heisler. In 1941 the Yankees trailed the Brooklyn Dodgers, 4-3, with two outs in the top of the ninth of Game Four. Yankees right fielder Tommy Henrich swung and missed for strike three but the ball got past Dodgers catcher Mickey Owen and rolled to the backstop. Instead of the game ending with a Dodgers win that would have evened the Series at two wins apiece, Henrich reached base and the Yankees rallied for a 7-4 win. The Yankees won the next day, 3-1, to win the Series.

9   Mike Littwin, "Astros Pitchers Had No Chance," *Los Angeles Times*, October 12, 1981: Part III, 1.

10 Vecsey.

DODGERS COMPLETE HOME SWEEP OF YANKEES TO TAKE DRIVER'S SEAT IN 78TH FALL CLASSIC

October 25, 1981: Los Angeles Dodgers 2, New York Yankees 1
(Game Five of the 1981 World Series)

by Chad Moody

On October 19, 1981, the Los Angeles Dodgers came from behind to defeat the Montreal Expos in the rubber match of the National League Championship Series. The next day, they found themselves in New York for Game One of the World Series against their long-time "bitter" adversary, the Yankees.[1] The well-rested Yankees had swept the Oakland A's in the ALCS five days earlier.

The Yankees held an 8-2 lead over the Dodgers in Series matchups, with each team boasting more October appearances than any other team in its league. The "wildest, most exciting World Series rivalry" dated back to 1941, when the then-crosstown Brooklyn Dodgers were "just a nickel subway ride" away from the Bronx.[2] The '81 Series would be the third time in the past five campaigns that the two teams battled for baseball's biggest prize, with the Yankees having won the previous two. No two teams had met in the fall classic more times.

Due to an extra playoff series added to the strike-shortened season, the 78th World Series was pushed later than ever into October. The home teams held serve in the first four contests to deadlock the Series at two games each. The critical Game Five, scheduled for Sunday, October 25, would be the last of a three-game set at Dodger Stadium before the Series headed back east to wrap up in the "city and venue that had not been all that kind to [the Dodgers] on many occasions in the past."[3] Dodgers shortstop Bill Russell said of playing in Yankee Stadium: "The fans unnerved us. They never let up on you. They have no courtesy at all. They're obnoxious. The worst."[4]

The Game Five pitching matchup featured Ron Guidry of New York against Jerry Reuss of Los Angeles. The same pair of fine southpaws had faced off in the Series opener, with the hard-throwing Guidry besting Reuss, who was knocked out of the box in the third inning. Despite his "tottering troops" – including prized free-agent acquisition Dave Winfield, who was hitless in the first four Series contests – having lost two in a row, demanding Yankees team owner George Steinbrenner delivered a pregame pep talk that was not of the expected fire-and-brimstone variety.[5] "It was more of a positive nature than anything," said slugging right fielder Reggie Jackson. "It was stressed on us that we haven't played well these past couple of days and that it was time we got back to doing the things that got us here. Time to start playing 'Yankee baseball.'"[6]

Pregame excitement was at a fever pitch in Chavez Ravine. "Breezy tailgate parties sprouted like weeds throughout the acres of parking lots," while many "frantic" fans were seen in desperate pursuit of tickets.[7] "It's very nice, actually," said Dodgers fan John Staves of the atmosphere outside the ballpark. "You get to meet a lot of nice people and throw food at Yankee fans."[8] However, some Angelenos' enthusiasm was perhaps tempered by their heroes' coming close but failing in several recent attempts to capture a championship with the same but now aging core talent. Indeed, Los Angeles's starting lineup was now chock full of veterans in their 30s. "If these Dodgers – in their current iteration, anyway – were going to win a title, they'd have to do it soon," wrote baseball author Jason Turbow.[9] With hope springing eternal, the third largest crowd in Dodger Stadium history to that point, 56,115 – including many Hollywood celebrities – packed the stands for the afternoon tilt.[10]

The visitors opened the scoring in the top of the second inning. Jackson led off with an opposite-field ground-rule double down the line in left field. He went to third when Bob Watson reached base on a bouncing ball that second baseman Davey Lopes bobbled for an error – his first of three fielding miscues in the game. Lou Piniella delivered a single to score Jackson. Despite the Yankees still threatening with no outs, Reuss escaped potential big trouble by getting Rick Cerone to hit into a double play and Aurelio Rodríguez to ground out.

New York's 1-0 lead held until the bottom of the seventh as Reuss and Guidry treated the crowd to a pitchers' duel. Considering that Guidry had not completed a game all season, Yankees manager Bob Lemon reportedly game-planned to pull his starter after seven innings and summon future Hall of Fame reliever Rich Gossage to begin the eighth.[11] In the end, Lemon did indeed stick to his plan but not before the Dodgers finally broke through against Guidry in his final scheduled frame. With one out and the bases empty, All-Star Pedro Guerrero homered and the next batter, catcher Steve Yeager, deposited a fastball into nearly the same spot in the left-center-field seats to give the Dodgers a 2-1 lead. "Guidry's tired," broadcaster Howard Cosell declared during the ABC telecast. "He's been tiring all year in the late innings."[12] After Yeager's blast, neither team scored the rest of the way to give Los Angeles a three-games-to-two lead as the Series returned to New York for Game Six.

Postgame commentary from Steinbrenner suggested that he and Lemon were not on the same page on how to handle the slightly built Guidry. "Ron Guidry pitched a great game," the owner said. "But I went over some numbers with Lem, and Guidry's earned-run average over the last three innings is 10-plus. We had a strategy – not to let him go more than six – and Lem didn't choose to go with it."[13]

Guidry's mound competition, Reuss, scattered five hits and three walks in going the distance to pick up the win. Deciding to "return to simplicity" after overthinking a mix of pitches in his ugly Series opener, the Dodgers' lefty went with his strength in giving the Yankees a "steady diet of fastballs."[14] "When I got

out on the mound here in Dodger Stadium, I said to myself, 'This is my valley and no one is going to tread on my valley,'" Reuss said after the game.[15]

The game's unlikely offensive hero, Reuss's weak-hitting batterymate Yeager, played so sparingly behind Mike Scioscia during the regular season that he requested a trade earlier in the year. "Their catcher [Yeager] had the game-winning hit and my catcher [Cerone] took us out of two game-winning rallies," Steinbrenner said in praising his opposition's backstop while being highly critical of his own.[16] Yeager had homered off Guidry in Game One and knocked in a key late-inning tiebreaking run a day earlier en route to Series co-MVP honors with teammates Guerrero and third baseman Ron Cey.

Nicknamed "Penguin" due to his waddling gait, Cey was involved in a frightening moment in the eighth inning when an errant 94-MPH fastball from Gossage struck him on the batting helmet. Cey fell to the ground as a "startled hush" swept through the ballpark.[17] "I was scared to death," admitted Dodgers manager Tom Lasorda.[18] Gossage was also "troubled by what his pitch had caused," despite being "booed heatedly" by the fans.[19] Cey never lost consciousness and was coherent during the few minutes he was down. Eventually he walked off with minimal assistance and was later diagnosed with a concussion. "No way was I throwing at him," Gossage said. "It was supposed to be down the middle. I usually try to throw my fastball down the middle, and against him I wanted to keep it up. Whew, it scares you."[20]

After the game, the colorful Lasorda sat in his office and joked about Cey with *Tonight Show* host Johnny Carson and "seemingly half of Southern California's show-business community," indicating that Cey was okay.[21] "He's coherent now," Lasorda laughingly said when asked about Cey's condition. "He was incoherent the last three weeks!"[22]

Drama was not limited only to the diamond, as Steinbrenner suffered a broken hand, swollen lip, and "an assortment of lumps and bruises" allegedly inflicted in a reported postgame scuffle with a pair of mouthy Dodger fans in a hotel elevator.[23] "I know he's missing three teeth and he's probably still looking for them," boasted The Boss of the supposed damage he inflicted on one of the assailants.[24]

However, Steinbrenner's victory in the elevator, if real, was his last during the baseball season; Los Angeles's momentum from its three-game sweep in Dodger Stadium could not be stopped.[25] The Dodgers marched into Yankee Stadium and cruised to a 9-2

Game Six win to take home the 1981 World Series trophy. It was their first Series title since 1965 and their first over the Yankees since 1963. "It wasn't just beating the Yankees, it was doing it with [Steve] Garvey and Lopes, Russell, Cey, the people I had been with for so long," Lasorda said of the first of his two titles. "We started together in the lowest minor leagues, and together we became world champions."[26]

SOURCES

The author accessed Baseball-Reference.com (https://www.baseball-reference.com/boxes/LAN/LAN198110250.shtml) for box scores/play-by-play information and other data, as well as Retrosheet.org. (https://www.retrosheet.org/boxesetc/1981/B10250LAN1981.htm). In addition to the sources cited in the Notes, the author also accessed GenealogyBank.com, NewspaperArchive.com, Newspapers.com, Paper of Record, and Stathead.com.

NOTES

1   Burton A. Boxerman and Benita W. Boxerman, *Ebbets to Veeck to Busch: Eight Owners Who Shaped Baseball* (Jefferson, North Carolina: McFarland & Company, 2003), 116.

2   Dan Hafner, "Dodgers-Yankees Rivalry Is Made for World Series," *Los Angeles Times*, October 20, 1981: Part III-3.

3   Richard J. Shmelter, *The Los Angeles Dodgers Encyclopedia* (Jefferson, North Carolina: McFarland & Company, 2017), 107.

4   Ross Newhan, "The Dodgers Say Bring on the Yankees, but Are They Ready for New York Fans?" *Los Angeles Times*, October 20, 1981: Part III-3.

5   Bill Madden, "Yanks Get Pep Talk from Steinbrenner," *New York Daily News*, October 26, 1981: C34.

6   Madden.

7   Mark A. Stein and Frank Spotnitz, "Outside Stadium, L.A.'s Faithful Party and Celebrate Ticket Deals," *Los Angeles Times*, October 26, 1981 Part II-8.

8   Stein and Spotnitz.

9   Jason Turbow, *They Bled Blue: Fernandomania, Strike-Season Mayhem, and the Weirdest Championship Baseball Had Ever Seen: The 1981 Los Angeles Dodgers* (New York: Houghton Mifflin Harcourt, 2019), xiii.

10   Glenn Schwarz, "Dodgers' Saga Like a Movie," *San Francisco Examiner*, October 26, 1981: F1. Games Three and Four of the 1981 World Series had drawn the two largest baseball crowds in the history of Dodger Stadium until they were topped by the 56,268 fans who attended Game Four of the 2004 National League Division Series.

11   Phil Pepe, "LA Lightning," *New York Daily News*, October 26, 1981: 53.

12   ABC television broadcast of the game as posted on YouTube, https://www.youtube.com/watch?v=BVDDAurAwWc, accessed August 31, 2023.

13   Murray Chass, "Steinbrenner Is Critical of Strategy in 5th-Game Loss," *New York Times*, October 26, 1981, https://www.nytimes.com/1981/10/26/sports/steinbrenner-is-critical-of-strategy-in-5th-game-loss.html, accessed on September 3, 2023.

14   Joseph Durso, "Dodgers Defeat Yankees, 2-1, and Take 3-2 Lead in Series," *New York Times*, October 26, 1981, https://www.nytimes.com/1981/10/26/sports/dodgers-defeat-yankees-2-1-and-take-3-2-lead-in-series.html, accessed on September 3, 2023; Jack Lang, "Turning Deaf Ear to Scouts, Reuss Has Fastball Festival," *New York Daily News*, October 26, 1981: 53.

15   Lang.

16   Chass.

17   Ross Newhan, "Cey Takes 94 M.P.H. Shot to the Head and Walks Away," *Los Angeles Times*, October 20, 1981: Part III-1.

18   "Cey Takes 94 M.P.H. Shot to the Head and Walks Away."

19   Joe Gergen, "Scary Reminder of the Unspoken," *Newsday* (Long Island, New York), October 26, 1981: 70; Newhan, "Cey Takes 94 M.P.H. Shot to the Head and Walks Away."

20   Gergen.

21   Schwarz, "Dodgers' Saga Like a Movie."

22   Dick Young, "Lasorda a Cutup – and That's No Baloney," *New York Daily News*, October 26, 1981: 51.

23   Eric Malnic, "Steinbrenner Claims a Victory," *Los Angeles Times*, October 26, 1981: Part II-8.

24   Dick Young, "Steinbrenner: Bloody but Unbowed," *New York Daily News*, October 27, 1981: C29.

25   Murray Chass, "Tales of '81: A Yankee Choke, a Boss Brawl," *New York Times*, June 17, 2004, https://www.nytimes.com/2004/06/17/sports/on-baseball-tales-of-81-a-yankee-choke-a-boss-brawl.html, accessed on September 3, 2023.

26   Tommy Lasorda and David Fisher, *The Artful Dodger* (New York: Avon Books, 1985), 293.

PEDRO GUERRERO SETS RECORD; STEVE HOWE ENDS DODGER CAREER

June 30, 1985: Los Angeles Dodgers 4, Atlanta Braves 3

by Jeff Findley

Pedro Guerrero was hitless in 11 consecutive at-bats. In a 162-game season, three games without hitting safely is not atypical, but Guerrero was wrapping up an exceptional month, already having hit 14 home runs, one short of the National League record for June.

Entering the final day of the month, the Los Angeles Dodgers trailed the division-leading and defending National League champion San Diego Padres by six games. The current series with the Atlanta Braves hadn't gone well; Guerrero was hitless in his previous three games, including two with the Braves. Although the Dodgers had pulled out a 3-2 win the previous day, they nearly squandered the lead in the top of the ninth when Bob Horner followed Dale Murphy's single with a home run. Tom Niedenfuer relieved Jerry Reuss to get the final out, moving to a Sunday afternoon series decider at Dodger Stadium.

The game pitted Pascual Pérez for Atlanta, winless in nine starts, against Dodgers righty and future Cy Young Award winner Bob Welch.

Welch had yet to hit his stride either, posting a 1-1 mark in four prior starts after missing time early in the season with a sore elbow.

As an additional distraction, pitcher Steve Howe was a no-show for the Dodgers.

If the midseason matchup between the National League West Division's third- and fifth-place teams was begging for a storyline, this one was unexpected. Howe had missed the entire 1984 season even though he was reinstated June 1, 1984, from a drug-related suspension, but returned to the Dodgers' major-league roster in 1985, achieving modest results, appearing in 19 games with a 4.91 earned-run average.

His absence, after he showed up late for a game a week before, was unexpected for Dodgers manager Tom Lasorda.

"It stuns me," Lasorda said. "I thought the young man was doing well. To see that happen is terrible.[1]

But as it turned out, Howe's vanishing act had little impact on the players.

"I didn't even know he wasn't here," Guerrero said. "I don't follow people who come here late. That's the manager's and the coaches' job."[2]

As play ensued, the early innings of the matchup were uneventful.

The Dodgers took a 1-0 lead in the second on three hits, with Steve Sax driving in first baseman Greg Brock. Guerrero was hitless in his first two at-bats, extending his streak to 13 at-bats without hitting safely.

It was the Braves' turn in the fifth. Through four innings, Welch had surrendered three hits and no runs, but home runs by Claudell Washington and Dale Murphy bookended Rafael Ramírez's single to give Atlanta a 3-1 lead. Lasorda stuck with Welch, who struck out to lead off the bottom of the inning as the Dodgers went down in order.

Rick Camp replaced Pérez in the bottom of the sixth, setting down the Dodgers in order, including a fly out by Guerrero for his third hitless trip to the plate. The score remained 3-1.

In the bottom of the seventh, the Dodgers mounted a challenge. With one out, Mike Scioscia walked and Sax reached on an error by Braves second baseman Glenn Hubbard. Lasorda removed Welch in favor of pinch-hitter Al Oliver, who singled to drive in Scioscia. The unearned run moved Los Angeles closer to the Braves. Dave Anderson hit into a double play to end the inning.

With Welch out of the game and Howe unavailable (he entered a few games earlier with an identical score against the Padres), Lasorda turned to Ken Howell. Howell had made 25 previous appearances and set the Braves down in order in the eighth without a ball leaving the infield.

In the bottom half of the inning with the heart of the order coming up for the Dodgers, Atlanta manager Eddie Haas brought in future Hall of Famer Bruce Sutter to replace Camp. Sutter retired Mariano Duncan, but Ken Landreaux singled, bringing Guerrero to the plate. Sutter had a streak of five saves in his five previous appearances.

"Our best against their best," Washington later commented.[3]

Guerrero smoked Sutter's second pitch into the left-field pavilion, tying the major-league record for homers in June, previously held by Babe Ruth (1930) and Roger Maris (1961) of the New York Yankees and Bob Johnson (1934) of the Philadelphia A's.

"I don't remember the last time I had a moment like this," said Guerrero, at this point 8-for-19 lifetime against Sutter. "To hit a homer in my last chance. … I have to sit back and think about it. How did I do it?"[4]

The record stood until Sammy Sosa shattered it with 20 home runs in June 1998.

The Braves had a final chance in the ninth when Gerald Perry led off with a walk against Howell. With Chris Chambliss pinch-hitting for catcher Bruce Benedict, Perry stole second as Chambliss struck out. With one out, Albert Hall, who entered the game in the eighth with Sutter, hit a slicing fly to left field that Guerrero ran down. Running on contact, Perry was doubled off second by Guerrero to end the contest.

The Braves left Los Angeles feeling shortchanged for their efforts.

"We made stupid mistakes that cost us these games," Braves third baseman Horner said. "Physical errors are one thing, but stupid mistakes. … We can't afford them in our position."[5]

Los Angeles dealt with the Howe situation promptly, promoting pitcher Dennis Powell from Albuquerque to fill his roster spot. Howe was released a couple of days later, with Los Angeles honoring the balance of his $325,000 salary, and offering to provide any medical assistance sought by Howe.

Most importantly, Lasorda lauded Guerrero, even though he thought Pedro was too conscious of hitting the record home run, accounting for his struggles the prior three games. "But he made contact with that ball," Lasorda said. "It jumped out of here. That's one of the great single achievements a hitter could ever accomplish, and it meant a lot to the team."[6]

Momentum from the win kick-started Los Angeles to a 20-7 record in July. The Dodgers overtook San Diego in the standings on July 13 and never relinquished the lead the rest of the season, winning the division by 5½ games over the Cincinnati Reds. San Diego finished in a third-place tie with Houston, 12 games back.

With Guerrero's hot June, he was selected for the All-Star Game but didn't show up in the box score. His slugging cooled down: He hit only 14 home runs the rest of the season, but he posted career highs in home runs (33), on-base percentage (.422), and slugging percentage (.577), leading the league in the latter two categories as well as on-base plus slugging (OPS) percentage (.999).

After winning the division, the Dodgers fell to the St. Louis Cardinals in the National League Championship series, four games to two.

SOURCES

In addition to the sources cited in the Notes, the author consulted Baseball-Reference.com, Retrosheet.org, and SABR.org.

https://www.baseball-reference.com/boxes/LAN/LAN198506300.shtml

https://www.retrosheet.org/boxesetc/1985/B06300LAN1985.htm

NOTES

1   Gordon Edes, "Guerrero Ends Month With a Game-Winner," *Los Angeles Times*, July 1, 1985: 29.

2   "Guerrero Ends Month With a Game-Winner."

3   Gerry Fraley, "Guerrero HR helps LA top Braves 4-3," *Atlanta Constitution*, July 1, 1985: 65.

4   "Guerrero HR helps LA Top Braves 4-3."

5   "Guerrero HR helps LA Top Braves 4-3."

6   "Guerrero Ends Month With a Game-Winner."

OCTOBER 12, 1988: DODGERS BEAT METS IN NLCS GAME SEVEN

Los Angeles Dodgers 6, New York Mets 0

by Thomas J. Brown Jr.

It all came down to this one game. The Dodgers and the Mets had battled through the first six games of the 1988 National League Championship Series. A crowd of 55,693 packed Dodger Stadium to see who would go to the World Series and face the Oakland A's, who had swept the Boston Red Sox to win the American League pennant.

The Dodgers had lost 10 of 11 games against the Mets during the season. But the Dodgers realized that those games did not matter at this point in the season. They just wanted to return to the World Series for the first time since 1981. The Mets were heavy favorites to go to the Series for the second time in three years. The Dodgers Dodger manager Tommy Lasorda said that his team was one "that everybody thought never belonged there."[1]

Mets manager Davey Johnson chose Ron Darling to take the mound for the Mets. Darling had pitched six innings in the third game of the series, giving up three runs in the Mets' 8-4 win. Darling pitched for the Mets in the seventh game of the 1986 World Series so he was no stranger to difficult situations. Before the game, he said, "That time, I was really excited to pitch. Then we had the rain delay and it took a lot of the emotion out of it for me. But that isn't going to happen this time. After all, it never rains in Southern California, does it?"[2]

Darling would face the Dodgers Orel Hershiser, who also started Game Three. Hershiser pitched seven innings and gave up three runs in that game. Hershiser had also started the first game of the series and lost a victory when the bullpen blew a save. He earned a save himself when he closed out the Dodgers' extra-innings win in Game Four. The only time Hershiser had been in a Game Seven situation was in a national amateur tournament before he turned pro. Like Darling, who

pitched only three innings in the 1986 game, Hershiser pitched only a couple of innings in that game.

Before this game, Davey Johnson told the media that he felt confident because Hershiser was pitching on short rest. It was his third start in nine days. Hershiser said later that Johnson's comments may have misfired. "We got [fired up] because Davey Johnson then joined the media parade as far as ripping on us," he said.[3]

After Lenny Dykstra led off and flied out to left field, Wally Backman singled and Keith Hernandez walked. Darryl Strawberry grounded to second and Hernandez was forced at second, leaving runners on first and third. But Kevin McReynolds lined out to third and the Mets lost their opportunity to take the lead.

In the bottom of the inning, the Dodgers wasted no time in scoring off Darling. Steve Sax led off with a single, Billy Hatcher doubled, and Kirk Gibson hit a sacrifice fly that scored Sax. It was redemption for Gibson, who had sabotaged the Dodgers' chances by popping out on a bunt the night before. The Dodgers led, 1-0. Darling struck out the next two batters. They were his only strikeouts, because he did not last through the second inning.

In the bottom of the second, the Dodgers continued their assault on Darling. Mike Scioscia, Jeff Hamilton, and Alfredo Griffin hit consecutive singles to load the bases. Hershiser then hit a grounder down the third-base line. Greg Jefferies fumbled the ball as he tried to throw home to get the lead runner. Scioscia scored and the bases remained loaded. Sax then hit his second single of the night, scoring Hamilton and Griffin.

Johnson had seen enough. Darling was removed after throwing just 35 pitches. Hoping to stop the bleeding, Johnson called on Dwight Gooden. Gooden had pitched solidly in Games One and Four but did not earn a win in either game. This was the first relief appearance of his career. Johnson reasoned that with "[w]ith Doc pitching, even 4-0, it's still within our grasp."[4]

After Hatcher grounded out, Gibson was walked intentionally to set up a double play. Mike Marshall hit a sharp groundball to the right side. Backman booted it, Hershiser scored, and the bases were still loaded. John Shelby then flied to left field to score the Dodgers' fifth run. By the time Gooden struck out Hamilton to end the inning, the Dodgers led 6-0.

After giving up a single to Dykstra in the third inning, Hershiser got Backman to fly out to left field and Hernandez to ground into a double play to end the inning. A similar situation happened in the fourth and again Hershiser kept the Mets hitters in check. He seemed to get stronger with each inning.

Gooden settled down and gave up only one hit in the third and fourth innings. Terry Leach took over in the fifth and scattered three hits over two innings. Rick Aguilera pitched the last two innings for the Mets and did not allow a hit.

After giving up a single in each of the first four innings, Hershiser didn't allow another until Jefferies doubled in the seventh inning. A wild pitch allowed Jefferies to reach third, but Hershiser again shut down the Mets as he got Gary Carter and Kevin Elster to fly out. Jefferies' double ended up being the last hit for the Mets.

Hershiser was just as amazed at his performance as the fans in Dodger Stadium. "I had no idea I could shut them out on only two days' rest," he said. "My mechanics were very bad for about the first two or three innings. Finally I got into a groove and made some adjustments."[5]

After the game, Lasorda told reporters: "What a job this guy has done for us. If he's not the Cy Young Award winner I want the FBI to investigate it."[6] The Dodgers were not expected to win the series but Lasorda was never in doubt, especially of Hershiser's

performance: "We definitely aren't a dominating team. We sometimes look like a high-school team. But when we fire on all cylinders, we win."[7]

"We have no excuse for losing," Johnson told reporters in the quiet Mets locker room. "We expected to win another world championship, and didn't. I've got a bad taste in my mouth. But I don't fault the guys for anything."[8]

Hershiser was named the most valuable player in the series. He started three games and relieved in one. With the Game Seven shutout, he had pitched seven shutouts in nine starts. During that time, he pitched himself into history by throwing 67 scoreless innings. Lasorda summed up his performance when he said, "[Y]ou have witnessed great pitching. Three times in this series, Orel started. Twice, he went to the bullpen. He's got great heart."[9]

SOURCES

In addition to the sources cited in the Notes, the author also used the Baseball-Reference.com, and Retrosheet.org websites for boxscore, player, team, and season pages, pitching and batting game logs, and other pertinent material.

https://www.baseball-reference.com/boxes/LAN/LAN198810120.shtml

https://www.retrosheet.org/boxesetc/1988/B10120LAN1988.htm

NOTES

1   Lyle Spencer, "Oral History of Epic Mets-Dodgers 1988 NLCS," MLB.com, October 5, 2015, found online at *mlb.com/news/oral-history-of-epic-mets-dodgers-1988-nlcs/c-152995440*.

2   Bill Dwyre, "Dodgers Leave It to the Bulldog," *Los Angeles Times*, October 13, 1988.

3   Spencer.

4   Joseph Durso, "Dodgers Win It as Hershiser Shuts Out Mets," *New York Times*, October 13, 1988.

5   "Hershiser Hurls Dodgers to 6-0 Flag Clincher," *Los Angeles Times*, October 13, 1988.

6   "Hershiser Hurls Dodgers to 6-0 Flag Clincher,"

7   Durso.

8   Durso.

9   Durso.

KIRK GIBSON'S HOMER WINS THE FIRST GAME OF THE 1988 WORLD SERIES

October 15, 1988: Los Angeles Dodgers 5, Oakland Athletics 4
(Game One of the 1988 World Series)

by Darren Gibson

The Los Angeles Dodgers weren't supposed to be there. Even after claiming the 1988 National League West crown by seven games, they were picked to fall to the heavily favored New York Mets in the National League Championship Series. The Mets, who won the NL East by 15 games, had beaten Los Angeles in 10 out of 11 regular-season contests. However, capped by a five-hit shutout by their magical ace Orel Hershiser in Game Seven, the Dodgers had surprisingly vanquished the vaunted Mets.

So here was the "Blue Crew," lined up on the third-base line, listening to 18-year-old pop sensation Debbie Gibson belt out the National Anthem on October 15, 1988, before Game One of the World Series. Their opponents across the diamond on the first-base line were the mighty Oakland A's, winners of 104 games in the regular season and coming off a sweep of the Boston Red Sox in the American League Championship Series. The A's were led by "Bash Brothers" outfielder Jose Canseco, the newly minted inaugural member of the 40-40 (homers and stolen bases) club, and second-year first baseman Mark McGwire.

The Dodgers' thoroughbred, left fielder Kirk Gibson, signed as a free agent before the season, had come up lame and was scratched, not even appearing or being announced during pregame on-field introductions. Gibson, signed after nine successful years with the Detroit Tigers, proved to be a bona fide star in LA in 1988, leading the team with 25 home runs and 28 doubles, on his way to a National League MVP award. He also belted two memorable home runs in the NLCS. His 12th-inning blast in Game Four in New York gave Los Angeles a dramatic 5-4 victory, while

his three-run shot the next day gave the Dodgers a 6-0 lead en route to a 7-4 win. However, Gibson had suffered a strained left hamstring and a sprained right knee ligament during the series. He received a cortisone shot in his right knee an hour before game time but could not answer the proverbial bell for the World Series opener. As NBC's Bob Costas lamented in the pregame analysis: "So the Dodgers brought in Debbie Gibson. Now if they only had Kirk Gibson."[1]

Gibson even admitted "I was trying to swing the bat in my living room this afternoon, and there was no way. Oh my Lord, there was no way."[2]

On top of not having Gibson in the starting lineup, the Dodgers matched up against 20-game winner Dave Stewart, buoyed by full rest after the ALCS sweep, as Oakland's Game One starter. It was a reunion of sorts, as Stewart joined teammates Rick Honeycutt, Bob Welch, and Matt Young (injured) as former Dodgers on the A's roster, while former A's Jay Howell, Mike Davis, and Alfredo Griffin now donned Dodger blue.

Replacing Gibson in left field and in the Dodgers' lineup was journeyman Mickey Hatcher, self-anointed leader of the "Stuntmen," a cadre of Dodgers role players who performed admirably throughout the season. Hatcher, in 212 at-bats over the regular season and playoffs, had hit exactly one home run. His three-run shot in the eighth inning in San Francisco on September 23 accounted for all of the Dodgers run in a 3-0 shutout and extended Hershiser's incredible scoreless inning streak to 49⅓ innings. Yet, here in the bottom of the first, Hatcher connected for an improbable two-run homer off Stewart, giving the underdog Dodgers an early 2-0 lead. (Hatcher would surprisingly club another two-run first-inning homer in the clinching Game Five.) The giddy Hatcher sprinted around the bases, prompting Dodgers third-base coach Joe Amalfitano to later quip, "It was as if he thought they would suddenly change their minds and take it back."[3]

The Dodgers' early lead would not last long. In the top of the second inning, rookie pitcher Tim Belcher, a mainstay starter for Los Angeles in 1988, allowed a single and two walks, including one to opposing pitcher Stewart, who had not made a plate appearance in five years. With the bases loaded and two outs, up stepped Canseco. In a prophetic bit of foreshadowing, the NBC television feed displayed the statistic that Canseco had never hit a grand slam among his 114 major-league homers (including the three in the ALCS). Two pitches later, that statistic would no longer be valid. Canseco "crunch(ed) a 1-and-0 slider from Tim Belcher on a frozen line, like a 2-iron shot, directly over the center-field fence. The ball caromed off an NBC camera and rolled between the two huge flagpoles. ... It was one of the lowest, hardest homers you'll see, clearing the fence like a comet, by about three feet."[4] The grand slam gave Oakland a 4-2 lead. (That was Canseco's only hit in the entire series in 19 at-bats.)

The scrappy Dodgers added a run in the sixth inning on Mike Scioscia's RBI single to close the gap to 4-3. However, all during this period, the Dodgers' leader, Gibson, was nowhere to be found on the bench. Even the inimitable Vin Scully pointed this out during the national broadcast, instructing his producer to pan the dugout, verifying Gibson's absence. But, as lore would have it, Gibby was not sitting idle. He had hobbled down into the bowels of Dodger Stadium, and started to hit off a tee, with clubhouse attendant Mitch Poole placing ball after ball on it.

The score remained 4-3 in favor of Oakland until the bottom of the ninth inning. A's manager Tony La Russa opted to remove starter Stewart after eight innings, summoning his lockdown closer, Dennis Eckersley. Eckersley notched 45 saves during the regular season and four more in the ALCS sweep, earning the ALCS MVP award.

Eckersley quickly dispatched Scioscia on a popup and Jeff Hamilton on a strikeout looking. Dodgers manager Tommy Lasorda then summoned Mike Davis, owner of a .196 regular-season batting average, to bat for shortstop Alfredo Griffin.

As the story was told, Gibson had sent word from the clubhouse to "Go tell Tommy that I can hit!"[5] So Lasorda indeed had Davis hit for Griffin, hopeful for Gibson to get a chance. Eckersley was aware of Davis's power potential, as the outfielder had hit 22 homers for Oakland the prior season. Davis eventually coaxed a two-out walk.

The crowd of 55,983 then erupted, while Dodgers play-by-play man Scully, working the national television broadcast for NBC, announced "[A]nd look who's coming up!" Gibson climbed the dugout steps and replaced infielder Dave Anderson in the on-deck circle. He applied tar to his bat, limbered up his arms with a few practice whirls, then strode ever so gingerly to home plate.

"You talk about a roll of the dice, this is it!" Scully commented before Gibson entered the box.

After Gibson awkwardly lunged and fouled off the first pitch, Scully remarked: "Not a bad opening act!" The *Los Angeles Times*'s Scott Ostler wrote that Gibson "seemed as steady at the plate as a rookie sailor walking the deck during his first storm."[6]

Gibson swung late on a second fastball, fouling it away. On the third pitch, Gibson cued a "little nubber" halfway up the first-base line that just barely turned foul before McGwire picked it up. The fourth pitch was a ball outside. The fifth pitch was a foul back of the plate, as Davis was on the move. Scully remarked that "Gibson (is) shaking his left leg, making it quiver like a horse trying to get rid of a troublesome fly. …"

The sixth pitch was a ball outside. The seventh pitch was a curveball outside, making the count full, with Davis successfully stealing second. So now if Gibson could only hit a long single, Davis could score to tie the game.

Until the errant curveball on that 2-and-2 pitch, Eckersley had thrown all fastballs. Now that the count was full, what would Eckersley throw Gibson? The injured Gibson had more than a hunch. Dodgers scout Mel Didier and the team's scouting department included in their report that Eckersley would throw a backdoor slider on a full count to a left-handed hitter.[7] On the eighth pitch of the at-bat, Eckersley threw that backdoor slider, Gibson swung with all arms and connected.

"Long fly ball to right field … she is GONE!" Scully's iconic TV call was followed by 69 seconds of silence as the crowd and viewers erupted while Gibson pumped his fist and circled the bases.

On the nationwide radio broadcast, Jack Buck exclaimed: "This is gonna be a home run! Unbelievable. … I don't believe what I just saw! I don't believe what I just saw!"

On the Dodgers radio broadcast, Dodgers pitching great Don Drysdale screamed: "WAY BACK! THIS BALL IS GONE!"[8]

Scully finally broke the television silence: "In a year that has been so improbable, the IMPOSSIBLE has happened!" Gibson's dramatic walk-off two-run home run to the right-field pavilion gave the underdog Dodgers an incredible 5-4 victory in Game One.

The irreplaceable Jim Murray of the *Los Angeles Times* simply titled his piece the next morning "This Could Happen Only in Hollywood."[9] He wrote, "This is John Wayne saving fort stuff. Errol Flynn taking the Burma Road. A guy who can hardly walk hits a ball where he doesn't have to. A few minutes before, he's sitting in a tub of ice like a broken-down racehorse. Kirk Gibson is the biggest bargain since Alaska. He should be on crutches – or at least a cane."[10]

Gibson did not make another game appearance in the Series, but it didn't matter. Hershiser tossed a three-hit shutout in Game Two, then another complete-game victory in the clinching Game Five as the Dodgers completed the improbable World Series win.

SOURCES

In addition to the sources cited in the Notes, the author consulted Baseball-Reference.com and Retrosheet.org, the feed of the NBC television broadcast, and the following:

Schiavone, Michael. *The Dodgers: 60 Years in Los Angeles* (New York: Sports Publishing, 2018).

https://www.baseball-reference.com/boxes/LAN/LAN198810150.shtml

https://www.retrosheet.org/boxesetc/1988/B10150LAN1988.htm

The final two at-bats of Game One can be seen on YouTube at https://www.youtube.com/watch?v=FERsNPyAUZM

NOTES

1   Bob Wisehart (McClatchy News Service), "Gibson's HR Saves So-So Effort by NBC," *Oakland Tribune*, October 16, 1988: 29.

2   Jon Rochmis, "No Movie Could Match Heroics Achieved by Gibson in Ninth," *Oakland Tribune*, October 16, 1988: 25.

3   Bill Plaschke, "Dodger Quarter Horse," *Los Angeles Times*, October 16, 1988: CC-3.

4   Scott Ostler, "Canseco Really Appreciates a Good Bash, Even One by Gibson," *Los Angeles Times*, October 16, 1988: CC-1.

5   Josh Suchon, *Miracle Men: Hershiser, Gibson, and the Improbable 1988 Dodgers* (Chicago: Triumph Books, 2013), 242.

6   Ostler.

7   Suchon, 250.

8   Radio calls pulled from Houston Mitchell, *If These Walls Could Talk: Stories from the Los Angeles Dodgers Dugout, Locker Room, and Press Box* (Chicago: Triumph Books, 2023), 110-117.

9   Jim Murray, "It Could Happen Only in Hollywood," *Los Angeles Times*, October 16, 1988: CC-1.

10 Murray.

PHENOM RAMÓN MARTÍNEZ REALIZES POTENTIAL

June 4, 1990: Los Angeles Dodgers 6, Atlanta Braves 0

By Thomas Baird

On the night of June 4, 1990, Ramón Martínez pitched one of the greatest games ever at Dodger Stadium. The achievement lacks the notoriety of a perfect game or even a no-hitter, but Martínez's masterful performance stands up well to almost any game pitched for or against the Dodgers.

The 22-year-old right-hander struck out 18 Atlanta Braves over nine innings, giving up only three hits and one walk. He tied Sandy Koufax for the most strikeouts thrown in one game by a Dodgers pitcher, but fell one strikeout short of the NL record held jointly by Steve Carlton and Tom Seaver, and two behind the major-league baseball record of 20 strikeouts by Roger Clemens. Koufax had struck out 18 batters on August 31, 1959, against the San Francisco Giants, and repeated the feat against the Chicago Cubs on April 24, 1962.[1] As of 2023 Martínez remained the only pitcher to strike out at least 18 in a game at Dodger Stadium,[2] and he did this in his first full big-league season.

Martínez is one of only 16 major-league pitchers to strike out 18 or more batters in a nine-inning game. The feat has been accomplished only 23 times, making it slightly rarer than a perfect game.[3] Martínez remarkably completed all 18 strikeouts in the eighth inning, with four outs remaining. Despite the opportunities to add to his total, Martínez could not retire another batter via strikeout, falling short of the NL record and major-league record.[4] The game serves as a microcosm of his injury-plagued career, reflecting his pitching brilliance while also prompting questions of what might have been.

The only other pitchers to record 18 strikeouts in the first eight innings are Roger Clemens (twice), Max Scherzer, Kerry Wood, Corey Kluber, and Randy Johnson (three times).[5] Of those six pitchers, only Johnson (September 27, 1992), Kluber, and Martínez were unable to add to their total in the ninth inning. Kluber was removed from his game after eight frames, and Johnson was the losing pitcher in an away game, so neither had an opportunity to chase the record in the ninth inning.[6]

The 6-foot-4-inch, 165-pound Martínez gave an admirable effort with his four remaining outs, reaching two strikes on a batter once in the eighth inning and twice in the ninth inning. Braves catcher Greg Olson said, "I looked at the scoreboard, I saw where he tied Koufax, and all I could tell myself was, great, here we go, I'm going to become the answer to a trivia question."[7] Olson drew two strikes before ending the inning on a groundout to first base. Despite receiving support from cheering fans and teammates, Martínez completed the ninth inning without recording an additional strikeout.[8] After the game, Martinez said, "I still got the complete game and the shutout and we won. And I am with a superstar like Sandy Koufax. I feel honored."[9]

Advanced stats have only increased the public's appreciation for the strikeout in the years since Martínez pitched this game. Weak contact is valuable, and low walk rate is helpful, but strikeouts leave less to chance.

When using Bill James's Game Score[10] as the primary metric for determining the greatest pitching performances at Dodger Stadium, this win ranks third all-time with a score of 98.[11] The game is eclipsed only by Clayton Kershaw's 15-strikeout no-hitter (102) in 2014, and Sandy Koufax's perfect game (101) in 1962. Jake Arrieta's no-hitter in 2015 is the only other Dodger Stadium pitching performance to match Martínez's game score of 98.

The game itself was not highly anticipated, but Martínez's emergence certainly was, and his performance that night only heightened expectations for the rest of the season. This Braves-Dodgers tilt became a ceremonial changing of the guard, as the young right-hander became the new face of a historically pitching-rich franchise. An underwhelming 22,097 fans were present to see the realization of Martínez's promise on June 4, but 36,800 would attend his next home start, followed by 31,000 on June 20. The Dodgers' Opening Day starter was a dominant Orel Hershiser, followed by young Tim Belcher, who struck out 200 batters the previous season and was expected to continue his ascent to ace status. Despite boasting a roster that still included Hershiser, Belcher, and team legend Fernando Valenzuela, the Dodgers would complete the season with a new bona fide ace in Martínez.

Martínez was named Pitcher of the Month for June[12] and made his first and only All-Star Game appearance in July. Pitching to batterymate Mike Scioscia, he threw one scoreless inning for the NL squad.[13] That year, he led the league in complete games and closed the season with a 20-6 record, finishing second to Doug Drabek in 1990 Cy Young Award voting. By September it was clear to Dodgers fans that Ramón's reign as top Dodgers hurler had officially begun. His star would never shine brighter than it did throughout the 1990 season.

Injuries intermittently derailed and disrupted his career for the next three seasons. Martínez won 17 games and threw a career-high four shutouts in 1991. An injury to his right hip and elbow cut his 1992 season short, but he rebounded in 1993 with another season with over 200 innings pitched.

After the players strike of 1994, Martínez had a renaissance in 1995, throwing a no-hitter at Dodger Stadium against the Marlins on July 14,[14] in the midst of a resurgent 17-win season. He was awarded a lucrative long-term contract but never threw 200 innings again. He retired as the second-winningest Dominican-born pitcher in major-league history, behind Juan Marichal, and as of 2024 ranked sixth on that list.

It is impossible to discuss this Braves-Dodgers game without mentioning the league-altering events of earlier that afternoon. The Braves and Dodgers organizations had already participated in the first round of the 1990 amateur draft by the time the first pitch was thrown at 7:37 P.M. The Dodgers took left-handed pitcher Ronnie Walden with the ninth pick. The Braves

took advantage of their first overall pick, choosing high-school slugger Chipper Jones over popular pitching prospect Todd Van Poppel.[15] Over the next decade and a half, the Braves would prove they won the day. The franchise-altering events of that afternoon would not impact the game that evening. Even so, it would be irresponsible to write a game story about the long-expected emergence of a hopeful Dodgers pitching powerhouse without also mentioning that the Braves were themselves on the precipice of a dynasty. For the Dodgers and their fans, June 4 felt like the beginning of a new era. It's a testament to this beautiful and unpredictable sport that this proved to be far truer for the lineup that struck out 18 times.

The Braves of the 1990s is associated with National League dominance, but this Atlanta team had not yet glimpsed that greatness. It team was coming off a last-place NL finish in 1989 and was on its way to another cellar-dwelling season in 1990. It was the last Atlanta team to finish anywhere but first until 2006. In fact, the Dodgers and Braves spent the summer of 1991 battling for first until the final days of the season, with the Braves ultimately seizing their first of 14 consecutive division championships.

Baseball players are constantly in development, and teams can only hope that their success will eventually be worth the wait. In 1984 a lanky 16-year-old Ramón Martínez pitched on the mound at Dodger Stadium as a member of the Dominican Republic Olympic baseball team.[16] Dodgers scouts originally thought he would be too skinny to develop an effective fastball, but chose to sign him shortly after the Olympics.[17] He rewarded the team six years later when he stood on that same mound and struck out 18 batters, including Braves legends Dave Justice, Jeff Blauser, Dale Murphy, Ron Gant, and Tom Glavine. It would be wrong to infer that Martínez was merely the older brother of Pedro Martínez, arguably his generation's greatest pitcher. This historic game serves as proof that Ramón Martínez was a genuine ace in his own right.

SOURCES

In addition to the sources cited in the Notes, the author consulted Baseball-Reference.com and Retrosheet.org.

https://www.baseball-reference.com/boxes/LAN/LAN199006040.shtml

https://www.retrosheet.org/boxesetc/1990/B06040LAN1990.htm

NOTES

1   Stathead Baseball, https://stathead.com/baseball/player-pitching-game-finder.cgi?request=1&ccomp%5B1%5D=gt&cval%5B1%5D=12&cstat%5B1%5D=p_so&team_id=LAD.

2   Stathead Baseball, https://stathead.com/baseball/player-pitching-game-finder.cgi?request=1&ccomp%5B1%5D=gt&cval%5B1%5D=12&cstat%5B1%5D=p_so&venue_id=LOS03.

3   Stathead Baseball, https://stathead.com/baseball/player-pitching-game-finder.cgi?request=1&ccomp%5B1%5D=gt&cval%5B1%5D=17&cstat%5B1%5D=p_so&ccomp%5B2%5D=lt&cval%5B2%5D=9&cstat%5B2%5D=p_ip.

4   Associated Press, "Martinez Strikes Out 18 as Dodgers Defeat Braves," *New York Times*, June 5, 1990: B19.

5   Stathead Baseball, https://stathead.com/baseball/player-pitching-game-finder.cgi?request=1&ccomp%5B1%5D=gt&cval%5B1%5D=17&cstat%5B1%5D=p_so&ccomp%5B2%5D=lt&cval%5B2%5D=9&cstat%5B2%5D=p_ip.

6   Stathead Baseball, https://stathead.com/baseball/player-pitching-game-finder.cgi?request=1&ccomp%5B1%5D=gt&cval%5B1%5D=17&cstat%5B1%5D=p_so&ccomp%5B2%5D=lt&cval%5B2%5D=9&cstat%5B2%5D=p_ip.

7   Bill Plaschke, "Martinez Strikes Out 18, Ties Koufax," *Los Angeles Times*, June 5, 1990: 1.

8   Plaschke.

9   Plaschke.

10 Explanation of Game Score can be found here: David Schoenfield, "The Best Pitching Performance Ever for All 30 Teams," ESPN.com, March 28, 2020, https://www.espn.com/mlb/story/_/id/23861547/the-best-pitching-performance-ever-all-30-teams. Accessed October 27, 2023.

11 Stathead Baseball, https://stathead.com/baseball/player-pitching-game-finder.cgi?request=1&order_by=p_game_score&ccomp%5B1%5D=gt&cval%5B1%5D=95&cstat%5B1%5D=p_game_score&ccomp%5B2%5D=lt&cval%5B2%5D=9&cstat%5B2%5D=p_ip&venue_id=LOS03.

12 "Pitcher of the Month," MLB.com, https://www.mlb.com/awards/pitcher-of-the-month (Accessed October 27, 2023).

13 "Ramon Martinez All-Star Stats," baseballalmanac.com, https://www.baseball-almanac.com/players/playerpost.php?p=martira02&ps=asg, accessed October 30, 2023.

14 Steve Dilbeck, "Martinez Throws 1st No-Hitter," *San Bernardino County* (California) Sun, July 15, 1995, https://newscomwc.newspapers.com/image/92362581/?terms=ramon%20martinez%20no-hitter&pqsid=jqnzgEpRpOCEHloGkXIXoQ%3A27472%3A1593193646, accessed October 27, 2023.

15 ESPN, "MLB First Round Draft Picks – 1990," https://www.espn.com/mlb/draft/history?year=1990, accessed October 21, 2023.

16 Sam McManis, "A Dandy Dominican," *Los Angeles Times*, February 26, 1988: III, 10.

17 McManis.

FERNANDO (SORT OF) PREDICTS NO-HITTER

June 29, 1990: Los Angeles Dodgers 6, St. Louis Cardinals 0

by Carter Cromwell

As predictions go, it doesn't rival Joe Namath's guarantee that his New York Jets would defeat Baltimore in Super Bowl III. In fact, it wasn't even a guarantee.

Nonetheless, it was right on the money.

A half-hour or so before he was to face the St. Louis Cardinals on June 29, 1990, Los Angeles Dodgers pitcher Fernando Valenzuela watched on television as former teammate Dave Stewart of Oakland completed a no-hitter against the Toronto Blue Jays. According to Dodgers manager Tommy Lasorda, Valenzuela said, "That's great. Now maybe we'll see another no-hitter."[1]

And they did.

Approximately three hours later, Valenzuela and a crowd of 38,583 saw Juan Samuel grab Pedro Guerrero's groundball, step on second to put out runner Willie McGee and throw to first to beat Guerrero by a step and clinch the only no-hitter of Valenzuela's career. It remains the only time since 1900 that two no-hitters have occurred on the same day.

And it's doubtful that anyone, except perhaps the man himself, had seen it coming.

Since 1987, Valenzuela had not been the same pitcher as in his previous six full seasons, when he was an All-Star each year, won 97 games, including a 21-win campaign, and ignited "Fernandomania" by sweeping the Rookie of the Year, NL Cy Young, and Silver Slugger Awards in 1981, in addition to being named Major League Player of the Year by *The Sporting News*. He posted a 29-35 won-lost record from 1987 to 1989 and, after going 255 games without missing a start, was on the shelf for a good part of 1988 because of shoulder trouble.[2]

When Valenzuela started against the Cardinals on that June night in 1990, he owned a 5-6 record and a 4.09 earned-run average. In his previous start, against Cincinnati, he had allowed eight earned runs in 5⅓ innings.[3] Announcers Joel Meyers and Ron Cey on the SportsChannel telecast of the game touched on this.

"The Dodgers, more than anything, are concerned about the lofty ERA," Meyers said. "It's been going up the last three or four weeks." Cey, the former Dodgers third baseman, added that Valenzuela had been "very inconsistent," adding, "In one game, he'll pitch extremely well and follow up with not a good game."[4]

On this night, he delivered the goods.

His teammates gave Valenzuela a quick lead in the first inning when Lenny Harris singled off St. Louis starter José DeLeón and later scored on a sacrifice fly by Hubie Brooks. The Dodgers added single runs in the fifth and sixth to lead 3-0. Harris singled and eventually scored on a squeeze bunt by Stan Javier for the fifth-inning run, and Brooks hit a solo home run in the sixth.

For his part, Valenzuela breezed through the first six innings – throwing 75 pitches and striking out five – with only Guerrero reaching base for the Cardinals on a dropped fly ball by left fielder Kirk Gibson in the first inning. There were no really close escapes, although Gibson did have to track down a hit into the left-center-field gap in the fourth.

Meyers told his TV audience that "Fernando is quietly walking into the fifth [inning] with a no-hitter." Cey opined that he "must be taking a tip from former teammate Dave Stewart, who threw a no-hitter tonight in Toronto." In the sixth inning, while talking in the booth with former Dodgers pitcher Carl Erskine – himself the author of two no-hitters – Meyers remarked, "We [now] may be watching another great moment in Dodger history."[5]

Valenzuela was doing it primarily with control and movement on his pitches.

Cey said, "Fernando has done an excellent job of getting in front of [the hitters on] just about every count. He hasn't given the Cardinals any opportunity to get started. And [because his control had been good] he's getting the calls on borderline strikes."[6]

He wobbled a bit in the seventh, walking Guerrero and Todd Zeile with one out and bringing third baseman Terry Pendleton to the plate. Pendleton, Cey noted, represented the tying run and "can occasionally hit the ball out of the ballpark."[7] Pendleton indeed came close, lifting the ball to the warning track in left field, where Gibson made the catch for the second out. Guerrero moved to third base on the play, but José Oquendo, a career 10-for-31 against Valenzuela at that point, grounded out to Harris at third to end the inning.

Los Angeles added to its lead in the bottom of the seventh inning when Valenzuela and Harris singled and Gibson drove in both with a single for a 5-0 Dodgers advantage.

Later, Lasorda mentioned a joke he played on Valenzuela – "I yelled for [Mickey] Hatcher to pinch-hit for Fernando. You should have seen the look on Fernando's face."[8]

By this time, too, superstition was taking hold in Dodger Stadium.

"Usually by the last innings, we have cleared all the players' workout clothes off their chairs, but we decided not to touch Fernando's stuff," said Dave Wright, assistant clubhouse manager. "And usually we turn off the clubhouse fan late in the game. But by the seventh inning, with the no-hitter still going, we decided to leave it going. Anything that might make a difference."[9]

And public-address announcer Pete Arbogast was concerned, as well. When announcing a seat location for a prize giveaway prior to the eighth inning, he said, "That's Row N, as in 'no-no.'" A "no-no," of course, means a no-hitter, and tradition holds that it's bad luck to mention it while the game is still going. "I didn't think I was doing anything wrong," Arbogast said. "But I guess if they had gotten a hit, I would have lost my job."[10]

But Valenzuela avoided the hex by retiring the Cardinals in order in the eighth, although there was a near-hiccup when pinch-hitter Craig Wilson drove an outside breaking pitch to left-center field that center fielder Javier had to run down on the warning track by the 385-foot sign.

"I was thinking, if a ball is hit to me, I've got to get a good jump on it," Javier said. "Then when he hit it, I didn't think, I just ran. And I ... had it all the way."[11]

The Dodgers then made it 6-0 on a home run by Samuel in the bottom of the inning and set up the climactic ninth.

"We all had goose bumps," Dodgers pitcher Mike Morgan said. "We were all just watching and hoping and waiting to charge the field."[12]

Valenzuela began by getting Vince Coleman with a borderline called strike on a 2-and-2 pitch, but he then walked McGee on four pitches to bring up Guerrero. With the count 0-and-2, Guerrero grounded back up the middle. Valenzuela ticked it with his glove, diverting it directly to Samuel standing by second base. Samuel simply touched the bag to get McGee and flipped to first to complete the game-ending double play.

"I was playing him to pull the ball, so I was right near second base and in a good position," Samuel said. "I don't know what happens if I'm not there."[13]

"Do you think if I don't touch that ball, it goes through for a single?" Valenzuela said afterward. "Whoooa. I think it does. I think [if] I don't touch it, I'm in trouble. I was just glad to see [catcher Mike] Scioscia running to the mound. Only then did I know it was over. This is a great moment for me."[14]

Valenzuela's agent, Tony DeMarco – in the stands with Fernando's sons Fernando Jr., 7, and Ricardo, 6 – said, "When it finally happened, I sat there crying like a stupid baby." And, he said, "[T]he boys were jumping up and down screaming, 'My pappy! My pappy!'"[15]

It was a last hurrah for Valenzuela as a Dodger. In what was his last season with Los Angeles, he finished 13-13 with a 4.59 ERA and led the National League with 104 earned runs allowed. He moved to the California Angels in 1991 and followed that with stops in the Mexican League, Baltimore, Philadelphia, and San Diego before finishing with five appearances for St. Louis in 1997. His only really successful season during that stretch was 1996, when he was 13-8 with a 3.62 earned-run mark for the Padres.

But this one night was a shining moment. As his teammates swarmed Valenzuela, legendary Dodgers announcer Vin Scully told his listeners, "If you have a sombrero, throw it to the sky!"[16]

Blue Heaven on Earth

SOURCES

In addition to the sources cited in the Notes, the author consulted Baseball-Reference.com.

https://www.baseball-reference.com/boxes/LAN/LAN199006290.shtml

NOTES

1   Bill Plaschke, "The Night of Two No-Hitters: Fernando Pitches One for the First Time as He Stymies Cardinals, 6-0," *Los Angeles Times*, June 30, 1990: https://www.latimes.com/archives/la-xpm-1990-06-30-sp-434-story.html.

2   Tom Callahan, "Valenzuela Toils On in Serene Obscurity," *Washington Post*, July 9, 1990: https://www.latimes.com/archives/la-xpm-1990-07-09-sp-111-story.html\.

3   Mark Langill, "OTD: A Tale of Two No-Hitters," *Dodger Insider*, June 29, 1990: https://dodgers.mlblogs.com/otd-a-tale-of-two-no-hitters-98ad5de9bc93.

4   Telecast of Game, SportsChannel, June 29, 1990: https://www.mlb.com/news/fernando-valenzuela-no-hitter-mlb-network.

5   Telecast of Game, SportsChannel, June 29, 1990.

6   Telecast of Game, SportsChannel, June 29, 1990. The home-plate umpire was Jerry Layne.

7   Telecast of Game, SportsChannel, June 29, 1990.

8   Bill Plaschke, "His Feat Is No-No Big Deal to Valenzuela: Day After Dodger Gets a Call from A's Stewart, but only Talks for a Minute. He Wants to Get On with Daily Routine," *Los Angeles Times*, July 1, 1990. https://www.latimes.com/archives/la-xpm-1990-07-01-sp-1087-story.html.

9   "His Feat Is No-No Big Deal to Valenzuela."

10 "His Feat Is No-No Big Deal to Valenzuela."

11 "His Feat Is No-No Big Deal to Valenzuela."

12 Plaschke, "The Night of Two No-Hitters: Fernando Pitches One for the First Time as He Stymies Cardinals, 6-0."

13 Plaschke, "His Feat Is No-No Big Deal to Valenzuela."

14 "His Feat Is No-No Big Deal to Valenzuela."

15 "His Feat Is No-No Big Deal to Valenzuela."

16 Ken Gurnick, "Rewatch Fernando Valenzuela's 1990 No-Hitter," MLB.com May 28, 2020: https://www.mlb.com/news/fernando-valenzuela-no-hitter-mlb-network.

DENNIS MARTÍNEZ'S PERFECT GAME

July 28, 1991: Montreal Expos 2, Los Angeles Dodgers 0

by Rory Costello

"El Presidente! El Perfecto!"

That was broadcaster Dave Van Horne's call on July 28, 1991, at Dodger Stadium, after Dennis Martínez completed the only perfect game in Montreal Expos history.

Other Montreal pitchers had thrown no-hitters – Bill Stoneman in 1969 and 1972, and Charlie Lea in 1981. Also, just two days before Martínez's gem, Mark Gardner went nine no-hit innings against Los Angeles – but Montreal could not score. Gardner then lost his no-no and the game in the 10th inning.[1] But Martínez became just the 13th man to throw a perfect game in major-league history.

Martínez's masterpiece symbolized his personal redemption. The pitcher, whose father was an alcoholic, became one too. It nearly derailed his career. As early as 1976, in Triple A, there were warning signs.[2] In 1983 his alcohol problem came to a head, and he got help. "It was a bad year," he later said, "but I got a new start."[3]

Though it took more than three years for Martínez to re-emerge fully, he became a master craftsman on the mound. The Expos acquired him from Baltimore in June 1986, and from June 1987 through 1993, Martínez was consistently among the best pitchers in the National League.

In 1988 he had said, "Before, when I was drinking, I used to think I was good. I didn't think about pitching. … I used to just try to throw the ball past the hitter. Now I think. I don't say it makes it easy, but it makes it easier."[4]

That thinking process made him a very crafty pitcher. He moved the ball around, changed speeds, focused on the weaknesses of the hitters, and made constant adjustments, setting up batters based on their reactions from pitch to pitch. He also hid the ball well with his motion and threw from varied arm angles. In some respects, Martínez had his finest season in 1991. He led

the NL in ERA at 2.39 – never rising above 2.42 – and finished fifth in the Cy Young Award voting.

"He's been this way all year," catcher Ron Hassey remarked after the perfect game. "There's been only one or two games when he hasn't had the kind of stuff he had today."[5]

However, as *El Presidente* took the hill at Dodger Stadium on July 28, he hadn't won since a complete-game 4-3 victory at Pittsburgh on July 5. In three starts after that, he had two no-decisions, sandwiched around one of his few shaky outings in '91, a loss to San Diego at home.

It was a typical summer Sunday afternoon in Los Angeles: 95 degrees and hazy. A big crowd of 45,560 was at the game. Martínez had attended Mass that morning, as he did each Sunday. "To me, that was the key point to the day," he later said.[6]

Never overpowering, Martínez fooled the Dodgers "with curveballs and sinkers and guts."[7] As Expos historian Jonah Keri wrote, "Though there weren't advanced pitch-tracking systems back then … you'd swear he threw 50 of his trademark knee-buckling curveballs."[8] Ken Singleton, the color commentator who teamed with Dave Van Horne on the TSN (Canada's only sports network at the time) telecast, said, "It's not your run-of-the-mill curveball that's coming up there today."[9]

Two of those benders came at critical junctures. As Bill Plaschke of the *Los Angeles Times* put it, "Hassey and Martínez combined on two big, bold pitches that may have saved the perfect game. With two out in the seventh inning and a full count on Eddie Murray, Martínez dared to throw a curveball. Murray jumped at it, grounding it to second base. With one out in the eighth inning and a full count on Kal Daniels, Martínez threw another curveball. Daniels swung through it for a strikeout."[10]

The Dodgers came close to a hit several times. With one out in the fourth, Montreal third baseman

Tim Wallach handled Juan Samuel's smash on the lip of the infield grass. With one out in the fifth, Daniels grounded to second base. Delino DeShields backed onto the outfield grass, waiting for a big hop. Daniels – once a fast runner, but slowed by several knee operations – got out of the box slowly but was still out by just half a step.

El Presidente also helped himself with one out in the seventh. The speedy Samuel pushed a bunt up the first-base line, but Martínez raced over, barehanded the ball, and threw out Samuel while falling forward. In the fourth inning, he had fought off a sore hip, caused by landing in a hole on the slippery mound dug by opposing pitcher Mike Morgan.

There was a play that almost led to an error. With one out in the sixth, DeShields fielded Alfredo Griffin's grounder, but his low throw to first nearly pulled Larry Walker off the bag.

Morgan also had a perfect game through five innings until Hassey led off the sixth with a single. The Expos' two runs – both unearned – came in the top of the seventh inning. Griffin, the Dodgers' shortstop, committed an error, and after a sacrifice bunt and a groundout, Walker got Montreal's big hit, a triple. Walker scored when Griffin made his second error of the inning on a Hassey groundball. Morgan went on to throw a complete game himself, allowing just four hits while walking one.

The last man between Martínez and perfection was pinch-hitter Chris Gwynn, younger brother of Tony. The lefty swinger almost ended the dream when he slapped a 1-and-1 pitch barely foul down the third-base line. Expos center fielder Marquis Grissom said, "I don't think anybody wanted the ball hit to them. I was so overexcited out there. I was just thinking, 'Please, no line drives, nothing hard.' I don't want to be the one to ruin history."[11]

Martínez left the 1-and-2 pitch up, and Gwynn lifted it to right-center. "I hit it well," said Gwynn, "but I knew it wasn't enough to get out."[12] Grissom said, "It was a routine fly ball. But I had to get over there and get it. I had to forget what was at stake."[13]

After Grissom gloved the ball, celebration ensued, led by Wallach. When the swarm abated, Martínez then enjoyed an interlude alone in the dugout. "There was nothing in my mind," he said. "I had no words to say, I could only cry. I didn't know how to express myself. I didn't know how to respond to this kind of game."[14]

Martínez's command was exceptional. He needed just 96 pitches, 66 of which were strikes. He went to a two-ball count on only eight hitters, and of these, only three went to a three-ball count. There were 17 groundouts, five strikeouts, two foul outs, and just three fair balls hit out of the infield.[15]

Hassey, who also caught Len Barker's perfect game of May 15, 1981, became the first major-league catcher to handle two of them. "This was a lot different than Lenny's," Hassey said. "Lenny was … a wild pitcher. Dennis is a pitcher's pitcher."[16]

The catcher added, "We had a game plan, and we went out and did it. You give the credit to Dennis. He's the guy who had to throw the pitches. I'm just the guy who's catching them and helping him."[17] Other Expos said, however, that Hassey was being too modest.[18]

Jonah Keri wrote, "In the clubhouse afterwards, Walker showered Martínez with beer, and the conquering hero carefully wiped it off his face. Later that night, teammates and friends toasted him with champagne; Martínez raised his glass, then set it down without taking a sip."[19] After the game, the sober man offered hope to others with drinking problems, saying, "It's never too late to do something about it."[20]

Martínez, the first player from Nicaragua to reach the majors, was already a hero in his homeland. He got the nickname *El Presidente* in 1979 from Ken Singleton, then a teammate with the Orioles. Tito Rondón, who in 1991 was sports editor of the Nicaraguan newspaper *La Prensa*, said, "Dennis Martínez was already the most popular man in the country before he pitched a perfect game. Now he's just more popular."[21]

"I thank God for this game that He gave me late in my career," said Martínez.[22] As it turned out, the veteran remained active through the 1998 season, when he turned 44. He threw eight more shutouts, including two of his six career two-hitters (he also had a one-hitter in 1985). He amassed 245 regular-season victories in the majors, which remained the record for Latin American hurlers until Bartolo Colón passed it in 2018 – but win number 174 was his finest hour.

SOURCES

In addition to the sources cited in the notes, another important article consulted by the author was:

"Perfect Sunday," W*ashington* (Pennsylvania) *Observer-Reporter,* July 29, 1991.

NOTES

1   Also worthy of mention are two rain-shortened performances. On April 21, 1984, David Palmer retired the first 15 St. Louis Cardinals he faced, but the game was called. On September 24, 1988, Pascual Pérez pitched five hitless innings against the Philadelphia Phillies, but that game was called in the top of the sixth. In September 1991 the Committee for Statistical Accuracy issued a retroactive ruling that these, among 50 games that had been listed as no-hitters, no longer qualified as such. The irony is that the committee made this decision after being asked to rule whether Mark Gardner's achievement deserved to be called a no-hitter.

2   Brian Bennett, *On a Silver Diamond: The Story of Rochester Community Baseball From 1956-1996* (Scottsville, New York: Triphammer Publishing, 1997), Chapter 4.

3   Gary Washburn, "Where Have You Gone, Dennis Martinez?" MLB.com, September 12, 2002.

4   Ian MacDonald, "Heeding Expos' Call for Arms," *The Sporting News*, September 12, 1988.

5   Wendy Lane, "Dennis Martinez: Simply Perfect," *Lexington* (North Carolina) *Dispatch*, July 29, 1991.

6   James Buckley Jr., *Perfect: The Inside Story of Baseball's Twenty Perfect Games* (Chicago: Triumph Books, 2012), 160.

7   Bill Plaschke, "Martinez Perfect Against L.A.," *Los Angeles Times*, July 29, 1991.

8   Jonah Keri, *Up, Up and Away* (Toronto: Random House Canada, 2014), 267.

9   TSN broadcast of the perfect game, accessed via YouTube.com.

10   Plaschke, "Notebook: Perfect Game Not New to Hassey," *Los Angeles Times*, July 29, 1991.

11   Plaschke, "Perfection Brings Expos' Martinez to Tears." (This is an alternate version of "Martinez Perfect Against L.A.")

12   Lane.

13   Plaschke, "Perfection Brings Expos' Martinez to Tears."

14   Plaschke, "Martinez Perfect Against L.A."

15   Plaschke, "Martinez Perfect Against L.A."

16   Plaschke, "Notebook: Perfect Game Not New to Hassey."

17   Lane.

18   Plaschke, "Notebook: Perfect Game Not New to Hassey."

19   Keri, 268.

20   Lane.

21   Buckley, *Perfect*, 169.

22   Lane.

AFTER SEASONS OF STRUGGLES, LA'S KEVIN GROSS DAZZLES FANS BY NO-HITTING THE GIANTS

August 17, 1992: Los Angeles Dodgers 2, San Francisco Giants 0

By Andrew Harner

Kevin Gross did not receive a warm welcome after signing with the Los Angeles Dodgers following the 1990 season. Within days, fans wrote to the *Los Angeles Times* and aired their displeasure; one dubbed the signing of the veteran right-hander "a Gross mistake."[1] After the Dodgers fell five games short of a playoff spot in '90, fans had hoped to see the franchise make a big splash in free agency, so they were understandably unmoved by the addition of a pitcher with an 80-90 career record and a 4.02 ERA. (In 1990 with the Montreal Expos, Gross had an underwhelming 9-12 record with a 4.57 ERA.)

Gross did not help his own cause by posting a dismal 13.50 ERA while losing his first three starts of 1991.[2] By the end of May, the Dodgers had demoted him to the bullpen, and he finished the season 10-11 with a 3.58 ERA. When fans booed him during a spot start on September 19, he angrily gestured in response. Going into the 1992 season, *Times* columnist Mike Penner asked if Gross could "truly be considered pennant-building material."[3]

"I think I put a lot of pressure on myself being in Los Angeles with a lot of good guys," Gross said during spring training in 1992 while self-assessing his first season on the West Coast. "I choked at the beginning, but the guys in the bullpen when I went down there were all for me and kind of kept me straight."[4]

Gross hoped the new campaign would play out differently, but he experienced a nearly identical story at the start of 1992. He lost three of his first four starts, and the Dodgers again sent him to the bullpen. Unlike in 1991, he returned to a regular spot in the rotation. He fired a shutout in his first start back, but suffered more losses than wins as the summer grew hotter. By the time he took the hill against the San Francisco Giants on August 17, he had not won in over a month and stood at 5-12 overall, though he boasted a respectable 3.59 ERA.[5] The Dodgers carried the National League's worst record (49-68) into the final game of the rivalry series.

But on that Monday night, 25,561 fans[6] at Dodger Stadium witnessed history: For the eighth time since the franchise relocated to California in 1958, a Dodgers pitcher threw a no-hitter.[7]

"It makes up for a not-so-good year for the Dodgers and myself," Gross said after throwing 71 of his 99 pitches for strikes in the major leagues' only no-hitter of the season. "It brought tears to my eyes, no doubt about it."[8]

Gross opened the night by inducing three routine groundouts on seven pitches in the first inning but lost his command a bit in the second, issuing a pair of walks before Kirt Manwaring grounded into a double play to end the inning. After Gross recorded two strikeouts as part of a one-two-three third inning, the Giants finally hit a ball out of the infield when Willie McGee led off the fourth with a fly out.

But Gross continued cruising. He retired 19 straight batters from Manwaring's double play to the end of the eighth inning. The game's top defensive highlight saw rookie shortstop José Offerman

make a leaping stab of Robby Thompson's sharp liner leading off the eighth. Offerman was arguably the most unlikely defensive hero on the field after racking up a major-league-worst 32 errors in his first 113 games, but his catch seemed to seal the Giants' fate.

"I hit that ball good," Thompson said. "I thought it was a hit. It seemed to be rising. He just made a great play. He told me he couldn't believe he caught it."[9]

As Gross recalled 30 years after the game: "When (Offerman) came into the dugout, he said, 'You're going to get this.' I said, 'Whatever. Let's just see what happens.' Everyone else in the dugout was quiet and didn't want to say anything. I was thinking, 'Who cares? If it happens, it happens.'"[10]

That Gross was due up to lead off the bottom of the eighth inning could have contributed to his indifference. He poked a single to center in support of his own cause, and he spent the entire inning on the basepaths, eventually making it to third before Mitch Webster flied out with the bases loaded in a failed rally.

With the victory in sight, Giants manager Roger Craig pulled out all the stops for the ninth. He pinch-hit Mark Leonard for light-hitting Mike Benjamin – who had one hit in his past 11 at-bats – bringing Leonard back into the fold for the first time since he received six stitches to close a gash on his left thigh after colliding with Mike Felder in the outfield three days earlier.

Gross's fourth pitch of the ninth hit Leonard on the left knee, and pitcher Bill Swift, a pinch-runner, nearly got to first base before Leonard did. But after another pinch-hitter, Greg Litton, hit into a fielder's choice and Felder flied out to left-center, Gross sat within one tough out of becoming the sixth Dodgers starter to throw a no-hitter at Dodger Stadium – the most recent being Fernando Valenzuela's outing on June 29, 1990.

"Willie McGee was the final hitter of the game," Gross recalled of the scrappy switch-hitter who also hit in the final inning of Valenzuela's no-hitter while with the Cardinals. "He's such a free swinger. He can hit any pitch from his toes to over his head."[11]

McGee swung through Gross's first offering – taking a cut at the first pitch of his third straight at-bat. As an energized crowd howled, Gross displayed obvious nervousness as he and catcher Mike Scioscia agreed on the one-strike pitch.

"We are a minute away from 10 o'clock," legendary Dodgers broadcaster Vin Scully announced over the airwaves before the final pitch of the night, "and Gross could be a minute away from a no-hitter."[12]

McGee lifted a weak fly to left, and Webster had to charge in only a few steps to track it down and preserve history. An emotional Gross broke down in tears on the mound as his teammates surrounded him. He directed a salute to his family on his way off the field – a contingent that included his mother, who was there when Gross threw a no-hitter in Little League in nearby Downey, California. His wife, Tamara, did not attend, instead celebrating her 27th birthday.[13]

Before the outing – the 13th time a pitcher had held the Giants hitless[14] – the fewest number of hits Gross had allowed in a game was three. He had done it three times, including when he struck out a career-high 13 batters as he returned to the rotation earlier in the season, on May 12. One start before facing the Giants, he pitched 4⅓ no-hit innings against the Reds.

"I told my coaches before the game I've never understood why this guy didn't win more ballgames," Giants manager Craig said. "He's a big, strong guy, and he's got outstanding stuff. His fastball's not what you'd call 93, 94, 95 (MPH), but it moves so good."[15]

In support of Gross, rookie Eric Karros led off the second with a home run to left-center against Giants starter Francisco Oliveras. It was the Dodgers' first homer since the second inning four days earlier, and the first since August 4 for Karros, the eventual NL Rookie of the Year.[16] In the fourth, Brett Butler doubled and scored on Henry Rodríguez's single, and those two runs helped the Dodgers avoid getting swept by the Giants in a four-game home series for the first time since 1923.[17]

San Francisco had squeaked out three straight one-run victories despite collecting only 13 total hits. For the series, the Giants collectively hit .109 with one extra-base hit and 29 strikeouts.

Perhaps inspired by Gross's outing, rookie Pedro Astacio fired a six-hit shutout the next night to outduel David Cone and the Mets.[18] Orel Hershiser pitched eight shutout innings the following night, giving the Dodgers 27 straight shutout innings.

The no-hitter remained the crowning jewel of Gross's career. He spent 15 seasons in the major leagues and compiled a 142-158 record with a 4.11 ERA. Gross pitched for the Dodgers from 1991 to '94, and he was arguably at his best in Southern California, posting a 40-44 record and a 3.63 ERA.[19]

"It's really strange how much you appreciate something like that later in life," Gross said in 2022. "Over the years, I get reminded of the no-hitter by lots of people, whether friends and family or fans. I went to the Home Run Derby this year at Dodger Stadium, and fans were congratulating me on the no-hitter. Some still have their ticket from the game or a card. It's really cool to have an achievement like that in a career like mine."[20]

SOURCES

In addition to the sources cited in the Notes, the author consulted the Baseball-Reference.com, Stathead.com, and Retrosheet.org websites for pertinent material and the box scores. He also used information from *The Sporting News* and numerous California newspapers.

https://www.baseball-reference.com/boxes/LAN/LAN199208170.shtml

https://www.retrosheet.org/boxesetc/1992/B08170LAN1992.htm

NOTES

1   "Readers Have a Name For It: Mike Downey," *Los Angeles Times*, December 8, 1990: C3.

2   Gross had an overall ERA of 12.19 by that time after pitching a scoreless inning in relief the day after his first start, which saw him allow five earned runs over 1⅓ innings.

3   Mike Penner, "On a Claire Day, You Can See All the Way Down to Anaheim," *Los Angeles Times*, January 15, 1992: C1.

4   Bill Boeding, "Gross Wants Starter's Role," *Vero Beach* (Florida) *Press Journal*, February 24, 1992: B1.

5   In Gross's 21 starts, the Dodgers scored an average of 3.38 runs, contributing to his poor won-lost record. In three of his losses, the offense failed to score, and in three others, the Dodgers scratched across a single run.

6   This attendance was the ballpark's third smallest of the season to that point. By season's end it was the 17th smallest.

7   Among those eight no-hitters, six were thrown at Dodger Stadium. Additional no-hitters at Dodger Stadium included Los Angeles Angels pitcher Bo Belinsky's 1962 no-hitter against the Baltimore Orioles and Montreal pitcher Dennis Martínez's perfect game in 1991.

8   Bill Plaschke, "Gross Chases Dodger Blues Away," *Los Angeles Times*, August 18, 1992: C1.

9   Nick Peters, "How Gross: Giants Are No-Hit," *Sacramento Bee*, April 18, 1992: E1.

10   Mark Langill, "30 Years Later: Gross Still Savors No-No," *Dodgers Insider*, August 17, 2022. Retrieved April 15, 2023 (https://dodgers.mlblogs.com/30-years-later-gross-savors-no-no-ea414d7567ac).

11   Langill.

12   MLB, "SF@LAD: Kevin Gross No-Hits the Giants," YouTube, August 9, 2013, Retrieved April 22, 2023 (https://www.youtube.com/watch?v=qQqDRnJeKVY).

13   Four days later, Bob Ojeda was scheduled to start on his wife's 29th birthday, and Gross jokingly suggested he needed to keep pace and throw a no-hitter for her. "I can't believe he was dropping that stuff on me," Ojeda said. "It isn't like he bought his wife a watch on her birthday, and so now I can buy the same watch. I've got no chance of pitching a no-hitter. Let's be serious." Ojeda allowed six hits over five innings against the Cubs. "Cost-Cutting Measures Considered," *Los Angeles Times*, August 19, 1992: C5.

14   The game marked the sixth time the Dodgers had no-hit the Giants. The most recent previous occurrence came from Jerry Reuss on June 27, 1980.

15   Associated Press, "Gross Nets a No-Hitter for Dodgers," *Thousand Oaks* (California) *News Chronicle*, August 18, 1992: D-1.

16   Karros famously kicked off a streak of five straight NL Rookies of the Year for the Dodgers, with Mike Piazza, Raul Mondesi, Hideo Nomo, and Todd Hollandsworth following from 1993 to '96.

17   The 1985 Philadelphia Phillies were the last previous team to sweep a four-game series in Dodger Stadium. Gross, then in his third big-league season, won one of the games for the Phillies.

18   Astacio became the 21st major-league pitcher to throw two shutouts in his first four appearances. The last pitcher to do so was Steve Rogers in 1973.

19   Gross earned an All-Star selection with the Philadelphia Phillies in 1988.

20   Langill, "30 Years Later: Gross Still Savors No-No."

DODGERS TURN THE TABLES
ON RIVAL GIANTS

October 3, 1993: Los Angeles Dodgers 12, San Francisco Giants 1

by Tom Schott

The 1993 Los Angeles Dodgers didn't win the World Series, the National League pennant, or the NL West Division. Truth is, they were a .500 ballclub. But after a season-ending 12-1 blitzkrieg of the rival San Francisco Giants leveled their record at 81-81, the Dodgers couldn't help but celebrate as though they had achieved something grander.

That's because the Dodgers prevented the Giants from reaching postseason play despite winning 103 games.[1] San Francisco finished one game behind the Atlanta Braves. Had the Giants beaten Los Angeles in the season finale, they would have hosted the Braves (104-58) in a one-game tiebreaker to determine the NL West champion.[2] It was the eighth time in major-league history that a 100-plus-win team finished in second place.

Before the game, Los Angeles general manager Fred Claire and manager Tom Lasorda educated their players on the fact that the Giants had spoiled Dodgers' playoff possibilities three times on this very date – October 3 – in 1951, 1962, and 1982, as well as more recently during the final weekend of the 1991 season.[3]

"They talked about those seasons, but I don't think they had to," said Dodgers center fielder Brett Butler, a Los Angeles native who played for the Giants from 1988 to 1990. "We wanted to beat them anyway."[4]

San Francisco had won the first three games of the four-game series at Dodger Stadium (3-1, 8-7, and 5-3), extending its surge to 14 victories in 16 games. But that came on the heels of an 11-18 stretch as the Giants went from leading the division by nine games over the Braves on August 11 to trailing by four games on September 17.[5]

The finale was played on a sun-splashed Sunday afternoon with a first-pitch temperature of 86 degrees. The Dodgers started 11-year veteran Kevin Gross, while the Giants countered with 21-year-old rookie

Salomón Torres, who was appearing in his eighth major-league game with a 3-4 record and a 3.70 ERA.[6] San Francisco boasted the NL's most potent offense,[7] buoyed by its heart of the order: first baseman Will Clark (.283 batting average for the season, 14 home runs, 73 RBIs); third baseman Matt Williams (.294, 38 homers, 110 RBIs); and left fielder Barry Bonds (.336 and league-highs of 46 homers and 123 RBIs).

Gross handcuffed the Giants from top to bottom, start to finish – allowing six hits (all singles) while pitching his third complete game of the season. He walked one and struck out five en route to finishing with a 13-13 record and a 4.14 ERA. Clark, Williams, and Bonds were a combined 2-for-11 with a walk and three strikeouts.

"I wanted to stick it to them one more time," said Gross, a native of Downey, California, in southeastern Los Angeles County, who no-hit the Giants on August 17, 1992. "It was our turn at payback after everything they've done to us."[8]

San Francisco's Dave Martinez and Royce Clayton singled with one out in the second inning, but Kirk Manwaring grounded into a 6-4-3 double play to thwart an early scoring threat.

The game was scoreless in the third when the Dodgers got to Torres. Gross singled leading off, took second on a sacrifice by Butler and third on a groundout by José Offerman, and scored on a single by Dave Hansen. All-Star rookie catcher Mike Piazza walked, and Eric Karros followed with a run-scoring double to deep left-center field to give Los Angeles a 2-0 lead.

An RBI bloop single by Offerman in the fourth scored Jody Reed, who had walked, making it 3-0 and knocking out Torres. In 3⅓ innings, Torres gave up five hits and walked five batters while recording one strikeout.

The Giants scored their lone run in the fifth. Clayton and Manwaring singled, and relief pitcher Trevor Wilson laid down a sacrifice bunt that put runners on second and third. Clayton scored as Darren Lewis grounded out to first.

It was all Dodgers the rest of the way. Piazza led off the bottom of the fifth with a first-pitch home run to the right-field pavilion off Dave Burba. Three batters later, Cory Snyder, who was born in Inglewood, California, in southwestern Los Angeles County, and played for the Giants the previous season, belted a two-run homer to the right-center pavilion, widening the gap to 6-1.

Karros made it 7-1 in the sixth with an RBI single off Michael Jackson, and the Dodgers put an exclamation point on the cockeyed victory in the eighth with a three-run homer by Piazza to deep right field off Dave Righetti and a two-run shot by rookie Raúl Mondesi to deep left off Jim Deshaies. With their .261 team batting average, the Dodgers ranked 10th in the NL, but they collected 14 hits and drew 10 walks against seven San Francisco pitchers.

"As it turned out, we ran out of pitchers," said first-year Giants manager Dusty Baker, an outfielder for the Dodgers from 1976 to 1983. "We had some tired guys. Everyone was running on empty."[9]

Meanwhile, Gross retired 15 of the last 16 Giants he faced, allowing only a sixth-inning leadoff single by Clark, in the 3-hour, 6-minute game.

Piazza, the Dodgers' 62nd-round draft pick in 1988, concluded his first full season in the majors with a Los Angeles-record 35 home runs[10] while also topping the team with a .318 batting average and 112 RBIs.[11] Among NL batters, Piazza ranked fourth in RBIs, sixth in homers, and seventh in batting average, and he joined Roy Campanella (three times), Gabby Hartnett, and Walker Cooper as the only major-league catchers to have at least a .300 average, 30 homers, and 100 RBIs. After warming up Gross in the ninth inning, Piazza was removed from the game so he could be acknowledged by the sellout crowd of 54,340.[12]

"Mike had a tremendous year," Lasorda said. "That ovation at the end by the fans was beautiful. He really deserved that."[13]

Piazza went on to be named NL Rookie of the Year and win a Silver Slugger Award.

"The whole year the guys helped a lot, keeping me focused and making me feel like I didn't have to produce, and that helped me to concentrate on catching," said Piazza, who enjoyed a 16-year big-league career and was inducted into the National Baseball Hall of Fame in 2016. "It's been a little overwhelming at times, all the attention and all, but I'm happy I established myself here."[14]

One year after finishing last in the NL West with 99 losses, Los Angeles moved up to fourth place (23 games behind the Braves). They won the season series over San Francisco, 7-6, for the first time since 1989.

"Maybe this won't make up for the season we had, but, for now, it means a lot," infielder Lenny Harris said. "It's a payback. We spoiled their party. There's nothing like returning the favor."[15]

Lasorda delighted in the moment, giving hugs and blowing kisses.

"I know it's a sad time for the Giants," Lasorda said. "They won 103 games and did a sensational job. But when we look back at what they did to us four times, we wanted to let them know what the feeling was like. We had to hang our heads a few times. Now it's their turn."[16]

For the Giants, the close-but-no-champagne ending marked the culmination of an 11-month roller-coaster ride. On November 10, 1992, his fellow NL owners rejected Bob Lurie's deal to sell the franchise to a group of Florida investors, who would have moved the Giants to St. Petersburg for the 1993 season. Ten days later, Lurie sold the team to a San Francisco group, led by Peter Magowan, and Al Rosen resigned as general manager. Roger Craig was fired as manager on November 30 and replaced by Baker, who had been the team's hitting coach the preceding four seasons. Magowan and new general manager Bob Quinn promptly made headlines by signing Bonds to a six-year contract worth a then-record $43.75 million on December 8, sparking the organization and its fans.

The Giants, who were in sole possession of first place from May 11 to September 10, became the first team to win 103 games and finish second since the 1954 New York Yankees and the first 100-win club to not finish first since the 1980 Baltimore Orioles. They won more games than any second-place NL team since the 1942 Brooklyn Dodgers.[17] [In 1994, the major leagues switched from two divisions to three and added a wild-card team (the nondivision winner with the best record) to the playoffs.]

"This has been a real team," said Baker, who was named NL Manager of the Year after piloting the Giants to a 31-game improvement over the 1992 season. "Everyone has contributed. We just fell one game short.

"This is like going to the prom and you can't go inside."[18]

SOURCES

In addition to the sources cited in the Notes, the author consulted the Baseball-Reference.com and Retrosheet.org websites for pertinent material and the box scores. He also reviewed a recording of the ESPN telecast posted on YouTube.

Https://www.baseball-reference.com/boxes/LAN/LAN199310030.shtml

Https://www.retrosheet.org/boxesetc/1993/B10030LAN1993.htm

Https://www.youtube.com/watch?v=uDhheliM-Y4

DODGER STADIUM

NOTES

1   The 103 wins were tied for the most in San Francisco Giants history and tied for third most in franchise annals at the time. The 1962 team also won 103 games (including two in a three-game tiebreaker series against the Dodgers), as did the 1912 New York Giants. The New York Giants won 106 games in 1904 and 105 games in 1905. Subsequently, the 2021 San Francisco Giants won 107 games.

2   The Braves beat the expansion Colorado Rockies, 5-3, in Atlanta on the season's final day – completing a 13-0 season sweep – and then watched the Giants-Dodgers game on ESPN in their clubhouse at Atlanta Fulton County Stadium.

3   In 1951 and 1962, the Giants won three-game tiebreaker series against the Dodgers to capture the NL pennant. In 1982, the Giants eliminated the Dodgers from NL West Division title contention. And on October 5, 1991, the Giants eliminated the Dodgers from the division race.

4   Terry Johnson, "One Giant Dose of Revenge," *San Pedro* (California) *News-Pilot*, October 4, 1993: B1.

5   The Giants' biggest division lead of the season was 10 games on July 22. The Braves went 54-19 after the All-Star break and won their third consecutive NL West title. They lost to the Philadelphia Phillies in the NLCS in six games.

6   Torres was the losing pitcher in the Giants' previous three defeats (September 15, 21, and 29), spanning 17 games.

7   In 1993, San Francisco led the NL with a .276 batting average and a .427 slugging percentage and ranked second with 808 runs.

8   Mark Langill, "L.A. Crushes Giants' Pennant Hopes, 12-1," *Pasadena Star-News*, October 4, 1993: C1.

9   Larry Stone, "100 Wins Not Enough," *San Francisco Examiner*, October 4, 1993: D-1.

10   The previous Los Angeles record for home runs was 33 by Steve Garvey (1977) and Pedro Guerrero (1985). Duke Snider held the franchise record at the time with 43 homers for the Brooklyn Dodgers in 1956.

11   Piazza's .318 batting average was the ninth highest in Los Angeles history, while his 112 RBIs were tied for the third-most by an NL rookie at the time.

12   The crowd was the largest for a Sunday afternoon game in Dodger Stadium history at the time.

13   "Dodgers Notebook," *Pasadena Star-News*, October 4, 1993: C4.

14   Maryann Hudson, "Dodgers Make It Worth Braves' Wait," *Los Angeles Times*, October 4, 1993: C1.

15   Terry Johnson, "One Giant Dose of Revenge."

16   "One Giant Dose of Revenge."

17   The 1954 Yankees went 103-51 and finished eight games behind the Cleveland Indians in the American League, while the 1980 Orioles went 100-62 and finished three games behind the Yankees in the AL East Division. The 1942 Dodgers went 104-50-1 and finished two games behind the St. Louis Cardinals in the NL.

18   Mike Waldner, "Baker's Boys Settle for Second," *San Pedro News-Pilot*, October 4, 1993: B1.

NOMO TAKES THE SPOTLIGHT WITH 17 K'S ON A BIG SPORTS NIGHT IN LOS ANGELES

April 13, 1996: Los Angeles Dodgers 3, Florida Marlins 1

by Bob Timmermann

It was a busy night for sports in the Los Angeles area on Saturday, April 13, 1996. The Dodgers had a home game with Japanese sensation Hideo Nomo starting, which usually meant a big crowd was on its way.

A few miles north of Dodger Stadium, the Los Angeles Galaxy were playing their first-ever Major League Soccer match at the Rose Bowl in Pasadena. That drew a crowd announced at 69,255, a number catching stadium authorities there by surprise; they had predicted about half that turnout. The Galaxy won 2-1 over the New York/New Jersey MetroStars.[1]

A few miles south of Dodger Stadium, the woebe-gone Los Angeles Clippers (28-49 at the time) drew a sellout crowd of 16,021 for a game against the Utah Jazz because of a high-school cheerleading promotion at the old Los Angeles Memorial Sports Arena. The Clippers prevailed, 91-81.[2]

All three events started at about the same time, turning the main thoroughfares connecting the three facilities, the Harbor and Pasadena Freeways, into parking lots. The traditionally late-arriving crowd at Dodger Stadium was coming in very late.

Hideo Nomo had made an immediate impression on his arrival to major-league baseball in the 1995 season. The first Japanese native to pitch in the majors since Masanori Murakami in 1965, Nomo won the Rookie of the Year Award in the National League with a 13-6 season, a 2.54 ERA, and a league-leading 236 strikeouts in 191 ⅓ innings. He also gave up the fewest hits (5.8) per nine innings.

Nevertheless, concerns were voiced over whether Nomo could pull off another season as good as his rookie year. Was Nomo's dominant debut season the result of a reduced spring training and limited scouting available for a player coming from Japan? Or was Nomo a legitimate pitching star?

After a bad start on the road at Houston (4 IP, 4 R, 7 H, 5 BB) to start the season, Nomo's own team-mates even raised questions. Second baseman Delino Deshields said, "I believe in Hideo, but I don't expect him to dominate like last year. People are going to make adjustments. This is the big leagues. These are big league hitters. And he's going to need that room to concentrate on what he needs to do."[3]

Nomo responded with a complete game, a three-hit shutout over World Series champion Atlanta in the home opener before 53,180. Another big crowd was anticipated for his next start, a Saturday night game against Florida. Although it was not a sellout, 46,059

Hideo Nomo threw two no-hitters (one with the Dodgers) and struck out 17 in April 1996 against the Marlins.

tickets were sold for an early-season game on a busy sports night in the city.

Nomo had a bit of a shaky start. Rookie leadoff man Quilvio Veras singled Jesus Tavarez drew a base on balls, putting two on with no outs for Florida's best hitter, Gary Sheffield. Nomo struck out Sheffield and catcher Mike Piazza gunned down Veras trying to steal third for a double play. Jeff Conine followed with a strikeout.

Two Marlins fanned in the second and the first two struck out in the third before Veras homered to give the Marlins a 1-0 lead. Veras's line drive hit the top of the wall in right field and bounced up in the air and back onto the field. First-base umpire Tom Hallion ruled it a homer.

The Dodgers tied the game on a solo homer by left fielder Billy Ashley in the third. A two-run homer by right fielder Raúl Mondesí in the fourth put the Dodgers ahead.

After five innings, Nomo was up to 10 strikeouts. He struck out two in the sixth sandwiched around a walk to Veras, who was subsequently picked off by Nomo and caught stealing at second. Nomo struck out the side in the seventh to bring his total to 15 K's.

By this time, Dodgers fans were aware that they could be seeing something special. The team record for strikeouts in a game was 18, done twice by Sandy Koufax (in 1959 and 1962) and matched by Ramón Martínez in 1990.

Shortstop Kurt Abbott was victim 16 to lead off the eighth, but the next two batters, pinch-hitter Joe Orsulak and Veras, were retired on a popout and a lineout, respectively.

Tavarez led off the ninth with a strikeout to bring Nomo's total to 17, one more than his previous best of 16, against the Pirates in 1995. A tiring Nomo had two chances left to get to 18 or 19. But Sheffield managed to ground out weakly to the box and Conine ended the game with a lineout to left. Even though it was not even a team record, the crowd roared its approval as Nomo pitched a game that put him in rarefied air among Dodgers pitchers.

With Nomo racking up the strikeouts and the game going by quickly (2:10), a large portion of the crowd stayed for the duration to cheer on the team's newest pitching hero.

After the game Abbott, Nomo's former teammate in Japan on the Kintetsu Buffaloes, said, "I just started laughing. It was so frustrating."[4]

Nomo downplayed the strikeouts after the game. "I didn't really think about it. The main point of the game is for the team to win instead of me setting records," he said through an interpreter. "It was fun. I was happy I was able to pitch in this kind of situation."[5]

Manager Tommy Lasorda said, "He was great. I can't put it any simpler. The man was great. I don't think there any doubts now."[6]

After the consecutive complete games, Nomo did not have another one until September 17, when he threw a no-hitter at Coors Field against the Rockies.

Nomo left the Dodgers in the middle of the 1998 season after requesting a trade instead of accepting a relief role. He then kicked around the majors, going to the Mets, Brewers, Tigers, and Red Sox. Nomo threw a second no-hitter, pitching for the Red Sox in 2001. He showed enough in 2001, leading the American League in strikeouts with 220, to get a return to the Dodgers, where he pitched well in 2002 and 2003, but fell off badly in 2004, going 4-11 with an ERA of 8.25, and was left off the postseason roster.

In seven Dodger seasons, Nomo was 81-66 with a 3.74 ERA.

After the Marlins game ended, the crowd filed out and got in their cars to head home, only to find out that the same sporting events that caused the traffic to get there had all ended around the same time too.

AUTHOR'S NOTE

The author attended this game and even for a lifelong Southern California resident found the traffic jams to be almost impenetrable.

SOURCES

In addition to the sources cited in the Notes, the author consulted Baseball-Reference.com and Retrosheet.org,

https://www.baseball-reference.com/boxes/LAN/LAN199604130.shtml

https://www.retrosheet.org/boxesetc/1996/B04130LAN1996.htm

NOTES

1   Grahame L. Jones, "Galaxy's Opener Is Fantastic: Soccer: Crowd of 69,225 at Rose Bowl watches 2-1 victory over MetroStars," *Los Angeles Times*, April 14, 1996; Shawn Hubler, "Soccer Surprise Stokes Debate on Rose Bowl," *Los Angeles Times*, April 18, 1996.

2   Scott Wolf, "Clippers Make Noise Against Jazz – Clippers 91, Utah 81," *Los Angeles Daily News*, April 14, 1996.

3   Bob Nightengale, "Astros Performance Takes Words Out of Nomo's Mouth," *Los Angeles Times*, April 4, 1996.

4   Bob Nightengale, "17 Marlins Join Nomo's Fan Club: Dodgers Pitcher Gets Career High in 3-1 Victory Over Florida," *Los Angeles Times*, April 14, 1996.

5   Nightengale, "17 Marlins Join Nomo's Fan Club."

6   Nightengale, "17 Marlins Join Nomo's Fan Club."

FERNANDO TATÍS TATTOOS TWO GRAND SLAMS IN THE SAME INNING

April 23, 1999: St. Louis Cardinals 12, Los Angeles Dodgers 5

By Mike Huber

The season was barely three weeks old. The visiting Cardinals were looking for their 10th victory of the season, while the hometown Dodgers were looking for win number nine. Before a crowd of 46,687 on a Friday night, St. Louis's José Jiménez squared off against Los Angeles' Chan Ho Park. Jiménez pitched seven innings to earn his second win of the season; Park did not last three innings. However, he did pitch enough of the third inning to make history. Each team mustered 11 hits in the game, but St. Louis put together six of theirs, two walks, a hit batsman, a batter who reached on a fielder's choice, and another batter who reached on an error – 11 baserunners – in an explosive third inning in which they scored 11 runs.

Powered by third baseman Fernando Tatís, the Cardinals sent up 14 batters in the top of the third. Tatís did something no other major leaguer has accomplished through the 2014 season. He slugged two grand slams in the same inning.

Los Angeles scored single runs in the first and second innings and led 2-0 as the Cardinals came to bat in the top of the third. The Cardinals had managed three baserunners and a stolen base in the first two innings but didn't score. For Los Angeles, Gary Sheffield hit a sacrifice fly to plate Eric Young in the first inning, and Todd Hundley hit a sacrifice fly to score Devon White in the second.

In the top of the third, the first three Cardinals (Darren Bragg, Edgar Renteria, and Mark McGwire) all reached to load the bases. Third-base coach Rene Lachemann held Bragg at third after McGwire's bloop single to right field. On a hitter's count, Tatís clobbered a 2-and-0 offering into the Dodgers' left-field bullpen, giving the Cardinals an instant lead. J.D. Drew grounded to first. Eli Marrero homered to deep left field. Pinch-hitter Plácido Polanco walked, as did Joe McEwing. Jiménez reached on a fielder's choice (a sacrifice bunt that Park threw wide to third base). Bragg, Renteria, and McGwire all came up with the bases loaded, and each at-bat ended with the bases still loaded, as Bragg reached on an error, Renteria singled with Jiménez holding at third, and McGwire popped out. This set the stage again for Tatís, who rocketed a full count pitch off Park, still laboring, into the pavilion past the left-center fence. Tatís had seen nine pitches in the inning and he had knocked in eight runs. After the second grand slam, Dodgers manager Davey Johnson pulled Park in favor of Carlos Pérez.

Until Tatís, Mark McGwire had been the only member of the 1999 Cardinals to have hit two home runs in the same inning.[1] However, McGwire had been with the Oakland Athletics at the time and only one of the home runs had been with the bases loaded. Describing Tatís's feat, a reporter for the *St. Louis Post-Dispatch* wrote, "Two swings of his bat, two thunder bolts into the Southern California night."[2] McGwire made both of the grand slams possible for Tatís. In his first at-bat in the third inning, McGwire singled to load the bases; in his second at-bat, he popped out to shallow right field, keeping the bases loaded for Tatís and the history books.

St. Louis added a run in the top of the sixth when Drew hit a two-out solo home run. Jiménez was cruising through the Dodgers lineup, at one point retiring nine in a row from the fourth through the sixth. In the seventh, however, he allowed three singles and a walk, giving up two more runs. Manny Aybar came on in the eighth to pitch for the Cardinals and allowed a run on a double and two groundouts. That ended the scoring in the game. The Cardinals cruised to a 12-5 victory over the Dodgers.

Dodgers broadcaster Vin Scully had been behind the mike for three perfect games and Hank Aaron's record-breaking 715th home run. After this game, Scully said, "When he came up the second time, I said, 'I'm not even going to look in the record book because I can't believe anybody could have ever (hit two slams in an inning),' and then damned if he didn't do it. What would it be comparable to? I don't know how you could compare it to anything. One inning is so preposterous."[3]

Sports Illustrated writers Tom Verducci and Jeff Pearlman noted that Dodgers pitcher Park had "served up both salamis to become the second pitcher after Whoa Bill Phillips to give up two slams in the same inning."[4] Phillips allowed two grand slams on August 16, 1890, pitching for the Pittsburgh Alleghenys against the Chicago Colts. Verducci and Pearlman wrote that the grand slams were Tatís's first in the major leagues; he "walloped a 2-and-0 fast-ball 450 feet into the Dodgers' bullpen for his first home run," then "double-Parked with two out by driving a 3-and-2 slider into the left-field pavilion."[5]

Since the American League began in 1901, only four major-league teams had hit two grand slams in the same inning, and these were by different batters.[6] No St. Louis Cardinal batter had ever hit two home runs in the same inning until this game.[7] In his historic feat, Fernando Tatís became the second National League player and the 10th major leaguer to hit two grand slams in one game.[8] The first National Leaguer was Atlanta Braves pitcher Tony Cloninger, who accomplished the task on July 3, 1966.[9] Tatís was the 20th major leaguer to homer twice in the same inning.[10]

AUTHOR'S NOTE

1. Tatís borrowed teammate Eric Davis's bat this night.[11]

2. McGwire had only six RBIs on the young season, but teammate Tatís had eight after two swings in this game's third inning.

3. The four previous teams to hit two grand slams in the same inning were the 1962 Minnesota Twins, the 1969 Houston Astros, the 1980 Milwaukee Brewers, and the 1986 Baltimore Orioles.

ACKNOWLEDGMENT

The author wishes to thank Ms. Rachel Hamelers, science librarian and reference services manager at Trexler Library, Muhlenberg College, for her assistance with obtaining sources.

SOURCES

In addition to the sources mentioned in the Notes, the author consulted Baseball-Reference.com, MLB.com, Retrosheet.org and SABR.org.

baseball-reference.com/boxes/LAN/LAN199904230.shtml

retrosheet.org/boxesetc/1999/B04230LAN1999.htm

NOTES

1. Rick Hummel, "It was Grand Night for Tatis; Cards Third Baseman Basks in 15 Minutes of Fame After Slams," *St. Louis Post-Dispatch*, April 25, 1999.

2. Bernie Miklasz, "Tatis Is Showing Ability to Handle Sudden Celebrity," *St. Louis Post-Dispatch*, April 26, 1999.

3. Rick Hummel, "Scully Relishes Tatis Slam Call." *St. Louis Post-Dispatch*, April 25, 1999.

4. Tom Verducci and Jeff Pearlman, "Slam Dancing," *Sports Illustrated*, May 3, 1999, 78.

5. Verduci and Pearlman.

6. Hummel, "It was Grand Night for Tatis; Cards Third Baseman Basks in 15 Minutes of Fame After Slams."

7. Tim Crothers, "In the Name of the Father," *Sports Illustrated*, June 14, 1999, 80.

8. "Two Grand Slams in One Game," baseball-almanac.com/feats/feats11.shtml.

9. Rick Hummel, "Tatis Hits Two Grand Slams in Third," *St. Louis Post-Dispatch*, April 24, 1999.

10. Hummel, "Tatis Hits Two Grand Slams in Third."

11. Crothers.

STEVE FINLEY GRAND SLAM ENDS DODGER PLAYOFF DROUGHT

October 2, 2004: Los Angeles Dodgers 7, San Francisco Giants 3

by Carter Cromwell

When Steve Finley came to bat with one out and the bases loaded in the bottom of the ninth inning on the afternoon of October 2, 2004, he had 35 home runs, tying a career high, and his Los Angeles Dodgers had just rallied to a 3-3 tie with their longtime rivals, the San Francisco Giants. Quickly, he snapped both ties and eliminated the potential of another.

Finley hit the second pitch from San Francisco's Wayne Franklin into the right-field stands at Dodger Stadium to lift his team to a 7-3 victory that clinched the National League West Division championship and extinguished the possibility of the teams finishing in a tie and needing a playoff.

And Finley's game-winning blast capped a regular season few had expected. The Dodgers hadn't made the playoffs since 1996 and had gotten a new owner in Frank McCourt and a new general manager in Paul DePodesta just before spring training. Still, they managed to lead the division for most of the opening months and made a key move by getting Finley from the Arizona Diamondbacks just minutes before the trade deadline.

Finley was a two-time All-Star who would retire with five Gold Glove Awards and more than 2,500 hits, and become one of only two major leaguers to hit at least 300 homers, 425 doubles, and 100 triples, and steal at least 300 bases. The other is Willie Mays.

At the time of the trade, Finley was batting .275 with 23 home runs, 48 RBIs, and an .828 OPS. He was still a good defender and played in all 162 games, despite being 39 years old. He had rejected deals to go to Florida and San Francisco. However, "right at the deadline came the opportunity to play in LA. I've always liked big markets, and this was just a perfect fit."[1]

Finley played in 58 games for his new team, posting a slash line of .263/.324/.491 with 13 home runs and 46 RBIs, and the last of his home runs pushed Los Angeles over the finish line in this next-to-last game of the regular season.

The Dodgers held a three-game lead over the Giants going into the final three-game series at Dodger Stadium – a classic matchup of heated rivals with the division title and playoff participation at stake. A crowd of 54,594 watched the action.

San Francisco had to sweep the series to force a playoff, and took the opener 4-2. In the second game, the Giants started Brett Tomko, who had gone 5-1 with a 1.64 ERA over his previous seven starts. The Dodgers countered with Elmer Dessens, who had done well in relief since being traded from Arizona on August 19 but was making his first start for Los Angeles because the rotation had lately suffered from injuries and ineffectiveness.

Former Dodger Eric Karros, color analyst on the Fox Sports telecast, predicted that "[i]f the Dodgers can get Tomko out early and get to that bullpen, they could fare a bit better."[2]

Tomko did not leave early, but the Dodgers did fare better when they finally got into the Giants' bullpen, which had been inconsistent all season. Tomko lasted 7⅓ innings, allowing just four hits and no runs. Meanwhile, San Francisco got a two-run single from Marquis Grissom in the fourth inning to help chase Dessens, and Grissom hit a solo homer off Duaner Sánchez in the seventh to make the score 3-0.

Tomko finally exited with one out in the eighth after Olmedo Sáenz and Jayson Werth had singled. Reliever Scott Eyre got Finley to ground out, and Giants manager Felipe Alou brought in closer Dustin Hermanson, who had earned the save the previous night, to face Adrián Beltré. The strategy worked, as Beltré grounded out on the first pitch to end the threat.

Hermanson, though, wasn't sharp in the dramatic ninth inning. Shawn Green led off by flaring an opposite-field single that Giants left fielder Barry Bonds just missed catching. Robin Ventura walked on a 3-and-2 pitch; Alex Cora struck out; and José Hernández walked on another 3-and-2 pitch to load the bases. Hee-Seop Choi pinch-hit for pitcher Yhency Brazobán and also went to 3-and-2 before walking to force in Ventura and make the score 3-1. At that point, Karros remarked, "You have to wonder if bringing in Hermanson in the eighth inning to face Beltré may have affected him. He came back out and had nothing left here in the ninth – no command."[3]

Hermanson was pulled in favor of Jason Christiansen after throwing 30 pitches in the inning, and Antonio Pérez ran for Choi. Christiansen induced César Izturis to ground a 1-and-1 pitch to the right of shortstop Cody Ransom, who had been inserted for defense. Ransom charged the ball, crossed over and tried to scoop it, but it went just under his glove for an error that enabled Ventura to score.

Reviewing the play, Karros said, "You've got to get one out here. [But it's] a tough play. You don't know if you can get the runner at second or the one at first. It's almost a do-or-die play, and ... he died."[4]

Right-hander Matt Herges then entered to face Jayson Werth, who fouled off several pitches and worked the count to 2-and-2.

"[Werth] is set up now," Karros said. "He's probably looking for a fastball away. If they come back with a fastball on the hands, they'll get him."[5]

However, though Giants catcher Yorvit Torrealba indeed set the target down and in, Herges' pitch leaked to the outside, and Werth reached out and lined it into right field for a single that scored Hernández, tied the game and sent the sellout crowd of 54,594 into another level of delirium.

Karros: "The idea was right, but the execution wasn't. Anything inside would have tied him up. Great job of hitting by Werth."[6]

That brought up Finley, who had had only four hits in his past 24 at-bats before the game. Giants manager Alou turned to Wayne Franklin, the fourth pitcher he called on in the ninth inning. A walk, a base hit or even a productive out would have won the game. The Dodgers just needed a fly ball deep enough to score Pérez from third base to win, but Finley provided much more.

"I was dreaming about it, and it happened," Finley said afterward. "I knew I was going to get it done. When I walked to the plate, I knew the game was over."[7]

Asked about it years later, Finley said, "I remember that Franklin in warm-ups didn't throw a pitch near the plate for a strike. Then the first pitch was right down the middle, and I thought, 'Are you kidding??'"[8]

But the next pitch was a fastball above the belt. Finley belted it, and Dodgers broadcaster Vin Scully exclaimed, "High fly ball to deep right field. Wherever it goes, the Dodgers have won!"[9]

It went over the 375-foot sign to give the Dodgers a franchise-record 53rd come-from-behind victory in the season and the division championship. Thirteen of the team's last 14 wins were comeback victories, and it won 26 in the final at-bats.[10]

"Can you believe this finish?!" Fox play-by-play announcer Thom Brennaman exclaimed.[11]

"We do it the Hollywood way – that's for sure," Dodger closer Eric Gagné said afterward. "It's amazing."[12]

Brennaman said, "[Finley was] unquestionably the biggest acquisition any team made at the deadline." Karros agreed: "Clutch hits, exciting defense, and he's a proven winner. He's been a godsend."[13]

The Dodgers lost to St. Louis in the National League Division Series, but that didn't dim the thrill of the division clincher.

One fan posted, "I was in Palm Desert after going to the previous 2 games. My wife [was] sleeping on (the) couch pregnant with my now 13 [year-old] daughter. When he hits that GS I quietly get up, go outside, walk about 25 feet away from the condo and scream[ed] like a little girl."

Another wrote, "That was the first game I ever went to. I remember everything about that game. ... Oh, good memories."[14]

SOURCES

In addition to the sources cited in the Notes, the author consulted Baseball-Reference.com and Retrosheet.org.

https://www.baseball-reference.com/boxes/LAN/LAN200410020.shtml

https://www.retrosheet.org/boxesetc/2004/B10020LAN2004.htm

NOTES

1   "Steve Finley and Shawn Green Relive Some Big Moments from the 2004 Dodgers Pennant Chase," IsoLate Night with Scott Rogowsky: https://www.youtube.com/watch?app=desktop&v=3yxEzhbfAck.

2   Fox Sports telecast of game, "Giants vs. Dodgers (10-2-2004, Dodgers clinch NL West," https://www.youtube.com/watch?v=8LbAGISAgTY.

3   Fox Sports telecast.

4   Fox Sports telecast.

5   Fox Sports telecast.

6   Fox Sports telecast.

7   "L.A. Wins West," *Washington Post*, October 3, 2004. https://www.washingtonpost.com/archive/sports/2004/10/03/la-wins-west/f150bdfe-03fe-44de-bcce-b627055389b2/.

8   IsoLate Night with Scott Rogowsky.

9   "Giants vs. Dodgers (10-2-2004, Dodgers clinch NL West," MLB, https://www.youtube.com/watch?v=d5NdnmQ_XSA.

10 "L.A. Wins West," *Washington Post*.

11 Fox Sports telecast.

12 Associated Press, "Finley's Slam Gives Dodgers West Crown," *Spokane Spokesman-Review*, October 3, 2004: https://www.spokesman.com/stories/2004/oct/03/finleys-slam-gives-dodgers-west-crown/.

13 Fox Sports telecast.

14 "Greatest Dodger Moments: A Grand Slam from Steve Finley for the NL West Crown," dodgersnation.com, March 3, 2013: https://dodgersnation.com/greatest-dodger-moments-a-grand-slam-from-steve-finley-for-the-nl-west-crown/2019/03/13/.

JOSÉ LIMA SHUTOUT BREAKS POSTSEASON DROUGHTS FOR DODGERS – AND DODGER STADIUM

October 9, 2004: Los Angeles Dodgers 4, St. Louis Cardinals 0
(Game Three of the 2004 National League Division Series)

by Joal Ryan

The drought at Dodger Stadium was serious. Heading into the 2004 season, a venue once flush with play-off and World Series games now came up dry year after year in October. The home team hadn't made the playoffs since 1996; Los Angeles, in fact, hadn't recorded a postseason win at Dodger Stadium since Orel Hershiser shut down the Oakland A's in Game Two of the 1988 World Series. The fault was not with the ballpark: The Dodgers hadn't won a postseason game *anywhere* since claiming the '88 title on the road. From 1989 to 2003, the ballclub either didn't make the playoffs or got swept out of them (as happened in back-to-back National League Division Series, in 1995 and 1996). The 15-year stretch of postseason futility was unprecedented for the Brooklyn-born franchise at Chavez Ravine.

With new owners (Frank and Jamie McCourt, taking the keys from the Fox Group[1]) and a new general manager (Paul DePodesta, fresh from the Oakland A's front office, and the pages of the best-selling *Moneyball*), the 2004 Dodgers looked primed to deliver storylines. They didn't, however, look primed to deliver postseason success. Writing for ESPN, baseball analyst Tom Tippett projected that the Dodgers would finish fourth in the NL West with a 77-85 record.[2]

Opening Day loss aside, the Dodgers got off to a fast start. Fueled by MVP candidate Adrián Beltré, putting up what would be career bests in home runs (48), RBIs (121), and batting average (.334), the Dodgers led the NL West at the All-Star break. The team kept rolling even after DePodesta overhauled the roster at the nonwaiver trade deadline, shipping out All-Star catcher Paul Lo Duca, premier set-up man Guillermo Mota, and two-thirds of its Opening Day outfield squadron, Dave Roberts and Juan Encarnación. In the next to last game of the regular season, the Dodgers clinched the NL West flag at home on a walk-off grand slam by Steve Finley, one of DePodesta's trade-deadline acquisitions. For the first time in the twenty-first century, Randy Newman's "Love L.A." was played at Dodger Stadium as the home team celebrated a division title.

In the four-team field that would determine the NL's World Series representative, the 93-win Dodgers were seeded third. They opened their best-of-five NL Division Series on the road against the top-seeded, 105-win St. Louis Cardinals. Game One at Busch Memorial Stadium[3] was a blowout 8-3 win for the resident NL Central champs. Albert Pujols, Larry Walker, and Jim Edmonds each homered off Odalis Pérez and chased the one-time Dodgers All-Star in the third inning. Game Two was a variation on the same theme: Dodgers starter Jeff Weaver surrendered six runs in 4⅔ innings; the Cardinals won 8-3. And just like that, as the series decamped to Los Angeles, the Dodgers faced elimination – and the prospect of another winless postseason.

For the must-win Game Three, José Lima was summoned as the Dodgers' starter. Once an All-Star and Cy Young vote-getter for the Houston Astros, Lima made eight starts in 2003 for the independent Atlantic League's Newark Bears. Before the 2004 season, the not-shy right-hander turned down a guaranteed deal from the Kansas City Royals, and bet on himself to make a bigger, better splash with the Dodgers.[4] "The magic is still there," he said at camp in Vero Beach, Florida.[5] True enough, the nonroster spring-training invitee made the Dodgers' starting rotation. He posted the second-best WHIP of the staff (1.245), and the third best of his roller-coaster career. He was especially effective at Dodger Stadium. He went 9-1 at home, with a 3.08 ERA (versus a 4-4 record and 5.56 ERA on the road). Tasked with bringing his self-proclaimed "Lima Time" show to Game Three, Lima had a plan. "I've got to come, and give my heart to this team," he said.[6]

Dodger Stadium, meanwhile, seemed to go all-out for its first postseason game in eight years. Its seats were full; the governor of California, Arnold Schwarzenegger, was in attendance. Even the Los Angeles weather was a Central Casting special: 70 degrees at game time. To the broadcast team calling the game for Fox, Thom Brennaman and Tim McCarver, the home team's shot at winning the do-or-die contest hinged on whether Lima could give the Dodgers six innings against the NL's highest-scoring team and shorten the bridge to LA's reigning Cy Young closer, Eric Gagné.

Lima opened the game with a strike to Tony Womack. One pitch later, Womack was on first after a line-drive single to right. Walker, Pujols, and Scott Rolen were due up. Lima struck out Walker, got a groundout from Pujols, struck out Rolen, and left Womack stranded on third. In the bottom of the first, Lima's counterpart, Matt Morris, a 15-game winner for St. Louis in the regular season, had an even easier time with the Dodgers' offense. He set down César Izturis, Jayson Werth, and Finley on 14 pitches.

In the second, Lima and Morris posted matching performances: Lima gave up a single to Edmonds; Morris surrendered one to Shawn Green; both got inning-ending double plays. The pitchers' paths diverged in the third. Lima got a one-two-three inning. Then, in the bottom of the frame, Dodger Stadium seemed to make Morris and the Cardinals pay for everything that had gone wrong for the boys in blue since '88.

Morris grazed leadoff batter Alex Cora on the right hand. According to the *Los Angeles Times*, Cardinals manager Tony La Russa appealed to the umpires that Cora didn't try to get out of the way of the pitch.[7] But the Dodgers infielder, who racked up the fourth-most HBPs in the major leagues in 2004, stayed at first. Brent Mayne, another Dodgers trade-deadline addition, followed with a single to center. With runners on the corners and no outs, Lima came to the plate,

and crouched for a sacrifice bunt. On a 1-and-0 count, he made contact. The TV broadcast showed that the batted ball bounced up and hit Lima's bat or hand before the Dodger took off down the line.[8]

The Gerry Davis-led umpire crew, which conferred on the matter but didn't have the benefit of replay, called Lima safe at first.[9] (After the game, Davis said the play should've been ruled a foul ball.)[10] Making matters worse for the Cardinals, catcher Mike Matheny, who'd jumped on the Lima ball and fired it to get Mayne, the lead runner, at second, failed to get the out call there. When the dust settled, the Dodgers had the bases loaded – and still no outs. The ballpark was a blizzard of white as fans, some sporting "It's Lima Time!" T-shirts, whirled rally towels. Still, Morris held his ground. He again got the Dodgers' one-two hitters, Izturis and Werth. With two outs, the bases still loaded, and the game still scoreless, Finley, the hero from the previous week, got a broken-bat hit into the left-field corner. The double scored Cora and Mayne. The Dodgers were up 2-0 – and though they'd add two more runs, thanks to solo homers in the fourth and sixth innings from Green, they'd handed Lima all the scoring he'd need.

Inning after inning, Lima kept the Cardinals off balance. St. Louis's biggest threat came in the fifth, when Edmonds and Matheny singled. But with two outs and the Dodgers ahead 3-0, the Cardinals allowed Morris to bat. The pitcher grounded out.

As the game went on, Lima grew more animated – a fist pump after getting Walker looking in the sixth; a bigger fist pump after getting Reggie Sanders to close out the seventh with a fly ball; a roar after getting the third out, a grounder from Walker, in the eighth. The Dodger Stadium faithful grew more animated, too. They roared along with Lima. They chanted his name. And likely anticipating a "Welcome to the Jungle"-accented appearance by Gagné in the ninth, they demanded a curtain call after the Walker groundout. But it was Lima, not Gagné, who stood on the mound as the Dodgers looked for the game's final three outs. Pitching with a hairline fracture in his right thumb,[11] and rarely touching 90 mph, Lima had managed eight scoreless innings on 99 pitches, walking only one and allowing five hits. He'd need only 10 more pitches to dispose of Pujols, Rolen, and Edmonds. The Dodgers won, 4-0.

Dodger Stadium was not only back in the postseason business, it was back in the postseason-win column. The drought was over. The next night, the Dodgers would be eliminated in Game Four, with a

6-2 loss, but the Lima Time triumph was not diminished. "The best game ever," Cora would recall in 2010 after Lima died of a heart attack at age 37. "I still remember 50,000 people going 'Lima, Lima' in the ninth inning."[12]

SOURCES

In addition to the sources cited in the notes, the author consulted Baseball-Reference.com for box scores/play-by-play information, and stats; SABR's José Lima biography by Rory Costello; and video of game at YouTube.com.

https://www.baseball-reference.com/boxes/LAN/LAN200410090.shtml

https://www.youtube.com/watch?v=CPMUI1gOSuk

NOTES

1   Andy McCue, "Los Angeles/Brooklyn Dodgers Team Ownership History," Society for American Baseball Research, last accessed on November 19, 2023: https://sabr.org/bioproj/topic/los-angeles-brooklyn-dodgers-team-ownership-history/.

2   Tom Tippett, "Projected Standings for 2004," ESPN, April 4, 2004, last accessed on November 19, 2023: https://www.espn.com/mlb/spring2004/news/story?id=1774245.

3   Busch Memorial Stadium (referred to as Busch Stadium II by Baseball-Reference.com) was the home of the St. Louis Cardinals from 1966 to 2005. The current (as of 2023) park for the Cardinals, Busch Stadium III, opened in April 2006.

4   Bill Shaikin, "Lima Feeling Content With Past and Future," *Los Angeles Times*, March 11, 2004: D11.

5   "Lima Feeling Content With Past and Future."

6   John Nadel (Associated Press), "Morris Has Chance to Finish Job," *Indiana* (Pennsylvania) *Gazette*, October 9, 2004: 19.

7   There was no mention, or shot of, Tony La Russa disputing the Cora HBP on the Fox broadcast. Bill Shaikin, "Umpires Say They Goofed," *Los Angeles Times*, October 10, 2004: D14.

8   The Fox broadcast refers to the ball as hitting Lima in fair territory, on the bat. "Umpires Say They Goofed."

9   "Umpires Say They Goofed."

10 "Umpires Say They Goofed."

11 Jason Reid, "Thumb Injury Sidelines Lima; Jackson to Start," *Los Angeles Times*, September 19, 2004: D5.

12 Ian Begley, "Mets' Reyes on Lima: 'A Great Guy,'" ESPN, May 23, 2010, last accessed on November 19, 2023: https://www.espn.com/new-york/mlb/news/story?id=5213357.

DODGERS TIE PADRES WITH 4 STRAIGHT HRS IN 9TH

September 18, 2006: Los Angeles Dodgers 11, San Diego Padres 10

by Bob Timmermann

The 2006 version of the Los Angeles Dodgers was one of the franchise's greatest offensive teams. The Dodgers had the second most runs scored by a Los Angeles team, 820 (22 behind the 1962 squad, which played three more games). They weren't known for hitting home runs, with only 153 for the season, second to last in the National League. But on September 18, with first place in the NL West on the line, the Dodgers put on an unprecedented power display in a game with repeated changes of fortune.

The Dodgers were finishing up a four-game series at home against the first-place San Diego Padres and were a half-game back. A 3-1 win in the series opener on September 15, behind 40-year-old Greg Maddux, had given Los Angeles a 1½-game lead over San Diego, but the Padres had responded by pounding the Dodgers, 11-2, in the series' second game and pushing across a ninth-inning run for a 2-1 win a night later, knocking Los Angeles from first place for the first time since August 9.

The Padres had won 13 of the 17 previous meetings with the Dodgers and their half-game lead in the NL West was viewed as almost their right. The Padres were battle-tested while the Dodgers relied on many rookies. "We're built for games like this," said the Padres' Dave Roberts. "We have guys who have been here before, who understand what happens when the pressure mounts."[1]

Brad Penny started for the Dodgers. Penny led the team in wins with 16 but had an ERA of 4.04. Jake Peavy, who was already 6-1 in his career against the Dodgers, started for the Padres. (Peavy would finish his career 15-3 against the Dodgers, the highest winning percentage of any pitcher against the Dodgers with more than 15 decisions.)

Night games at Dodger Stadium are known for being low-scoring affairs, in which home runs are infrequent because of the infamous Marine Layer, a term used to describe the cooler weather that prevails in parts of the region that get onshore breezes from the Pacific.[2] However, the Marine Layer is seasonal, most commonly occurring in May and June. September and October are often some of the hottest months in California.

And on September 18, 2006, the game-time temperature was a balmy 80. It would cool off at night, but not all that much.

The Padres scored four runs in the top of the first off Penny, who appeared to have little to offer in the way of fooling San Diego hitters. However, the Dodgers started pecking away at Peavy and thanks to RBI doubles from Jeff Kent and J.D. Drew and solo homers by Marlon Anderson and Rafael Furcal, the Dodgers tied the game at 4-4 after three innings.

The bullpens were in charge from the sixth inning on – normally a strength for each team. But not on this night. The Padres scored five runs off Jonathan Broxton and Takashi Saito and the Dodgers managed a run off Scott Linebrink. The Padres led, 9-5, going into the bottom of the ninth.

The four-run lead meant that it was not a save situation. So Padres manager Bruce Bochy decided not to call on his future Hall of Fame closer, Trevor Hoffman. Instead, he brought in Jon Adkins.

The first batter Adkins faced was Jeff Kent. On the second pitch to him, Kent homered deep to center to make it 9-6. J.D. Drew followed: Four pitches later, it was 9-7 after another homer, this one landing two-thirds of the way up in the right-field pavilion. The remnants of the Dodger Stadium crowd began making U-turns and heading back to their seats.[3]

Bochy brought in Hoffman to replace Adkins. Up to bat was rookie catcher Russell Martin, whose father had flown in from Montreal to watch the game.[4] Martin hit Hoffman's first pitch for a home run just over the left-field fence to make it 9-8.

The crowd was now extremely interested, and quite loud despite the late hour on a school night.[5] Up to bat was Marlon Anderson, an August 31 acquisition from the Washington Nationals. He had been 12-for-28 so far in his short time in Los Angeles, and Dodgers manager Grady Little had given Anderson the left-field job over rookie Andre Ethier to keep his bat in the lineup.

Hoffman threw one pitch to Anderson. Anderson hit it just over the right-field fence to tie the game at 9-9. For the first time in major-league history, a team down four runs in the ninth had tied the game on four straight solo home runs. It was the first save Hoffman had blown against the Dodgers since 2001. Hoffman got fly outs from Julio Lugo, Ethier, and Furcal and managed to preserve the tie.

In the 10th, the next man up for the Dodgers on the mound was veteran Aaron Sele. San Diego catcher Josh Bard tagged him for a two-out RBI double to give San Diego a 10-9 lead.

Bochy did not like to use Hoffman for more than one inning, so he brought in Rudy Seanez, who was in his fourth of four stints with San Diego. (He would also have two different tours with the Dodgers.) "We could have pushed [Hoffman], but I would have felt worse if we had pushed him and something would have happened," Bochy said after the game.[6]

Seanez walked Kenny Lofton to lead off the inning. That brought up first baseman Nomar Garciaparra, who was a relatively quiet 1-for-5 in the game. Seanez fell behind 3-and-1 and then left a pitch over the plate. Garciaparra swung, dropped the bat and admired a shot that went into the left-field pavilion. The Dodgers had come all the way back to win, 11-10, and move into first place. "When I was rounding the bases, I couldn't wait to get home and hug everybody. It was like a group hug, because it was a group effort," Garciaparra said.[7]

"It's definitely the greatest game I've ever played in," said Marlon Anderson.[8]

The Dodgers finished with 19 hits, including seven home runs. None of the Padres' 15 hits were homers, but they benefited from eight walks (three of them intentional) from Dodgers pitching. Despite scoring 11 runs, the Dodgers were just 3-for-13 in at-bats with runners in scoring position.

The next day the Dodgers lost to the Pirates, 10-6, to fall back into second. They finished the regular season tied with the Padres for first at 88-74, with San Diego being declared division champs because of the teams' head-to-head record. The Dodgers went on to face the Mets in the playoffs as the wild card and were swept in three games. The Padres fell to the eventual World Series champion Cardinals in four games.

SOURCES

In addition to the sources cited in the Notes, the author relied on the Baseball-Reference.com and Retrosheet.org websites for pertinent material and the box scores noted below. The author also reviewed a video of the Dodgers' four ninth-inning home runs and Garciaparra's game-winner in the 10th, available at the YouTube link noted below.

https://www.baseball-reference.com/boxes/LAN/LAN200609180.shtml

https://www.retrosheet.org/boxesetc/2006/B09180LAN2006.htm

https://www.youtube.com/watch?v=KJ-SHQ3cbKA

NOTES

1   Bill Plaschke, "Here's Why Half a Game Back Is a Tough Way to Go," *Los Angeles Times*, September 18, 2006: D1.

2   California-Nevada Applications Program, Scripps Institute of Oceanography, "What Are Marine Layer Clouds and How Do They Form?," available at http://meteora.ucsd.edu/~iacob/ml_formation.html (last accessed July 5, 2021).

3   Bill Plaschke, "Even Fans Were Part of the Comeback," *Los Angeles Times*, September 2006: D1.

4   "Even Fans Were Part of the Comeback."

5   "Even Fans Were Part of the Comeback."

6   Bill Shaikin, "What Are the Chances? Players Tell What It Was Like to Be a Part of Monday's Power Performance, Which Ranks High in Dodgers Lore," *Los Angeles Times*, September 20, 2006: D1.

7   Shaikin.

8   Shaikin.

DODGERS DEFEAT ANGELS
DESPITE GETTING NO HITS

June 28, 2008: Los Angeles Dodgers 1, Los Angeles Angels of Anaheim 0

by Mike Huber

"Zero hits and 50,000 cheers."[1] That's the best way to describe what took place on June 28, 2008, in a game between the Los Angeles Dodgers and the Los Angeles Angels of Anaheim at Dodger Stadium. Los Angeles manager Joe Torre described the game as "about as bizarre as you can get"[2] but added, "It was magical."[3] Broadcaster Vin Scully called it "unbelievable."[4] Whatever the descriptions, this game defied the odds, as the Dodgers beat the Angels, 1-0, without getting a single hit.

After playing 72 games against National League opponents to open the 2008 season, the Dodgers had a nine-game homestand against American League teams. They lost two series (to the Cleveland Indians and Chicago White Sox) before welcoming the Angels for a three-game set. Although they held second place in the NL West, the Dodgers (37-41) were struggling to score runs as they prepared to host Anaheim.

The Angels (48-31) were atop the AL West standings as they faced the Dodgers. This was their fifth consecutive series against NL foes, and after losing the first two series (to the Atlanta Braves and New York Mets), they had won five of their past six games (against the Philadelphia Phillies and Washington Nationals).

Chan Ho Park's strong start led to a four-hit shutout, as the Dodgers took the first game against the Angels, 6-0. Game Two was set for Saturday, June 28.

A crowd of 55,784 turned out for the crosstown rivalry, and a pair of right-handers faced off on the mound. For the Dodgers, it was 23-year-old Chad Billingsley, in his third major-league season. He had split his time in 2007 as both starter and reliever, but in 2008 he had become an integral part of LA's starting rotation. Billingsley had pitched at least five innings in 14 consecutive starts coming into this contest, and

he was in search of his seventh win of the season. Opposing him was Jered Weaver. The younger brother of former Dodgers hurler Jeff Weaver, Jered was also in his third ML season, always a starter. He had won five of his past seven decisions and was trying for season win number eight.

This proved to be a pitchers' duel from the start. Billingsley faced the minimum through the first two innings, notching two strikeouts. Weaver walked Andre Ethier in the opening inning but stranded him on the bases, and he retired three straight in the second, also recording two strikeouts.

Anaheim's Howie Kendrick led off the top of the third with a single to center. Jeff Mathis walked, and the Angels suddenly had a mini-rally. Because this was interleague play in a National League ballpark, Weaver had to bat. He struck out, and Billingsley retired both Maicer Izturis and Erick Aybar to end the inning.

Both teams had a baserunner in the fourth, as each pitcher gave up a base on balls. Billingsley was in a groove, though, and he fanned two more Angels in the fifth, giving him six through five innings.

The pivotal play of the game occurred in the bottom of the fifth inning. After taking a ball, Matt Kemp hit a "spinning squibber"[5] toward the right of the pitcher's mound. Weaver charged off the mound and reached down with his glove but could not pick up the ball. Scully described the path of the baseball: "That looked like a runaway gyroscope."[6] Kemp was safe on the play; Weaver was charged with a fielding error. Two pitches later, Kemp stole second base took third on catcher Mathis's throwing error, and scored the lone run of the game on Blake DeWitt's sacrifice fly to deep right field (on the very next pitch). Therefore, over the course of just four pitches, none of which turned into a Dodgers hit, Kemp reached first and came around to score. The Angels had made two errors. Angel Berroa flied out after Kemp scored. Weaver walked Billingsley, his third free pass of the game, before Juan Pierre grounded out to end a most unusual half-inning

Don Hartack, the official scorer, ruled that Kemp had indeed reached on an error. Hartack told reporters, "My thinking was, it really wasn't a bang-bang play. I looked at the replay once. Weaver had plenty of time to make the out."[7] When asked after the game, Kemp agreed with the ruling, saying, "He could have made the play, but he just dropped the ball. It was an error."[8] On air, Scully said, "He's gotta make that play, and he doesn't."[9]

The Angels threatened in the sixth. With one out, Aybar lined a single to right but was thrown out trying to stretch it into a double. Billingsley walked Garret Anderson. Vladimir Guerrero reached on an error by second baseman Jeff Kent. Billingsley recovered and again left the runners on base, striking out Torii Hunter. In the home half, Weaver hit Kent with a pitch, but he retired the side, still having not allowed a hit in the game.

Casey Kotchman led off the top of the seventh for the Angels with a single. Kendrick flied out, and then Angels manager Mike Scioscia inserted pinch-hitters for both Mathis and Weaver, the two players who had made the critical errors in the fifth. Billingsley induced two groundball outs, keeping the Angels off the scoreboard.

The Angels had a two-out single in the eighth, but again, the runner was stranded. José Arredondo relieved Weaver to pitch the seventh and eighth, and he retired all six batters he faced. The Dodgers still did not have a hit.

The Angels threatened to tie the game in the top of the ninth. Leading up to this point, the Angels were 0-for-5 with runners in scoring position. In a double-switch, Takashi Saito came on in relief to close out the game, and Luis Maza replaced Kent at second base. Saito struck out Hunter for the first out. Then second sacker Maza (who had replaced Kent) made a diving stop of Kotchman's grounder for the second out. The Angels still had some hope when Kendrick lined a pitch down the left-field line for a double. Mike Napoli walked, putting the go-ahead runner on base. If the Angels could tie the game, at least three more Dodgers batters would have to bat in the bottom of the ninth.

Reggie Willits entered as a pinch-hitter for Arredondo, and Saito struck him out swinging. Both Los Angeles batterymates pumped their fists in triumph. The Angels could not believe they had lost. The Dodgers could not believe they had won.

Weaver had nothing to show for his six innings of hitless work – except a loss. Billingsley struck out seven Anaheim batters in his seven innings on the mound. No Angels runners made it past second base. In fact, only four runners made it into scoring position. Billingsley was credited with the win, even though his own team did not get any hits. This marked the first time in 30 games that the Dodgers had won the contest while scoring two or fewer runs.[10]

The Angels were shut out for the second consecutive game. They did go on to win the series finale, beating the Dodgers 1-0 and holding them to three hits. Anaheim's run came on Napoli's RBI single in the second.

Angels hurlers Weaver and Arredondo were not credited with a no-hitter, since they pitched only a combined eight innings, one inning shy of the required nine for an official no-hit game. Weaver and Arredondo's combined feat resulted in only the fourth time in major-league history that a visiting team's pitcher(s) did not yield a hit but were not credited with the no-no.[11] To make the case more "bizarre" (to quote Torre), the winning run was unearned, meaning that neither team's pitchers gave up any earned runs.

SOURCES

In addition to the sources mentioned in the Notes, the author consulted Baseball-Reference.com, MLB.com, Retrosheet.org, and SABR.org.

https://www.baseball-reference.com/boxes/LAN/LAN200806280.shtml

https://www.retrosheet.org/boxesetc/2008/B06280LAN2008.htm

A YouTube video of the game (with broadcaster Vin Scully) can be found at https://www.youtube.com/watch?v=1T3thxbd7hY.

NOTES

1   Bill Plaschke, "Held hitless, Dodgers Still Win," *Los Angeles Times*, June 29, 2008: 61, 72.

2   Associated Press, "A No-Hitter That Wasn't (Wasn't Even a Victory)," *New York Times*, June 30, 2008, found online at https://www.nytimes.com/2008/06/30/sports/baseball/30nohitter.html. Accessed April 2023.

3   Plaschke.

4   "Angels vs Dodgers," YouTube video of the game. See https://www.youtube.com/watch?v=1T3thxbd7hY.

5   "A No-Hitter That Wasn't (Wasn't Even a Victory)."

6   "Angels vs Dodgers," YouTube video of the game. See https://www.youtube.com/watch?v=1T3thxbd7hY.

7   ESPN.com news services, "Weaver, Arredondo Hold Dodgers Hitless but Angels Still Lose," June 28, 2008, found online at https://www.espn.com/mlb/recap/_/gameId/280628119. Accessed April 2023.

8   "Weaver, Arredondo Hold Dodgers Hitless but Angels Still Lose."

9   "Angels vs Dodgers," YouTube video of the game. See https://www.youtube.com/watch?v=1T3thxbd7hY.

10   Plaschke.

11   The other three instances are: Charles "Silver" King, Chicago Pirates, lost to the Brooklyn Wonders (Players League) on June 21, 1890, by a score of 1-0; Andy Hawkins, New York Yankees, lost to the Chicago White Sox (American League) on July 1, 1990, by a score of 4-0; and Matt Young, Boston Red Sox, lost to the Cleveland Indians (American League) on April 12, 1992, by a score of 2-1.

ANDRE ETHIER HITS MAJOR-LEAGUE RECORD FOURTH WALK-OFF HOME RUN OF THE SEASON

September 15, 2009: Los Angeles Dodgers 4, Pittsburgh Pirates 3 (13 innings)

by Joseph Wancho

"Fastball ... High drive into deep right!
Back goes Jones! Is gone!"
– Vin Scully[1]

When Charles Dickens wrote, "It was the best of times, it was the worst of times, it was the age of wisdom, it was the age of foolishness …" to begin his classic book *A Tale of Two Cities*, he could have been referring to the Pittsburgh Pirates and Los Angeles Dodgers in 2009, which was 150 years after Dickens' masterpiece hit the bookshelves in bookstores and libraries.

Coming into the September 15, 2009, game, the Pirates were not only going through a tough stretch, having lost 15 of their last 17 games, they could have written a "how-to" guide" book on the subject. Since 2004 Pittsburgh had finished either last or fifth in the six-team National League Central Division. In 2009 they were in line to land in the cellar for the third straight season.

Los Angeles was shooting for its second straight NL West Division title and fourth postseason appearance since 2004. With 17 games left to play, the Dodgers held a four-game lead over the Colorado Rockies.

The 2009 season was winding down as Pittsburgh arrived in Los Angeles for a three-game set beginning on September 14. The Pirates (55-86) lost the opener to LA (85-59), 6-2. Dodgers starter Jon Garland pitched six strong innings while the bullpen threw shutout baseball for the final three frames. The Dodgers' hitting attack was led by Andre Ethier and Orlando Hudson. Each drove in two runs, with Either hitting his 29th home run of the season.

The pitching matchup for the second game of the series featured a pair of southpaws. Pittsburgh's Zach Duke (10-14, 4.02 ERA) opposed the Dodgers' Randy Wolf (10-6, 3.22). Like the teams they played for, the starting pitchers were having different levels of success in 2009. Duke had losing streaks of three and four games. He was named to the NL All-Star squad in 2009, although he did not appear in the game. He was tied with Cincinnati's Aaron Harang for the most losses in the NL.

Wolf began the season 5-6 before enjoying a four-game win streak from August 11 to 26 that upped his record to 9-6. Wolf was the workhorse of the LA staff, which would have three pitchers start 30 or more games: Wolf, Chad Billingsley, and Clayton Kershaw.

Pittsburgh scored first, three runs in the top of the second inning. With one down, Lastings Milledge walked. Steve Pearce, who was batting .225, lined his fourth home run of the season to left field to give the Pirates a 2-0 advantage. Ronny Cedeño followed with a double to center field and moved to third base on a groundout off the bat of Luis Cruz. Pitcher Duke singled him home to give Pittsburgh a 3-0 lead.

The lead was remarkable in that it provided Duke something he had lacking all year: "[T]he Pirates offense failed to score as many as three runs in 16 of his 28 previous starts."[2]

The score held until the bottom of the fifth inning, when Matt Kemp led off with a double to left field. He came home on a triple by Casey Blake. Mark Lorretta then lifted a fly ball to deep left field to bring home Blake. The Pirates' lead was sliced to 3-2.

Both starting pitchers were effective. Duke, in addition to collecting an RBI, pitched 7⅓ strong innings. He gave up two runs on four hits and struck out seven batters with no walks. Wolf hurled seven innings, surrendering three earned runs on five hits. He struck out five and walked two Pirates batters.

The question was whether Pittsburgh's relief corps could hold the one-run lead. The answer was no. Matt Capps, the Pirates' closer, entered the game in the bottom of the ninth with 25 saves. But he could not shut the door on LA. The Dodgers scored a run to knot the score, 3-3. With one away, Ethier doubled to right and scored on Kemp's single. It was the fifth blown save of the season for Capps, and the third in his past eight attempts.

The 52,562 spectators were cheering loudly. The Rockies were nipping at the Dodgers' heels. The crowd knew every win counted, especially against a team like the Pirates that was struggling so much.

The game moved into extra innings. Both managers, LA's Joe Torre and Pittsburgh's John Russell, strategized through their bullpens to secure a victory.

Los Angeles received a big boost from James McDonald. The right-handed hurler threw three scoreless innings. The Pirates' Joel Hanrahan pitched two innings of no-hit relief.

However, both pitchers had exited from the game when the 13th inning began. Ronald Belisario entered the game for the Dodgers after McDonald was lifted for a pinch-hitter in the bottom of the 12th. Leadoff hitter Andrew McCutchen reached base on a throwing error by LA third baseman Blake. Andy LaRoche sacrificed McCutchen to second base. The Dodgers intentionally walked Garrett Jones to face catcher Ryan Doumit. The strategy backfired and Doumit, who struck out three times in the game, laced a single to left field to bring home McCutchen with the unearned, go-ahead run.

Russell brought Chris Bootcheck into the game in the bottom of the inning. The righty was sporting a whopping 11.57 ERA as he made his way to the center of the diamond. Leadoff batter Rafael Furcal reached first base on an infield single, a liner that Bootchck couldn't handle. Russell Martin flied out and John Russell went to his bullpen again. He summoned Phil Dumatrait to the mound. The maneuver set up a lefty-lefty matchup with Dumatrait facing Ethier.

But the plan did not work: Ethier smashed his 30th home run into the right-field pavilion at Dodger Stadium, his major-league-leading sixth walk-off hit of the season, four of them home runs. It was the 37th time this year that the Dodgers grabbed a come-from-behind win.[3]

"As Yogi would say, 'It's déjà vu all over again'" said Torre, quoting Yankees great Yogi Berra. "You've seen him do it, you want to visualize it, and when he does it, it's just surreal."[4]

"You pinch yourself," said Ethier. "If there's a heartbeat left, we can come by and try to win it. I was just looking for a good pitch to hit and put a good swing on something."[5]

Dumatrait had thrown just one pitch, but it made all the difference. "I wanted to get ahead of him," he said. "I threw a two-seam (fastball) in. It was just above the knees on the black, maybe even in a little bit. All the scouting reports said you can get him in. I made my pitch. But he beat me."[6]

"I went and looked at the video and it was just above the knees and a little bit off the plate," said Dumatrait. "I made my pitch and he just kind of dropped the head of the bat on it and put a good swing on it, and unfortunately it went out of the park. It's frustrating. He just beat me on that one pitch."[7]

Belisario, despite giving up the go-ahead run, was the beneficiary of Ethier's blast. He improved his record to 4-3. Dumatrait (0-1) took the loss.

The Dodgers (95-67) won the NL West Division by three games over Colorado. They swept St. Louis in three games in the NLDS. However, they were ousted in five games against Philadelphia in the NLCS.

Pittsburgh (62-99) finished in last place in the Central Division and would suffer the same fate in 2010.

SOURCES

In addition to the Sources cited in the Notes, the author used the Baseball-Reference.com and Retrosheet.org websites.

https://www.baseball-reference.com/boxes/LAN/LAN200909150.shtml

https://www.retrosheet.org/boxesetc/2009/B09150LAN2009.htm

NOTES

1   Emma Amaya, "Mr. Miracle, Andre Ethier: The King of Walk-Offs," Dodger Blue World, September 16, 2009, https://mlblogscrzblue.wordpress.com/2009/09/16/mr-miracle-andre-ethier-the-king-of-walk-offs/, accessed March 27, 2024.

2   Chuck Finder, "Another Duke Gem Wasted," *Pittsburgh Post-Gazette*, September 16, 2009: D1, D5.

3   Jim Peltz, "Ethier Shows He's Still King of Walk-Off," *Los Angeles Times*, September 16, 2009: C1.

4   Associated Press, "Ethier's League-Leading Sixth Walk-Off Lifts Dodgers," September 16, 2009.

5   "Ethier's League-Leading Sixth Walk-Off Lifts Dodgers."

6   Rob Biertempfel, "Dodgers Drop Pirates in 13 Innings with Walk-Off Homer," *Pittsburgh Tribune-Review*, September 16, 2009.

7   "Ethier's League-Leading Sixth Walk-Off Lifts Dodgers.

LORETTA'S HIT COMPLETES DODGERS' NINTH-INNING RALLY

October 8, 2009: Los Angeles Dodgers 3, St. Louis Cardinals 2
(Game Two of the 2009 National League Division Series)

by Kevin Snyder

A generational talent made his first postseason start in Game Two of the 2009 National League Division Series. A veteran big leaguer, extending his career for a few days, struck the game-winning hit. From beginnings to endings, Game Two between the Dodgers and St. Louis Cardinals had all the elements of a great postseason game, including a ninth-inning comeback from a near-certain loss.

The 2009 Dodgers won 95 games, more than any other in the Frank McCourt era. McCourt's ownership had some success on the field but was better characterized by what did and did not happen off the field.[1] Investments in star players and upgrades to the ballpark were frequently discussed but rarely materialized due to an eventual bankruptcy that led to the sale of the club.[2] Despite this, a well-stocked farm system fueled the Dodgers' run of playoff berths led by outfielders Andre Ethier and Matt Kemp, catcher Russell Martin, and pitcher Clayton Kershaw. The Dodgers entered the 2009 season with high expectations following a season in which they won the National League West and a playoff series for the first time since their 1988 World Series championship. Of note, the Cardinals had eliminated the Dodgers in the 1985 and 2004 postseasons.

The Cardinals won the NL Central Division championship and returned to the playoffs for the first time since they won the World Series in 2006. Featuring Albert Pujols, the National League MVP for the second consecutive season, and two aces in Chris Carpenter and Adam Wainwright, the Cardinals were a veteran team with a chance to win it all. Although the bullpen had been a concern, the team hoped to ride the strength of its starting pitching to a long October run.

That plan got off to a shaky start in Game One of the NLDS with Los Angeles scoring five times off Carpenter, including a first-inning two-run home run by Kemp en route to a 5-3 victory. Opposing Wainwright for Game Two was the relative newcomer Kershaw, making his first postseason start. The 21-year-old had had a strong first full season in the majors, amassing a 2.79 ERA and 185 strikeouts over 171 innings. On the rare occasions in which he struggled, command was a problem; he walked 13 percent of the batters he faced. Although this was his introduction to many baseball fans, Kershaw had been the Dodgers' top prospect a year earlier, rising as high as number 5 in all of baseball.[3]

Kershaw and Wainwright were brilliant, dueling through six innings, with each allowing only a solo home run. Matt Holliday homered for the Cardinals in the second inning, while Ethier homered for Los Angeles in the fourth.

Kershaw was in full command on this afternoon, mixing in a 95-MPH fastball with a sharp curve and striking out four while walking only one. Finally, the Cardinals broke through. Tiring after approaching the 100-pitch barrier, Kershaw conceded a bloop single by Mark DeRosa to lead off the seventh, followed by Colby Rasmus's double off the center-field wall that gave the Cardinals a 2-1 lead. Wainwright pitched a clean seventh and stranded three runners in the eighth inning to finish allowing only one run on three hits while striking out seven against only one walk. The Cardinals lined up their bullpen as desired with lefty specialist Trever Miller and All-Star closer Ryan Franklin, a right-hander.

Los Angeles countered in the ninth with the heart of the order, starting with Ethier, who had led the team with 31 home runs. Cardinals manager Tony La Russa elected to start the inning with Miller. After eight pitches, several left dangerously close to the middle of the plate, Ethier popped out to second base. As was his reputation, La Russa immediately went to the bullpen again to match up with the forthcoming right-handed Dodgers hitters. Franklin, attempting to complete his first postseason save after registering 38 in the regular season alongside a sparkling 1.92 ERA, entered to face Manny Ramírez.

A lazy fly ball to center field brought the Cardinals to within an out of gaining control of the Series.

The Dodgers' last hope was James Loney, a solid hitter but not the same threat as Ethier and Ramirez. On a 2-and-2 pitch, Loney hit a looping liner to Holliday in left field. The ball sailed far enough for Holliday to make a catch but was sinking fast. In a full sprint and stuck between catching the fly with his glove up or down, Holliday did neither as the ball ricocheted off his glove onto the grass, giving the Dodgers life. Holliday had made only one error for St. Louis after arriving from Oakland in July and the Cardinals had among the best outfield defenses in baseball.[4] The mistake was as unlikely as it was untimely.

With Loney reaching second on the misplay and pinch-runner Juan Pierre taking his place, Dodgers third baseman Casey Blake came to the plate. After falling behind 1-and-2, Blake fought back to earn a nine-pitch walk. Given new life, the Dodgers, who led the majors with 22 last-at-bat wins in 2009, now had the winning run on base.[5] Down to the bottom of the lineup and the end of the bench, the Dodgers turned to second baseman Ronnie Belliard, a trade-deadline acquisition from Washington. On the first pitch, a curveball down in the strike zone, Belliard served a single into center field, scoring the speedy Pierre from second to tie the game.

The stunned Cardinals were reeling. Dodger Stadium was now raucous, thumping from the cheers of the elated fans. Meanwhile, Franklin walked catcher Russell Martin on four pitches far from the zone, bringing up the pitcher's spot in the lineup and a need for a Dodgers pinch-hitter. Enter Mark Loretta. Although he was a two-time All-Star, the 38-year-old Loretta returned to Los Angeles to join his fourth team in five years, hoping to squeeze every moment out of a productive big-league career. A forgettable regular season ended with a .232 batting average and without a home run. Loretta, who grew up in La Cañada, 12 miles from Dodger Stadium, stepped into the batter's box with a chance to give his hometown team a commanding two-game lead in the Series.

On the second pitch, Loretta floated a hit just beyond the infield, settling softly on the outfield grass. Blake crossed the plate with the winning run as the Dodgers streamed from the dugout, sprinting past the shell-shocked Cardinals players. Listeners to the radio broadcast across Southern California heard Vin Scully call out the winning hit:

"0-and-1 the count to Mark Loretta … out of a stretch goes Franklin's strike one pitch, Loretta gets one into left center. Dodgers win 3-2!"[6]

Ever attuned to the moment, Scully let the radio listeners hear the delirious Dodger crowd for 32 seconds before recapping the rally – a dropped fly ball, two walks, and two soft singles that found their way into center field. Instead of one thunderous blow, the comeback was initiated from the bottom of the Dodgers' lineup battling to extend the game to the next batter until they finally broke through.

Two nights later, the Dodgers eliminated the Cardinals in a 5-1 victory at Busch Stadium in St. Louis. However, Los Angeles' season came to an end in the NLCS: The Dodgers lost for the second straight year to the Philadelphia Phillies in five games. Although Loretta came to bat twice in that round, his game-winning single in Game Two of the NLDS was his final major-league hit. Kershaw's first postseason start was the opening act of a Hall of Fame-worthy pitching career. Kershaw's beginning and Loretta's ending propelled the Dodgers to one of the most dramatic wins in club history.

SOURCES

In addition to the sources cited in the Notes, the author consulted Baseball-Reference.com and Retrosheet.org for pertinent information, including the box score and play-by-play.

https://www.baseball-reference.com/boxes/LAN/LAN200910080.shtml

https://www.retrosheet.org/boxesetc/2009/B10080LAN2009.htm

The game itself can be seen on YouTube: https://www.youtube.com/watch?v=cUEyvo2HwEs

NOTES

1   Dodger Blue, "Dodgers History: Timeline of Dodger Stadium Renovations." https://dodgerblue.com/dodgers-history-timeline-dodger-stadium-renovations/.

2   Bill Shaikin, "Dodgers New Owners See Winning Business Model; Others See Trouble," *Los Angeles Times*, May 2, 2012. https://www.latimes.com/sports/la-xpm-2012-dec-15-la-sp-dodgers-guggenheim-20121216-story.html.

3   Brandon Heikooop, "Clayton Kershaw: Most Hyped Dodgers Prospect," *Bleacher Report*, May 25, 2008. https://bleacherreport.com/articles/25344-clayton-kershaw-most-hyped-los-angeles-dodgers-prospect.

4   Dylan Hernandez, "Rally is out of left field; Dodgers come back in the ninth for 2-0 series lead after the Cardinals' Holliday drops what would have been the third out," *Los Angeles Times*, October 9, 2009. https://www.proquest.com/docview/422233412/8932AC06A03C4550PQ/2?accountid=3783

5   "Game 2 NLDS Cardinals vs. Dodgers," Major League Baseball, Fox, October 8, 2009. Broadcast at https://www.youtube.com/watch?v=cUEyvo2HwEs

6   "Game 2 NLDS Cardinals vs. Dodgers," Los Angeles Dodgers radio broadcast, KABC, October 8, 2009. Broadcast at https://www.youtube.com/watch?app=desktop&v=MU49T3ch7yM

OPENING DAY PITCHERS' DUEL ULTIMATELY DECIDED BY KERSHAW'S BAT

April 1, 2013: Los Angeles Dodgers 4, San Francisco Giants 0

by Greg King

As part of its Opening Day lineup of nationally televised games aired on April 1, 2013, ESPN featured for one of its marquee matchups the defending World Series champion San Francisco Giants going head-to-head with their ancient arch-nemesis, the Los Angeles Dodgers.

On a sunny Southern California afternoon, and in a ballpark that was unveiling a $100 million offseason renovation, an exuberant crowd of 53,136 settled into their seats. Among pregame festivities, Hall of Fame 77-year-old left-hander Sandy Koufax walked to the pitcher's mound at Dodger Stadium, where he had last pitched in 1966, and tossed a ceremonial ball to Orel Hershiser, the MVP of the 1988 World Series.[1]

Taking the mound for the Dodgers this afternoon was 25-year-old Dodgers southpaw Clayton Kershaw, beginning his sixth season with the ballclub, and making his third consecutive Opening Day start. In the top of the first inning, after the first two Giants made out, third baseman Pablo Sandoval, the 2012 World Series MVP, singled and then reached second base on a wild pitch. Catcher Buster Posey, the reigning NL batting champion, hitting in the cleanup spot, was caught looking at a Kershaw curveball and struck out.[2]

It was the Dodgers' turn to take their first at-bats of the new season. The Giants handed the Opening Day assignment to Matt Cain for the first time in his career. The 28-year-old right-hander, who had begun his big-league career with San Francisco in 2005, forged a 16-5 won-lost record in 2012, helping his team get to the World Series. One of the pitcher's gems the previous season had been one for the record books: a perfect game against the Houston Astros on June 13, 2012.

In this game, however, Cain immediately ran into some trouble. In the bottom of the first inning, batting in the leadoff spot, left fielder Carl Crawford, who was making his Dodgers debut, banged a single. He moved up a bag when second baseman Mark Ellis was nicked by a pitch. The next batter, center fielder Matt Kemp, promptly found himself in an 0-and-2 hole, but he patiently worked to a full count. He saw 11 pitches before being finally called out on a third strike looking. Crawford made the second out of the inning when a laser throw from the arm of the catcher Posey, 2012 National League MVP, nailed him trying to steal third. First baseman Adrián González walked, but Cain eventually got out of the jam by striking out right fielder Andre Ethier on a swing and miss. The Giants hurler had thrown 29 pitches in the opening frame, but he would largely settle down going forward.

As the game progressed, Cain continued to handcuff Dodgers batters, tossing six scoreless innings. Over that span he struck out eight, scattered four hits, and walked one. He got out of trouble in the fourth inning, when with one out Gonzalez and Ethier hit back-to-back singles, and again in the sixth inning, when Mark Ellis led off with a double. Each time Cain skillfully plied his craft, ultimately stranding the baserunners and getting back to the Giants dugout unscathed.

Meanwhile, Kershaw's blend of fastballs and curves, coming in at different speeds and angles, worked masterfully against the Giants lineup.[3] With two outs in the top of the third, center fielder Ángel Pagán singled, but the inning concluded when he was easily thrown out by catcher A.J. Ellis attempting to steal second. Then Kershaw set down 10 consecutive batters before Sandoval singled with one out in the top of the seventh. Posey, however, hit a line-drive bullet to the third baseman, Luis Cruz, and outfielder Hunter Pence flied out to center field to end the threat.

With each pitcher clearly on his game and baffling opposing hitters, the game moved along at a fast clip. The score was still 0-0 in the bottom of the seventh inning when Giants manager Bruce Bochy decided it was time to lift his starter. Cain had thrown 93 pitches. "It was his first outing. It's a long season. You always look at the big picture," Bochy later explained.[4] Reliever George Kontos was brought in from the bullpen and he retired each of the three Dodgers he faced in the seventh inning.

Kershaw retired the side in the top of eighth, three Giants up and three Giants down, and was due to bat first in the bottom of the eighth. He hadn't proved himself much of a hitter in his first five seasons. In fact, Kershaw had mustered just one extra-base hit and carried a .144 batting average (38 hits in 263 at-bats) over the course of his major-league career, including striking out in his first two plate appearances against Cain this afternoon. But Dodgers manager Don Mattingly was alert to his left-hander having thrown only 85 pitches and still possessing pinpoint accuracy. He chose to leave his ace in the game to pitch another inning rather than remove him for a pinch-hitter, and he would let him hit for himself.

On Kontos's first pitch, a fastball in the middle of the strike zone, Kershaw rewarded his manager's decision. Vin Scully, then beginning his 64th consecutive season in the Dodgers broadcast booth, told listeners, "And a high fly ball to center. Pagan going back. It is over his head! It is over the fence!"[5]

The 400-foot blast was Kershaw's first major-league home run. He rounded the bases quickly and high-fived his joyous teammates when he entered the dugout. The highly partisan fans erupted; "the thunder set the press box to jiggling," wrote the veteran sportswriter Scott Ostler of the *San Francisco Chronicle*.[6] It was the first time a Dodgers pitcher had hit a home run on Opening Day since 1965, when Hall of Famer Don Drysdale homered against the New York Mets, and the first time any pitcher in the major leagues had accomplished it in an opening game since 1988, when Joe Magrane of the St. Louis Cardinals went deep against the Cincinnati Reds.[7]

But despite the general hysteria among the fans in attendance in Los Angeles, the Dodgers still had but a 1-0 lead. The Kershaw blast, however, seemed to ignite the team. Crawford next stepped up to the plate and sliced a double down the left-field line, his second hit of the game. Mark Ellis followed with a bunt single, also for his second hit. Kontos, who had given up three consecutive hits and would eventually

be tagged with the loss, was lifted for Santiago Casilla, whose wild pitch scored Crawford for a Dodgers 2-0 lead. After Kemp walked, Bochy called on his third fireman of the inning, Jeremy Affeldt. The strategy continued to misfire. Two more runners reached base: Gonzalez was hit in the shoulder by a pitch, then an intentional pass issued to Cruz loaded the bases. The Dodgers tallied their final two runs on groundout RBIs from Ethier and A.J. Ellis.

Staked to a 4-0 lead, Kershaw went back out to the pitcher's mound in the ninth inning and recorded a shutout; the game ended when Sandoval was thrown out at first on his groundball to third base. As it turned out, Kershaw's bomb would have been plenty, after all.

In tossing his sixth career shutout, his third against the Giants, Kershaw was a model of efficiency, throwing only 94 pitches in a game that lasted 2 hours and 25 minutes. He surrendered four hits, two each to Pagan and Sandoval, while walking none. The only runner to reach second base was Sandoval in the first inning.

Kershaw was creating an impressive record in pitching Opening Day games. In his three consecutive starts from the 2011 through 2013 seasons, facing the Giants, Padres, and Giants again, totaling 19 innings, he hadn't allowed a run and had fanned 19.

Baseball fans also witnessed something that had not been achieved in 60 years: Kershaw became the first pitcher on Opening Day to hit a home run and throw a shutout since Hall of Famer Bob Lemon accomplished the feat for the Cleveland Indians in 1953.[8]

In postgame interviews, several Dodgers looked back on a frustrating first inning in which they missed an opportunity to take an early lead, but found some solace once the victory had been secured. Kemp's 11-pitch duel with Cain, albeit ultimately resulting in a strikeout, had seemingly paid dividends later when the Giants starter had to be lifted for a reliever after completing only six innings, due to a high pitch count, while he was still pitching a shutout. "You look at the good of what comes out of something like that," said Ethier. "Guys went out there and had tough at-bats."[9]

Cain, whose performance that afternoon certainly deserved better than getting a no-decision, remained the gracious player he had always been throughout his career. After the game he reflected on his first-ever Opening Day start. "It was great to have," the Giants pitcher said. "I've seen some guys do it, and I wondered what it felt like. There's always a lot of hype, maybe a little over-reporting leading up to the game.

But that's the fun part of it. It was a great experience. I enjoyed it."[10]

After the game, Kershaw's batterymate A.J. Ellis told a reporter, "This was one of those games everyone is going to say they were at the game." He hastened to add, "I'll never forget it."[11]

This initial win by Kershaw was followed by 15 more during the 2013 regular season, and in leading the NL both with 232 strikeouts and a 1.83 ERA, he would be selected as the NL Cy Young Award winner, his second. The Dodgers went on to claim the Western Division in 2013, their first division title since 2009.

SOURCES

In addition to the sources cited in the Notes, the author consulted Baseball-reference.com and Retrosheet.org.

https://www.baseball-reference.com/boxes/LAN/LAN201304010.shtml

https://www.retrosheet.org/boxesetc/2013/B04010LAN2013.htm

NOTES

1   Bill Plaschke, "New Blue Harmony," *Los Angeles Times*, April 2, 2013: A1. On April 14, 1964, Koufax pitched the first Opening Day shutout in Dodger Stadium, beating the St. Louis Cardinals, 4-0.

2   The game's highlights can be viewed in a YouTube.com video uploaded on July 18, 2013, accessed at youtu.be/U9d5O6GVeAM.

3   Beth Harris, "Giants Drop L.A. Opener," *San Francisco Examiner*, April 2, 2013: 19.

4   Dylan Hernandez, "Working the Count Works Out Nicely," *Los Angeles Times*, April 2, 2013: C3.

5   Scully's call of Kershaw's home run can be viewed in a YouTube.com video uploaded on April 9, 2013, accessed at youtu.be/E8pZiV03YYM.

6   Scott Ostler, "Uh-Oh – Looks Like Things Are Getting Serious in L.A.," *San Francisco Chronicle*, April 2, 2013: B1.

7   *Los Angeles Times*, April 2, 2013: C3. Drysdale also hit an Opening Day home run in 1959, against the Chicago Cubs; Mike Hiserman, "Kershaw Is Money - Again," *Chicago Tribune*, April 2, 2013: 3-1.

8   Lemon pitched a one-hitter against the Chicago White Sox on April 14, 1953.

9   Hernandez.

10 Henry Schulman, "Too Much Kershaw," *San Francisco Chronicle*, April 2, 2013: B1.

11 Plaschke.

URIBE HOME RUN ADVANCES DODGERS TO NLCS

October 7, 2013: Los Angeles Dodgers 4, Atlanta Braves 3
(Game Four of the 2013 National League Division Series)

by Theo Tobel

On a clear, 71-degree October night in the hills above downtown Los Angeles, the Atlanta Braves, one loss from postseason elimination but also one win from forcing a winner-take-all game on their home field, lined up to face the Los Angeles Dodgers in Game Four of the 2013 National League Division Series.

The Dodgers' manager, Don Mattingly, on thin ice in the third and final year of his contract, had only two options: Clayton Kershaw, bound for his second career Cy Young Award and coming off a 12-strikeout masterpiece in Game One of the series, or journeyman Ricky Nolasco.[1] With 54,438 at Dodger Stadium eagerly waiting in anticipation of the first pitch at 6:38 P.M., Kershaw jogged out to the mound. In his sixth major-league season, it was the 25-year-old left-hander's first career start on three days' rest.

But the Braves would be no easy foe for Kershaw: They had led the NL in home runs and were second in wins (96, to the Dodgers' 92). Each team had won its respective division. In this series the Dodgers had seized a two-games-to-one lead, winning 13-6 a day earlier to push Atlanta to the brink of elimination.

On the opposing side, 37-year-old Freddy García, a back-to-back All-Star more than 10 years earlier, was entrusted with the ball. García, with a high-80s fastball, a sharp slider, and a deceiving splitter, planned to take down the Dodgers by filling up the zone and forcing soft contact.[2]

The game did not start off well for García, who allowed Carl Crawford a leadoff home run on a hanging breaking ball – giving the 32-year-old left fielder home runs in back-to-back games. García ran into more trouble later in the inning, surrendering a single and stolen base to Hanley Ramírez before getting dynamic rookie

Yasiel Puig to fly out to the warning track to end the inning.

In the bottom of the third, Crawford hit another solo shot, just inside the right-field foul pole, to put the Dodgers ahead 2-0.

Meanwhile, Kershaw was breezing through the Braves' hitters, touching 95 mph, with only one scare – when García launched a ball that was caught five feet short of the left-field wall. But the Braves capitalized on the Dodgers' poor defense in the fourth to tie the game: a single by Freddie Freeman followed by a crucial throwing error by first baseman Adrian González, a wild pitch, a single, and a fielder's choice. Both runs were unearned.

A Dodgers rally in the bottom of the sixth was quelled quickly by a 5-4-3 double play, punctuated by Freeman's incredible scoop at first to get Puig by a half-step. At the end of the sixth, Kershaw, his pitch count at 91, was removed from the game with the score still tied, 2-2.

Once Kershaw exited, Atlanta's offense attacked reliever Ronald Belisario in the top of the seventh. Second baseman Elliot Johnson roped a ball down the right-field line, where Puig misplayed it, resulting in a standup triple, Johnson's first hit of the series. A pinch-hit single by José Constanza, batting for García, put the Braves in the lead for the first time all night.[3]

As the game headed to the bottom of the eighth, the Braves, with right-hander David Carpenter, their third pitcher of the night, on the mound, were six outs from moving the series back home to Turner Field for Game Five. After stranding men in scoring position in the sixth and seventh innings, however, the Dodgers started the eighth with a leadoff double by Puig.

Juan Uribe, at age 34 in his third season as a utility infielder in Los Angeles, with World Series rings from the 2005 Chicago White Sox and 2010 San Francisco Giants, stepped up to bat. Mattingly called for a bunt, intending to advance Puig to third for a better chance at scoring the tying run.

But Dodgers fans, looking for Uribe to knot the game himself after a double in his previous at-bat, roared their disapproval, hurling insults in Mattingly's direction.

On the first pitch, Uribe squared up … and his bunt rolled foul. The crowd booed Mattingly: "Let him hit!"

On the second pitch, Uribe squared around again, and the fans groaned in disbelief at another foul bunt.

With two strikes, Uribe had no choice but to swing away.

After taking two balls, he did just that on the fifth pitch, raising both hands to the sky as he finished the swing, dropping the bat and watching the ball soar farther and farther until it landed in the Dodgers bullpen, just over the outfield wall in left. The Dodgers now led, 4-3.

TV cameras panned to Craig Kimbrel standing in Atlanta's bullpen – with his 1.21 ERA and league-leading 50 saves – hands on his hips, still waiting to be called in … too late.[4]

The fans, who had been relatively quiet since the third inning, exploded into ecstasy and excitement. They continued to roar as Uribe rounded the bases, celebrated with his teammates pouring out of the dugout, and came out for a curtain call.

In the top of the ninth, 26-year-old closer Kenley Jansen wasted no time in finishing the Braves' offense, striking out all three hitters he faced. His second strikeout was aided by a favorable call from the home-plate umpire on a pitch outside the strike zone to Jason Heyward, and then Jansen finished Justin Upton off with a high cutter, his signature pitch, sending the Dodgers to the National League Championship Series. Ultimately, the Dodgers fell to the St. Louis Cardinals in six games, due to poor performances by Kershaw and Jansen, along with below-average hitting.

But for the second time in his career, Uribe's home run had made the difference in the final game of a postseason series. His eighth-inning homer off Ryan Madson of the Philadelphia Phillies in Game Six of the 2010 NLCS had put the Giants in the World Series.

When asked about his heroic 2013 feat in a postgame interview, Uribe said, "You know, when they gave me the bunt sign … I'm thinking … I need to do my job: try to move the runner. [But] they gave me a hanging breaking ball. … [I saw] the ball, and hit it."[5]

So how did the two stars of the game, Juan Uribe and Carl Crawford, end their careers? Uribe had an under-the-radar season in 2014, the year after his famous homer, collecting a 4.0 Wins Above Replacement, as determined by Baseball-Reference.com (bWAR), in only 103 games. Sadly, this was his last good season, as in the remaining two years of his career his bWAR never surpassed 1.0; in 2015 he played for three teams before ending his career in 2016, playing in only 73 games prior to his release. Still, he solidified his place in Dodgers lore with the home run.

Crawford's career ended similarly to Uribe's. Crawford, who had been traded to the Dodgers from the Boston Red Sox in a nine-player deal in August 2012, less than two years after signing a seven-year, $142 million contract with Boston, had an above-average season in 2014, but he was both unhealthy and inconsistent in 2015 and 2016, leading to his release with $35 million left on his contract.

As for the Braves, the 23-year-old Freeman turned into one of the most consistent hitters in the league. The Braves' third-base coach in 2013, Brian Snitker, became the manager in 2016, replacing Fredi González, who had managed Atlanta since 2011.

The Braves-Dodgers rivalry remained heated, as the former NL West divisional foes faced off in a seven-game Championship Series in 2020, which the Dodgers won en route to their first World Series title since 1988, with Kershaw and Jansen the only players remaining in Los Angeles from the 2013 team.

The Braves extracted their vengeance in 2021 – managed by Snitker and with Freeman their only on-field link to 2013 – beating the Dodgers in six games in the NLCS en route to winning the World Series and breaking a 26-year title drought of their own.

AUTHOR'S NOTE

This game was the first postseason game I ever attended. I was 8 years old and will always remember jumping up and down with my father after the two-run blast.

ACKNOWLEDGMENTS

This article was fact-checked by Ray Danner and copy-edited by Len Levin.

DODGER STADIUM

SOURCES

The author accessed Baseball Reference and Retrosheet for general game information and play-by-play data. The author also watched the full game on YouTube.

https://www.baseball-reference.com/boxes/LAN/LAN201310070.shtml

https://www.retrosheet.org/boxesetc/2013/B10070LAN2013.htm

https://www.youtube.com/watch?v=Tuzl34F_bG0

The author obtained the photo from Flickr. It was taken by Derral Chen (attribution required per Creative Commons license).

https://www.flickr.com/photos/derra1029/10132141214/

NOTES

1   Eric Stephen, "On Clayton Kershaw, Ricky Nolasco & Game 4." True Blue LA.com. October 6, 2013. Accessed February 6, 2022. https://www.truebluela.com/2013/10/6/4809712/clayton-kershaw-ricky-nolasco-game-4-dodgers-braves.

2   García's 1.9 walks per nine innings (BB/9) in 2013 were far below the league average 3.02. By the end of his career, García was purely a contact pitcher; his opponent's contact percentage, and his first-pitch strike percentage, were greatly above average, according to Fangraphs.com.

3   At this point, the Braves had a Win Expectancy of 72 percent, according to Baseball-Reference.com, meaning that teams leading under similar circumstances (score, inning, etc.) win 72 percent of the time.

4   Consistent with standard bullpen roles and use in 2013, the Braves used Kimbrel in only one game during the eighth inning in the regular season that year. In all other regular-season appearances, he entered in the ninth inning or during extra innings. Three days earlier, however, in Game Two of the NLDS on October 4, Braves manager Fredi González called on Kimbrel, with a one-run lead, to retire Uribe for the third out of the eighth inning. Kimbrel closed out the game in the ninth to complete the four-out save.

5   "Oct. 7 Juan Uribe Postgame Interview," MLB.com. October 8, 2013. Accessed January 17, 2022. https://www.mlb.com/news/oct-7-juan-uribe-postgame-interview/c-62678892.

CLAYTON KERSHAW THROWS NO-HITTER AGAINST ROCKIES

June 18, 2014: Los Angeles Dodgers 8, Colorado Rockies 0

by Glen Sparks

The game ended with one more strikeout and a roar from the crowd. The celebration began with a starting pitcher who raised his arms in triumph and hugged his catcher, who had raced to the mound. About his no-hit performance on June 18, 2014, Los Angeles Dodgers left-hander Clayton Kershaw said, "It was just so much fun I can't explain it."[1]

The 26-year-old struck out 15 batters, walked no one, and needed just 107 pitches to beat the Colorado Rockies, 8-0, at Dodger Stadium. A.J. Ellis, behind the plate for this masterpiece, told reporters, "That's probably the best combination he's had of his slider and curveball working on the same night. When you've got those things going, nights like this are possible."[2]

Only a Hanley Ramírez throwing error in the seventh inning kept the no-hitter from being a perfect game. According to Mark Saxon of espn.com, Kershaw pitched with "almost-effortless dominance." He added that "when Kershaw has everything working, it doesn't matter if he's facing Paul Bunyan."[3]

This was Kershaw's seventh season in the majors, and he already had won two National League Cy Young Awards and three ERA titles. Thus far in 2014, he was 6-2 with a 2.93 ERA after missing all of April with a back injury. In his most recent start, on June 13 in Arizona, Kershaw gave up one run in seven innings as the Dodgers beat the Diamondbacks, 4-3. Of note, he did not allow a run over his final 4⅓ innings.

LA began the day 39-34 and in second place, 5½ games behind the San Francisco Giants. The Rockies, meanwhile, were 34-38, and in third place, 10 games out of the top spot. Jorge De La Rosa, a left-hander like Kershaw, started for the Rockies. The 11-year-veteran had a 6-5 record and a 4.12 ERA.

A crowd of 46,069 filed into Dodger Stadium on a Wednesday night. Rockies manager Walt Weiss penciled in an all-righty lineup, except for the lefty Corey Dickerson, who had a .333 batting average. Dickerson struck out to lead off the game, Brandon Barnes flied out, and Troy Tulowitzki grounded out.

The Dodgers scored twice in the bottom of the first. Dee Strange-Gordon led off with a walk and stole second. De La Rosa also walked the Dodgers' number-2 hitter, Ramírez. Both runners advanced one base after De La Rosa fired an attempted pickoff throw into center field. Yasiel Puig followed with a sacrifice fly. After Adrián González grounded out, Matt Kemp

Clayton Kershaw has won 210 games for the Dodgers through 2023 and has struck out nearly 3,000 batters.

knocked an RBI single into left field. Scott Van Slyke lined out to end the inning.

LA broke the game open in the third inning with a five-run outburst. Puig began the rally with a two-out walk. González hit an RBI double and ran to third on the throw home. The next batter, Kemp, added another run-scoring two-base hit.

Both Van Slyke and Ellis walked to fill the bases. Up to the plate stepped Miguel Rojas, the third baseman and eighth batter in the order. Known more for this glove than his bat, Rojas hit a line-drive double into deep left field that cleared the bases and gave LA a 7-0 lead. Kershaw grounded out to complete the frame.

The Dodgers scored their eighth and final run in the fourth inning. After Gordon struck out, Ramírez singled and Puig doubled. Those hits ended De La Rosa's evening and brought reliever Franklin Morales into the game. González, the first batter Morales faced, lofted a pitch into left-center field deep enough for Ramírez to score. The next hitter, Kemp, grounded into a double play.

Kershaw, meanwhile, had struck out six Rockies through the first four innings. Dodgers legendary broadcaster Vin Scully provided some memorable play-by-play for television viewers. After Wilin Rosario struck out to lead off the second inning, Scully said, "Sloooow curveball. See ya later. Oh, that's not fair." When D.J. LeMahieu fanned on a similar pitch for the second out in the sixth, after Kyle Parker had struck out to begin the frame, Scully said, "Curveball got him. Big, overhand downer. Wow."[4] Ryan Wheeler, pinch-hitting for Morales, whiffed to end the inning.

Dickerson led off the Rockies' half of the seventh and hit a slow roller to the shortstop Ramírez, who charged the ball and made a throw that eluded González at first base. The scorekeeper ruled an error, ending the perfect game but keeping the no-hitter intact. Kershaw looked at Ramírez and shrugged "as if to tell him not to worry."[5] Later, Ramírez told reporters, "You just have to catch the ball and throw it. In that situation, you would rather have the error than just let it go."[6] Kershaw said, "It was a pretty tough play. Under normal circumstances, that's pretty close to a hit."[7]

Pitching from the stretch for the first time, Kershaw struck out Barnes swinging. That brought up Tulowitzki, who began the evening with a lofty .361 batting average. He grounded a ball down the line to Rojas, who made a long throw on one bounce that González scooped for an out. "That's the bullet

we dodged," catcher Ellis said in a 2021 interview. Rosario struck out to end the inning.

After a scoreless bottom half of the seventh, with Adam Ottavino now on the mound for Colorado, Carlos Triunfel took over for Ramírez at shortstop to start the eighth. Kershaw struck out Drew Stubbs and did the same to Josh Rutledge. Kyle Parker grounded out to end the inning.

Rex Brothers replaced Ottavino in the bottom of the eighth and retired the side in order. LeMahieu led off for Colorado in the top of the ninth and grounded out, González to Kershaw covering at first base. Next, Charlie Culberson hit a shallow fly ball to Puig for the second out. Ellis joked later that "it was probably the only time Yasiel used two hands to catch a ball."[8] Now only Dickerson separated Kershaw from glory. As Scully said, "There is one out to go. One miserable, measly out."[9] Dickerson swung through a 94-mph fastball for strike one and fouled off the next two pitches. He missed a fastball for strike three.

Scully told TV viewers, "He's got it!"[10] Radio play-by-play announcer Charlie Steiner exclaimed, "The greatness of Clayton Kershaw shown off again. ... Another sparkling chapter in the career of Clayton ... Edward ... Kershaw."[11]

Los Angeles Times sportswriter Bill Shaikin, who called Kershaw "the most intense of competitors," described how the pitcher, after the final out, "allowed himself a rare smile, and an awfully wide one, when Ellis handed him the game ball." Kershaw accepted the souvenir. "He tucked it into his pocket," Shaikin wrote.[12]

Dodger players mobbed Kershaw and gave him the obligatory Gatorade bath. The drenched but exhilarated star of the game told television reporter Alana Rizzo, "As far as individual games go, this is pretty special. I'll remember this the rest of my life. To do it at home is even better. This is amazing."[13]

Just a few weeks earlier, on May 25, Dodgers veteran Josh Beckett threw a no-hitter against the Philadelphia Phillies at Citizens Bank Park. The right-hander struck out six and walked three. "Beckett told me he was going to teach me how to do it," Kershaw said.[14]

No teammates had thrown a no-hitter in the same season since the Chicago Cubs' Burt Hooton and Milt Pappas in 1972. The last two Dodgers to accomplish that feat were Carl Erskine and Sal Maglie in 1956.[15]

Kershaw rolled up a game score of 102, the second highest in a nine-inning game since 1914, just behind the 105 that Kerry Wood posted with a 20-strikeout, one-hit performance against the Houston Astros in 1998.[16] He also recorded the third most strikeouts in a no-hitter, behind Nolan Ryan, who fanned 17 in his no-no on July 15, 1973, and 16 on May 1, 1991, at the age of 44.[17]

According to Grosnick, "It wasn't quite a perfect game, at least statistically, but it was one of the finest pitching performances we've ever seen."[18] Dave Cameron from Fangraphs.com wrote that Kershaw gave "one of the most dominant performances in the history of baseball. … It might not have been perfect. It was better."[19]

In his next start, Kershaw could not match the nearly impossible and throw a second straight no-hitter, something only Johnny Vander Meer has done. Facing the Kansas City Royals, he gave up a single to the second batter of the game, Eric Hosmer. Kershaw did, however, throw eight shutout innings before giving way to a reliever. In his two starts after that, he threw a combined 15 scoreless innings. Finally, on July 10, the San Diego Padres' Chase Headley homered off him with two outs in the sixth inning. Kershaw had kept teams from scoring for 41 innings, the seventh-longest streak in the Live Ball Era.[20]

Kershaw ended the 2014 season with a 21-3 record and a league-leading 1.77 ERA. He won his third Cy Young Award and NL MVP honors.

SOURCES

In addition to the sources cited in the Notes, the author consulted Baseball Reference.com and Retrosheet.org for general game information and play-by-play data.

https://www.retrosheet.org/boxesetc/2008/B05250LAN2008.htm

https://www.retrosheet.org/boxesetc/2014/B06180LAN2014.html

NOTES

1   https://www.youtube.com/watch?v=_fgX3ODoCb8.

2   Steve Dilbeck, "No One Better," *Los Angeles Times*, June 20, 2014: 25.

3   https://www.espn.com/mlb/story/_/id/11106270/clayton-kershaw-pulls-inevitable-no-hitter-los-angeles-dodgers.

4   "Scully Calls Every Out of Kershaw's No-Hitter," https://www.youtube.com/watch?v=xxspKrnpMFE.

5   Everett Scott, "Ramirez Doesn't Blame Injury," *Los Angeles Times*, June 19, 2014: 25.

6   "Ramirez Doesn't Blame Injury."

7   "Ramirez Doesn't Blame Injury."

8   https://podcasts.apple.com/us/podcast/extra-innings-episode-12/id1562950135?i=1000525777962.

9   "Scully Calls Every Out of Kershaw's No-Hitter."

10 "Scully Calls Every Out of Kershaw's No-Hitter."

11 https://podcasts.apple.com/us/podcast/extra-innings-episode-12/id1562950135?i=1000525777962.

12 Bill Shaikin, "Near Perfection," *Los Angeles Times*, June 19, 2014: 25.

13 https://www.youtube.com/watch?v=_fgX3ODoCb8.

14 Bill Shaikin, "Near Perfection."

15 https://www.espn.com/blog/statsinfo/post/_/id/91774/top-10-facts-on-kershaws-no-hitter.

16 Mike Axisa, "Clayton Kershaw's No-Hitter Was as Close to Perfect as It Gets," CBSsports.com. https://www.cbssports.com/mlb/news/clayton-kershaws-no-hitter-was-as-close-to-perfect-as-it-gets/. Max Scherzer of the Washington Nationals moved into second place when he recorded a game score of 105 in a no-hit performance against the New York Mets on October 3, 2015. https://www.baseball-reference.com/boxes/NYN/NYN201510032.shtml.

17 https://www.espn.com/blog/statsinfo/post/_/id/91774/top-10-facts-on-kershaws-no-hitter. Scherzer tied Ryan's mark when he struck out 17 in his October 3, 2015, no-hitter.

18 https://www.beyondtheboxscore.com/2014/6/19/5823800/clayton-kershaw-throws-the-greatest-modern-no-hitter.

19 https://www.beyondtheboxscore.com/2014/6/19/5823800/clayton-kershaw-throws-the-greatest-modern-no-hitter.

20 Andrew Simon, "The 10 Longest Scoreless-Inning Streaks," https://www.mlb.com/news/longest-scoreless-inning-streaks-in-history.

VIN SCULLY BIDS FAREWELL TO LA FANS

September 25, 2016: Los Angeles Dodgers 4, Colorado Rockies 3

by Thomas Baird

Vin Scully was hired at the age of 22 by Dodgers broadcaster Red Barber, and broadcast his first game at Shibe Park in Philadelphia on April 18, 1950. Scully became the team's primary announcer when Barber joined the New York Yankees in 1954.[1] Scully was on the call when the team won its first championship in 1955. He remained with the Dodgers when they relocated from Brooklyn to Los Angeles in 1958, and spent the next four years describing baseball games from the LA Coliseum.

Scully created an unparalleled dynamic between himself and the Los Angeles fan base, inspiring fans to bring transistor radios to the ballpark so they could experience the game as though sitting alongside him. The device became a household necessity just as the Dodgers arrived from Brooklyn, and Scully's storytelling became a part of the ballpark experience. In the massive Coliseum, where the team played from 1958 to 1961, fans found that a familiar voice could bring them closer to the game than their binoculars could. Scully once famously asked fans to join him in saying Happy Birthday to umpire Frank Secory, and the Coliseum crowd erupted with a unified "Happy Birthday!"[2] With their transistor radios in hand, they were no longer just spectators. *Los Angeles Times* writer Bill Shaikin called this "the greatest communal experience in Southern California sports history."[3]

Scully introduced fans to Dodger Stadium on Opening Day, April 10, 1962. In the decades between his first and final broadcasts at Dodger Stadium, he nurtured the growing bond between this team and its city. The World Series championships in 1959, 1963, and 1965 certainly helped endear the team to LA fans, but Scully would engage listeners in the midst of losing seasons as well. His tenure in Los Angeles included the 99-loss season of 1992, which occurred in the midst of social unrest and violent riots.

Transistor radios eventually gave way to digital streaming platforms. His voice no longer echoed through the concession stands as it had in the 1960s, but Scully remained an integral part of the fan experience until his final game. He continued to broadcast games without a partner in the booth, in order to maintain a "one-on-one" dynamic with listeners. "If I want to sell you a car, is it better for me to talk to you about the merits of the car or talk to so-and-so and have you listen to our discussion about the merits of the car? Red [Barber] always felt that it was better to talk one on one."[4] Scully wanted fans to know that he was talking directly to them.

Despite all the drama surrounding the team's playoff push, Scully's farewell tour took center stage in September 2016. In the final months of the season, opponents honored Scully with tributes. Multiple teams silenced their own broadcast team for an inning to provide their own fan base an opportunity to experience Scully's play-by-play calls.[5] The Dodgers held their own ceremony for Scully on September 23, with guest speakers Sandy Koufax and Kevin Costner.[6]

Dodgers games were not typically like this. Scully had always removed himself from the on-field drama, broadcasting as an unbiased fellow spectator. Scully had been advised by Barber to never root from the broadcast booth.[7] This became a trait beloved by fans. In a *Sports Illustrated* article in 1964, Robert Creamer wrote of a fan's perspective on Scully: "A Scully admirer has said, 'I can never tell from the tone of Vin's voice whether the Dodgers are ahead or behind. … It doesn't get gleeful, it doesn't get dull and flat. I like baseball, and I think he does, too.'"[8] When asked about his approach to calling his final home game, Scully responded, "I don't think I'm going to stress anything about me, I'll try to just do the game. I really will."[9]

At the opening of the broadcast, Scully issued a statement harkening back to his early days in Los Angeles. He said, "Since 1958, you and I have really grown up together. Through the good times and the bad."[10] The statement was released publicly prior to the game. True to form, Scully reserved personal sentiment for the moments before and after the game.

The Dodgers came up to bat in the bottom of the first inning, and each Dodger tipped his cap toward the press box as he stepped to the plate. First, it was Howie Kendrick. Justin Turner followed. Corey Seager did the same. Vin was unaware of the tribute until the second inning. Once he noticed what was happening, he made an effort to wave back to each player.[11] Turner and Adrián González, who had both grown up in Southern California, planned this salute. Turner said after the game, "We just wanted to make sure he knew how special he is to us."[12] The game proceeded in this way, with periodic reminders from players, fans, and Scully himself that this was the last time they would all be able to do this together.

In the second inning, Rockies shortstop Cristhian Adames singled and then scored when Dustin Garneau doubled to left field. Garneau took third base on a groundball to the left side, and came home on a fly ball by Charlie Blackmon. The Rockies led, 2-0.

Scully's impartiality and anecdotal style always lent itself well to tough losses and close games. He could celebrate baseball on behalf of either dugout, or find levity in a child's smile, so he would have no difficulty guiding fans through a loss if the Rockies were to hold their lead. Scully specialized in bringing comfort, even when the loss occurred beyond the baseball field. News broke early that morning that Miami Marlins star pitcher José Fernández had died in a boating accident at age 24. It was shocking, heartbreaking news. Fernández had been a friend of fellow Cuban Yasiel Puig, and Puig had given a tearful interview mourning the loss of his friend.[13] Scully honored Fernández by reading aloud a comment made on social media by the Marlins pitcher the previous year: "If you were given a book with the story of your life, would you read the end?"[14] It was brief, poignant, and fitting.

The Dodgers were trailing 2-1 as the game reached the seventh-inning stretch. In the bottom half of the inning, Justin Turner singled and Corey Seager drove him home with a triple to the right-field wall. With the score tied 2-2 in the top of the ninth inning, manager Dave Roberts called on closer Kenley Jansen. Outfielder David Dahl had struck out in his two previous appearances against Jansen,[15] but this time hit a home run to center field after falling behind, 0-and-2.

The game could have ended with a 3-2 Rockies victory, without additional drama. Vin Scully would have undoubtedly redeemed the low moment with a gracious farewell to Dodgers fans, and this game would still be fondly remembered. Thanks to Corey Seager, that never happened.

In the Dodgers ninth, Rockies closer Adam Ottavino struck out the first two batters but fell behind 2-and-0 to Seager. With the next pitch, Seager fully revived the fans still there, plus those listening to Scully on the drive home. Seager homered to right field and the crowd erupted.

In the bottom of the 10th inning, Rockies reliever Boone Logan got two outs and then faced Charlie Culberson, a defensive specialist journeyman with only 67 major-league at-bats since the end of the 2014 season. Culberson would finish the 2016 season with a career batting line of .234/.272/.327, with 5 home runs. He had not hit a home run since 2014, when he was playing for the Rockies.

The rest of the game reads like a bedtime story. On Logan's second pitch to him, Culberson hit a home run to left field, giving the Dodgers a walk-off victory and clinching the NL West Division championship.

The moment belonged to Vin Scully as much as it belonged to Culberson. As fans watched the ball land, Scully exclaimed, "A high fly ball to deep left field … the Dodger bench empties, and would you believe a home run?"[16]

After the excitement died down, the Dodgers gathered on the field and raised their caps to the press box. Manager Dave Roberts, who was being interviewed on the field, proclaimed "Vin, we love you, and this is for you, my friend." Scully, with his wife and family beside him, motioned a hug to Roberts and the team. Scully closed the game by playing his rendition of "Wind Beneath My Wings" over the PA system.

The communal gathering of players, coaches, fans, and family served as a fitting farewell for the Transistor Kid. Scully's voice echoed throughout the ballpark once again, for one last time.

SOURCES

In addition to the sources cited in the Notes, the author consulted Baseball-Reference.com and Retroheet.org.

https://www.baseball-reference.com/boxes/LAN/LAN201609250.shtml

https://www.retrosheet.org/boxesetc/2016/B09250LAN2016.htm

A full video of the game is available on YouTube at: https://www.youtube.com/watch?v=xPpa2200xWY

Scully's final call may also be seen at: https://www.youtube.com/watch?v=HayOXW09kl8

NOTES

1   Robert Creamer, "The Transistor Kid," *Sports Illustrated*, May 4, 1964.

2   Bill Shaikin, "Vin Scully, Dodger Fans and the Transistor Radio," *Los Angeles Times*, July 15, 2022. https://www.latimes.com/sports/dodgers/story/2022-07-15/vin-scully-dodgers-los-angeles-fans-transistor-radio-dodger-stadium-coliseum.

3   "Vin Scully, Dodger Fans and the Transistor Radio."

4   Jeffrey Brown. "Vin Scully, 'One on One' From the Booth," PBS News Hour. October 5, 2009. https://www.pbs.org/newshour/show/dodgers-vin-scully-one-on-one-from-the-booth

5   Bill Shaikin, "After 67 Years of Greatness Calling Dodgers Games, Vin Scully Just Wants to be Remembered as a Good Man," *Los Angeles Times*, September 25, 2016. https://www.latimes.com/sports/dodgers/la-sp-scully-career-20160924-snap-story.html.

6   Jesse Dougherty, "In His Words: Vin Scully Shares His 'Thanksgiving' with Dodger Stadium Crowd," *Los Angeles Times*, September 23, 2016.

7   Creamer.

8   Creamer.

9   Ted Berg, "Here's Literally Everything Vin Scully Said in One of His Last Conference Calls, " *USA Today*, August 3, 2022, Accessed January12, 2024. https://ftw.usatoday.com/2022/08/vin-scully-conference-call-dodgers-giants-retirement-playoffs-mlb

10   Andrew Joseph, "Vin Scully Delivers an Incredible Open Before His Last Broadcast at Dodger Stadium," *USA Today*, September 25, 2016. https://ftw.usatoday.com/2016/09/vin-scully-dodger-stadium-dodgers-final-broadcast-intro-mlb.

11   Pedro Moura, "Vin Scully's Last Broadcast at Dodger Stadium Has a Fitting Ending," *Los Angeles Times*, September 25, 2016. Accessed October 28, 2023, https://www.latimes.com/sports/dodgers/la-sp-dodgers-report-20160925-snap-story.html.

12   Andrew Joseph.

13   Pedro Moura, "A Shaken Yasiel Puig Dedicates Sunday's Game to Fallen Friend Jose Fernandez," *Los Angeles Times*, September 25, 2016. Accessed October 28, 2023, https://www.latimes.com/sports/mlb/la-sp-fernandez-puig-reaction-20160925-snap-story.html.

14   Sammy Roth, "Vin Scully's Last Dodgers Games: What I'll Remember About the Man Behind the Voice," *Palm Springs* (California) *Desert Sun,* September 28, 2016.

15   Ken Gurnick and Thomas Harding. "Vinning Tribute! LA Walks Off to Clinch West," MLB.com, September 25, 2016. Accessed October 28, 2023, https://www.mlb.com/news/dodgers-walk-off-in-10th-clinch-nl-west-title-c203311116.

16   Gurnick and Harding.

JUSTIN TURNER HOMERS ON ANNIVERSARY OF GIBSON'S '88 HOME RUN

October 15, 2017: Los Angeles Dodgers 4, Chicago Cubs 1
(Game Two of the 2017 National League Championship Series)

by Glen Sparks

On the night that Kirk Gibson hit his epic home run into the right-field pavilion at Dodger Stadium to end Game One of the 1988 World Series, a little red-headed boy squealed with delight at his grandmother's house in the Los Angeles suburbs.

Justin Turner, not yet 4 years old, watched as family members jumped up and down and the Stadium crowd cheered at such a dramatic finale. Turner has called that game "one of my earliest baseball memories."[1]

On October 15, 2017, exactly 29 years after Gibson's blast, Turner hit a three-run homer in the bottom of the ninth inning to give the Dodgers a 4-1 win in Game Two of the National League Championship Series. It was only the second walk-off postseason home run in Dodgers history.[2]

Turner thrust his arms outward as he rounded first base and tossed away his helmet when he rounded third and headed for home plate, where he was greeted by jubilant teammates. Cole Roberts, the teenage son of Dodgers manager Dave Roberts, described the game-winning hit as "the slickest thing ever."[3] Turner said, "That was the coolest thing I've ever done in my baseball career."[4]

The victory gave the Dodgers a two-games-to-none lead in the best-of-five NLCS, with the teams headed to Wrigley Field in Chicago. The Dodgers made it to this point after going 104-58 in the regular season and winning the West Division by 11 games over the runner-up Arizona Diamondbacks. Los Angeles swept Arizona in the three-game Division Series. The Cubs, meanwhile, won the Central Division with a 92-70 mark and beat the NL East Division champion Washington Nationals in the division series. The Cubs

were coming off a World Series championship in 2016, the team's first since 1908.

The NLCS began on October 14 in Los Angeles. The Dodgers won, 5-2. Yasiel Puig drove home two runs and Kenta Maeda earned the win in relief of starter Clayton Kershaw, who allowed two runs in five innings. Kenley Jansen picked up the save.

Rich Hill started Game Two for the Dodgers. The 6-foot-5-inch left-hander went 12-8 with a 3.32 ERA in his first full season in Los Angeles. The Massachusetts native was 37 years old and with his eighth big-league team.

Jon Lester, 6-feet-4 and a lefty like Hill, took the ball for the Cubs. Lester had completed a so-so campaign. He went 13-8 but with a 4.33 ERA after going 19-5 with a 2.44 ERA in 2016, his sophomore season in Chicago.

It was a warm day in Los Angeles. The temperature at first pitch, 3:20 P.M., was 92 degrees. A crowd of 54,479 filed into Dodger Stadium. John Jay led off against Hill by singling to left field. Kris Bryant flied out, and Anthony Rizzo and Willson Contreras struck out.

Lester retired the Dodgers in order in the bottom half of the first. Hill did the same to the Cubs in the top of the second and added another strikeout. Enrique "Kiké" Hernández drew a walk to start the LA second, and, with two out, Puig also walked. Charlie Culberson lined out to end the threat.

The Cubs got a runner as far as third base in the third inning. Hill walked Javier Báez to begin the frame. After Lester struck out, Baez stole second base with Jay at bat. Next, Hill unfurled a wild pitch and Baez dashed ahead another 90 feet. Jay hit a weak groundout to first base, though, and Bryant struck out swinging.

The Dodgers put together a rally of their own in the bottom half of the third. Turner walked with two outs and made it to third base on Cody Bellinger's double. The inning ended when Hernandez flied out to Jason Heyward in right field.

Chicago scored the game's first run in the fifth inning after going down in order in the fourth. Hill, who by now had seven strikeouts, gave up a leadoff homer to Addison Russell.

The 1-0 lead lasted for just a few minutes. Culberson lined a double into left field to start the Los Angeles fifth. That hit ended Hill's evening. Roberts elected to lift his starter, who had given up the solo run but just two other hits and had eight strikeouts. The pinch-hitter, Curtis Granderson, fouled out to third baseman Bryant. Chris Taylor grounded out but advanced Culberson to third. That brought Turner to the plate.

He was in his fourth season with the Dodgers and had long red hair and a long red beard. The Cincinnati Reds had selected him in the seventh round of the 2006 amateur draft out of Cal State-Fullerton, where he played on the 2004 College World Series championship team. Cincinnati traded Turner to the Baltimore Orioles on December 9, 2008. After a couple of short stints with the Orioles – he mostly played in the minor leagues – Turner was claimed off waivers by the New York Mets. He spent parts of four seasons with New York before being nontendered after the 2013 season.

Tim Wallach, the Los Angeles third-base coach and a former standout third baseman (260 home runs in 17 seasons), saw Turner play in a Cal-State Fullerton alumni game in early 2014 and recommended him to the Dodgers. Thanks in part to a retooled swing, Turner batted .340 in 2014. He batted .322 in 2017 with a .945 OPS and made his first All-Star team.

In his third at-bat against Lester, Turner grounded a single into right field, and Culberson came home. Bellinger walked, and Cubs skipper Joe Maddon brought in Carl Edwards Jr., a slender right-hander at 6-feet-3, 165 pounds. Edwards fanned Chase Utley for the third out. About being lifted despite allowing just one run, Lester said, "The game has definitely changed."[5]

Both teams went down one-two-three in the sixth inning, the Cubs facing Brandon Morrow, who relieved Hill, and the Dodgers batting against Edwards. Morrow pitched another perfect frame in the seventh, while Pedro Strop took over pitching duties for Chicago. After getting the first two batters to ground out, he walked Taylor. Turner flied out to center field.

Josh Fields and Tony Watson combined to throw a perfect eighth inning for Los Angeles, while the Dodgers put two runners on base but could not score against Brian Duensing in the bottom of the inning.

Jansen hit Rizzo with a one-out pitch in the top of the ninth before striking out Willson Contreras and getting Albert Almora to ground out. Puig led off the bottom of the ninth by drawing a walk and Culberson sacrificed him to second. Kyle Farmer, pinch-hitting for Jansen, struck out swinging. Maddon lifted Duensing for John Lackey with Taylor coming up to bat. Usually a starter, Lackey had pitched 1⅔ innings of relief in Game One and gave up an RBI single to Turner, the first hitter he faced.

Lackey also ran into trouble right away in Game Two. He walked Taylor to put runners on first and second. Turner stepped into the batter's box, took the first pitch, and belted the second one into the left-center-field pavilion. As he took his 360-foot run around the bases, he recalled, "I felt like I was floating."[6] He decided against duplicating Gibson's famous fist pump from '88. "We'll wait until the World Series to do that," he said.[7] Andy McCullough of the *Los Angeles Times* wrote that "the noise inside the stadium felt volcanic." Minutes after the homer, McCullough added, "the aisles at Dodger Stadium still were packed."[8]

Maddon answered some pointed postgame questions from reporters. Why, for instance, did the skipper call on Lackey for the second straight game rather than his three-time All-Star closer Wade Davis? "I liked (Lackey) a lot on the first guy, Taylor," Maddon said. "Once that walk occurred, all bets were off against Turner. Nobody is a really great matchup against Turner."[9]

About the pitch, Lackey said, "Bad location, bad selection. You want to be in those games. It's not typical (a starter being called to relieve), but you still have to try to get the job done."[10]

Turner's heroics put the Dodgers within one victory of going to the World Series for the first time since that magical year of 1988. "The most important thing was helping us get another win," Turner said. "But (the homer) is something down the road, hopefully many years from now, I will get to tell stories about."[11]

Keith Hupp, a longtime Dodgers fan and a retired police officer, caught Turner's home-run ball. He traded the souvenir for some memorabilia. Turner said, "He actually told me, 'This ball means so much to me, you have no idea. I said, 'Yeah, it means kind of a lot to me, too.'"[12] The Dodgers went on to beat the Cubs in five games in the NLCS before losing the World Series to the Houston Astros.

SOURCES

In addition to the sources cited in the Notes, the author consulted Baseball-Reference.com for pertinent information, including the box score and play-by-play.

https://www.baseball-reference.com/boxes/LAN/LAN201710150.shtml

Video of Turner's home run is available on YouTube.com: https://www.youtube.com/watch?v=7gKyto7CIgU

NOTES

1   Mike Puma, "Justin Turner Makes Dodger Stadium Explode with Thrilling Walkoff," nypost.com, October 15, 2017.

2   Andy McCullough, "Turner Joins Gibson in Dodgers Lore, Homers for 2-0 Lead," *Los Angeles Times*, October 16, 2017: D1.

3   McCullough.

4   McCullough.

5   Mark Gonzales, "It's a Smash Ending," *Chicago Tribune*," October 16, 2017: 3.

6   McCullough.

7   https://www.facebook.com/watch/?v=358714688513764.

8   McCullough.

9   Dylan Hernandez, "Maddon's Bullpen Call is Costly," *Los Angeles Times*, October 16, 2017: D2.

10   Gonzales.

11   Puma.

12   Eric Stephen, "Justin Turner Got His Home Run Ball Back From the Dodgers Fan Who Caught It," truebluela.com, October 16, 2017. https://www.truebluela.com/2017/10/16/16485998/justin-turner-home-run-ball-fan-great-catch-dodgers-nlcs.

KERSHAW, TURNER, MOTHER NATURE BRING THE HEAT TO SERIES OPENER

October 24, 2017: Los Angeles Dodgers 3, Houston Astros 1
(Game One of the 2017 World Series)

by John Bauer

The average high temperature in Los Angeles on October 24 is 76 degrees Fahrenheit.[1] The weather for Game One of the 2017 World Series at Dodger Stadium did not follow historical trends. Rather, the Los Angeles Dodgers hosted the Houston Astros with the thermometer reading 103 degrees at the 5:11 P.M. starting time, making for the hottest game in World Series history.[2] Greeting the early arrivals who sought the shaded areas of the grandstand, the organist played 1960s classics like "Heat Wave" and "Summer in the City."[3] Given the temperature, there were questions about how the unusual heat would affect the flight of the baseball, with one columnist observing that the heat "thinned the usually thick marine air that rolls into Chavez Ravine in the evening."[4] Without the drag, might the ball carry in atypical ways. If so, which team might benefit?

The Series itself had the promise of a classic, being the first to match 100-game winners since 1970.[5] The Dodgers (104-58) swept the Arizona Diamondbacks (3-0) in the NL Division Series and smothered the defending champion Chicago Cubs (4-1) in the Championship Series. Houston (101-61) faced a stiffer challenge from AL opposition, but used a 6-0 home record to take out the Boston Red Sox in the Division Series (3-1) and the New York Yankees (4-3) in the Championship Series.

The World Series Game One pitching matchup featured the sort of duel that often marked the great Series games. Houston's Dallas Keuchel was two years removed from his AL Cy Young Award-winning season, but the left-hander still enjoyed an All-Star-caliber season in 2017 with a 14-5 record and a 2.90 ERA. Keuchel recognized the challenge of pitching to the NL pennant winners. He noted, "They'll be the deepest team that we've played, hands down. You don't win a hundred-plus games for just luck of the draw."[6] Keuchel led the AL in ground ball to fly ball ratio,[7] suggesting that his pitching style was well-suited to the ball staying inside the ballpark. Dodgers manager Dave Roberts made clear the team's offensive strategy: "Light air today ... so I think for us to try to get underneath it and try to put the ball in the air. With him obviously, it's a tall task."[8]

Clayton Kershaw led the NL in wins and ERA (18-4, 2.31) and exceeded 200 strikeouts for the seventh time. By this stage in his career, Kershaw had an unfortunate association with postseason mediocrity, entering the game with a 6-7 postseason record with a 4.40 ERA.[9] There was some question whether the infield behind Kershaw would be at full strength. Justin Turner was held out of a recent workout, but the Dodgers third baseman assured that the absence was only maintenance-related. The availability of All-Star shortstop Corey Seager for the Series was a greater concern. Seager injured his back on a seemingly routine slide into second base in Game Three of the Division Series, and was inactive for the Championship Series. Rehabilitation work paid off, and Seager was restored to the active roster for the World Series.

The October 24 date of the game had greater significance than record-shattering temperatures. It was the 45th anniversary of Jackie Robinson's death, and his widow, Rachel Robinson delivered the ceremonial first pitch accompanied by her family. Then Kershaw faced Astros center fielder George Springer to open the game, and Springer swung and missed at strike three for the first out. Kershaw made short work of Alex

Bregman (fly out to Kiké Hernández) and José Altuve (grounder to Seager) to complete the top of the first on only nine pitches.

Multidimensional Chris Taylor, starting in center field, led off the bottom of the first. Roberts' pregame words seemed immediately prescient when Taylor blasted Keuchel's first pitch into the left-field pavilion. Taylor said after the game that pouncing on Keuchel was his plan. He said, "I didn't overthink it. I was just going up there trying to get the barrel to the ball, thinking without being aggressive, and be ready to hit the first one."[10] In his excitement, Taylor broke one of baseball's unwritten rules by flipping his bat, although the act was not necessarily included in his plan. He said, "I wasn't trying to do a bat flip or anything, just kind of almost like a fist pump-bat flip."[11] Whatever Taylor's motive, the Dodgers had a quick 1-0 lead. Keuchel permitted no further damage, striking out Turner then getting groundouts from Cody Bellinger and Yasiel Puig.

Kershaw and Keuchel both cruised through the second. Leading off the Dodgers third and starting in place of Yasmani Grandal in his role as Kershaw's personal catcher, Austin Barnes singled on a grounder to left field. Kershaw sacrificed his batterymate to second base. Taylor hit a liner to shortstop Carlos Correa, who tossed the ball to Altuve at second to double off Barnes.

Leading off the fourth, Bregman connected with a Kershaw fastball and sent it soaring six rows deep into the left-field pavilion. Game One was now tied, 1-1. If Kershaw was fazed by Bergman's solo shot, he did not show it: He struck out Altuve, Correa, and Yuli Gurriel to retire the Astros. Keuchel and Kershaw faced the minimum number of batters for each of the next two innings, as the game clipped along at a breakneck pace by the standard of twenty-first century postseason baseball before the pitch clock. (In fact, this game was the fastest World Series game since 1992.)

In the Dodgers sixth Barnes and Kershaw hit grounders to shortstop Correa for easy outs. Taylor walked on five pitches to keep the inning alive and bring Turner to the plate. Turner, whose career had taken off in Los Angeles, made his first All-Star Game appearance at age 32 in 2017. He took Keuchel's first pitch low and inside, then swung and missed to even the count. Keuchel went low and outside on the next pitch; Turner held off but umpire Phil Cuzzi judged the pitch a strike. Keuchel threw twice to first baseman Gurriel to keep Taylor honest. His next throw was an 87-mph cutter that appeared designed to jam the right-handed Turner, who adjusted to meet the ball with enough of the bat to loft the ball into left-center field. Marwin González tracked the ball until he conceded it was beyond his reach. The ball cleared the fence and landed in front of the pavilion seats. Bellinger flailed at the third strike for the final out, but the Dodgers led, 3-1.

Seventh innings had provided the greatest source of Kershaw's postseason anguish. He took the mound for this seventh inning, bringing from the dugout a career postseason seventh-inning ERA of 25.50.[12] Altuve led off with a grounder that found a hole between Seager and Turner for a single. Correa's bouncer to Turner forced Altuve at second. Gurriel grounded to shortstop Seager for a potential inning-ending double-play ball. Seager, though, fumbled the exchange from glove to hand. But he managed to scoop the ball to Logan Forsythe for the force at second. There was no seventh-inning jinx for Kershaw this time. Brian McCann flied to Taylor for the third out.

Although his pitch count sat at a relatively modest 83 pitches, Kershaw's evening reached its end with one earned run, three hits, zero walks, and 11 strikeouts; Kershaw joined Don Newcombe as the only Dodgers pitchers to achieve 11 strikeouts with no walks in a World Series game. The Dodgers bullpen possessed the best ERA in the regular season, and they carried that success to the postseason with a 0.94 mark.[13] Roberts trusted the lead to Brandon Morrow and Kenley Jansen. The pair had combined for a scoreless innings streak that stretched back to Game Two of the NLDS.[14] Roberts' confidence was well placed. Morrow retired the Astros in order in the eighth, and Jansen earned the save by doing the same in the ninth. Cue Randy Newman's "I Love L.A.," and the Dodgers claimed the early advantage in the World Series.

About his deciding home run, Turner nodded to the weather. He said, ""[I]f it's 10 degrees cooler, that's probably a routine fly ball."[15] Keuchel seemed to agree, commenting, "I didn't think it was going out by any mean. … I was trying to get in on him and I thought I did. He didn't square it up by any means."[16]

For Kershaw, Game One was an evening of redemption. He flipped the narrative into a gem, or as teammate Brandon McCarthy said, "That, to me, was his masterpiece."[17]

DODGER STADIUM

SOURCES

In addition to the sources cited in the Notes, the author consulted Baseball-Reference.com and Retrosheet.org, and viewed the Fox broadcast of the game accessible at youtube.com.

https://www.baseball-reference.com/boxes/LAN/LAN201710240.shtml

https://www.retrosheet.org/boxesetc/2017/B10240LAN2017.htm

https://www.youtube.com/watch?v=F2QVELDu_Y4

NOTES

1   Weather Spark, accessed at https://weatherspark.com/d/1705/10/24/Average-Weather-on-October-24-in-Los-Angeles-California-United-States#Figures-Temperature.

2   Bill Plaschke, "A Scorching Hot Opener," *Los Angeles Times*, October 25, 2017: A1.

3   Associated Press, "Kershaw, Dodgers Beat Astros 3-1 in Hot World Series Opener," ESPN.com, October 24, 2014. https://www.espn.com/mlb/recap/_/gameId/371024119. Accessed December 30, 2023.

4   Billy Witz, "Game One Is No Sweat for Dodgers," *New York Times*, October 25, 2017: B-11.

5   The 1970 World Series matched the 108-54 Baltimore Orioles and the 102-60 Cincinnati Reds. The Orioles won the Series in five games.

6   Pedro Moura and Kevin Baxter, " Keuchel Recalls the Lean Years in Houston," *Los Angeles Times*, October 24, 2017: V13.

7   Witz.

8   Witz.

9   "Kershaw, Dodgers Beat Astros 3-1 in Hot World Series Opener."

10 Witz.

11 Plaschke.

12 Plaschke.

13 Moura and Baxter.

14 Andy McCullough and Kevin Baxter, "Roster Move Is Not a Stunner," *Los Angeles Times*, October 25, 2017: D3.

15 Witz.

16 Witz.

17 Plaschke.

ROOKIE RIGHT-HANDER BEATS ROCKIES, DODGERS WIN NL WEST TITLE

October 1, 2018: Los Angeles Dodgers 5, Colorado Rockies 2

by Paul Hofmann

After falling nine games off the pace on May 8 and treading water during the month of August, the Los Angeles Dodgers battled back to finish the 2018 season with a record of 91-71, tied for first in the National League West Division with the Colorado Rockies. The Rockies won nine of their final 10 games to force a one-game tiebreaker at Dodger Stadium. At stake was a trip to the National League Division Series.

The Monday afternoon winner-take-all matchup pitted a pair of young up-and-coming right-handers against each other. The Dodgers started right-hander Walker Buehler. The 24-year-old rookie and former first-round draft pick out of Vanderbilt University was 7-5 with a 2.76 ERA. Before the game, Dodgers manager Dave Roberts referred to Buehler as his team's "best." He described the decision to start him as "a no-brainer."[1]

"I believe he's the right guy for this moment," Roberts said.[2]

Buehler was opposed by the Rockies' 23-year-old Venezuelan right-hander Germán Márquez, who was 14-10 with a 3.76 ERA. Márquez entered the game with a string of 12 consecutive quality starts and a 2.14 earned-run average in September.[3]

The game drew an announced crowd of 47,816 and was played under nearly ideal conditions. The temperature was 90 degrees with sunny skies and a gentle breeze blowing out to center field when Buehler delivered the first pitch at 1:09 P.M.

Buehler retired the Rockies in order in the top of the first. Márquez did the same to the Dodgers in the bottom of the inning before Buehler tossed a second one-two-three inning in the top of the second. Márquez navigated his way around a second-inning leadoff single by Manny Machado to keep the game scoreless.

Buehler, displaying his imprecise command, hit Rockies first baseman Ian Desmond with a pitch to start the third inning. After Rockies catcher Tony Wolters grounded into a fielder's choice, Márquez sacrificed Wolters to second and Charlie Blackmon drew a walk. With runners on first and second, Buehler retired the side on DJ LeMahieu's grounder to shortstop. Márquez walked Buehler but pitched a scoreless bottom of the third. The game appeared to be shaping up as a pitching duel.

The Dodgers caught a sizable break against Márquez in the fourth, when catcher Wolters dropped a third strike and allowed Max Muncy to reach first base after striking out on a 98-mph fastball. Márquez stuck out the next two batters he faced – effectively striking out the side – but still had to face Cody Bellinger.[4] The Dodgers center fielder unloaded on a fastball, depositing a two-run homer into the pavilion in right-center field to give the Dodgers a 2-0 lead. It was Bellinger's 25th home run of the year. Yasiel Puig doubled to deep left-center and Kiké Hernández was intentionally walked, but Márquez stuck out Buehler, his fourth strikeout of the inning, to retire the side.

Buehler continued his mastery of the Rockies in the fifth inning, retiring the side in order on 10 pitches before the Dodgers struck again. Left fielder Joc Pederson led off the bottom of the fifth with a double to center. Two batters later, Muncy hit his 35th home run of the season, a shot to left-center, to extend the Dodgers' lead to 4-0. After Machado flied out to deep left, Rockies manager Bud Black called on left-hander Harrison Musgrave to face catcher Yasmani Grandal. Musgrave, who entered the game with a 2-3 record and a 4.57 ERA, retired Grandal on a groundout to short.

The Rockies finally touched Buehler for a hit when Blackmon singled to right field with one out in the sixth. Buehler retired the next two batters of ground-balls and Blackmon was stranded at second base. The score remained 4-0.

The Dodgers added a run in the bottom of the sixth. Hernández hit a two-out ground-rule double to right and Buehler helped his own cause with an RBI single to right. The Dodgers now led 5-0.

Buehler retired the first two Rockies on fly balls to right-center to start the seventh inning. After he walked right fielder Carlos González, Roberts decided to go to the bullpen. "Buehler showed his surfeit of talent across 6⅔ innings of one-hit baseball,"[5] silencing the bats of the Rockies, who had averaged more than 7 runs per game over their last 10 games. Right-hander Pedro Báez, who was 4-3 with a 2.91 ERA, walked Ian Desmond but got Matt Holliday on a popup to shortstop for the last out of the seventh inning.

Scott Oberg relieved to start the bottom of the eighth for the Rockies. An unsung hero of the Rockies bullpen, the right-handed Oberg entered the game with a record of 8-1 and a 2.48 ERA. After giving up back-to-back singles to Justin Turner and Muncy to lead off the inning that put runners at the corners, Oberg got Machado to ground into a double play with Turner holding at third. With the switch-hitting Grandal due up, the Rockies went the bullpen once again, bringing in veteran Jake McGee. The situational left-hander, who had struggled for much of the season and was 2-4 with an inflated 6.62 ERA, struck out Grandal swinging to end the inning.

The Dodgers used three pitchers in the eighth inning. Baez, who recorded the last out of the seventh, started the inning by getting Chris Iannetta to line out to third. Left-hander Scott Alexander, making his 73rd appearance of the season, gave up a single to Blackmon, his second hit of the day. Roberts then turned to Japanese right-hander Kenta Maeda, who recorded the final two outs of the inning.

McGee came back out to start the bottom of the eighth. He retired Bellinger and Puig on groundouts to first and third, respectively, before being replaced by DJ Johnson. The right-handed-throwing Johnson retired Hernández on the first pitch, a grounder to third base. After eight innings, the score remained 5-0.

Although it was not a save opportunity, the Dodgers turned to closer Kenley Jansen for the bottom of the

ninth. The right-hander was 1-5 with a 2.80 ERA and 38 saves. The Rockies finally got on the scoreboard when third baseman Nolan Arenado sent Jansen's first offering into the left-field pavilion, his 38th home run of the season. Shortstop Trevor Story then won a nine-pitch battle with Jansen, sending his 37th home run to right-center, cutting the Dodgers lead to 5-2. Jansen quickly recovered, getting Gonzalez to ground out to first on the next pitch, then striking out to final two batters to preserve the victory and send the Dodgers to a NLDS matchup against the Atlanta Braves.

With the victory, Buehler improved his record to 8-5 and lowered his ERA to 2.62. Márquez finished with a record of 14-11. His 14 victories were a career high. The time of the game was 3 hours and 21 minutes.

After the game, a reporter asked the brash Buehler if he knew he was going to win the game. Buehler curled his upper lip into a grin. "I won't say yes," Buehler said. "But, yes."[6]

The Dodgers went on to beat the Braves in the NLDS three games to one and advanced to the National League Championship Series. They won the National League pennant by beating the Milwaukee Brewers four games to three before dropping the World Series to the Boston Red Sox four games to one.

SOURCES

In addition to the sources cited in the Notes, the author relied on Baseball-reference.com, Retrosheet.org, and Baseball-Almanac.com.

https://www.baseball-reference.com/boxes/LAN/LAN201810010.shtml

https://www.retrosheet.org/boxesetc/2018/B10010LAN2018.htm

NOTES

1   Tribune Content Agency, "Walker Buehler Leads Dodgers to NL West Title and the NLDS," *Fairfield* (California) *Daily Republic,* October 1, 2018. Retrieved on October 4, 2023, from www.dailyrepublic.com/sports/walker-buehler-leads-dodgers-to-nl-west-title-and-the-nlds/article_ca00f848-4a6b-5e55-82fc-1bd82586b83d.html.

2   Tribune Content Agency.

3   Tribune Content Agency.

4   Andy McCullough, "Walker Buehler Leads Dodgers to NL West Title and into NLDS, *Los Angeles Times,* October 1, 2018. Retrieved on October 3, 2023, from https://www.latimes.com/sports/dodgers/la-sp-dodgers-rockies-20181001-story.html.

5   McCullough.

6   McCullough.

TWO GAMES IN ONE – DODGERS PREVAIL OVER RED SOX IN LONGEST WORLD SERIES GAME EVER

October 26, 2018: Los Angeles Dodgers 3, Boston Red Sox 2 (18 innings) (Game Three of the 2018 World Series)

by Bill Nowlin

Because the third game of the 2018 World Series was being played in a National League city, NL rules applied – which meant there was no designated hitter. Red Sox manager Alex Cora elected to have J.D. Martinez play left field and Andrew Benintendi remain on the bench.

Both teams started right-handers, Walker Buehler for the Dodgers and Rick Porcello for the Red Sox. The Dodgers put their power hitters into the lineup. None of their four top homer hitters had started in either Game One or Game Two – Joc Pederson, Max Muncy, Cody Bellinger, and Yasmani Grandal.[1]

Buehler had started 23 games for the Dodgers and finished the season 8-5 with a 2.62 ERA and a WHIP of 0.961.[2] He had struggled in his first two postseason outings but had started Game Seven of the NLCS and allowed just one run in 4⅔ innings. He set down the first six Red Sox batters in order, though it took him 26 pitches to get through the first inning.

Porcello walked Muncy in the first inning, but he was the only batter who reached base in the first two. Porcello (a Cy Young Award winner for Boston in 2016) had been 17-7 in the regular season, but with a 4.28 ERA and a WHIP of 1.176.[3]

In the third inning, the Sox singled twice, but Jackie Bradley Jr. was out trying to steal second after the first single. Porcello laid down a sacrifice bunt to move Christian Vázquez to second, but Buehler got Mookie Betts to fly out to center.

In the bottom of the third, with two outs, the Dodgers took a 1-0 lead when Joc Pederson swung at the first pitch and homered down the right-field line.

No one reached base for either team in the fourth, nor in the Red Sox fifth. When Pederson came up again in the bottom of the fifth, with two outs and no one on, lefty Eduardo Rodriguez relieved Porcello and struck out the Dodgers batter.

Buehler worked through the sixth and seventh, one-two-three in both innings. He had thrown seven shutout innings with just two hits and had not walked a man. The Red Sox had Joe Kelly work the sixth and Ryan Brasier the seventh. Matt Kemp pinch-hit for Buehler and grounded out for the third out of the bottom of the seventh.

Chad Finn of the *Boston Globe* wrote of Buehler's effort that when he "came out after 108 pitches, it felt like a reprieve for the Red Sox."[4]

Kenley Jansen took over pitching for Los Angeles. He'd had extraordinary bad luck in 2018, the team's closer with a season ERA of 3.01 but a record of 1-5. After getting two outs, he served up a 2-and-0 pitch to Jackie Bradley Jr., which the Red Sox center fielder pounded a few rows deep into the right-field seats.

Matt Barnes pitched the bottom of the eighth for the Red Sox. A single was the only base hit.

Jansen retired all three Red Sox batters in the top of the ninth. Alex Cora turned to David Price to pitch the bottom of the ninth.

The Red Sox were doing a great deal of defensive shifting, starting in the eighth. When right-hander Manny Machado came to bat with two outs, center fielder Bradley had moved to left, Mookie Betts moved from right to center, and J.D. Martinez moved from left over to right. Machado struck out. In the ninth, the three outfielders all moved back to their original positions, but with two outs and a runner on, and Craig Kimbrel – who took over for Price – walked Chris Taylor, they all shifted again with pinch-hitter Brian Dozier at the plate. Dozier fouled out to the catcher and the game went into extra innings.

J.D. Martinez left for a pinch-runner in the top of the 10th. No one scored, thanks to a terrific throw home from Bellinger in center field.[5] There was more shifting come the bottom of the 10th.[6]

Both teams worked a base on balls in the 11th. No one scored. The 12th inning saw three-up, three-down for both teams.

In the 13th, the Red Sox scored a go-ahead run. Leading off, Brock Holt walked. And stole second. Eduardo Núñez hit a ball that took a high chop and came down in the no-man's land between the pitcher's mound and first base. Both ran to field it, pitcher Scott Alexander grabbing it and then tossing to the second baseman covering the bag at first. Holt easily made it to third. Nunez was safe on a close play and the throw went astray (error on Alexander); Holt ran home. It was 2-1, advantage Red Sox. Despite a later double and an intentional walk, the Red Sox couldn't add to their score. Xander Bogaerts ended the inning by grounding a ball about two feet in front of the plate. The catcher picked up the ball and stepped on the plate to force out the runner coming from third.

Sandy Leon came in to catch for Boston, with Vazquez taking over at first base. Scheduled Game Four starter Nathan Eovaldi was pressed into action. He pitched an eventless 12th, but ran into some trouble in the 13th with a walk. With one out, Bellinger hit a foul ball that third baseman Nunez caught – but fell into the stands while doing so.[7] Muncy alertly tagged up at first and took second base on the play. But there were two outs. Yasiel Puig came up. He hit an infield grounder toward the middle that could have produced the third out, but Ian Kinsler stumbled on the some-what "cushiony" turf (the word was Roberts's) and threw the ball well wide of first base – an error that allowed Muncy to score, tying the game, 2-2.[8]

Each team had scored one run in the 13th, and both runs came on errors.

The game kept going. Dylan Floro had gotten the Dodgers out of the 13th; he set the Red Sox down in order in the 14th. Eovaldi gave up a single, but no more.

Kenta Maeda pitched the 15th for Los Angeles. David Freese had pinch-hit for Floro. He took over at first base, Muncy moved to play second, and Enrique Hernández moved to left field. With an infield single and a walk, the first two runners got on. Vazquez laid down a very good bunt, but Maeda pounced on it and fired to third base for an out. Maeda then struck out the next two Red Sox. Eovaldi struck out two (though a foul ball by Muncy came close to going out) and got a popup to second base.

Maeda struck out all three Red Sox he faced in the top of the 16th, and Eovaldi retired the side in order, too. The game passed the seven-hour mark. The Red Sox had only one pitcher left in the bullpen, Drew Pomeranz. Eovaldi was the ninth pitcher Boston had used.

Julio Urías relieved Maeda in the 17th. The only one to reach base was Bradley, on a two-out walk. Eovaldi retired the three batters he faced, one of whom was Clayton Kershaw, pinch-hitting for Maeda. He made contact, but lined out to right field.

It was the 18th inning. Alex Wood took the mound for the Dodgers, their ninth pitcher of the game. He walked Leon. The Red Sox had two good hitters up – Mookie Betts and Xander Bogaerts. Eovaldi was the next one due up. Betts grounded into a force play at second base. Eovaldi had already pitched six innings. The Red Sox were going with him all the way. They had no one up in the bullpen and he was in the on-deck circle. Bogaerts hit into a 6-4-3 double play.

Eovaldi faced Max Muncy leading off the bottom of the 19th. He had already thrown 90 pitches in relief, but he was still throwing heat. Fox announcer Joe Buck noted pitches of 97 and 98 miles per hour. The count went to 3-and-2. On his seventh pitch of the at-bat, Muncy homered to left-center. The game was over. Angelenos who had stayed up past midnight (gasp!) could finally go to bed. In New England, the game ended at 3:30 A.M.

It had been the longest World Series game of all time, both in terms of innings played and in time elapsed (7 hours 20 minutes). Between them, the two teams had used 18 pitchers. Most of the Dodger Stadium crowd had stayed until the end.

"We're feeling pretty good about ourselves right now," Dave Roberts said after the game. "Considering where we're at … I think there's a little bit of momentum on our side."[9]

Back in Boston, Eovaldi was lionized for his heroic effort.[10]

SOURCES

In addition to the sources cited in the Notes, the author consulted Baseball-Reference.com, Retrosheet.org, and a YouTube broadcast of the game.

https://www.baseball-reference.com/boxes/LAN/LAN201810260.shtml

https://www.retrosheet.org/boxesetc/2018/B10260LAN2018.htm

https://www.youtube.com/watch?v=5cB6SUqDlR4

NOTES

1   All four of them had appeared in both games, though, coming in as pinch-hitters or defensive replacements. In those games, they batted a combined 1-for-11. Three of them were left-handed hitters; Grandal was a switch-hitter. The quartet had hit 109 regular-season home runs.

2   His ERA was a starter was 2.31, fifth-best in the majors.

3   In 2018 the Red Sox team ERA was 4.40. He had won Game Four of the ALDS against the Yankees. It's of some interest that, as a batter in 2018, Porcello hit for a .429 average; he was 3-for-7 with two doubles and three RBIs.

4   Chad Finn, "It Had Just About Everything," *Boston Globe*, October 27, 2018: C8.

5   "I was glad I had a chance to redeem myself," he said after the game. "I would not have been able to sleep." He was referring to his baserunning gaffe in the bottom of the ninth. Bill Plaschke, "Max Muncy and the Dodgers' 18-Inning World Series Victory Changed Everything," *Los Angeles Times*, October 27, 2018. search-proquest-com.mcpl.idm.oclc.org/latimes/docview/2126136143/4F290E1B95CC4DB3PQ/11?accountid=69.

6   Ian Kinsler had been the pinch-runner. He stayed in the game to play second base. Brock Holt, who'd been at second, went out to left field. Eduardo Núñez, who had pinch-hit for Rafael Devers and hit into an inning-ending double play, played third base. Bradley moved from left back to center, and Betts moved over from center to right. After Muncy hit a two-out double, Bradley moved to left, Betts to center, and Holt from left to right. Machado popped up to short. By the end of the game, Betts – to name one fielder— had been shifted six times.

7   Nunez was taking a beating. It was the third time in the game that the trainer had to come out to look at Núñez - – and he'd only come into the game in the 10th. Before tumbling into the seats, he'd earlier been knocked over by the catcher at the plate and had later fallen while running over first base. Rick Porcello said he jokingly told Nunez, "Get up. We're tired of watching you roll around in the dirt and then be fine.'" After the game, Núñez said, in Spanish, "I'm a little injured but we don't have any other options. We have to play. We have to win two more games. … You have to give it your all." See Maria Torres, "Eduardo Nunez Has a Rough Time in Game 3," *Los Angeles Times*, October 27, 2018. search-proquest-com.mcpl.idm.oclc.org/latimes/docview/2126136273/84D83AA3DF4449CDPQ/17?accountid=69\ Torres quoted Nunez after the game: "We have three months to recuperate."

8   Needless to say, an opponent scoring from second on an error in a World Series game reminded many Red Sox fans of Game Six of the 1986 World Series. Dan Shaughnessy, "After This Stunner, It's a Series," *Boston Globe*, October 27, 2018: A1, C4. As to the turf quality, see Peter Abraham, "David Price Announced as the Game 5 Starter," *Boston Globe*, October 28, 2018: C16.

9   Bill Plaschke.

10 See, for instance, Nick Cafardo, "Eovaldi Heroic in Defeat," *Boston Globe*, October 27, 2018: C1. "Never been more proud of a teammate than I am right now," wrote David Price on Instagram. See Peter Abraham, "David Price Announced as the Game 5 Starter." Abraham quoted Rick Porcello as saying, "After the game I started crying, because that was … I mean, he's grinding. Every pitch. He literally gave everything he had on every pitch. … That's the epitome of reaching down deep."

DODGERS SMACK EIGHT HOMERS IN RECORD-BREAKING OPENING DAY AT HOME

March 28, 2019: Los Angeles Dodgers 12, Arizona Diamondbacks 5

by Bryan Dietzler

The start of the 2019 season came on March 28, when the Arizona Diamondbacks traveled to Dodger Stadium to take on the previous year's National League champions. In 2018, the 82-80 Diamondbacks ended up 9½ games behind the Dodgers in the National League West race.

Perhaps the breakout should not have been too much of a surprise. The Dodgers had led the National League with 235 home runs in 2018. But this game showed just how powerful their lineup was and what kind of damage it could do.[1]

Before a crowd of 53,086, the Dodgers entered the history books with a bevy of home runs that no one had ever seen since the ballpark opened in 1962.

Above Dodger Stadium were "picturesque puffy white clouds on a 68-degree afternoon."[2] It was perfect baseball weather. The day also included a tribute to Don Newcombe, the Dodgers pitcher who had died at the age of 92 on February 16.[3]

The pitching matchup saw Arizona put former Dodger Zack Greinke on the mound against the Dodgers' Hyun-Jin Ryu. Longtime Opening Day starter Clayton Kershaw was on the 10-day disabled list with shoulder inflammation. He had been the starting pitcher the eight previous Opening Days, with five wins, one loss, and two no-decisions.[4]

The Diamondbacks were scoreless in the first, though Ryu allowed a single to Eduardo Escobar. The Dodgers scored in the bottom of the inning on Max Muncy's groundout to first base that drove in Joc Pedersen, who had doubled and taken third on a groundout.

The Diamondbacks were cold in the top of the second inning and the Dodgers maintained their lead.

In the bottom of the second, Pedersen hit a homer with Austin Barnes on base. That made it 3-0.

Neither team scored in the third inning. The Dodgers enjoyed an offensive explosion in the fourth. Enrique Hernández hit a two-run homer, Barnes and Corey Seager added solo shots, and the Dodgers jumped ahead, 7-0. (Seager had missed a lot of time the previous season with injuries; he had not played a game for the Dodgers in 333 days thanks to several ailments, including hip surgery and a torn ulnar collateral ligament.[5]

After the Seager home run, Diamondbacks manager Torey Lovullo pulled Greinke and replaced him with Matt Koch. Justin Turner lined to right field to end the inning.

The Diamondbacks posted a run in the sixth inning when Adam Jones hit a solo home run to make it 7-1. The Dodgers answered by tacking on two runs in the bottom half on a two-run homer by Pedersen that gave LA a 9-1 advantage.

Arizona added another run on Christian Walker's home run in the top of the seventh inning off Yimi Garcia. In the bottom of the frame, Muncy, Cody Bellinger, and Hernández all hit solo homers and Los Angeles pushed ahead, 12-2.

The Dodgers pulled Garcia and had Brock Stewart pitch the final two innings. In the eighth Stewart didn't allow any runs and the score remained 12-2. The Dodgers failed to score in the bottom of the eighth.

The Diamondbacks mounted a comeback of sorts in the ninth inning as Walker doubled to score Wilmer

Flores, Ketel Marte hit a sacrifice fly that brought home David Peralta, and a sacrifice fly by Nick Ahmed drove in Walker. The game ended with the Dodgers in front, 12-5.

No major-league team had ever had so many home runs on Opening Day. Through 2023 the record still stood.[6] The previous record, six, was set by the New York Mets in 1988 and tied by the Chicago White Sox in 2018.[7]

In addition, the Dodgers tied their record for the most home runs in a game. They had hit eight homers on May 23, 2002, against the Milwaukee Brewers at Milwaukee's Miller Park.[8] (The Toronto Blue Jays hold the record for most home runs hit in a single game, with 10 on September 14, 1987.)

Not to be lost was the pitching performance of Ryu, who struck out eight and set down 13 straight Diamondbacks at one point.

Greinke had a horrible game and said, "Yeah it was bad. Not really much to build off because all that stuff was bad, so that's probably the most disappointing thing."[9]

The game was the kickoff moment in a season that saw the Dodgers go 106-56, the second-best record in the major leagues that season (Houston was one win better, at 107-55) and advanced to the National League Division Series, where they were eliminated by the Washington Nationals, the eventual World Series winners.

The Diamondbacks went on to have an 85-77 record, slightly better than their previous season. They didn't make the postseason.

SOURCES

In addition to the sources cited in the Notes, the author consulted Baseball-Reference.com and Retrosheet.org.

https://www.baseball-reference.com/boxes/LAN/LAN201903280.shtml

https://www.retrosheet.org/boxesetc/2019/B03280LAN2019.htm

NOTES

1   Jorge Castillo, "Blasts from Cast; Six Dodgers Hit Eight Homers to Tie Team Record in First Game," *Los Angeles Times*, March 29, 2019: D-1.

2   Hailey Branson-Potts, "A Smashing Opening Day; Fans at Dodger Stadium Start the Season Brimming with High Hopes, Missing Some Favorite Players and Witnessing Eight L.A. Home Runs," *Los Angeles Times*, March 29, 2019: B-1.

3   Bill Plaschke, "Blasts from the Cast; a Great Day to be Back, Back, Back, Back, Back, Back, Back, Back," *Los Angeles Times*, March 29, 2019: B-1.

4   Matthew Moreno, "History of Clayton Kershaw's Streak Opening Day Starts for Dodgers," *Dodger Blue*, March 28, 2019, retrieved on January 2, 2024 from https://dodgerblue.com/dodgers-history-clayton-kershaw-franchise-record-opening-day-starts-streak-snapped/2019/03/28/.

5   Andy McCullough, "Seager Makes Immediate Impact; After Two Surgeries and 11 Months Away, Shortstop Joins In on Home Run Parade," *Los Angeles Times*, March 29, 2019: D-7.

6   Associated Press, "Power Surge! Dodgers Hit 8 Homers in 12-5 Win Over Arizona," ESPN.com, March 29, 2019. Retrieved on January 1, 2024, from https://www.espn.com/mlb/recap/_/gameId/401074733.

7   Associated Press, "Dodgers Set Opening Day Record with Eight Home Runs," *New York Times*, March 28, 2019. Retrieved on July 12, 2023, from https://www.nytimes.com/2019/03/28/sports/dodgers-eight-home-runs.html.

8   Associated Press, "Dodgers Set Opening Day Record with Eight Home Runs."

9   "Power Surge! Dodgers Hit 8 Homers in 12-5 Win Over Arizona."

THIRD STRAIGHT GAME WITH A WALK-OFF HOME RUN BY A ROOKIE

June 23, 2019: Los Angeles Dodgers 6, Colorado Rockies 3

by Joey Elledge

Three rookies took turns hitting walk-off home runs in three straight games for the Dodgers in June 2019. No major-league trio had ever pulled off such an unlikely feat. Matt Beaty, Alex Verdugo, and Will Smith did it in a weekend series against the Colorado Rockies at Dodger Stadium. Each game attracted more than 50,000 fans.

The Dodgers, coming off their second straight World Series appearance, entered the series in first place with a record of 51-25. They led the National League West by 10 games over the second-place Colorado Rockies, who were 40-34.

Beaty was the first to send LA fans home happy. He hit a two-out, two-run homer off Jairo Diaz that led his team to a 4-2 victory on June 21, on the same night right-hander Walker Buehler struck out 16 batters and walked no one. The next day Verdugo hit a walk-off solo home run in the 11th inning off Jesus Tinoco that gave the Dodgers a 5-4 win. It was his fourth hit of the game. The next afternoon, Smith, who had just been recalled from the minors, hit a walk-off, three-run homer to beat the Rockies, 6-3. It was a monumental accomplishment for all three rookies.

Beaty was a 12th-round pick by the Dodgers out of Belmont University in Nashville, Tennessee.[1] Beaty's calling card at Belmont was his remarkable eye for the strike zone, as he walked more than he struck out in his junior year. However, this walk-off home run almost did not happen.

Three days earlier, on June 20, Beaty had been demoted to Triple-A Oklahoma City. An injury to pitcher Josh Sborz, though, kept Beaty in Los Angeles and allowed him to hit a 402-foot walk-off home run against the Rockies.

Alex Verdugo, a high-school draft pick from Arizona, was a pitcher and a fielder. Most teams had evaluated him as a pitcher, but the Dodgers liked him as a hitter. Verdugo rewarded the Dodgers by batting .329 in 91 games for Oklahoma City in 2018. He made LA's Opening Day roster in 2019 after getting call-ups the two previous years and was batting .294 when the Colorado series began. Verdugo's walk-off homer was his seventh round-tripper of the season.

The next game's hero, Will Smith, was sitting in the Oklahoma City Dodgers' clubhouse and watched Verdugo's home run on television.[2] Smith's own shining moment was less than 24 hours away.

The Sunday afternoon game began on a scary note. In the first inning, a woman at Dodger Stadium was struck in the head by a foul line drive struck by Los Angeles star Cody Bellinger.[3] She was sitting four rows from the field along the first-base line, just beyond the protective netting that extends to the end of the visiting dugout. Bellinger checked on her between innings. After first aid was administered, the woman was taken to a hospital for precautionary tests but was later released.

Smith was a supplemental first-round draft pick (32nd overall) from the University of Louisville in 2016, where he was known for stellar defense behind the plate. In the minors, Smith's bat helped him advance through the farm system. He was promoted to Los Angeles from Oklahoma City on the day of the game. Smith, who had been called up earlier in the season for six games (going 6-for-21 with two home runs), caught a 6 A.M. flight to Los Angeles and gave the 50,023 at Dodger Stadium a chance to watch history.

Colorado took an early lead with a first-inning home run by right fielder David Dahl. Second baseman Ryan McMahon hit an RBI single in the third to give the Rockies a 2-0 lead.

Right-hander Antonio Senzatela held the Dodgers scoreless into the seventh inning, when pinch-hitter Chris Taylor greeted reliever Chad Bettis with a three-run homer to left field and gave the Dodgers a 3-2 lead. The Rockies tied the game in the top of the eighth on Tony Wolters' RBI double to right field. In the Rockies' ninth, Dodgers closer Kenley Jansen got Charlie Blackmon to fly out and struck out Raimel Tapia before giving up a single to center fielder Garrett Hampson. Hampson stole second base but was stranded when David Dahl struck out.

With Jansen due up as the fifth batter in the bottom of the ninth, Dodgers manager Dave Roberts was prepared to send up a pinch-hitter.

Scott Oberg took over from Jake McGee and became the fourth pitcher of the game for the Rockies. The first Dodger he faced was Beaty, the hero from two nights earlier, who reached first base a throwing error by second baseman McMahon. Kiké Hernández fouled out to the first baseman. With Chris Taylor batting, Beaty took second on a wild pitch by Oberg, who then struck out Taylor. With first base open, Rockies manager Bud Black made the textbook move and had Oberg walk Russell Martin.

Smith batted for Jansen and hit a 1-and-0 pitch into the right-field seats, giving the Dodgers a walk-off victory in his seventh game played for the team. After his opposite-field home run, Smith told reporters, "We were saying that's a record that's probably never going to be broken."[4]

Taylor said, "That was sick, I think we're all still in shock. Three nights in a row, walk-off homers by three rookies. It's special to be able to do that. I think it takes some serious nerve to calm yourself in those situations, and [Smith] has done it twice. Was it a walk-off? It's pretty impressive."[5] Smith hit his first walk-off home run on June 1, 2019.

Dodgers manager Roberts said, "We talk about these young players not being afraid of the moment. For Will to get a pitch in and carry it to the opposite part of the field is impressive."[6]

SOURCES

In addition to the sources cited in the Notes, the author consulted Baseball-Reference.com and Retroheet.org.

https://www.baseball-reference.com/boxes/LAN/LAN201906230.shtml

https://www.retrosheet.org/boxesetc/2019/B06230LAN2019.htm

Some highlights of the game may be seen on YouTube: https://www.youtube.com/watch?v=6lyl5OCR7do

A compilation, "All the Los Angeles Dodgers Walk-Offs from 2019!" shows the other walk-offs, as well as the one on June 23: https://www.youtube.com/watch?v=qC1yTHOyqdI.

NOTES

1   David Schoenfield, "Real or Not? Even the Dodgers' Rookies Are Out of This World," ESPN.com, June 23, 2019. https://www.espn.com/mlb/story/_/id/27041089/real-not-even-dodgers-rookies-this-world.

2   Mike DiGiovanna, "BASEBALL; DODGERS 6, COLORADO 3; Third Rookie Stars in L.A.'s Summer Rerun; Smith's Blast Gives the Dodgers Three Straight Walk-Off Homers From a First-Year Player." *Los Angeles Times*, June 24, 2019: D-1.

3   Associated Press, "Fan Taken to Hospital After Struck by Bellinger's Foul," SpectrumNews1, June 23, 2019. https://spectrumnews1.com/oh/toledo/ap-online/2019/06/23/fan-taken-to-hospital-after-struck-by-bellingers-foul.

4   Joe Reedy, "Dodgers Win on Walk-Off Home Run for 3rd Straight Game," NBC Los Angeles, June 23, 2019. https://www.nbclosangeles.com/news/sports/dodgers-rookie-will-smith-hits-walk-off-home-run/149048/.

5   DiGiovanna.

6   Reedy.

DODGERS HIT 8 HRS AND SCORE DODGER STADIUM RECORD 22 RUNS

July 10, 2021: Los Angeles Dodgers 22, Arizona Diamondbacks 1

by Paul Hofmann

A crowd of 44,645 came to Dodger Stadium on a picture-perfect Southern California Saturday evening. The game-time temperature was 75 degrees under clear skies, and there was a gentle breeze of 7 MPH blowing out to left field. The typically large LA crowd was treated to a record-setting offensive performance by the Dodgers as the team broke out of its recent offensive funk.[1]

The Dodgers, who had dropped four of their past five contests, had a record of 54-35 and were trailing the San Francisco Giants by two games in the tightly contested NL West Division when play started. The Diamondbacks were in the middle of one of the worst seasons in franchise history and were in last place, 30 games off the pace with a record of 26-64. Through it all, the Diamondbacks endured a 17-game losing streak, another 13-game skid, and a record 24-game road drought.[2]

Left-hander Caleb Smith was making his ninth start of the season for the Diamondbacks, his eighth since joining the rotation in June. He was 2-5 with a 3.45 ERA. He was opposed by right-hander Walker Buehler, who was enjoying a breakout season. He was 8-1 with a 2.49 ERA.

Buehler held the Diamondbacks scoreless in the top of the first as he struck out three while navigating his way around a one-out double by Pavin Smith and two-out walk to Christian Walker.

The Dodgers jumped on Smith from the outset. Mookie Betts led off with a walk and advanced to second on a groundball single by Chris Taylor that found its way through the hole between third base and shortstop. After Justin Turner flied out to short right field, Max Muncy lined a double down the right-field line that scored Betts and Taylor. Albert Pujols struck out for the second out of the inning before Cody Bellinger hit a two-run home run to deep left, his fourth of the season. A.J. Pollock followed by hitting his second homer of the season, a drive that landed deep into the left-field pavilion. Austin Barnes flied out to David Peralta in left-center to end the inning. At the end of the first, the score was 5-0.

Buehler needed only 11 pitches to get through a one-two-three second inning, bringing a battered Smith back out to the mound after he threw 35 pitches in the first. Buehler helped his own cause with a line-drive single to right-center. Betts and Taylor both walked to load the bases with no outs and Turner sent a 3-and-2 pitch over the wall in left-center for a grand slam, ending the night for Smith. Turner's blast extended the Dodgers' lead to 9-0 before many of the traditionally late-arriving Los Angeles fans had settled into their seats.

Diamondbacks manager Torey Lovullo called on right-hander Matt Peacock to relieve Smith. Peacock, who was making his 21st appearance of the season, had a record of 3-6 with a 5.59 ERA. He retired the next three Dodgers hitters to end the second inning.

Buehler and Peacock traded scoreless innings in the third and fourth. Buehler tossed a scoreless top of the fifth before the Diamondbacks turned to left-hander Alex Young to replace Peacock, who had been lifted for a pinch-hitter in the top of the inning. Young, who hadn't pitched in 12 days, was 2-6 with a 5.82 ERA.

Young walked Pollock to start the bottom of the fifth. After getting Barnes to ground into a 4-6-3 double play, he struck out Buehler to end the inning.

Buehler continued to make short work of the Diamondbacks and retired the side in order in the top of sixth before turning it over to the Dodgers bullpen. In the bottom of the sixth, Young navigated around a leadoff single by Betts and a one-out single by Turner to keep the score at 9-0.

Right-hander Phil Bickford, whom the Dodgers selected off waivers from the Milwaukee Brewers in late May, was a dependable middle reliever during the

2021 season. In 21 games he had a 2.25 ERA. Bickford pitched a perfect seventh before the Dodgers erupted once again.

Young returned to the mound for his third inning of work in the bottom of the seventh. With one out, Pollock singled through the hole on the left side of the infield. Barnes was hit by a pitch and Matt Beaty, who was now playing right field and hitting in Buehler's spot in the order, beat out a dribbler back to the mound to load the bases before Betts hit his 12th home run of the season and the Dodgers' second grand slam of the evening. The score now stood at 13-0.

However, the Dodgers were not done. With two outs, Peralta misplayed a fly ball off the bat of Zach Reks, allowing Reks to get to second. Zach McKinstry followed with a two-run homer to deep left-center, his seventh of the season. Pujols then crushed his 12th homer of the season, to left-center, to make the score 16-0. Bellinger grounded out to first to end the inning.

Left-hander Garrett Cleavinger started the eighth inning for the Dodgers. He was 2-3 with a 1.80 ERA.

The Diamondbacks finally got on the board when second baseman Andrew Young, who had entered the game as a pinch-hitter for Peacock in the top of the fifth, led off the inning with his fifth home run of the season. Cleavinger retired the next three hitters, striking out two of them.

Leading 16-1, the Dodgers were not yet finished. The Diamondbacks called on right-hander Jordan Weems, who five days earlier had been claimed off waivers from the Oakland A's, to pitch the eighth and hopefully finish the game for the Arizona.

Pollock greeted Weems with a home run to left, his second of the game. Barnes followed with a walk, Beaty singled to right, and Betts walked to load the bases. Gavin Lux, who had replaced Taylor at shortstop in the top of the fourth, hit a bases-clearing triple to increase the Dodgers' lead to 20-1. After Weems struck out Reks for the inning's first out, veteran outfielder Josh Reddick came off the bench to pitch. It was Reddick's first and only appearance as a pitcher in a major-league game.

After McKinstry was retired on a liner to right, Pujols hit a two-run homer to left. It was his second home run of the game, the 675th of his career, and the Dodgers' record-tying eighth of the night. Cleavinger, batting for himself, doubled to left, the first major-league hit of his career. After a walk to Pollock, Barnes grounded into an unassisted force out at second. The score was now 22-1.

Rookie right-hander Jake Reed came in to pitch the ninth inning for the Dodgers. He had pitched in only three prior major-league games and had a 9.00 ERA. Reed retired the Diamondbacks in order, ending the game.

The Dodgers' eight home runs matched a franchise record.[3] The grand slams by Turner and Betts marked the second time the Dodgers had hit two grand slams in a game that season.[4] It was the first time in major-league history that a team had two games in a season with two grand slams.[5] Add the two sets of back-to-back home runs and it was a historic night.

The Dodgers were the first team in baseball history to hit eight home runs, two grand slams, and two separate sets of back-to-back home runs in the same game. To put that in historical perspective, no team has ever accomplished those three things in a season, let alone all in one game.[6]

LA's 22 runs matched a Los Angeles Dodgers record for runs scored.[7] It was also the most runs scored by the team at Dodger Stadium. The franchise record for runs scored is 25.

The winning pitcher was Buehler. He improved his record to 9-1 and lowered his ERA to 2.36 on his way to being named to the NL All-Star team for the first time. Smith took the loss and dropped to 2-6. The time of the game was 3 hours and 19 minutes.

SOURCES

In addition to the sources cited in the Notes, the author relied on Baseball-reference.com, Retrosheet.org, and Baseball-Almanac.com.

https://www.baseball-reference.com/boxes/LAN/LAN202107100.shtml

https://www.retrosheet.org/boxesetc/2021/B07100LAN2021.htm

NOTES

1   The Dodgers had scored multiple runs in just four different innings in their previous five games.

2   Doug Padilla, "Dodgers Break Multiple Records in 22-1 Rout of Diamondbacks," NBCLosAngeles.com, July 21, 2021, retrieved on September 9, 2023, from https://www.nbclosangeles.com/news/sports/dodgers-break-multiple-records-in-22-1-rout-of-diamondbaacks/2635627/.

3   The Dodgers hit eight home runs in a game on two previous occasions. On May 23, 2002, they hit eight home runs against the Milwaukee Brewers at Miller Park and on March 28, 2019 (Opening Day), also against the Arizona Diamondbacks, at Dodger Stadium.

4   Pollock and Beaty hit grand slams against the Milwaukee Brewers on May 2 that year.

5   Padilla.

6   Padilla.

7   The Dodgers scored 22 runs on July 21, 2001, against the Colorado Rockies at Coors Field.

CHRIS TAYLOR HITS THREE HOME RUNS TO PROPEL DODGERS TO CRUCIAL WIN IN NLCS

October 21, 2021: Los Angeles Dodgers 11, Atlanta Braves 2 (Game Five of the National League Championship Series)

by Frank Ittner

The Los Angeles Dodgers had every reason to feel confident as they approached the 2021 National League Championship Series. Not only were they the defending World Series champions (albeit in the pandemic-shortened 2020 season), but they had also amassed an impressive 106-56 regular-season record, second only to their division rivals, the San Francisco Giants (107-55). Furthermore, in the National League Division Series, the Dodgers had turned the tables on the Giants by taking the series in a tense fifth and deciding game, scoring the winning run in the top of the ninth inning to win 2-1.

By contrast, the Dodgers' NLCS opponents, the Atlanta Braves, had mustered only an 88-73 regular-season record, a full 18 wins fewer than Los Angeles. However, since the Braves had won the NL East, they had earned home-field advantage for the best-of-seven series. In addition, the Braves had more quickly dispatched their Division Series opponent, the Milwaukee Brewers, three games to one.

Coming off an emotional Division Series involving the two teams with the best records in baseball, Dodgers manager Dave Roberts reflected on the possibility of a letdown going into the NLCS: "I have all the confidence we wouldn't be a victim of that. Knowing I don't have to worry about that, it just gives me added confidence in our guys."[1]

The first two games of the tightly contested NLCS in Atlanta were won by the Braves, both in walk-off fashion in the bottom of the ninth. Once the series shifted to Los Angeles, the Dodgers came back to win Game Three by a 6-5 score, but then suffered a decisive 9-2 loss in Game Four, as 20-game winner Julio Urías was roughed up for five runs and eight hits in five innings and the Dodgers managed only four hits off six Braves pitchers. Even more daunting, the Braves' starting pitcher for Game Five would be their ace, Max Fried, who had won 14 games with a 3.04 ERA during the regular season. On the other hand, because the Dodgers were missing one of their key starters, Clayton Kershaw, they were relegated to planning a "bullpen game," choosing reliever Joe Kelly as the opening pitcher.

One of the Dodgers' most versatile and valuable players during the 2021 season was 31-year-old utilityman Chris Taylor. The ultimate team player, Taylor saw action at six positions during the regular season (second base, shortstop, third base, and all three outfield positions) and even made the 2021 All-Star team as a utilityman. Dodgers manager Roberts had campaigned for Taylor's inclusion on the All-Star squad, saying, "[H]is versatility and offensive contributions are often overlooked."[2]

In the 2021 postseason Taylor had clinched the Dodgers' wild-card game win over St. Louis with a dramatic two-run home run in the bottom of the ninth inning. Already in the first four games of the NLCS, Taylor had made starts at three different positions (third base, left field, and center field) and would prove to be the key player for Los Angeles in Game Five.

The game did not begin well for the Dodgers, as the Braves' Ozzie Albies singled with one out in the top of the first inning and Freddie Freeman followed with a 425-foot home run to give the visitors a quick 2-0 lead.[3] After retiring the next hitter, Kelly was then forced to leave the game with a right biceps strain and was replaced by Evan Phillips, who struck out Adam Duvall to end the inning.

The Dodgers failed to score in the first inning but quickly grabbed the lead in the bottom of the second. AJ Pollock led off with a home run off Fried, and the next batter, veteran Albert Pujols, lined a single to left. That brought up Taylor, starting at third base because Justin Turner had been removed from the playoff roster due to a hamstring injury.[4] Taylor jumped on the first pitch from Fried and hammered it to left for a two-run homer.

One inning later, consecutive singles by the same triumvirate (Pollock, Pujols, and Taylor) produced the fourth run of the game for the Dodgers. The lead was further extended in the bottom of the fifth inning after Fried walked two of the first three batters he faced (the first of whom had been eliminated on a double-play ball). Fried was then lifted in favor of right-hander Chris Martin, who faced Taylor in his third at-bat of the game. After falling behind 0-and-2, Taylor responded by slamming a home run to right-center field, putting the Dodgers up 6-2.

On the pitching side, once Kelly had exited the game, the Dodgers' group of relievers combined to keep the Braves in check in innings two through five. Phillips retired the side in order in the top of the second, followed by scoreless frames for Alex Vesia in the third and Brusdar Graterol in the fourth and fifth innings.

As the game reached the later innings, the Dodgers continued to add to their lead. (Later, Braves manager Brian Snitker admitted, "After a while, it got out of control.")[5] Already with two homers and five RBIs, Taylor came up with two outs in the seventh inning against the Braves' Dylan Lee. With the crowd roaring, Taylor blasted his third home run of the game, to left field, extending the Dodgers' lead to 7-2 and resulting in a curtain call from the Dodgers faithful, the first of Taylor's career.[6] Los Angeles then added four more runs in the bottom of the eighth inning, the first on an RBI single by Trea Turner and three more on Pollock's second homer of the game. That outburst enabled Taylor to bat one last time with a chance to make postseason history with a fourth homer, but he struck out against Jacob Webb.

When closer Kenley Jansen set down the Braves in order in the ninth inning, the Dodgers had earned a decisive 11-2 win that cut the Braves' series lead to three games to two, with the Series now shifting back to Atlanta. In the process, Taylor became only the 11th major leaguer to hit three home runs in a playoff game and the first to do so in an elimination game for his team.[7] He also became only the second player in postseason history to have at least three home runs, four hits, and six RBIs in a game, joining Pujols, who accomplished the feat in Game Three of the 2011 World Series as a member of the St. Louis Cardinals.[8] Finally, the Dodgers became only the fourth team to win a postseason elimination game when their starting pitcher did not make it through the first inning, joining the 2017 New York Yankees (AL wild-card game), the 1924 Washington Senators (World Series Game Seven), and the 1925 Pittsburgh Pirates (World Series Game Seven).[9]

After the game, the understated Taylor commented: "It's definitely a surreal feeling for me. I never thought I was going to hit three homers in a game, let alone a postseason game. It just still hasn't really sunk in." He added, "When you're feeling good, it's more just see the ball, hit the ball."[10] Still down three games to two in the NLCS, the Dodgers certainly hoped that those good feelings would carry over to Game Six.

Postscript: In Game Six, a three-run homer by NLCS MVP Eddie Rosario in the fourth inning proved to be the difference as the Braves won 4-2 to advance to the World Series. Despite Taylor's Game Five heroics, the Dodgers' bid to reach their fourth World Series in five years had fallen short.

SOURCES

In addition to the sources cited in the Notes, the author consulted Baseball-Reference.com and Retrosheet.org.

https://www.baseball-reference.com/boxes/LAN/LAN202110210.shtml

https://www.retrosheet.org/boxesetc/2021/B10210LAN2021.htm

NOTES

1 Dylan Hernandez, "Hangover? Try More Champagne," *Los Angeles Times*, October 16, 2021: D1.

2 Caroline Darney, "Chris Taylor Earns Spot on NL All-Star Team," July 4, 2021, http://www.streakingthelawn.com/2021/7/4/22563396/chris-taylor-national-league-mlb-all-star-team-los-angeles-dodgers.

3 Anthony DiComo, "Final Hurrah? Freeman Driven to Win with ATL," MLB.com, October 22, 2021, https://www.mlb.com/news/freddie-freeman-homers-in-nlcs-game-5.

4 Jorge Castillo, "The Dodgers Belt Five Home Runs in a Rout to Stay Alive," *Los Angeles Times*, October 22, 2021: D1.

5 Bill Plaschke, "Taylor Lifts Dodgers with Their Season on the Line," *Los Angeles Times*, October 22, 2021: A1.

6 Castillo.

7   Manny Randhawa, "October Power Surge: Most Homers in Playoff Game,"
     MLB.com, October 21, 2021, https://www.mlb.com/news/most-home-runs-
     in-one-mlb-postseason-game-c296424904.

8   Castillo.

9   AJ Cassavell, "Kelly (Biceps Injury) Out for Postseason," MLB.com,
     October 22, 2021, www.mlb.com/news/joe-kelly-injury-nlcs-game-5-
     biceps-tightness.

10   Plaschke.

DODGERS' UNBEATEN GONSOLIN UNABLE TO STOP AL FROM 9TH CONSECUTIVE ALL-STAR WIN

July 19, 2022: AL All-Stars 3, NL All-Stars 2

by Richard Cuicchi

Forty-two years after the first major-league baseball All-Star Game was played in Dodger Stadium, the third oldest major-league ballpark still in use (after legendary Fenway Park and Wrigley Field), hosted the 92nd midsummer classic in 2022. Two hometown pitchers, Clayton Kershaw and Tony Gonsolin, played integral roles in the game, although their National League team failed to achieve the outcome they hoped for – a win, to break the American League's eight-game winning streak.

Despite being 60 years old, Dodger Stadium has retained its regal status as one of the classic ballparks in the majors. It easily fit into the classification of "baseball cathedral" that has been attached to several major-league parks over the years. Tucked away in a spacious parkland surrounded by Chavez Ravine and just north of downtown, it had the largest capacity of all big-league stadiums in 2022. Dodger Stadium was no stranger to momentous events, having hosted numerous World Series, concerts, and more in its rich history.

Dodger Stadium was to have hosted the All-Star Game in 2020, but the COVID-19 pandemic forced cancellation of the event.

Dodgers third baseman Justin Turner observed about the upcoming game and his hometown fans, "[The All-Star Game] is long overdue. That energy and that buzz and that atmosphere that is created here, which has a lot to do with our fan base, makes it an exciting place to play."[1]

It seemed fitting that Dodgers ace pitcher Kershaw would make his first career All-Star start in his home ballpark. Despite being the league's premier pitcher from 2011 to 2017, he had never drawn the starting assignment in eight prior selections. In the 2022 regular season, he was having a typical Kershaw season, with a 7-2 record and a 2.13 ERA for the first-place Dodgers.

Much of the attention in the days leading up to the game was focused on Kershaw's outing, including a potential pitcher/batter matchup with Los Angeles Angels' two-way star Shohei Ohtani. In a news conference on the day before the game, the usually humble Kershaw offered, "Hopefully, I don't screw it up too bad."[2] Perhaps he was referring to his past two All-Star Game appearances (2019 and 2015), in which he was charged with the losses.

As good as Kershaw had been in the first half of the season, his teammate Gonsolin was even better. The first-time All-Star could have easily been named the starter instead of Kershaw, since he had fashioned an 11-0 record and a 2.02 ERA in 17 starts. The batting line against him was a stingy .168/.230/.308.

The National League's AL opponents were headlined by Aaron Judge, who was already projecting to challenge Babe Ruth's American League home-run record, with 33 home runs and 70 RBIs at midseason. Additionally, Shohei Ohtani was doing his best to repeat his MVP Award season of 2021, with 19 homers and 56 RBIs, while also posting a 9-4 record and a 2.38 ERA.

In only his second major-league season, Tampa Bay Rays lefty Shane McClanahan drew the starting pitcher assignment for the American League. His challenge would be containing a potent NL lineup whose first five batters were Ronald Acuña Jr., Mookie Betts, Manny Machado, Paul Goldschmidt, and Trea Turner.

One of the other novel backstories involved the All-Star Contreras brothers achieving a family milestone. With a 5½-year difference in age, Willson and William Contreras had never played on the same team. They finally got their chance on one of baseball's biggest stages, when the brothers were in the National League's starting lineup batting sixth and seventh respectively.

Willson, a catcher with the Chicago Cubs, was making his third All-Star Game appearance, while William was making his All-Star debut as a catcher with the Atlanta Braves. (William's game appearance was as the designated hitter.) The last time two brothers appeared in the same All-Star Game was 2003. Cincinnati Reds infielder Aaron Boone donned a National League jersey, while his brother Bret, a Seattle Mariners infielder, represented the American League. The last time a pair of brothers started together in an All-Star Game was in 1992, when Sandy Alomar Jr. and Roberto Alomar were both in the American League's starting lineup.

The day before the game, Ohtani said, "To be able to face [Kershaw] in an All-Star Game in Dodger Stadium isn't a chance that comes often. I'd like to swing with everything I have." He said his goal was to hit a home run.[3]

Before a sellout crowd of 52,518, pregame ceremonies included the celebration of the 100th birthday of Rachel Robinson, Jackie's wife. Former Dodgers hurler Fernando Valenzuela threw out the first pitch, allowing fans to recall memories of Fernandomania days he had inspired 41 years earlier.

When asked in an on-field interview before the game what he was looking forward to in the game, Ohtani replied in English, "First pitch, first swing. That's it."[4]

Kershaw faced leadoff designated hitter Ohtani to start the game. They had previously opposed each other in eight at-bats in regular season games, with Kershaw holding Ohtani hitless.

On Kershaw's first pitch to Ohtani, he gave the left-handed hitter the pitch he wanted — a waist-high 91-MPH fastball on which Ohtani delivered a broken-bat, flare single to center field.[5] After two pitches to the ominous 6-foot-7 Judge, Kershaw picked off Ohtani at first base and then came back to strike out Judge. After walking Rafael Devers, Kershaw escaped the inning by inducing Vlad Guerrero Jr. to ground out.

Of his pickoff move to get Ohtani out, Kershaw said, "I just kind of lobbed it over there. I didn't know what pitch to throw yet, so kind of giving myself a second and I got him." Ohtani went back to his dugout with a smile, acknowledging that Kershaw won their confrontation.[6]

McClanahan wasn't as fortunate in his first inning. After Ronald Acuña Jr. led off with a ground-rule double, Betts drove him in with a single. After Machado grounded into a double play, Goldschmidt added another score with a solo home run to deep left-center field.

In the bottom of the second, Blue Jays pitcher Alek Manoah struck out the side, retiring William Contreras, Joc Pederson, and Acuna.

Following relievers Sandy Alcantara and Joe Musgrove, who held the American League scoreless in the second and third innings, Gonsolin yielded a single to José Ramirez to start the fourth inning. After retiring Guerrero on a fly ball, Gonsolin gave up back-to-back home runs to Giancarlo Stanton and Byron Buxton to put the American League ahead 3-2. It was the seventh set of back-to-back home runs in All-Star Game competition.[78]

The remainder of the game was scoreless, marked by only four total hits by both sides. The American League managed three more (by Ramirez, Jose Trevino, and Luis Arraez), while the National League could muster only one more, by Austin Riley in the eighth.

Cleveland Guardians reliever Emmanuel Clase closed out the American League's victory by striking out the side in the ninth.

The American League collected eight hits while whiffing 12 times. The National League managed five hits, with 10 strikeouts.

Undefeated during the regular season before the All-Star Game, Gonsolin was in unfamiliar territory in absorbing the loss. He had somewhat of an aftereffect in his first start after the All-Star Game when he suffered his first loss of the regular season on July 25. However, he finished the season with a 16-1 record.

Houston Astros pitcher Framber Valdez got credit for the AL win, as he retired the formidable hitting trio of Juan Soto, Manny Machado, and Freddie Freeman on groundballs in the third inning. Giancarlo Stanton was named the game's Most Valuable Player.

The Contreras brothers failed to contribute offensively to the NL's cause. Together, they were hitless in three plate appearances. However, the brothers cherished their outing. "Having my brother along my side is a blast," Willson told reporters. "We got to talk a lot about the game."[9]

In claiming its ninth consecutive All-Star Game win, the American League extended its dominance over it counterparts since 1988. During that stretch, the National League had won only six times (2010-2012) and (1994-1996).[10]

SOURCES

In addition to the sources cited in the Notes, the author consulted the following:

Montemurro, Meghan. "All-Star Game a Family Affair," *Chicago Tribune*, July 13, 2022: Section 3, 3.

baseball-reference.com/allstar/2022-allstar-game.shtml.

retrosheet.org/boxesetc/2022/B07190NLS2022.htm.

NOTES

1   Jack Harris, "At 60 Years Young, Still Looking Great," *Los Angeles Times*, July 17, 2022: V6.

2   Jack Harris, "Kershaw Gets the Nod for the NL," *Los Angeles Times*, July 19, 2022: B10.

3   Dylan Hernandez, "Ohtani Gives All Against Kershaw," *Los Angeles Times*, July 20, 2022: B10.

4   Hernandez, B6.

5   Hernandez.

6   Hernandez.

7   LaMond Pope, "Sox, Cubs Players Make Some Impact," *Chicago Tribune*, July 21, 2022: Section 3, 3.

8   The other six occurrences of back-to-back home runs in All-Star Games are: 1954 (Al Rosen and Ray Boone), 1956 (Ted Williams and Mickey Mantle), 1975 (Steve Garvey and Jim Wynn), 1989 (Bo Jackson and Wade Boggs), 2001 (Derek Jeter and Magglio Ordóñez), and 2018 (Alex Bregman and George Springer). Baseball Almanac. https://www.baseball-almanac.com/asgbox/all_star_game_home_runs.shtml. Accessed April 29, 2023.

9   Pope, "Sox, Cubs Players Make Some Impact."

10   The NL dominated between 1960 and 1985, as the AL won only three times (1962 Game Two, 1971, and 1983) in that span.

Leaving Dodger Stadium in 2001.

DODGER STADIUM CONTRIBUTORS

Marc Z Aaron is a lifelong Yankees fan, having grown up in the Bronx. Despite this fact, he idolized Sandy Koufax and had the thrill of speaking with Sandy in connection with the biography of Koufax he authored for SABR's BioProject. Marc has been to games in Dodger Stadium and has contributed numerous bios to the BioProject. He now resides in Pinehurst, North Carolina, where he does not play golf, but continues to play competitive tournament tennis.

Thomas Baird is a social worker, adjunct professor, and lifelong baseball enthusiast living in California. He attributes his baseball obsession to his parents and brothers, with whom he attended countless Dodgers games as a child. In 2006 he threw out the first pitch at a minor-league game in Trenton, New Jersey. Unfortunately, scouts were not in attendance, and the team did not allow him to keep pitching once the game started.

John Bauer resides with his wife and two children (although one is now at college) in Bedford, New Hampshire. By day, he is general counsel of an insurance group headquartered in Manchester, New Hampshire, with specialties in corporate and regulatory law. By night, he spends many spring and summer evenings staying up too late to watch the San Francisco Giants, and he is a year-round avid reader of baseball, history, and baseball history. He is a past and ongoing contributor to various SABR projects.

Dr. Jeff Barto has been teaching about baseball at UNC Charlotte since 1992. He has created several baseball-related courses. These include Baseball History, Baseball Through Critical Thinking, and, most recently, Baseball Analytics, a course for the University's Sports Analytics Certificate. Dr. Barto is a lifelong Pittsburgh Pirates fan and often centers his Game and BioProject contributions on the team. Currently, he is interested in Rick Monday. He wrote about Monday's Flag-Saving game and his "Blue Monday" blast that stunned the Expos to send the Dodgers to the 1981 World Series. He plans to complete his trilogy on Monday by authoring his BioProject biography.

When **Mike Bell** was 12 years old, he wrote his first baseball article in 1973 as a budding sportswriter in Southern California. Fifty years later, he has written his first SABR article. Mike's journalism career was sidetracked by a 42-year stint as a firefighter and 9-1-1 Communications director. Mike grew up watching games at Dodger and Angel Stadiums. He witnessed Mickey Mantle's 527th career home run in a game against the Angels in 1968. He played a year of college baseball at Cal-Poly Pomona for legendary coach John Scolinos. Mike hosts a podcast called *Baseball Journeys,* which explores the impact the game has had on people who have played or been associated with baseball at any level.

Kurt Blumenau is a frequent contributor to the SABR Games Project and Biography Project. He grew up in the Rochester, New York, area, following the Mets and the Triple-A Rochester Red Wings. He works in corporate communications in the Boston area.

Thomas J. Brown Jr. retired as a national board certified high-school science and ELL teacher after 34 years. Despite being retired, he still mentors many former students. Thomas enjoys traveling with his wife and has visited five continents and all 50 states. He also enjoys cooking and keeps a blog about the recipes he makes called Cooking and My Family. He has also enjoyed writing game stories and biographies for SABR after his retirement.

Warren Campbell is a Toronto-based entertainment industry executive. For 30 years he's avoided being on a stage and spends his free time searching through old publications for curious baseball stories. He still has dreams of owning an Independent baseball team.

Alan Cohen has been a SABR member since 2011. He chairs the BioProject fact-checking committee, serves as vice president-treasurer of the Connecticut Smoky Joe Wood Chapter, and is a datacaster (MiLB stringer) with the Eastern League Hartford Yard Goats, the Double-A affiliate of the Colorado Rockies. He also works with the Retrosheet Negro Leagues project and serves on SABR's Negro League Committee. His biographies, game stories, and essays have appeared in more than 70 baseball-related publications. He had the opportunity to visit Dodger Stadium in 1964 after graduating from high school. He has four children, nine grandchildren, and one great-grandchild, and resides in Connecticut with wife Frances, their cats, Zoe and Ava, and their dog, Buddy.

Rory Costello has been to Dodger Stadium just once, back in 1986. He lives in Brooklyn, New York – the home that the team forsook – with his wife, Noriko, and son, Kai.

Carter Cromwell was formerly a sportswriter for daily newspapers, covering a wide variety of athletics at all levels. In a later life, he was a public-relations professional in the high-tech world. Since 2019, he has worked with an independent-league professional baseball team, the San Rafael Pacifics, doing the play-by-play and coordinating the in-game statistics. A SABR member, he also writes baseball-related articles for various websites and has contributed to multiple book projects. When not doing that, he has a passion for world travel, photography, and rescue dogs.

Bryan Dietzler is an established writer who has written about all kinds of sports over the last 24 years and has more recently concentrated on baseball as his writing passion. His favorite professional baseball team is the Chicago White Sox and he enjoys attending minor-league games locally with his favorite team being the Cedar Rapids Kernels. Bryan is originally from North Dakota but calls Iowa home, having lived there most of his life. He currently works in the educational technology industry. His first loves are family, sports, and writing.

Richard Cuicchi joined SABR in 1983 and is an active member of the Schott-Pelican Chapter. Since his retirement as an information technology executive, Richard authored *Family Ties: A Comprehensive Collection of Facts and Trivia about Baseball's Relatives*. He has contributed to numerous SABR BioProject and Games Project publications. He does freelance writing and blogging about a variety of baseball topics on his website, TheTenthInning.com, and CrescentCitySports.com. Richard lives in New Orleans with his wife, Mary.

Joseph "Joey" Elledge is a professor of sport management at Erskine College. As an avid baseball fan, Joey is a lifelong Chicago Cubs fan and a big supporter of minor league baseball. Joey became a baseball

fan by attending games of the Capital City Bombers (former Single-A affiliate for the New York Mets) with his family, and holds partial season tickets to minor-league games in Columbia, South Carolina, with his mother, sisters, and his wife. He works with the Lexington County Blowfish (Coastal Plain League) in sales. He is a new contributor to SABR projects and studies the business side of baseball in his free time. Joey resides in Lexington, South Carolina, with his wife, Katie, and three dogs, Cookie, Sammy (named after Sammy Sosa), and Boone.

Jeff Findley has been a member of SABR since 2009. A native of Eastern Iowa, he did the only logical thing growing up in the heart of the Cubs/Cardinals rivalry – he embraced the 1969 Baltimore Orioles and became a lifelong fan. When he's not watching baseball, he works as an information security professional for a Fortune 50 financial services company in central Illinois. He enjoys doing historical research and contributing to both the SABR Biography Project and Games Project.

Zak Ford is chair of the Dusty Baker-Sacramento SABR Chapter and serves on the advisory committee of the Pacific Coast League Historical Society. He is the author of *Called Up: Ballplayers Remember Becoming Major Leaguers*. Ford lives in Cameron Park, California.

John Fredland is an attorney and retired Air Force officer. As an undergraduate at Rice University, he covered Rice's nationally ranked baseball teams for the school newspaper, the *Rice Thresher*. John received his law degree at Vanderbilt University, then served as an active-duty attorney in the Air Force's Judge Advocate General's Corps for 20 years. He lives in San Antonio, Texas, and chairs SABR's Baseball Games Project Research Committee.

October 15, 1988, began, and ended, as a very important Southern California sports day in author **Darren Gibson**'s life. On that day, his school's football team, the UCLA Bruins, vaulted into the number-1 spot in the polls for the first time in 21 years. This freshman economics major and subpar lefty first baseman, recently cut from his UCLA baseball tryout, was elated as he sat to catch Game One of the World Series involving his beloved Dodgers. Although no relation to the subject, Darren jumped at the chance to write about the unforgettable 1988 Kirk Gibson World Series home-run game. Darren has authored over 35 SABR biographies and is a middle-school math teacher in Orange County, California.

Michael Green is chair of the history department and professor of history at the University of Nevada, Las Vegas, and president of the Las Vegas Maddux Brothers Chapter of SABR.

A love of baseball was instilled in **Andrew Harner** from childhood, but since he had next to no athletic skills, he instead dove into the game's history and pored over box scores as often as he could. And because baseball history wasn't offered as a college major, he settled for the next best thing – a bachelor's degree in sports journalism with a minor in history. He graduated from Bowling Green State University in 2010 and spent nearly seven years as a sports editor before leaving the newspaper industry to pursue a career in hospitality management. Andrew has since published baseball research for *HowTheyPlay*, spent a little over a year producing online NFL content for *Sports Illustrated*, and he currently serves as a content writer in the sports card industry. He has been married to his wife, Elizabeth, since 2011, and they have two daughters.

Paul Hofmann has been a SABR member since 2002. He has contributed to more than 30 SABR publications and co-edited *The 1883 Philadelphia Athletics: American Association Champions*. Paul is currently the associate vice provost for international affairs at the University of Louisville and teaches in the College of Management at National Changhua University of Education in Taiwan. A native of Detroit, Paul is an avid baseball card collector and lifelong Detroit Tigers fan. He currently resides in Lakeville, Minnesota.

Mike Huber, a longtime SABR member, is a professor of mathematics at Muhlenberg College in Allentown, Pennsylvania. He routinely teaches a course titled Reasoning With Sabermetrics or mentors students with sabermetrical research. His first major-league-baseball memories are of the Dodgers and Orioles in the 1966 World Series.

Frank Ittner is a retired accountant and New England native now living in suburban Washington, DC. He is a lifelong Red Sox fan, a contributor to the SABR Games Project, and keenly interested in baseball history, trivia, and visiting major and minor-league ballparks and sites throughout the country. He is forever indebted to his daughter, Claire, for introducing him to SABR and purchasing his initial membership in 2015.

Greg King is a California-based public historian who attended his first game at Dodger Stadium in 1962, a 13-inning affair that produced a 2-1 LA win over the Reds and featured both managers being tossed. He and the late Woody Wilson co-founded SABR's Dusty Baker – Sacramento Chapter in 1994.

Norm King (1957-2018) of Ottawa, Ontario, joined SABR in 2010 and became a prolific contributor to the SABR BioProject and Games Project until his untimely death from a rare form of bile duct cancer in 2018. He was the lead editor and author of *Au jeu/Play Ball: The 50 Greatest Games in the History of the Montreal Expos*, published in 2016, and wrote chapters for a number of other SABR books, including *Thar's Joy in Braveland: The 1957 Milwaukee Braves*; *Winning on the North Side: The 1929 Chicago Cubs*; and *A Pennant for the Twin Cities: The 1965 Minnesota Twins*. He was an active member of SABR's Quebec Chapter and a friendly face at the SABR national convention each year.

David Krell is the chair of SABR's Elysian Fields Chapter and the author of *1962: Baseball and America in the Time of JFK*; *Our Bums: The Brooklyn Dodgers in History, Memory and Popular Culture*; and *The Fenway Effect: A Cultural History of the Boston Red Sox*.

A 15-year member of the Halsey Hall Chapter of SABR, **Dave Lande** served four years on the chapter's board of directors and currently co-chairs the chapter's research committee. Growing up in a single-parent home, he owes his love of baseball and the Minnesota Twins to his mother, who tuned in Twins games in on the radio, Topps baseball cards from the '60s, and *The Baseball Encyclopedia*. He experienced his first serious baseball heartbreak when Sandy Koufax, pitching on two days' rest, defeated the Twins in a shutout in the last game of the 1965 World Series.

Len Levin is a longtime newspaper editor in New England, now retired. He lives in Providence with his wife, Linda, and an overachieving orange cat. He now (Len, not the cat) is the grammarian for the Rhode Island Supreme Court and copy-edits its decisions.

He also copy-edits many SABR books, including this one. He is just down the interstate from Fenway Park, where he has spent many happy – and not-so-happy – hours.

Andy McCue, a former president of SABR, won the Seymour Medal for *Mover and Shaker: Walter O'Malley, the Dodgers, and Baseball's Westward Expansion*. He is also the author of *Baseball by the Books: A History and Complete Bibliography of Baseball Fiction* and *Stumbling Around the Bases: The American League's Mismanagement in the Expansion Eras* (University of Nebraska Press, 2022). He is a retired newspaper reporter, editor, and columnist and a winner of SABR's highest honor, the Bob Davids Award.

Chad Moody is a nearly lifelong resident of the Detroit area, where he has been a fan of the Detroit Tigers from birth. An alumnus of the University of Michigan and Michigan State University, he has spent 30-plus years working in the automotive industry. Chad has contributed to numerous SABR and Professional Football Researchers Association projects. He and his wife, Lisa, live in Plymouth, Michigan, with their dog, Daisy.

Bill Nowlin has been known to call Fenway Park his second home. The attachment that many fans have to their home ballpark is often very real and it is a pleasure to work with a few dozen SABR members on helping edit a book such as this one on Dodger Stadium. A Boston native, and co-founder of the Rounder Records label, he spends much of his time researching and writing about baseball.

Tony S. Oliver is a native of Puerto Rico currently living in Sacramento, California, with his wife and daughter. While he works as a Six Sigma professional, his true love is baseball and he cheers for both the Red Sox and whoever happens to be playing the Yankees. He is fascinated by baseball cards and is currently researching the evolution of baseball tickets. He believes there is no prettier color than the vibrant green of a freshly mown grass on a baseball field.

Tim Otto grew up in northeast Ohio 35 miles from Cleveland's Municipal Stadium. His first memories of major-league baseball date to the spring of 1960 when, as a second-grader, he was fascinated by the controversy surrounding the trade of Rocky Colavito to the Tigers for Harvey Kuenn. Shortly thereafter, he started monopolizing the sports section of the *Cleveland Plain Dealer* each morning at breakfast and that June attended his first major-league game. He remembers closely following the 1962 Dodgers-Giants pennant race and was excited to learn that his article on the deciding playoff game would be included in this book.

Zac Petrillo holds a Bachelor of Arts from Hunter College and a Master of Fine Arts from Chapman University's Dodge College of Film and Media Arts. His experience spans directing multiple short films and producing content for networks like Comedy Central and TruTV. In 2016 Zac played a pivotal role in the launch of Vice Media's 24/7 cable network, Vice TV. As an active member of SABR, he dedicates his research to exploring the realm of post-1980s baseball, particularly examining its intersection with the media industry. Currently, he serves as the director of technical operations at A+E Networks and imparts his knowledge in television studies as a lecturer at Marymount Manhattan College.

Bill Pruden has been a teacher of American history and government for almost 40 years. A SABR member for over two decades, he has contributed to SABR's BioProject and Games Project as well as some book projects. He has also written on a range of American history subjects, an interest undoubtedly fueled by the fact that as a 7-year-old he was at Yankee Stadium to witness Roger Maris's historic 61st home run.

Carl Riechers retired from United Parcel Service in 2012 after 35 years of service. With more free time, he became a SABR member that same year. Born and raised in the suburbs of St. Louis, he became a big fan of the Cardinals. He and his wife, Janet, have three children and he is the proud grandpa of two.

Joal Ryan has written for the *New York Times* (Motherlode), the *Los Angeles Times*, CBS News, CNET, Yahoo! and more. She contributed to the SABR book *The First Negro League Champion: The 1920 Chicago American Giants*. A Southern California native, she was 9 when her uncle Mike took her to her first game at Dodger Stadium. She's been a not-infrequent visitor ever since, and was on hand for the José Lima shutout game she writes about for this collection.

Jason Scheller is a professor of history at Vernon College in Wichita Falls, Texas. He is a graduate of

Texas Tech University. His graduate work has been featured in the books *The Empire Strikes Out: How Baseball Sold U.S. Foreign Policy and Promoted the American Way Abroad*, by Robert Elias, and *The Boys Who Were Left Behind: The 1944 World Series Between the Hapless St. Louis Browns and the Legendary St. Louis Cardinals*, by John Heidenry and Brett Topel. He joined the Dallas-Fort Worth Banks-Bragan chapter of SABR in 2018. His interests are in World War II baseball, the Negro Leagues, the minor leagues, the Texas Rangers, the Los Angeles Dodgers, and the Boston Red Sox. He enjoys attending minor-league baseball games throughout the country with his wife and daughter each summer. A Red Sox fan since 1986, he follows them every season and relishes the opportunity to attend games at Fenway Park whenever he gets a chance.

Tom Schott joined SABR in 2020 and has written for the BioProject and Games Project. He got his start in sports journalism at age 12 when he co-founded his own magazine called *The Redbird Chirps*, interviewing nearly 100 major-league players, managers, coaches, and broadcasters from 1981 to 1986. A native of St. Louis, Schott has been a contributing writer for the Cardinals media guide, the Hall of Fame induction program, and website (Cardinals.com). He is co-author of *The Giants Encyclopedia* and *The Giants Encyclopedia: Second Edition* – the definitive history of the New York and San Francisco Giants franchise. He also has written for the Giants website (SFGiants.com), the Atlanta Braves media guide and website (Braves.com), and the National Baseball Hall of Fame and Museum website (BaseballHall.org). Schott resides in West Lafayette, Indiana, with his wife, Jane. They have two sons, August and Sam.

Curt Smith's 18 books include *The Presidents and the Pastime, Long Time Gone*, and what *Esquire* Magazine calls "among the 100 Best Baseball Books Ever Written" – *Voices of The Game*. Smith has hosted or keynoted Smithsonian Institution series, the Cooperstown Symposium on Baseball and American Culture, the NINE Conference, and the Great Fenway Writers Series. The Senior Lecturer of English at the University of Rochester and former *Saturday Evening Post* senior editor also wrote more speeches than anyone for former President George H.W. Bush, including Bush's address at Pearl Harbor on the 50th anniversary of December 7, 1941.

Kevin Snyder is a professor of sport management at Southern New Hampshire University and teaches classes on statistics and sports. He resides in Nashua, New Hampshire, and enjoys traveling to see baseball throughout the country. Kevin's additional research interests include innovation, sustainability, and corporate strategy. He has been a SABR member since 2023 and looks forward to eventually seeing the Pirates win the World Series.

Glen Sparks has many fond memories of going to Dodger Stadium. While he now lives far away from California, he still follows the team that plays its home games in a ballpark that sits on a hill. Sparks is a graduate of the Santa Monica Little League program and has a bachelor's degree in journalism from the University of Missouri. He worked at a newspaper for several years and wrote a full-length biography of Hall of Fame shortstop Pee Wee Reese, published in 2022 by McFarland. He has co-edited several books for SABR (including this one) and has written many articles. He is married to his wife, Pam.

Russ Speiller lives in Cincinnati with his wife, Lisa, and their two children. A lifelong Yankees fan whose father filled him with stories of the 1961 "M&M boys," Russ holds a chemical engineering degree from the University of Pennsylvania. Having joined SABR in February of 2023, Russ has discovered the pure joy of researching and writing about the great game of baseball. He completed his first BioProject work (Pat Venditte), submitted multiple articles to the *Turnstyle* literary arts journal, and is proud to make his first SABR book contribution, the start of many more to come!

As a young Yankees fan, **Mark S. Sternman** had his bar mitzvah on October 24, 1981, the date of Game Four of the World Series at Dodger Stadium. New York had won the first two games of the championship but lost Game Three and then dropped Game Four, too, blowing 4-0 and 6-3 leads. Sternman has since had the opportunity to attend games at Dodger Stadium and while he enjoys the park as an adult, he still retains a twinge of his teenage disappointment from Game Four of 1981 (as well as the rest of that sad series).

Alan Stowell is a retired lawyer and journalist now living in Florida with his wife, Patricia. He is a lifelong Dodgers fan and a devoted Nationals fan since their relocation to Washington in 2005. Among his baseball accomplishments is happily attending games in 46 different major-league ballparks.

Bob Timmermann is a librarian who lives in Tujunga, California. He has made multiple contributions to the SABR Games Project and the SABR BioProject, as well as other SABR publications.

Theo Tobel is a first-year student at Harvard College, where he is studying psychology and statistics. In his spare time, Theo enjoys watching Dodgers baseball, hiking, and playing bass guitar.

Joseph Wancho lives in Sheffield Lake, Ohio. He has been a SABR member since 2005. Wancho is an occasional contributor to various SABR projects.

Bob Webster grew up in northwestern Indiana and has been a Cubs fan since 1963. After moving to Portland, Oregon, in 1980, Bob now spends his time working on baseball research and writing and is a contributor to quite a few SABR projects. He worked as a stats stringer on the MLB Gameday app for three years

and is a member of the Pacific Northwest Chapter of SABR and the Oregon Sports Hall of Fame, and is on the board of directors of the Old-Timers Baseball Association of Portland.

John Zinn is an independent historian with a special interest in the history of baseball. He is the chairman of the board of the New Jersey Historical Society and was the chair of New Jersey's Committee on the Sesquicentennial of the Civil War. John is the author of five books including three about the Brooklyn Dodgers as well as numerous essays and articles. He also writes a baseball history blog entitled A Manly Pastime. John holds BA and MBA degrees from Rutgers University and is a Vietnam veteran. He is the scorekeeper for the Flemington Neshanock vintage baseball team. John and his wife Carol are the parents of Paul Zinn and the grandparents of Sophie and Henry Zinn.

Become a SABR member today!

If you're interested in baseball — writing about it, reading about it, talking about it — there's a place for you in the Society for American Baseball Research.

SABR memberships are available on annual, multi-year, or monthly subscription basis. Annual and monthly subscription memberships auto-renew for your convenience. Young Professional memberships are for ages 30 and under. Senior memberships are for ages 65 and older. Student memberships are available to currently enrolled middle/high school or full-time college/university students. Monthly subscription members receive SABR publications electronically and are eligible for SABR event discounts after 12 months.

Here's a list of some of the key benefits you'll receive as a SABR member:

- Receive two editions (spring and fall) of the *Baseball Research Journal*, our flagship publication
- Receive expanded e-book edition of *The National Pastime*, our annual convention journal
- 8-10 new e-books published by the SABR Digital Library, all FREE to members
- "This Week in SABR" e-newsletter, sent to members every Friday
- Join dozens of research committees, from Statistical Analysis to Women in Baseball.
- Join one of 70+ regional chapters in the U.S., Canada, Latin America, and abroad
- Participate in online discussion groups
- Ask and answer baseball research questions on the SABR-L e-mail listserv
- Complete archives of *The Sporting News* dating back to 1886 and other research resources
- Promote your research in "This Week in SABR"
- Diamond Dollars Case Competition
- Yoseloff Scholarships

- Discounts on SABR national conferences, including the SABR National Convention, the SABR Analytics Conference, Jerry Malloy Negro League Conference, Frederick Ivor-Campbell 19th Century Conference, and the Arizona Fall League Experience
- Publish your research in peer-reviewed SABR journals
- Collaborate with SABR researchers and experts
- Contribute to Baseball Biography Project or the SABR Games Project
- List your new book in the SABR Bookshelf
- Lead a SABR research committee or chapter
- Networking opportunities at SABR Analytics Conference
- Meet baseball authors and historians at SABR events and chapter meetings
- 50% discounts on paperback versions of SABR e-books
- Discounts with other partners in the baseball community
- SABR research awards

We hope you'll join the most passionate international community of baseball fans at SABR! Check us out online at SABR.org/join.

- - ✂ -

SABR MEMBERSHIP FORM

	Standard	Senior	Young Pro.	Student
Annual:	❑ $65	❑ $45	❑ $45	❑ $25
3 Year:	❑ $175	❑ $129	❑ $129	
5 Year:	❑ $249			
Monthly:	❑ $6.95	❑ $4.95	❑ $4.95	

(International members wishing to be mailed the Baseball Research Journal should add $10/yr for Canada/Mexico or $19/yr for overseas locations.)

Participate in Our Donor Program!

Support the preservation of baseball research. Designate your gift toward:
❑ General Fund   ❑ Endowment Fund   ❑ Research Resources   ❑_____
❑ I want to maximize the impact of my gift; do not send any donor premiums
❑ I would like this gift to remain anonymous.

Note: Any donation not designated will be placed in the General Fund.
SABR is a 501 (c) (3) not-for-profit organization & donations are tax-deductible to the extent allowed by law.

Name _____

E-mail* _____

Address _____

City _____ ST_____ ZIP_____

Phone _____ Birthday _____

* Your e-mail address on file ensures you will receive the most recent SABR news.

Dues $_____

Donation $_____

Amount Enclosed $_____

Do you work for a matching grant corporation? Call (602) 496-1460 for details.

If you wish to pay by credit card, please contact the SABR office at (602) 496-1460 or sign up securely online at SABR.org/join. We accept Visa, Mastercard & Discover.

Do you wish to receive the *Baseball Research Journal* electronically? ❑ Yes   ❑ No
Our e-books are available in PDF, Kindle, or EPUB (iBooks, iPad, Nook) formats.

Mail to: SABR, Cronkite School at ASU, 555 N. Central Ave. #416, Phoenix, AZ 85004

10/19

The SABR Digital Library

Available wherever books are sold

The First Negro League Champion: The 1920 Chicago American Giants

Edited by Frederick C. Bush and Bill Nowlin

Paperback $29.95 244 pages • Ebook $9.99

This book chronicles the team which won the title of champion in the Negro National League's inaugural season. Rube Foster, a Hall of Famer, and his White business partner John Schorling are featured along with biographies of every player on the team include Cristóbal Torriente, a member of both the National Baseball Hall of Fame and the Cuban Baseball Hall of Fame, as well as early Blackball stalwarts Dave "Lefty" Brown, Bingo DeMoss, Judy Gans, Dave Malarcher, Frank Warfield, and Frank Wickware. A comprehensive timeline of the 1920 season and a history of the founding of the Negro National League are included.

We Are, We Can, We Will: The 1992 World Champion Toronto Blue Jays

Edited by Adrian Fung and Bill Nowlin

Forewords by Buck Martinez and Dave Winfield

Paperback US $34.95/Canada $41.95 394 pages • Ebook $9.99

The 1992 Toronto Blue Jays will always be remembered as the first World Series-winning club from Canada. After a near miss in 1991, the 1992 club confidently adopted "We Are, We Can, We Will" as their team motto. This book features biographies of every player who played for the 1992 Toronto Blue Jays including Hall of Famers Dave Winfield, Jack Morris, and Roberto Alomar. Manager Cito Gaston, Hall of Fame general manager Pat Gillick, and radio broadcaster Tom Cheek are also included, as well as a "ballpark biography" of SkyDome. Ten reports describe significant games from the 1992 season illustrating Toronto's championship journey from Opening Day to the last game of the World Series.

From Shibe Park to Connie Mack Stadium: Great Games in Philadelphia's Lost Ballpark

Edited by Gregory H. Wolf
Paperback $39.95 398 pages • Ebook $9.99

This collection evokes memories and the exciting history of the celebrated ballpark through stories of 100 games played there and several feature essays. The games included in this volume reflect every decade in the ballpark's history, from the inaugural game in 1909, to the last in 1970.

Shibe Park was the home of the Philadelphia A's from 1909 until their relocation to Kansas City and the Philadelphia Phillies from 1938 until the ballpark's closure at the end 1970. In 1953 it was renamed Connie Mack Stadium. The ballpark hosted big-league baseball for 62 seasons and more than 6,000 games—over 3,500 games by the A's and 2,500 by the Phillies—and was home to Frank Baker, Del Ennis, Chief Bender, and Robin Roberts.

¡Arriba!: The Heroic Life of Roberto Clemente

edited by Bill Nowlin and Glen Sparks

Paperback $34.95 338 pages • Ebook $9.99

2022 marks the 50th anniversary year of Roberto Clemente's passing. This book celebrates his life and baseball career. Named to 15 All-Star Game squads, Clemente won 12 Gold Gloves, four batting titles, and was the National League's Most Valuable Player in 1966. The first Latino inducted into the National Baseball Hall of Fame, Clemente played 18 seasons for the Pittsburgh Pirates and became the 11th player to reach the 3,000-hit milestone, hitting number 3000 on the season's last day. At the time no one knew he would never play baseball again. Clemente was known for his charitable work. He lost his life on the final day of 1972 while working to provide relief for victims of an earthquake in Nicaragua.

The Stars Shone on Philadelphia: The 1934 Phila. Stars
ISBN 978-1-960819-04-8 $9.99 ebook
ISBN 978-1-960819-05-5 $29.95 paperback
Biographies of Ed Bolden's 1934 Negro National
League champions, including Biz Mackie and Jud
Wilson.

Yankee Stadium: America's First Modern Ballpark
ISBN 978-1-960819-16-8 $9.99 ebook
ISBN 978-1-960819-21-5 $39.95 paperback
Essays about the history of Yankee Stadium and
recaps of over 50 historic games and other events
there, including papal visits, football, and more.

*Ebbets Field: Great, Historic, and Memorable Games at
Brooklyn's Lost Ballpark*
ISBN 978-1-960819-16-1 $9.99 ebook
ISBN 978-1-960819-17-8 $39.95 paperback
Relive Jackie Robinson's and Sandy Koufax's debuts,
and over 90 other heartbreaks and triumphs in
Brooklyn, plus essays on the ballpark.

Nichibei Yakyu: Volume II: 1960-2019
ISBN 978-1-960819-14-7 $9.99 ebook
ISBN 978-1-960819-15-4 $34.95 paperback
Fascinating recaps of the exhibition tours and
MLB games by US baseball teams in Japan.

Sox Bid Curse Farewell: The 2004 Boston Red Sox
ISBN 978-1-960819-18-5 $9.99 ebook
ISBN 978-1-960819-19-2 $34.95 paperback
Biographies of every player and coach on the 2004
World Championship team, as well as essays about
the season, effects of the win on fans, and more.

Dodger Stadium: Blue Heaven on Earth
ISBN 978-1-960819-20-8 $9.99 ebook
ISBN 978-1-960819-21-5 $29.95 paperback
Essays about the history of Dodger Stadium and
recaps of over 50 historic games there, from
Fernandomania to Vin Scully's bow.

One-Win Wonders
ISBN 978-1-960819-13-0 $39.95 paperback
ISBN 978-1-960819-12-3 $9.99 ebook
Biographies of 78 players whose entire major league
pitching record consisted of just one win, from the
tragic, like Nick Adenhart, to the improbable, like
catcher Brent Mayne.

Willie Mays: Five Tools
ISBN 978-1-960819-02-4 $9.99 ebook
ISBN 978-1-960819-03-1 $29.95 paperback
Twenty essays on Mays' life and career, plus
recaps of 30 historic games.